Lecture Notes in Artificial Intelligence 9571

Subseries of Lecture Notes in Computer Science

More information about this series at http://www.springer.com/series/1244

Michael Rovatsos · George Vouros
Vicente Julian (Eds.)

Multi-Agent Systems and Agreement Technologies

13th European Conference, EUMAS 2015
and Third International Conference, AT 2015
Athens, Greece, December 17–18, 2015
Revised Selected Papers

 Springer

Editors
Michael Rovatsos
University of Edinburgh
Edinburgh
UK

Vicente Julian
Technical University of Valencia
Valencia
Spain

George Vouros
Department of Digital Systems
University of Piraeus
Piraeus
Greece

ISSN 0302-9743   ISSN 1611-3349 (electronic)
Lecture Notes in Artificial Intelligence
ISBN 978-3-319-33508-7   ISBN 978-3-319-33509-4   (eBook)
DOI 10.1007/978-3-319-33509-4

Library of Congress Control Number: 2016936984

LNCS Sublibrary: SL7 – Artificial Intelligence

Printed on acid-free paper

This Springer imprint is published by Springer Nature
The registered company is Springer International Publishing AG Switzerland

Preface

This volume contains revised versions of the papers presented at the 13th European Conference on Multi-Agent Systems (EUMAS 2015) and the Third International Conference on Agreement Technologies (AT 2015), which were both held in Athens during December 17–18, 2015.

EUMAS 2015 followed the tradition of previous editions (Oxford 2003, Barcelona 2004, Brussels 2005, Lisbon 2006, Hammamet 2007, Bath 2008, Agia Napa 2009, Paris 2010, Maastricht 2011, Dublin 2012, Toulouse 2013, Prague 2014) in terms of aiming to provide the prime European forum for presenting and discussing agents research as the annual designated event of the European Association of Multi-Agent Systems (EURAMAS).

AT 2015 was the third installment in a series of events (after Dubrovnik 2012 and Beijing 2013) to focus on bringing together researchers and practitioners working on computer systems in which autonomous software agents negotiate with one another, typically on behalf of humans, in order to come to mutually acceptable agreements.

This year, for the first time, both events were co-located and run as a single, joint event. This joint organization aimed to encourage cross-fertilization among the broader EUMAS and the more specialized AT communities, and to provide a richer and more attractive program to participants. While the technical program was put together by their independent committees into conference-specific thematic sessions, they shared keynote talks and aligned their schedules to minimize overlap and enable participants to make the best possible use of the combined program of the two conferences.

Traditionally, both conference series have always followed a spirit of providing a forum for discussion and an annual opportunity for primarily European researchers to meet and exchange ideas. For this reason, they have always encouraged submission of papers that report on both early and mature research. They also permitted submission of papers for oral presentation of previously published work, although these contributions have not been included in the present volume, which only contains original contributions.

The peer-review processes carried out by both conferences put great emphasis on ensuring a high quality of accepted contributions. The EUMAS Program Committee accepted 15 submissions (34.8 %) as full papers and another 10 submissions (23.2 %) as short papers out of a total of 43 submissions. The AT review process resulted in the acceptance of seven full (31.8 %) and seven short papers (31.8 %) out of 22 submissions overall.

This volume is structured as follows: In the first part, we include invited papers from the two keynote speakers, Michael Luck (King's College London, UK) and Onn Shehory (IBM Haifa Research Lab, Israel). The remaining 36 papers are grouped together in thematic areas on the following topics:

- Coordination and planning
- Learning and optimization

- Argumentation and negotiation
- Norms, trust, and reputation
- Agent-based simulation and agent programming

Each of these thematic sections contains a mix of papers from EUMAS 2015 and AT 2015, where full papers are followed by short papers.

The editors wish to thank the Program Committee members (over 100 of them for the two conferences combined) and the additional reviewers they recruited for helping EUMAS and AT put together a program of high-quality papers that gives an up-to-date overview of the breadth and excellence of agents research in Europe.

We also thank the local organizers for their hard work in ensuring the event ran as smoothly as it did – all aspects of the conference organization received unanimous praise. Their help with publicizing the conference through the conference website and by producing print publicity was also much appreciated.

Finally, we would like to express our gratitude to the sponsors of the conference, the European Coordinating Committee for Artificial Intelligence (ECCAI), the University of Piraeus Research Center (KEPP), and the *Artificial Intelligence* journal for their generous support, without which this event would not have been possible.

March 2016   Michael Rovatsos
                                                              George Vouros
                                                              Vicente Julian

Organization

EUMAS 2015 Organization

Conference Chairs

Michael Rovatsos	University of Edinburgh, UK
George Vouros	University of Piraeus, Greece

Local Organization

George Vouros	University of Piraeus, Greece
Alexander Artikis	NCSR Demokritos, Greece
George Santipantakis	University of Piraeus, Greece

Program Committee

Natasha Alechina	University of Nottingham, UK
Luis Antunes	Universidade de Lisboa, Portugal
Alexander Artikis	NCSR Demokritos, Greece
Katie Atkinson	University of Liverpool, UK
Bernhard Bauer	University of Augsburg, Germany
Ana L.C. Bazzan	Universidade Federal do Rio Grande do Sul, Brazil
Elizabeth Black	King's College London, UK
Olivier Boissier	ENS Mines Saint-Etienne, France
Nils Bulling	Delft University of Technology, The Netherlands
Cristiano Castelfranchi	Institute of Cognitive Sciences and Technologies, Italy
Sofia Ceppi	University of Edinburgh, UK
Georgios Chalkiadakis	Technical University of Crete, Greece
Massimo Cossentino	National Research Council of Italy, Italy
Mehdi Dastani	Utrecht University, The Netherlands
Paul Davidsson	Malmö University, Sweden
Tiago de Lima	University of Artois and CNRS, France
Frank Dignum	Utrecht University, The Netherlands
Malcolm Egan	Czech Technical University in Prague, Czech Republic
Amal El Fallah Seghrouchni	LIP6 - University of Pierre and Marie Curie, France
Nicola Gatti	Politecnico di Milano, Italy
Valentin Goranko	Stockholm University, Sweden
Michal Jakob	Czech Technical University in Prague, Czech Republic
Matthias Klusch	DFKI, Germany
Franziska Klügl	Örebro University, Sweden
Joao Leite	Universidade Nova de Lisboa, Portugal
Brian Logan	University of Nottingham, UK
Alessio Lomuscio	Imperial College London, UK

AT 2015 Organization

Conference Chairs

Vicente Julian Inglada   Technical University of Valencia, Spain
George Vouros   University of Piraeus, Greece

Local Organization

George Vouros   University of Piraeus, Greece
Alexander Artikis   NCSR Demokritos, Greece
George Santipantakis   University of Piraeus, Greece

Program Committee

Giulia Andrighetto   ISTC CNR, Italy
Estefania Argente   Universitat Politècnica de València, Spain
Javier Bajo   Universitat Politècnica de Madrid, Spain
Olivier Boissier   ENS Mines Saint-Etienne, France
Pompeu Casanovas   Universitat Autònoma de Barcelona, Spain
Cristiano Castelfranchi   Institute of Cognitive Sciences and Technologies, Italy
Carlos Chesevar   Universidad Nacional del Sur, Argentina
Paul Davidsson   Malmö University, Sweden
Maria Ganzha   University of Gdańsk, Poland
Mirjana Ivanović   University of Novi Sad, Serbia
Gordan Jezic   University of Zagreb, Croatia
Jeroen Keppens   King's College London, UK
Matthias Klusch   DFKI, Germany
Ryszard Kowalczyk   Swinburne University of Technology, Australia
Mario Kusek   University of Zagreb, Croatia
Lea Kutvonen   University of Helsinki, Finland
Viorel Negru   West University of Timisoara, Romania
Paulo Novais   University of Minho, Portugal
Eugénio Oliveira   University of Porto, Portugal
Eva Onaindia   Universitat Politècnica de València, Spain
Sascha Ossowski   Rey Juan Carlos University, Spain
Marcin Paprzycki   IBSPAN, Polish Academy of Sciences, Poland
Axel Polleres   WU Vien, Austria
Miguel Rebollo   Universidad Politécnica de Valencia, Spain
Jordi Sabater Mir   IIIA-CSIC, Spain
Marco Schorlemmer   IIIA-CSIC, Spain
Michael Ignaz Schumacher   University of Applied Sciences Western Switzerland,
                             Switzerland
Carles Sierra   IIIA-CSIC, Spain
Francesca Toni   Imperial College London, UK

Denis Trcek   University of Ljubljana, Slovenia
László Zsolt Varga   Hungarian Academy of Sciences, Hungary
Antoine Zimmermann   ENS Mines Saint-Etienne, France

EUMAS 2015/AT 2015 Sponsors

European Coordinating Committee for Artificial Intelligence

University of Piraeus Research Center

Artificial Intelligence Journal

Abstracts of Invited Talks

Excerpts from the Study of Coalitions: From Social Behavior to Computer Science

Onn Shehory

IBM Research – Haifa, Israel

onn@il.ibm.com

From the very early days of human society, people have engaged in coalitions. Individuals in the context of others typically have to interact and collaborate to meet their goals. Collaboration can take place in diverse ways, and indeed various collaboration mechanisms have emerged across history. Science has attempted to study the collaborative phenomenon of coalescing. Philosophical and social studies were conducted first, followed by game theoretic and mathematical research. Computer science, and in particular the multi-agent systems discipline attempted to leverage the game theoretic coalitional solutions and relax them.

As asserted by *Aristotle* in *Politics*, *"people always act in order to obtain that which they think good"*, and *"every partnership is established with a view to some good"*. In other words, coalition formation is a natural human action that attempts to maximize some value. While that philosophical study is dated back to the 4th-century BC, modern science has begun studying coalitions only in the 20th century, with Game Theory and Social Science leading that research, and later on Computer Science and specifically Multi-agent Systems leveraging the theoretical foundations to generate practical coalition formation solutions.

The goal of the social science approach was to establish a coalition theory that describes, explains, and possibly predicts coalitional behavior. Researchers have examined coalition formation and dissolution in contexts where cooperation is necessary to maximize value. The focus was on observations based on which models and theories were developed. Social science research has included two main approaches. The first approach - *"office-seeking"* - focuses on coalition size. That is, coalitions that form are such that they are large enough to win, but not larger than that. This is well documented in *The theory of political coalitions*, Riker, 1962. The second approach - *"policy-seeking"* - attempts to minimize ideological heterogeneity within formed coalitions. This is well documented in *Coalition theories and cabinet formations*, De Swaan, 1973.

The assumption made by social scientists according to which actors behave rationally set the ground for game theoretic approaches. These, in turn, developed mathematical modeling of bargaining behaviors which were initially observed and reported in social science. Game theory has initially focused on normative aspects of coalitions and not on behavioral ones as commonly dome in social science. That is, it aimed to compute the actions players should perform to reach a desired outcome of a coalition formation process. While social science focused on experimentation and observation, initial studies in game theory suggested that *"lab experiments contribute noting to game theory*", as stated in *Games and Decisions, Luce & Raiffa*, 1957. However, Maschler challenges this viewpoint suggesting that normative aspects can benefit from lab experiments as documented in *"Playing an n-person game, an experiment"*, *Maschler*, 1965.

Computer science has attempted to rely on game theory as a basis for practical coalitions formation. While game theoretic solutions are elegant and stable, their computational complexity is hyper-exponential. Additionally, game theory rarely provides player algorithms to practice coalition formation, and solutions are sensitive to small changes. Hence, feasible algorithmic approaches were called for.

Indeed, multiple coalitional games have been considered to facilitate collaboration, and many mechanisms have been devised. Within such coalitions, software agents may jointly perform tasks that they would otherwise be unable to perform, or will perform poorly. To allow agent collaboration via coalitions, one should devise a coalition formation mechanism that exhibit desirable properties such as stability, fairness, optimality, and computational tractability. Agents that take part in those mechanisms should be provided with algorithms to guide their activity within. Yet, no solution can concurrently address all of these requirements. This problem intensifies when the number of agents increases. These issue have opened up a field of research that focuses on algorithmic coalition formation. The author of this paper has published multiple articles on such research, e.g. [1, 2]. These were discussed at EUMAS&AT 2015, Athens, Greece, in a keynote lecture delivered by the author.

In his lecture, the author has presented excerpts from coalitions' research from the early days of Aristotle to contemporary computer science. The lecture discussed agent attributes and mechanism properties and their effect on agent interaction. It presented some games that facilitate interaction as well as algorithms that implement feasible solutions to such games. It has finally presented coalition formation challenges in the context of social networks, big data and security risks.

Acknowledgement. We would like to thank ECCAI for supporting this EUMAS&AT 2015 keynote lecture.

References

1. Shehory, O., Kraus, S.: Methods for task allocation via agent coalition formation. Artif. Intell. J. **101**(1-2), 165–200 (1998)
2. Shehory, O., Kraus, S.: Feasible formation of coalitions among autonomous agents in non-super-additive environments, Comput. Intell. **15**(3), 218–251 (1999)

Probationary Contracts: Reducing Risk in Norm-Based Systems

Chris Haynes, Simon Miles and Michael Luck

Department of Informatics, King's College London, UK
christopher.haynes@kcl.ac.uk

Abstract. In human organisations, it is common to subject a new employees to periods of probation for which additional restrictions or oversight apply in order to reduce the consequences of poor recruitment choice. In a similar way, multiagent organisations may need to employ agents of unknown trustworthiness to perform services defined by contracts (or sets of norms), yet these agents may violate the norms for their own advantage. Here, the risk of employing such agents depends on the agents trustworthiness and the consequences of norm violation. In response, in this paper we propose the use of probationary contracts, generated by adding obligations to standard contracts in order to further constrain agent behaviour. We evaluate our work using agent-based simulations of abstract tasks, and present results showing that using probationary roles reduces the risk of using unknown agents, especially where violating a norm has serious consequences.

Contents

Invited Keynote

Probationary Contracts: Reducing Risk in Norm-Based Systems   3
   Chris Haynes, Simon Miles, and Michael Luck

Coordination and Planning

From Public Plans to Global Solutions in Multiagent Planning   21
   Jan Tožička, Jan Jakubův, and Antonín Komenda

Intelligent People Flow Coordination in Smart Spaces   34
   Marin Lujak and Sascha Ossowski

Customized Document Research by a Stigmergic Approach
Using Agents and Artifacts.   50
   Zina El Guedria and Laurent Vercouter

Collaborative Framework for Monitoring Reliability of Distributed
Components of Composed Services.   65
   Hisain Elshaafi, Steven Davy, and Dmitri Botvich

Graph Patterns, Reinforcement Learning and Models of Reputation
for Improving Coalition Formation in Collaborative Multi-agent Systems. . . .   74
   Predrag T. Tošić

Multiagent Model for Agile Context Inference Based on Articial Immune
Systems and Sparse Distributed Representations   82
   Radu-Casian Mihailescu, Paul Davidsson, and Jan Persson

Learning and Optimization

Factored MDPs for Optimal Prosumer Decision-Making in Continuous
State Spaces.   91
   Angelos Angelidakis and Georgios Chalkiadakis

Composing Swarm Robot Formations Based on Their Distributions
Using Mobile Agents.   108
   Ryotaro Oikawa, Munehiro Takimoto, and Yasushi Kambayashi

Group-Based Pricing to Shape Demand in Real-Time Electricity Markets. . . .   121
   *Rahul Agrawal, Anirban Chakraborti, Karamjit Singh, Gautam Shroff,
and Venkatesh Sarangan*

Human Rating Methods on Multi-agent Systems.   129
   Chairi Kiourt, Dimitris Kalles, and George Pavlidis

Learning in Multi Agent Social Environments with Opponent Models   137
   Chairi Kiourt and Dimitris Kalles

A Particle Swarm Optimization Metaheuristic for the Blocking Flow Shop
Scheduling Problem: Total Tardiness Minimization   145
   Nouri Nouha and Ladhari Talel

Argumentation and Negotiation

Towards an Agent-Based Negotiation Scheme for Scheduling Electric
Vehicles Charging.   157
   *Andreas Seitaridis, Emmanouil S. Rigas, Nick Bassiliades,
   and Sarvapali D. Ramchurn*

Agreement Technologies Applied to Transmission Towers Maintenance.   172
   *Pablo Chamoso, Fernando De la Prieta,
   Juan Francisco De Paz Santana, Javier Bajo Pérez,
   and Ignacio Belacortu Arandia*

TugaTAC Broker: A Fuzzy Logic Adaptive Reasoning Agent
for Energy Trading   188
   *Thiago R.P.M. Rúbio, Jonas Queiroz, Henrique Lopes Cardoso,
   Ana Paula Rocha, and Eugénio Oliveira*

A Dialectical Approach to Enable Decision Making in Online Trading   203
   Wei Bai, Emmanuel Tadjouddine, and Terry Payne

What Should an Agent Know Not to Fail in Persuasion?   219
   Shizuka Yokohama and Kazuko Takahashi

Argumentation-Based Hybrid Recommender System
for Recommending Learning Objects.   234
   *Paula Rodríguez, Stella Heras, Javier Palanca, Néstor Duque,
   and Vicente Julián*

How to Share Knowledge by Gossiping.   249
   Andreas Herzig and Faustine Maffre

Norms, Trust, and Reputation

Identifying Malicious Behavior in Multi-party Bipolar Argumentation
Debates   267
   Dionysios Kontarinis and Francesca Toni

Probabilistic Argumentation, a Small Step for Uncertainty, a Giant Step
for Complexity   279
    Xin Sun and Beishui Liao

Modeling Social Deviance in Artificial Agent Societies   287
    J. Octavio Gutierrez-Garcia and Emmanuel Lopez-Neri

Modeling and Enforcing Semantic Obligations for Access Control   303
    Fabio Marfia, Nicoletta Fornara, and Truc-Vien T. Nguyen

Coupling Regulative and Constitutive Dimensions in Situated
Artificial Institutions   318
    Maiquel de Brito, Jomi Fred Hübner, and Olivier Boissier

Trust-Based Multiagent Credit Assignment (TMCA)   335
    Samira Nazari and Mohammad Ebrahim Shiri

Information Sources About Hydrogeological Disasters: The Role of Trust . . .   350
    Rino Falcone, Alessandro Sapienza, and Cristiano Castelfranchi

Trust, Negotiations and Virtual Currencies for a Sharing Economy   363
    Dave de Jonge and Carles Sierra

Logic and Games for Ethical Agents in Normative Multi-agent Systems   367
    Xin Sun and Livio Robaldo

Agent-Based Simulation and Agent Programming

Human-in-the-Loop Simulation of a Virtual Classroom   379
    Jesper Nilsson and Franziska Klügl

Applying Agent Based Simulation to the Design of Traffic Control Systems
with Respect to Real-World Urban Complexity   395
    Andreea Ion, Cristian Berceanu, and Monica Patrascu

Towards Smart Open Dynamic Fleets   410
    Holger Billhardt, Alberto Fernández, Marin Lujak, Sascha Ossowski,
    Vicente Julián, Juan F. De Paz, and Josefa Z. Hernández

A Concurrent Architecture for Agent Reasoning Cycle Execution in Jason . . .   425
    Maicon R. Zatelli, Alessandro Ricci, and Jomi F. Hübner

Hardware Architecture Benchmarking for Simulation of Human Immune
System by Multi-agent Systems   441
    Fábio Rodrigues Martins, Alcione de Paiva Oliveira,
    Ricardo Santos Ferreira, and Fábio Ribeiro Cerqueira

Automating Personalized Learning Through Motivation   449
  Patricia Gutierrez, Nardine Osman, and Carles Sierra

Agent Based Simulation to Evaluate Adaptive Caching in Distributed
Databases   455
  Santhilata Kuppili Venkata, Jeroen Keppens, and Katarzyna Musial

Analysing Incentive Strategies to Promote Participation
in Crowdsourcing Systems   463
  E. del Val, G. Martínez-Cánovas, V. Botti, and P. Hernández

Author Index   473

Invited Keynote

Probationary Contracts: Reducing Risk in Norm-Based Systems

Chris Haynes, Simon Miles, and Michael Luck$^{(\boxtimes)}$

Department of Informatics, King's College London, London, UK
{christopher.haynes,Michael.Luck}@kcl.ac.uk

Abstract. In human organisations, it is common to subject a new employees to periods of probation for which additional restrictions or oversight apply in order to reduce the consequences of poor recruitment choice. In a similar way, multi-agent organisations may need to employ agents of unknown trustworthiness to perform services defined by contracts (or sets of norms), yet these agents may violate the norms for their own advantage. Here, the risk of employing such agents depends on the agents trustworthiness and the consequences of norm violation. In response, in this paper we propose the use of probationary contracts, generated by adding obligations to standard contracts in order to further constrain agent behaviour. We evaluate our work using agent-based simulations of abstract tasks, and present results showing that using probationary roles reduces the risk of using unknown agents, especially where violating a norm has serious consequences.

1 Introduction

In recent years, advances in hardware and software have held out the promise of very large scale networks of devices that interact in order to solve distributed problems as envisaged in the related paradigms of the Internet of Things, Ambient Intelligence or Ubiquitous Computing [2]. If these devices, or *agents*, are autonomous with respect to the network and to each other, then they can be flexible and creative in their problem solving. However, such autonomy can lead to problems with coordination, and asocial behaviour, as agents may prioritise their own needs and goals at the expense of others and even the system itself. Yet in these paradigms, it is desirable that agents work together without conflict, do not obstruct others, use only their fair share of resources, and respect privacy where appropriate, in a fashion analogous to the concept of being a *good citizen* in human societies. The question therefore arise as to how to control the behaviour of such autonomous agents and ensure that they are good citizens within the vast, open networks in which they reside.

One approach that has witnessed a growing interest in recent years is the use of *norms* to regulate and coordinate agent behaviour. Norms specify the actions that an agent may, should or should not undertake, and the states of affairs that an agent may, should or should not allow to occur. They impart obligations to agents, or specify what is permitted or prohibited within a system.

© Springer International Publishing Switzerland 2016
M. Rovatsos et al. (Eds.): EUMAS 2015/AT 2015, LNAI 9571, pp. 3–18, 2016.
DOI: 10.1007/978-3-319-33509-4_1

In this context, there are two approaches to controlling the behaviour of agents: *regulation* and *enforcement*. In a regulation approach, such as that embodied by *electronic institutions* [11], the system itself imposes constraints on what an agent can do, but this severely restricts autonomy, and thus reduces system flexibility. In contrast, an enforcement approach specifies what an agent ought to do (or not do) and relies on *enforcement* of the rules so that violators are punished. This allows agents to retain their autonomy, but it also requires an enforcement mechanism to monitor agent behaviour for norm violations in order to motivate agent compliance.

Of course, in this latter enforcement approach, agents must be informed of the applicable norms, so that they can comply with them, and one way of doing this is through formalising norms as *contracts* and ensuring that agents are aware of them. Then, activity within a system can be made contingent on agreeing to a contract, in the same way that using a service can require agreeing to a set of terms and conditions. As suggested by Modgil et al. [16], a *contract* is a set of *clauses* describing the normative behaviour expected of given agents, the *contract parties*, where a contract clause specifies an obligation, prohibition or permission. Unlike *social norms*, which are usually informal and often hard even for adherents to articulate, contracts are formal expressions of expectations that explicitly detail what behaviour is expected, by whom, and under what circumstances. The penalties for breaking a contract are also usually explicit, either within the contract itself, or in the body of regulations that govern contracts in general. Contract parties can thus determine the actions they must perform, and others can clarify what constitutes a violation.

Yet, just as in human societies, in this approach computational autonomous agents may choose to violate norms even after agreeing to comply with a contract specifying them. Such non-compliance can be a risk to the system or organisation in which these agents operate, the extent of the risk depending on the likelihood of an agent failing to perform its assigned task and the consequence of such a failure. While agents can be monitored and norm violations may be detected, this detection may not prevent the consequences of the norm violation; for example, if the violation is due to an atomic action that can only be detected once it has been performed then monitoring cannot prevent the consequences of the violation.

In response, in this paper we address the risk involved in non-compliance with norms and contracts by proposing our the use of *probationary contracts* to reduce the consequences of uncertain trust in normative multi-agent systems.

The remainder of the paper is organised as follows. First, we discuss organisations and roles as the basis for considering probationary contracts to mitigate risk. Then, we detail our concept of probationary contracts in terms of tasks and task graphs, and how these probationary contracts may be created from standard contracts via the addition of sub-goal obligations. Finally, we consider a somewhat abstract scenario to evaluate the use of these probationary contracts using simulated random tasks, before reviewing related literature and concluding.

2   Organisations, Risk and Probationary Contracts

We can consider any multi-agent system or, more generally, any system in which multiple entities interact in support of some broader overall goal or objective, to be an *organisation*. Within organisations, these entities or agents play particular *roles*, or units of functionality, each of which has a set of responsibilities and tasks to perform. If roles have been correctly devised then, when these tasks are performed successfully, the organisational goals are achieved. It is thus agents playing roles that bring the rewards associated with organisational goals. In other words, roles allow agents to contribute to organisational performance. For example, the OperA organisation modelling language [9] defines a role in terms of its goals (which may include sub-goals) and norms (both obligations and permissions).[1] Similarly, in the MOISE+ model roles are defined in terms of missions (plans to reach specific goals) and norms (obligations to perform missions) [12]. Both models also describe the communication and authority links between roles.

Now, if a role imposes an obligation to perform one or more *tasks*, each of which has a goal state, then each task can also be specified as a contract that explicitly details the norms applicable to the agents performing the task. A role is thus sensibly represented as a set of contracts in which it participates. In this context, employing unknown agents of uncertain motivations in an organisation has an inherent risk: they may put their own desires above that of the organisation and violate the norms specified in their contract. Trust and reputation mechanisms can increase the likelihood that an organisation will select a trustworthy (and competent) agent, but such mechanisms are frequently uncertain due to lack of sufficient information about a candidate [18,20]. If tasks need to be performed, then organisations may need to take a chance on possibly untrustworthy agents, increasing the risk of failure. While agents can be monitored and norm violations detected, this may not prevent the *consequences* of norm violation, either due to the nature of the violation (which may occur too quickly to prevent) or the monitoring (which may only detect a violation after the consequences are apparent).

In contrast, human organisations have developed mechanisms to mitigate against this, and it is common for new recruits to be subject to additional restrictions for a probationary period in order to reduce the consequences of a poor recruitment choice. To mitigate the risk of employing possibly untrustworthy agents, therefore, we propose the computational analogue of this approach through the use of *probationary contracts*, which are special contracts with additional obligations. In this view, a probationary contract has the same goal as a standard contract, but the additional obligations restrict the way in which the task should be performed, so that an agent bound by it has less autonomy in the way it carries out the task. For example, in the case of the design and manufacture of a 100 widgets, a standard contract might specify the desired properties of the widgets, such as cost and functionality, and the deadline for delivery, on the

---

[1] In OperA a role's goals are termed *objectives* and permissions are termed *rights*.

basis that a trustworthy agent will design and build the widgets to specification. However, when dealing with possibly untrustworthy agents, it may be desirable to create additional obligations: allowing the design to be examined for approval before manufacturing begins, or the delivery of a prototype widget for similar approval. These additional obligations restrict the contracted agent, but reduce the consequences of employing an untrustworthy agent since any contract violations will be detected earlier (before the delivery of 100 defective widgets) or prevented entirely. Such additional obligations must be monitored for compliance (like any other norm), and this may add to the cost of employing an agent in the role, and so reduce the eventual reward to the organisation.

To elaborate probationary contracts, we first need to consider roles, agents and risk further. First, we must introduce the concept, for each role, of an *ideal agent*, which is one that will fulfil a contract to the best of its ability and not pursue personal goals that conflict with organisational ones; that is, it is not tempted to violate norms in order to gain personal benefit. This benevolence does not prevent an agent from violating norms in order to achieve organisational goals in the face of unexpected events—indeed, the possibility of such violation gives norms their flexibility. An ideal agent may not actually exist in reality, but an organisation will seek to fill each role with an agent as close to ideal as possible.

In this context, we can define the *risk* of failure as the probability of a loss occurring due to a specified risk factor (where each risk factor can be understood as a distinct source of risk) multiplied by the consequence of that loss[2]: $risk = p \times c$. For example, the risk involved in betting \$6 on the toss of a fair coin is \$3 ($0.5 \times \$6$), while the risk of betting that a fair six-sided die will land on a one, is \$5 ($0.833 \times \$6$). So we can say that betting on the die is *riskier* than betting on the coin.

More specifically in our case, there is a possibility of a loss due to an agent failing to comply with norms specified in a contract, due to incompetence or selfishness. The consequences of this potential loss may even exceed the possible rewards from simply performing the task correctly, since an incompetent or selfish agent performing a role may be worse than leaving the role empty. For example, in the case of a delivery firm, an incompetent driver may get lost or crash a truck, while a selfish driver may take excessive breaks or steal a truck. These norm violations have an effect on organisational performance according to the nature of the violation.

Quantifying the consequences of a norm violation for an organisation may not be straightforward. In a situation with explicit costs, such as an industrial process, it may be possible to calculate it directly; for example, if the consequence of a norm violation is the shut-down of a production line for an hour, then the cost can be calculated. Otherwise, it may be possible to evaluate the norms via observation of their effect on the quality of agent interactions [17]. However, even if this is impossible, it may be possible to estimate it using simulation techniques [13] or, if the norm has been developed using an evolutionary approach [3], then its fitness value may be a reasonable estimate.

---

[2] This definition is common in the literature, for example [10].

The risk of allowing a non-ideal agent to play a role is therefore related to the probability of that agent violating one or more of the contractual norms and the consequences of the violation. The problem for an organisation is that while the consequences may be known, the probability is not. In the next section, we present the notion of task risk in order to quantify the level of risk involved in allowing an agent of uncertain trust to perform a role, and discuss how using probationary contracts can reduce this risk.

3   Tasks and Task Risk

3.1   Task Graphs, Risk and Reward

The tasks that agents must perform can be represented as directed graphs, with the nodes representing states and the edges transitions between those states. Figure 1 shows a simple task represented in this way: the initial state is S_0, the task is completed in state S_8, and state S_4 is prohibited by a norm.

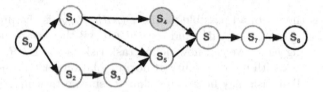

Fig. 1. A state graph for a task.

Such graphs can be constructed using Hierarchical Task Analysis [19], where tasks are decomposed into a series of steps. The granularity of the decomposition can be determined by the needs of the organisation and the nature of the task, so long as decision points where an agent would have a choice of actions are captured, and the prohibited states identified. Representing the task as a graph facilitates the estimation of the risk of allowing an agent of unknown motivation to perform it as we will see below. The purpose of this is two-fold: first, it enables an organisation to assess the risk of allowing an agent of uncertain trustworthiness to perform a task; second, it allows two tasks to be compared with respect to their risk, and so the relative risk of possible probationary contracts can be assessed.

Now, to capture the risk inherent in any particular agent not complying with a norm, without detailing the underlying mechanisms, we use a simple property (with a value from 0 to 1 inclusive), P_{viol}, that determines the probability of it violating the contract norms. An agent thus begins in the initial state and moves through the task graph towards the goal state. When it reaches the goal, and completes the task, the agent generates a reward for the organisation. This reward is reduced if norms are violated: the exact amount of the reduction depends on the consequences of the norm violation.

The *task risk* varies according to the topology, the position of the prohibited states in the graph, the consequences of entering those prohibited states, and also the agent behaviour as it traverses the task graph. For example, if by traversing the task graph an agent has a low probability of being placed in a position where it is tempted to violate a norm, then the inherent risk is low, regardless of P_{viol}. If the only path to the goal is filled with temptation, even an agent with a low P_{viol} value may eventually succumb due to the number of times it must resist. We can also specify an *expected performance reward* (EPR) of each task based on the probability of an agent traversing each path and the reward gained from that path. The expected performance from a single path through the graph is calculated by multiplying the probability of selecting that path by the reward generated by that path. The EPR for a task is then the sum of all the possible expected performances for a given P_{viol}, and we sum across the possible values of P_{viol} and normalise by dividing by the maximum possible reward:

$$EPR = \frac{\int_{P_{viol}=0}^{1} \left(\sum_{path \in Paths} P(path, P_{viol}) \times reward(path) \right) dP_{viol}}{\sum_{path \in Paths} P(path, 0) \times reward(path)}$$

where $Paths$ is the set of all possible paths, $P(path, P_{viol})$ is the probability of an agent with P_{viol} traversing $path$, and $reward(path)$ is the reward generated by an agent traversing $path$. We can now define task risk as $1 - EPR$. A task risk of 0 indicates a task with no probability of norm violation (or no consequence of such violation). Task risk may be greater than 1, since a task may have norms with severe consequences.

3.2 An Illustrative Example

To illustrate our notion of task risk, consider the task graph in Fig. 1. Now, suppose that completion of the task generates a reward to the organisation of 100, but S_4 is a prohibited state and a path that traverses through S_4 only yields a reward of 50. Note that these rewards are for the organisation, not the agent, with P_{viol} encapsulating this reward to the agent. The agents employed to perform the task are simple ones, and each has the following behaviour. An agent will always travel along a compliant path toward the final goal unless there is an opportunity to violate a prohibition norm, in which case it will violate the norm (and travel to the prohibited node) with a probability determined by its P_{viol} value. If there are multiple compliant ongoing paths (and it is not violating a norm) it chooses one at random. It is opportunistic in nature and may violate norms for its own benefit if the opportunity arises, but will not actively seek out the prohibited state. So, even a very selfish agent may decide to go to S_2, even though it makes it impossible to reach S_4. In total, there are three paths through the graph, shown in Table 1, with the reward gained for following them and the probability in terms of the agent's P_{viol} value. The first path, p_1, traverses S_4, and the probability of traversing that path is 0.5 (from the first random choice between S_1 and S_2) multiplied by P_{viol} from traversing the link to S_4 with no further choices.

Table 1. Paths for task represented in Fig. 1

Path	Nodes	Reward	Probability
p_1	$S_0, S_1, S_4, S_6, S_7, S_8$	50	$0.5 \times P_{viol}$
p_2	$S_0, S_1, S_5, S_6, S_7, S_8$	100	$0.5 \times (1 - P_{viol})$
p_3	$S_0, S_2, S_3, S_5, S_6, S_7, S_8$	100	0.5

We can calculate the expected reward:

$$ER(P_{viol}) = (100 \times 0.5) + (100 \times 0.5 \times (1 - P_{viol})) + (50 \times (0.5 \times P_{viol}))$$

and simplify it to $ER(P_{viol}) = 100 - 25 \times P_{viol}$. From this we can calculate the definite integral with respect to P_{viol} from 0 to 1 and normalise to obtain the value of EPR = 0.875, giving a task risk of 0.125. If entering the prohibited state rendered the task worthless (reward = 0) then the task risk would be 0.25. If it harmed the organisation further (reward = −100), then the task risk would be 0.5.

3.3 Probationary Contracts via Sub-goal Obligations

In light of the discussion on tasks and task risk, here we explicate the concept of probationary contracts, special contracts that include extra conditions or norms to restrict the behaviour of an agent performing the probationary role that commits to the contract. To do this, we simply insert an additional sub-goal (or intermediate goal state) that must be achieved during a task in order to restrict a choice between paths, such as that between S_1 and S_2 in Fig. 1, where we want the agent to avoid the path that traverses S_4 (and hence S_1). In this way, a sub-goal can act as an adjunct to existing norms to make their violation impossible or less likely (unless the sub-goal obligation is itself violated).

As we have seen, Fig. 1 shows a task expressed in a directed acyclic graph (DAG), with the nodes representing environment states and the edges representing transitions caused by agent actions. An agent begins in state S_0, and the task contract requires achieving the goal of reaching S_8 (which we could also consider as a norm), while complying with the prohibition against bringing about state S_4. These should ensure that an ideal agent will choose a path to S_8 that does not pass through S_4. However, for selfish reasons a non-ideal agent may choose to violate the norm and bring about S_4. While the violation may be detected, there will still be a reduction to organisational performance and under certain circumstances this may be severe (for example, where violation causes loss of resources or damage to the system). To reduce the risk of reaching S_4, a sub-goal obligation to reach S_2 can be added. Of course, this can still be violated by an agent with a high P_{viol} value, but it would be noticed earlier and would not damage organisational performance. If monitoring is effective, the organisation could remove the agent from the role before reaching S_4 and before the damage.

Now, using our task risk analysis, it is possible for an organisation to calculate the risk of a proposed probationary contract. One approach to determining what kind of probationary contract to use (or where to add a sub-goal obligation) is thus to iterate through the possible states in the graph adding a sub-goal obligation as above, calculate the risk for each contract and choose the lowest. This distinguishes between different probationary contracts corresponding to different probationary roles. However, the probationary contract with the lowest risk may not be the best choice, because while an organisation may wish to reduce risk, it must also distinguish between trustworthy and untrustworthy agents by means of observing their performance in probationary roles. Here, if a probationary contract removes too much risk, then performance of agents is hard to distinguish.

Indeed, by constraining agent behaviour with an additional sub-goal obligation, perfectly trustworthy agents may be rejected because of their range of capability. For example, the standard role for the task in Fig. 1 allows two ways to perform a task, but if an agent is only capable of performing it via S_1, then it will not be able to fulfil a probationary contract that obliges S_2. Therefore, an organisation must be mindful of the capabilities of the candidate agents when it selects a probationary contract.

4   Evaluation

4.1   An Evaluation Scenario

Consider an abstract organisation that requires external agents to perform services and uses a *gatekeeper* to allocate these service provider roles. Each role has a single task (specified by a single contract), and the organisation has norms targeting these roles in order to improve organisational performance. For clarity, we consider only the case in which an organisation seeks to reduce the risk of an agent violating a norm to save effort or otherwise increase its personal reward at the expense of organisational performance.

In our evaluation, we assume we have a pool of 400 agents, which are homogenous except for their P_{viol} value which is chosen from a uniform random distribution from 0 to 1, $P_{viol} \in \mathbb{R} | 0 \leq P_{viol} \leq 1$. To ensure some dynamism, every 100 units of time, each idle agent is removed from the pool with probability 0.002, so it is likely that there will always be unknown agents in the pool. Now, our example organisation requires 40 agents at any one time to fill roles and perform tasks. When it has a vacancy, the organisation's gatekeeper chooses an agent from the pool at random and assesses it using a simple trust mechanism based on previous interactions to decide whether to allow an agent to play the role. After an agent completes a task, an interaction value, iv, is generated, where $iv = \frac{perceived\ performance}{possible\ performance}$. Possible performance is the maximum performance accrued from a job completed with no violations, and perceived performance is calculated by reducing the possible performance by the impact of detected norm violations (undetected violations do not count against an agent). The interaction value has a maximum value of 1.0, but the minimum is open-ended, since violating norms may result in organisational performance being reduced sufficiently to result in a negative value. The trust value is calculated as the mean of the interaction values. For an agent a the trust value is

$$trust_a = \frac{1}{|I_a|} \sum_{iv_i \in I_a} iv_i$$

where I_a is the set of previous interactions for agent a, and iv_i is one of the inter-actions in that set. The gatekeeper uses two trust thresholds: accept, τ_{accept}, and reject, τ_{reject}. If $trust_a \geq \tau_{accept}$ then the agent is accepted for a standard role, and if $trust_a < \tau_{reject}$ it is rejected outright. Otherwise, the agent is accepted for a probationary role. If an agent is rejected for a role, another agent is selected from the pool for assessment. We use $\tau_{accept} = \tau_{reject} = 0.9$ when not using pro-bationary roles, and $\tau_{accept} = 0.9, \tau_{reject} = 0.8$ when using probationary roles. An unknown agent is accepted for the standard role when not using probationary roles, otherwise it is accepted for a probationary role.

Both probationary and standard tasks are represented by graphs as previ-ously described. Some state nodes are prohibited by norms, and each norm has an associated impact value denoting the reduction in performance that accrues if an agent violates it and enters the state. While violations harm organisational performance, they benefit individuals, so an agent could violate a norm in line with its P_{viol} value. The organisation monitors agent activity, with violations being detected with a probability of 0.8.

As we have seen, probationary contracts are based on standard contracts, but with additional sub-goal obligations that are monitored (like prohibition violations); if an agent enters a state from which a sub-goal state is unreachable without having first achieved the sub-goal, then it is deemed to be in violation. We assume that the organisation can always detect if a sub-goal is achieved, since an agent has no incentive to conceal this and, indeed, a strong incentive to make it apparent. To represent the additional monitoring effort, the reward generated by a probationary contract is 80 % that of a standard contract. In our experiments, we generated probationary contracts using a brute force approach: each possible probationary contract was tried for each standard contract in the evaluation, and the best performing one was used.

As a consequence of the agent behaviour described previously and formalised as Algorithm 1, an agent will not leave a compliant path no matter how selfish it is, unless given the choice to immediately violate a prohibition norm. For example, in Fig. 1 with a sub-goal of S_2, no agent will ever go to S_1. We base this behaviour on the assumption that an agent only benefits from violating the prohibition norms, not from missing sub-goals, and that it is opportunistic in nature—it may violate norms for its own benefit if the opportunity arises but will not actively seek out prohibited states.

When an agent reaches the goal, the organisational performance is increased by the contract's reward value minus the effect of any norm violations, and the gatekeeper updates the agent's trust value based on the perceived performance of the agent (as described above). The agent then re-applies for the role, and is re-assessed by the gatekeeper. Agents only leave if their trust value becomes too low for the organisation to accept them in the role. If the agent leaves, the organisation seeks another agent from the pool at random to fill the vacant role.

Algorithm 1. Agent control algorithm used to select next node

---

Require: Set of remaining goal states, G
Require: Set of prohibited states, P
Require: Agent's P_{viol} value
  1: Get set of successor states, SN
  2: Get empty set of successor prohibited states, SP
  3: Get empty set of successor goal states, SG
  4: Get empty set of successor compliant states, SC
  5: **for all** $node$ in SN **do**
  6:    **if** $node \in P$ **then**
  7:       Add $node$ to SP
  8:    **else if** $node \in G$ **then**
  9:       Add $node$ to SG
 10:    **else if** $reachable(node, G)$ **then**
 11:       Add $node$ to SC
 12:    **end if**
 13: **end for**
 14: **if** $Rnd(0,1) < P_{viol}$ AND $SP \neq \emptyset$ **then**
 15:    $NextNode = pickRnd(SP)$
 16: **else if** $SG \neq$ **then**
 17:    $NextNode = pickRnd(SG)$
 18: **else**
 19:    $NextNode = pickRnd(SC)$
 20: **end if**

In our evaluation, we measure the success of the method by examining the overall performance of the organisation using probationary roles compared to not using probationary roles. In order to evaluate the effectiveness of our technique, we randomly generated task graphs using the JGraphT Java library[3]. Each task graph is a DAG with 25 nodes representing states (including initial and goal states) and norms that prohibit five states. Reaching the final goal state gives a reward of 100, entering any of four of the prohibited states reduce this reward by 20, and entering one of them reduces the reward by 120 (to represent a serious situation to be especially avoided). Therefore, the maximum reward per task is 100, and the minimum is -100 if all prohibited states are entered *en route* to the final goal. The prohibited states are randomly chosen; if necessary, edges are added to ensure that there is always a compliant path from the initial state to the goal. Figure 2 shows the graph for an example task, where the initial state is node 0 and the goal state is node 24. The task risk for this example can be determined to be 0.505, using the $1 - EPR$ formula specified earlier.

4.2   Experimental Results

In this section, we present our evaluation of the probationary contract method. For each random role, the performance is calculated for each possible sub-goal

---

[3] http://jgrapht.org/.

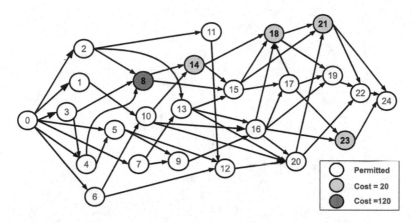

Fig. 2. State graph for an example task. There are 25 nodes, 5 of which represent prohibited states.

node, and the best was used for the evaluation. We examine the results for 700 random tasks, each with 25 nodes, to get a generalised picture of how the method affects performance and then we examine selected individual roles to obtain a more detailed view. Each experiment was run for 10000 time units.

Figure 3 shows the results. The points show the average ratio of the performance when using the probationary contract method to the performance when not using one, with results binned in a bin width of 0.1 risk. A value greater than 1.0 indicates that there is some benefit, and a value less than 1 indicates that use of a probationary contract reduces performance. Error bars show the standard deviation. The response of individual roles is quite variable, but there is a trend for probationary contract to become more useful as the task risk increases. While some low risk roles benefit from the approach, most do not, while the reverse is true for higher risk roles.

In order to examine the probationary method more closely, we examined a single representative role (but omit the task graph for reasons of space). Figure 4 shows the expected performance of the standard and probationary contracts for agents of varying P_{viol}. The standard contract is a high risk one, since even an agent with $P_{viol} = 0.4$ will, on average, contribute nothing to organisational performance. In contrast, the probationary contract has a much lower risk—even an agent with $P_{viol} = 1$ will contribute on average over 40 % of the performance of an ideal agent.

Figure 5 shows the performance ratio of the probationary contract method over time. When all agents are unknown, using probationary contracts is very useful, since an organisation allowing unknown agents to work in a standard contract suffers performance losses from violated norms. Over time, the benefit of using probationary contracts is reduced since the organisation builds up enough information about each agent and retains those agents that have proven to be trustworthy. However, using probationary contracts continues to have some benefit, albeit a less dramatic one.

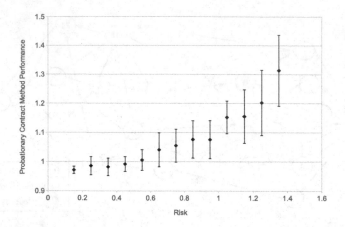

Fig. 3. Probationary method performance versus task risk.

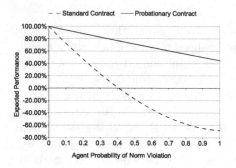

Fig. 4. Expected performance of standard and probationary contracts.

Fig. 5. Performance ratio over time.

Finally, Fig. 6 shows the average selfishness of the agents working under the standard contract. Recall that the organisation does not know the value of P_{viol}, and can only assess it based on interactions. This graph, therefore, allows us to examine how successfully the gatekeeper mechanism assesses the agents. While, over time, the average P_{viol} value of the workers is reduced for both methods as the organisation learns which agents are trustworthy, probationary contracts enable more selfish agents to be rejected before they are offered a standard contract.

5   Related Work and Conclusions

While we have focussed in this paper on the issues surrounding questions of risk and a means to address them through probationary contracts, there are broader questions to be answered in relation to establishing effective interaction in open systems of the kind we are increasingly starting to see. Norms can provide one way to give some degree of confidence in these interactions but, just as in human societies, the results of using them cannot be guaranteed. In these conclusions, we cover first a consideration of risk and how to manage it through trust, second an examination of emergent contracts or norms, which may become increasingly important in the new open world of thousands (if not millions) of interacting devices, and finally a summary of the key points of our work.

5.1 Mitigating Risk

Since risk arises from the probability of a risk factor and its consequences, risk mitigation can involve reducing either the probability or the consequences. Research here has concentrated on reducing the probability of recruiting an unsuitable agent.

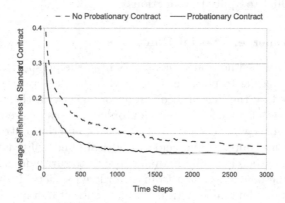

Fig. 6. Average selfishness of agents working under a standard contract.

There has been a great deal of work on computational trust and reputation systems (Sabater and Sierra provide a good review [18]). Such systems can be used to assess the suitability of a candidate agent either by direct interaction, or by gathering information from other agents. While trust systems can be very useful, they suffer from a bootstrapping problem; reputation systems allow the experience of other agents (referees) to contribute to the assessment, but these too require knowledge of previous interactions and also introduce the problem of whether to trust the referees.

As an alternative, a multi-agent organisation may use *gatekeeping* mechanisms to assess an agent's suitability for a role. Alderwereld et al. propose the use of a gatekeeper agent to match an agent's professed capabilities to the needs of a role within the OperA organisational modelling language [1]. They suggest using trust and reputation in order to judge whether an agent has the capability it is claiming, and monitoring to verify the claims. Stereotyping has been suggested as a means to swiftly bootstrap trust, by comparing the external characteristics of unknown agents to those of known agents in order to gauge their trustworthiness [5], but this depends on the existence of characteristics that correlate to capability and benevolence.

Monitoring and verification may allow an organisation to detect poorly performing, or selfish, agents. Modgil et al. propose a framework for monitoring norm compliance [16]. Such a system may allow an unsuitable agent to be identified, but this may only detect the consequences of failure rather than reduce those initial consequences. The use of reputational incentives have also been proposed [4], both positive (to encourage agents to be benevolent), and negative (to discourage agents tempted to violate norms), as part of an overall system of control. Along with more concrete incentives for success and penalties for failure, these could form part of a role specification as an explicit contract [15] that an agent agrees to comply with as a condition of accepting a role within an organisation. However, these reputational incentives rely upon the agent caring about its wider reputation, and sanctions for poor performance rely on the organisation's ability to apply the sanctions.

5.2   Towards Emergent Social Contracts

So far, we have discussed normative contracts from the perspective of an organisation employing agents to perform a task, with the expectation that the contracts are designed by the organisation in accordance with their requirements. However, norms are also useful in complex open systems where agents seek to pursue their own goals while coexisting with others, and the contract model may also be useful in this context. The field of political philosophy uses the concept of a *social contract*, whereby an individual consents to surrender some autonomy in exchange for the benefits gained from an ordered society. Leaving aside the philosophical issues in human societies, a social contract in a multi-agent system could be a concrete set of norms to which agents explicitly agree.

Generating the social contract itself is a challenge due to the conflicting goals of the agents and the complexity of the possible interactions. One option is to observe the agent society to determine behaviour that is beneficial and to promote that via explicit norms, while discouraging behaviour that is not. In this way, norms can be allowed to *emerge* in society in response to agent interactions, with each other and with the system environment. For example, Mahmoud et al. [14] have considered mechanisms for establishing emergent norms in distributed computational systems. The detection and evaluation of these emergent norms [6,7], their formalisation into social contracts [8], and the monitoring and enforcement of those contracts [16] represent a challenge, but each of these issues has separately been the subject of a research effort, and it seems likely that bringing these threads together could yield benefits in the future.

5.3   Conclusions

In this paper, we have presented our concept of probationary contracts in agent systems, where an organisation adds obligations in order to reduce the consequences of recruiting untrustworthy agents. By representing tasks as graphs, we have introduced the notion of a quantified task risk, which allows an organisation to assess the relative risks of a particular role and to compare these risks. We have evaluated the use of probationary contracts using randomly generated abstract tasks and shown that they can be effective where the task risks are high. Our work is limited in a number of respects. First, our probationary contracts use only a single additional sub-goal; second, we do not provide an automatic way to generate a probationary contract; third, we assume that the agents are opportunistic and rather simple in behaviour. It seems likely that a more sophisticated approach with multiple sub-goals would render probationary roles more useful. Also, a mechanism to balance the need to reduce risk against the necessity to detect untrustworthy agents is required.

Acknowledgements. This paper is based on work supported by the UK's Engineering and Physical Sciences Research Council (EPSRC) and the US Air Force Office of Scientific Research, Air Force Materiel Command, USAF under Award No. FA9550-15-1-0092. We also thank ECCAI for supporting the keynote talk, by the last author, on which this paper is based.

References

1. Aldewereld, H., Dignum, V., Jonker, C.M., van Riemsdijk, M.B.: Agreeing on role adoption in open organisations. Künstl. Intell. **26**(1), 37–45 (2012)
2. Atzori, L., Iera, A., Morabito, G.: The Internet of Things: a survey. Comput. Netw. **54**(15), 2787–2805 (2010)
3. Bou, E., López-Sánchez, M., Rodríguez-Aguilar, J.-A.: Towards self-configuration in autonomic electronic institutions. In: Noriega, P., Vázquez-Salceda, J., Boella, G., Boissier, O., Dignum, V., Fornara, N., Matson, E. (eds.) COIN 2006. LNCS (LNAI), vol. 4386, pp. 229–244. Springer, Heidelberg (2007)
4. Burnett, C.: Trust assessment and decision-making in dynamic multi-agent systems. Ph.D. thesis, University of Aberdeen (2011)
5. Burnett, C., Norman, T.J., Sycara, K.: Bootstrapping trust evaluations through stereotypes. In: Proceedings of the 9th International Conference on Autonomous Agents and Multiagent Systems, pp. 241–248 (2010)
6. Chen, C.-C., Nagl, S.B., Clack, C.D.: A formalism for multi-level emergent behaviours in designed component-based systems and agent-based simulations. In: Aziz-Alaoui, M.A., Bertelle, C. (eds.) From System Complexity to Emergent Properties. UCS, vol. 1, pp. 101–114. Springer, Heidelberg (2009)
7. Cranefield, S., Savarimuthu, B., Meneguzzi, F., Oren, N.: A Bayesian approach to norm identification. In: Proceedings of the 14th International Conference on Autonomous Agents and Multiagent Systems, pp. 1743–1744 (2015)
8. Dellarocas, C., Klein, M.: Contractual agent societies. In: Conte, R., Dellarocas, C. (eds.) Social Order in Multiagent Systems. Multiagent Systems, Artificial Societies, and Simulated Organizations, vol. 2, pp. 113–133. Springer, New York (2001)
9. Dignum, M.V.: A model for organizational interaction: based on agents, founded in logic. Ph.D. thesis, Universiteit Utrecht (2003)
10. Dimmock, N.: How much is "enough"? Risk in trust-based access control. In: Proceedings of the 12th IEEE International Workshop on Enabling Technologies: Infrastructure for Collaborative Enterprises, pp. 281–282. IEEE (2003)

11. d'Inverno, M., Luck, M., Noriega, P., Rodriguez-Aguilar, J., Sierra, C.: Communicating open systems. Artif. Intell. **186**, 138–94 (2012)
12. Hannoun, M., Boissier, O., Sichman, J.S., Sayettat, C.: MOISE: an organizational model for multi-agent systems. In: Monard, M.C., Sichman, J.S. (eds.) SBIA 2000 and IBERAMIA 2000. LNCS (LNAI), vol. 1952, pp. 156–165. Springer, Heidelberg (2000)
13. Haynes, C., Miles, S., Luck, M.: Monitoring the impact of norms upon organisational performance: a simulation approach. In: Balke, T., Dignum, F., van Riemsdijk, M.B., Chopra, A.K. (eds.) COIN 2013. LNCS, vol. 8386, pp. 103–119. Springer, Heidelberg (2014)
14. Mahmoud, S., Griffiths, N., Keppens, J., Taweel, A., Bench-Capon, T.J.M., Luck, M.: Establishing norms with metanorms in distributed computational systems. Artif. Intell. Law **23**(4), 367–407 (2015)
15. Miles, S., Groth, P., Luck, M.: Handling mitigating circumstances for electronic contracts. In: Proceedings of the AISB 2008 Symposium on Behaviour Regulation in Multiagent Systems, pp. 37–42 (2008)
16. Modgil, S., Oren, N., Faci, N., Meneguzzi, F., Miles, S., Luck, M.: Monitoring compliance with e-contracts and norms. Artif. Intell. Law **23**(2), 161–196 (2015)
17. Morales, J., Lopez-Sanchez, M., Rodriguez-Aguilar, J.A., Vasconcelos, W., Wooldridge, M.: Online automated synthesis of compact normative systems. ACM Trans. Auton. Adapt. Syst. **10**(1), 2 (2015)
18. Sabater, J., Sierra, C.: Review on computational trust and reputation models. Artif. Intell. Rev. **24**(1), 33–60 (2005)
19. Stanton, N.A.: Hierarchical task analysis: developments, applications, and extensions. Appl. Ergon. **37**(1), 55–79 (2006)
20. Teacy, W.T.L., Luck, M., Rogers, A., Jennings, N.R.: An efficient and versatile approach to trust and reputation using hierarchical Bayesian modelling. Artif. Intell. **193**, 149–185 (2012)

Coordination and Planning

From Public Plans to Global Solutions in Multiagent Planning

Jan Tožička$^{(\boxtimes)}$, Jan Jakubův, and Antonín Komenda

FEE, Department of Computer Science, Agent Technology Center,
Czech Technical University in Prague, Prague, Czech Republic
{jan.tozicka,jan.jakubuv,antonin.komenda}@agents.fel.cvut.cz

Abstract. Multiagent planning addresses the problem of coordinated
sequential decision making of a team of cooperative agents. One possible approach to multiagent planning, which proved to be very efficient
in practice, is to find an acceptable public plan. The approach works in
two stages. At first, a public plan acceptable to all the involved agents
is computed. Then, in the second stage, the public solution is extended
to a global solution by filling in internal information by every agent. In
the recently proposed distributed multiagent planner, the winner of the
Competition of Distributed Multiagent Planners (CoDMAP 2015), this
principle was utilized, however with unnecessary use of combination of
both public and internal information for extension of the public solution.

In this work, we improve the planning algorithm by enhancements of
the global solution reconstruction phase. We propose a new method of
global solution reconstruction which increases efficiency by restriction
to internal information. Additionally, we employ reduction techniques
downsizing the input planning problem. Finally, we experimentally evaluate the resulting planner and prove its superiority when compared to
the previous approach.

1 Introduction

Intelligent agents cooperatively solving a problem in a shared environment are
required to coordinate their activity and preserve their local private knowledge.
Deterministic multiagent planning (DMAP), an established sub-area of the planning research, provides formal and practical tools to solve such problems.

The commonly used model for DMAP is MA-STRIPS [2] proposed by Brafman
and Domshlak as a minimalistic extension of the classical planning model
STRIPS [7]. MA-STRIPS begins with a set of cooperative agents, each capable of a different set of abilities described in the form of deterministic actions.
The shared environment the agents act in is defined over a finite set of possible
states, each state represented as a set of possibly holding facts. If a fact influences
and/or is influenced only by a single agent, there is no need for the other agents
to consider it, therefore it is *private* (or *internal*) for the given agent. Actions
and states form a global transition system modeling the target planning problem. In order to execute an action, its preconditions have to be satisfied in the

© Springer International Publishing Switzerland 2016
M. Rovatsos et al. (Eds.): EUMAS 2015/AT 2015, LNAI 9571, pp. 21–33, 2016.
DOI: 10.1007/978-3-319-33509-4_2

current state of the environment. Conversely, after execution of an action, the environment is transformed into a new state according to effects of the action (under the close-world assumption). A solution of MA-STRIPS problem is an ordered sequence of agents' actions – a multiagent plan – which after execution transforms the environment from a predefined initial state to one of predefined goal states.

MA-STRIPS planning is domain independent, therefore the real-world motivation spans over a wide variety of problems [16], similarly to classical planning [14]. Representative examples, presented in our benchmarks are: the logistics domain modeling a heterogeneous fleet of vehicles transporting goods among predefined places; the rovers and satellites domains modeling teams of autonomous rovers and satellites conducing experiments around and on the surface of a distant planet; and a multi-robot variant of the classical Sokoban puzzle, where crates has to be pushed (pulls are not allowed) from their initial positions to predefined storage (goal) positions in a grid maze.

Following the historical development of classical planners, currently in DMAP, plan-space and state-space search techniques compete what approach is the more efficient. Our presented planning technique follows the principle of plan-space search to find a valid public plan, which can be consequently extended by local planning to a global solution of the planning problem. This principle was proposed in the first MA-STRIPS planner Planning First [17], using transformation of the plan-space search to a Distributed Constraint Satisfaction Problem, which solution represented the public plan. The transformation was superseded by Fabre et al. in [6] by public plans represented as Finite State Machines (FSMs). This idea inspired our line of work [11,19–21] on satisficing (i.e., a correct plan is sufficient, cf. optimal plan) DMAP by intersection of Planning State Machines (PSMs), which are FSMs representing compactly a set of plans of different agents.

DMAP problems are hard to solve. Particularly, planning of MA-STRIPS problems is exponential in (the tree-width of) the interaction graph among the agents [3] to the size of the planning problem. This inherent complexity cannot be in general tackled tractably (unless $P = NP$), therefore as in classical planning, we had to utilize automatically derived heuristics. In our recent work, we used the LAMA planner comprising forward-search planning heuristics (Fast-Forward [10] and LAMA landmarks [18]) to solve the local planning problems of particular agents. The local planning extends public plans towards a global solution. Additionally, we used the concept of planning landmarks to direct the plan-space search for the public plan in [19].

Besides the heuristics, which help to navigate the search, a special form of complexity can be reduced by an appropriate transformation of the planning problem. Such reductions can remove *accidental complexity* [8], i.e., superfluous complexity of planning caused by inappropriate formulation of problems. In classical planning, the most frequently used reduction technique is reachability analysis (e.g., in [9,10]), that is removal of a subset of actions which can be proved to be inapplicable during the search. Problem reduction by reachability analysis is one of transition system reduction techniques [1,4,5,8,13,15]. Recently, we have proposed first steps towards reductions for DMAP in [12].

In this paper, we propose a new method of global solution reconstruction, which increases efficiency by restriction to internal information. This combined with reductions for DMAP increases efficiency of the best performing distributed multiagent planner PSM-RVD [21] in the Competition of Distributed Multiagent Planners (CoDMAP 2015)[1]. On average, the improvement by proposed techniques in the coverage of solved problems is 13 %.

2   Multiagent Planning

This section provides a condensed formal prerequisites of multiagent planning based on MA-STRIPS formalism [2].

MA-STRIPS *planning problem* Π is a quadruple $\Pi = \langle F, \{\alpha_i\}_{i=1}^n, I, G\rangle$, where F is a set of facts, α_i is the set of actions of i-th agent[2], $I \subseteq F$ is an initial state, and $G \subseteq F$ is a set of goal facts. We define selector functions $\mathsf{facts}(\Pi)$, $\mathsf{agents}(\Pi)$, $\mathsf{init}(\Pi)$, and $\mathsf{goal}(\Pi)$ such that the following holds.

$$\Pi = \langle \mathsf{facts}(\Pi), \mathsf{agents}(\Pi), \mathsf{init}(\Pi), \mathsf{goal}(\Pi)\rangle$$

An *action* an agent can perform is a triple of subsets of $\mathsf{facts}(\Pi)$ called *preconditions, add effects, delete effects*. Selector functions $\mathsf{pre}(a)$, $\mathsf{add}(a)$, and $\mathsf{del}(a)$ are defined so that $a = \langle \mathsf{pre}(a), \mathsf{add}(a), \mathsf{del}(a)\rangle$.

A *planning state* s is a finite set of facts and we say that fact f *holds in* s, or that f *is valid in* s, iff $f \in s$. When $\mathsf{pre}(a) \subseteq s$ then *state progression* function γ is defined classically as $\gamma(s, a) = (s\backslash\mathsf{del}(a)) \cup \mathsf{add}(a)$.

In MA-STRIPS, out of computational or privacy concerns, each fact is classified either as *public* or as *internal*. A fact is *public* when it is mentioned by actions of at least two different agents. A fact is *internal for agent* α when it is not public but mentioned by some action of α. A fact is *relevant for* α when it is either public or internal for α. MA-STRIPS further extends this classification of facts to actions as follows. An action is *public* when it contains a public fact (as a precondition or effect), otherwise it is *internal*. An action from Π is *relevant for* α when it is either public or owned by (contained in) α.

We use $\mathsf{int\text{-}facts}(\alpha)$, $\mathsf{pub\text{-}facts}(\alpha)$, and $\mathsf{rel\text{-}facts}(\alpha)$ to denote in turn the set of internal, the set of public, and the set of relevant facts of agent α. Moreover, we write $\mathsf{pub\text{-}facts}(\Pi)$ to denote all the public facts of problem Π. We write $\mathsf{pub\text{-}actions}(\alpha)$ and $\mathsf{int\text{-}actions}(\alpha)$ to denote in turn the set of public, and the set of internal actions of agent α. Finally, we use $\mathsf{pub\text{-}actions}(\Pi)$ to denote all the public actions of all the agents in problem Π. The notation is summarized in Fig. 1.

In multiagent planning with external actions, a *local planning problem* is constructed for every agent α. Each local planning problem for α is a classical STRIPS problem where α has its own internal copy of the global state and where

---

[1] See http://agents.fel.cvut.cz/codmap for more info about CoDMAP'15.

[2] Note, that agents are defined only by their actions and thus α_i represents both the agent and the actions it can perform.

each agent is equipped with information about public actions of other agents called *external actions*. These local planning problems allow us to divide MA-STRIPS problem to several STRIPS problems which can be solved separately by a classical planner.

The *projection* $F \triangleright \alpha$ of set of facts $F \subseteq \mathsf{facts}(\Pi)$ to agent α is the restriction of F to the facts relevant for α, representing F as seen by α. The *projection* $a \triangleright \alpha$ of action a to agent α is obtained by restricting the facts in a to facts relevant for α, that is, hiding internal facts of other agents. The *public projection* $a \triangleright \star$ of action a is obtained by restricting the facts in a to public facts. Projections are extended to sets of actions element-wise.

A *local planning problem* $\Pi \triangleright \alpha$ of agent α, also called *projection of* Π *to* α, is a classical STRIPS problem containing all the actions of agent α together with external actions, that is, public projections other agents public actions. The local problem of α is defined only using the facts relevant for α. Formally,

$$\Pi \triangleright \alpha = \langle \mathsf{facts}(\Pi) \triangleright \alpha, \alpha \cup \mathsf{ext\text{-}actions}(\alpha), I \triangleright \alpha, G \rangle$$

where the set of external actions $\mathsf{ext\text{-}actions}(\alpha)$ is defined as follows.

$$\mathsf{ext\text{-}actions}(\alpha) = \bigcup_{\beta \neq \alpha} (\mathsf{pub\text{-}actions}(\beta) \triangleright \star)$$

In the above, β ranges over all the agents of Π. The set $\mathsf{ext\text{-}actions}(\alpha)$ can be equivalently described as $\mathsf{ext\text{-}actions}(\alpha) = (\mathsf{pub\text{-}actions}(\Pi) \backslash \alpha) \triangleright \star$. To simplify the presentation, we consider only problems with public goals and hence there is no need to restrict goal G.

3   Multiagent Planning by Plan Set Intersection

The previous section allows us to divide MA-STRIPS problem into several classical STRIPS local planning which can be solved separately by a classical planner. Recall that local planning problem of agent α contains all the actions of α together with α's external actions, that is, with projections of public actions of other agents. This section describe conditions which allow us to compute a solution of the original MA-STRIPS problem from solutions of local problems.

A *plan* π is a sequence of actions. The state progression function can then be iteratively extended to $\gamma^\star(s_0, \pi)$ defined on plans instead of actions. A *solution* of Π is a plan π whose execution transforms the initial state into a state in the set of goals, i.e. $\gamma^\star(I, \pi) \in G$. A *local solution* of agent α is a solution of $\Pi \triangleright \alpha$. Let $\mathsf{sols}(\Pi)$ denote the set of all the solutions of MA-STRIPS or STRIPS problem Π. A *public plan* σ is a sequence of public actions. The *public projection* $\pi \triangleright \star$ of plan π is the restriction of π to public actions. To avoid confusions possibly arising when two different actions have the same projection, we consider actions to have assigned unique ids which are preserved by projections. We omit ids from formal development in this work.

$\mathsf{facts}(a)$	$=$	$\mathsf{pre}(a) \cup \mathsf{add}(a) \cup \mathsf{del}(a)$	*facts of action a*
$\mathsf{facts}(\alpha)$	$=$	$\bigcup_{a \in \alpha} \mathsf{facts}(a)$	*facts of agent α*
$\mathsf{facts}(\Pi)$	$=$	$\bigcup_{\alpha \in \mathsf{agents}(\Pi)} \mathsf{facts}(\alpha)$	*all facts*
$\mathsf{actions}(\alpha)$	$=$	α	*actions of agent α*
$\mathsf{actions}(\Pi)$	$=$	$\bigcup_{\alpha \in \mathsf{agents}(\Pi)} \mathsf{actions}(\alpha)$	*all actions*
$\mathsf{pub\text{-}fact}(f)$	$\Leftrightarrow$	$\exists \alpha \neq \beta : f \in (\mathsf{facts}(\alpha) \cap \mathsf{facts}(\beta))$	*public fact (predicate)*
$\mathsf{pub\text{-}facts}(\Pi)$	$=$	$\{f \in \mathsf{facts}(\Pi) : \mathsf{pub\text{-}fact}(f)\}$	*all public facts*
$\mathsf{pub\text{-}action}(a)$	$\Leftrightarrow$	$(\mathsf{facts}(a) \cap \mathsf{pub\text{-}facts}(\Pi)) \neq \emptyset$	*public action (predicate)*
$\mathsf{pub\text{-}actions}(\Pi)$	$=$	$\{a \in \mathsf{actions}(\Pi) : \mathsf{pub\text{-}action}(a)\}$	*public actions*
$\mathsf{pub\text{-}facts}(\alpha)$	$=$	$\mathsf{facts}(\alpha) \cap \mathsf{pub\text{-}facts}(\Pi)$	*public facts of agent α*
$\mathsf{int\text{-}facts}(\alpha)$	$=$	$\mathsf{facts}(\alpha) \setminus \mathsf{pub\text{-}facts}(\Pi)$	*internal facts of agent α*
$\mathsf{rel\text{-}facts}(\alpha)$	$=$	$\mathsf{facts}(\alpha) \cup \mathsf{pub\text{-}facts}(\Pi)$	*relevant facts of agent α*
$\mathsf{pub\text{-}actions}(\alpha)$	$=$	$\mathsf{actions}(\alpha) \cap \mathsf{pub\text{-}actions}(\Pi)$	*public actions of agent α*
$\mathsf{int\text{-}actions}(\alpha)$	$=$	$\mathsf{actions}(\alpha) \setminus \mathsf{pub\text{-}actions}(\Pi)$	*internal actions of agent α*

Fig. 1. MA-STRIPS privacy classification of facts and actions of problem Π.

A public plan σ is *extensible* when there is $\pi \in \mathsf{sols}(\Pi)$ such that $\pi \triangleright \star = \sigma$. Extensible public plans are also called *public solutions*. Similarly, σ is α-*extensible* when there is $\pi \in \mathsf{sols}(\Pi \triangleright \alpha)$ such that $\pi \triangleright \star = \sigma$. Extensible public plans give us an order of public actions which is acceptable for all the agents. Thus extensible public plans are very close to solutions of Π and it is relatively easy to construct a solution of Π once we have an extensible public plan. That is why, in our previous work, the procedure of reconstruction of a global solution of Π from a public plan received little attention. In this work, we elaborate this procedure in detail.

The following Lemma [19] establishes the relationship between extensible and α-extensible plans. Its direct consequence is that to find a solution of Π it is enough to find a local solution $\pi_\alpha \in \mathsf{sols}(\Pi \triangleright \alpha)$ which is β-extensible for every agent β.

Lemma 1 ([19])**.** *Public plan σ of Π is extensible if and only if σ is α-extensible for every agent α.*

Our previous multiagent planning algorithms [12,19,20] work in two-stages. In the first stage, a public solution is found, while, in the second stage, the public solution is extended to a global solution. Simple public solution search is described in Algorithm 1. Every agent executes the loop from Algorithm 1, possibly on a different machine. Every agent keeps generating new solutions of its local problem and stores public projections of local solutions set Φ_α. These sets are exchanged among all the agents so that every agent can compute their intersection Φ. Once the intersection Φ is non-empty, the algorithm terminates yielding Φ as the result. Hence Algorithm 1 yields a set of extensible public plans.

Algorithm 1. Public solution distributed search.

---

1 **Function** MaPublicPlan($\Pi \rhd \alpha$) **is**
2      $\Phi_\alpha \leftarrow \emptyset$;
3   **loop**
4   generate new $\pi_\alpha \in \mathsf{sols}(\Pi \rhd \alpha)$;
5         $\Phi_\alpha \leftarrow \Phi_\alpha \cup \{\pi_\alpha \rhd \star\}$;
6   exchange public plans Φ_β with other agents;
7         $\Phi \leftarrow \bigcap_{\beta \in \mathsf{agents}(\Pi)} \Phi_\beta$;
8   **if** $\Phi \neq \emptyset$ **then**
9   **return** Φ;
10   **end**
11   **end**
12 **end**

Algorithm 2. Multiagent planning algorithm.

---

1 **Function** MaPlan(Π) **is**
2   **foreach** $\alpha \in \mathsf{agents}(\Pi)$ **do**
3   execute MaPublicPlan($\Pi \rhd \alpha$);   // Algorithm 1
4   **end**
5      $\Phi \leftarrow$ the result of MaPublicPlan($\Pi \rhd \alpha$);   // of an arbitrary agent α
6      $\sigma \leftarrow$ any public solution from Φ;
7      $\pi \leftarrow$ global solution reconstruction from σ;   // Sections 4 &5
8   **return** π;
9 **end**

Once an extensible public plan is found, it needs to be extended to a global solution. The reconstruction of a global solution of the original MA-STRIPS problem Π is described in details in the following sections. The overall procedure covering both public plan search and global solution reconstruction is depicted in Algorithm 2.

4 Global Solution from Local Solutions

This section summarizes methods of global solution reconstruction used in our previous work [12,19,20]. In multiagent planning algorithms based on the idea of plan set intersection sketched in Algorithm 2, every agent keeps generating local solutions until every agent generates a local solution with the same public projection as other agents. A global solution is then reconstructed from these local solutions utilizing Lemma 1. Its constructive proof [19, Lemma 1] suggests a method for reconstruction of a global solution from local solutions by their merging.

The above method can be used in situations when local solutions with an equal public projection were generated during the public plan search. Our successor planning algorithms [12,20] can, however, arrive at a public solution σ

without generating local solutions with public projection σ. In [20], public projections of local solutions generated by individual agents are stored in structures called *Planning State Machines* (PSM). In some cases, plans stored by a PSM are combined together giving rise to new plans which were not explicitly generated. Moreover, analysis of dependencies of public actions [12] can yield a public solution without generating any local solution at all. Hence in these cases, a different approach needs to be used to reconstruct a global solution from σ.

Suppose we have a public plan σ and we know that σ is a public solution, that is, we know that σ is extensible. For every agent α, a local solution of $\Pi \triangleright \alpha$ with public projection σ can be found by a method originally used to test α-extensibility [19]. For a public plan σ, we construct a classical STRIPS problem $\alpha \circ \sigma$ which contains public actions from σ together with α's internal actions. Public actions from σ are extended with special *mark facts* which ensure that every solution of $\alpha \circ \sigma$ contains all the actions from σ in the right order, possibly interleaved with α-internal actions. When $\sigma = \langle a_1, \ldots, a_k \rangle$, then we use $k + 1$ distinct mark facts $\{m_0, \ldots, m_k\}$. The meaning of fact m_i is that actions $a_1, \ldots, a_i$ has been used in the right order, and that action a_{i+1} should be used now. This behavior is achieved by adding m_{i-1} to the precondition and the delete effect of a_i, and by adding m_i to the add effect. For convenience, we define function mark-act$(a, from, to)$, which adds mark facts *from* and *to* to action a as follows.

$$\text{mark-act}(a, from, to) = \langle \text{prc}(a) \cup \{from\}, \text{add}(a) \cup \{to\}, \text{del}(a) \cup \{from\} \rangle$$

The following formally defines the STRIPS problem $\alpha \circ \sigma$. Note that the first mark m_0 is added to the initial state, and that m_k is added to the goal. The goal mark fact m_k ensures that all the actions were used. Also note that, as opposed to $\Pi \triangleright \alpha$, problem $\alpha \circ \sigma$ does not contain external actions.

Definition 1. *Let* $\alpha \in$ agents(Π) *and let* $\sigma = \langle a_1, \ldots, a_k \rangle$ *be a public plan. Let* marks $= \{m_0, \ldots, m_k\}$ *be a set of facts distinct from* facts(Π). *The* α-*extensibility check of* σ, *denoted* $\alpha \circ \sigma$, *is the* STRIPS *problem* $\langle F_0, A_0, I_0, G_0 \rangle$ *where*

1. $F_0 = ($facts$(\Pi) \triangleright \alpha) \cup$ marks, *and*
2. $A_0 =$ int- actions$(\alpha) \cup \{$mark-act$(a_i \triangleright \alpha, m_{i-1}, m_i) : 0 < i \leq k\}$, *and*
3. $I_0 = ($init$(\Pi) \triangleright \alpha) \cup \{m_0\}$, *and*
4. $G_0 = G \cup \{m_k\}$.

The following lemma relates the STRIPS problem $\alpha \circ \sigma$ with α-extensibility of σ.

Lemma 2 ([19]). *Let* $\alpha \in$ agents(Π) *and let* σ *be a public plan. Then* σ *is* α-*extensible iff* sols$(\alpha \circ \sigma) \neq \emptyset$.

Suppose we have a public solution σ. It is easy to see that every solution of $\alpha \circ \sigma$ is also a local solution of $\Pi \triangleright \alpha$, provided mark facts are removed. Hence problems $\alpha \circ \sigma$ can be used to generate local solutions with public projection σ. These local solutions can in turn be used to reconstruct a global solution as described above.

5   Global Solution from Public Solution

The previous section defines the α-extensibility check problem $\alpha \circ \sigma$ which can be used either to (1) verify that a public plan σ is α-extensible, or to (2) find a local solution of $\Pi \rhd \alpha$ with public projection σ. In this section we concentrate on task (2) in situations where an extensible public plan σ is given. The extensibility check problem $\alpha \circ \sigma$ contains public facts in public actions coming from σ. These public facts increase the complexity of planning task $\alpha \circ \sigma$. We propose an improved method for finding a local solution with a given public projection σ, provided we know that σ is (α-)extensible.

Every public solution σ is α-extensible and hence there is a solution π of $\Pi \rhd \alpha$ with public projection σ. Recall that π contains all the actions from σ possibly interleaved with α-internal actions. Public preconditions of public actions in π can not be affected by internal actions, and hence the public preconditions must be satisfied by actions coming from σ. Thus, when extending a public solution σ to a local solution, we can omit public facts and concentrate only on internal facts (public actions can have additional internal preconditions and effects).

Given a public solution σ, we define the α-*reconstruction problem*, denoted $\sigma \bullet \alpha$, similar to the α-extensibility check problem $\sigma \circ \alpha$. The only difference is that the reconstruction problem further restricts the facts to internal facts. Recall that α-projection ($\rhd$) is the restriction to the facts relevant for α. We define *internal α-projection* ($\blacktriangleright$) as the restriction to α-internal facts. For convenience, Fig. 2 summarizes definitions of different projections.

$$
\begin{aligned}
F \rhd \alpha &= F \cap \mathsf{rel\text{-}facts}(\alpha) &&\quad \textit{facts } \alpha\textit{-projection} \\
F \blacktriangleright \alpha &= F \cap \mathsf{int\text{-}facts}(\alpha) &&\quad \textit{facts internal } \alpha\textit{-projection} \\
F \rhd \star &= F \cap \mathsf{pub\text{-}facts}(\Pi) &&\quad \textit{facts public projection} \\[4pt]
a \rhd \alpha &= \langle \mathsf{pre}(a) \rhd \alpha, \mathsf{add}(a) \rhd \alpha, \mathsf{del}(a) \rhd \alpha \rangle &&\quad \textit{action } \alpha\textit{-projection} \\
a \blacktriangleright \alpha &= \langle \mathsf{pre}(a) \blacktriangleright \alpha, \mathsf{add}(a) \blacktriangleright \alpha, \mathsf{del}(a) \blacktriangleright \alpha \rangle &&\quad \textit{action internal } \alpha\textit{-projection} \\
a \rhd \star &= \langle \mathsf{pre}(a) \rhd \star, \mathsf{add}(a) \rhd \star, \mathsf{del}(a) \rhd \star \rangle &&\quad \textit{action public projection}
\end{aligned}
$$

Fig. 2. Different projections of facts and actions.

The α-reconstruction problem of σ is formally defined as follows. Note that only the last mark fact constitutes the goal because all the other goal facts are public.

Definition 2. *Let $\alpha \in \mathsf{agents}(\Pi)$ and let $\sigma = \langle a_1, \ldots, a_k \rangle$ be a public plan. Let $\mathsf{marks} = \{m_0, \ldots, m_k\}$ be a set of facts distinct from $\mathsf{facts}(\Pi)$. The α-reconstruction problem of σ, denoted $\alpha \bullet \sigma$, is the STRIPS problem $\langle F_0, A_0, I_0, G_0 \rangle$ where*

1. $F_0 = (\mathsf{facts}(\Pi) \blacktriangleright \alpha) \cup \mathsf{marks}$, and

2. $A_0 = \text{int-actions}(\alpha) \cup \{\text{mark-act}(a_i \blacktriangleright \alpha, m_{i-1}, m_i) : 0 < i \leq k\}$, and
3. $I_0 = (\text{init}(\Pi) \blacktriangleright \alpha) \cup \{m_0\}$, and
4. $G_0 = \{m_k\}$.

The following lemma relates solutions of $\sigma \bullet \alpha$ with α-extensibility of σ. When compared with the similar result for the extensibility check problem $\sigma \circ \alpha$ (Lemma 2), only one implication can be proved.

Lemma 3. *Let $\alpha \in \text{agents}(\Pi)$ and let σ be a public plan. If σ is α-extensible then $\text{sols}(\alpha \bullet \sigma) \neq \emptyset$.*

Proof. By Lemma 2, there is $\pi \in \text{sols}(\alpha \circ \sigma)$. A solution of $\alpha \bullet \sigma$ can be obtained from π by internal α-restriction of actions (preserving mark facts). $\square$

There is a relationship between solutions of $\sigma \bullet \alpha$ and local solutions of agent α. When σ is α-extensible then every solution of $\sigma \bullet \alpha$ is also a solution of the local problem $\Pi \triangleright \alpha$. Formally as follows.

Lemma 4. *Let $\alpha \in \text{agents}(\Pi)$ and let σ be an α-extensible public plan. Then $\text{sols}(\sigma \bullet \alpha) \subseteq \text{sols}(\Pi \triangleright \alpha)$ (up to the mark facts).*

Proof. Let $\pi \in \text{sols}(\sigma \bullet \alpha)$. Let π' be π with mark facts removed from the actions. Hence π' contains only actions from $\Pi \triangleright \alpha$. Let $I = \text{init}(\Pi \triangleright \alpha)$ and let us prove that $\gamma^*(I, \pi')$ is defined. Every α-internal precondition of every action from π' is satisfied because it was satisfied in π, and other actions in π' do not affect α-internal facts. Hence, it is enough to prove that public preconditions are satisfied. It, however, follows from extensibility of σ. Finally, $\gamma^*(I, \pi') \subseteq \text{goal}(\Pi \triangleright \alpha)$ because all the goals are public and σ is α-extensible. $\square$

Hence α-reconstruction problems of σ can help us to construct local solutions with public projection σ. These local solutions can in turn be used to reconstruct a global solution. The following theorem put the pieces together, that is, it provides a constructive way to construct a global solution from a public solution. Given a public solution σ, a local solution with public projection σ is computed using α-reconstruction by every agent α. All these local solutions contain the same public actions given by σ. These public actions naturally split the plans into parts which are merged together giving rise to a global solution.

Theorem 1. *Let $\text{agents}(\Pi) = \{\alpha^1, \ldots, \alpha^n\}$ and let $\sigma = \langle a_1, \ldots, a_k \rangle$ be an extensible plan of Π. Then*

1. *there is $\pi^i \in \text{sols}(\alpha^i \bullet \sigma)$ for every $0 < i \leq n$, and*
2. *for every π^i, there are $\pi^i_1, \ldots, \pi^i_k$ such that π^i can be written as*

$$\pi^i = \pi^i_1 \cdot \langle a'_1 \rangle \cdot \cdots \cdot \pi^i_k \cdot \langle a'_k \rangle \quad \text{where} \quad a'_j = \text{mark-act}(a_j \blacktriangleright \alpha^i) \quad (\text{for } 0 < j \leq k)$$

3. *and, plan*

$$\pi = \pi_1 \cdot \langle a_1 \rangle \cdot \cdots \cdot \pi_k \cdot \langle a_k \rangle \quad \text{where} \quad \pi_j = \pi^1_j \cdot \cdots \cdot \pi^n_j \quad (\text{for } 0 < j \leq k)$$

is a solution of Π.

Proof. Claim (1) is by Lemmas 1 and 3. For Claim (2), let $\pi^i \in \mathsf{sols}(\alpha \bullet \sigma)$ be given. Due to the marks, π^i contains all the actions from σ in the right order. We can consider (α^i-projection of) a_k to be the last action of π^i because it is the only action fulfilling the goal of $\alpha^i \bullet \sigma$. Hence π_j^i are simply the (α^i-internal) actions between (projections of) a_j and a_{j-1} in π^i. For Claim (3), let $I = \mathsf{init}(\Pi)$. Now $\gamma^\star(I, \pi)$ is defined following the same arguments as in the Proof of Lemma 4. Finally, $\gamma^\star(I, \pi) \subseteq \mathsf{goal}(\Pi)$ because all goals are public and σ is extensible.   □

6   Experiments

This section experimentally evaluates the impact of improved global solution reconstruction. In order to undertake the experiments, we use our PSM-RVD planner [21] which performs public solution search utilizing Planning State Machines (PSM) [20] enhanced with analysis of internal dependencies of public actions [12]. In the Competition of Distributed Multiagent Planners (CoDMAP 2015), PSM-RVD solved 180 problems out of total 240 problems within the 30 min time limit, achieving the best results in the *distributed* track.

Planner PSM-RVD submitted to CoDMAP 2015 implemented global solution reconstruction using *extensibility check problems* (○) described in Sect. 4. To undertake the experiments, we have implemented global solution reconstruction using *reconstruction problems* (●) from Sect. 5. We use 220 benchmark problems from 11 domains[3], with the time limit of 5 min.

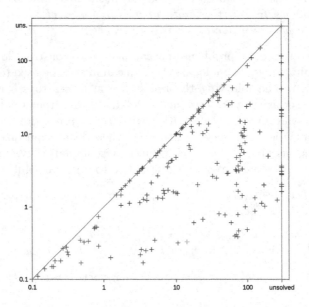

Fig. 3. Impact of improved global solution reconstruction on the runtime of PSM-RVD on CoDMAP benchmark problems (logarithmic scales).

---

[3] The last *Wireless* domain is not supported by the planner parser.

Table 1. Impact of improved global solution reconstruction on the coverage of PSM-RVD on CoDMAP benchmark problems.

Domain	Solved problems [count]		Reconstruction phase [avg. % of runtime]	
	(○)	(●)	(○)	(●)
Blocksworld (20)	18	**19**	92 %	**47 %**
Depot (20)	8	**15**	86 %	**24 %**
Driverlog (20)	19	**20**	18 %	**14 %**
Elevators (20)	7	**12**	3.0 %	**2.4 %**
Logistics (20)	12	**18**	86 %	**35 %**
Rovers (20)	6	**7**	2.3 %	**1.3 %**
Satellites (20)	8	8	4.1 %	4.1 %
Taxi (20)	20	20	82.8 %	**35.9 %**
Sokoban (20)	15	15	83 %	**29 %**
Woodworking (20)	18	18	35 %	**20 %**
Zenotravel (20)	10	10	5.5 %	**4.4 %**
Total (220)	141	**162**	45.2 %	**19.7 %**

Figure 3 evaluates the impact of improved global solution reconstruction on CoDMAP benchmark problems. For each problem, a point is drawn at the position corresponding to the runtime with extensibility check problems ○ (x-coordinate) and the runtime with reconstruction problems ● (y-coordinate). Hence points below a diagonal constitute improvements. We can see that for all the problems, the runtime was either improved or unchanged.

Table 1 shows (1) the impact of improved global solution reconstruction on the coverage of solved problems, and (2) the impact on a relative length of global solution reconstruction phase. The relative length of global reconstruction phase is measured in the percentage of runtime. We can see that the relative length of a reconstruction phase was shorten even in the cases where it has no effect on total coverage.

7   Conclusions

We have formally and practically enhanced the winning planner of recent competition of distributed and multiagent planners. The global solution reconstruction phase was limited to use only of private facts, which increased efficiency of the algorithm. We have formally proved that such narrowing preserves extensibility of the plan, and therefore the soundness and completeness of the planner. Additionally, we have used recently proposed static reductions of the planning problems for multiagent planning. The practical experiments show improvements of coverage of solved problems by 13 % and strong domination over to the original variant of the planner.

Acknowledgments. This research was supported by the Czech Science Foundation (grant no. 13-22125S) and by the Ministry of Education of the Czech Republic within the SGS project (no. SGS13/211/OHK3/3T/13). Access to computing and storage facilities owned by parties and projects contributing to the National Grid Infrastructure MetaCentrum, provided under the program "Projects of Large Infrastructure for Research, Development, and Innovations" (LM2010005), is greatly appreciated.

References

1. Bäckström, C., Jonsson, A., Jonsson, P.: Macros, reactive plans and compact representations. In: Raedt, L.D., Bessière, C., Dubois, D.,Doherty, P., Frasconi, P., Heintz, F., Lucas, P.J.F. (eds.) ECAI 2012. Frontiers in Artificial Intelligence and Applications, vol. 242, pp. 85–90. IOS Press (2012). http://dx.doi.org/10.3233/978-1-61499-098-7-85
2. Brafman, R., Domshlak, C.: From one to many: planning for loosely coupled multi-agent systems. In: Proceedings of ICAPS 2008, vol. 8, pp. 28–35 (2008)
3. Brafman, R.I., Domshlak, C.: From one to many: planning for loosely coupled multi-agent systems. In: Proceedings of ICAPS 2008, pp. 28–35 (2008)
4. Chen, Y., Yao, G.: Completeness and optimality preserving reduction for planning. In: Proceedings of 21st IJCAI, pp. 1659–1664 (2009)
5. Coles, A., Coles, A.: Completeness-preserving pruning for optimal planning. In: Proceedings of 19th ECAI, pp. 965–966 (2010)
6. Fabre, E., Jezequel, L., Haslum, P., Thiébaux, S.: Cost-optimal factored planning: promises and pitfalls. In: Proceedings of the 20th International Conference on Automated Planning and Scheduling, ICAPPS 2010, Toronto, Ontario, Canada, May 12–16, 2010, pp. 65–72 (2010)
7. Fikes, R., Nilsson, N.: STRIPS: a new approach to the application of theorem proving to problem solving. In: Proceedings of the 2nd International Joint Conference on Artificial Intelligence, pp. 608–620 (1971)
8. Haslum, P.: Reducing accidental complexity in planning problems. In: Proceedings of 20th IJCAI, pp. 1898–1903 (2007)
9. Helmert, M.: The fast downward planning system. J. Artif. Intell. Res. **26**, 191–246 (2006)
10. Hoffmann, J., Nebel, B.: The FF planning system: fast plan generation through heuristic search. JAIR **14**, 253–302 (2001)
11. Jakubův, J., Tožička, J., Komenda, A.: Multiagent planning by planset intersection and plan verification. In: ICAART 2015 - Proceedings of the International Conference on Agents and Artificial Intelligence, Lisbon, Portugal, 10–12 January, 2015, vol. 2, pp. 173–182 (2015)
12. Jakubův, J., Tožička, J., Komenda, A.: On internally dependent public actions in multiagent planning. In: Proceedings of 3rd DMAP Workshop (ICAPS 2015) (2015)
13. Jonsson, A.: The role of macros in tractable planning. J. Artif. Intell. Res. **36**, 471–511 (2009)
14. Nau, D., Ghallab, M., Traverso, P.: Automated Planning: Theory & Practice. Morgan Kaufmann Publishers Inc., San Francisco (2004)
15. Nissim, R., Apsel, U., Brafman, R.: Tunneling and decomposition-based state reduction for optimal planning. In: Proceedings of 20th ECAI, pp. 624–629 (2012). http://www.cs.bgu.ac.il/~apsel/files/decomp_ecai12.pdf

16. Nissim, R., Brafman, R.: Distributed heuristic forward search for multi-agent planning. JAIR **51**, 293–332 (2014)
17. Nissim, R., Brafman, R.I., Domshlak, C.: A general, fully distributed multi-agent planning algorithm. In: Proceedings of AAMAS, pp. 1323–1330 (2010)
18. Richter, S., Westphal, M.: The lama planner: guiding cost-based anytime planning with landmarks. J. Artif. Intell. Res. **39**(1), 127–177 (2010)
19. Tožička, J., Jakubův, J., Durkota, K., Komenda, A., Pechoucek, M.: Multiagent planning supported by plan diversity metrics and landmark actions. In: ICAART 2014 - Proceedings of the 6th International Conference on Agents and Artificial Intelligence, ESEO, Angers, Loire Valley, France, 6–8 March, 2014, vol. 1, pp. 178–189 (2014). http://dx.doi.org/10.5220/0004918701780189
20. Tožička, J., Jakubův, J., Komenda, A.: Generating multi-agent plans by distributed intersection of finite state machines. In: ECAI 2014 - 21st European Conference on Artificial Intelligence, 18–22 August 2014, Prague, Czech Republic - Including Prestigious Applications of Intelligent Systems (PAIS 2014), pp. 1111–1112 (2014)
21. Tožička, J., Jakubův, J., Komenda, A.: PSM-based planners description for CoDMAP 2015 competition. In: Proceedings of the Competition of Distributed and Multi-agent Planners (CoDMAP 2015), pp. 29–32 (2015)

Intelligent People Flow Coordination
in Smart Spaces

Marin Lujak$^{(\boxtimes)}$ and Sascha Ossowski

CETINIA, University King Juan Carlos, Madrid, Spain
marin.lujak@urjc.es

Abstract. In this paper, we present a short overview of the people flow coordination methods and propose a multi-agent based route recommender architecture for smart spaces which considers the influence of stress on human reactions to the recommended routes. The objective of the architecture is to ensure that people can efficiently move in and among smart spaces while at the same time improve the overall system performance. The functioning of the architecture is demonstrated on a case study. The proposed approach can be used, among others, in route recommendation in smart cities, large public events, and emergency evacuations.

1 Introduction

Present people flow guidance approaches are mostly static and preassigned. In the case of congestion in closed spaces, frequently no coordination is used except for building evacuation where inhabitants should consult predefined evacuation maps. In the case of open spaces, on the other hand, human coordinators are introduced mostly on isolated critical parts of traffic networks such as road intersections. Such myopic and fragmented approaches can seriously jeopardize the inhabitants' safety and can contribute to congestion and related problems at a larger scale since by incorporating the local people flow coordination solution in a broader context, the flow from the local may surmount the feasibility of the global flow. This is why real time route recommendation systems applicable to large densely inhabited cities today are urgently needed.

A promising direction to this challenge lies in the paradigm of smart spaces which are meant to provide assistance to inhabitants in everyday activities. The smart space can be modelled as an agent able to acquire and apply knowledge about itself and about its inhabitants in order to improve their experience in the same. Moreover, by implementing smart spaces at a larger scale, a city may be seen as a system of smart spaces and their inhabitants. In such a complex system, by using the information of the both, intelligent route recommendation is aimed at guiding people to their destinations considering individually optimal routes while optimizing the global people flow based on the infrastructure conditions. The resulting interaction of a multitude of space agents and humans requires a scalable and responsive people flow coordination approach.

© Springer International Publishing Switzerland 2016
M. Rovatsos et al. (Eds.): EUMAS 2015/AT 2015, LNAI 9571, pp. 34–49, 2016.
DOI: 10.1007/978-3-319-33509-4_3

In this paper, we present a short overview of the State-of-the-Art people flow coordination methods. The overview does not have the purpose of being exhaustive; its aim is to present main issues in this topic and the achievements so far in solving them. Moreover, we propose a multi-agent based route recommender architecture which considers the influence of stress on human reactions to the recommended routes.

The proposed architecture is composed of the newly proposed route optimization module and a human factor module. The route optimization module is made of a newly proposed optimization model for computing the safest routes integrated with a System Optimal (SO) decomposition model with fairness guarantees similar to [15,16]. The route optimization module aims to simultaneously optimize conflicting objectives of the network's makespan and individual path travel times subject to the availability and reliability of the infrastructure, while the human factor module inspired by [2,13] includes user response to the suggested routes influenced by stress-related irrational behaviors. The functioning of the architecture is demonstrated on a case study.

The presented approach facilitates the movement of people in and among smart spaces as smoothly and safely as possible. We design it with a long-term objective of the usage in times of rush hours and in large events such as, e.g., football games, large concerts, but also in emergency building, urban and ship evacuations.

The rest of the paper is organized as follows. In Sect. 2, we consider State-of-the-Art methods for people flow coordination. We treat human factor and irrational behaviors in emergency evacuation in Sect. 3. In Sect. 4, we formally define the people flow coordination problem. The proposed route-recommender architecture is presented in Sect. 5. The performance of the architecture is demonstrated on a case study in Sect. 6. We conclude the paper in Sect. 7.

2   People Flow Coordination Methods

People route recommendation systems rely on pedestrian flow models which can be divided into microscopic and macroscopic by their dimension. Microscopic people flow models consider pedestrians as discrete individuals and focus on the individual speed and interaction with the environment. The objective is to realistically simulate how human communication and individual behavior affect other individuals and a group as a whole. Most of the present State-of-the-Art microscopic models are a good representation of people behavior especially describing a human factor and panic state in the case of emergencies. Those models, however, are not scalable and there is still a gap between microscopic models of people flows in corridors and rooms and the macroscopic models of people flows on a larger scale.

In most of the macroscopic models, on the other hand, pedestrian movement is seen as a homogeneous and continuous fluid flowing with a specified rate. Individuals are considered as identical stream-following particles of the flow that interact with one another over some generally applied rules. Also called network-flow models, these models focus on the aggregate representation of pedestrian movements in a crowd through flow, density and speed relationships in a fundamental diagram for traffic flow.

In the fundamental diagram, maximal flow Q occurs at some critical combination of velocity and density and separates the free flow ($q \leq Q$) from the congested one ($q > Q$). When $q > Q$, velocities decrease until jam density where there is no more flow. In densely populated areas with increased movement velocities these conditions can result in trampling, stampeding, and related casualties. However, the level of describing the laws of human interaction in crowds over fundamental diagrams is not still sufficiently detailed. By representing the particle (pedestrian) as unthinking elements, these models do not account for the fact that varied behaviour of individual particles can significantly change the way in which the fluid (crowd) as a whole behaves especially in emergency situations. This is why Hughes in [10] proposed a theory for the flow of pedestrians based on continuum modelling which attempts to model the flow of pedestrians as an "intelligent fluid" based on certain predefined hypotheses. The theory has been designed for the development of general techniques to understand the motion of large crowds with the potential to be used as a predictive tool.

To bridge the gap between microscopic and macroscopic crowd models, a probabilistic graphical model was presented in [14, 24]. Both works focus on group behavior and establish a macroscopic network-flow model where fire, smoke, and psychological factors evoke a group's desired flow rate. They integrate fire propagation effects on crowd behaviors in stressful conditions with consequences on egress capacities and crowd flow rates. Egress routes for groups are optimized by using a combination of stochastic dynamic programming and the rollout scheme. A divide-and-conquer approach is developed for groups' competing for passages. The approaches were shown over simulations to be more efficient than the strategy of using nearest exits. Testing results demonstrate also that, compared with the method ignoring crowd behaviors, their methods evacuate more people and faster. However, those methods do not consider the system optimality and fairness in people flow coordination.

3   Human Factor and Irrational Behaviors

In the focus of people flow coordination methods research is the emergency evacuation in large buildings. Some methods assume that crowd behaviors are independent of emergency situations and are fully controllable under guidance, e.g., [24]. However, the psychology of the behavior of an individual in a group is complex and these assumptions preclude the consideration of irrational behaviors.

The behavior of crowds can be explained through the collective behaviour and consensus decision making. Couzin et al. in [4] used computer simulations to investigate the mechanisms behind these two factors. Individuals in groups tend to suppress independent thinking. Thus, the actions of the crowd are usually different from what the actions of the majority in the crowd would be independently of the crowd [7]. However, assuming that a crowd is unorchestrated, it can be modeled as a thinking and rational fluid and, as such, can follow scientific rules of behavior [11].

In general, building evacuation due to imminent danger is accompanied by considerable physical and psychological stress. When individuals perceive life threatening risk in hazardous environmental conditions, multiple negative psychological factors such as, e.g., nevousness, fear, anxiety, frustration, and panic may emerge [8]. The latter may result in irrational behaviors (e.g., denial or enduring) or in the behaviors that are neither rational nor irrational as they may involve the use of trust, emotion, and intuition. In the case of incomplete information, trust, emotion, and intuition in combination can facilitate more effective decision making. What's more, frustration might occur when performed actions do not result in a desired outcome. Excessive stress might diminish sensory functioning and reduce situation awareness while increasing disorientation [12]. General disorientation with excessive frustration may burst into mass panic where panicking agents run toward the exit thus crowding other agents [18].

Panic disasters can be the result of trampling to death in mobile crowds before crushing, asphyxiation by others tripping and falling on top, or crushing resulting in asphyxiation while still standing. These crowd behaviors are related to the herding and stampeding behaviors in very high crowd densities.

Herding occurs when individuals surrender their ability to function as individuals and choose to follow others rather than behave independently on the basis of their own information [13,22]. Those individuals move toward the exit where the majority of the nearest neighbors are heading to. This may lead people to a dead end or cause blockages of some exits even though other exits are not fully utilized [21]. Various herding models are present in literature, e.g., [22] but their validation has been scarce.

One of the most known models for crowd egress in the presence of panic was made by Helbing et al. in [9]. They investigated the mechanisms and conditions that lead to panic and jamming through uncoordinated motion in human crowds. A mixture of individualistic and collective behaviour is the optimal strategy for escaping a smoke filled room. Individualistic behaviour allowed some individuals to successfully locate exits, and collective (herding) behaviour ensured that the behaviour was imitated. However, they mislabled a generic term of irrational behavior with a narrow concept of panic. Moreover, in [19], Moussaid et al. summarized the typical features of escape panics. People under panic are usually willing to move along known routes, even if this means they run towards the fire, which may lead to more fatalities.

For all the above reasons, traditionally, emergency management plans and policies considered evacuees as unthinking or instinctive masses rather than as groups of rational, social beings, excluding them, thus, from the evacuation decision making [5,8]. Those plans and policies relied on specialized emergency individuals such as firefighters, trained to make decisions in a dynamically changing environment. Furthermore, they often intentionally concealed information to public to prevent people from overreacting. Subsequently, very little attention was put on communication technologies that might provide updated emergency information and, in this way, help evacuees make informed decisions about their own safety.

Newer research results emphasize that panic outreach in crowds is not as common as the traditional approaches to emergency management imply [6]. The latter overemphasize the psychological effects of disasters and propose practices that may increase fear and undermine the crowd's shared social identity developed during the common experience of an emergency [6]. Cocking et al. conducted two interview-based studies of survivors' experiences of different emergencies in [3]. It was found that being in an emergency can create a common identity that promotes solidarity amongst affected. This causes people to be cooperative and altruistic towards others even if strangers in life-threatening situations and results in coordinated and beneficial actions [3]. Those actions include such features as mutual support and coordination, which in turn provide a basis for collective agency and adaptive action [5].

Furthermore, Drury and Reicher in [6] indicate that individuals not only behave sensibly in emergencies but also display solidarity. Therefore, solutions that facilitate self-organizing behavior of evacuees are needed rather than the traditional emergency approaches that seek to herd groups of people as if they were unintelligent and instinctive. Ordinary people should, therefore, be viewed as "first responders" and given practical information about their situation so that they can make rational choices [6].

4   People Flow Coordination Problem Formulation

In this paper, we concentrate on finding and recommending to persons the safest paths with minimum costs such that we keep track of the related fairness considerations among the paths assigned to individuals of the same and different origin-destination (O-D) pairs. Furthermore, we consider the person's reactions to these paths including human factor. With this aim, we consider a network of smart spaces in static flow conditions where flow represents people transit pattern at steady state. Even though the assumption on the steady state flow is constraining, it can be applied to transit networks and public edifices like shopping malls, sports stadiums, etc. in time windows when people transit exhibits a flow-like behavior, e.g. in rush hours and building evacuations.

If real-time infrastructure information is available to pedestrians, and they can negotiate their routes, it becomes possible to provide a selection of safe fair routes considering individual preferences. Therefore, we assume that the infrastructure and pedestrians are monitored by strategically positioned cameras. The monitoring permits us both to recognize the inhabitants' behavior in respect to the suggested route and time window as to perceive the traffic and safety conditions of the infrastructure.

Furthermore, we assume that the people flow demand (i.e., O-D requests) for a specific time window is known at the beginning of the time window. In rush hours, this can be performed through a reservation system where each person reserves his/her O-D pair and the relatively short time range in which he/she plans to start the travel at his/her origin, while in evacuation, the destinations are near safe exits for all building occupants at their momentary positions.

In this way, each individual is seen as a unit element (particle) of the total people flow. The behavior of individuals can be conditioned and monitored in real time but it cannot be fully controlled. This is the reason why we consider subjective route evaluation, anxiety, and other human factors' effects on people flow coordination and model them in Sect. 5.1. We assume, furthermore, that the variations of the O-D pair people transfer demands are negligible in an observed time window.

Starting from the above stated assumptions, let $G = (N, A)$ be a connected digraph representing the building infrastructure network where N is the set of n nodes representing rooms, offices, halls, and in general, any portion of space within a building or other structure, separated by walls or partitions from other parts. In the case of larger open spaces, for simplicity, the same are divided into regions represented by nodes.

Let A be the set of m arcs $a = (i, j)$, $i, j \in N$ and $i \neq j$, representing corridors or passages connecting nodes i and j. To simplify the notation, we assume that there is at most one arc in each direction between any pair of nodes. Furthermore, $x_a \geq 0$ is the flow of people in a unit time period on arc $a \in A$, which is limited from above by the arc capacity $u_a \geq 0$ being the maximum arc flow.

Nodes represent origins and destinations of people transit. We assume that there are n_O origin nodes $o \in O$, and n_D destination nodes $d \in D$, $n_O, n_D \leq n$. In the case of evacuation, evacuation destinations are defined as the final locations at which evacuees are considered to be safe. Furthermore, let w represent a generic O-D pair and W the set of all O-D pairs such that $w \in W$. By acceptable in terms of duration cost, we mean the paths for O-D pair considering the upper bound in respect to the minimum duration among the paths for that O-D pair. Moreover, let R be a $n_O \times n_D$ matrix representing O-D demands where $R_{od} = R_w$ entry indicates the demand of inhabitants in unit time period who request to leave origin node $o \in O$ to go to destination node $d \in D$.

Let $\overline{P}_w$ denote the set of available (simple) paths acceptable in terms of duration cost for each O-D pair $w \in W$ taking into account fairness considerations. Furthermore, let $\overline{P}_W$ be the set of all such paths. Then, all the path flows in $\bar{P}_W$ can be gathered in the global path flow vector $\mathbf{x}_W = (x^1, \ldots, x^r)$, where $r = |\overline{P}_W|$. Moreover, we define a feasible flow $\mathbf{x}_w$ as a subvector of flows of paths $k \in \bar{P}_w$ and x^k the flow along path $k \in \overline{P}_w$. For describing the people flows over the whole road network in terms of path flows, we introduce the $[|W| * |\overline{P}_W|]$ O-D pair-path incidence matrix Ψ with rows indexed by $w \in W$ and columns indexed by paths $k \in \bar{P}_W$. Furthermore, let Φ be the $[|A| * |\overline{P}_W|]$ arc-path incidence matrix.

Moreover, let us assume that safety status S_a is given for each arc $a \in A$ as a function of safety conditions as, e.g., temperature, humidity, space consistency, etc. We normalize it to the range $[0, 1]$, such that 1 represents perfect conditions while 0 represents conditions impossible for survival, with a critical level for survival depending on the combination of the previously mentioned parameters $0 < S_a^{cr} < 1$.

Furthermore, for every arc $a \in A$, there is an arc cost function $f_a(x_a)$. Path duration cost $f^k(x^k, \{x^l\}_{l \in \mathcal{L}(k)})$ of each path $k \in \overline{P_w}$, where $w \in W$ is the sum of the duration costs of its arcs $f_a(x_a)$, i.e., $f^k(x^k, \{x^l\}_{l \in \mathcal{L}(k)}) = \sum_{(i,j) \in k} f_a(x_a)$ and is strictly convex. Since the arc duration cost $f_a(x_a)$ is influenced by the total flow of persons passing through the arc, path duration cost depends not only on a local path flow x^k but also on flows of other paths $\{x^l\}_{l \in \mathcal{L}(k)}$, where $\mathcal{L}(k)$ is the set of paths that use the same arc(s) as path k and are therefore coupled with it. Similarly, we introduce the set of coupled O-D pairs $\mathcal{M}(w)$ whose paths use one or more same arc(s) as O-D pair $w \in W$.

Arc cost function $f_a(x_a)$ is, without loss of generality, assumed to be proportional to average travel time $T_a(x_a)$. The latter is experienced by a walking person when traversing arc $a \in A$ and is in general an increasing nonlinear function due to the congestion effects on the arc travel time. Different functions for travelling time can be considered, but for simplicity and without loss of generality, we consider the average travel time function inspired by the U.S. Federal Highway Administration [17] and accommodate it with desired flow $T_a(x_a) = t_a(1 + 0.15(\frac{x_a}{u_a(x_a^d)})^4)$.

In building evacuation, people desire to move faster as they perceive urgent threats [23]. In this light, we model the arcs' (passage and corridors') capacity u_a as a function of the desired flow x_a^d of people who desire to move through a passage per time unit. Therefore, $u_a(x_a^d)$ is defined, inspired by [14], through the two following distinguished parts separating the free flow from the congested one:

a. If $x_a^d \leq |u_a|$, i.e., if the desired flow is lower than the free flow nominal arc capacity (related with critical density), then $u_a(x_a^d)$ maintains its free flow nominal value $|u_a|$.

b. If $x_a^d > |u_a|$, the probability of disorder and blocking increases as the difference between x_a^d and $|u_a|$ increases, influencing, thus, arc's capacity $u_a(x_a^d)$ i.e.,

$$u_a(x_a^d) = \begin{cases} 1 - \exp\left(\frac{-\alpha}{x_a^d - |u_a|}\right), & \text{if } u_a^{Blc} > x_a^d > |u_a| \\ \exp\left(\frac{-\alpha}{x_a^d - |u_a|}\right), & \text{if } x_a^d \geq u_a^{Blc} \end{cases}. \quad (1)$$

Here, $|u_a|$ denotes the free flow capacity where the density of people on arc a is $k_a < k_a^{cr}$, i.e., people can walk without adapting their speed to the crowd movement. On the other hand, u_a^{Blc} denotes the capacity when the arc is blocked, i.e., people density on arc k_a reached its maximum value.

Routes' Safety Optimization. The safety optimization problem is related with minimizing the risks caused by possible threats present on the arcs of the paths towards travellers' destinations. Path safety S^k, for each path $k \in \bar{P}_w$, $w \in W$ is defined by the safety of its constituent arc with the worst safety conditions $a_k^{cr} = \arg\min_{a \in k} S_a$, where $S^k = \min_{a \in k} S_a$. If $S^k < S^{cr}$, then path k is not safe for passage. When safety on path S^k, $k \in \bar{P}_w$ falls behind threshold value S^{cr}, its harmful effects may threaten the evacuees' lives. Therefore, proposed routes $k \in \bar{P}_w$ for $w \in W$ should all satisfy safety conditions $S^k \geq S^{cr}$.

Egalitarian social welfare optimization provides a good solution when the minimum safety requirements of all paths should be satisfied. Unfortunately, by optimizing system's safety based on the worst-off performance, we deteriorate its efficiency and thus, the utilitarian welfare. Utilitarian social welfare on the other hand, sums up the paths' safeties in a given allocation and thus gives us a measure of the overall and average benefit for the system. However, it is not applicable in the safety context since in utilitarian systems, the optimum is paid by (usually a few) paths with the worst off safeties possibly underneath critical safety value.

The balance between egalitarian and utilitarian social welfare is given by the maximization of the Nash product which, in this context, is the product of the paths' individual safeties. A high Nash value, when it is defined in terms of benefits, is an indication of both good utility value and a good egalitarian value, i.e. allocation solutions with a high Nash value are both locally and globally good solutions. Furthermore, Nash product combines utilitarian and egalitarian social welfare since it reaches the maximum when the utilities realized are high and distributed equally over all the paths.

However, Nash product optimization doesn't work when defined through the minimization of the overall cost since it is sufficient that only one of the paths obtains the safety value close to zero for it to have the overall value close to zero. This is why we propose reciprocal values of the costs which multiplied together will result in high Nash product values. Hence, the risk is calculated by

$$\min T\left(\mathbf{S}^k\right) = \sum_{k \in P_w} \prod_{a \in k} \frac{1}{\left(S^{cr} - S_a\right)^+}, \ \forall w \in W, \tag{2}$$

where $(S^{cr} - S_a)^+$ is considered if $S^{cr} > S_a$ and the product in the equation is the value of risk probability related with the safety of path k.

Routes Travel Cost Optimization. Criteria of equity include fairness and *no-envy* criteria. In travel cost optimization, we use the optimization procedure and envy-minimization criterion introduced in [16]. For the autosufficiency of this work, we bring the most important details of the procedure in the following.

We use a normalized mean path duration cost $\gamma_w(x_w, \{x^l\}_{l \in \mathcal{M}(w)})$ of O-D agent $w \in W$ defined as:

$$\gamma_w(x_w, \{x^l\}_{l \in \mathcal{M}(w)}) = \sqrt[|\bar{P}_w|]{\prod_{k \in \bar{P}_w} f^k \cdot x^k}. \tag{3}$$

We propose the mathematical programming model for Nash product minimization with included envy-freeness and fairness parameters as in [16]:

$$\min z(\mathbf{x}_W) = \sum_{w \in W} \log \gamma_w = \sum_{w \in W} \log \left[\sqrt[|\bar{P}_w|]{\prod_{k \in \bar{P}_w} \sum_{a \in A} f_a(x_a) \cdot \phi_{ak} x^k} \right] \tag{4}$$

subject to:

$$\sum_{w \in W} \sum_{k \in \overline{P}_w} \phi_{ak} \cdot x^k \leq u_a \ , \forall a \in A \tag{5}$$

$$\gamma_w \geq \gamma_{w'}^{\alpha}, \ \forall w, w' \in W | w \neq w' \tag{6}$$

$$\sum_{k \in \overline{P}_w} \psi_{wk} \cdot x^k = R_w, \ \forall w \in W \tag{7}$$

$$x^k \geq 0 \ , \ \forall k \in \overline{P}_w, w \in W \ , \tag{8}$$

where α is a maximum tolerance factor for non-enviousness such that $0 < \alpha \leq 1$ and (6) expresses the constraint that there is no agent w' that envies any other agent w for paying less than α^{th} power of the cost paid by w'.

The objective of the problem definition (4)-(8) is, therefore, to achieve a requested normalized person path flow over arcs $a \in A$ of minimum Nash product cost such that each person goes through one route from its origin and terminates at the destination position with the constraints on arc flow (5), envy-freeness (6), O-D demand (7), and admissible paths in $\overline{P}_W$ (8) satisfied.

5 Proposed Route-Recommender Architecture

The proposed route recommendation architecture is composed of the human factor and the route optimization module. The latter, furthermore, includes routes' safety optimization, and routes' travel time system optimization with fairness model, Fig. 1. The proposed architecture considers three different agent categories: persons, person travel route origins, and infrastructure agents. No a priori global assignment information is available and the information is exchanged among the persons, O-D agents and infrastructure agents through the neighbor to neighbor communication. The persons exchange the information only with the closest intfrastructure agent. In this way, we obtain a dynamic network which can dynamically recalculate person routes based on the actual traffic load and person demand.

The objective of the optimization module is to find safe and efficient routes for all the system users. The routes' safety optimization model maximizes the proposed routes' safety based on the real time safety situation in the infrastructure of concern. Moreover, the module of routes' travel time system optimization with fairness finds the shortest paths on the safe graph topology given by the safety optimization module. Finally, human factor module integrates the reactions of people based on their frustration and stress level into the recommended routes.

The input to the architecture are O-D demands and the infrastructure information including the topology, arcs' safety, capacities and distances. The architecture computes the route recommendation solution in iterations based on the infrastructure information and the people flow O-D demand. The iterative process stops when the termination condition on the solution error or the maximum number of iterations is satisfied.

In the following we describe individually each of the modules.

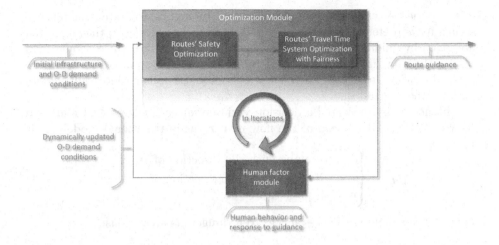

Fig. 1. Proposed route recommender architecture considering human factor

5.1 Human Factor Module

The desired flow rate x_a^d can be defined as $x_a^d = \sum_{w \in W} \sum_{k \in \bar{P}_w} \phi_{a,k} \cdot x_{des}^k$ for all $a \in A$, where x_{des}^k is the flow of individuals desiring to move on path $k \in \bar{P}_w$, where $w \in W$. It depends on the safety conditions of the path S^k and recommended flow x^k:

$$x_{des}^k = f(x^k, S^k) = \begin{cases} x^k/S^k, & \text{if } S^k \geq S^{cr} \\ 0, & \text{otherwise} \end{cases} \tag{9}$$

With high frustration level, evacuees feel uncertain and anxious which intensifies herding behavior and makes people depend more on familiarity. The herding and familiarity behaviors are modelled in the following subsections.

We model frustration Δ^k on path $k \in \bar{P}_w$, $\forall w \in W$ through the level of achievement of a desired flow $x^{k_{des}}$. The nominal value of flow x^k is given by the routing solution of the SO model with included fairness conditions. Then, if the desired flow, based on people's reaction to the recommended route and the safety conditions on the same, is higher than the nominal flow, the frustration increases with the increase of the desired flow, while otherwise, the frustration level is zero:

$$\Delta^k = f(x^k, x^{k_{des}}) = \begin{cases} 1 - \frac{x^k}{x^{k_{des}}}, & if \, x^{k_{des}} \geq x^k \geq 1 \\ 0, & \text{otherwise.} \end{cases} \tag{10}$$

Guidance. The guidance system enables the users to follow a proposed path by following visual, tactile, acoustic or audio-haptic signals. The main challenge here is the adaptation to the dynamically changing environment and individual user's behaviors such that the users trust it. This trust depends on the prior user's experience with the system's accuracy. In highly accurate and reliable systems, users prefer to trust the provided information. However, the suggested route given by guidance may not be evacuees' familiar route. Since people tend to use paths they are familiar with, if the information system is less accurate, users will attempt to exploit their knowledge about familiar routes, ultimately preferring the shortest one.

Guidance g_a^k is considered a decision variable for each edge $a \in A$ and each path $k \in \bar{P}_w$, $w \in W$ instead of the flow rate x_a as in traditional models. It is defined as:

$$g_a^k = \begin{cases} +1, & \text{if along with the direction of arc } a \\ -1, & \text{if opposite to the direction of arc } a \\ 0, & \text{otherwise.} \end{cases} \tag{11}$$

The guidance should not lead evacuees to a dangerous area. Thus:

$$g_a^k = 0 \text{ if } S_{a' \in A_{out}} \leq S^{cr}, \ \forall a \in A, \tag{12}$$

where A_{out} is a set of outgoing adjacent arcs of $a \in A$. Vector $\mathbf{g}_A^k = [g_1^k, \ldots, g_{|E|}^k]$ specifies an egress decision at each passageway for routes $k \in \bar{P}_w, \forall w \in W$. These decisions, when filtered for each route $k \in \bar{P}_w$ for each O-D pair $w \in W$ provide an individual's route plan that can be communicated through, e.g., mobile phones.

Herding. Inspired by [13], we model the herding behavior in the following way. Evacuees' route changes due to herding on every path $k \in \bar{P}_w$, $w \in W$ are interpreted as a result of being affected by their trust in the outgoing arc $a^{max} \in A_a^{out}$ with the largest flow, where $A_a^{out} \subset A$ is a set of outgoing arcs of arc $a \in A$. Let $t_h^{a_i}$ be herding trust on arc $a_i \in A_a^{out}$ defined as the probability of selecting an outgoing arc a_i of the set of all outgoing arcs A_a^{out}:

$$t_h^{a_i} = Pr(a_i) = \frac{x_{a_i}}{\sum_{a \in A_a^{out}} x_a}, \forall a_i \in A_a^{out}, \ a \in A, \tag{13}$$

where x_{a_i} is the flow of evacuees that in their route use arc a_i and $\sum_{a \in A_a^{out}} x_a$ is the total flow of evacuees on the outgoing arcs of arc a. Moreover, to balance the influence of herding on the resulting evacuees' behavior, we introduce weight of herding behavior w_h^k shared among all the individuals on path $k \in \bar{P}_w$. w_h^k increases as frustration Δ^k shared among the individuals on the same path k caused by external safety conditions S^k increase, i.e., $w_h^k = f(\Delta^k)$.

This herding model is inline with the herding model in [2] which defines certain critical tie-breaking assumptions which we modify to our egress people flow case:

Assumption A. Whenever a decision maker has no egress information on arc $a \in A$ and the largest flow of the agents present on the arc is towards arc $a_{out}^{max} = \arg \max \left(x_{a_i} \in A_a^{out} \right)$, then the former always chooses a_{out}^{max}.

Assumption B. When a decision maker is indifferent between relying on its internal egress emergency information and following someone else's egress choice, it always decides independently, relying on its own information.

Assumption C. When a decision maker is indifferent between following more than one of the outgoing arcs $a_i \in A_a^{out}$ of arc $a \in A$, it chooses to follow the one which has the highest flow $a_{out}^{max} = \arg\max \left(x_{a_i} \in A_a^{out} \right)$.

Familiarity. Based on Assumption B, if familiar exits are available, then the familiarity with an escape route results in agent's increased probability to use it. To derive this probability, similar to [13], let t_f^i be evacuees' trust in route $i \in \bar{P}_w$, $w \in W$ ranging from 0 to 1 where 0 represents distrust and 1 full trust. Because evacuees' trust in route i is positively correlated with the probability $Pr(i)$ of selecting it, then we model this probability as:

$$Pr(i|t_f^{k \in \bar{P}_w}) = \frac{t_f^i}{\sum_{k \in \bar{P}_w} t_f^k}, \ \forall i \in \bar{P}_w, w \in W. \tag{14}$$

Another behavior related to selecting a route is exploration behavior, and occurs when evacuees have few ideas about the escape route. This behavior will be eliminated if evacuees receive proper guidance to follow.

Combining Guidance, Familiarity, and Herding. We model the interplay between guidance and familiarity in the following way similar to [13]. Let $t_g^i \in [0, 1]$ denote evacuees trust in route i that is indicated by guidance. Then, given a guidance g_w, for every O-D pair $w \in W$, each individual is assumed to follow guidance route $i \in \bar{P}_w$ with probability:

$$Pr(i|t_f^{k \in \bar{P}_w}, t_g^i) = \frac{\omega_f t_f^i + \omega_g t_g^i}{\omega_f \sum_{k \in \bar{P}_w} t_f^k + \omega_g t_g^i}, \ \forall i \in \bar{P}_w, w \in W. \tag{15}$$

where ω_f and ω_g are weights assigned to the trust in familiar routes and guidance respectfully to combine the effects of familiarity and guidance with the notion of trust. Those weights change dynamically based on the frustration level caused by safety conditions of the egress layout. For example, guidance weight ω_g will be high for path $k \in \bar{P}_w$ for frustration value $\Delta^k = 0$, i.e., if evacuees are not stressed and they rely on guidance even they are familiar with other routes.

The infrastructure topology, safety status $\mathbf{S}$, arcs' capacity $\mathbf{u}$ and O-D flow demand x^w, $\forall w \in W$ are the input parameters to this model. The actual people flow $\mathbf{x}^k$ distributed over paths $k \in \bar{P}_w$ is the output variable. We expand the model from Eq. (15) with herding similar to [13] to obtain the overall probability model for using route i:

$$Pr(i|t_f^{k \in \bar{P}_w}, t_g^i, t_h^i) = \frac{\omega_f t_f^i + \omega_g t_g^i + \omega_h t_h^i}{\omega_f \sum_{k \in \bar{P}_w} t_f^k + \omega_g t_g^i + \omega_h t_h^i}. \tag{16}$$

5.2   Optimization Module

Optimization module is made of two models: routes' safety optimization, and travel time system optimization with fairness, Fig. 1.

Routes' Safety Optimization Model. Our objective is not only to find routes with satisfied minimal safety conditions, but also to increase the chances of survival, we need to find routes that maximize the Nash social welfare of the safety of the routes. Therefore, the safety optimization problem including Nash product of arcs' safeties (2) is solved. The solution of the safety optimization model is a connected graph with the routes' safeties S^k above the critical value S^{cr}.

Routes' Travel Time SO with Fairness. The details of the routes' travel time SO with fairness modules can be found in [16]. However, for the self-completeness of this work, we bring the basic idea of the module. To decompose the network optimization problem, the route's travel time SO with fairness model is divided in two layers. On the upper layer, Nash social welfare maximization problem with included envy-freeness and fairness constraints (4)–(8) is decomposed at four levels to reach a subproblem which can be optimized individually locally by every O-D pair independently of other O-D pairs.

Moreover, on the upper layer, person agents inform of their traveling preferences the intersection agent closest to the origin of their travel (origin agent o). Based on the total demand for each time period expressed in terms of person flow per time unit, each origin agent o tries to achieve a sufficient number of shortest paths considering fairness for all its destinations d_o. Those destinations are requested by the persons starting the travel on o and the paths are computed through, e.g., k-shortest path routing algorithm. Since problem (4)–(8) is not easily decomposable and O-D objective functions are dependent on each other, we use dual decomposition at four levels where each origin agent o negotiates for each of its O-D pairs path flows, path, envy-freeness, consistency, and demand distribution dual prices. Intersection agents then distributively optimize arcs' prices influenced by the arcs congestion obtained through O-D paths flow requests.

Interconnected intersection "auctioneer" agents iteratively calculate arcs' shadow prices in terms of arc penalty λ minimizing the congestion effects. Lagrange multipliers are calculated through a distributed dual-decomposition based algorithm which decouples coupled objectives (4) and coupled constraint sets (5) that are not readily decomposable. On the other hand, each origin agent calculates shortest paths to its destinations with arcs' prices updated and given by the intersection agents, envy-freeness prices ζ, consistency dual prices ξ, and person demand distribution over paths prices μ and thus decides upon the amount of persons to be routed on assigned paths depending on the arcs' prices. The network decomposition method used here was inspired by [20].

After the traffic assignment is made for O-D pairs on the first level of the optimization model, the latter decide, on the second level, of the persons' assignment to the paths based on relevant social welfare parameters that guarantee equality through an iterative auction. The negotiation through auctions at the second level is local between each origin agent and the persons starting their travel at that origin. The person disutility is seen as a function of some nominal and the actual travel time.

6   Case Study

We demonstrate the functionality of the proposed architecture on a simple case study example and show how the route recommendation changes when the flow of the people following the suggestions changes based on the herding and familiarity behavior.

We consider the example in Fig. 2 which appears in [1] without the route's safety optimization. In the example, there are two O-D pairs, (s_1, t_1) and (s_2, t_2), the demand of (s_1, t_1) being 10, and of (s_2, t_2) 20. The arcs' capacities u_{ij}, costs of transverse c_{ij} and safeties S_{ij} can be seen in Fig. 2. The flows of (s_1, t_1) is colored in red, and of (s_2, t_2) in black.

In finding safe paths and minimizing O-D demands paths' costs across the network, we are concerned about the dynamics of the persons' average travel times in respect to the user responses to recommended paths influenced by irrational behaviors. The parameters for the routes travel time optimization model were taken from [16].

The optimal flow Nash product solution is 4.57, obtained in 4 iterations with flow over arcs shown in Fig 2. The best set of routes for this problem when there is no frustration ($\Delta = 0$) is as follows. For O-D pair $s_1 - t_1$, $s_1 - t_1$ with cost 5, $s_1 - 3 - 4 - t_1$ with cost 70, and for $s_2 - t_2$, $s_2 - 3 - 4 - t_2$ with cost 70, and $s_2 - t_2$ with cost 30. when $\Delta = 1$, and the herding behavior dominates, the probability of any of the two paths for O-D pair $s_1 - t_1$ is equal and depends on the first pedestrian's path decision. O-D pair $s_2 - t_2$ will always choose path $s_2 - 3 - 4 - t_2$ influenced by the larger flow volume on this path. With $\Delta = 1$, in a full panic state, a crowd is insusceptible of any route recommendation. However, with $\Delta < 0.5$, i.e., a majority of the flow being susceptible to the guidance, we can influence the flow and the solution will gradually stabilize to the flow with $\Delta = 0$.

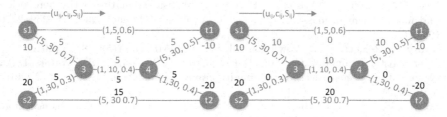

Fig. 2. Left: The case study network with people flow when $\Delta = 0$; Right: The network flows when $\Delta = 1$.

7   Conclusions

In this work we studied people flow coordination problem with the focus on smart spaces. We considered how stress and frustration affect the desired flow rate and how these factors further affect the physical movement of crowds. In this context, we proposed a multi-agent based route recommender architecture composed of the route optimization and the human factor module. The former, furthermore, includes routes' safety optimization, and travel time system optimization with fairness models. The architecture considers the rational and irrational behavior caused by excessive stress and frustration that can lead to familiarity and herding behaviors. The architecture's functioning is demonstrated on a case study. Moreover, if we consider multiple communicating open and closed spaces, this coordination model can be potentially applied to different scales in emergency evacuation at a building, district, and urban level. In the future work, we plan to perform a thorough scalability analysis and validate the model in relevant simulated scenarios.

Acknowledgements. This work has been partially supported by the Spanish Ministry of Economy and Competitiveness through grant TIN 2012-36586 -C03-02 ("iHAS") as well as by the Autonomous Region of Madrid through grant P2013/ICE-3019 ("MOSI-AGIL-CM", co-funded by EU Structural Funds FSE and FEDER), and through the Excellence Research Group GES2ME (Ref. 30VCPIGI05) co-financed by the University King Juan Carlos and Santander Bank.

References

1. Ahuja, R.K., Magnanti, T.L., Orlin, J.B.: Networks Flows: Theory, Algorithms, and Applications. Prentice Hall, New Jersey (1993)
2. Banerjee, A.V.: A simple model of herd behavior. Q. J. Econ. **107**(3), 797–817 (1992)
3. Cocking, C., Drury, J., Reicher, S.: The psychology of crowd behaviour in emergency evacuations: results from two interview studies and implications for the fire and rescue services. Ir. J. Psychol. **30**(1–2), 59–73 (2009)
4. Couzin, I.D., Franks, N.R.: Self-organized lane formation, optimized traffic flow in army ants. Proc. R. Soc. Lond. B Biol. Sci. **270**(1511), 139–146 (2003)
5. Drury, J., Novelli, D., Stott, C.: Psychological disaster myths in the perception and management of mass emergencies. J. Appl. Soc. Psychol. **43**(11), 2259–2270 (2013)
6. Drury, J., Reicher, S.D.: Crowd control. Sci. Am. MIND **21**(5), 58–65 (2010)
7. Dyer, J.R.G., Ioannou, C.C., Morrell, L.J., Croft, D.P., Couzin, I.D., Waters, D.A., Krause, J.: Consensus decision making in human crowds. Anim. Behav. **75**(2), 461–470 (2008)
8. Fahy, R.F., Proulx, G., Aiman, L.: Panic or not in fire: clarifying the misconception. Fire Mater. **36**(5-6), 328–338 (2012)
9. Helbing, D., Farkas, I., Vicsek, T.: Simulating dynamical features of escape panic. Nature **407**(6803), 487–490 (2000)
10. Hughes, R.L.: A continuum theory for the flow of pedestrians. Transp. Res. Part B Methodol. **36**(6), 507–535 (2002)

11. Hughes, R.L.: The flow of human crowds. Annu. Rev. Fluid Mech. **35**(1), 169–182 (2003)
12. Koo, J., Kim, B.-I., Kim, Y.S.: Estimating the effects of mental disorientation and physical fatigue in a semi-panic evacuation. Expert Syst. Appl. **41**(5), 2379–2390 (2014)
13. Lu, X., Luh, P.B., et al.: Guidance optimization of building evacuation considering psychological features in route choice. In: 11th World Congress on Intelligent Control and Automation (WCICA), pp. 2669–2674. IEEE (2014)
14. Luh, P.B., Wilkie, C.T., Chang, S.-C., Marsh, K.L., Olderman, N.: Modeling, optimization of building emergency evacuation considering blocking effects on crowd movement. IEEE Trans. Autom. Sci. Eng. **9**(4), 687–700 (2012)
15. Lujak, M., Giordani, S., Ossowski, S.: Fair route guidance: bridging system and user optimization. In: IEEE 17th International Conference on Intelligent Transportation Systems (ITSC), pp. 1415–1422. IEEE (2014)
16. Lujak, M., Giordani, S., Ossowski, S.: Route guidance: bridging system and user optimization in traffic assignment. Neurocomputing **151**, 449–460 (2015)
17. Traffic Assignment Manual: Bureau of public roads. US Department of Commerce (1964)
18. Mawson, A.R.: Understanding mass panic and other collective responses to threat and disaster. Psychiatry **68**(2), 95–113 (2005)
19. Moussaïd, M., Helbing, D., Theraulaz, G.: How simple rules determine pedestrian behavior and crowd disasters. Proc. Nat. Acad. Sci. **108**(17), 6884–6888 (2011)
20. Palomar, D.P., Chiang, M.: A tutorial on decomposition methods for network utility maximization. IEEE J. Sel. Areas Commun. **24**(8), 1439–1451 (2006)
21. Pan, X., Han, C.S., Dauber, K., Law, K.H.: Human and social behavior in computational modeling and analysis of egress. Autom. Constr. **15**(4), 448–461 (2006)
22. Raafat, R.M., Chater, N., Frith, C.: Herding in humans. Trends Cogn. Sci. **13**(10), 420–428 (2009)
23. Staal, M.A., Bolton, A.E., Yaroush, R.A., Bourne Jr., L.E.: Cognitive performance and resilience to stress. In: Lukcy, B.J., Tepe, V. (eds.) Biobehavioral Resilience to Stress, pp. 259–299. Taylor & Francis Group (2008)
24. Wang, P., Luh, P.B., Chang, S.-C., Sun, J.: Modeling and optimization of crowd guidance for building emergency evacuation. In: IEEE International Conference on Automation Science and Engineering, CASE 2008, pp. 328–334. IEEE (2008)

Customized Document Research by a Stigmergic Approach Using Agents and Artifacts

Zina El Guedria$^{(\boxtimes)}$ and Laurent Vercouter

Normandie University, INSA Rouen, LITIS, 76000 Rouen, France
{zina.el_guedria,laurent.vercouter}@insa-rouen.fr

Abstract. Document research in a digital corpus can be considered as a browsing process driven by some information needs. Such browses requires the use of traditional information retrieval tools to select relevant documents based on a query. But they can be improved by the use of customization and adaptation mechanisms in order to refine the representation of information needs. Several factors are useful to influence this customization: user profiles, browsing profiles, semantic proximity of documents, recommendations from other similar users, ... We propose in this article to treat this diversity of influence by a multiagent system interacting with a shared environment representing the users navigation. We follow a stigmergic approach in which the agents implement different customization factors and modify their shared environment to influence the representation of users needs and the browsing. This multiagent system has been implemented using an artifact layer for the environment.

Keywords: Customized document research · Agent and artifact · Stigmergic approach · Information need

1 Introduction

Accessing documents from a digital corpus raises problems related to information retrieval, visualisation of query results and navigation between documents. Some of these problems are similar to those encountered in the field of information retrieval on the web (e.g. the calculation of the relevance of documents in response to a query) but others are specific to the fact that we consider a closed, finite corpus in which documents, queries and users are specific to a given thematic. In this context, the recognition of distinctive users or uses may be interesting to improve the documents retrieval process.

We are interested in this article in the customization of browsing inside a digital document corpus. There are many factors that can be taken into account for customizing: a user-specific profile, a recognized browsing use case, a semantic proximity between documents or a recommendation built on the navigation history. We propose in this article to treat this diversity of influence by a multiagent system interacting with a shared environment representing the users navigation. We follow a stigmergic approach in which the agents implement different

© Springer International Publishing Switzerland 2016
M. Rovatsos et al. (Eds.): EUMAS 2015/AT 2015, LNAI 9571, pp. 50–64, 2016.
DOI: 10.1007/978-3-319-33509-4_4

customization factors and modify their shared environment to influence the representation of users needs and the browsing. This environment, implemented in a layer of artifacts, is thus an object built and adapted by the collective activity of agents and the user, implementing the decision layer. The contributions described in this article are:

- An agent-artifact model of a multiagent system to achieve customized browsing;
- A representation of a browsing profile including a query reformulation process;
- A recommendation process based on similar profiles.

This article is organised as follows: Sect. 2 provides an overview of research being carried out concerning customized information retrieval. In particular, we present researches using a multiagent approach for information retrieval and customization. Section 3 presents our multiagent model of a customized browsing platform composed by two layers: a browsing layer and a decision layer. Section 4 presents an application case that have been realized for a High-Normandy regional project, PlaIR 2.0, using a digital corpus from the field of international transportation law. Finally, the conclusion summarizes the work described in this article and our prospects for future work.

2 Information Retrieval and Multiagent Systems

2.1 Multiagent System for Information Retrieval

The first multiagent approaches for information retrieval have focused on the distribution of information retrieval tasks. Generally, these tasks are assigned to different agents that can execute them in sequence or in competition. These multiagent models proposes distinct agents in charge of different entities: users, resources, ontology etc. Among the first multiagents systems for information retrieval we can cite for example: InfoSleuth [1], the NetSA system [2], the digital library UMDL [3], RETSINA model [7] and the AgentSeek system [8].

Customization has been addressed in more recent approaches such as SARI-POD (An Intelligent Possibilistic Web Information Retrieval using multiagent system) [4]. This multiagent model offers a collaboration between different actors and implements all the features of the information retrieval system for the web. It is based on two Hierarchical Small-Worlds (HSW) Networks and a Possibilistic Networks (PN): The first HSW consists in structuring the found documents in dense zones of Web pages, which strongly depend on each other. The second HSW consists in considering the query as multiple in the sense that we don't seek only the keyword in the Web pages but also its semantically close substantives. The PN generates the mixing of these two HSW in order to organize the searched documents according to user's preferences.

The SWAPP platform (Search based Web AdaPtive Platform) proposes a self-adaptive and interactive system by a self-organising multiagent system applied to customize information access [9]. It uses the AMAS approach (Adaptive multiagent System) to propose a customized and adaptative assessment of implicit user feedback using the UIM (User Interest Manager) as well as the adaptive construction of his profile based on the UPM (User Profile Manager) using textual documents representing its interests.

2.2   Customized Information Retrieval

Customized information retrieval is required when the expression of an information need may be imprecise or erroneous. Indeed, to refine their information needs, users may be unable to find the right terms for a query [10] that may also be ambiguous [11]. This task is difficult even for experienced users [12]. Several works in the field of information retrieval have been interested by the issue of customization. We can distinguish individual and collaborative customization. Individual customization [13,14] considers the user as isolated and the user model is built on the basis of its content preferences or activities and mobility through applications. Collaborative customization [15,16] considers the user as a member of a group of users and the user model is built on the basis of its content preferences or activities through applications as well as models of other similar users.

There are three forms of customization: explicit, implicit and hybrid customization. When it is explicit, the collection of descriptive data to build a profile is provided by the user. For example, demographic data (age, sex, tongue [17,18]), the choice of preferences (language, kind of documents [14]), the topic of interest [19] and qualitative judgments about the information (I like, I dislike) [13,20]. The aforementioned data can be collected through forms (boxes, key words entry), developed interfaces (votes, notes, annotations) or questionnaires. Concerning implicit customization, data is collected by analyzing user interactions and activity [21] writing styles [22] or queries [23]. Situational data that depends on the place and time of issue of the query [24,25], the user's social environment such as his friends [26], or physically close persons [27] as a source of data. We also include the user's social data such as annotations, posts, blogs, messages, signals, etc. [28–30]. User activity is a primary source for implicit customization. This activity can be determined on the one hand from the visited documents, queries past [13,31] navigation data [32,33], used applications [33,34], bookmarks [34] and the user locations history [35]. On the other hand the interactions of the user such as eye movements; clicks [36]; actions on documents (opening, closing, printing, reading etc.) [37]; messages (emails) sent or received [38]; social annotations and bookmarks [28,29].

Finally hybrid customization uses both implicit and explicit customization. This hybrid customization can begin with the explicit collection and refine with an implicit approach (System WAIR [39]) or it can start by an implicit collection that has to be validated by an explicit action of users.

Another axis of customization deals with the duration of search session namely; customization based on the current context (short term) and passed context-based customization (long-term). In the short-term customization, a memory of the customization is equal to the duration of the session. In this case, one encounters a problem of delimitation of the search session. Either a delimitation based on time (e.g. 30 min in [40]), a delimitation based on the similarity of successive queries [41,42] or a delimitation based on the similarity of the search results [43]. customization based on the past context (long term) where customization memory is equal to the duration of the user account. In these systems, we can define the search sessions [6,14], or not [13].

Each of the systems shown above, propose a multi agent model for a specific information retrieval system. Thus, they are designed for a specific use and resources and the agents and their interactions are defined according to the information systems component. Int his article, we propose a more general approach, based on the general information retrieval process, but that allows open customization by adding customization factors according to the current needs.

3   A Multiagent System for Customized Corpus Browsing

This section describes the proposed multiagent system to achieve customized browsing in a digital corpus of documents. A multiagent approach has been adopted to represent the heterogeneity of customization factors. Thus, each agent applies a different influence on the selection of documents to be presented to the user. The first part of this section presents the overall architecture of the system. Then the shared environment, representing browsing processes is described. At last, we present the agents specifications for the decision layer.

3.1   Multiagent Architecture

The aim of our platform is to allow users to browse sequentially through a closed, finite corpus by visualising various documents and refining or adapting their query progressively. First, It is necessary to use traditional information retrieval mechanisms to select relevant documents based on a query. We propose to complete these tools with customization and adaptation mechanisms to refine the representation of the information need. This evolution is dynamic since it is performed during a browsing session based on the users profile, their actions and their previous browsings. For that reason we use the term *information need* to describe the overall objective that the platform must meet rather than *query*, specific to a punctual search for information.

To achieve a customized browsing, the stigmergic approach [46] allows carrying out an open browsing system that supports independent addition of new customization factors.

Stigmergy is a mechanism of indirect coordination between agents or actions [47]. The principle is that the trace left in the environment by an action stimulates the performance of a next action, by the same or a different agent. In that way, subsequent actions tend to reinforce and build on each other, leading to the spontaneous emergence of coherent, apparently systematic activity.

Stigmergy is a form of self-organization. It produces complex, seemingly intelligent structures, without need for any planning, control, or even direct communication between the agents. As such it supports efficient collaboration between extremely simple agents, who lack any memory, intelligence or even individual awareness of each other [47].

Direct coordination wastes a lot of time and resources to discuss and argue the discussions. In a stigmergic system, all agents have full autonomy to act as they wish. In this system based on action, what counts is action on the environment, i.e. the trace left by an agent on the environment leads further actions of this agent or other agents.

We represent the informational needs within a virtual environment shared by agents. This need, initially expressed by a query composed of a set of terms is modified through the actions of agents. The evolution of the informational need is thus the result of a co-building process involving agents and the user to integrate various sources of customization and user control. In addition, the shared environment includes necessary tools for navigation (index, information search engine, user interface), as well as all documents judged relevant for the current navigation.

In order to distinguish the decision layer and operational layers of the platform, we have chosen the Agent-artifact approach [44]. Decisions about the modification of the information need are made by the multiagent system, sometimes in interaction with the user. Storage of information related to navigation and the execution of queries are the responsibility of the artifacts of the environment. This architecture is shown in Fig. 1.

In the *Browsing* layer, five types of artifacts are used. An *Interface* artifact encapsulates the capabilities of direct interaction with the user. Each instance of *Browsing* artifacts represents the informational need of a browsing session. For each session, an instance of *Search* artifact is created to run a search for information on the corresponding need. The result of a search is stored in a *Document* artifact. Finally, *Profile* artifacts collect information on user behaviours.

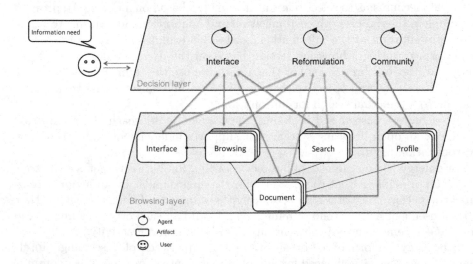

Fig. 1. Agent-Artifact proposed architecture

The *Decision* layer contains agents that will decide to act on the Browsing layer in order to modify the information need or the documents provided to the user. The *Interface* agent serves as entry point to the user to create an initial query and change it during navigation. The *Reformulation* agent proposes to add terms to the information need on the basis of documents selected by previous searches. Finally the *Community* agent proposes to add documents considered as relevant during past similar sessions.

3.2   Browsing Layer

The five artifacts in the browsing layer are specified in this subsection.

We note $\mathcal{D}$ the set of documents provided by a digital corpus. The queries are performed by a set of keywords taken from the whole set of possible keywords noted $\mathcal{K}$. Among these keywords, a subset $\mathcal{T} \subset \mathcal{K}$ is the set of terms used to index documents of the corpus. Finally, we make the assumption that the terms indexing a document are accessed by an *Index* function such as:

$$Index : \mathrm{D} \mapsto P\left(\mathrm{T}\right) \tag{1}$$

Browsing Artifact. A Browsing artifact encapsulates an informational need for a user. Let $\mathcal{N} = \{\mathrm{N}_1, ..., \mathrm{N}_m\}$ be the set of all browsings, for each browsing N_i, a user u_{N_i} has a current query K_{N_i} composed of several terms $\mathrm{k}_{N_i}^j$.

$$\mathrm{N}_i = (\mathrm{K}_{N_i}, \mathrm{u}_{N_i}) \tag{2}$$

Where

$$\mathrm{K}_{N_i} = \left\{\mathrm{k}_{N_i}^1, ..., \mathrm{k}_{N_i}^l\right\} \tag{3}$$

Document Artifact. A Document artifact contains a reference to the documents considered as relevant for a given browsing N_i. This set is brought to evolve during browsing by the actions of agents and by the user. The set of document D_i for the browsing N_i is the union of documents resulting from information search $\mathrm{D}_{i,RI}$ and those recommended by the Community agent, $\mathrm{D}_{i,REC}$:

$$\mathrm{D}_i = (\mathrm{D}_{i,RI}, \mathrm{D}_{i,REC}) \tag{4}$$

Where

$$\mathrm{D}_{i,RI} = \left\{\mathrm{d}_{i,RI}^1, ..., \mathrm{d}_{i,RI}^n\right\}, \tag{5}$$

$$\mathrm{D}_{i,REC} = \left\{\mathrm{d}_{i,REC}^1, ..., \mathrm{d}_{i,REC}^p\right\} \tag{6}$$

Profile Artifact. The profile P_i of a user involved in a browsing session N_i is composed by its initial query $\mathrm{K}_{P_i}^{INIT} \subset \mathcal{K}$, the proposed terms during reformulation $\mathrm{T}_{P_i}^{ACC} \subset \mathcal{T}$ (accepted by the user) and $\mathrm{T}_{P_i}^{REJ} \subset \mathcal{T}$ (rejected by the user), and finally the references of documents deemed as relevant by the user $D_{P_i}^{REL} \subset D_i$. As a profile is related to a browsing session, there may be several Profile artifacts attached to a same user.

$$P_i = \left(K_{P_i}^{INIT}, T_{P_i}^{ACC}, T_{P_i}^{REJ}, D_{P_i}^{REL} \right) \tag{7}$$

Where

$$K_{P_i}^{INIT} = \left\{ k_{P_i}^1, ..., k_{P_i}^n \right\} \tag{8}$$

$$T_{P_i}^{ACC} = \left\{ t_{P_i}^{ACC,1}, ..., t_{P_i}^{ACC,p} \right\} \tag{9}$$

$$T_{P_i}^{REJ} = \left\{ t_{P_i}^{REJ,1}, ..., t_{P_i}^{REJ,q} \right\} \tag{10}$$

$$D_{P_i}^{REL} = \left\{ d_{P_i}^{REL,1}, ..., d_{P_i}^{REL,r} \right\} \tag{11}$$

and

$$K_{P_i}^{INIT} \cap T_{P_i}^{ACC} \cap T_{P_i}^{REJ} = \emptyset \tag{12}$$

Search Artifact. The Search artifact serves as an information search engine. We use for our platform the *Lucene*[1] engine which is a free open source application for full text searching and analysis of textual content. The objective of the artifact is to take as input a set of terms coming from a query and provide the references of documents deemed relevant as output.

$$Search : (K) \mapsto P(D) \tag{13}$$

Interface Artifact. The function of the Interface artifact is to manage the user interactions. It covers the query input process as well as user feedback collect on behalf of Interface agents and Reformulation agents, and displays the results of research carried out by the agents.

3.3   Decision Layer

The decision layer is composed of three agents who have the ability to perceive and act on their shared environment representing a current navigation process.

Interface Agent. There is an interface agent per user, in charge of monitoring its navigation. A user u starts a navigation by entering a query $K_u = \left\{ k_u^1, ..., k_u^n \right\}$ composed by a set of keywords.

   If the user has no browsing session in the browsing layer, a new one is created for this initial query. If there are existing browsing information for this user, the interface agent has to determine whether this is the beginning of a new browsing or the insertion of new terms in the continuity of a current session. For this

---

[1] http://lucene.apache.org/core/.

purpose, the agent calculates a similarity measure $Sim(K_u, K_{N_i})$ between the query terms and those of all previous browsing artefacts attached to the user u.

We assume that such a function exists without limiting us to a precise calculation of similarity (for examples of similarity between queries, see [41,42]). If the similarity is below a threshold θ for all past navigations, the agent considers that a new browsing session starts, otherwise it considers to be a continuation of the most similar browsing session.

$$\exists N_i \in \mathcal{N} | u = u_{N_i}, Sim(K_u, K_{N_i}) > \theta, \tag{14}$$

$$K_{N_i} = K_{N_i} \cup K \tag{15}$$

Otherwise, a new browsing artifact is created:

$$\nexists N_i \in \mathcal{N} | u = u_{N_i}, Sim(K_u, K_{N_i}) < \theta, \tag{16}$$

$$N_m = (K, u) \tag{17}$$

Each time a browsing artifact is created or updated (let us note it N_j) the agent performs a search by the corresponding artifact $Search(N_j)$ with the result of creating or updating the document artifact with a set $D_{N_j, RI}$.

Finally, the Interface agent sends the document set D_j to the Interface artifact for displaying it to the user.

Reformulation Agent. A Reformulation agent is associated to each user of the platform. The functioning of the Reformulation agent is based on the observation of artifacts. It reacts to the perception that a browsing N_i and a set of documents D_i were created. In this case the first action of the Reformulation agent is to create a Profile artifact:

$$P_i = (K_{N_i}, \emptyset, \emptyset, \emptyset) \tag{18}$$

The second part of the functioning of the Reformulation agent is based on the user's relevance feedback from the interface artifact. In our system we have chosen an explicit feedback by asking user to press a button "is relevant" to express his relevance judgment. All the documents selected as relevant constitute the set $D_{P_i}^{REL}$ which is added to P_i.

The proposed reformulation is based on the frequent terms indexing documents deemed as relevant. These terms are obtained by $Index(D_{P_i}^{REL})$.

The set $Proposition(N_i)$ containing a set of terms proposed by Reformulation agent to the user is constructed as:

$$\forall d \in D_{P_i}^{REL}, \forall t \in Index(d) | t \notin K_{P_i}^{INIT} \cup T_{P_i}^{ACC} \cup T_{P_i}^{REJ}, \tag{19}$$

$$t \in Proposition(N_i) \tag{20}$$

This set is proposed to the user who can choose to accept (set T_{acc}) or reject them (set T_{rej}). The profile is updated by the Reformulation agent where:

$$T_{P_i}^{ACC} = T_{P_i}^{ACC} \cup T_{acc} \tag{21}$$

$$\mathrm{T}_{P_i}^{REJ} = \mathrm{T}_{P_i}^{REJ} \cup \mathrm{T}_{rej} \tag{22}$$

If $\mathrm{T}_{P_i}^{ACC}$ has been modified, the Reformulation agent launches a new search using the new query:

$$Search\left(\mathrm{K}_{P_i}^{INIT} \cup \mathrm{T}_{P_i}^{ACC}\right) \mapsto \mathrm{D}' \tag{23}$$

then updates all the relevant documents based on the information retrieval.

$$\mathrm{D}_i = \left(\mathrm{D}_{i,RI} \cup \mathrm{D}', \mathrm{D}_{i,REC}\right) \tag{24}$$

This process of reformulation, described here after the first result of a query will be repeated each time the user selects the documents proposed as relevant (these may have been derived from a query already re-formulated).

Community Agent. The decision layer contains one Community agent whose role is to suggest documents which were considered relevant by users of nearest navigation profiles. When creating a profile P_i, the community agent analyses all other profiles P_j to compare their initial terms and accepted to those of P_i. If all terms of P_i are included in those of a profile P_j, documents deemed relevant for P_j will be recommended for P_i

The construction of the set D_{AJ} representing all documents to be added to those recommended is as follows

$$\forall \mathrm{P}_j \in \mathcal{P} | \mathrm{K}_{P_i}^{INIT} \subset \mathrm{K}_{P_j}^{INIT} \cup \mathrm{T}_{p_j}^{ACC}, \mathrm{D}_{P_j}^{REC} \subset \mathrm{D}_{AJ} \tag{25}$$

$$\mathrm{D}_j = (\mathrm{D}_{j,RI}, \mathrm{D}_{j,REC} \cup \mathrm{D}_{AJ}) \tag{26}$$

4 Application to a Digital Corpus on Transportation Law

The customized browsing multiagent platform, modeled in the previous section, is intended to be implemented for an access to a digital prototype corpus of international transport law. We describe in this section, the corpus used for the prototype implementation in progress with the platform Cartago [45] then a usage scenario.

4.1 The IDIT Corpus

A prototype of a platform of navigation in a digital corpus in the field of international transport law is in development under the PlaIR 2.0 project (Regional Indexing Platform) in collaboration with the Institute of International Transport Law (IDIT).

The corpus constituted by IDIT [5], contains over 40 000 numbered references in all fields of Transport (Rail, Road, Maritime, Air, Multimodal and Logistic) of different type of document (Court Cases, Doctrine, Legislation...) These documents are indexed using a terminology and a full text analysis of the documents.

Customization based on the observation of users' browsing is very interesting in this type of corpus. On the one hand users do not have the same needs for a the same query due to different levels of expertise. On the other hand, the "typical" browsings are held without being precisely formalised by frequent practices as comparative case studies, court-case, specific research ...

4.2   The Artifacts

The modeling of the artifacts of the system for their implementation in Cartago [45] is shown in Fig. 2.

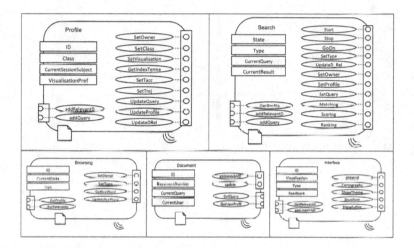

Fig. 2. The artifacts

An artifact is defined by its operations and its observable properties. As examples, we cite some operations in the Profile artifact that allow agents to update the information it contains: *SetOwner*, *UpdateQuery*, *SetTacc* and *SetTrej* respectively used to change the user, the terms of his current information need, accepted and rejected terms. Furthermore, the observable properties provide information to the agents. For example, the Search artifact *currentQuery* and *currentResult* respectively contain the keywords of a query and documents obtained as result.

The concept of links between artifacts (Links in Cartago) enables sharing of operations between artifacts. In the Profile artifact, the agent can access and add relevant documents as well as the user's information needs *AddReleventD*, *AddQuery*. For lack of space, we can not detail here all the artifacts of the model.

The decision layer is implemented in Jason, which allows us to use the integrated platform *JaCa* (Jason+Cartago).

4.3   Execution Scenario

In this section, we describe a browsing scenario within the IDIT corpus.

Initial Query. Suppose a user, Paul, initiates a navigation seeking all legal decisions involving trucks. His initial query is $K_{N_1}^{INIT} = \{trucks\}$. The Interface agent creates a Browsing artifact defined by $N_1 = (\{trucks\}, Paul)$.

The Interface agent launches a first query: $Search(trucks)$ via the Search artifact, which returns two documents $D_{N_1,RI} = \{Decision_1, Decision_{10}\}$. It follows the creation of a Document artifact $D_1 = \{\{Decision_1, Decision_{10}\}, \emptyset\}$.

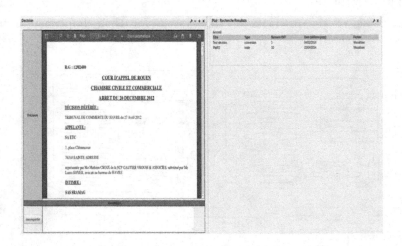

Fig. 3. Relevance feedback

Reformulation. The user chooses to visualise two documents (Fig. 3). He considers the $decision_{10}$ as a relevant result. This relevance feedback, and the first results, involves the creation of an Profile artifact by the Reformulation agent initialised to $P_1 = (\{trucks\}, \emptyset, \emptyset, \{Decision_{10}\})$. The Reformulation agent retrieves the index terms of the $decision_{10}, Index(Decision_{10})$, that returns {motorised vehicles, trucks, fruits, foods, accidents, motorcycles, car}.

Let's assume that the terms having the most important weight and that are not in the initial query are: *motorised vehicles, accidents* and *fruits*.

The Reformulation agent suggests then these terms to the user who has the choice to accept or reject them. Suppose that Paul accepts the last two, his navigation profile then became:
$P_1 = \{\{trucks\}, \{accidents, fruits\}, \{motorised vehicles\}, \{Decision_{10}\}\}$.

The Reformulation agent launches a new Search:
$Search(trucks, accidents, fruits)$ which returns as results the decisions (1, 10, 15, 20 and 19). The user consults the decisions (20, 19 and 15) and judges the decisions 15 and 19 as relevant.

$P_1 = (\{trucks\}, \{accidents, fruits\}, \{motorised vehicles\}, \{Decision_{10}, Decision_{15}, Decision_{19}\})$.

The terms of the index of $decision_{15}$ and the $decision_{19}$ are: *fruits, trucks, damages, goods, percentage of damage* and *delivery time*.

The terms accepted by the user will bring new documents, that may be marked as relevant, bringing new terms proposed and so on until the set of terms remains stable.

Community Recommandation. Suppose a new user, Jean uses the platform after Paul.

The associated browsing artifact is $N_2 = (\{\text{fruits}, \text{delivery time}\}, Jean)$. Alongside the documents proposed by Interface and Reformulation agents, the Community agent compares this initial information need with other known profiles.

As a result he finds $\{\text{fruits}, \text{delivery time}\} \subset \{K^{INIT} \cup T^{ACC}, Paul\}$. He proposes as recommended documents, relevant documents judged by *Paul* for this information need namely decisions (27, 15, 19 and 10). The result to be displayed to the user includes the results of the interface agent and the recommendations of the Community agent: Decision_1, Decision_{51}, Decision_{11}, Decision_{19} et Decision_{27}, Decision_{15}, Decision_{10} and Decision_{19}.

5   Conclusion and Perspectives

We presented through this article a multiagent model to accompany browsing in a digital corpus of documents. The corpus of International Transport Law documents, considered in the PlaIR 2.0 project, represents a case of access to information where customization is a crucial aspect to be considered and includes different points of view namely a user profile, a use case for browsing, semantic proximity between documents or recommendation built on the history of browsing.

We have proposed a model as a layer of artifacts to represent a shared user browsing environment, and as a decision layer, the agents who will, together with the user, influence the browsing by evolving their environment. A browsing scenario illustrates how the agents will proactively propose reformulations of queries or documents deemed relevant in past browsings. As perspective, we plan an experimental validation on a panel of users.

Acknowledgments. The work carried out this article receives funding from the *Grand Réseau de Recherche: Logistique, Mobilité, Numérique* Haute-Normandie Region (PlaIR 2.0 project 2013-2016).

References

1. Nodine, M., Fowler, J., Ksiezyk, T., Perry, B., Taylor, M., Unruh, A.: Active information gathering in infosleuthTM. Int. J. Coop. Inf. Syst. **9**(01n02), 3–27 (2000)
2. Côté, M., Troudi, N.: NetSA: Une Architecture Multiagent pour la Recherche sur Internet. Expertise Informatique **3**(3) (1998)
3. Chaib-draa, B., Jarras, I., Moulin, B.: Systèmes multiagents: Principes généraux et applications. Edition Hermès (2001)

4. Bilel, E.: SARIPOD: Système multiagent de Recherche Intelligente POssibiliste de Documents Web. Thèse de doctorat en informatique. Université de Toulouse, Toulouse (France) (2009)
5. Institut du Droit International des Transports. Site. http://www.idit.asso.fr/
6. Sieg A., Mobasher, B., Lytinen, S., Burke, R.: Using concept hierarchies to enhance user queries in web-based information retrieval. In: Artificial Intelligence and Applications (AIA) (2004)
7. Sycara, K., Decker, K., Pannu, A., Williamson, M., Zeng, D.: Distributed intelligent agents. IEEE Expert **11**, 36–46 (1996)
8. Grey, D.J., Dunne, G., Ferguson, RI.: A mobile agent architecture for searching the WWW. In: Proceedings of Workshop on Agents in Industry, 4th International Conference of Autonomous Agents, Barcelona (2000)
9. Lemouzy, S.: Systèmes interactifs auto-adaptatifs par systèmes multiagents auto-organisateurs: application à la personnalisation de l'accès à l'information. Thèse de doctorat en informatique. Université Paul Sabatier - Toulouse III, Toulouse (France) (2011)
10. Jansen, B.J., Spink, A., Saracevic, T.: Real life, real users, and real needs: a study and analysis of user queries on the web. Inf. Process. Manage. **36**(2), 207–227 (2000)
11. Spink, A., Jansen, B.: Web Search: Public Searching of the Web. Kluwer Academic Publishers, Netherlands (2004)
12. Leake, D.B., Scherle, R.: Towards context-based search engine selection. In: Paper Presented at the International Conference on Intelligent User Interfaces, Santa Fe, New Mexico, United States, 14–17 January 2001
13. Liu, F., Yu, C., Meng, W.: Personalized web search for improving retrieval effectiveness. IEEE Trans. Knowl. Data Eng. **16**(1), 28–40 (2004)
14. Sieg, A., Mobasher, B., Burke, R.: Web search personalization with ontological user profiles. In: Proceedings of the Sixteenth ACM Conference on Information and Knowledge Management, pp. 525–534. ACM, November 2007
15. Teevan, J., Morris, M.R., Bush, S.: Discovering and using groups to improve personalized search. In: Proceedings of the Second ACM International Conference on Web Search and Data Mining, pp. 15–24. ACM, February 2009
16. Morris, M.R., Teevan, J., Bush, S.: Enhancing collaborative web search with personalization: groupization, smart splitting, and group hit-highlighting. In: Proceedings of the 2008 ACM Conference on Computer Supported Cooperative Work, pp. 481–484. ACM, November 2008
17. Hupfer, M.E., Detlor, B.: Gender and web information seeking: a self-concept orientation model. J. Am. Soc. Inf. Sci. Technol. **57**(8), 1105–1115 (2006)
18. Weber, I., Castillo, C.: The demographics of web search. In: Proceedings of the 33rd International ACM SIGIR Conference on Research and Development in Information Retrieval, pp. 523–530. ACM, July 2010
19. Cheverst, K., Davies, N., Mitchell, K., Friday, A., Efstratiou, C.: Developing a context-aware electronic tourist guide: some issues and experiences. In: Proceedings of the SIGCHI Conference on Human Factors in Computing Systems, pp. 17–24. ACM, April 2000
20. Chen, L., Sycara, K.: WebMate: a personal agent for browsing and searching. In: Proceedings of the Second International Conference on Autonomous Agents, pp. 132–139. ACM, May 1998
21. Hu, J., Zeng, H.J., Li, H., Niu, C., Chen, Z.: Demographic prediction based on user's browsing behavior. In: Proceedings of the 16th International Conference on World Wide Web, pp. 151–160. ACM, May 2007

22. Argamon, S., Koppel, M., Fine, J., Shimoni, A.R.: Gender, genre, and writing style in formal written texts. To appear in Text **23**(3) (2003)
23. Jones, R., Kumar, R., Pang, B., Tomkins, A.: I know what you did last summer: query logs and user privacy. In: Proceedings of the Sixteenth ACM Conference on Information and Knowledge Management, pp. 909–914. ACM, November 2007
24. van Setten, M., Pokraev, S., Koolwaaij, J.: Context-aware recommendations in the mobile tourist application COMPASS. In: Bra, P.M.E., Nejdl, W. (eds.) AH 2004. LNCS, vol. 3137, pp. 235–244. Springer, Heidelberg (2004)
25. Abowd, G.D., Atkeson, C.G., Hong, J., Long, S., Kooper, R., Pinkerton, M.: Cyberguide: a mobile context-aware tour guide. Wireless Netw. **3**(5), 421–433 (1997)
26. Church, K., Neumann, J., Cherubini, M., Oliver, N.: SocialSearchBrowser: a novel mobile search and information discovery tool. In: Proceedings of the 15th International Conference on Intelligent User Interfaces, pp. 101–110. ACM, February 2010
27. Rhodes, B.: Using physical context for just-in-time information retrieval computers. IEEE Trans. **52**(8), 1011–1014 (2003)
28. Karweg, B., Huetter, C., Böhm, K.: Evolving social search based on bookmarks and status messages from social networks. In: Proceedings of the 20th ACM International Conference on Information and Knowledge Management, pp. 1825–1834. ACM, October 2011
29. Hecht, B., Teevan, J., Morris, M.R., Liebling, D.J.: SearchBuddies: bringing search engines into the conversation. ICWSM **12**, 138–145 (2012)
30. Vallet, D., Cantador, I., Jose, J.M.: Personalizing web search with folksonomy-based user and document profiles. In: Gurrin, C., He, Y., Kazai, G., Kruschwitz, U., Little, S., Roelleke, T., Rüger, S., van Rijsbergen, K. (eds.) ECIR 2010. LNCS, vol. 5993, pp. 420–431. Springer, Heidelberg (2010)
31. Shen, X., Tan, B., Zhai, C.: Context-sensitive information retrieval using implicit feedback. In: Proceedings of the 28th Annual International ACM SIGIR Conference on Research and Development in Information Retrieval, pp. 43–50. ACM, August 2005
32. Speretta, M., Gauch, S.: Personalized search based on user search histories. In: Proceedings of the 2005 IEEE/WIC/ACM International Conference on Web Intelligence, pp. 622–628. IEEE, September 2005
33. Yau, S.S., Liu, H., Huang, D., Yao, Y.: Situation-aware personalized information retrieval for mobile internet. In: Proceedings of the 27th Annual International Computer Software and Applications Conference, COMPSAC 2003, pp. 639–644. IEEE, November 2003
34. Dumais, S., Cutrell, E., Cadiz, J.J., Jancke, G., Sarin, R., Robbins, D.C.: Stuff I've seen: a system for personal information retrieval and re-use. In: Proceedings of the 26th Annual International ACM SIGIR Conference on Research and Development in Informaion Retrieval, pp. 72–79. ACM, July 2003
35. Ying, J.J.C., Lu, E.H.C., Lee, W.C., Weng, T.C., Tseng, V.S.: Mining user similarity from semantic trajectories. In: Proceedings of the 2nd ACM SIGSPATIAL International Workshop on Location Based Social Networks, pp. 19–26. ACM, November 2010
36. Sun, J.T., Zeng, H.J., Liu, H., Lu, Y., Chen, Z.: Cubesvd: a novel approach to personalized web search. In: Proceedings of the 14th International Conference on World Wide Web, pp. 382–390. ACM, May 2005
37. Pretschner, A., Gauch, S.: Ontology based personalized search. In: Proceedings of the 11th IEEE International Conference on Tools with Artificial Intelligence, pp. 391–398. IEEE (1999)

38. Bellotti, V., Begole, B., Chi, E.H., Ducheneaut, N., Fang, J., Isaacs, E., Walendowski, A.: Activity-based serendipitous recommendations with the Magitti mobile leisure guide. In: Proceedings of the SIGCHI Conference on Human Factors in Computing Systems, pp. 1157–1166. ACM, April 2008
39. Zhang, B.T., Seo, Y.W.: Personalized web-document filtering using reinforcement learning. Appl. Artif. Intell. **15**(7), 665–685 (2001)
40. Silverstein, C., Marais, H., Henzinger, M., Moricz, M.: Analysis of a very large web search engine query log. ACM SIGIR Forum **33**(1), 6–12 (1999). ACM
41. He, D., Göker, A., Harper, D.J.: Combining evidence for automatic web session identification. Inf. Process. Manage. **38**(5), 727–742 (2002)
42. Jones, R., Klinkner, K.L.: Beyond the session timeout: automatic hierarchical segmentation of search topics in query logs. In: Proceedings of the 17th ACM Conference on Information and Knowledge Management, pp. 699–708. ACM, October 2008
43. Daoud, M., Lechani, L.T., Boughanem, M.: Towards a graph-based user profile modeling for a session-based personalized search. Knowl. Inf. Syst. **21**(3), 365–398 (2009)
44. Omicini, A., Ricci, A., Viroli, M.: Artifacts in the A&A meta-model for multiagent systems. Auton. Agent. Multi-Agent Syst. **17**(3), 432–456 (2008)
45. Ricci, A., Viroli, M., Omicini, A.: CArtAgO: an infrastructure for engineering computational environments in MAS. In: Weyns, D., Parunak, H.V.D., Michel, F. (eds.) Proceedings of the E4MAS, pp. 102–119. Hakodate, Japan (2006)
46. Grassé, P.-P.: La reconstruction du nid et les coordinations interindividuelles chez Bellicositermes natalensis et Cubitermes sp. la théorie de la stigmergie: Essai d'interprétation du comportement des termites constructeurs. Insectes Sociaux **6**(1), 41–80 (1959)
47. Leslie, M., Christian, O.: Stigmergic epistemology, stigmergic cognition. Cogn. Syst. Res. **9**(1), 136–149 (2008)

Collaborative Framework for Monitoring Reliability of Distributed Components of Composed Services

Hisain Elshaafi$^{(\boxtimes)}$, Steven Davy, and Dmitri Botvich

Waterford Institute of Technology, Waterford, Ireland
{helshaafi,sdavy,dbotvich}@tssg.org

Abstract. In this paper we describe a collaborative agent-based framework that allows service providers to monitor and evaluate component reliability using reports of the results of composed service executions. In the framework, service providers share reliability data with each other to mutually maintain the reliability of their services and protect them from unreliable components. Consumers rate success or failure of the composed service after each transaction. In service environments, providers can utilise component services offered by other providers to create new enterprise services. Therefore, a distributed component service can be executed simultaneously by several composed services. Since a composed service is offered as an integrated service, it is not possible for consumers to directly recognise a component that causes the service to fail. Collaborating agents use the association between component and composed services to monitor the reliability of the components and identify those that are unreliable.

1 Introduction

In service-oriented environments, a service can act as a component of the business processes of multiple providers where it is jointly executed in those processes. Each business process is exposed externally to the consumers as a Web service. Meanwhile, *composed services* (*CSs*) may contain several component services. This association between composed and component services can benefit the CS providers and their consumers. The correlation between the reliability of CSs sharing components allows the evaluation of the reliability of their components. Therefore, CSs can collaboratively achieve better reliability during component selection and using adaptation by substituting unreliable components.

Service *reliability* is an important attribute of trustworthy services [1,2]. The reliability of a CS depends on the successful execution of its components. We measure reliability as the percentage of successful executions over a specified period of time. We describe novel framework and mechanisms for the monitoring and evaluation of component service reliability based on the consumer reports on the reliability of CSs. The CSs invoke distributed component services. Despite the possible varying process structure and allocation of components between

© Springer International Publishing Switzerland 2016
M. Rovatsos et al. (Eds.): EUMAS 2015/AT 2015, LNAI 9571, pp. 65–73, 2016.
DOI: 10.1007/978-3-319-33509-4_5

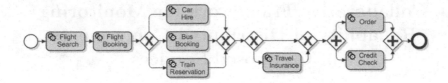

Fig. 1. Example Travel service sharing distributed components.

CSs, our solution assumes some degree of sharing of components between them. The CS providers set up contract agreement between each other to ensure fair collaboration and sharing of reliability data to mutually maintain their reliability. In order to evaluate the reliability for a set of component services, we find a system of equations in which the number of equations equals the number of variables. The linear or nonlinear system of equations can then be solved to provide a unique solution. Each equation corresponds to the structure of a particular CS. The variables in those equations correspond to component reliabilities.

Figure 1 shows an example travel CS modelled using BPMN [3]. The CS is orchestrated from distributed component services to perform eight tasks. The illustrated CS is offered by one provider while other variations of the composition are available from other providers e.g. offering flight and hotel services only. Therefore, services offered by component providers are used jointly by the travel services. A CS is offered to consumers as a whole service and component providers are unrecognisable. The services are implemented as a process with a Web portal for the consumers to collect the required data to be processing. The consumers are requested to submit a reliability report. The reliabilities of components computed by the agents are utilised by the CS providers to maintain their reliability. Business processes consist of constructs as in Fig. 1, including *Sequence, Synchronised Parallel* and *Exclusive Choice*. In BPMN, *AND merge/split* parallel gateway is indicated by '+' and the exclusive *XOR* gateway by '×'. Process structure can affect reliability, and the evaluation of components as a result. Other constructs include *Unsynchronised Parallel* construct and *Multi-choice with Synchronised Merge* construct. We use an empty gateway '◇' in merging Unsynchronised Parallel paths to indicate that it has to wait for one incoming branch in order to proceed to the next flow. *Inclusive* gateways ' ◈ ' are used to split and merge the process flow in Multi-Choice with Synchronised Merge. In this construct a subset of the construct's services are executed in parallel and the outgoing flow is triggered only when all parallel executions are completed. Constructs in business processes are described by researchers e.g. [4].

The rest of the paper is structured as follows. Section 2 describes the framework. Section 3 discusses the reliability computation. Section 4 describes examples and experiments to examine the approach. Related work is discussed in Sect. 5 and Conclusions in Sect. 6.

2   Collaborative Framework

Our proposed framework for the exchange of reliability data between CS providers and reliability computation by agents is illustrated in Fig. 3. The CSs correspond to those in Fig. 2. Each provider orchestrates a subset of components and invokes them by its execution engine. When a consumer executes a CS he or she submits a reliability report that indicates either success or failure of the execution. Each CS agent exchanges reliability data and CS models with corresponding agents and computes component reliability. The bus connecting agents exemplifies the communication chan-
nel to exchange the data. Mutual collab-
oration through the sharing of reliability
data is ensured through a contract-based
agreement between CS providers. Details of
establishing the agreement are outside the
scope of this paper. Coordination agents are
proposed to have the responsibility of coordinating and controlling the scope of col-

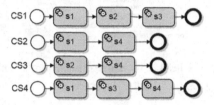

Fig. 2. CSs sharing components.

laboration between local agents to ensure scalability and effectiveness of the multi-agent system. Following a CS execution, a reliability rating $R_i \in \{0,1\}$ is recorded, where i is an index number for the rating. The reliability of a CS is measured based on the number of successful executions to the total executions l over a specified period of time $(1 \leq i \leq l)$. A CS Failure indicates that a component service has not completed execution successfully. Figure 4 models the procedure for identifying unreliable components performed by CS agents. A failure reported by a consumer triggers the computation of the component reliabilities. The agent continuously updates the state by collecting reliability statistics from peer agents. The statistics are used to evaluate components' reliabilities. The data includes BPMN models of the related CSs in XML. Based on the data, the agent checks if it can set up enough equations where each equation represents own or peer composed service. The unknowns are the component reliabilities. The number of equations should equal the number of unknowns in order to find a unique and accurate solution. If not, the server can solve the

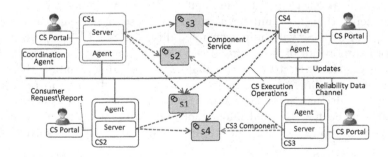

Fig. 3. Collaborative framework to monitor component reliability.

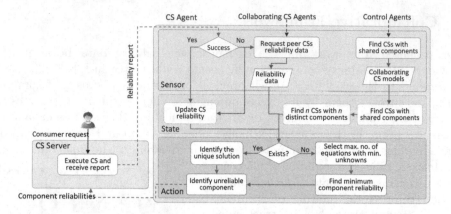

Fig. 4. Procedure of identifying unreliable component service by a CS agent.

problem by finding a local solution. In the next sections we focus on the case where it is possible to find equal equations and variables. The computation of reliability of component services is carried out locally by the local agents.

3   Computation Approach

The agent's computation of reliabilities of CS components has to consider the following aspects of the collaborating CSs: *(i)* The CS process constructs which determine the structure of the equation representing the CS and its linearity. *(ii)* The level of sharing and distribution of components among collaborating CSs. This affects the accuracy of results. *(iii)* The probability that some components are executed in constructs with optional components such as Exclusive Choice and Multi-choice with Synchronised Merge constructs. The following steps describe the set-up of required equations by a CS agent to evaluate reliability of CS components. The next sections detail the computation and provide examples.

Step (1) Find equal number of CSs and Components: Assemble a set of equations whose size m is at least equal to the number of their variables z i.e. provider's CS components that have unknown values. We use $\bar{S}$ to indicate the set of components of all CSs with unknown reliability, i.e. $\bar{S} = \bigcup_{j=1}^{m} S_j$ where S_j is the set of components of a composed service CS_j and j is a numeric identifier for the CS. In order to achieve equal equations and variables there must be $|\bar{S}|$ linear or nonlinear equations (i.e. $m = z = |\bar{S}|$). If this can be achieved then unique solutions can be found and the computation process ends. These are detailed in Sect. 3. If equal number of equations and variables cannot be achieved, go to step (2). If all equations are linear, the problem is solved using a linear solution for better accuracy and speed. The reliability r_{cs_j} of CS_j with n Sequence components is calculated as product of reliabilities of its components as in Eq. (1) due to the dependency between components.

$$r_{cs_j} = \prod_{i=1}^{n} r_i \tag{1}$$

Consequently, the component reliabilities can be computed using the equation $\sum_{i=1}^{n} \log(r_i) = \log(r_{cs_j})$. The equations apply also to some other constructs such as Synchronised Parallel. The boolean function $g(s_i, CS_j)$ is a function that indicates whether s_i is a component of CS_j. If S_j is the set of components of CS_j then

$$g(s_i, CS_j) = \begin{cases} 1 & if \ s_i \in S_j \\ 0 & if \ s_i \notin S_j \end{cases} \tag{2}$$

The component reliabilities can then be calculated using matrix multiplication as in Eq. 3. Alternatively, if the equations are nonlinear the problem is solved as a nonlinear system. In such cases, if $\bar{S}$ is the set of all variables (i.e. components of all CSs) then we must have $|\bar{S}|$ nonlinear equations. Therefore, to calculate component reliabilities, the equation for CS_j can be represented as $r_{cs_j} = f(R_j)$ where f is a nonlinear function that is defined by the structure of CS_j, S_j is the set of components of CS_j (i.e. $S_j \subset \bar{S}$) and R_j is the set of S_j reliabilities.

$$\begin{pmatrix} g(s_1, CS_1) & g(s_2, CS_1) & \cdots & g(s_z, CS_1) \\ g(s_1, CS_2) & g(s_2, CS_2) & \cdots & g(s_z, CS_2) \\ \vdots & \vdots & \ddots & \vdots \\ g(s_1, CS_m) & g(s_2, CS_m) & \cdots & g(s_z, CS_m) \end{pmatrix} \cdot \begin{pmatrix} log(r_{s_1}) \\ log(r_{s_2}) \\ \vdots \\ log(r_{s_z}) \end{pmatrix} = \begin{pmatrix} log(r_{cs_1}) \\ log(r_{cs_2}) \\ \vdots \\ log(r_{cs_m}) \end{pmatrix} \tag{3}$$

Step (2) Consider only a subset of components: Assemble a set of equations whose size is not equal to the number of CS components but equals the number of the equations' variables and includes a subset of the CS components. The equation for the local CS is not included in the set of equations i.e. $S_j \not\subset \bar{S}$ but $S_j \cap \bar{S} \neq \emptyset$. The set of considered components may also include some that are not in the local CS. This also provides a unique solution that includes the values for some of the CS components. If this step is achieved and some of the component reliabilities become known, return to step (1) to compute the remaining CS component reliabilities. Otherwise, go to step (3).

Step (3) Find a local solution instead: If equal number of equations and variables cannot be achieved ($z > m$), then assemble best possible set of equations which is where there would be the least number of variables and maximum number of equations and $z \approx m$. This provides local optimal solutions. In order to increase the evidence that the solution indicates the actual reliabilities of the components, multiple sets of equations can be solved and their solutions are compared.

4   Examples and Experiments

We first use as an example the set of four Sequence-based CSs in Fig. 2. The services share components indicated by numbers. Each equation represents reliability of a corresponding CS in Fig. 2 according to the CS components e.g. equation $r_{cs_1} = r_{s_1} \cdot r_{s_2} \cdot r_{s_3}$ represents CS1.

Example 1. Based on the aggregated reliability reports, the following are reliabilities for CS1 to CS4 respectively; $\{0.78, 0.96, 0.97, 0.80\}$. We aim to evaluate the reliability of their components. Since we have equal number of equations and variables, there is one solution to this problem. Accordingly, we can calculate the reliabilities of the components based on Eq. (3). This results in the values $\{0.96, 0.97, 0.84, 1.0\}$ for r_{s_1} to r_{s_4} respectively. Figure 5 presents how component reliabilities changes as a result of the change of CS reliabilities. In each case one CS changes while the rest of the CS are fixed at values used in Example (1). The shaded area is where the computed results are feasible i.e. all component reliabilities are between 0 and 1.0. The feasible solution range indicates where solutions are valid i.e. all reliabilities between 0 and 1. As mentioned earlier, this depends on the shared components in the changing CS and the distribution of components among all CSs. As a CS reliability increases the net result of multiplication of its component reliabilities components must also increase i.e. at least one component reliability has to increase. The changes in the component reliabilities must also satisfy other equations for which the CS reliability does not change. As a result, the changes of component reliabilities affect the size of the feasible solutions. The unreliable component may not always be affected by the change but that it can be identified even when the CS reliabilities are not precise. The solution to Example (1) is shown by the dashed line.

Composed services can contain more complex constructs. The linear solution described in the previous example applies also to CSs with Synchronised Parallel constructs because Eq. (1) applies to this construct as well. Composed services CS5 to CS8 in Fig. 6 contain more complex constructs including Unsynchronised Parallel in CS5, Exclusive Choice in CS6 and Multi-choice with Synchronised

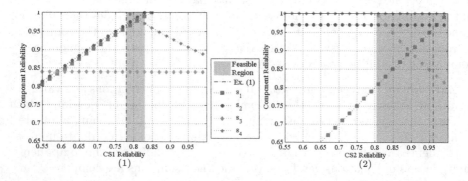

Fig. 5. Evaluation results of component reliabilities based on their CSs.

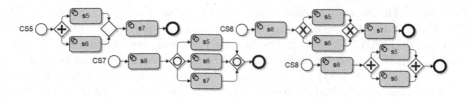

Fig. 6. More complex CSs sharing multiple components.

Merge construct in CS7. The additional complexity requires more elaborate procedure for the evaluation of component reliabilities. The reliabilities of the CSs in Fig. 6 can be represented with a system of nonlinear equations that based on reliability aggregation techniques for each type of construct. Because an Unsynchronised Parallel construct fails when the execution of all its components fail, its reliability r_θ is aggregated as $r_\theta = 1 - \prod_{i=1}^{n}(1 - r_i)$, where θ signifies the construct and n is the number of construct components. For Exclusive choice construct, reliability is the sum of reliabilities of the exclusive components multiplied by the respective probability of execution ρ_i (i.e. $r_\theta = \sum_{i=1}^{n} \rho_i \cdot r_i$). For a Multi-choice with Synchronised Merge construct containing a set of components S and two or more subsets k of those components that may be executed in parallel, reliability is aggregated as in Eq. (4).

$$r_\theta = \sum_{k \subset S} \left(\rho_k \cdot \prod_{i \in k} r_i\right) \tag{4}$$

In our example, we assume that there is equal percentage of executions between exclusive components of Exclusive Choice. We also assume the percentage executions of subsets $\{s_5, s_6\}$, $\{s_6, s_7\}$ and $\{s_5, s_6, s_7\}$ of Multi-choice with Synchronised Merge is 30 %, 30 % and 40 % respectively. Accordingly, for CSs in Fig. 6 we set up a system of nonlinear equations. For example, for CS5 the equation is $r_{cs_5} = (1 - (1 - r_{s_5})(1 - r_{s_6})) \, r_{s_7}$. As we have four equations and four unknowns there is only one solution to this non-linear system of equations.

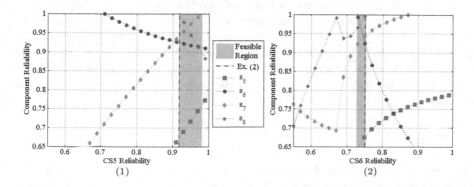

Fig. 7. Evaluation results of component reliabilities in more complex CSs.

Example 2. The following reliabilities are aggregated for CS5, CS6, CS7 and CS8; {0.92, 0.75, 0.68, 0.62} respectively. Using the nonlinear system solver *fsolve* in MATLAB. The starting points for the component reliabilities in the algorithm are set at 0.5 for each variable. The solver provides the correct result i.e. {0.67, 0.92, 0.94, 0.99} for r_{s_5} to r_{s_8}. The solution indicates low reliability of the component s_5. Figure 7 presents the change in the computed component reliabilities when the reliability of one CS (CS5 and CS6 respectively) gradually changes while the other CSs stay at the reliability specified in this example.

5   Related Work

There is a wide range of research in the area of reliability of component-based systems and services. However, to our knowledge, no existing work addresses the collaborative monitoring of reliability of component services based on the reliability of their compositions. Our collaborative solution also has advantages over related work. For example, Nepal et al. [5] only consider the evaluation of component reliability based on individual CS. Researchers such as in [6–8] discuss how to aggregate component Quality of Service (QoS) and how to select component services for new composition but do not examine how the QoS of a component is pre-evaluated except through direct interaction of consumers with the component. However, component services may not always have direct business value as atomic services unless used in a composition. Therefore, our solution addresses an important problem that has not been addressed yet. The method proposed by Nepal et al. aims to fairly distribute QoS (e.g. reliability) values from a CS to its components. It includes exchange of data between entities in the service community, but does not support correlation between reliability data from different sources to derive component reliabilities. Their algorithm does not consider collaborations between providers. Other attempts to solve the problem of distributing feedback from CSs to components include the work by Wen et al. [9] who distribute the scores based on the contribution of each component in the service's success and failure. Zheng and Lyu [10] propose a reliability prediction approach for services that utilises past failure data of similar users to predict service failure probabilities for a current user. In our previous work [11] we describe the aggregation techniques for trustworthiness attributes. In [12] we introduce the topic of determining component reliability from their CSs in the case of unequal number of CSs and their components. This paper builds on and complements our previous work. Grassi and Patella [13] present reliability prediction method that aims to address decentralization and autonomy.

6   Conclusion

The paper describes a multi-agent framework and a detailed methods to collaboratively evaluate the reliability of joint distributed components of multiple composed services in service environments where components are highly shared between CSs. In addition to the characteristics of reliability in CSs, local agents also consider other aspects in computing reliabilities of components. Comparison of results to those from the related work indicate that our results are more accurate. The approach can discover unreliable components with some tolerance to inaccuracies in CS reliability reports. However, it is limited by the existence of joint components between CSs and the data exchange regarding structure and reliability.

Acknowledgement. The research leading to these results has partly received funding from the EU Seventh Framework Programme under grants no. 257930 (Aniketos) and no. 619682 (Mas2tering).

References

1. Tan, W., Li, S., Zhang, Q., Chen, S., Tang, A., Hu, X.: Reliable service computing platform architecture for cross-organizational workflows. In: Proceedings of the 2014 IEEE International Conference on Systems, Man and Cybernetics (SMC), pp. 3066–3071, October 2014
2. Li, H., Suomi, R.: A proposed scale for measuring e-service quality. Int. J. U- E-Serv. **2**(1), 1–10 (2009)
3. Object Management Group, Business Process Model and Notation (BPMN) 2.0. http://www.omg.org/spec/BPMN/2.0
4. Weske, M.: Business Process Management. Concepts, Languages, Architectures, 2nd edn. Springer, Heidelberg (2012)
5. Nepal, S., Malik, Z., Bouguettaya, A.: Reputation propagation in composite services. In: Proceedings of the 7th IEEE International Conference on Web Services, July 2009
6. Paradesi, S., Doshi, P., Swaika, S.: Integrating behavioral trust in web service compositions. In: 2009 IEEE International Conference on Web Services, pp. 453–460 (2009)
7. Hang, C.-W., Singh, M.P.: Trustworthy service selection and composition. ACM Trans. Auton. Adapt. Syst. **6**(1), 1–18 (2011)
8. Hwang, S.-Y., Lim, E.-P., Lee, C.-H., Chen, C.-H.: Dynamic web service selection for reliable web service composition. IEEE Trans. Serv. Comput. **1**(2), 104–116 (2008)
9. Wen, S., Li, Q., Yue, L., Liu, A., Tang, C.: Reputation distribution based on structure-related importance in services composition. In: Proceedings of the IEEE 8th International Conference on e-Business Engineering, October 2011
10. Zheng, Z., Lyu, M.R.: Personalized reliability prediction of web services. ACM Trans. Softw. Eng. Methodol. **22**(2), 12.1–12.25 (2013)
11. Elshaafi, H., McGibney, J., Botvich, D.: Trustworthiness Monitoring and Prediction of Composite Services. In: Proceedings of the 17th IEEE Symposium on Computers and Communications (ISCC), pp. 580–587, July 2012
12. Elshaafi, H., Botvich, D.: Optimisation based collaborative determination of component trustworthiness in service compositions. J. Secur. Commun. Netw. **9**(6), 513–527 (2016). Wiley
13. Grassi, V., Patella, S.: Reliability prediction for service-oriented computing environments. Int. Comput. **10**(3), 43–49 (2006)

Graph Patterns, Reinforcement Learning and Models of Reputation for Improving Coalition Formation in Collaborative Multi-agent Systems

Predrag T. Tošić[✉]

School of Electrical Engineering and Computer Science,
Washington State University, Pullman, WA, USA
predrag.tosic@wsu.edu

Abstract. We outline a new model of *multi-agent coalition formation* which focuses on how collaborative agents can improve their coalition formation skills over time, learning from their prior interactions. The proposed research direction builds on our prior work on *distributed coalition formation* in collaborative *multi-agent systems* (MAS), centered at partitioning the underlying network of agents into non-overlapping cliques. At the core of that prior research is the MCDCF algorithm which provides a semantically simple, fully decentralized, local and (for sufficiently sparse networks) scalable mechanism for multi-agent coalition formation [1–3]. Our goal is to extend the MCDCF-based coalition formation along several new dimensions. First, we want to consider candidate coalitions that (i) no longer have to be cliques but can be more general types of (connected) subgraphs, and (ii) that also satisfy additional, more complex "compatibility" properties stemming from individual agents' capabilities and preferences. Second, we begin exploration of semantically more rich and versatile ways of capturing this inter-agent compatibility than what's found in the existing literature. In particular, we propose applying *graph pattern* techniques to capture a variety of qualitative "compatibility relationships" among agents. Next, we revisit approaches to and benefits of *reinforcement learning* (RL) in the context of autonomous agents repeatedly engaging in coalition formation. Last but not least, we discuss benefits of each agent maintaining other agents' *reputations* that quantify those agents' coalition formation effectiveness in the past. With these extensions, we argue that the resulting modeling framework adequately captures core aspects of a much richer class of multi-agent coalition formation scenarios, as well as, more broadly, of a variety of distributed consensus reaching problems in collaborative MAS.

1 Introduction: Coalition Formation in Collaborative MAS

Distributed *coalition formation* is an important and frequently encountered problem in a broad variety of collaborative multi-agent systems (MAS). Autonomous agents may need to self-organize into coalitions in order to divide-and-conquer tasks, share resources, and/or reach consensus on various matters of common interest. Not surprisingly, mathematical models and scalable algorithms for effective coalition formation have been intensely researched by the Distributed AI community for over 20 years.

© Springer International Publishing Switzerland 2016
M. Rovatsos et al. (Eds.): EUMAS 2015/AT 2015, LNAI 9571, pp. 74–81, 2016.
DOI: 10.1007/978-3-319-33509-4_6

In most MAS applications that necessitate fully decentralized multi-agent coordination, the interacting agents are both physically and logically distributed. Moreover, in cyber-physical collaborative multi-agent domains such as autonomous micro unmanned (aerial, ground or underwater) vehicles or smart wireless sensors, agents might be prone to failures and are severely resource-bounded, including in terms of limited ranges of their sensing and communication capabilities [3, 4]. These constraints have important implications for the design of practical MAS coalition formation protocols. One, such protocols need to be decentralized and, ideally, strictly local. Two, the computational and communication loads per-agent should be rather modest; this applies to the semantics of inter-agent communication, the number and size of exchanged messages, and the overall cost of local computations carried out by each agent. Three, such protocols need to ensure system-level robustness in the presence of multiple individual node and/or communication link failures [3].

One general framework which captures all of these key aspects of decentralized MAS coalition formation, formulates coalition formation as a *distributed constraint optimization or satisfaction problem over a graph*, where the graph nodes represent agents and graph edges usually capture either communication links between agents, or some aspect of inter-agent pair-wise mutual compatibility (e.g., [5, 6]). When all explicitly captured constraints on allowable coalitions are derived from the structure of such a graph, the coalition formation problem boils down to design of an appropriate *distributed algorithm* for graph partitioning or graph covering.

2   Distributed Graph Partitioning Based Coalition Formation

In graph-based models of multi-agent coalition formation, most common approaches model the coalition formation process as (i) *graph covering* (when a single agent is allowed to simultaneously belong to more than one coalition) or (ii) *graph partitioning* (when each agent can belong to only one coalition at a time). Local communication constraints and desire to achieve the highest level of system-level robustness and fault-tolerance have motivated the (maximal) clique based solutions, in which the resulting coalitions are required to be (maximal) cliques of the graph capturing the underlying *ad hoc* network topology of interacting agents. One such fully distributed and local graph partitioning algorithm for coalition formation, MCDCF, was originally proposed by us back in 2004 [1, 2]. That algorithm has been demonstrated to be scalable and efficient on fairly large networks of cooperating agents (made of hundreds or even thousands of nodes), as long as those networks are *sparse* [1, 2, 7, 8]. Further, the MCDCF algorithm, originally inspired by coordinating micro-UAVs [4], has a number of desirable properties relevant to a much broader range of collaborative MAS domains. Those desirable properties include simple semantics of communication and local reasoning, scalability and good "convergence in practice" properties (as long as certain general, fairly reasonable in practice assumptions about the underlying network topology hold), and good fault-tolerance in the presence of "gracious" (that is, non-malicious, non-Byzantine) failures [3]. Software simulations on interesting types of underlying graphs have confirmed theoretically established scalability and convergence properties, under the sole assumption of sufficient sparseness [7, 8].

However, in many important collaborative MAS applications, the requirement that each coalition be a clique in the underlying communication network topology may be too stringent. One practical danger is that MCDCF may end up resulting in too many small coalitions rather than more preferable fewer but larger ones [7, 8]. In our renewed interest in coalition formation via distributed graph partitioning, we relax the cliqueness requirement to merely insisting that each coalition be a *connected (sub)graph*. This ensures that messages from any member of a coalition can reach any other member without assistance from a central controller – as long as the connectedness of such a coalition is maintained, in the presence of possible individual agent and/or communication link failures [3].

Communication connectedness within a coalition, however, is merely a necessary, but in general not a sufficient condition for a coalition to be effective. An effective coalition is comprised of agents that are mutually compatible with each other, and whose combined capabilities and resources will enable them to complete high-payoff tasks. A number of models capturing mutual (in)compatibility and resourcefulness of agents forming coalitions with each other have been proposed in the MAS literature (see, e.g., [6, 9, 10]). In the graph-based models, these constraints on coalition properties translate into which subgraphs are most desirable (optimization) or, at least, acceptable (constraint satisfaction) as candidate coalitions. The second key modification we introduce to the MCDCF framework is to explicitly capture the desirability of different candidate coalitions in terms of each agent's capabilities and preferences, and agents' mutual compatibility w.r.t. those capabilities and preferences, beyond those implied by the network topology. To illustrate, let's consider the following scenario: a multi-agent, multi-task environment comprised of multiple autonomous agents and mutually independent tasks. We will assume, an agent can work on only one task at a time, and belong to only one coalition at a time. Let's focus on a "single shot" problem where, rather than planning to optimize its performance over multiple stages and multiple tasks, each agent is striving to maximize the gain or utility stemming from the selection of a single task, based on how preferable that task is (this, basically, defines each agent's objective function) and what are each task's resource requirements (which essentially defines applicable sets of constraints).

Within this general setting, let's consider a concrete example. Assume that *Task1* requires agent resources or capabilities {A,B,C}, *Task2* requires {A,D,E} and *Task3* requires {D,E,F}. Consider the coalition-formation problem from a local viewpoint of an agent, call it **Agent1**, which has capabilities [A,B,D]. To form an effective coalition for tackling *Task1*, **Agent1** needs to team up with one or more other agents at least one of whom has the capability {E}. However, if (based on estimated expected utility and/or other metrics) **Agent1** prefers *Task3*, it needs to team up with agent(s) that have capabilities {E,F}. Therefore, if an agent can partially or totally order known to it tasks from most to least preferable, such preference ordering of tasks implies a similar preference ordering of how desirable are different other agents as candidate coalition partners.

This model of tasks' requirements in terms of tuples of resources [5, 6] can be further generalized in various ways to more realistically capture the requirements on combined capabilities of a coalition or team of agents so that such a coalition can successfully complete a given task and be rewarded the payoff associated with that task. We emphasize that, whatever the exact meaning of agents' capabilities, preferences and mutual compatibility in a particular scenario, all of those are assumed *intrinsic properties* of individual agents in terms of each agent's "skillset"; see, e.g., [4, 6, 11] for some specific examples. In particular, these agents' properties are *independent of the network topology* which, in most cyber-physical applications, is cf. a consequence of the agents' physical distances from each other, and practical limitations on communication and sensing ranges. We note that, in the model outlined above, (i) an agent's capabilities are mapped in a 1-to-1 manner to a task's resource requirements (hence, we basically use the terms "capability" and "resource" interchangeably); and (ii) each such capability (or, equivalently, resource) is *binary*, in a sense that an agent either has a particular capability or does not have it (and likewise with tasks' resource requirements). More general models, where capabilities and resources can take on more general (discrete or continuous) values, can be readily formulated and indeed a number of such models are found in the existing literature. Such more refined models of capabilities and resources naturally lead to more general *distributed constraint satisfaction or optimization* formulations of coalition formation for task and/or resource allocation (see, e.g., [6, 9]).

To obtain a more flexible framework than previously proposed models of resources and capabilities [5, 6, 9], we take advantage of recent progress in *graph pattern mining*. We specify the network of agents not merely as a "traditional" graph – that is, an ordered pair $G = (V, E)$, where V is the set of nodes (agents) and E is the set of edges (links that connect pairs of agents). Instead, we model a network of agents as a *labeled graph $G = (V, E, L)$*, where L is a set of semantics-carrying labels that are applied to the nodes (or, more generally, to both nodes and edges). Then coalition formation can be formalized as a (labeled) *graph pattern mining* problem: an acceptable candidate coalition is a connected subgraph of G such that all hard constraints as specified by sentences over L are satisfied, and a desirable coalition is one that, in addition to satisfying hard topological (connectedness) and semantic (a set of expressions over L) constraints, also "ranks high" with respect to the soft constraints (i.e., the preferences). The soft constraints and, when appropriate, an objective function, can also be specified as an appropriate set of expressions over L. This formulation of graph-based coalition formation allows us to take advantage of efficient algorithms and heuristics in graph pattern mining (see, e.g., [12]), while providing much more flexibility, versatility and expressive power than our original MCDCF – or, indeed, other frameworks defined on unlabeled graphs.

We are currently exploring various possible specifications of the label set L and constraints specified as statements about those labels, and how different choices of L and statements over L "map" into particular collaborative MAS scenarios of interest. One such scenario is an ensemble of micro-UAVs on a multi-task mission [4, 11]. Another, rather different application domain, that in particular necessitates very different "semantics" of vertex and edge labels, are *networks of search engines* or other "experts on the Web" that provide search, relevance ranking and recommendation services to the end user [15]. These two sample applications differ in more than semantics of graph labels; the natures of constraints as well as what exactly constitutes inter-agent mutual (in)compatibility are also rather different. We will report new insights from the generalized coalition formation framework as outlined herein in our future work.

3 Learning to Form Better Coalitions and Value of Reputation

Highly dynamic collaborative MAS such as ensembles of micro-UAVs often necessitate repeated engagement in coalition formation and other coordination activities. Therefore, programming such agents to be able to learn from their past experience is highly desirable. Various *Reinforcement Learning* techniques have been successfully applied to micro-UAVs, team robotics and other collaborative multi-agent domains for many years. More recently, the need as well as the opportunities for more complex, multi-tiered learning spanning the levels of individual agents, small subgroups of agents and entire large ensembles have been investigated [11, 13].

The MAS environments we are interested in are typically only *partially observable*: what agents sense about their tasks (and about each other) is in general noisy and incomplete [4]. Further, these environments tend to be highly dynamic; in particular, changes to the inter-agent communication network topology or the distribution, resource requirements and/or (estimated) values of tasks may necessitate that the agents need to engage in coalition formation repeatedly. Moreover, those subsequent interactions of an agent may have to be with candidate coalition partners with whom that agent has not formed coalitions before. However, even in such complex, non-episodic environments, an agent should be able to learn over time, based on the feedback (typically, in the form of received utility or payoff) from the previous interactions. In our coalition formation for distributed task and/or resource allocation setting, this payoff comes from the utility associated with a completed task (or multiple tasks), that an agent was capable of completing as a member of a coalition it has joined [2, 5]. That is, how successful an agent has been in striving to join best possible coalitions, is measured by the value (and implicitly, the success rate) of tasks that have been completed by the coalitions that this agent was a part of.

To provide for the necessary adaptability, flexibility and ability to cost-effectively learn over time in such complex circumstances, we propose that each agent maintains its own local, cognitively simple model of *reputation* of other agents. As such an agent engages in repeated coalition formation interactions with some of the other agents, it updates its reputation evaluation of those other agents based on (i) successfulness of prior attempts to form coalition with those agents and (ii) whenever the coalition formation has indeed succeeded, on effectiveness of thus formed coalitions (recall our comments earlier in this section and see, e.g., references [3, 5, 6]). So, in the future rounds of coalition formation, each agent will try to form coalitions preferably with those (near-by and/or otherwise compatible) other agents (i) that provide the capabilities required for completing the desired task (or set of tasks) and (ii) whose reputation based on the past interactions is the highest.

Decision-making of goal- or utility-driven autonomous agents based on those agents' view of other agents' reputation has been studied in the context of economics-centric applications of MAS and AI such as, for instance, e-Commerce [16]. However, we argue that quantifying and maintaining reputation of other agent is potentially very beneficial for autonomous agents in a much broader variety of MAS applications, including but not limited to the traditional collaborative domains such as team robotics and ensembles of autonomous unmanned vehicles [3, 4]. In particular, individual agent as well as agent ensemble reinforcement learning and meta-learning in such collaborative MAS applications, as proposed for example in [11, 13, 17], can be also applied to how an agent maintains and updates its model of other agents' reputations, and then uses the information on those reputations in order to get better at choosing candidate coalition partners in the future rounds of coalition formation.

Setting aside the details of how an agent models other agents' reputation, we observe that, from an individual agent's standpoint, the perceived utility of various available tasks and the perceived reputation (and therefore suitability, trustworthiness, reliability, etc.) of various other agents can be assumed to be two independent, mutually orthogonal properties. Therefore, there are many possible ways of balancing out and trading off between two qualitatively distinct, and potentially competing, objectives. On one hand, a utility-driven self-interested agent will wish to complete the task with the highest (expected) utility – and therefore, this agent will aim for the coalition partners potentially enabling the completion of the most valuable task. On the other hand, a risk-averse agent will strive to form coalition with most reliable among other agents, that is, with those agents whose reputations are the highest – even if a coalition with those most reputable agents enables completion of less valuable tasks. We argue that ultimately, these considerations boil down to the familiar paradigm of maximizing expected payoff (as the most common goal for risk-taking rational agents) vs. minimizing the variance (as the most common objective for risk-averse agents). Therefore, the usual machinery from mathematical economics can be fruitfully applied in this context, in order to design boundedly-rational agents with the desired level of risk-tolerance, and in particular achieve a suitable tradeoff between aiming for coalition partners that have the potential to ensure the highest possible payoff (but perhaps also have a higher risk of failure) on one hand, and preferring coalition partners that are most trustworthy to not fail (thus ensure some payoff while minimizing the likelihood of failed coalition), on the other. Theoretical and experimental investigation on how to establish the right tradeoff, given the properties of a particular coalition formation scenario, as well as the risk tolerance level of a particular agent or group of agents, is the subject of our ongoing research.

4   Summary

We revisit some approaches to distributed multi-agent coalition formation for the purposes of task or resource allocation. Our focus is on scalable graph partitioning algorithms for coalition formation. Within that framework, we expand on the prior arts (including our own research) and initiate investigating the semantic enrichment of such graphs or networks of agents in order to more faithfully capture the most relevant properties of both the individual agents and the inter-agent interaction patterns. One promising novel direction of such semantic enrichment is via graph patterns and pattern mining, which can enable discovering non-obvious (in)compatibility relationships among agents. We also briefly revisit some proposed reinforcement learning approaches that enable agents to improve their coalition formation effectiveness over time; to enhance such learning, we propose that each agent maintains and dynamically updates a model of other agents' reputations. We argue that maintaining reputations of other agents holds many potential benefits in a broad variety of multi-agent encounters, including but not limited coalition formation and other types of distributed problem solving, as well as across a range of negotiation-based interactions among either strictly cooperative or self-interested autonomous agents (see, e.g., [3, 11, 14]).

With the proposed extensions to the modeling frameworks of distributed coalition formation found in the existing literature, we argue that the most important aspects of a rich class of multi-agent coalition formation and other distributed consensus problems can now be adequately captured. Our future work will focus on making the abstract ideas outlined in this short paper concrete, followed by pursuing a rigorous theoretical and experimental investigation that will quantify the benefits arising from the proposed enrichments of mathematical and computational models of distributed multi-agent coalition formation.

References

1. Tosic, P., Agha, G.: Maximal clique based distributed group formation for autonomous agent coalitions. In: Proceedings of Coalitions and Teams Workshop (W10), pp. 1–8. Within the 3rd International Joint Conference on Agents and Multi Agent Systems (AAMAS 2004), New York City, New York, USA (2004)
2. Tošić, P.T., Agha, G.: Maximal clique based distributed coalition formation for task allocation in large-scale multi-agent systems. In: Ishida, T., Gasser, L., Nakashima, H. (eds.) MMAS 2005. LNCS (LNAI), vol. 3446, pp. 104–120. Springer, Heidelberg (2005)
3. Tosic, P.: Distributed coalition formation for collaborative large-scale multi-agent systems. MS thesis, University of Illinois at Urbana-Champaign, Urbana, Illinois, USA (2006)
4. Tosic, P., et al.: Modeling a system of UAVs on a mission, invited session on agent-based computing. In: Proceedings of the Seventh World Multiconference on Systemics, Cybernetics, and Informatics (SCI 2003), pp. 508–514 (2003)
5. Shehory, O., Kraus, S.: Task allocation via coalition formation among autonomous agents. In: Proceedings of the International Joint Conference on Artificial Intelligence (IJCAI 1995), Montréal, Canada, pp. 655–661 (1995)
6. Shehory, O., Sycara, K., Jha, S.: Intelligent agents IV multi-agent coordination through coalition formation. In: Singh, M.P., Rao, A., Wooldridge, M.J. (eds.) ATAL 1997. LNCS (LNAI), vol. 1365, pp. 143–154. Springer, Heidelberg (1997)
7. Tosic, P., Ginne, N.K.: Distributed coalition formation for collaborative multi-agent systems: a performance case study on random graphs. In: Proceedings of the 9th European Workshop on Multi-agent Systems (EUMAS 2011), Maastricht, The Netherlands, December 2011
8. Tosic, P., Ginne, N.K.: Challenges in distributed coalition formation among collaborative multi-agent systems: an experimental case study on small-world networks. In: Proceedings of the International Conference on Artificial Intelligence (ICAI 2011), Las Vegas, Nevada, USA (2011)

9. Sandholm, T., et al.: Coalition structure generation with worst case guarantees. AI J. **111**(1–2), 209–238 (1999)
10. Cerquides, J., et al.: A tutorial on optimization for multi-agent systems. Comput. J. **57** (6), 799–824 (2014). British Computer Society, UK
11. Tosic, P., Vilalta, R.: A unified framework for reinforcement learning, co-learning and meta-learning how to coordinate in collaborative multi-agent systems. In: Proceedings of the International Conference on Computational Science ICCS-2010 (Track on Cognitive Agents: Theory and Practice), Amsterdam, The Netherlands, June 2010. In: Procedia Comput. Sci. **1** (1), 2217–2226 (2010)
12. Fan, W., et al.: Association rules with graph patterns. In: Proceedings of the International Conference on Very Large Data Bases (VLDB 2015), pp. 1502–1513. Kohala Coast, Hawai'i, USA (2015)
13. Soh, L.K., Li, X.: An integrated multilevel learning approach to multiagent coalition formation. In: Proceedings of the International Joint Conference on Artificial Intelligence (IJCAI 2003), pp. 619–624. Acapulco, Mexico (2003)
14. Tošić, P.T., Ordonez, C.: Distributed protocols for multi-agent coalition formation: a negotiation perspective. In: Huang, R., Ghorbani, A.A., Pasi, G., Yamaguchi, T., Yen, N.Y., Jin, B. (eds.) AMT 2012. LNCS, vol. 7669, pp. 93–102. Springer, Heidelberg (2012)
15. Tosic, P., Wu, Y.: Towards networks of search engines and other digital experts: a distributed intelligence approach. In: Proceedings of the 8th International Conference on u- and e-Service, Science and Technology (UNESST 2015), pp. 35–38. IEEE Computer Society (2015)
16. Tran, T.T.: Reputation-oriented reinforcement learning strategies for economically-motivated agents in electronic market environments. Ph.D. thesis, University of Waterloo, Waterloo, Ontario, Canada (2004)
17. Tosic, P., Vilalta, R.: Learning and meta-learning for coordination of autonomous unmanned vehicles - a preliminary analysis. In: Proceedings of the European Conference on Artificial Intelligence (ECAI-2010), pp. 163–168. Lisbon, Portugal, August 2010

Multiagent Model for Agile Context Inference Based on Articial Immune Systems and Sparse Distributed Representations

Radu-Casian Mihailescu[1,2]([✉]), Paul Davidsson[1,2], and Jan Persson[1,2]

[1] School of Technology, Malmö University, Malmö, Sweden
[2] Internet of Things and People Research Center, Malmö, Sweden
{radu.c.mihailescu,paul.davidsson,jan.a.persson}@mah.se

Abstract. The ubiquity of sensor infrastructures in urban environments poses new challenges in managing the vast amount of data being generated and even more importantly, deriving insights that are relevant and actionable to its users and stakeholders. We argue that understanding the context in which *people* and *things* are connected and interacting is of key importance to this end. In this position paper, we present ongoing work in the design of a multiagent model based on immunity theory concepts with the scope of enhancing sensor-driven architectures with context-aware capabilities. We aim to demonstrate our approach in a real-world scenario for processing streams of sensor data in a smart building.

1 Context-Awareness in Distributed Sensor-Driven Systems

Automatically acquiring context models from distributed data sources is an important open research issue in the realm of sensor-driven systems [7]. In contrast to existing distributed system, the problem is exacerbated due to a high device heterogeneity, a large-scale deployment, as well as the dynamically appending or removing of devices. In this sense, context-awareness can enable systems to operate in a more flexible and adaptable manner and switch between different modes and configurations in response to dynamics in the environment or to user requests.

In this paper we propose a multiagent (MAS) architecture that draws inspiration from immunity theory in order to represent, acquire and infer context information. Existing solutions are typically limiting in the sense that they attempt to map incoming sensor data to predefined high-level context descriptions [8,14]. In our approach, we construct context models that emphasize patterns in the data in a bottom-up fashion, without the assumption of predefined system rules or other built-in understanding of the structure of the data. Moreover, we provide a novel approach to represent data within an artificial immune system (AIS) based on sparse distributed representations (SDRs), which is instrumental for context modelling.

Work partially supported by the Knowledge Foundation through the Internet of Things and People research profile.

© Springer International Publishing Switzerland 2016
M. Rovatsos et al. (Eds.): EUMAS 2015/AT 2015, LNAI 9571, pp. 82–87, 2016.
DOI: 10.1007/978-3-319-33509-4_7

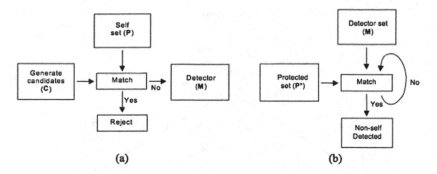

Fig. 1. Negative selection: (a) generating the detector set and (b) monitoring via non-self pattern recognition [16]

2   An Agent-Based Model Using the Artificial Immune System Approach

Artificial immune systems represent biologically-inspired mechanisms that replicate some of the observed immune functions, principles and models, applying them for various problem solving purposes. From a computational perspective, the vertebrate immune system exhibits a number of particularly interesting characteristics: *(i)* distributed information management using no central organ for controlling the functioning of the system; *(ii)* dynamic, parallel processing involving autonomous system components performing complementary roles; *(iii)* self-adaptation and self-learning capability allowing the system to remain stable in a continuously changing environment. Artificial immune systems have already been designed and successfully applied in different application domains, including network security [11,12], intrusion detection [6,13], fault diagnosis [10] or fraud detection [3,9].

2.1   The Biological Immune System

Succinctly, the main role of the immune system is to perform forensic monitoring of the host organism in search for foreign disease causing elements, called *antigens* (*non-self*), in a process termed *self/non-self discrimination*. In order to do so, during the *maturation* process *T-cells* migrate into the *thymus*, where they are exposed to elements that are considered representative for the *self*. A process termed *negative selection* (see Fig. 1) ensures that only *T-cells* that are tolerant to *self* leave the *thymus* and are circulated through the body. Mature cells either evolve into so-called *memory cells* or die once they exceed their life-cycle.

Complementary, the *clonal selection* process is responsible for proliferating *antibodies* in order to cope with the invading non-self antigen, in proportion to the affinity with which the antigen is recognized. Moreover, clones undergo a *hypermutation* procedure, whereby a selective pressure causes the resulting

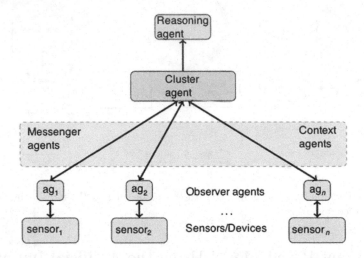

Fig. 2. MAS architecture overview

antibodies to have a higher affinity with the selective antigen. For a detailed discussion, background and terminology, we refer the reader to [5].

2.2 A MAS-Based Approach to AIS and Sensor-Driven Systems

Our approach builds upon the AIS metaphor in relation to the task of context acquisition and inference in the following manner. We propose a multiagent model to represent the structure of a sensor-driven system. We base this choice on the fact that MAS allows to address challenges of autonomous and decentralized decision-making in a flexible manner, by decomposing complex tasks and assigning subproblems to loosely coupled components that interact and coordinate autonomously to solve system-level design goals ([17]), much like in the case of an AIS. Also, MAS solutions have been employed to tackle a wide spectrum of applications, ranging from the energy domain [15], to transportation [4], to healthcare [2]. Now, our proposed functional architecture depicted in Fig. 2 consists of several agent roles:

- *Observer agents* are running on sensor devices and are responsible for monitoring the environment and collecting sensor data. The role of the observer agents is to inspect the incoming data stream for abnormal behavioral patterns. *Negative selection* is applied here for discriminating between the current context (self) and the emergence of a new one (non-self). This can be regarded as an alternative paradigm to pattern recognition, by means of capturing information about the complement set of the patterns to be recognised, without prior knowledge of the structure of these patterns. Moreover, observer agents are organized into clusters that reflect in some way their spatial distribution (i.e. floor levels in a building).

- *Messenger agents*. Once a change of pattern is detected by the observer agent, messenger agents, encapsulating this data (i.e. context features), are created proportionally to the level of stability displayed by the emerging pattern. This procedure is akin to the *clonal selection* phase of the immune system. In contrast to observer agents which reside at the sensor level, messenger agents are mobile in the sense that they migrate within their cluster to other sensor devices. In effect, messenger agents carry out the role of antibodies in the AIS, acting as a distributed short-term memory. Thus, within a fixed lifecycle, if they match sensor patterns exceeding a certain threshold, they are evolved to context agents. Otherwise, they are eliminated from the system.
- *Context agents* act as a long-term distributed memory of stable context patterns encountered throughout the system. In addition, the population of context agents can be differentiated in relation to the time-point when an agent has last been matched, which adds a temporal dimension for context analysis.
- *Cluster agents* are responsible for aggregating data regarding the population of messenger and context agents within their designated cluster, reflecting its current state, alongside the level of stability of the existing contexts. Notably, a spatio-temporal generalization of the observed lower-level patterns can be carried out at this stage.
- *Reasoning agent* provides support for performing system-wide reasoning about the state of the system, given that patterns are expected to emerge at the global level from the interplay of different context patterns. Additionally, the reasoning agent can act as a gateway for querying information about the system.

2.3   Properties of Sparse Distributed Representations

A generally accepted way to represent data in an AIS is using Hamming shape-spaces, where an attribute string $s = \langle s_1, \dots s_L, \rangle$, built upon the set of binary elements, in an L-dimensional shape-space, represents an immune cell, while the degree of match is determined using the Hamming distance. In this work we propose a different approach based on SDRs ([1]) for encoding and manipulating the data, while maintaining the binary format, which is required for certain processes of the AIS (i.e. hypermutation). In short, a context is denoted by an attribute string $\|s\| = n$, which is a high-dimensional binary vector, where only a small percentage of the bits are active $\|s\|_1 = w$, $w \ll n$. Then, we define a

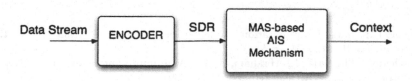

Fig. 3. Context inference procedure

match between strings s_1 and s_2 as the *overlap* in the number of bits that are active: $overlap(s_1, s_2) = s_1 \cdot s_2$. Encoding the data in SDR form gives rise to several desired properties.

First, SDRs achieve a high tolerance to noise in the input data, which is a typical occurrence in sensor readings. Suppose that the overlap between two attribute strings s_1 and s_2 is considered a match if the number of bits w, that are active in the same locations in both strings, exceeds a predefined threshold θ. It follows that, by lowering θ in contrast to w, we can increase the noise robustness of the system. Clearly though, a certain level of parameter tuning is required at this stage, since by lowering θ we could also influence the probability of a false match with another random string. Second, SDRs exhibit a high reliability in recognizing a larger pattern based on matching only a subset of the active bits of that pattern. This is an important property for inferring a context match given that a context is generally based on data gathered from multiple, often different sensors. Thus, a specific sensor reading can be perceived as a subset of its associated context. We refer to this property as *spatial pooling*. Third, SDRs have the interesting property of reliably storing a set of binary patterns as a single fixed representation, by performing an OR operation over the set of patterns. Then, to determine if a new pattern is a member of the initial set, we simply perform the overlap function and asses whether there is a match. We term this feature *temporal pooling* because it allows to represent a context as a sequence of sensor readings observed over a certain time interval. The overall data flow is captured in Fig. 3. Finally, it is important to point out that under the right set of parameters, SDR can enable massive capacity for representing spatio-temporal sequences, while exhibiting robustness to noise.

3   Discussion and Future Work

In this position paper we introduced a MAS architecture for modelling context inference based on biologically inspired computing mechanisms in the immune system. This work is currently being carried out within the *CoSIS* project[1] and a test scenario is planned to be deployed in one of the buildings at Malmö University in collaboration with several industry partners. The main goal is to leverage contextual information inferred from monitoring smart buildings in order to foster services that increase user satisfaction through value added services for smart environments.

References

1. Cheng, H.: Sparse Representation, Modeling and Learning in Visual Recognition. Springer, London (2015)
2. Corchado, J.M., Bajo, J., Abraham, A.: GerAmi: improving healthcare delivery in geriatric residences. IEEE Intell. Syst. **23**(2), 19–25 (2008)

---

[1] http://iotap.mah.se/cosis/.

3. Dasgupta, D., Senhua, Y., Nino, F.: Recent advances in artificial immune systems: models and applications. Appl. Soft Comput. **11**(2), 1574–1587 (2011)
4. Davidsson, P., Friberger, M.G., Holmgren, J., Jacobsson, A., Persson, J.A.: Agreement technologies for supporting the planning and execution of transports. Agreement Technologies. Law, Governance and Technology Series, vol. 8, pp. 533–547. Springer, The Netherlands (2013)
5. De Castro, L., Timmis, J.: Artificial Immune Systems: A New Computational Intelligence Approach. Springer Science, London (2002)
6. de Paula, F.S., de Castro, L.N., de Geus, P.L.: An intrusion detection system using ideas from the immune system. In: Proceeding of IEEE Congress on Evolutionary Computation (CEC), vol. 1, pp. 1059–1066 (2004)
7. Dey, A.K.: Understanding and using context. Pers. Ubiquitous Comput. **5**(1), 4–7 (2001)
8. Fonteles, A.S., Neto, B.J.A., Maia, M., Viana, W., Andrade, R.M.C.: An adaptive context acquisition framework to support mobile spatial and context-aware applications. In: Liang, S.H.L., Wang, X., Claramunt, C. (eds.) W2GIS 2013. LNCS, vol. 7820, pp. 100–116. Springer, Heidelberg (2013)
9. Gadi, M.F.A., Wang, X., do Lago, A.P.: Credit card fraud detection with artificial immune system. In: Bentley, P.J., Lee, D., Jung, S. (eds.) ICARIS 2008. LNCS, vol. 5132, pp. 119–131. Springer, Heidelberg (2008)
10. González, F.A., Dasgupta, D.: Anomaly detection using real-valued negative selection. Genet. Program. Evolvable Mach. **4**(4), 383–403 (2003)
11. Hofmeyr, S., Forrest, S.: Architecture for an artificial immune system. Evol. Comput. **8**(4), 443–473 (2000)
12. Kim, J., Bentley, P.J.: An evaluation of negative selection in an artificial immune system for network intrusion detection. In: Proceedings of the Genetic and Evolutionary Computation Conference (GECCO), pp. 1330–1337 (2001)
13. Kim, J., Bentley, P.J., Aickelin, U., Greensmith, J., Tedesco, G., Twycross, J.: Immune system approaches to intrusion detection - a review. Nat. Comput. **6**(4), 413–466 (2007)
14. Kramer, D., Kocurova, A., Oussena, S., Clark, T., Komisarczuk, P.: An extensible, self contained, layered approach to context acquisition. In: Proceedings of the Third International Workshop on Middleware for Pervasive Mobile and Embedded Computing (M-MPAC 2011), pp. 6:1–6:7. ACM (2011)
15. Mihailescu, R.-C., Klusch, M., Ossowski, S.: eCOOP: privacy-preserving dynamic coalition formation for power regulation in the smart grid. In: Chesñevar, C.I., Onaindia, E., Ossowski, S., Vouros, G. (eds.) AT 2013. LNCS, vol. 8068, pp. 19–31. Springer, Heidelberg (2013)
16. Nossal, G.J.: Negative selection of lymphocytes. Cell **76**(2), 229–239 (1994)
17. Woolridge, M.: Introduction to Multiagent Systems, 2nd edn. Wiley, New York (2009)

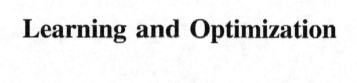

Learning and Optimization

Factored MDPs for Optimal Prosumer Decision-Making in Continuous State Spaces

Angelos Angelidakis$^{(\boxtimes)}$ and Georgios Chalkiadakis

School of Electronic and Computer Engineering, Technical University of Crete,
Chania, Greece
aggelos@intellingence.tuc.gr

Abstract. The economic profitability of Smart Grid *prosumers* (i.e., producers that are simultaneously consumers) depends on their tackling of the decision-making problem they face when selling and buying energy. In previous work, we had modelled this problem compactly as a factored Markov Decision Process, capturing the main aspects of the business decisions of a prosumer corresponding to a community microgrid of any size. Though that work had employed an exact value iteration algorithm to obtain a near-optimal solution over discrete state spaces, it could not tackle problems defined over continuous state spaces. By contrast, in this paper we show how to use approximate MDP solution methods for taking decisions in this domain without the need of discretizing the state space. Specifically, we employ fitted value iteration, a sampling-based approximation method that is known to be well behaved. By so doing, we generalize our factored MDP solution method to continuous state spaces. We evaluate our approach using a variety of basis functions over different state sample sizes, and compare its performance to that of our original "exact" value iteration algorithm. Our generic approximation method is shown to exhibit stable performance in terms of accumulated reward, which for certain basis functions reaches 98 % of that gathered by the exact algorithm.

Keywords: Energy · Smart Grid · Factored MDPs · Decision-Making · Approximation methods · Continuous state spaces

1 Introduction

In the emerging Smart Grid, prosumers are entities that both produce and consume energy, and which could be of utmost importance for the effectiveness and the stabilization of the electric networks [3,14,15]. A prosumer could correspond to a single residence, a specific industry, or to whole neighbourhoods of houses, that may or may not be connected to the rest of the electricity Grid. Already today, in Europe alone, there exist dozens of *energy cooperatives* encompassing hundreds of thousands of electricity prosumers [18]. The prosumer we consider in this work corresponds to a *microgrid* distributing power to a community. As such, he produces energy by means of *renewable energy sources*, and

© Springer International Publishing Switzerland 2016
M. Rovatsos et al. (Eds.): EUMAS 2015/AT 2015, LNAI 9571, pp. 91–107, 2016.
DOI: 10.1007/978-3-319-33509-4_8

is responsible for the needs of *residential consumers*. Moreover, the prosumer has access to *storage devices (batteries)*, which he can use to store energy for future use. Our prosumer is connected to the wider Grid, and he has to take decisions regarding the amounts of energy to purchase from or sell to utility companies. The economic viability of such an entity therefore relies entirely on its business decisions regarding buying, selling, or storing energy; the prosumer aims to maximise profits, while covering the electricity needs of its consumers. Prosumers like the one we consider here are set to become commonplace in the near future [3].

There has been much recent interest in decision making regarding selling and buying electricity in the Smart Grid. There are many competitors in the well-known PowerTAC research competition, for instance, pitting autonomous brokers that compete with each other in order to maximize profits through energy trading.[1] Most of published work in the domain, however, does not deal with prosumers; and papers that do, do not focus on micro-grid consumers. As an example, Nikovski and Zhang [13], propose a method for finding the optimal conditional operational schedule for a set of power generators, assuming stochastic electricity demand and stochastic generator output. However, they do not tackle the problem of selling or storing the power generated. Kanchev *et al.* [10], on the other hand, propose an energy management system for prosumers managing photovoltaic generators, storage units, and gas micro-turbines; but their system is deterministic, and does not consider any uncertainties or perceivable failures.

To the best of our knowledge, our recent work in [2] is the only one tackling the decision-making problem faced by a micro-grid prosumer, modelling him as a *factored Markov Decision Process (FMDP)* [4]. In this way, the problem can be represented compactly, and an exact solution can be provided via dynamic programming, notwithstanding its large size. Our FMDP representation enabled a simple *value iteration* [16] method to outperform a state-of-the-art method for stochastic planning in very large environments [2]. However, the state space in [2] was finite, and as a result its *generalisation* to large state spaces is problematic [16]. In our work here we remove this limitation, and adopt an alternative solution method that approximates the value function, and can thus be employed in continuous state spaces.

Specifically, in this paper we employ *fitted value iteration*, a sampling-based approximation method that is known to perform well in a large class of MDPs [8,12]. This enables us to provide a near-optimal solution to the problem faced by a prosumer corresponding to a microgrid of *any* size, when the problem is modelled as a continuous-state FMDP. Representing the approximate value function requires the use of certain parameters and basis functions [5,12]. We use some well known polynomial and non-polynomial basis-functions, and estimate the optimal approximate value function parameters via employing off-the-shelf optimization algorithms.

In a nutshell, our contribution in this paper lies in proposing and evaluating, for the first time, the use of an approximate factored MDP solution method to

---

[1] See http://www.powertac.org/node/11 for a list of related publications.

continuous state decision problems faced by Smart Grid prosumers. We test-evaluate our approach using a variety of basis functions over different state sample sizes, and compare its performance to that of our original "exact" value iteration algorithm. Our generic approximation method is shown to exhibit stable performance in terms of accumulated rewards, reaching about 98 % of the performance of the exact algorithm in some cases.

The rest of this paper is organized as follows. Section 2 provides a brief background on factored MDPs and reviews related work; Sect. 3 then describes our model, while our approximate value iteration algorithm is described in Sect. 4; Sect. 5 presents our evaluation; and, finally, Sect. 6 concludes this paper and outlines future work.

2 Background

Algorithms for approximate value iteration fall into three different categories: model-based value iteration with parametric approximation, model-free value iteration with parametric approximation, and value iteration with non-parametric approximation. First, we describe the value iteration with parametric approximation approaches in some detail. Specifically, in Sect. 2.1 we present model-based algorithms, and in Sect. 2.2 we describe offline and online model-free algorithms. Then, in Sect. 2.3, we present value iteration with non-parametric approximation.

2.1 Model-Based Value Iteration with Parametric Approximation

This section considers Q-iteration with a parametric approximator. Q-iteration [16] is a model-based algorithm for approximate value iteration. Approximate Q-iteration [5] is an extension of the exact Q-iteration algorithm. Exact Q-iteration starts from a Q-function Q_0 and at each iteration i updates the Q-function:

$$Q_{i+1} = T(Q_{i+1}) \tag{1}$$

where T is the mapping between the states and the Q_{value}. In approximate Q-iteration, the Q-function cannot be represented exactly. Instead, an approximation is compactly represented by a parameter vector $\theta_i \in \rho^n$, using a appropriate approximation mapping F: $R^n \rightarrow Q$:

$$\hat{Q}_i = F(\theta_i) \tag{2}$$

This approximate Q-function replaces Q_i, as an input to the Q-iteration mapping T. So, the Q-iteration update becomes:

$$\hat{Q}_{i+1} = (T \circ F)(\theta_i) \tag{3}$$

The Q-function $\hat{Q}_{i+1}$ cannot be explicitly stored. Instead, it must also be represented approximately. A new parameter vector θ_{i+1} is used. This parameter

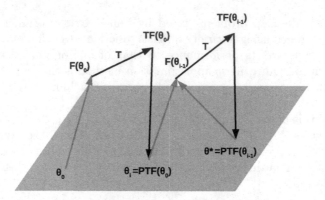

Fig. 1. An illustration of approximate Q-iteration. At each iteration, the approximation mapping F is applied to the current parameter vector to obtain an approximate Q-function, which is then passed through the Q-iteration mapping T. The result of T is then projected back onto the parameter space with the projection mapping P. The algorithm converges to a fixed point θ^*, when passing through $P \circ T \circ F$ leads back to itself. Q-function $F(\theta^*)$ is the approximated solution [5].

> $i \leftarrow 0$
> **repeat**
> > **for** $k=1,\ldots,n_s$ *samples* **do**
> > > $Q_{i+1}(x_k, u_k) \leftarrow \rho(x_k, u_k) + \gamma max_{u'}\{F(\theta_i)\}$
> >
> > **end**
> > $\theta_{i+1} \leftarrow argmin_\theta \sum(Q(x_k, u_k) - F(\theta)(x_k, u_k))^2$
> > $i \leftarrow i+1$
>
> **until** θ *is satisfactory*;

Algorithm 1. Least-squares approximate Q-iteration for deterministic MDPs [5].

vector is calculated by a projection mapping $P: \hat{Q} \rightarrow R^n$. Least-squares regression can be used to choose P, which produces:

$$p(Q) = \theta, where \tag{4}$$

$$\theta = argmin_\theta \sum(Q(x_i, u_i) - F(\theta)(x_i, u_i))^2 \tag{5}$$

The most common problem is ensuring convexity, and some care is required to ensure that θ exist. For example, when the approximator F is parametrized as a linear function, it is a convex quadratic optimization problem, and the respective techniques must be used in order solve the problem and find the θs. Figure 1 illustrates approximate Q-iteration, and the relations between the mappings of T and P, and Q-functions. Then, Algorithm 1 presents an example of approximate Q-iteration for a Markov decision process (MDP), using the least-squares projection. (We refer to [5] for more details.)

Another well known model-based value iteration algorithm is *fitted value iteration (FVI)* [8,12]. This algorithm is known to be well-behaving, in the sense that by using a sufficiently large number of samples for a large class of MDPs, good performance can be achieved with high probability, as convergence rate results indicate [12]. *FVI* was the algorithm of choice for us in this paper.

2.2 Model-Free Value Iteration with Parametric Approximation

Model-free algorithms for approximate value iteration do not have any prior knowledge for the transition and reward model. Algorithms from that class are can be cast as either *offline model-free approximate value iteration* or *online model-free value iteration*.

Offline Model-Free Approximate Value Iteration. The transition dynamics f and the reward function ρ are unknown in the case of offline model-free approximation. Only some transition samples are available:

$$(x_i, u_i, x_i', r_i)|i = 1, ..., n_s$$

where the next state x_i' and the reward r_i are observed after taking action u_i in the state x_i. The *fitted Q-iteration* method of Algorithm 2 is an example of a model-free version of approximate Q-Iteration. There are two changes wrt. the original algorithm. First, a sample based projection mapping is taking place using only the samples (x_i, u_i), via least-squares regression. Second, due to the fact that F and ρ are not available, the updated Q-function $Q_{i+1} = (T \circ F)(\theta_i)$ cannot be computed exactly. Hence, the Q-values $Q_{i+1}(x_i, u_i)$ are approximated using some parameter variables θ_i s.t. $F(\theta_i) \approx Q_{i+1}$.

---

i ← 0
repeat
    for *k=1,... , n_s samples* **do**
$$Q_{i+1}(x_k, u_k) \leftarrow r(x_k, u_k) + \gamma max_{u'}\{F(\theta_i)\}$$
    end
    $\theta_{i+1} \leftarrow argmin_\theta \sum (Q_{i+1,k} - F(\theta)(x_k, u_k))^2$
    i ← i+1
until θ *is satisfactory*;

Algorithm 2. Least-squares fitted Q-iteration with parametric approximation [5].

Online Model-Free Approximate Value Iteration. The original Q-learning updates the Q-function with:

$$Q_{i+1}(x_i, u_i) = Q_i(x_i, u_i) + \alpha_i[r_{i+1} + \gamma max_{u'} Q_i(x_{i+1}, u') - Q_i(x_i, u_i)] \quad (6)$$

after observing the next state x_{i+1} and reward r_{i+1}, as a result of taking action u_i in state x_i. A straightforward way to integrate approximation in Q-learning is by using gradient descent [5]. For simplicity, we denote the approximate Q-function at time i by:

$$\hat{Q}_i(x_i, u_i) = [F(\theta_i)](x_i, u_i) \tag{7}$$

The algorithm aims to minimize the squared error between the optimal value Q^* and the current Q-value:

$$\theta_{i+1} = \theta_i - \frac{1}{2}\alpha_i \frac{\partial}{\partial \theta_i} \left[Q^*(x_i, u_i) - \hat{Q}(x_i, u_i) \right]^2 \tag{8}$$

However, in reality $Q^*(x_i, u_i)$ is not available, and it is thus replaced by an estimate derived from the Q-iteration mapping:

$$r_{i+1} + \gamma max'_u \hat{Q}_i(xi + 1, u')$$

The approximate Q-learning update then takes the form:

$$\theta_{i+1} = \theta_i - \frac{1}{2}\alpha_i \frac{\partial}{\partial \theta_i} \left[r_{i+1} + \gamma max'_u \hat{Q}_i(xi + 1, u') - \hat{Q}(x_i, u_i) \right]^2 \tag{9}$$

Actually an approximation of the temporal difference is computed. With a linearly parameterized approximator: $\phi^T(xi + 1, u')\theta_i$ and $\phi^T(xi, u_i)\theta_i$, the update simplifies to:

$$\theta_{i+1} = \theta_i - \frac{1}{2}\alpha_i \frac{\partial}{\partial \theta_i} \left[r_{i+1} + \gamma max'_u \left(\phi^T(xi + 1, u')\theta_i \right) - \phi^T(xi, u_i)\theta_i \right]^2 \tag{10}$$

Approximate Q-learning requires exploration. As an example, Algorithm 3 presents gradient-based Q-learning with a linear parametrization and ϵ-greedy exploration. Basically, at each time-step of this algorithm, with some small probability an exploratory action is chosen uniformly at random.

---

for $i=1,\ldots$, N *time-step* **do**

$$u_i \leftarrow \begin{cases} u \in argmax'_u(\phi^T(x_i, u_i)\theta_i), & \text{if probability } 1 - \epsilon_i. \\ \text{a uniform random action in U,} & \text{with probability } \epsilon_i. \end{cases}$$

apply u_i, measure next state x_{i+1} and reward r_{i+1}

$$\theta_{i+1} \leftarrow \theta_{i+1} = \theta_i - \frac{1}{2}\alpha_i \frac{\partial}{\partial \theta_i} \left[r_{i+1} + \gamma max'_u \left(\phi^T(xi + 1, u')\theta_i \right) - \phi^T(xi, u_i)\theta_i \right]^2$$

end

Algorithm 3. Q-learning with a linear parametrization and ϵ-greedy exploration [5].

2.3   Value Iteration with Non-parametric Approximation

In the non-parametric case, fitted Q-iteration can no longer be described using approximation and projection mappings that remain unchanged from one iteration to the next. Instead, non-parametric approximators are generated at each new iteration. Algorithm 4 outlines fitted Q-iteration with non-parametric approximation. The non-parametric regression of the algorithm is responsible for generating a new approximator Q_{i+1} that represents the updated Q-function, using information provided by the available samples.

$i \leftarrow 0$
repeat
 | **for** $k=1,\ldots,n_s$ *samples* **do**
 | $Q_{i+1}(x_k,u_k) \leftarrow R(x_k,u_k) + \gamma max_{u'}\{Q_i(x'_k,u')\}$
 | **end**
 | find Q_{i+1} using non-parametric regression on $(x_k,u_k),Q_{i+1,k}$
 | $i \leftarrow i+1$
until Q_{i+1} *is satisfactory*;
Algorithm 4. Fitted Q-iteration with non-parametric approximation [5].

3   A Factored MDP Model for Buying and Selling Energy

Factored Markov Decision Processes (FMDPs) [4] provide a *compact* alternative to standard MDP representation. Specifically, they decompose states into sets of *state variables* in order to represent the transition and model compactly—since transitions and rewards may rely on specific model aspects, corresponding to subsets of variables only. Thus, the set of states in a factored MDP representation correspond to multivariate random variables, $s = \langle s_i \rangle$, with the s_i variables taking on values in their corresponding $DOM(s_i)$ domains. Intuitively, state variables correspond to a selection of *features* which are sufficient to describe the system state. In FMDPs, actions are also quite often described as random variables, while reward functions used are assumed to be factored into specific (usually additive) components. Furthermore, FMDP models allow for *external signals*, described by *signal variables*, affecting state variables; while *temporal Bayesian networks (TBNs)* and *influence diagrams* can be employed to represent the effects of actions on state transitions and rewards. A multitude of techniques that exploit the resulting representational structure can then be used to solve large problems, at least approximately (e.g., linear value functions, approximate linear programming, stochastic algebraic decision diagrams, and so on) [4,9].

 The FMDP model in our work here is as in [2], with the only difference that the state space is not finite. We provide a summarized description of this model here, and refer to [2] for more details. The model assumes that the Grid is represented by some utility company that can specify time–specific tariffs determining the sell and buy prices of electricity, to which the prosumer can subscribe to. The tariffs available to prosumers for the day-ahead are announced by the utility company at the beginning of each day. Then, the problem facing the prosumer is taking the right decisions as to which tariff to subscribe to, and what amounts of energy to buy, sell, or store at any given interval of the day-ahead—so as to meet demand at a minimum cost, and make a profit by selling the electricity to the utilities. We note that all factored variables in our formulation are independent of the size of the prosumer microgrid–i.e., they are not affected by the number of generators or homes populating it.

Factored States, Actions, and Signals. The factored states are described as a multivariate random variable $s = \langle s_i \rangle$, where each variable s_i can take a value in its domain $\text{DOM}(s_i)$. The first one, *tms*, represents the time steps at which the prosumer takes decisions. Its domain is set to $[1 \ldots 24]$, one for each hour in the day-ahead (for which we perform our actions scheduling). The second variable, *bat*, represents the amount of energy available in the batteries, and its domain is $[0 \ldots Battery_{max}]$, with $Battery_{max}$ refers to the maximum capacity of the batteries. This state variable takes on continuous values. Finally, *tf* represents the tariff the prosumer subscribes to at each *tms* and its domain is the tariffs that the utility announces during the day. Its domain is $\text{DOM}(tf) = \{tf_1, \cdots, tf_i, \cdots, tf_K\}$, with K corresponds to the number of tariffs available on a specific day. Each tf_i tariff is described by a $buying_i$ and a $selling_i$ price.

Then, actions can be described as a multivariate random variable $a = \langle a_i \rangle$ where each variable a_i affects the transition from a factored state to another, and takes a value in its domain $\text{DOM}(a_i)$. The discretization for each $\text{DOM}(a_i)$ is based on the discretization of the $\text{DOM}(s_i)$ domains, in a way that from any given state, actions can lead to any other. There are three factored actions. First, action *buy*, which corresponds to the amount of energy bought or sold to the electric utility. $Load_{max}$ denotes the maximum total predicted residential consumption load of the prosumer, and RES_{nom} denotes the nominal power generating capacity of the renewable energy sources. The domain for *buy* is set to $[-RES_{nom} \ldots Load_{max}]$. Negative *buy* values signify the selling of energy. Second, factored action *chg*, represents the attempt to charge or discharge the batteries. Its value range is $[-Battery_{max} \ldots Battery_{max}]$. Finally, the third action, sel_{tf}, corresponds to a selection of tariff by the prosumer. Its domain is $[0 \ldots K]$. The value 0 corresponds to the choice of the prosumer to remain to its current tariff, while values 1 to K corresponds to a choice to select one of the other K tariffs.

Now, there are three types of external signals received by the prosumer and can be described as multivariate random variable $sg = \langle signal_i \rangle$. Each variable $signal_i$ can take a value in its domain $\text{DOM}(signal_i)$. *prod* and *cons* signify the prediction about the production and consumption of the prosumer at a specific time step *tms*. Their domains are $\text{DOM}(prod) = [0 \ldots RES_{nom}]$ and $\text{DOM}(cons) = [0 \ldots Load_{max}]$, and corresponds to the variables RES_{nom} and $Load_{max}$ respectively. The third signal, $price_{tf}$, represents, the buy and sell prices ($buying_i$ and $selling_i$) for each one of the K tariffs.

Finally, we note that there exist certain *physical constraints* that need to be respected at all times [2]. A battery cannot be charged over its capacity, and there should not be an attempt to discharge an energy quantity higher than that currently stored in the unit. Moreover, the battery storage level must always be kept between 20% and 80%. Finally, it is crucial that the *balance energy constraint* [1,11] must be respected at all times. This means that, at any time step t, power produced (including that bought) should match power consumed (including that stored):

$$prod_t - cons_t - chg_t + buy_t = 0 \qquad (11)$$

Transition Model. State transitions in our model are stochastic, since faults may occur while taking actions. The variable *tms* is an exception to this rule–since one specific time step is always followed by the next one. For the rest of the variables, we define certain *bounded regions* which include a subset of the state space lying close to the factored state intended to transition to by performing a factored action taken at time t. The boundaries can be set to any values required. Actions are successful with some probability p while, with probability $1-p$, they transition (uniformly at random) to some state within the bounded region.

Factored Reward Representation. The reward function is associated with *(a)* either the gain from selling power to the utility or the cost of buying power in a certain price; *(b)* the running costs for being subscribed to a tariff; and *(c)* the operation costs of using the storage devices. As such, we choose to represent the reward function as a cost function with three main components. The function describing the immediate cost for a transition from state s_t to s'_{t+1} by executing some a_t at time-step t:

$$Cost(s_t, a_t, s'_{t+1}) = C_{energy} + C_{period} + C_{bl}$$

C_{energy}, captures the cost per Wh for buying electricity given the buy/sell rates prescribed by the tariff in effect:

$$C_{energy}(tf_{t+1}, buy_t) = \begin{cases} buy_t \cdot \text{buying}_{tf_{t+1}} & \text{if } buy_t \geq 0 \\ buy_t \cdot \text{selling}_{tf_{t+1}} & \text{if } buy_t < 0 \end{cases}$$

C_{period} captures the periodic cost for being subscribed into a tariff:

$$C_{period}(tf_{t+1}, price_{tf}^{t+1}) = C_1 \exp\{-C_2 \cdot (\text{buying}_{tf}^{t+1} - \text{selling}_{tf}^{t+1})\}$$

where $C_1 = 0.013$, $C_2 = -2.7$ [2]. C_{bl}, captures the costs associated with *battery life losses*. That is, the costs of charging (or discharging) the storage devices (batteries). The C_{bl} cost of an attempted *chg* action can then be viewed as a fraction of the C_{init} *initial investment cost* for the batteries:

$$C_{bl} = L_{loss} \cdot C_{init}$$

The "life loss" L_{loss} factor in the above equation is affected by the *effective throughput* A_c of the battery over a certain charge period, measured in Ah (see [2, 17] for details):

$$L_{loss} = \frac{A_c}{A_{total}}$$

A_{total} is the total cumulative throughput (in Ah) during the battery's lifetime.

4   Solving the Factored Continuous-State MDP

With the above model at hand, we solve the prosumer decision problem using a model-based value iteration approximation method. Model-based value iteration is appropriate for the task, due to our prior knowledge of the transition and reward models. Specifically, our method of choice is *fitted value iteration (FVI)* [8,12], a sampling-based approximation method that is known to be well-behaving, as explained in Sect. 2.1 above. We now describe the method in some detail.

The decision problem of the prosumer has a continuous state space $S = R^n$, but we will assume that the action space A is discrete. In traditional, exact value iteration, one needs to perform the following update:

$$V(s) \leftarrow \max_a \int_{s'} Pr(s' \,|\, a, s) \cdot (R(s, a, s') + V(s')).$$

The main idea of fitted value iteration is to approximately carry out this step, over a finite sample of states $s^{(1)}, \ldots, s^{(m)}$. Specifically, we can use a supervised learning algorithm–linear regression in our description below–to approximate the value function as a linear function of the states:

$$V(s) = \theta^T \phi(s)$$

Thus, to approximate the value function, one needs to obtain the parameters θ and the basis functions ϕ, where ϕ is some appropriate feature mapping of the states. For each state s in our finite sample of m states, fitted value iteration will first compute a quantity y, which will be our approximation to

$$\int_{s'} Pr(s' \,|\, a, s) \cdot (R(s, a, s') + V(s'))$$

Then, it employs some supervised learning algorithm, for instance linear regression, to get $V(s)$ close to y. In detail, the method is as described in Algorithm 5.

Fitted value iteration does not provably always converge. However, in practice, it often does converge (or at least approximately converge) [12]. If one uses a deterministic MDP model, then fitted value iteration can be simplified by setting $k = 1$ in the above algorithm. This is because the expectation becomes an expectation over a deterministic distribution, and so a single iteration is sufficient to exactly compute that expectation.

Randomly sample m states $s^{(1)}, \ldots, s^{(m)} \in S$
for *k iterations* **do**
    for *each horizon h* **do**
        for *each sampled state s* **do**
            for *each action a* **do**
                sample state transitions s'
                $q(a) = \frac{1}{m} \sum (R_h(s,a) + \gamma V_{h-1}(s'))$
            end
            $y_h(s) = \min(q(a))$ % min because reward corresponds to costs
        end
        $\theta \leftarrow argmin_\theta \frac{1}{2} \sum (\theta^T \phi_h(s, a) - y_h(s))^2$
        $V_h(s) = \theta^T \phi_h(s, a)$
    end
end

Algorithm 5. Fitted Value Iteration with finite horizon. Algorithm description based on the pseudo-code in Andrew Ng's lecture notes in http://cs229.stanford.edu/notes/cs229-notes12.pdf.

Now, in order to find the optimal parameters θ, we have to solve the equation:

$$\theta \leftarrow argmin_\theta \frac{1}{2} \sum (\theta^T \phi_h(s, a) - y_h(s))^2$$

This is an optimization problem and we employ least linear square optimization to this purpose. IBM CPLEX provides us with a high performance optimizer to solve such optimization problems. Selecting the basis functions ϕ, on the other hand, can require extensive experimentation, in order to choose the ones whose use results to the best performance in a given setting. In our case, we evaluated several candidate basis functions, as we report in Sect. 5 below.

5 Evaluation

We evaluate our model by examining a residential prosumer at New Hampshire, New England, north-eastern United States. Our simulated prosumer serves 30 households and includes 20 photovoltaic modules with nominal power 60 kW, 2 wind-turbines with nominal power 1000 kW and 24 deep cycle 12 Volts batteries 212AH C20/FMD200 – VRLA/AGM, with cost of each battery 269,00 €. Estimated battery lifetime is 10–12 years. All experiments were conducted on a 2.10 GHz × 4 Intel Core i3-2310 M processor, with 8 GB of memory.

We initially adopted the following discretisation for our state and action variables. The discretisation step size is shown inside the range of the factored state *bat* (corresponding to the prosumer's batteries' array), and the action *chg* below:

$$bat = [0kWh \; : \; 1kWh \; : \; 60kWh]$$

$$chg = [-60kWh \; : \; 1kWh \; : \; 60kWh]$$

We also defined nine tariffs, which are as follows:

$$tf_1 = \{0.1\text{€}, 0.1\text{€}\} \quad tf_4 = \{0.2\text{€}, 0.1\text{€}\} \quad tf_7 = \{0.3\text{€}, 0.1\text{€}\}$$

$$tf_2 = \{0.1\text{€}, 0.2\text{€}\} \quad tf_5 = \{0.2\text{€}, 0.2\text{€}\} \quad tf_8 = \{0.3\text{€}, 0.2\text{€}\}$$

$$tf_3 = \{0.1\text{€}, 0.3\text{€}\} \quad tf_6 = \{0.2\text{€}, 0.3\text{€}\} \quad tf_9 = \{0.3\text{€}, 0.3\text{€}\}$$

which thus give rise to 10 possible sel_{tf} tariff selection actions (nine corresponding to choosing one of the tariffs, plus one for staying with their current one). The transition boundaries for our state variables were set to bound$_{bat}$ = 1kWh and bound$_{tf}$ = 0.1€.

The discretisation above results to a state space size of $|S| = 13,176$, when the values of the state variable tms are also taken into account. However, tms can be incorporated into the problem's horizon, by setting the horizon to be equal to the number of time steps at which the prosumer is required to act; this effectively reduces the size of the finite state space. Without tms, the $state$ space contains 549 discrete states, while the size of $state$-$action$ $space$ is $|S \times A| = 664290$. This is the finite space upon which the exact value iteration algorithm of [2] operates.

Now, in order to learn the approximate value function for this problem and generalise to the continuous state spaces, we use (progressively increasing) fractions of the aforementioned finite state space as the m samples required by the FVI method of Algorithm 5 for learning the $V_h(s)$. Specifically, we learned 11 different approximate value functions, using sample sizes of 5 % and $\{10\%, 20\%, 30\% \ldots 100\%\}$ of the finite state space, and then we evaluated the performance of their corresponding resulting policies, by observing the actual rewards they accumulate, and by calculating their $root$ $mean$ $squared$ $error$ $(RMSE)$ [7] with respect to the rewards accumulated by the exact value iteration algorithm of [2]. In order to assess the effect of different basis functions on approximation quality, we tested 9 different basis functions at each one of our 11 approximation settings. These functions are the well-known $sigmoid$, $gaussian$, $inverse$ $quadratic$, $thin$ $plate$ $spline$, and five $polynomials$ of 1st to 5th degree.

All the FVI variants thus obtained, compute value functions that constitute $generalised$ solutions; these can then be used to provide the optimal (greedy wrt. the value function) policies, given any particular state space discretisation. Here we assume a discretisation that is as the one presented above, and evaluate the performance of each FVI variant as follows. Once the approximate value functions and their corresponding approximate optimal policies are calculated, we execute the policies 1,000 times each—and compute their accumulated rewards over a complete horizon, and its average value over the 1,000 runs. We can thus assess the various variants in terms of average performance $wrt.$ accumulated rewards. We present our findings in Table 1. Moreover, we calculate the $RMSE$ of the rewards derived from policies corresponding to the approximate and non–approximate value function. The $RMSE$ values are presented in Table 2.

We see in those tables that, with the exception of the $inverse$ $quadratic$ variants, all methods exhibit good performance, which is also quite stable across

Table 1. Accumulated reward when using different basis functions and different sample sizes of the finite state space for learning the approximate value function. All numbers in the 5 % to 100 % columns are averages over 1000 runs and discount factor $\gamma=1$. We also report that the average actual reward when running the exact value iteration (EVI) method of [2] is *1850* for the entire finite state space. Values shown in **bold** are those that are over $1820 = \mathbf{98\%} \cdot 1850$€.

		Percentage of Sampling											
		5 %	10 %	20 %	30 %	40 %	50 %	60 %	70 %	80 %	90 %	100 %	Average
Functions	Sigmoid	1321	1641	1641	1641	1641	1641	1641	1641	1641	1641	1641	1613
	Gaussian	1483	1778	1805	1807	1816	1817	1818	1817	1818	1818	1818	1781
	Inverse quadratic	581	585	580	576	578	580	585	586	585	586	581	582
	Thin plate spline	1469	636	1205	1205	1206	1207	1206	1207	1206	1206	1207	1179
	1st polynomial	**1821**	**1824**	**1824**	**1824**	**1824**	**1825**	**1825**	**1826**	**1826**	**1826**	**1827**	**1825**
	2nd polynomial	**1824**	**1825**	**1824**	**1826**	**1823**	**1826**	**1826**	**1826**	**1826**	**1826**	**1829**	**1826**
	3rd polynomial	1350	1241	1141	1346	1347	1346	1346	1346	1347	1347	1268	1312
	4th polynomial	1350	1241	1143	1347	1346	1347	1347	1347	1347	1347	1268	1312
	5th polynomial	**1821**	**1824**	**1824**	**1826**	**1823**	**1826**	**1827**	**1827**	**1827**	**1826**	**1830**	**1826**

most sample sizes used for learning. The *gaussian* and the $1^{st}, 2^{nd}$ and 5th *polynomial* variants, in particular, are doing very well, often exhibiting performance that reaches or exceeds 95 % of that of the exact value iteration (EVI for short) algorithm used in [2]. Moreover, they appear to be able to do quite well even with small sample sizes. By contrast, the sigmoid method does exhibit stable performance, regularly at 85 % of that of EVI. The fact that most variants, and the *polynomial* variants in particular, are good approximations of the exact value function is further exhibited in Figs. 2, 3, 4, 5, 6, 7, 8, 9 and 10, where blue line presents the approximate value function while the red line presents the EVI value function.[2] We observe there that the graphs of their approximate value functions in general follow closely those of EVI for a large part of the state space, even though the expected values calculated do not match those calculated by EVI. Indeed, what is important for a good approximation is that the graph slope and the *relative ranking* of the state values are as those in the EVI value function graph, while the actual values do not matter. The graphs for the value functions of certain polynomial variants and of the *gaussian*, exhibit this behaviour. By contrast, the graph of the *thin plate spline* and the *inverse quadratic* variants depart from that of EVI, which is consistent with the fact that their performance wrt. *RMSE* and accumulated rewards is not as satisfactory as that of the rest of our methods. In conclusion, the variants that exhibit the strongest and more stable performance are those employing *gaussian* and the $1^{st}, 2^{nd}$ and 5th *polynomial* basis functions, with the 2nd and 5th *degree polynomial* variants, doing slightly better, regularly reaching a performance that is at about 98.7 % of that achieved by EVI.

---

[2] States on the x axis in these figures are ranked in reverse order wrt. steps-to-go in the horizon: states with small indices occur early in the day-ahead, and the ones to the right late.

Table 2. RMSE with respect to the EVI [2] policy reward for discount factor $\gamma = 1$.

		\multicolumn{12}{c}{Percentage of Sampling}											
		5%	10%	20%	30%	40%	50%	60%	70%	80%	90%	100%	Average
	sigmoid	1050	458	340	407	236	275	275	275	275	275	236	373
	gaussian	1371	648	109	68	132	135	135	135	135	135	189	291
	inverse quadratic	1488	1487	1488	1488	1488	1488	1488	1488	1488	1488	1488	1488
	thins plate spline	$3.9\,10^5$	$7.2\,10^6$	$2.8\,10^6$	$9.8\,10^5$	$1.9\,10^5$	$1.2\,10^5$	$1.2\,10^5$	$1.2\,10^5$	$1.2\,10^5$	$1.2\,10^5$	$6.1\,10^4$	$1.1\,10^6$
Functions	1st polynomial	24	26	24	143	229	206	206	206	206	206	226	155
	2nd polynomial	18	23	23	144	230	202	202	202	202	202	227	153
	3rd polynomial	2341	7829	7585	4694	4249	4254	4254	4254	4254	4254	4358	4757
	4th polynomial	2341	7829	7585	4694	4249	4254	4254	4254	4254	4254	4358	4757
	5th polynomial	27	26	24	144	230	203	203	203	203	203	227	154

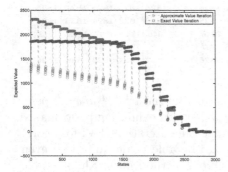

Fig. 2. Approximate value function with a sigmoid basis function (Color figure online).

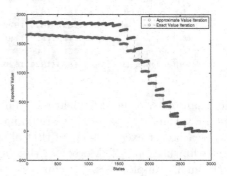

Fig. 3. Approximate value function with a gaussian basis function (Color figure online).

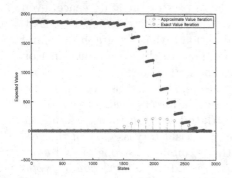

Fig. 4. Approximate value function with an *inverse quadratic* basis function (Color figure online).

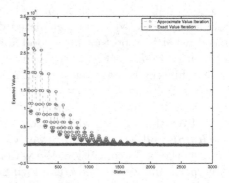

Fig. 5. Approximate value function with a *thin plate spline* basis function (Color figure online).

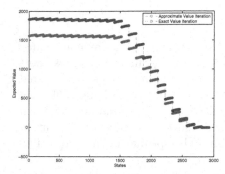

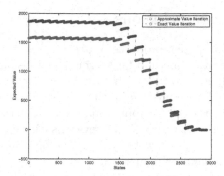

Fig. 6. Approximate value function with a $1^{st} degree$ $poly$ basis function (Color figure online).

Fig. 7. Approximate value function with a $2^{nd} degree$ $poly$ basis function (Color figure online).

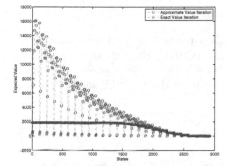

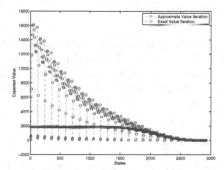

Fig. 8. Approximate value function with a $3^{rd} degree$ $poly$ basis function (Color figure online).

Fig. 9. Approximate value function with a $4^{th} degree$ $poly$ basis function (Color figure online).

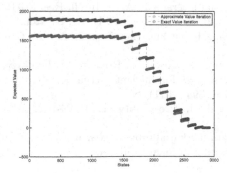

Fig. 10. Approximate value function with a $5^{th} degree$ $poly$ basis function (Color figure online).

6   Conclusions

This paper proposes and evaluates, for the first time, an approximate value iteration method for solving the decision problem facing Smart Grid prosumers when operating within an environment modelled as a continuous-state factored MDP. We provided a thorough evaluation of various functions that might form the basis of the approximate value function, and demonstrated that our approach performs very well for several such functions. As such, our model and solution technique allow the determination of approximately optimal policies regarding the main prosumer activities.

Future work includes incorporating more prosumer actions into our model, such as altering the projected production and consumption levels to increase the economic turnouts; and testing alternative MDP solution methods. Finally, we plan to incorporate our model within *renewable energy sources cooperatives*, the emergence of which is of extremely high economic, social, and environmental importance [6,18].

Acknowledgements. The work presented in this paper was supported by the Greek General Secretariat for Research and Technology (GSRT) through the funding of research project "AFORMI – Reconfigurable Systems for scientific research" with proposal code 2427 within the context of action "ARISTEIA" of the Lifelong Learning Program.

References

1. Ackermann, T. (ed.): Wind Power in Power Systems. Wiley, Chichester (2005)
2. Angelidakis, A., Chalkiadakis, G.: Factored MDPs for optimal prosumer decision-making. In: Proceedings of AAMAS-2015, pp. 503–511 (2015)
3. Asmus, P.: Microgrids, virtual power plants and our distributed energy future. Electr. J. **23**(10), 72–82 (2010)
4. Boutilier, C., Dean, T., Hanks, S.: Decision-theoretic planning: structural assumptions and computational leverage. J. Artif. Intell. Res. (JAIR) **11**, 1–94 (1999)
5. Busoniu, L., Babuska, R., De Schutter, B., Ernst, D.: Reinforcement Learning and Dynamic Programming Using Function Approximators. CRC Press, Boca Raton (2010)
6. Chalkiadakis, G., Robu, V., Kota, R., Rogers, A., Jennings, N.: Cooperatives of distributed energy resources for efficient virtual power plants. In: Proceedings of AAMAS-2011, pp. 787–794 (2011)
7. DeGroot, M., Schervish, J.: Probability and Statistics. Addison-Wesley, Reading (2002)
8. Gordon, G.J.: Stable function approximation in dynamic programming. In: Proceedings of the 12th International Conference on Machine Learning, pp. 261–268 (1995)
9. Guestrin, C., Koller, D., Parr, R., Venkataraman, S.: Efficient solution algorithms for factored MDPs. J. Artif. Intell. Res. (JAIR) **19**, 399–468 (2003)
10. Kanchev, H., Lu, D., Colas, F., Lazarov, V., Francois, B.: Energy management and operational planning of a microgrid with a PV-based active generator for Smart Grid applications. IEEE Trans. Ind. Electron. **58**(10), 4583–4592 (2011)

11. Kirschen, D., Strbac, G.: Fundamentals of Power System Economics. Wiley, Chichester (2005)
12. Munos, R., Szepesvári, C.: Finite-time bounds for fitted value iteration. J. Mach. Learn. Res. **9**, 815–857 (2008)
13. Nikovski, D., Zhang, W.: Factored markov decision process models for stochastic unit commitment. In: IEEE Conference on Innovative Technologies for an Efficient and Reliable Electricity Supply (CITRES), pp. 28–35 (2010)
14. Ramchurn, S.D., Vytelingum, P., Rogers, A., Jennings, N.: Putting the 'smarts' into the Smart Grid: a grand challenge for artificial intelligence. Commun. ACM **55**(4), 86–97 (2012)
15. Rogers, A., Ramchurn, S., Jennings, N.: Delivering the Smart Grid: challenges for autonomous agents and multi-agent systems research. In: Proceedings of AAAI-2012, pp. 2166–2172 (2012)
16. Sutton, R.S., Barto, A.G.: Reinforcement Learning: An Introduction. The MIT Press, Cambridge (1998)
17. Zhao, B., Zhang, X., Chen, J., Wang, C., Guo, L.: Operation optimization of standalonemicrogrids considering lifetime characteristics of battery energy storage system. IEEE Trans.Sustain. Energ. **4**(4), 934–943 (2013)
18. Federation of European renewable energy cooperatives. http://www.rescoop.eu

Composing Swarm Robot Formations Based on Their Distributions Using Mobile Agents

Ryotaro Oikawa[1]([✉]), Munehiro Takimoto[1], and Yasushi Kambayashi[2]

[1] Department of Information Sciences, Tokyo University of Science,
2641 Yamazaki, Noda 278-8510, Japan
{oikawa,mune}@cs.is.noda.tus.ac.jp
[2] Department of Computer and Information Engineering,
Nippon Institute of Technology, 4-1 Gakuendai, Miyashiro-machi,
Minamisaitama-gun 345-8501, Japan
yasushi@nit.ac.jp

Abstract. This paper presents a control algorithm for composing formations of swarm robots. The composed formations represent specific symbols. The algorithm is based on our mobile software agent based control model where robots acquire any control program as necessary. The robots start working with just generic control programs and they acquire control programs for specific tasks from outside as mobile software agents. Since the mobile software agents can migrate from one robot to another autonomously, they can migrate to the most conveniently located robot for a specific task. This control model eliminates unnecessary movements of physical robots, contributing to suppressing the total costs of any multi-robot systems. Our control algorithm for composing formations takes the advantages of this mobile agent model. We have implemented our algorithm in a simulator and conducted experiments to demonstrate the feasibility of our approach.

Keywords: Mobile agent · Formation control · Multiple robots · Swarm intelligence

1 Introduction

In the last decade, robot systems have made rapid progress not only in their behaviors but also in the way they are controlled. In particular, a control system based on multiple software agents can control robots efficiently [1]. Multi-agent systems introduced modularity, reconfigurability and extensibility to control systems. It has made the development of control systems easy on distributed environments such as multi-robot systems.

On the other hand, the excessive interactions among agents in the multi-agent system may cause problems in the multiple robot environments. In order to mitigate the problems of excessive communication, mobile agent methodologies

© Springer International Publishing Switzerland 2016
M. Rovatsos et al. (Eds.): EUMAS 2015/AT 2015, LNAI 9571, pp. 108–120, 2016.
DOI: 10.1007/978-3-319-33509-4_9

have been developed for distributed environments. In a mobile agent system, each agent can actively migrate from one site to another site. Since a mobile agent can bring the necessary functionalities with it and perform its tasks autonomously, it can reduce the necessity for interaction with other sites. In the minimal case, a mobile agent requires that the connection is established only when it performs migration [2].

The model of our system is a set of cooperative multiple mobile agents executing tasks by controlling a pool of multiple robots [3]. The property of inter-robot movements of the mobile agents contributes to the flexible and efficient use of the robot resources. A mobile agent can migrate to the robot that is the most conveniently located to a given task, e.g. the nearest robot to a physical object such as a soccer ball. Since the agent migration is much easier than the robot motion, the agent migration contributes to saving power consumption [1]. We took the advantage of the fact that any agents on a robot can disappear as soon as they finish their tasks. If the agent has a policy of choosing idle robots rather than busy ones, in addition to the power-saving effect, it would result in more efficient use of robot resources.

We proposed our model in a paper and have shown the effectiveness of saving power consumption [1] and the efficiency of our system for searching targets [4,5], transporting them to a designated collection area [6], clustering robots [7], and serialization of them [8,9]. Choosing idle robots is a new feature we have introduced in the current system. In our system, all the robots have no specific tasks; they are all general purpose. In such a system, the same robot can perform various tasks such as mentioned above and when the robot completes a task it can proceed another task immediately or become idle state waiting for the next task. Our mobile agent system can work efficiently in such a situation because mobile agents can select the suitable robot for the current task without central control and do not burden other robots working for different tasks.

In the previous paper, we focus our attention on the formation control of robots [10]. Formation control is one of the most important tasks in the multi-robot applications, especially when individual robot has limited abilities and a given task requires collective actions. For example, robots may aggregate for coordinated search and rescue, collectively transporting large objects, exploring and mapping unknown area, or maintaining formations for area defense or flocking [11].

We have utilized the concept of the ant colony optimization (ACO) for the formation control. ACO is a swarm intelligence-based method and a multi-agent system that exploits artificial stigmergy for the solution of combinatorial optimization problems. In fact, we have implemented both the ants and the pheromone as mobile software agents. They are Ant agents (AAs) to drive robots and Pheromone agents (PAs) to attract AAs. Each AA creates PA at the locations for its neighbor robots to occupy, which diffuses to attract neighbor AAs through migrations. Once a PA reaches the AA to attract, the AA migrates to the robot nearest to the target location, and then drives the robot to the location, following the guidance of the PA. The control manner achieved distributed formation without any leader, and the migration properties of the agents contribute to suppressing the total cost of the formation.

In this paper, we propose an improved algorithm for multi-robot formations. In forging the new algorithm, we have focused on the efficiency. The new algorithm calculates the locations suitable for efficiently composing a formation so that the robots can suppress the duration time and energy consumption. In this algorithm, we introduce two kinds of mobile agents; the guide agent and node agents. The guide agent migrates among the robots in order to collect the locations of the robots and calculates the optimal locations of the robots for the formation based on the conceptual barycenter of them. The node agents drive the robots to the locations that the guide agent calculates.

The structure of the balance of this paper is as follows. In the second section, we describe the background. The third section describes the mobile agent model and the algorithm for our formation control. In the fourth section, we report the results of the numerical experiments using a simulator based on our algorithm. Finally, we conclude our discussions in the fifth section.

2   Background

Kambayashi and Takimoto have employed mobile agent system for our framework [3]. The framework helps users to construct intelligent robot control software by migration of mobile agents. They have implemented a team of cooperative search robots in order to show the effectiveness of their framework [5]. At the same time they have demonstrated that their framework contributes to energy saving of multiple robots [1,4]. They have achieved significant energy saving for search robot applications.

Formation control strategies can be classified into three strategies [12]; behavior-based, virtual-structure, and leader-following. Behavior-based strategy defines simple behaviors or motion primitives for each robot. Balch and Arkin [13] proposed the motor scheme control. In virtual-structure strategy, virtual structure considers the entire formation as a rigid body. The motion of each robot is translated from the motion of the virtual structure, which is determined by the definition of the dynamics of virtual structure. Lewis and Tan [14] proposed one of pioneering works. In leader-followed strategy, some robots are selected as leaders, and the other robots follow the leaders. Das et al. [15] proposed one of the most popular control techniques using a feedback linearization control method. Cheng [11] proposed not only a formation control algorithm but also a formation generation algorithm using Contained Gas Model in which robots act like a particle in a container.

We proposed distributed formation control algorithm using mobile agents that is inspired by ant colony optimization [10]. In the approach, the guide agent plays the role as the leader. Unlike leader-followed strategy, however, the guide agent does not drive robots to compose formations. Instead, the guide agent has the virtual-structure of the objective formation and calculates the optimal locations of the formations. After calculating the locations to which the swarm robots are supposed to move, the guide agent generates node agents and makes them drive the robots to the locations. Our approach assumes that each robot knows the shape of the formation.

3   The Mobile Agents

Our system model consists of robots and two kinds of mobile software agents. We assume that the robots have simple capabilities of locomotion such as driving wheels, measuring distance and angle through an optical camera and a sensor as well as some communication devices with which they can communicate each other through a communication network such as a wireless LAN.

In our algorithm, all the controls for the mobile robots are achieved through the mobile agents. They are a guide agent (GA) and node agents (NAs). There is one GA in the system, which calculates the location of the conceptual barycenter of the formation and all the locations for the robots to occupy, based on the conceptual barycenter. NAs physically drive the robots to the locations to compose the formation. Here, consider that several formations are continuously performed. In that case, the distribution of robots in the field would be different every time. In order to efficiently adapt the formation to each distribution, while suppressing the duration time for composing a formation and the total length of traces of robot movements, the GA determines the target locations of the robots based on the center coordinate, i.e. the conceptual barycenter, of each distribution.

To determine the center coordinate of the formation, we use the concept of the barycenter of all robots in the field. The GA migrates among robots in order to collect locations of the robots and calculate the barycenter of them as if they are connected into one object. Upon the completion of GA's calculation, NAs drive the robots to the locations that the GA determines based on the conceptual barycenter. We assume that the objective shape is represented as a set of point coordinates. We also assume that the mobile agents on the robots do not know the absolute coordinates of robots but they can measure the relative coordinate of neighbor robots using sensors or cameras. In our algorithm, all mobile agents uses relative coordinate from the base robot that is selected by the GA. Each relative coordinate is represented as a vector value. When an mobile agent migrates from the base robot R_1 to the robot R_n along the path $(R_1, \cdots, R_n)$, the relative coordinate $\boldsymbol{p}_n$ of robot R_n are calculated as follows:

$$\boldsymbol{p}_n = \sum_{i=1}^{n-1} \boldsymbol{v}_i \tag{1}$$

$\boldsymbol{v}_i$ is the vector value from robot R_i to robot R_{i+1}. The $\boldsymbol{v}_i$ can be measured by sensors or cameras.

3.1   Guide Agent

In this section, we describe the algorithm for the GA. The GA can migrate to robots through communication networks. First, the GA visits robots scattered in the field to find an idle robot. Once the GA finds an idle robot, the GA appoints that idle robot to be the base robot to calculate the relative coordinates. Then, the GA traverses all the reachable idle robots one by one in order to collect their locations. When the GA visits all the reachable idle robots, the GA calculates the conceptual barycenter g as follows:

$$g = \frac{1}{n} \sum_{i=1}^{n} p_i \qquad (2)$$

n is the number of robots and p_i is the relative coordinate of each robot from the base robot, which is calculated by (1). The information of the original formation F is represented as follows:

$$F = \{f_1, f_2, \cdots, f_i, \cdots, f_n\}$$

We assume that f_i is the vector value from the conceptual barycenter f_o of the original arrangement of nodes in formation F. Henceforth we call the conceptual barycenter as just the barycenter. The GA translates them to the vectors from the base robot. The GA uses the barycenter g in the field instead of barycenter of the original formation. Thus, the vectors from g are identical to the vectors from f_o. To translate the vectors from g to the vectors from the base robot, the GA adds g to each f_i as follows:

$$p_{f_i} = f_i + g, f_i \in F \qquad (3)$$

Since each f_i is identical to the vector value from g, each p_{f_i} becomes the target locations for robots to move. Upon completion of the calculation of all the vector values, the GA generates NAs that drive robots to p_{f_i}.

Example 1 (Calculating locations). Consider that the objective shape is the square as shown in Fig. 1. The vector f_i in this figure is a relative coordinate from the barycenter of the original formation that is represented as a small circle at the center in the figure. Figure 2 shows the initial state of the positions of robots and the pale color circle in the figure represents the base robot that becomes the base coordinate of the positions of robots. That is, the base robot has coordinate $(0,0)$. The GA calculates the barycenter g by (2), which is the vector (or the relative coordinate) from the base robot (Fig. 3). After that, the GA overlaps the barycenter of the original formation and the barycenter g in the field as shown in Fig. 4, where f_i is the relative coordinate from the barycenter of the original formation. To translate f_i to the vector from the base robot (p_{f_i} in Fig. 4), the GA add g to f_i followed by (3), so that the relative coordinate p_{f_i} is calculated.

3.2   Node Agent

In this section, we describe the algorithm for NAs. The GA calculates the relative coordinates $(p_{f_1}, \cdots, p_{f_n})$ from the base robot. n is the number of robots of the formation. For each robot, the GA generates the corresponding NA, and gives each NA the relative coordinate p_{f_i} as the target location to which it

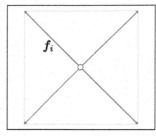

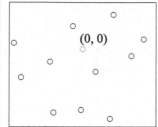

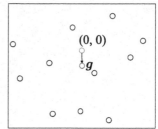

Fig. 1. Objective formation.

Fig. 2. Initial state. (Color figure online)

Fig. 3. Barycenter.

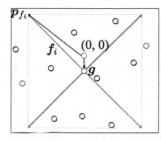

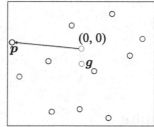

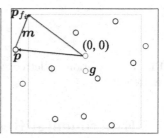

Fig. 4. Translation.

Fig. 5. Location of an NA.

Fig. 6. The movement.

should drives the robot. The NA calculates the movement vector m to the target location as follows:

$$m = p_{f_i} - p \tag{4}$$

Coordinate p is the current coordinate of the NA from the base robot as shown in Fig. 5, and movement vector m is a relative coordinate from current robot to target location as shown in Fig. 6. If a NA finds some robots that are nearer to the target location than the current robot, the NA migrates to the nearer robot instead of driving the current robot in order to suppress the duration time and energy consumption for composing the formation. After each migration, the coordinate p of NA is updated as follows:

$$p \leftarrow p + v$$

Vector v is the vector from the current robot to the nearest robot that is measured by sensors or cameras.

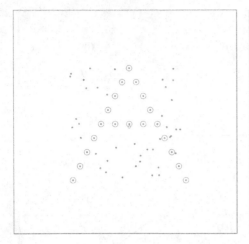 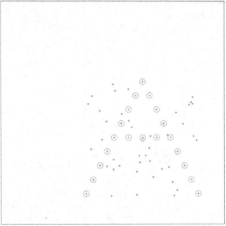

Fig. 7. Formation of letter A. (Color figure online)

Fig. 8. Formation of letter A (2). (Color figure online)

4   Experimental Results

In order to demonstrate the correctness and effectiveness of our method, we have implemented our algorithm on a simulator, and conducted numerical experiments. In the experiments, we assume the following conditions.

1. Robots are scattered in an 800×800 square field in the simulator.
2. The view range of each robot is 150 units, and the range of wireless network is wider than the view range.
3. Each robot can move 2 units in each step in the simulator.
4. The initial locations of robots are randomly set without overlapping.
5. Each robot is represented as a circle on the grid field.

First, we conducted experiments for formation of letter A in different initial arrangements of robots as shown in Figs. 7 and 8. In the figures, where small black circles represent robots, large circles represent robots with a NA, and the small pale color circle represents the barycenter, both formations are composed around the center of the area where robots scatter. The results show that GA calculates the barycenter and the NAs compose the formation around it correctly.

4.1   Comparison to the Other Algorithm

We also conducted experiments to compare this novel approach with our previous approach [10] in terms of efficiency we gain and the total cost we reduce. We investigated the efficiency by the duration time, and the total cost by the total length of traces of robots for composing formations. In the algorithm, when all the NAs arrive at the target locations means that the formation task is completed. On the other hand, in our previous work, robots gradually compose a formation, and then continue fine adjustments after the formation composing is mostly completed. Thus, it was hard to decide when the task ends in our previous work. Therefore, we have to decide allowable deviation, and check whether the current locations of robots are under it in every time steps.

In order to show the preciseness in our new algorithm, we measured gaps between the current locations and the objective ideal positions, and calculated the average of them. First, we calculated the barycenter of points for both actual and ideal points, and then calculated all the coordinate of robots relative to the barycenter. After that, we measured the distances between the relative coordinates of actual robots and the ideal relative coordinates, and calculated the averages D of them for various shapes with the difference numbers of robots as follows:

$$D = \frac{1}{n} \sum_{i=1}^{n} \|I_i - A_i\| \tag{5}$$

In the equation, I_i is the ideal relative coordinate of a robot from the barycenter, A_i is the actual relative coordinate of the robot from the barycenter and n is the number of NAs composing the shape. Figure 9 shows the average distances of this algorithm and the previous work for convergence time, where the horizontal axis is time and the vertical axis is the average distance calculated by (5). In the experiment, the objective formation is a circle with radius 150 units, the number of nodes of the formation is 20, and the number of robots that are scattered in the field is 40. We assume that NAs that compose a formation are generated after the GA calculates the barycenter and the target locations based on it, and hence, the line chart for the newly proposed approach, which represents the change of average distances, starts from 100 time steps after calculation of the barycenter. As shown in the figure, the experimental result shows our newly proposed approach is remarkably more efficient than the previous approach even if it includes the time for calculating the barycenter and the target locations. This is because each NA knows its own target location to move, so that NAs can go straight to the locations.

On the other hand, the previous approach determines the target locations dynamically. It continuously adjusts the current locations once they arrive around the targets. Indeed, in most cases, all NAs completed their task by the 140 steps, while the previous approach took approximately 600 time steps to settle down. Also, for the same reason, the total length of traces of the newly proposed approach becomes much shorter than the previous approach. The trace of the newly proposed approach is 30 times as short as the previous approach. Previous approach takes 25000 units and newly proposed approach 800 units.

4.2   Migration

Migrations to other robots can contribute to suppressing the duration time and energy consumption for composing formations. To show this effect, we conducted

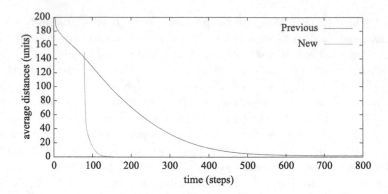

Fig. 9. Comparison to our previous approach.

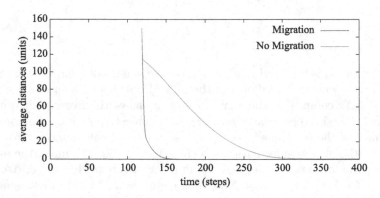

Fig. 10. Effect of migration.

an experiment under the condition where NAs continue to stay on initial robots without migrating to other robots. We compare the result with an experiment in which NAs use the migration to make robots move to their target locations, where the objective shape is a circle whose radius is 150 units. The number of nodes of the shape is 20, and the number of robots is 60. Therefore only 20 out of 60 robots are used to compose the shape. Figure 10 shows the average distance of the experiments. In the case with migration, the whole task was completed at 150 time steps, where the GA completed its task at 120 time steps and then NAs moved to their target in 30 time steps.

On the other hand, in the case without migration, it took 310 time steps to complete the whole task, where the total time of the task of NAs was 190 time steps that was 6 times as much as the case with migration. Also, as shown by the bar named "60" in Fig. 11, the total length of traces of robots for composing the formation was 600 for the case with migration, and 2700 for the case without migration. This result shows the traces with migration are 4.5 times as short as ones without migration in average. These results show the superiority of the migration.

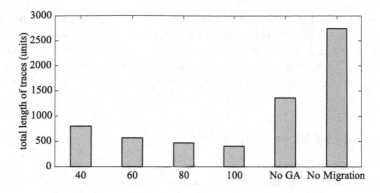

Fig. 11. Total length of traces for different condition.

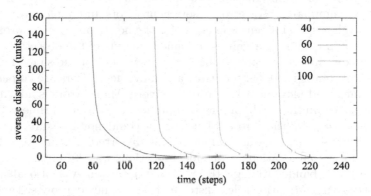

Fig. 12. Effect of the number of robots.

Finally, in order to check the influences of the number of robots to the duration time and energy consumption, we conducted experiments with the cases of the number of robots: 40, 60, 80 and 100. Like the other experiments, the objective shape is a circle whose radius is 150 units, and the number of nodes of the shape is 20. Figure 12 shows the average distances of these experiments. As shown the figure, the GAs completed their tasks at time steps 80, 120, 160 and 200, respectively. This means that the cost of GAs is in proportion to the number of robots. On the other hand, NAs complete their tasks at 60, 30, 25 and 20 time steps, respectively. Also, as shown in Fig. 11, the total lengths of traces are 800, 570, 470 and 410, which is in inverse proportion to the number of robots. The result shows that the migration is suppressing energy consumption more effectively as the number of robots increases. In our simulator, mobile agents are able to migrate to other robots in one time step and robots move 2 units in one time step. Hence, the faster network speed is, the more important the number of robots becomes.

Conversely, when network speed is slow, visiting robots for collecting their locations might become a bottleneck of the task in terms of total time. The bar named "No GA" in Fig. 11 shows the experiment where the GA does not collect any locations of robots. In this case, where the number of robots is 60 and the barycenter is not calculated, the length of traces becomes twice as long as the case with GA. These experiments show that the newly proposed approach can suppress energy consumption in proportion to network speed and the number of robots without sacrificing the total time.

4.3   Accuracy of Movement and Sensors

We have conducted experiments in the simulator assuming the ideal conditions. In such a condition, robots can move correctly with no error and sensors or cameras can measure precise distances and directions to other robots. In the real world, there are some movement errors and sensor errors caused by imperfect hardware. We simulate sensor errors, movement errors and angle errors.

Figure 13 shows the influences of errors for the newly proposed approach and the previous approach in the same error condition, where the objective shape is a circle whose radius is 150 units. The number of nodes of the shape is 20, and the number of robots is 60. Sensor errors and movement errors are 20 percent of sensed distance and movement length respectively. Angle errors is added within [−10, 10] degrees. In the newly proposed approach, the duration time of the task was not influenced by the errors. Since robots could not measure the precise locations, however, the eventual formation was distorted. The average distance of robots from actual locations to the ideal locations was 20 units.

On the other hand, although the previous approach was also affected by errors, the eventual formation is less distorted than the newly proposed approach. This arises from the difference of the distance between attractor and attractee. In the newly proposed approach, NAs that are attractors tend to move to the target locations that are attractees in a long way repeating migrations, so that errors are accumulated. On the other hand, in the previous approach, each agent just attracts other agents to neighbor locations. Thus, the newly proposed approach

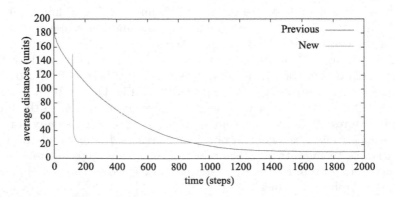

Fig. 13. Influence of error.

would be suitable for composing formations with not so many nodes for not so big shape.

5   Conclusions and Future Works

We have proposed a control algorithm for composing formations of swarm robots based on their distributions using many mobile software agents. In this approach, we introduced two kinds of mobile software agents, a guide agent (GA) and node agents (NAs). The GA traverses all the robots and calculates the conceptual barycenter of them, and then, calculates the suitable locations of the formation using the barycenter. The GA generates NAs that drive robots to the calculated locations. Each NA migrates to the robot that is nearest to the target location, and drives that robot to the location.

In order to show the effectiveness of our algorithm, we have implemented it on a simulator. And then we have conducted numerical experiments on the simulator. We have shown that our algorithm suppresses the duration time for a given formation task and energy consumption compared with our previous approach, and composes the formation at a suitable location based on the distribution of robots. Furthermore, we have shown that increasing the number of robots is effective to suppress energy consumption. We have simulated the errors caused in the real world, and shown that the proposed approach in this paper is not affected by the errors in term of the duration time of the formation task, while it tends to accumulate errors in the migration process compared with the previous approach.

As a future direction, we plan to conduct a control experiment. We will implement another multi-robot system where message-based approach being employed, and compare the result with that of our current agent-base system to show superiority of our agent-based approach. Also we plan to invent a new algorithm that adjusts the each location at certain intervals at low network cost in order to mitigate the problem of error accumulation.

Acknowledgments. This work is supported in part by Japan Society for Promotion of Science (JSPS), with the basic research program (C) (No. 26350456), Grant-in-Aid for Scientific Research.

References

1. Takimoto, M., Mizuno, M., Kurio, M., Kambayashi, Y.: Saving energy consumption of multi-robots using higher-order mobile agents. In: Nguyen, N.T., Grzech, A., Howlett, R.J., Jain, L.C. (eds.) KES-AMSTA 2007. LNCS (LNAI), vol. 4496, pp. 549–558. Springer, Heidelberg (2007)
2. Binder, W., Hulaas, J.G., Villazon, A.: Portable resource control in the J-SEAL2 mobile agent system. In: Proceedings of the Fifth International Conference on Autonomous Agents (AGENTS 2001), pp. 222–223. ACM (2001)
3. Kambayashi, Y., Takimoto, M.: Higher-order mobile agents for controlling intelligent robots. Int. J. Intell. Inf. Technol. (IJIIT) 1(2), 28–42 (2005)

4. Nagata, T., Takimoto, M., Kambayashi, Y.: Suppressing the total costs of executing tasks using mobile agents. In: 42nd Hawaii International Conference on System Sciences, 2009 (HICSS 2009), pp. 1–10, January 2009

5. Abe, T., Takimoto, M., Kambayashi, Y.: Searching targets using mobile agents in a large scale multi-robot environment. In: O'Shea, J., Nguyen, N.T., Crockett, K., Howlett, R.J., Jain, L.C. (eds.) KES-AMSTA 2011. LNCS, vol. 6682, pp. 211–220. Springer, Heidelberg (2011)

6. Shibuya, R., Takimoto, M., Kambayashi, Y.: Suppressing energy consumption of transportation robots using mobile agents. In: Proceedings of the 5th International Conference on Agents and Artificial Intelligence (ICAART 2013), pp. 219–224. SciTePress (2013)

7. Mizutani, M., Takimoto, M., Kambayashi, Y.: Ant colony clustering using mobile agents as ants and pheromone. In: Nguyen, N.T., Le, M.T., Świątek, J. (eds.) ACIIDS 2010. LNCS, vol. 5990, pp. 435–444. Springer, Heidelberg (2010)

8. Shintani, M., Lee, S., Takimoto, M., Kambayashi, Y.: Synthesizing pheromone agents for serialization in the distributed ant colony clustering. In: ECTA and FCTA 2011 - Proceedings of the International Conference on Evolutionary Computation Theory and Applications and the Proceedings of the International Conference on Fuzzy Computation Theory and Applications [Parts of the International Joint Conference on Computational Intelligence (IJCCI 2011)], pp. 220–226. SciTePress (2011)

9. Shintani, M., Lee, S., Takimoto, M., Kambayashi, Y.: A serialization algorithm for mobile robots using mobile agents with distributed ant colony clustering. In: König, A., Dengel, A., Hinkelmann, K., Kise, K., Howlett, R.J., Jain, L.C. (eds.) KES 2011, Part I. LNCS, vol. 6881, pp. 260–270. Springer, Heidelberg (2011)

10. Oikawa, R., Takimoto, M., Kambayashi, Y.: Distributed formation control for swarm robots using mobile agents. In: Proceedings of the Tenth Jubilee IEEE International Symposium on Applied Computational Intelligence and Informatics, pp. 111–116 (2015)

11. Cheng, J., Cheng, W., Nagpal, R.: Robust and self-repairing formation control for swarms of mobile agents. In: Proceedings of the 20th National Conference on Artificial Intelligence AAAI 2005, vol. 1, pp. 59–64. AAAI Press (2005)

12. Kanjanawanishkul, K.: Formation control of mobile robots: survey. eng.ubu.ac.th 50–64 (2005)

13. Balch, T., Arkin, R.: Behavior-based formation control for multirobot teams. IEEE Trans. Robot. Autom. 14(6), 926–939 (1998)

14. Lewis, M., Tan, K.H.: High precision formation control of mobile robots using virtual structures. Auton. Robots 4(4), 387–403 (1997)

15. Das, A., Fierro, R., Kumar, V., Ostrowski, J., Spletzer, J., Taylor, C.: A vision-based formation control framework. IEEE Trans. Robot. Autom. 18(5), 813–825 (2002)

Group-Based Pricing to Shape Demand in Real-Time Electricity Markets

Rahul Agrawal[1], Anirban Chakraborti[2], Karamjit Singh[1(✉)],
Gautam Shroff[1], and Venkatesh Sarangan[1]

[1] TCS Research, New Delhi, India
karamjit.singh@tcs.com
[2] Jawaharlal Nehru University, New Delhi, India

Abstract. Maintaining the balance between electricity supply and demand is one of the major concerns of utility operators. With the increasing contribution of renewable energy sources in the typical supply portfolio of an energy provider, volatility in supply is increasing while the control is decreasing. Real time pricing based on aggregate demand, unfortunately cannot control the non-linear price sensitivity of deferrable/flexible loads and leads to other peaks [4,5] due to overly homogenous consumption response. In this paper, we present a day-ahead group-based real-time pricing mechanism for optimal demand shaping. We use agent-based simulations to model the system-wide consequences of deploying different pricing mechanisms and design a heuristic search mechanism in the strategy space to efficiently arrive at an optimal strategy. We prescribe a pricing mechanism for each groups of consumers, such that even though consumption synchrony within each group gives rise to local peaks, these happen at different time slots, which when aggregated result in a flattened macro demand response. Simulation results show that our group-based pricing strategy out-performs traditional real-time pricing, and results in a fairly flat peak-to-average ratio.

Keywords: Demand side management · Demand response · Market segmentation · Energy consumption scheduling · Energy pricing · Demand shaping · Smart grid · Multi agent systems

1 Introduction

The electricity grid is undergoing transformation from a centralised unidirectional transmission system to a "smart grid" that facilitates the two way flow of electricity *and* information. As a result there are opportunities to mitigate the need for scaling infrastructure (both generation capacity and transmission lines) to accommodate (i) Deficiency in supply peaks, (ii) Integration of more renewables, and (iii) Fault tolerable redundancy in unreliable infrastructure. Utilities and grid operators have to maintain sufficient capacity and infrastructure to be able to cater to the expected peak, which most of the time is under-utilised. For example, let us suppose that on some day the renewable energy is at a minima:

M. Rovatsos et al. (Eds.): EUMAS 2015/AT 2015, LNAI 9571, pp. 121–128, 2016.
DOI: 10.1007/978-3-319-33509-4_10

This causes a deficit in supply, which in turn causes wholesale prices to rise. However, this higher wholesale price cannot generate further renewables. Moreover, due to flat prices at the user-end, the customers do not have any incentive to curtail or shift their demand. This condition forces the utilities increase generation from expensive non-renewable sources in order to meet the demand.

The smart grid promises an alternative wherein customer can *actively* participate (altering their consumption profile) in response to "information" (pricing, incentives, frequency, etc.) from suppliers, and empowers the grid operators to shape demand so as to minimize their cost price. In particular, 'smart pricing' drives users are encouraged to voluntarily manage their loads, e.g., by reducing their consumption at peak hours or by shifting their consumption to different cheaper time interval [2,3,6]. In this regard, critical-peak pricing (CPP), time-of-use pricing (ToUP), and real-time pricing (RTP) are amongs the popular practices. In RTP tariffs, the price of electricity varies at different hours of the day. However, the challenges that the RTP faces are: (i) Additional information and decision making burden is thrust upon the customers, (ii) All customers are geared to respond simultaneously (e.g., every user switching on the air conditioning at the same time), thus generating other peaks in demand [4,5,7].

In this paper, we consider a scenario where a source of energy (utility) is shared among several consumers, each of whom are equipped with 'smart agents' that make optimal load curtailment and scheduling decisions based on published day-ahead prices that may vary by time-of-day, while respecting user-defined constraints. We present a simple market segmentation technique that can be utilised by grid operators to make users coordinate their consumption pattern [1], in order to have the macro demand mimic the expected supply of the following day. We use agent-based simulations to model the system-wide consequences of deploying different pricing-mechanisms. We design a heuristic search mechanism in the strategy space to efficiently arrive at an optimal strategy. We prescribe a pricing mechanism for each groups of consumers, such that even though there exists a consumption synchrony within each group which gives rise to a local peak, these happen at different time slots such that the aggregate results in a flattened macro demand response. The remainder of the paper is organised as follows: We introduce the system and model in Sect. 2. The DSM based on individual and group interactions peak to average ratio cost minimisation problems are formulated in Sect. 3. Greedy search algorithms used for simulations are presented in Sect. 4. Our simulation results are in Sect. 5, and our concluding remarks in Sect. 6.

2   System Model

In this section, we describe and define the system model of a centralised Electric utility and several residential consumers.

2.1 Residential Consumers

Throughout the paper, we use $N \doteq \{1, 2, 3, ...\}$ to denote the set of residential consumers. Each of the residential consumer loads/appliances as per their price sensitivity, categorised in two groups of loads: (i) Fixed (load level is price sensitive - we call this 'curtailment' type of sensitivity), and (ii) Flexible (schedule is price sensitive, we call this 'deferrable' sensitivity).

Fixed Load: For each user $n \in N$, let A_n^{fixed} represents a set of fixed non-deferrable household appliances and $x_{n,a^{fixed}}^{h}$ denote consumption value for hour h, of the nth user, for each non-deferrable appliance $a^{fixed} \in A_n^{fixed}$. For simplicity, we assume the time granularity to be of one hour. Fixed load consumption vector for 24 h for n^{th} user can be written as $X_{n,a^{fixed}} \doteq \{x_{n,a^{fixed}}^{1}, x_{n,a^{fixed}}^{2}, \cdots, x_{n,a^{fixed}}^{24}\}$. Fixed loads exhibit load level price sensitivity, which we model by using a sigmoid function for the price sensitivity of the fixed loads using below equation. Here The b denotes unregulated base price, $x_{n,a^{fixed}}^{i}(b)$ denotes the base consumption level.

$$x_{n,a^{fixed}}^{i}(p) = x_{n,a^{fixed}}^{i}(b)[\frac{1}{2} + \frac{1}{1 + e^{(p-b)}}]. \qquad (1)$$

Flexible Load: For each user $n \in N$, let A_n^{flexi} represent set of deferrable loads and $X_{n,a^{flexi}} \doteq \{x_{n,a^{flexi}}^{1}, x_{n,u^{flexi}}^{2}, \cdots, x_{n,a^{flexi}}^{24}\}$ denotes a flexible load consumption vector for n^{th} user for $a^{flexi} \in A_n^{flexi}$. Flexible loads can be scheduled anywhere within consumers preferences without much effect on their life style. If $[a_n, b_n]$ is the preferences of nth user, then the smart agent depending upon the set of 24 h day-ahead prices advertised $C_H \doteq \{c^1, c^2, ..., c^{24}\}$, will schedule load $load_{a^{flexi}}$ to the lth hour where minimum price is advertised within user preferences and for all hours excluding the lth hour flexible load consumption vector will be zero.

2.2 Electric Utility

An electric utility is assumed to be well-connected to all residential consumers via the electric grid and communication link. Electric utility advertises price to each user, who then responds accordingly. Uniform 24 h day-ahead pricing advertised to all users, results in a synchronization in their responses, and leads to a peak in another time interval. To avoid this type of a peak, and also for more optimal demand shaping, we propose that the utility segments the market customers into different groups, and then advertises different prices to the different groups. The following nomenclature will be used throughout the paper to represent the set of groups and pricing advertised in each group: **R:** Set of groups/region $\doteq \{r^1, r^2, ...\}$ and **CR:** Set of pricing strategies in each group $\doteq \{cr^1, cr^2, ...\}$. Energy cost function that may be the cost of generating or distributing by utility or artificial cost tariff used for load control is assumed to be increasing piecewise linear increasing function, as shown in Fig. 1, where (p, d) are base price and base supply.

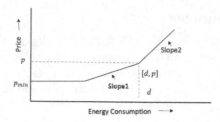

Fig. 1. Plot of energy cost function of utility

3   Optimization Problem

In this section, we formulate the two different optimization problems: (i) DSM based on Individual Interactions, and (ii) DSM based on Group Interactions (Group-based pricing strategy). In system for DSM based on individual interactions, each consumer responds rationaly to same pricing strategy advertised by the utility and in system for DSM based on group interactions, Rational consumers are segmented into groups with each group advertised a representative pricing strategy which ensures local peaks of each group to different time. The main objective of a utility is to minimize peak in macro demand with respect to that of supply, and increase the average consumption to match supply. The performance function, Peak-to-Average ratio (PAR), captures this perfectly and can be mathematically expressed as:

$$PAR \doteq \frac{H \max\limits_{h \in H} \sum_{n \in N} \sum_{a \in A_n} x_{n,a}^h}{\sum_{h \in H} \sum_{n \in N} \sum_{a \in A_n} x_{n,a}^h}, \tag{2}$$

DSM Based on Individual Interations: In day-ahead real-time pricing based on past demand, supply, price sensitivity of customer, and corresponding external parameters (weather, public events, festivals, etc.), the following day's (future) demand and supply, as functions of external parameters can be predicted and each consumer can be modelled for price sensitivity. That is then used to decide what price is to be advertised for each hour of next day. This problem of finding the optimal real time pricing, given predicted demand and supply, can be mathematically formulated as: $\min\limits_{C^H \in C} PAR$.

If we assume that k types of pricing can be advertised for any particular hour, then the above search problem can be solved exhaustively in $O(k^{24})$ steps, which is of the dimension of the pricing strategy space C. Intuitively, based on the predicted demand and supply curves, the pricing strategy of increasing (or decreasing) price for that hour deviates from the base price by an amount proportional to the difference between the demand and supply. We find that this model works well for fixed load scenario only, and the non-linear price sensitivity cannot be controlled by this simple linear strategy for flexible load scenario.

DSM Based on Group Interactions: In the flexible load scenario, the coordination amongst the users comes into play, which sometimes synchronize their deferrable behaviour to same time slot, often leading to large peaks in demand. The problem with the above formulation is that the aggregate demand results in inaccurate and suboptimal decisions because of non-linear effects. However, with huge computational power and data analysis, it is possible to solve the optimization problem, which takes care of the individual utility optimal decisions and grouping of people having the same advertised strategy, mathematically represented as $\min\limits_{cr^j, r^j \, \forall j} Segmented \ PAR.$, where Segmented PAR is given by:

$$Segmented \ PAR \doteq \frac{H \max\limits_{h \in H} \sum\limits_{i \in R} \sum\limits_{n \in r^i} \sum\limits_{a \in A_n} x_{n,a}^h(cr^i)}{\sum\limits_{h \in H} \sum\limits_{i \in R} \sum\limits_{n \in r^i} \sum\limits_{a \in A_n} x_{n,a}^h(cr^i)}, \tag{3}$$

Again, if we assume that k types of pricing can be advertised for any particular hour, then the above problem can be solved exhaustively in $O(N^{k^{24}})$ steps.

4   Greedy Algorithm

Instead of an exhaustive search in this huge space, we used a *greedy* approach, similar to the gradient descent with the error as an approximation to slope (as we do not know the slope of the objective function). The main aim is to exploit the price sensitivity (reaction to price changes) of residential consumers in the best way, in order to give demand a desired shape. The price sensitivity of a typical residential customer can be characterised by two types: deferrable and curtailment. The latter, because of linearity, can be easily controlled for optimal pricing strategy search using gradient descent type algorithm with gross demand as reference. The former cannot be controlled using gross demand, because of its non-linear nature. In order to control the flexible load, we divided the customers into 24 groups, with each advertised lowest price in group i^{th} hour; as per its effect on gross demand, the group size is determined. Detailed greedy algorithms for controlling both fixed and flexible load, are presented below.

Fixed load demand shaping: The gradient descent (greedy) algorithm for fixed load demand shaping, is represented in Algorithm 1 and depicted schematically in Fig. 2a. First, take the seed 24 h vector pricing strategy, as $c^h = $ base_price $\forall \ h \ \epsilon \ H$. Second, simulate the assumed multi agent model to give gross demand. This is then used with previous step demand to calculate Estimated Demand (ED), which is then used for deciding the pricing strategy for the next step as the earlier assumed superposition of $(0.8 \times$ current strategy) plus $(0.2 \times$ demand charge (shown in Fig. 1)) parameterised by estimated demand. This is repeated till demand converges to the supply, as close as desired.

Flexible load demand shaping: The gradient descent (greedy) algorithm for flexible load demand shaping, is represented Algorithm 2 and depicted schematically in Fig. 2b. Each of the 24 groups is characterised by a representative 24 h day-ahead pricing advertised. First of all, each group is assigned a pricing based group id, gross demand for base pricing strategy and supply. For i^{th} group, the mechanism of deciding pricing strategy is as follows: For any hour, if demand leads the supply $(1.5 \times base\_price)$ is advertised, else $(base\_price)$ is advertised. The ith element of the strategy vector is then replaced by $(0.5 \times base\_price)$ to give the final pricing to be advertised in i^{th} group. Then, the Error (E) is calculated as {Supply (S) - Demand (D)}, if supply is greater than demand, else {zero}. The size for each group is determined to be $E(i)$, as fraction of $\sum\limits_{i \in H} E(i)$ and normalised to the total number of customers (n). Now, the 24 different groups are assigned random customers (with similar characteristics) as per calculated size. The resulting demand is then compared with supply to get the error, which is then used to update each group size till demand converges very close to supply.

Algorithm 1. Gradient descent control for fixed load demand shaping

```
1: procedure PRESCRIBE–PRICING STRATEGY
2:     c^h = base_price ∀ h ∈ H.
3:     for Demand not converged to Supply do
4:         Got gross demand(D) = Σ_{n∈N} Σ_{a∈A_n} x^h_{n,a}.
5:         Error(E) = k_p × ( Demand (D) - Supply (S) ) + k_d × (Prev_Error - Error(E)) + k_I × Integral_Error.
6:         Prev_Error = E.
7:         Integral_Error = Integral_Error + E.
8:         Estimated Demand (ED) = S + E.
9:         Update c^h ∀h∈ H as function of ED in demand charge (Fig. 1).
10:    end for
11: end procedure
```

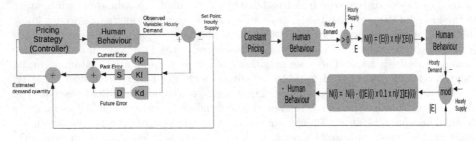

(a) Fixed load demand shaping.   (b) Flexible load demand shaping

Fig. 2. Schematic diagram of gradient descent control mechanism

Algorithm 2. Market Segmentation for flexible load demand shaping

```
1: procedure PRESCRIBE–PRICING STRATEGY
2:     Initialise c^h = base_price.
3:     Got gross demand(D) = Σ_{n∈N} Σ_{a∈A_n} x^h_{n,a}.

4:     for i in H do
5:         cr^i[i] = 0.5 × base_price.
6:         if D[j] > S[j] ∀ j ∈ H/i then
7:             cr^i[j] = 1.5 × base_price
8:         else
9:             cr^i[j] = base_price
10:        end if
11:    end for
12:    Error(E) = ((Supply (S) - Demand (D)) > 0 ? 1:0) * (S - D).
13:    r^i = (E(i) × N)/ Σ_{i∈H} E(i).
14:    Compute Demand Σ_{i∈R} Σ_{n∈r^i} Σ_{a∈A_n} x^h_{n,a}.
15:    for Demand not converged to Supply do
16:        Calculate |Error(e)| = |S - D|.
17:        Update r^i = r^i - (e(i) × N × 0.1)/ Σ_{i∈H} |e(i)|
18:        Got gross demand(D) = Σ_{n∈N} Σ_{a∈A_n} x^h_{n,a}.
19:    end for
20: end procedure
```

5   Simulation Results

In this section, we present the simulation results for each approach and their quantitative comparison. In our simulations, there are $n = 1000$ consumers. Each user is assumed to have four curtailment type sensitivity load (Fan, Refrigerator, Light, AC) and four deferrable type sensitivity load (Dishwasher, Washing Machine, Dryer, Electric Vehicle). Each of the curtailment type load is assumed to be a different harmonic of a sinusoid basis function i.e. different Amplitude, DC Offset, and Time Period for each curtailment type. Flexible load is characterised by the consumption value (load) and user preference range $[a, b]$. Different load and user preference is assumed for each appliance.

Fixed load demand shaping: For simulating fixed load only case, all the flexible loads were assumed to be zero. The demand for the assumed settings with constant base pricing strategy (2 Units for all hours), pricing strategy vector prescribed by proposed heuristic search. As mentioned earlier, the basic gradient descent search algorithm based on gross demand, cannot control deferrable load non-linearity and leads to other peaks, as shown in Fig. 3.

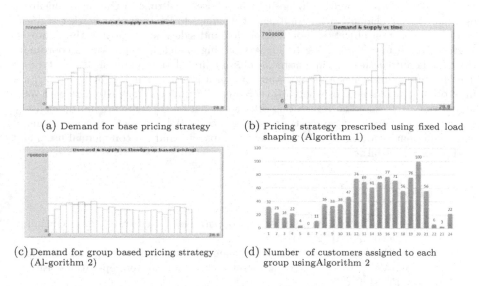

(a) Demand for base pricing strategy

(b) Pricing strategy prescribed using fixed load shaping (Algorithm 1)

(c) Demand for group based pricing strategy (Al-gorithm 2)

(d) Number of customers assigned to each group usingAlgorithm 2

Fig. 3. Fixed and flexible load demand shaping simulation results

Flexible load demand shaping: For simulating flexible load only case, the fixed load price sensitivity was assumed to be zero. Demand for the assumed settings with constant base pricing strategy (2 Units for all hours) is used; the corresponding demand is shown in Fig. 3. For quantitative performance comparison, we use Peak to average ratio, Root mean square error, and Cosine distance. Table 1 shows the results obtained when Algorithms 1 and 2 are used for fixed and flexible loads. Algorithm 1 works fine in case of only fixed loads, but it cannot control when deferrable loads are introduced. Whereas, Algorithm 2 results in very good coordination among flexible loads resulting in flatter (closer to unity) peak-to-average ratio, lesser mean square error and cosine distance closer to unity, as evident from Table 1 for the different cases (CP: constant pricing, PP: prescribed pricing).

Table 1. Quantitative performance measures

Measure	Fixed load control		Flexible load control	
	CP	PP	CP	PP
Peak to average ratio	1.6236	1.1826	1.5059	1.283
Root mean square error	823908	621301	592932	477405
Cosine distance	0.9442	0.9758	0.9777	0.9967

6   Concluding Remarks and Future Directions

In this paper, we presented a day-ahead group-based real-time pricing mechanism for optimal demand shaping in the multi-agent framework. We proposed market segmentation optimisation objective function for demand side management rather than an aggregated optimisation leading to a smart pricing model driving users to coordinate their loads automatically. Simulation results confirmed the potential of this type of demand side management strategy. Our approach is also amenable for generalisation in to other related scenarios where (a) there are different types of customers with individual load profiles and corresponding price sensitivities, (b) there are multiple energy sources with different energy cost, or even (c) residential users who can store energy at certain hours with battery, PHEV, heat pumps, etc. and (d) commercial users and load in an industrial region.

References

1. Akasiadis, C., Chalkiadakis, G.: Agent cooperatives for effective power consumption shifting. In: AAAI (2013)
2. Centolella, P.: The integration of price responsive demand into regional transmission organization (RTO) wholesale power markets and system operations. Energy **35**, 1568–1574 (2010)
3. Herter, K.: Residential implementation of critical-peak pricing of electricity. Energy Policy **35**, 2121–2130 (2007)
4. Mohsenian-Rad, A.H., Leon-Garcia, A.: Optimal residential load control with price prediction in real-time electricity pricing environments. IEEE Trans. Smart Grid **1**, 120–133 (2010)
5. Ramchurn, S.D., Vytelingum, P., Rogers, A., Jennings, N.: Agent-based control for decentralised demand side management in the smart grid, vol.1, pp. 5–12 (2010)
6. Triki, C., Violi, A.: Dynamic pricing of electricty in retail markets. 4OR **7**, 21–36 (2009)
7. Zois, V., Frincu, M., Chelmis, C., Saeed, M.R., Prasanna, V.: Efficient customer selection for sustainable demand response in smart grids. In: 2014 International Green Computing Conference (IGCC), pp. 1–6. IEEE (2014)

Human Rating Methods on Multi-agent Systems

Chairi Kiourt[1,2(✉)], Dimitris Kalles[1], and George Pavlidis[2]

[1] School of Science and Technology,
Hellenic Open University, 26335 Patras, Greece
{chairik,kalles}@eap.gr
[2] "Athena" Research Centre,
University Campus at Kimmeria, 67100 Xanthi, Greece
gpavlid@ceti.gr

Abstract. Modern artificial intelligence approaches study game-playing agents in multi-agent social environments, in order to better simulate the real world playing behaviors; these approaches have already produced promising results. In this paper we present the results of applying human rating systems for competitive games with social activity, to evaluate synthetic agents' performance in multi-agent systems. The widely used *Elo* and *Glicko* rating systems are tested in large-scale synthetic multi-agent game-playing social events, and their rating outcome is presented and analyzed.

Keywords: Multi-agent systems · Rating systems · Game playing

1 Introduction

Since complex problems began to be studied as Multi-Agent Systems (MAS), the study of Social Learning (SL) has become more exciting [1, 2]. Diverse scientific areas such as sociology, economics, computer science, mathematics and marketing use social learning as an Artificial Intelligence (AI) tool for developing MAS [2]. Ferber [3] shows that the two extremes of the Social Organizations (SO), *cooperation* and *competition*, may be studied autonomously or as a combined social organization, which depends on the case study. As it is quite usual in such cases, the social environments are being populated with game playing agents [4]. For a game agent, social environment is represented by a game with all its components and entities [3, 4]. Learning in a game is said to occur when an agent changes a strategy choice in response to new information, and thus mimicking human behavior [4–6]. All those studies and many others support that the simulation of complex social environments and the analysis of their data become an intractable problem of agent social learning mechanisms. In addition, due to the continuous evolution of the dynamic systems that attempt to better simulate the human behaviors and habits, there have been some attempts to apply human rating systems to evaluate virtual agents and assess their performance [7]. Among the most widely used human rating systems are *Elo* [8] and *Glicko* [9]. Generally, different rating systems may disagree about players' absolute performance but

© Springer International Publishing Switzerland 2016
M. Rovatsos et al. (Eds.): EUMAS 2015/AT 2015, LNAI 9571, pp. 129–136, 2016.
DOI: 10.1007/978-3-319-33509-4_11

could report similar ranking results with small deviations on specific events, like tournaments, for example [10].

The contribution of the study presented in this paper is to demonstrate how these two human rating systems perform in multi-agent systems which try to enhance the potential of the social events for the purposes of learning in unknown environments. Our study shows that although these rating systems seem to be adequate and useful for MAS evaluation, they also tend to not always be consistent. Also, it should be highlighted that the simulation of human behavior with synthetic agents is far from being accurate. By comparing the selected rating systems in MAS, it was found that they do not agree in several agents' ratings. Since Glicko (*v2*) was introduced as an improvement of Elo it was expected that the two ratings would be fairly similar, but, as it turned out, various inconsistencies have been recorded in the experimentations, such the large deviations in various agents' ratings players, which presents an ambiguity for their effectiveness in multi agents systems.

The rest of this paper is structured in three sections. The next two sections provide a brief background of the selected rating systems, the game used for the experiments and the game-playing social environment. The fourth section describes our experimentation on multi agent systems, also highlights the comparison of the rating systems. The last section presents our conclusions and our scheduled future work.

2 Performance Rating

Rating systems were first used in chess to calculate an estimate the strength of a player, based on player's performance against the opponent. The Ingo and Harkness system was the first chess player rating system [11]. It was first used to allow the members of the United States Chess Federation (USCF) to track their individual progress in terms other than tournament wins and losses [11].

The *Elo rating system* was first introduced by Arpad Elo in 1960 as a simple skill calculation of players, based on their wins and losses, and of their opponents in chess [8]. Chess, however, is a competitive two-agent system, where each agent's performance is based solely on its skill. In multi-agent systems, it is used as a calculation of fitness for many different learning or search algorithms, with promising results [7].

The Elo system assumes that each player has a skill that is drawn from a random distribution (an agent may have a "good" game or may have a "bad" game); it attempts to find the center of that distribution and converge to that value. The calculation is performed after each match, in a game between two agents A and B. Each agent has a current rating, R_A for agent A and R_B for agent B. Unrated players, generally start with a rating of *800 Elo*, which is associated to bad playing or a beginner level. Rating also depends on the tournament type and the players' attributes.

The *Glicko rating system* was first introduced by Mark Glickman in 1995 as an improvement of the Elo rating system [9]. The Glicko (*v2*) rating system is a method for assessing a player's strength in games of skill, such as *chess* and *go*. The main contribution of this measurement method is "ratings reliability", the so-called *ratings deviation* (RD). RD measures the accuracy of players rating. After a game, the amount of the ratings change depends on the RD: the change is smaller when the players' RD is low, and also when their opponents' RD is high. The RD itself decreases after playing a game, but increases slowly over time of inactivity.

The Glicko rating system was improved by its inventor and was named Glicko-2. This newer version introduces the *rating volatility* σ [9]. A slightly modified version of the Glicko-2 rating system is used by the Australian Chess Federation.

In the Glicko rating systems, unrated players start with rating set to 1500 and RD set to 350. A player's most recent rating is used to calculate the new RD from the previous with a specific set of formulas provided by the Glicko rating systems.

3 The Game-Based Multi-agent System

Our workbench, *RLGame* [12], was initially presented as a purely competitive test environment. It is a tool for studying multi-agent systems via its tournament version, *RLGTournament* [4, 15] that implements a *round-robin tournament* scheme (combinations, repetitions not allowed) to pair participants against each other. RLGTournament fits the description both of an autonomous organization [3] and of a social environment [2, 3].

The RLGame board game is played on an $n \times n$ square board by two players and their pawns. Two $a \times a$ square bases on opposite board corners are initially populated by β pawns for each player, with the white player starting from the lower left base and the black player starting from the upper right. The goal for each player is to move a pawn into the opponent's base or to force all opponent pawns out of the board (it is the player and not the pawn that acts as an agent in this scenario). The base is considered to be a single square, therefore a pawn can move out of the base to any adjacent free square. Players take turns and pawns move one at a time, with the white player moving first. A pawn can move vertically or horizontally to an adjacent free square, provided that the maximum distance from its base is not decreased (so, backward moves are not allowed).

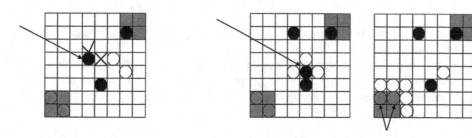

Fig. 1. Examples of game rules application.

The rightmost boards demonstrate the loss of pawns, with arrows showing pawn casualties. A "trapped" pawn automatically draws away from the game; thus, when there is no free square next to the base, the rest of the pawns of the base are lost. The leftmost board in Fig. 1 demonstrates a legal ("tick") and an illegal ("cross") move for the pawn pointed to by the arrow, the illegal move being due to the rule that does not allow decreasing the distance from the home (black) base.

Each agent is an autonomous system, which acts according to its characteristics and knowledge. The learning mechanism of each agent is based on approximating its (reinforcement-learning-inspired) value function with a neural network [2, 3], with similar techniques already documented in the field [13]. Each autonomous (back propagation) [14] neural network is trained depending on its customization and the next possible moves. The board positions for the next possible move along with some flags on overall board coverage are used as input-layer nodes. The hidden layer consists of half as many hidden nodes. A single node in the output layer denotes the extent of the expectation to win when one starts from a specific game-board configuration and then makes a specific move.

RLGame was transformed into a tool for studying multi-agent systems via its tournament version, RLGTournament. *RLGTournament fits the description both of an autonomous organization and of a social environment* [3]. Depending on the number of the agents, social categories can be split into sub-categories of micro-social environment, environment composed of agent groups and global societies, which are the next level of the cooperation and competition extremes of the social organizations [2, 3].

4 Experimentations and Results

In order to study the human rating systems Elo and Glicko applied onto MAS and analyze the performance and learning rate of the agents using as many reliable data as possible, a large scale tournament was configured as follows: 126 agents, all with different characteristics, were used in a round-robin tournament with 100 games per match (each match was repeated 100 times). Each agent played 125 matches against different agents, resulting in a total number of

$$\binom{126}{2} \times 100 = \frac{126!}{124! \times 2!} \times 100 = 787.500$$

experiments, which have been repeated twice. Both experiments are identical in terms of agent configurations and flow of execution.

A first comparison between the Elo and Glicko ratings obtained by the experiments is shown in Fig. 2, which shows the graph of the *Elo-Glicko signed difference*[1] (top) and the corresponding *histogram of signed differences* (bottom). The signed difference is simply

$$d_i = R_i^E - R_i^G \qquad i = 1 \ldots 126$$

where R_i^E is the rank of the *i-th* agent according to the Elo rating and R_i^G is the rank of the same agent according to the Glicko rating. It turned out the in our experiments these

---

[1] We are not considering here the L_1 distance but rather the simple subtraction of the rankings.

differences fall within [–94, 68] and, apparently, the two rating systems "disagree" in how they rank the agents in most cases, with a "strong disagreement" in many cases. The histogram shows that the distribution of this "disagreement" is similar to a normal distribution with zero mean (denoted 'm' in the graphs) and large variance. The standard deviation (denoted in the graphs as 's') is about 33 ($\sigma = 32.716$), which means that most of the Elo-Glicko rank differences can be expected to fall within a region that spans a range of about 66 rank positions. This spanning range is quite high (more than half of the total range) if one considers that there are 126 total rank positions, which is a strong indication that the two ranking systems treat the experiments in a quire different way and they are not expected to produce consistent rankings.

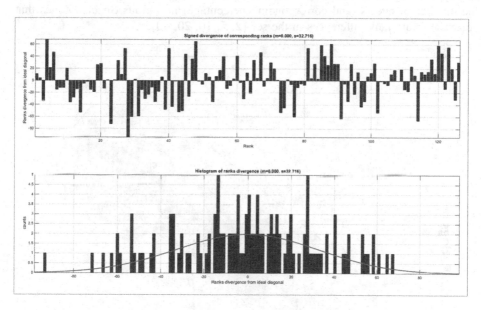

Fig. 2. Divergence between Elo and Glick ratings and the corresponding histogram

Further study of the results included the usage of the *Spearman's rank correlation coefficient (ρ)* [16], which measures the statistical dependence between two variables, and is specifically efficient at capturing the monotonic (non-linear, in general) correlation on ranks. As known, the range of the coefficient falls within [−1, 1], with high negative values representing strong negative correlation, low absolute values representing small or no correlation and high positive values representing strong positive correlation. In our experiments it was estimated that

$$\rho = 0.5987$$

which indicates a typical positive correlation, which is not strong enough to support a consistent behavior of the two ranking methods.

Figure 3 presents a graph of the Elo rankings vs. the Glicko rankings. Ideally, if the two ranking systems would agree, we would expect to find all point on the diagonal. In our case we see that there are many agents off-diagonal. If we adopt a scenario that we are error-tolerant (i.e. we accept rank differences with specific limits) we may define various *Special Zones* centered around the diagonal that would represent various zones of ranking "agreement". These Zones are presented in various shades of gray in Fig. 3. If for example agent X was ranked in the 26th position by the Glicko system and in the 36th position by the Elo system, then the error (disagreement) is ten positions, which corresponds to about 8 % error relative to the total range of 126. In addition, the green and red lines make a heuristic distinction of "good", "moderate" and "bad" playing, by simply dividing the total ranking scale to three regions of equal lengths. Table 1 reports the number of agents (and corresponding percentage) in various Special Zones that accept absolute rank differences in the set {2, 5, 10, 20, 40}.

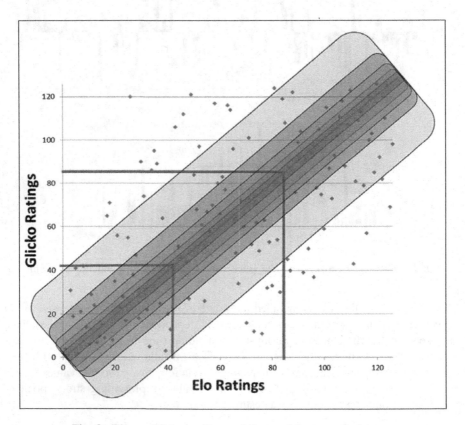

Fig. 3. Elo vs. Glicko ranking and the special zones of tolerance

It is evident that even one adopts a fault-tolerant approach the two ranking methods produce consistent rankings only for a very small number of agents.

Table 1. Various special zones of Elo-Glicko absolute rank difference tolerance

Rank difference	#agents	% agents
2 (1.67%)	10	7.94
5 (4.03%)	21	16.67
10 (8.06%)	33	26.19
20 (16.13%)	64	50.79
40 (32.26%)	95	75.39

Table 2 presents a more detailed view of the difference in the ranks obtained by the two rating methods for the identified Special Zones and playing performance. Specifically, it shows how many of the agents fall within a Special Zone either for both methods (rows "Agree for") or for just one of the methods (rows "Disagree for"); it also presents those results using the heuristic classification as "Good", "Moderate" or "Bad" produced by uniformly dividing the total rank scale in three equal parts.

Table 2. Agreement and disagreement of the two methods within the special zones

Playing perfor-mance	Agreement / disagreement of methods	2 ranks dif-ference #agents	5 ranks dif-ference #agents	10 ranks dif-ference #agents	20 ranks dif-ference #agents	40 ranks dif-ference #agents
Good	Agree for	4	7	9	21	31
	Disagree for	38	35	33	21	11
Moderate	Agree for	4	10	18	23	33
	Disagree for	38	32	24	21	9
Bad	Agree for	2	4	7	20	31
	Disagree for	40	38	35	20	11
SUM	Agree for	10 (7.94%)	21 (16.67%)	34 (26.98%)	64 (50.79%)	95 (75.39%)
	Disagree for	116 (92.06%)	105 (83.33%)	92 (73.02%)	62 (49.21%)	31 (24.61%)

5 Conclusions

As more and more multi-agent systems with social organization and advanced learning mechanisms are being studied, synthetic agent-rating mechanisms are starting to be applied and tested. Among the choices for agent rating there are the rating methods for human performance, such as Elo and Glicko, which have initially been developed to rank human players performance on games like chess and go. Extensive experiments have shown that the rankings produced be the two methods show excessive ranking inconsistencies and rise doubts on the applications of both methods in synthetic worlds.

By developing a simpler method as a substitute to existing rating methods, we also hope to use it as a benchmark to calculate the extent to which these two methods differ as regards score calculation in a series of multi-agent competitions. Such simpler methods may rely on just adding up the number of wins, maybe discounted over time, and still provide adequate information as to the quality of individual agents. In our future work we are planning to develop and compare more suitable rating mechanisms that would be efficient in assessing the performance of synthetic agents in multi-agent systems with social organization.

References

1. Gilbert, N., Troitzsch, K.G.: Simulation for the Social Scientist, 2nd edn. Open University Press, Maidenhead (2005)
2. Shoham, Y., Leyton, K.B.: Multiagent Systems: Algorithmic, Game-Theoretic and Logical Foundations. Cambridge University Press, New York (2009)
3. Ferber, J.: Multi-agent Systems: An Introduction to Distributed Artificial Intelligence. Addison-Wesley, Boston (1999)
4. Kiourt, C., Kalles, D.: Social reinforcement learning in game playing. In: IEEE International Conference on Tools with Artificial Intelligence, Athens, Greece, pp. 322–326 (2012)
5. Marivate, V.N.: Social learning methods in board game agents. In: IEEE Symposium Computational Intelligence and Games, Perth, Australia, pp. 323–328 (2008)
6. Caballero, A., Botia, J., Gomez-Skarmeta, A.: Using cognitive agents in social simulations. Eng. Appl. Artif. Intell. 24(7), 1098–1109 (2011)
7. Logan, Y., Kagan, T.: Elo ratings for structural credit assignment in multiagent systems. In: Twenty-Seventh AAAI Conference on Artificial Intelligence (Late-Breaking Developments) (2013)
8. Elo, A.E.: The Rating of Chess Players, Past and Present. Arco Publishing, New York (1978)
9. Glickman, E., Albyn, J.C.: Rating the chess rating system. Chance 12(2), 21–28 (1999)
10. Glickman, M.E.: A comprehensive guide to chess ratings. Am. Chess J. 3, 59–102 (1995)
11. Harkness, K.: Official Chess Handbook. McKay, New York (1967)
12. Kalles, D., Kanellopoulos, P.: On verifying game design and playing strategies using reinforcement learning. In: Proceedings of ACM Symposium on Applied Computing, Special Track on Artificial Intelligence and Computation Logic, Las Vegas (2001)
13. Tesauro, G.: Practical issues in temporal difference learning. Mach. Learn. 4, 257–277 (1992)
14. Sutton, R., Barto, A.: Reinforcement Learning - An Introduction. MIT Press, Cambridge (1998)
15. Kiourt, C., Kalles, D.: Building a social multi-agent system simulation management toolbox. In: 6th Balkan Conference in Informatics, Thessaloniki, Greece, pp. 66–70 (2003)
16. Spearman, C.: The proof and measurement of association between two things. Am. J. Psychol. 15(1), 72–101 (1904)

Learning in Multi Agent Social Environments with Opponent Models

Chairi Kiourt[(✉)] and Dimitris Kalles

School of Science and Technology, Hellenic Open University, Patras, Greece
{chairik,kalles}@eap.gr

Abstract. We examine how synthetic agents interact in social environments employing a variety of agent training strategies against diverse opponents. Such agent training and playing methods indicate that quality playing relies more on the correct set-up of the learning mechanism than on experience. The experimentation provides valuable insight into the potential of an agent to compete against other agents in its environment and yet manage to also co-operate so that this particular environment allows for the emergence of a competitive champion agent, which will represent its group in further contests. Additionally, by investigating performance while constraining the number of moves we gain interesting insight into competitive learning and playing with resource constraints.

Keywords: Multi-agent systems · Social learning · Opponent based learning

1 Introduction

Computer social simulation and agent-based simulation began to be used widely in the 1990s, as a way of modeling and understanding social processes [1–3]. Many agents in a common location, each one usually acting selfishly, produce Multi-Agent Systems (MASs), sometimes mimicking traits of human behavior [1, 4, 5] and one can show that agent differentiation improves playing behavior [7]. Moreover, learning occurs when an agent changes its tactic or strategy in response to new information [1, 2, 4, 5]. Agent differentiation in game based multi-agent systems is a key aspect of social environments, with other parameters being the size of the environment, rules, pay offs and penalties, amongst others [1–5].

Using a metaphor, we note that in a school courtyard, pupils play against each other with the aim to top their local ranking table but they also hope to, collectively, improve their performance when their school faces off an adversary and individual matches can be scheduled. Chess players in clubs participate in a series of intra-club matches before leading to chess club tournaments, where each club fields only some of its members. Football teams participate in national tournaments and, then, champions get a chance to represent their leagues at international events. These are all examples of individual agents working for their own purposes but also sharing a common goal of group improvement. For all these contexts, an abstraction is evident: one needs to optimize the effort to be spent with colleagues, who act as competitors, before one tries to tackle

© Springer International Publishing Switzerland 2016
M. Rovatsos et al. (Eds.): EUMAS 2015/AT 2015, LNAI 9571, pp. 137–144, 2016.
DOI: 10.1007/978-3-319-33509-4_12

opponents from another group. There exists, therefore, an interesting co-operation/ competition dilemma: you need to practice effectively and efficiently, before you actually challenge an unknown opponent.

To translate the metaphor in the context of multi-agent systems endowed with learning capabilities, we introduce a game to allow for two opponents (of varying strength, tactics and motives) to compete against each other, then we create an environment where arbitrary collections of agents compete against each other and, then we design an evaluation toolkit to measure how two distinct groups of agents manage their intra-group training with respect to their inter-group face off. There may even exist restrictions on the amount of learning resources (time, allowable number of practice games, allowable number of defeats: one can readily think of several such resources). Additionally, there exist quite a few allowable degrees of freedom for such experiments; besides learning resources, one can experiment with a variety of learning mechanism configurations (thus, simulating different characters; for example, fast vs. slow learners, risky vs. conservative learners, exploiters vs. explorers, etc.), as well as a variety of opponent selection mechanisms (opting to play against a stronger or a weaker opponent, opting to play against an opponent of unknown stature, etc.), all of which lead to a wealth of social interactions. Such interactions can be recorded and subsequently analyzed with the objective of identifying interesting (or promising) behaviors.

To facilitate the research above, one needs to address two broad directions. On one hand, one needs to design, experiment and analyze the results of various learning and interaction mechanisms, to investigate the emergence of social hierarchies and of "best" individuals. This direction is best served by machine learning, data mining and analytics at large, and is the focus of this paper, with an emphasis on the formation of clusters of agent behavior within a society. On the other hand, all these activities require the utilization of high performance computing infrastructures and tools to manage the experimentation life cycle (in this paper we make extensive use of a home-grown platform for this purpose).

So, our paper focuses on benchmarking the performance of synthetic agents and profiling that performance across a range of properties.

The main contribution of the paper is to highlight the effect of the initial diverse configuration of agents on the eventual ranking within a society and to present the best learning strategy against diverse synthetic agents in the same society group. Those experiments generally suggest that powerful agents can be created across a range of learning behavior configurations and that inexperienced playing agent need to have a positive predisposition to learning.

The rest of this paper is structured in three sections. The next section provides a brief background of game-playing social learning aspects and the synthetic agents' characters. The third section describes our experimentation on socially trained synthetic agents and some attributes for better learning and training in inter-group contests. The last section presents our conclusions and sets out future work.

2   A Brief Background

As originated in the MAS domain, social organizations are environments where more than two agents act autonomously, each with its own information about the world and the other agents [2, 4]; the concept also applies to games [4, 5, 9]. There are two extremes regarding the interactions between agents in MAS environments [2, 3]: **Cooperation**, where agents cooperate for a common goal (sometimes sharing utility functions and knowledge) and **Competition**, where an agent can only win when another agent loses (zero-sum game).

To demonstrate our approach and our results, we use RLGame; a strategy board game [10] which features two players and their pawns and is played on an $n \times n$ square board. Two $a \times a$ square bases are on opposite board corners; these are initially populated by β pawns for each player. A pawn can move out of the base to any adjacent free square, by starting the game with the first move of the white player from the lower left base towards the upper right base of the black player. The black player follows the exactly opposite direction. A pawn can move vertically or horizontally to an adjacent free square, provided that the maximum distance from its base is not decreased (thus, backward moves are not allowed). Players can move a pawn at a time and take turns to move. A pawn that cannot move is lost. A player also loses by running out of pawns. Each player's goal is to move a pawn into the opponent's base or to force all opponent pawns out of the board.

Each agent-player is autonomous and acts according to its characteristics and knowledge. The learning mechanism of each agent is based on approximating its (reinforcement learning inspired [13]) value function with a back propagation neural network [2, 3]. A neural network takes as input a game board snapshot and outputs a value that reflects the expectation to win by making a specific move.

The agent's goal is to learn an optimal policy that will maximize the expected sum of rewards in a specific time, determining which action should be taken next given the current state of the environment. The policy to select between moves is an ε-Greedy policy, with ε denoting the probability to select the best move (exploitation), according to present knowledge, and 1-ε denoting a random move (exploration) [14]. The learning mechanism is associated with two additional learning policies, Gamma (γ) and Lambda (λ). Risky or conservative agent behavior is associated with the γ discount rate parameter, which specifies the learning strategy of the agent and determines the values of future payoffs, with values in $0..1$; effectively, we associate large values with long-term strategies. The speed and quality of agent learning is associated with Lambda, which is the learning rate of the neural network, also taking values in $0..1$. Small values of λ can result in slow, smooth learning, whereas large ones could lead to accelerated, unstable learning. These properties are what we, henceforth, term as "characteristic values" for the playing agents.

For our social organization experiments we evolved RLGame to its tournament variant, RLGTournament [4, 6], implementing a Round-Robin scheme to pair participants against each other; this set-up corresponds to the competition extreme. Similar techniques have also been used in similar contexts [5, 9] and earlier experiments have demonstrated that self-playing trained agents are, generally speaking, weaker than socially trained ones [4, 6]. This concurs with similar findings, which report that the efficiency of an agent in a social environment is better than the corresponding one of a self-playing agent; as a result, the population and the number of the games are important attributes of social learning environments [5].

3   Experimental Investigation

3.1   Testing Inexperienced Agents

The first part of the experiments pits inexperienced agents against experienced ones, for studying their progress under a variety of constraints on the number of pawn moves, with each "experienced" having already played about 12,000 games [15]. Table 1(a) presents the agents' configurations, ratings (also using the Elo [16] and Glicko [17] systems, widely used for rating chess players) and rankings. There are twenty-one experienced agents from three different classes, Good Playing (GP), Moderate Playing (MP) and Bad Playing (BP), with Good-Moderate-Bad playing being classified as such by the researchers who actually analyzed the results of previous RLGame tournaments [15]. Additionally, seven inexperienced agents were initialised, in correspondence to the experienced agents and a further trivial agent was added (*PlrxN*). A further default rating system is also reported, based on the *grades* earned by each player; this is the sum of games won by each agent during the tournament, with each win contributing +1 and each loss contributing −1.

Table 1.   (a) Agent setup and statistics (b) initial results.

Group	Class	ε	γ	λ	Name	Pr.Ra.	Ranking	Elo	Glicko	Grades
Agents with 12,500 Games, Experience	Good Playing (GP)	0.6	0.6	0.8	Plr3	1	1	943	1612	4004
		0.6	0.7	0.6	Plr6	2	2	773	1665	4002
		0.6	0.7	0.7	Plr7	3	3	888	1664	3974
		0.6	0.7	0.8	Plr8	4	4	904	1714	3556
		0.6	0.99	0.8	Plr23	5	5	825	1758	3548
		0.6	0.6	0.6	Plr1	6	6	888	1857	3484
		0.6	0.6	0.7	Plr2	7	7	962	1963	3076
	Moderate Playing (MP)	0.8	0.9	0.8	Plr68	60	8	756	1357	-206
		0.9	0.6	0.6	Plr76	61	9	807	1518	-244
		0.9	0.8	0.7	Plr87	62	10	777	1569	-268
		0.8	0.9	0.9	Plr69	63	11	699	1296	-276
		0.9	0.8	0.6	Plr86	64	12	761	1605	-308
		0.9	0.7	0.6	Plr81	65	13	792	1784	-328
		0.9	0.9	0.7	Plr92	66	14	876	1702	-346
	Bad Playing (BP)	0.8	0.9	0.99	Plr70	120	15	729	1476	-2554
		0.7	0.8	0.99	Plr40	121	16	751	1625	-2844
		0.7	0.6	0.99	Plr30	122	17	708	1302	-2850
		0.6	0.9	0.99	Plr20	123	18	568	1358	-2926
		0.7	0.7	0.99	Plr35	124	19	712	1299	-3140
		0.7	0.9	0.99	Plr45	125	20	746	1582	-3264
		0.6	0.8	0.99	Plr15	126	21	713	1286	-3328
Inexperienced Agents, Expected to be	GP	0.6	0.6	0.8	Plr1N	no	no	800	1500	0
		0.6	0.7	0.6	Plr2N	no	no	800	1500	0
	MP	0.8	0.9	0.9	Plr3N	no	no	800	1500	0
		0.9	0.8	0.6	Plr4N	no	no	800	1500	0
	BP	0.7	0.9	0.99	Plr5N	no	no	800	1500	0
		0.6	0.8	0.99	Plr6N	no	no	800	1500	0
		0.99	0.99	0.99	PlrxN	no	no	800	1500	0

Group	Agent	Elo	Glicko	Grades	Ranked	Old Ra.
Good Playing	Plr6	841	1617	832	1	2
	Plr8	880	1654	776	2	4
	Plr7	967	1759	772	3	3
	Plr1N	812	1470	736	4	No
	Plr2N	1070	1957	720	5	No
	Plr2	879	1743	598	6	7
	Plr3	905	1821	524	7	1
Moderate Playing	Plr68	752	1489	142	8	8
	Plr76	738	1411	86	9	9
	Plr69	986	1713	12	10	11
	Plr3N	775	1574	4	11	No
	Plr1	740	1526	0	12	6
	Plr4N	817	1553	-20	13	No
	Plr86	640	1320	-128	14	12
	Plr87	743	1512	-130	15	10
	Plr92	779	1542	-146	16	14
	Plr81	796	1485	-232	17	13
	PlrXN	854	1732	-262	18	No
	Plr30	811	1494	-322	19	17
	Plr20	730	1368	-418	20	18
	Plr23	730	1368	-418	21	5
Bad Playing	Plr5N	765	1467	-436	22	No
	Plr70	737	1480	-466	23	15
	Plr15	673	1332	-578	24	21
	Plr35	616	1317	-584	25	19
	Plr40	768	1466	-618	26	16
	Plr6N	607	1291	-724	27	No
	Plr45	609	1257	-794	28	20

We report on five experiments (Table 2) featuring the same agent configurations (Table 1(a)) but subject to different RLGame pawn-move constraints. With an 8×8 board size and a 2×2 base size, RLGame cannot be concluded in fewer than 10 pawn moves; we thus set the lowest allowable number of moves at 16 and then double the limit, with the last constraint effectively imposing no limit at all (as Table 2 shows, unlimited moves always result in one side winning over the other).

Table 2. Results from first 5 experiments.

Max Moves per Tournament	Average Values					Min and Max Values					
	Moves	Draws	elo	glicko	Grades	min Elo	maxElo	min Glicko	max Glicko	min Grades	max Grades
16	12.24	142	796	1548	5	594	947	1288	1769	-552	380
32	17.10	21	788	1555	-35	569	981	1130	1920	-648	606
64	22.81	8	788	1530	-38	683	955	1341	1741	-872	844
128	29.25	2	786	1525	-38	607	1070	1257	1957	-794	832
10000	45.29	0	787	1539	-46	574	939	1262	1746	-868	888

Results, in particular for the inexperienced agents, confirm that a well-tuned learning mechanism is more efficient than the experience (Table 1(b)). Note that all three rating systems produce relatively similar rankings of the agents, though there do exist deviations. A notable singularity is observed with player Plr23, which demonstrates a huge difference between its old and new ranking. This position difference probably arises from the combination of a quite large γ value and a low ε value, which are associated with the discount rate parameter and the policy of selecting the next move, suggesting that a long-term strategy coupled with a stronger exploration bias may cause instability.

The inexperienced MP agent only has positive results when facing lower level class agents, while when it faces agents from the same class, the contest seems to be resolved based on the importance of the experience. The BP inexperienced agent lost nearly 90 % of the matches only scoring wins against similar level agents.

3.2 Successive Training of Agents in Intra-group and Inter-group Settings

We now report on a series of experiments to simulate the preparation of an agent in intra-group matches to represent its group in subsequent tournaments against agents coming from other ("hostile") groups. For this reason, a GP agent configuration is chosen to determine the best intra-courtyard training against experienced and inexperienced agents of different configurations and classes. This agent is trained with six different classes in intra-group matches, experienced and inexperienced agent, in order to determine the best training evolution strategy for a good playing agent (which is starting to compete based on zero experience). Experiment configurations are shown in the left sub-table of Table 3. We developed two categories of experiments composed of three different experiment set-ups for each one. The first category contains experiments with inexperienced opponents of three different classes and the second category features experienced opponents, with all other configurations kept to the values of the first category. In both experiments, the subject agent (Plr1N) begins as an inexperienced one and, after those experiments, is tested in further different configurations, as shown in the two sub-tables to the right of Table 3.

Table 3. Plr1N training and tournament playing, experiments setup.

Tournament Sessions

Plr1N Experience	Experiment	Opp.	Wins
Plr1N (A-1)	Experienced	Various Agents 3 - (GP), 3 - (MP), 3 - (BP) ⇧	66%
Plr1N (A-2)		⇧	65%
Plr1N (A-3)		⇩	60%
Plr1N (A-1)	Inexperienced	Various Agents 3 - (GP), 3 - (MP), 3 - (BP) ⇩	57%
Plr1N (A-2)		⇧	63%
Plr1N (A-3)		⇨	59%

Inter-Courtyard Training Session

	Exp.		Opp.	Wins
Plr1N	A-1	Experienced	9 - (GP) ⇩	52%
	A-2		9 - (MP) ⇨	63%
	A-3		9 - (BP) ⇧	69%
	B-1	Inexperienced	9 - (GP) ⇩	56%
	B-2		9 - (MP) ⇨	63%
	B-3		9 - (BP) ⇧	68%

Tournament Sessions

Plr1N Experience	Experiment	Opp.	Wins
Plr1N (B-1)	Experienced	Various Agents 3 - (GP), 3 - (MP), 3 - (BP) ⇧	64%
Plr1N (B-2)		⇩	61%
Plr1N (B-3)		⇧	64%
Plr1N (B-1)	Inexperienced	Various Agents 3 - (GP), 3 - (MP), 3 - (BP) ⇩	61%
Plr1N (B-2)		⇩	62%
Plr1N (B-3)		⇧	67%

Initial results of the agent from the inter-courtyard (right side of Table 3) experiments show that there performance does not seem to be affected by the experience level of the intra-courtyard opponents (as seen in the left side of Table 3). Some details appear in Fig. 1, which shows the progress (Grades) of Plr1N form the inter-courtyard training sessions. The lines refer to the experienced three different agent classes (opponents) whereas the dashed lines refer to the inexperienced three different agent classes (opponents); we denote GP opponents with rhombus symbol, MP opponents with triangle symbol and BP opponents with square symbol.

Player Plr1N has the best evolution against a weaker opponent, regardless of such an opponent's experience. The main difference occurs when playing with a same class experienced agent, where the player's Plr1N performance clearly deteriorates.

Inter-courtyard experiments are setup for testing player Plr1N after its intra-courtyard training; Plr1N variants are then tested in twelve tournaments with different opponent configurations, as shown in the two sub-tables to the right of Table 3.

In general, the Plr1N, after training, performed good in almost all cases. Based on these results we observe that: a GP agent trained with experienced opponents performs better against experienced opponents in tournaments, a GP agent trained with experienced MP opponents always performs better, and a GP agent trained against inexperienced BP opponents performs better than one trained with BP experienced opponents.

With regard to those strategies, it seems that when an agent faces opponents of corresponding strength, it does face some instability in its progress, which is not the case

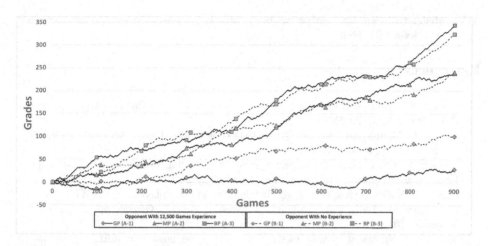

Fig. 1. Training Plr1N inter-courtyard with different classes.

when training with lower level opponents, where progress is more stable. In general, the strength of the opponents influences the power of the learning-to-play agent. Still, there do exists anomalies in this relatively clear pattern which need to be resolved (at the top left graph of Fig. 1, we observe that Plr1N coped better against some experienced agents compared to some inexperienced ones).

4   Conclusions and Future Work

The results of these experiments suggest that an opponent is an important key point on an agent's learning progress in a social environment. We have also demonstrated that intra-courtyard training is necessary for preparing inexperienced members of a group for inter-courtyard matches. Some important highlights of those experiments are: when an inexperienced agent meets equivalent agents (i.e. good playing), regardless of whether the latter are experienced or not, it faces serious problems on its progress. Additionally, training with lower level opponents produces more stable evolving agents, which, however, are at the low end of the performance spectrum and may be unable to improve with a satisfactory pace.

Based on these outcomes, we plan to investigate how agents may decide to select their opponents to improve their (individual and collective) learning (and playing) behavior. This may also take place under resource constraints (for example, given only 10 games to play and given access to the performance rankings of all agents in the tournament, an agent might decide to play against an opponent and skip another one). In addition, the dynamic manipulation of the characteristic values could produce more powerful agents, which dynamically match their effort to their opponents. Our experimental platform [15] allows us to investigate such social learning aspects of the agents and simulate powerful social environments.

Acknowledgment. The first author has been partially supported by the Hellenic Artificial Intelligence Society (EETN).

References

1. Gilbert, N., Troitzsch, K.G.: Simulation for the Social Scientist, 2nd edn. Open University Press, Maidenhead (2005)
2. Ferber, J.: Multi-agent Systems: An Introduction to Distributed Artificial Intelligence. Addison-Wesley, Boston (1999)
3. Shoham, Y., Leyton, B.K.: Multiagent Systems: Algorithmic, Game-Theoretic, and Logical Foundations. Cambridge University Press, Cambridge (2009)
4. Kiourt, C., Kalles, D.: Social reinforcement learning in game playing. In: IEEE International Conference on Tools with Artificial Intelligence, Athens, Greece, pp. 322–326, 7–9 November 2012
5. Marivate, V.N.: Social learning methods in board game agents. In: IEEE Symposium on Computational Intelligence and Games (CIG 2008), Perth, Australia, pp. 323–328 (2008)
6. Kiourt, C., Kalles, D.: Building a social multi-agent system simulation management toolbox. In: 6th Balkan Conference in Informatics, Thessaloniki, Greece, pp. 66–70 (2013)
7. Lockett, J.A., Miikkulainen, R.: Evolving opponent models for Texas Hold 'Em. In: IEEE Symposium on Computational Intelligence and Games, Perth, Australia, pp. 31–38 (2008)
8. Carmel, D., Markovitch, S.: Opponent modeling in multi-agent systems. In: Weiss, G., Sen, S. (eds.) IJCAI-WS 1995. LNCS, vol. 1042, pp. 40–52. Springer, Heidelberg (1996)
9. Al-Khateeb, B., Kendall, G.: Introducing a round robin tournament into evolutionary individual and social learning checkers. In: Developments in E-Systems Engineering, Dubai, United Arab Emirates, December 2011
10. Kalles, D., Kanellopoulos, P.: On verifying game design and playing strategies using reinforcement learning. In: Proceedings of ACM Symposium on Applied Computing, Special Track on Artificial Intelligence and Computation Logic, Las Vegas (2001)
11. Tesauro, G.: Programming backgammon using self-teaching neural nets. Artif. Intell. **134**, 181–199 (2002)
12. MacNamee, B., Cunningham, P.: Creating socially interactive non player characters. The μ-SIC system. Int. J. Intell. Games Simul. **2**(1), 28–35 (2003)
13. Sutton, R., Barto, A.: Reinforcement Learning - An Introduction. MIT Press, Cambridge (1998)
14. March, J.G.: Exploration and exploitation in organizational learning. Organ. Sci. **2**(1), 71–87 (1991)
15. Kiourt, C., Kalles, D.: Development of grid-based multi agent systems for social learning. In: IEEE International Conference on Information Intelligence, Systems and Applications (IISA 2015), Corfu, Greece, 04–07 July 2015
16. Elo, A.E.: The Rating of Chess Players, Past and Present. Arco Publishing, New York (1978)
17. Glickman, E.M., Albyn, J.C.: Rating the chess rating system. Chance **12**(2), 21–28 (1999)

A Particle Swarm Optimization Metaheuristic for the Blocking Flow Shop Scheduling Problem: Total Tardiness Minimization

Nouri Nouha[1]([✉]) and Ladhari Talel[2]

[1] Ecole Supérieure des Sciences Economiques et Commerciales de Tunis,
University of Tunis, Tunis, Tunisia
nouri.nouha@yahoo.fr
[2] College of Business, Umm Al-Qura University, Umm Al-Qura, Saudi Arabia
talel_ladhari2004@yahoo.fr

Abstract. In this research, the blocking permutation flow shop problem is invoked where the Particle Swarm Optimization algorithm (PSO) is used to minimize the total tardiness criterion. Indeed, particles constructing the swarm and their corresponding velocities are encoded as a job-permutation lists. Initially, the population is formed using a new NEH heuristic version and then updated based on some fixed neighborhood search method. The computational evaluation carried out on the well-known benchmark sets of Ronconi and Henriques has shown that the proposed technique is very effective in comparison with other state-of-the-art algorithms. New best solutions for the fixed instances are reported.

Keywords: Flow shop · Blocking · Total tardiness · PSO algorithm

1 Introduction

The permutation flow shop problem is one of the leading problem that has been explored as a machine scheduling models since Johnson's paper appearance that solves the 2-machine flow shop problem [1]. The main query is to specify for each machine the same complete sequence of all jobs minimizing some fixed criterion. The most likely studied optimization measure is the makespan (C_{max}) which defines the time at which the last job in the sequence is completed. Other scheduling objectives have been tackled: the maximum lateness, the maximum tardiness, the maximum earliness, the total flow time and others. In any case, it is assumed that buffer storage capacity between machines is infinite.

When we assert that no intermediate buffer exists between consecutive machines, then the problem becomes a Blocking Permutation Flow Shop (BFSP) [2]. If there are no buffers, then the job blocks the machines till its next machine becomes free. In such situation, we are talking about some blocking context namely 'Release when Starting Blocking (RSb)'. One of the pioneering works on this problem is [20] who revealed that the $F2|blocking|C_{max}$ instance may be

© Springer International Publishing Switzerland 2016
M. Rovatsos et al. (Eds.): EUMAS 2015/AT 2015, LNAI 9571, pp. 145–153, 2016.
DOI: 10.1007/978-3-319-33509-4_13

reduced to a special case of the traveling salesman problem which may be solved using Gilmore and Gomory algorithm [7]. When $m > 2$, the problem belongs to the class of strongly NP-hard [11]. Likewise, the two-machine flow shop under total flow time and/or tardiness is NP-hard [3, 21].

Among the proposed constructive heuristics for the BFSP under makespan, we refer basically to the Profile Fitting (PF) [15] and the NEH (Nawaz-Enscore-Ham)[16] heuristics. Under total flow time, we cite the modified NEH heuristic (NEH-WPT) [25]. As an improvement heuristics, we mention the Genetic Algorithm (GA) proposed in [5], the (Ron) algorithm in [22], the Tabu search (TS) algorithms used in [8], and the Hybrid Discrete Differential Evolution (HDDE) algorithm proposed in [24]. Later, a Discrete Artificial Bee Colony algorithm (DABC_D) is proposed [6] and compared with other algorithms including DABC [23] and HDDE. Hybrid DABC algorithms are proposed in [12], and a Revised Artificial Immune Systems (RAIS) algorithm is used in [14]. In [17], a three-phase algorithm is presented, and a Discrete Particle Swarm Optimization is proposed in [26]. Next, a Memetic Algorithm (MA) is appeared in [18], and a chaos-induced discrete self organizing migrating algorithm is applied in [4]. Unfortunately, there is a huge work dedicated to developing both exact and heuristic algorithms for both makespan and total flow time criteria, it seems that little work has dealt with the total tardiness criterion until recently. In [27], a TS procedure is proposed, and in [2] a new NEH-based method called (FPDNEH) and a Greedy Randomized Adaptive Search Procedure (GRASP) were proposed. In [28], an efficient Iterated Local Search algorithm (ILS) coupled with a Variable Neighborhood Search (VNS) is presented. Concretely, in this work, the Particle Swarm Optimization algorithm (PSO) is used to solve the blocking permutation flow shop scheduling problem. This method is adopted to minimize the total tardiness criterion. We hybridize the algorithm with a local search technique and provide new schemes for all particles and their corresponding velocities. Computational experiments are done using the well known Ronconi and Henriques's benchmark sets.

Thus, the paper is organized as follows. Section 2 roughly introduce the BFSP problem. In Sect. 3 we detail the proposed blocking PSO algorithm. The experiments results are reported in the next section and finally, Sect. 5 includes some concluding remarks.

2   The Blocking Flow Shop Scheduling Problem

This study investigates the blocking problem minimizing the total tardiness in the M-machine permutation flow shop environment. The problem may be stated as follows. Consider N independent jobs to be processed sequentially on M different machines with zero intermediate storage. So that in-between queues of jobs waiting in the system for their subsequent operation are prohibited. Besides, when processed, all jobs follow the same route in the machines. Each job may be processed on exactly one machine at any time, and each machine can process only one job at a time. Jobs are ready for processing at time zero and have no precedent constraints among them. Indeed, there is exactly one task corresponding to the processing of job i ($i = 1, 2, ..., N$) on each machine j ($j = 1, 2, ..., M$) which needs a processing time p_{ij}, and could have some fixed due date D_i (the time point at which the job should finish). Anyway, a job cannot leave a machine until the next machine downstream is free. Based on the afore-stated definition, the objective is to meet a final sequence processing all jobs on all declared machines under tardiness. The blocking instance considered in this study is the $Fm|block|\sum T_j$ representing the BFSP under tardiness [10]. Let: $\Pi := (\pi_1, \pi_2, ..., \pi_N)$ be a solution for the problem, where π_i denotes the ith job in the considered sequence; $d_{\pi_i,j}$ ($i = 1, 2, ..., N; j = 0, 1, 2, ..., M$) represents the departure time of job π_i on machine j, where $d_{\pi_i,0}$ denotes the time job π_i starts its processing on the first machine. The corresponding values of makespan of Π may then be calculated as $C_{max}(\Pi) = C_{\pi_N,M}(\Pi)$, where $C_{\pi_i,M} = d_{\pi_i,M}$ is the completion time of job π_i on machine M that can be deduced using the following expressions [19]:

$$d_{\pi_1,0} = 0 \tag{1}$$

$$d_{\pi_1,j} = \sum_{k=1}^{j} p_{\pi_1,k} \quad j = 1, 2, ..., M - 1 \tag{2}$$

$$d_{\pi_i,0} = d_{\pi_{i-1},1} \quad i = 2, ..., N \tag{3}$$

$$d_{\pi_i,j} = max\{d_{\pi_i,j-1} + p_{\pi_i,j}, d_{\pi_{i-1},j+1}\} \quad i = 2, ..., N; j = 1, 2, ..., M - 1 \tag{4}$$

$$d_{\pi_i,M} = d_{\pi_i,M-1} + p_{\pi_i,M} \quad i = 1, 2, ..., N \tag{5}$$

Using one more time the afore recursion, we may calculate the total tardiness (TT) as $TT(\Pi) = \sum_{i=1}^{N}(T_i)$ where $T_i = max\{0, (C_{\pi_i} - D_i)\}$. We choose to calculate the due dates D_i following the Total Work content (TWK) rule [9]: $D_i = \tau \times (\sum_{j=1}^{M}(p_{\pi_i,j}))$. τ is the due date tightness factor and $\sum_{j=1}^{M}(p_{\pi_i,j})$ is the total processing time of job π_i on all machines. τ is taken randomly in the range [1–3] to make the job's due date loose, medium or tight.

3   The Blocking PSO Algorithm

PSO algorithm is a population-based stochastic optimization technique first introduced by Kennedy and Eberhart [13]. Each member in the swarm is called a particle and has a velocity V_i^t to explore the solution space iteratively thus to update its current position X_i^t. This update is done based on two factors: the local best P_i^t and the global best G^t. The first factor represents the personal best position of the ith particle and the second refers to the global best solution obtained by the population at the tth iteration. During the search, there is interaction between particles in the neighborhood where they share information. After a fixed number of iterations, the swarm looses its heterogeneity and the algorithm is headed straight for the optimal solution. Mathematically, the new position of the ith particle is updated as follows:

$$X_i^t = V_i^t + X_i^{t-1} \tag{6}$$

Meanwhile, the velocity update is performed as:

$$V_i^t = w^{t-1}V_i^{t-1} + c_1 r_1 (P_i^{t-1} - X_i^{t-1}) + c_2 r_2 (G^{t-1} - X_i^{t-1}) \tag{7}$$

where w^t is the inertia weight, constants c_1 and c_2 are two learning factors, and r_1, r_2 are random numbers between $(0,1)$. The key concept in applying successfully PSO algorithm is thus to provide an effective decoding mechanism to change the continuous solution into a discrete one. To the best of our knowledge, there is no published paper employing the PSO algorithm to minimize the BFSP under tardiness.

3.1   Solution Representation

A particle in the swarm is encoded as a job-permutation list of N jobs. That is, a particle at the tth iteration is denoted as $X_i^t = \{x_{i1}^t, x_{i2}^t, ..., x_{iN}^t\}$ where x_{ij}^t is the index of the job arranged at position j. Similarly, the velocity of that particle is defined as a permutation of all jobs.

3.2   Population Initialization

The swarm is constructed based on the NEH heuristic [16]. This technique generates only one sequence at each run. We need to generate several permutations to form the initial swarm. The steps of our revised-NEH algorithm are described as follows. After initializing the seed sequences, α random jobs are picked up randomly and exchanged in the α first positions in each particle's permutation instead of changing the two first jobs. Among the α generated sequences only the best one is retained. Stage 3 is the iterative process of the classic NEH. So, for each particle a sequence is generated depending on the α random number drawn. Besides, for each particle i, the personal best position P_i^t is initialized the same as its current position X_i^t and its initial velocity V_i^t is fulfilled randomly. The swarm is evaluated using the objective function $TT(X_i)$ and the global best G^t equals to the best position among the whole swarm is memorized.

3.3   Particle Enhancement Scheme

A neighborhood search technique is needed to evolve the position values of particles in the solution space. This position update is based on discrete job permutations. In fact, in the iteration t, the 'otimes' operator is used to update the position of one particle using the following equations:

$$V_i^{t+1} = V_i^t \otimes P_i^t \otimes G^t \tag{8}$$

$$X_i^{t+1} = V_i^{t+1} \otimes X_i^t \tag{9}$$

where '$\otimes$' denotes the two-point crossover operator. The implementation of these formulas consists of two phases. First, the particle's personal best position is crossed over the current global position in the swarm. Then, one of the two resulting solutions is picked randomly and crossed over the current velocity. These equations are simple and easy to implement but after some iterations there is a risque to be trapped in local optima. To solve this problem, we performed a referenced local search technique for that particle as in [17] and where the new velocity is introduced as a reference. Indeed, if a particle's current position coincides with the global best position, then this particle will stop moving. The referenced local search is used to search its neighborhood.

$$X_i^{t+1} = Referenced\ local\ search(X_i^t, V_i^{t+1}). \tag{10}$$

3.4   Final Blocking PSO Algorithm (BPSO)

Based on the solution representation, the population initialization, and the particle enhancement scheme the structure of the BPSO algorithm is summarized. The algorithm is stopped when it reaches the Maximal Cycle Number of generation (MCN) or the maximum computation time allowed in milliseconds ('T').

Algorithm. BPSO

Stage 1: Initialization

- Initialize the parameters: PS, T, and MCN.
- Generate the initial swarm: apply the Revised-NEH heuristic to produce PS particles and initialize their velocities randomly.
- Evaluate each particle in the swarm using the objective function $TT(\Pi)$.
- Set the personal best of each particle to be the particle itself, and the global best to be the best one among the swarm.
- Set $t = 0$ and $cp = T$.

Stage 2: Update the current global best position G^t

   For each particle i *Do*

- If $TT(P_i^t) < TTG^t)$ then $G^t = P_i^t$

   End For

Stage 3: Stopping criterion

- If $(t = MCN)$ or $(cp = 0)$ Then return the obtained global best position and Stop

Stage 4: Swarm evolution

   For each particle i *Do*

- If $X_i^t = G^t$ Then pick randomly another particle
- Set $V_i^{t+1} = V_i^t \otimes P_i^t \otimes G^t$
- Set $X_i^{t+1} = Referenced\ local\ search(X_i^t, V_i^{t+1})$
- If the objective value $TT(X_i^{t+1})$ has not been improved Then replace the X_i^{t+1} by another random position
- Update the personal best position

Stage 5: Update iteration counter: $t = t + 1$ and $cp = cp - 1$ then go to *Stage 2*

---

4   Computational Results

In this section we describe the computational experiments conducted to evaluate the performance of the BPSO algorithm based on the well-known test problems of Ronconi and Henriques [2]. In such benchmark, there are 5 groups of job sizes: 20, 50, 100, 200, and 500. In each job subset (20,50,100), there are 5, 10, and 20 machines to process the jobs, respectively. The job subset (200) has 10 and 20 machines, and the job subset (500) has only 20 machines to process the jobs. 10 different matrices of processing times were generated for each of the 12 sizes, and for each of those matrices 4 scenarios were built. Each instance is independently executed ten replications, and in each replication the Relative Percentage Deviation (RPD) is computed. TT^A defines the objective value reached by the BPSO, and TT^{Min} defines the minimum objective value obtained among all the compared algorithms.

$$RPD(A) = \frac{(TT^A - TT^{Min}) \times 100}{TT^{Min}} \qquad (11)$$

The BPSO algorithm is coded in Visual C++ and run on an Intel Pentium IV 2.4 GHz PC with 512 MB of memory. On the basis of a set of preliminary experiments, best results were achieved using the following parameters (Table 1).

Table 1. Parameters values used for the BPSO after calibration

Parameter	MCN	PS	T
Value	100	50	$N \times (M/10)$ ms

4.1   Comparison of Ronconi and Henriques's Benchmarks

In this subsection we present the performance evaluation of the BPSO with respect to minimization of the total tardiness. We have used the already announced benchmark set of Ronconi and Henriques where due dates are uniformly distributed between $P(1-T-R/2)$ and $P(1-T+R/2)$ [30]. Accordingly, each one of the four scenarios correspond to a combination of $T = \{0.2, 0.4\}$ and $R = \{0.6, 1.2\}$. Table 2 summarizes the results of the comparison of the algorithms under the fixed criterion. The effectiveness of the reported methods against the GRASP metaheuristic [2] and the GA based on the path relinking technique GA_PR [29] was measured by listing again the ARPDs values, where TT^{Min} defines the total tardiness value obtained by GRASP algorithm. Based on Table 2, BPSO obtained the same results as the GRASP in 55 problems. These performances are much more better than those obtained by GA_PR (110 problems). We report the average of improvement percentage of each class with 10 problems. For all test instances, BPSO achieved the highest improvement with N*M varying from (20*5) up to (500*20).

Table 2. ARPD values on Ronconi and Henriques's instances under total tardiness

Inst	BPSO				GRASP				GA_PR				All Scenario		
	Sc. 1	Sc. 2	Sc. 3	Sc. 4	Sc. 1	Sc. 2	Sc. 3	Sc. 4	Sc. 1	Sc. 2	Sc. 3	Sc. 4	BPSO	GRASP	GA_PR
20*5	0,000 %	0,000 %	0,000 %	0,000 %	6,841 %	1,847 %	2,826 %	2,278 %	2,540 %	0,604 %	0,761 %	0,562 %	0,000 %	3,448 %	1,117 %
20*10	0,000 %	0,000 %	0,000 %	0,000 %	2,241 %	3,345 %	1,910 %	1,913 %	0,973 %	0,817 %	0,435 %	0,510 %	0,000 %	2,352 %	0,684 %
20*20	0,000 %	0,000 %	0,000 %	0,000 %	2,038 %	0,905 %	0,656 %	1,003 %	0,413 %	0,345 %	0,164 %	0,255 %	0,000 %	1,152 %	0,294 %
50*5	0,000 %	0,000 %	0,000 %	0,000 %	16,414 %	2,581 %	5,407 %	4,312 %	4,610 %	2,581 %	1,066 %	0,902 %	0,000 %	7,178 %	2,290 %
50*10	0,000 %	0,000 %	0,000 %	0,000 %	15,592 %	28,227 %	4,780 %	4,444 %	5,743 %	8,788 %	1,411 %	2,634 %	0,000 %	13,261 %	4,644 %
50*20	0,000 %	0,001 %	0,000 %	0,000 %	7,655 %	5,492 %	3,274 %	2,483 %	4,425 %	2,904 %	1,058 %	0,907 %	0,000 %	4,726 %	2,323 %
100*5	0,000 %	0,000 %	0,000 %	0,000 %	19,029 %	9,141 %	2,125 %	4,587 %	5,022 %	6,625 %	1,524 %	3,976 %	0,000 %	8,745 %	2,787 %
100*10	0,000 %	0,000 %	0,000 %	0,000 %	11,889 %	13,075 %	3,480 %	5,356 %	4,370 %	35,525 %	1,118 %	1,344 %	0,000 %	8,376 %	10,589 %
100*20	0,000 %	0,000 %	0,000 %	0,000 %	13,749 %	19,604 %	3,280 %	2,370 %	8,454 %	17,037 %	1,766 %	1,897 %	0,000 %	9,826 %	7,289 %
200*10	0,000 %	0,000 %	0,000 %	0,000 %	18,814 %	54,987 %	8,596 %	11,682 %	11,678 %	18,926 %	7,302 %	9,914 %	0,000 %	23,520 %	11,955 %
200*20	0,000 %	0,000 %	0,000 %	0,000 %	20,260 %	30,594 %	9,452 %	8,472 %	13,837 %	25,804 %	6,762 %	5,893 %	0,000 %	17,120 %	13,074 %
500*20	0,000 %	0,000 %	0,000 %	0,000 %	25,862 %	142,695 %	19,746 %	38,961 %	18,071 %	63,174 %	16,799 %	34,072 %	0,000 %	56,821 %	33,029 %
Average	0,000 %	0,000 %	0,000 %	0,000 %	13,365 %	26,041 %	5,461 %	7,307 %	6,678 %	14,761 %	3,347 %	5,239 %	0,000 %	13,044 %	7,506 %

5   General Conclusion

In this paper we have proposed a new variant of PSO algorithm to the permutation flow shop scheduling problem under blocking such to minimize the total tardiness criterion. This population-based technique was hybridized with local search to much more intensify the exploration and so diversify the search. Initial population is generated based on a new revised-NEH heuristic by changing the step 1 of the original NEH algorithm. Computational results attest that BPSO algorithm is very competitive when compared with leading algorithms. Improvements occur in all Ronconi and Henriques's instances from (20×5) to (500×20) test sets.

References

1. Johnson, S.M.: Optimal two- and three-stage production schedules with setup time included. Nav. Res. Logistics Q. **1**, 61–68 (2013)
2. Ronconi, D.P., Henriques, L.R.S.: Some heuristic algorithms for total tardiness minimization in a flowshop with blocking. Omega **37**(2), 272–281 (2009)
3. Koulamas, C.: The total tardiness problem: review and extensions. Oper. Res. **42**, 1025–1041 (1994)
4. Davendra, D., Bialic-Davendra, M., Senkerik, R., Pluhacek, M.: Scheduling the flowshop with blocking problem with the chaos-induced discrete self organising migrating algorithm. In: Proceedings of the 27th European Conference on Modelling and Simulation, pp. 386–392 (2013)
5. Caraffa, V., Ianes, S., Bagchi, T.P., Sriskandarajah, C.: Minimizing makespan in a flowshop using genetic algorithms. Int. J. Prod. Econ. **2**, 101–115 (2001)
6. Deng, G., Xu, Z., Gu, X.: A discrete artificial bee colony algorithm for minimizing the total flow time in the blocking flow shop scheduling. Chin. J. Chem. Eng. **20**, 1067–1073 (2012)
7. Gilmore, P., Gomory, R.: Sequencing a one state variable machine: a solvable case of the traveling salesman problem. Oper. Res. **5**, 655–679 (1964)
8. Grabowski, J., Pempera, J.: The permutation flowshop problem with blocking. a tabu search approach. Omega **3**, 302–311 (2007)
9. Baker, K.R., Bertrand, J.W.M.: An investigation of due date assignment rules with constrained tightness. J. Oper. Manage. **3**, 109–120 (1984)
10. Graham, R., Lawler, E., Lenstra, J., Rinnooy, K.: Optimization and approximation in deterministic sequencing and scheduling: a survey. Ann. Discrete Math. **5**, 287–362 (1979)
11. Hall, N., Sriskandarajah, C.: A survey of machine scheduling problems with blocking and no-wait in process. Oper. Res. **44**, 510–525 (1996)
12. Han, Y.-Y., Liang, J., Pan, Q.-K., Li, J.-Q., Sang, H.-Y., Cao, N.: Effective hybrid discrete artificial bee colony algorithms for the total flowtime minimization in the blocking flowshop problem. Int. J. Adv. Manuf. Technol. **67**, 397–414 (2013)
13. Kennedy, J., Eberhart, R.: Particle swarm optimization. Proc. IEEE Int. Conf. Neural Netw. **4**, 1942–1948 (1995)
14. Lin, S., Ying, K.: Minimizing makespan in a blocking flowshop using a revised artificial immune system algorithm. Omega **41**, 383–389 (2013)
15. McCormick, S., Pinedo, M., Shenker, S., Wolf, B.: Sequencing in an assembly line with blocking to minimize cycle time. J. Oper. Res. **37**(6), 925–935 (1989)

16. Nawaz, M., Enscore, J., Ham, I.: A heuristic algorithm for the m-machine, n-job flow-shop sequencing problem. Omega **11**, 91–95 (1983)
17. Pan, Q., Wang, L.: Effective heuristics for the blocking flowshop scheduling problem with makespan minimization. Omega **2**, 218–229 (2012)
18. Pan, Q., Wang, L., Sang, H., Li, J., Liu, M.: A high performing memetic algorithm for the flowshop scheduling problem with blocking. IEEE Trans. Autom. Sci. Eng. **10**, 741–756 (2013)
19. Pinedo, M.: Scheduling: Theory, Algorithms, and Systems. Pretice Hall, U.A.S (2008)
20. Reddi, S., Ramamoorthy, C.: On the flow-shop sequencing problem with no wait in process. Oper. Res. Q. **3**, 323–331 (1972)
21. Rock, H.: Some new results in flow shop scheduling. Zeitschrift fur Oper. Res. **28**, 1–16 (1984)
22. Ronconi, D.: A branch-and-bound algorithm to minimize the makespan in a flow-shop problem with blocking. Ann. Oper. Res. **1**, 53–65 (2005)
23. Tasgetiren, M., Pan, Q., Suganthan, P., Chen, A.: A discrete artificial bee colony algorithm for the total flow time minimization in permutation flow shops. Inform. Sci. **16**, 3459–3475 (2011)
24. Wang, L., Pan, Q., Suganthan, P., Wang, W., Wang, Y.: A novel hybrid discrete differential evolution algorithm for blocking flowshop scheduling problems. Comput. Oper. Res. **3**, 509–520 (2010)
25. Wang, L., Pan, Q., Tasgetiren, M.: Minimizing the total flow time in a flowshop with blocking by using hybrid harmony search algorithms. Expert Syst. Appl. **12**, 7929–7936 (2010)
26. Wang, X., Tang, L.: A discrete particle swarm optimization algorithm with self-adaptive diversity control for the permutation flowshop problem with blocking. Appl. Soft Comput. **12**, 652–662 (2012)
27. Armentano, V.A., Ronconi, D.P.: Minimização do Tempo Total de Atraso No Problema de Flowshop Com Buffer Zero através de Busca Tabu. Gestao and Produçao **7**(3), 352–363 (2000)
28. Ribas, I., Companys, R., Tort-Martorell, X.: An efficient iterated local search algorithm for the total tardiness blocking flow shop problem. Int. J. Prod. Res. **51**, 5238–5252 (2013)
29. Januario, T.O., Arroyo, J.E.C., Moreira, M.C.O.: Nature Inspired Cooperative Strategies for Optimization (NICSO 2008). Springer, Heidelberg, pp. 153–164 (2009)
30. Potts, C.N., Van Wassenhove, L.N.: A decomposition algorithm for the single machine total tardiness problem. Oper. Res. Lett. **1**, 177–181 (1982)

Argumentation and Negotiation

Towards an Agent-Based Negotiation Scheme for Scheduling Electric Vehicles Charging

Andreas Seitaridis[1], Emmanouil S. Rigas[1(✉)],
Nick Bassiliades[1], and Sarvapali D. Ramchurn[2]

[1] Aristotle University of Thessaloniki, 54124 Thessaloniki, Greece
{andrseit,erigas,nbassili}@csd.auth.gr
[2] Electronics and Computer Science,
University of Southampton, Southampton SO17 1BJ, UK
sdr1@soton.ac.uk

Abstract. We consider the problem of scheduling Electric Vehicle (EV) charging within a single charging station aiming to maximize the number of charged EVs, as well as the amount of charged energy. In so doing, we propose one offline optimal solution using Mixed Integer Programming (MIP) techniques, and two online solutions which incrementally execute the MIP algorithm each time an EV arrives at the charging station. Moreover, we apply agent based negotiation techniques between the station and the EVs in order to service EVs when the MIP problem is initially unsolvable due to insufficient resources (i.e., requested energy, charging time window). We evaluate our solutions in a setting partially using real data, and we show that when applying negotiation techniques, the number of EVs charged increases on average by 7 %, energy utilization by 6.5 %, while there is only a small deficit (about 10 %) on average agent utility which is unavoidable due to the fact that the initial incremental demand-response problem is unsolvable.

1 Introduction

Electric vehicles (EVs) are an efficient alternative to internal combustion engined ones when it comes to running costs, environmental impact and quality of driving. However, these advantages come with a certain cost, as EVs suffer from short range and long charging times. In order such problems to be reduced, a large number of charging stations with state of the art facilities (i.e., fast chargers, or battery swappers) should exist. However, here there is a quandary problem, as drivers will not buy EVs if charging stations are not available, and companies, organizations, or even countries will not invest in charging facilities unless many EV-customers exist.

In this paper, we claim that multi-agent systems can be proved useful in partially solving such problems and making EVs popular. In particular, we study a setting where EVs arrive at a single charging station and need to charge. The EVs are self-interested agents that need to maximize their profit (i.e., maximize energy charged and minimize waiting time), while the charging station aims to maximize the number of serviced EVs and the utilization of the available energy.

© Springer International Publishing Switzerland 2016
M. Rovatsos et al. (Eds.): EUMAS 2015/AT 2015, LNAI 9571, pp. 157–171, 2016.
DOI: 10.1007/978-3-319-33509-4_14

To date, a number of papers trying to solve similar problems exist in the literature [9]. For example, Bayram et al. [1] assumes a large number of charging points, each of them having pre-ordered a certain amount of energy. They use a centralized mathematical programming algorithm to optimally allocate the energy to EVs, so as to service the maximum number of EVs. The authors evaluate the mechanism in a setting where both selfish (want to charge at the nearest charging point), and cooperative EVs exist, and verify the performance of their algorithms. In turn, [6] propose dynamic programming algorithms that schedule the charging of EVs according to the availability of energy while guaranteeing the intended journeys can be completed. They also show that their solutions can adapt to fluctuations in energy generation from renewable sources thus increasing EV penetration to the grid. Instead, in [4], agents state time windows within which they will be available to charge, and bid for units of electricity in a periodic multi-unit auction (one auction per time step). In order to ensure truthfulness, the authors developed a mechanism that occasionally leaves units of electricity unallocated (burned), even if there is demand for them. In addition, using more traditional agent-based negotiation techniques, Gan et al. [3], implement an iterative procedure to allow EVs to negotiate the charging rate (at different time points) with a utility company (that broadcasts a price signal to control charging). Crucially, they show that, should the charging characteristics of all EVs be known, an optimal solution is reached in a decentralized fashion. Finally, the authors in [2,5] propose methodologies for coping with the important problem of placing the charging stations in such places so that the number of EVs they service can be maximized.

The common characteristic of the majority of the work in this field is that the preferences of the EVs, once communicated to the charging station(s) are taken for granted (e.g., to [1,4,6]). In other words, the preferences of the EVs do not change. The main difference of our approach is that here, we propose an agent-based scheme where in case an EV's preferences cannot be fulfilled, the station can negotiate with it and suggest a different charging plan. In contrast to [3], charging characteristics of all EVs are not assumed to be known. Note that, negotiation techniques [7] have already been considered as an efficient method to increase the participation of various actors within the smart grid [8].

We advance the state of the art as follows:

1. We propose an offline optimal solution to schedule the charging of EVs in a single charging station aiming to maximize energy utilization and EV satisfaction (i.e., number of serviced EVs).
2. We propose an online algorithm, which incrementally uses the aforementioned optimal formulation, for EV charging scheduling.
3. We extend the aforementioned algorithm with the ability to start a negotiation procedure with the EVs (by making counter offers to them) in case a charging plan based on their initial preferences cannot be calculated. In this vein, we propose three algorithms for calculating the offers that are made to the EVs during the negotiation procedure.

4. Finally, we empirically evaluate our proposed algorithms in a setting partially using real data (renewable energy generation) and we prove the efficiency of the negotiation technique in increasing EVs satisfaction and energy utilization.

2   Problem Definition

In this paper, we study a setting where a number of EVs arrive at a single charging station over time and need to charge. We assume that each EV has his own agent which communicates to the charging station the EV's needs and constraints and tries to satisfy them in the best possible way. In a real scenario, such an agent could reside on the navigation system of the car. At the same time, the charging station aims to serve as many clients as possible in order to maximize its profit, as well as the total welfare of the agents. In so doing, it takes into consideration its available resources (i.e., charging slots, available energy (both renewable and non-renewable energy is assumed to be available to the charging station)), as well as the EVs' constraints.

In more detail, we denote the set of EV-agents $a_i \in A$, and the charging station c which has a number of charging slots $s_j \in S$. Moreover, we assume a set of discrete time points $t \in T$ to exist. At each time point, the charging station has $e_t \in E$ energy units available for EV charging (note that, energy storage is not supported). The number of charging slots, as well as the amount of energy set an upper limit to the number of EVs that can charge simultaneously. Now, for each EV we define a tuple $p_i = \left\langle a_i, t_i^{sys}, t_i^{arr}, t_i^{dep}, e_i^{max}, e_i^{min} \right\rangle$. In more detail, upon its arrival to the system at time point t_i^{sys}, each EV i informs the charging station about its arrival time at the station $t_i^{arr} \geq t_i^{sys}$ (i.e., the EV can inform the charging point about its preferences the time it arrives to it, or earlier), the preferred departure time t_i^{dep}, as well as the maximum e_i^{max} and minimum e_i^{min} energy that it prefers to charge.

Now, once an EV has informed the charging station about its preferences, the station applies a scheduling algorithm to decide on its charging schedule. In case, given the EV's and station's constraints, such a schedule is impossible to be computed, the station begins a negotiation procedure with the EV, during which a number of counter offers/suggestions are communicated to it. During this procedure, the EV can either accept or reject the offers. This procedure is presented in detail in Sect. 3.3.

3   EV Scheduling Algorithms

To solve the problem of EV charging scheduling, three approaches are considered. In more detail, the charging station's parameters (i.e., number of chargers, and available energy) are assumed to be known in advance, while the EVs' preferences can either be known in advance (offline approach - see Sect. 3.1) or can be made known dynamically (online approaches - see Sects. 3.2 and 3.3).

3.1   Offline Optimal Solution

In this section we present a centralized, static, optimal Mixed Integer Programming (MIP) formulation of the problem (developed using IBM ILOG CPLEX 12.5) which is used for benchmarking purposes, but it also acts as an important building block for the online algorithms presented in the following sections. The aim of this formulation is to find the optimal charging plan such that both the number of EVs serviced, and the amount of energy charged are maximized. Thus, the objective function to be maximized (Eq. 1) is a weighted sum of these two values. The weights show the priority that the station gives to the two values. The formulation contains two binary decision variables: (1) decision variable $a_{i,t} \in \{0, 1\}$ denoting whether an EV i is charging at time point t, and (2) $b_i \in \{0, 1\}$ denoting whether an EV is serviced or not. The objective function is maximized under a number of constraints:

Objective Function:

$$w_1 \times \sum_{a_i \in A} \sum_{t \in T} a_{i,t} + w_2 \times \sum_{a_i \in A} b_i \tag{1}$$

$$\text{where } w_1 + w_2 = 1$$

Constraints:

$$\forall a_i \in A, \ \sum_{t=t_i^{arr}}^{t_i^{dep}} a_{i,t} \times b_i \leq e_i^{max} \tag{2}$$

$$\forall a_i \in A, \ \sum_{t=t_v^{arr}}^{t_v^{dep}} a_{i,t} \times b_i \geq e_i^{min} \tag{3}$$

$$\forall t, \ \sum_{a_i \in A} a_{i,t} \leq |S| \tag{4}$$

$$\forall t, \ \sum_{a_i \in A} a_{i,t} \leq e_t \tag{5}$$

In more detail, every vehicle i must charge a number of energy units between its minimum and maximum preferred values (Eqs. 2 and 3), while the number of the vehicles that charge simultaneously must not exceed the total number of charging slots (Eq. 4). Finally, the total number of energy units charged at one time point, should not exceed the total number of the available energy units (Eq. 5). From now on, we will refer to the MIP formulation of the problem as *Optimal* which takes as input parameters all tuples $p_i, \forall a_i$.

3.2   On-Line Scheduling Algorithm Without Suggestions

To this point, the number and the preferences of the EVs were assumed to be known in advance. However, here, the EVs inform the charging station about their preferences dynamically, the time they arrive at the system (see Algorithm 1). Once the station receives a new charging request, it calls the optimal scheduling algorithm giving as input the preferences of the new EV as well as the charging plan of the EVs that have already arrived at the past, while constraints 6 and 7 are added to the MIP formulation. In more detail, the EVs $a_i \in charged \subseteq A$ that have already been scheduled to charge are constrained to receive the number of energy units (i.e., e_i^{total}) that was decided the first time (Eq. 6), within the predefined departure time (Eq. 7). What can change is the time points that the EV will actually charge. Regarding the new EV, the charging station is free to decide whether or not it will be charged, as well as the time points the charging will take place. Note that, the case where an EV can book a slot for charging and then cancel it, or leave the charging station earlier than its predefined time is not studied.

$$\forall a_i \in charged, b_i = 1 \tag{6}$$

$$\forall a_i \in charged, e_i^{total} = \sum_{t \in T} a_{l,t} \tag{7}$$

Algorithm 1. Dynamic EVs Scheduling Algorithm Using MIP

---

    for $\forall t \in T$ **do**

        for $\forall a_i \subset A : t_i^{arr} = t$ **do**

            {All EVs arriving at t are assigned to set *current*.}

            current ← *current* + p_i

        end for

        Call Algorithm 2(*current*)

    end for

    Return: $\forall a_i \in A$, $a_{i,t}$, e_i^{total} and *charged*

3.3   On-Line Approach with Suggestions

Similarly to the previous algorithm, here EVs' preferences become available dynamically, the moment the EV arrives at the system. However, in addition to what has been studied so far, here the charging station has the ability to make counter offers/suggestions to the EVs in case it is impossible to cover their needs as they are communicated to it at first. In more detail, once an EV arrives at the system and communicates its needs to the station, it applies the optimal scheduling algorithm as this has been described in Algorithm 1. In case a feasible solution does not exist and a schedule cannot be calculated, then the station

Algorithm 2. EVs Scheduling Algorithm
***
Require: *current*
    Call *Optimal(current)*
    {Each EV that has charged and is not in set *charged*}
    for $\forall a_i \in A$ **do**
        if $(b_i = 1)$ AND $(a_i \notin charged)$ **then**
            $charged \leftarrow charged + a_i$
            $e_i^{total} = \sum_{t \in T} a_{i,t}$
        end if
    end for
    Return: $(\forall a_i, t\ a_{i,t},\ e_i^{total},\ b_i)$ and *charged*
***

starts a negotiation procedure and makes a number of counter offers to the EV, which can either be accepted or rejected (see Algorithm 3 and Fig. 1). In order to capture the EV's reply, variable $r_i \in \{0,1\}$ is defined which is actually drawn from a probabilities distribution. In the next section, the algorithms that are used in order to calculate the station's suggestions to the EVs are presented.

Algorithm 3. EVs Scheduling Algorithm with Suggestions.
***
    for $\forall t \in T$ **do**
        for $\forall a_i \in A : t_i^{arr} = t$ **do**
            $current \leftarrow current + p_i$
        end for
        Call Algorithm 2(*current*)
        {For the EVs that couldn't be scheduled for charging}
        for $(\forall a_i \in current : b_i = 0)$ **do**
            $count = 4$
            while $(accepted! = 1)$ AND $(count \leq 6)$ **do**
                {We call Algorithms 4, 5, 6 consecutively (see Figure 1).}
                Call Algorithm count
                $accepted = r_i$
                $count = count + 1$
            end while
        end for
    end for
    Return: $\forall a_i \in A,\ a_{i,t},\ e_i^{total}$ and *charged*
***

3.3.1 Suggestions Calculation Algorithms

Here, we describe how the charging station calculates the offers made to the EVs during the negotiation procedure. As one can see in Fig. 1, this negotiation phase has up to three steps. In each one, the station is making an offer to the EV, which can either be accepted or rejected. This negotiation starts from the stations' most preferred solution, where the proposed amount of energy is identical to the original, thus its utilization is maximized, but the charging time

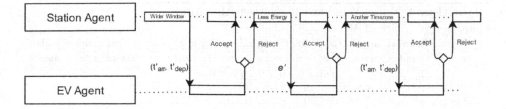

Fig. 1. EV-station negotiation procedure

window is widened, then, at the second step the time window remains the same but the amount of proposed energy is reduced (the maximum available energy should be at least equal to the minimum amount asked by the EV), and finally a totally different time window but with the initially desired amount of energy is proposed to the EV.

1. Step 1: Here the station calculates a **wider time window** (see Algorithm 4) in order to provide to the EV at least the minimum energy it has asked for. In so doing, the station aims to widen the predefined time window until the necessary energy becomes available. Firstly, the window is widen to the right (i.e., future time points) and if enough energy is still not available, it is also widen to the left, given that the EV's arrival time at the system is different (smaller) compared to the arrival time at the station. For every time point that an available energy unit is found, variable $energy \in N$ is increased by one. If such a time window is not found, or the new time window has a not $acceptable_\tau \in \{0, 1\}$ size ($acceptable_\tau$ is defined by the user), or the EV rejects the offer, the station goes to the next step.

2. Step 2: In case enough energy is not available within the time window defined by the EV, the station calculates whether a **smaller amount of energy** (see Algorithm 5) can be provided within these time limits. In so doing, the station has already decided a percentage $acceptable_e \in [0, 1]$ of the initial energy within which an offer can be made to the EV. In other words, the station searches within the time window if $e_i^{min} \times acceptable_e$ energy units are available. In case enough energy is not found, or the EV rejects the offer, the station goes to the next step.

3. Step 3: Finally, the station can calculate a **different time zone** (see Algorithm 6) for an EV to charge. In so doing, the time window within which the EV will charge is shifted across the set of time points (constrained so as the arrival time of the EV is not violated), while the tightness of the window is also taken into consideration (i.e., the first and the last time points at which an EV will charge should not be too far from each other). Note that, the main difference with Algorithm 4 is that here the time window can be completely different compared to the initial one, while in Algorithm 4 the initial window acts as a pivot, and is always part of the offer.

Algorithm 4. Wider Window Calculation Algorithm.

Require: $\forall i, p_i,$ *acceptable*

    {First widen window to the right. If desired energy not found, widen window to the left. If acceptable window is found suggest to EV. Initial window acts as a pivot}

    $t_i'^{arr} = t_i^{arr}; \; t_i'^{dep} = t_i^{dep}; \; found = 0; \; energy = 0$

    {The available energy in the initial time window is calculated.}

    for $(\forall t \in T : (t \geq t_i^{arr})$ AND $(t \leq t_i^{dep}))$ **do**

        if $(e_t > 0)$ AND $(\sum_{a_i \in A} a_{i,t} < |S|)$ {If enough energy and chargers exist} **then**

            $energy = energy + 1$

        end if

    end for

    {$t_i'^{dep}$ is increased by 1 until necessary energy found, or final time point is reached.}

    while $energy < e_i^{min}$ **do**

        $t_i'^{dep} := t_i'^{dep} + 1;$

        if $(e_{t_i'^{end}} > 0)$ AND $(\sum_{a_i \in A} a_{i,t_i'^{end}} < |S|)$ **then**

            $energy = energy + 1;$

        end if

    end while

    {$t_i'^{arr}$ is decreased by 1 until necessary energy is found, or t_i^{sys} is violated.}

    while $energy < e_i^{min}$ **do**

        $t_i'^{arr} := t_i'^{arr} - 1;$

        if $(e_{t_i'^{end}} > 0)$ AND $(\sum_{a_i \in A} a_{i,t_i'^{end}} < |S|)$ **then**

            $energy = energy + 1$

        end if

    end while

    {If energy is found and time window not too large.}

    if $(energy \geq e_i^{min})$ AND $((t_i'^{dep} - t_i'^{arr}) \div (t_i^{dep} - t_i^{arr}) > acceptable)$ **then**

        $found = 1;$

    end if

    Return: $t_i'^{arr}, t_i'^{dep}, energy, found$

Algorithm 5. Less Energy Calculation Algorithm.

Require: $\forall i, p_i,$ *acceptable*

    {Searches in given window how much energy is available. If more than acceptable percentage, then suggest to EV.}

    $energy = 0$

    for $(\forall t \in T : (t \geq t_i^{arr})$ AND $(t \leq t_i^{dep}))$ **do**

        {If enough energy and chargers exist.}

        if $(e_t > 0)$ and $(\sum_{a_i \in A} a_{i,t} < |S|)$ **then**

            $energy = energy + 1$

        end if

    end for

    $percentage = energy \div e_i^{min}$

    if $percentage \geq acceptable$ **then**

        $found = 1$

    end if

    Return: $energy, found$

Algorithm 6. Another Time Zone Calculation Algorithm.

Require: $\forall i, p_i, acceptable$
$\quad t_i^{\prime arr} = t_i^{sys}, t_i^{\prime dep} = t_i^{sys} - 1$
$\quad$ {If the longest time window based on $t_i^{\prime arr}$ is large enough for the station to provide the minimum required energy.}
$\quad energy = 0, penalty = 0$
$\quad$ **while** $(|T| - t_i^{\prime arr}) \geq (e_i^{min})$ **do**
$\quad\quad$ **while** $((energy < e_i^{min})$ and $(t_i^{\prime dep} < (|T| - 1)))$ **do**
$\quad\quad\quad t_i^{\prime dep} = t_i^{\prime dep} + 1$ {Increase new window to the left}
$\quad\quad\quad$ **if** $(e_t > 0)$ and $(\sum_{a_i \in A} a_{i,t} < |S|)$ **then** {If enough energy, chargers exist}
$\quad\quad\quad\quad energy = energy + 1$
$\quad\quad\quad$ **else**
$\quad\quad\quad\quad penalty = penalty + 1$
$\quad\quad\quad$ **end if**
$\quad\quad$ **end while**
$\quad\quad$ {If $t_i^{\prime dep}$ has reached the final time point, no window can be found}
$\quad\quad$ **if** $(t_i^{\prime dep} = |T|)$ **then**
$\quad\quad\quad$ Break
$\quad\quad$ **else**
$\quad\quad\quad$ {If a window containing the desired energy is found check if it sparse}
$\quad\quad\quad$ **if** $(penalty \div (t_i^{dep} - t_i^{start} + 1) \leq acceptable)$ **then**
$\quad\quad\quad\quad found = 1;$ break
$\quad\quad\quad$ **end if**
$\quad\quad$ **end if**
$\quad\quad$ {If a legitimate window was not found, increase start time by one and continue}
$\quad\quad$ **if** $(e_{t_i^{\prime arr}} > 0)$ and $(\sum_{a_i \in A} a_{t,t} < |S|)$ **then**
$\quad\quad\quad energy = energy - 1$
$\quad\quad$ **else**
$\quad\quad\quad penalty = penalty - 1$
$\quad\quad$ **end if**
$\quad\quad t_i^{\prime arr} = t_i^{\prime arr} + 1$
$\quad$ **end while**
$\quad$ Return $t_i^{\prime arr}, t_i^{\prime dep}, found$

4 Evaluation

We evaluate our algorithms according to execution times (see Sect. 4.1), performance (i.e., EVs charged, EVs' utility, and energy utilization) (see Sect. 4.2), and sensitivity (i.e., dependence of the performance on the number of charging slots) (see Sect. 4.3).

Throughout the evaluation, we assume the charging station to operate 24 h a day (we want to show how the system operates in a full day) and 288 time points to exist (i.e., 1 time point = 5 min - as our energy data was measured every 5 min). The day is divided into 4 zones, each one with 72 time points where the zones are equivalent to: (1) morning to noon, (2) afternoon, (3) evening to night, (4) early morning of the next day. Also, the charging station has 5 chargers (this is a number that fits our EVs data so as the scenario to be realistic).

On top of this, we assume that all EVs have the same charging rate, which is one unit of energy at each time point. Moreover, EVs arrival times are generated by Gaussian distributions, where the probability for an EV to arrive during the first and third time zones is higher compared to the rest, and energy demand is generated by a uniform distribution. Also, the weights in our objective function are 50-50, which means that the station tries to maximize the serviced EVs and its profit with the same priority. Finally, we use real data regarding energy production from renewable energy sources (photovoltaic), generated by the International Hellenic University's solar panel park (energy, measured in kilowatts per hour, generated by a single solar panel with a five-minute interval). We assume that in every five minutes (i.e., 1 time point) an EV uses 0.6 kW/h (1 energy unit) for charging. Finally, the collected data is transformed from kW/h to energy units, and it is multiplied by 5, as we also assume that the station contains five solar panels (energy that fits the EVs data).

4.1   Execution Times

Execution time and scalability is a major factor in the usability of a given scheduling algorithm. For this reason, here, keeping all parameters but the number of EVs fixed, we measure the execution time of both the online and the offline algorithms. For a setting with 30–300 EVs (see Fig. 2), we could argue that for the optimal algorithm the execution time increases near linearly, while for the online without suggestions increases super-linearly with a rather low rate of growth, while for the online with suggestions the execution time increases super-linearly with a rather high rate of growth. However, in the worst case, the average execution time does not exceed the 100 s, thus making even the online with suggestions usable for large settings. Remember, that the online algorithms call the optimal one incrementally when an EV arrives at the system, and therefore their larger execution times were expected. Also note, that the online algorithm with suggestions has an even larger execution time as it includes also the execution of the algorithms for calculating the suggestions. Finally, we should mention that the execution time of the online algorithm with suggestions depends on the number of EVs that accept an offer and the negotiation round that this happens, as the calculation of the offers is time consuming (i.e., calculation of fewer offers leads to lower execution time).

4.2   EV Satisfaction and Energy Utilization

Here, we evaluate the performance of our proposed algorithms in terms of EV satisfaction (i.e., number of serviced EVs and average utility), as well as energy utilization (see Figs. 3, 4, 5 and Table 1). In terms of EV satisfaction, the offline algorithm is better than the online one without suggestions. This was expected given the fact that in the offline approach full knowledge of EV demand is assumed to be known in advance. Now, in terms of energy utilization, the gap between the two approaches is smaller, as even though the online algorithm charges less EVs, it uses about the same amount of energy. This happens because

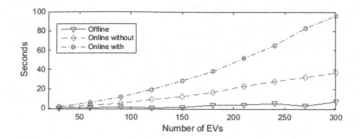

Fig. 2. Algorithms' execution time

the online algorithm decides to charge more vehicles with high needs for energy compared to the offline one. Thus, the station still has a good profit, but many agents are unsatisfied. When it comes to the online algorithm with suggestions, in settings with 30–100 EVs, is clearly ahead of the online without suggestions and close to the optimal solution, while from 100 until 150 EVs remains ahead of the online without suggestions but with a smaller gap. Here, we can point out the fact that the online algorithm shows the bigger improvement in settings with small to medium number of EVs. For larger number of EVs, the station starts becoming too congested and therefore the negotiation procedure becomes less effective. If you see this in correlation with the high execution times when the number of EVs increases, we could argue that the online with suggestions may not worth being used for large number of EVs. Regarding energy utilization, the online with suggestions has a clear advantage for small and medium number of EVs where more available charging slots exist, while later it starts leveling off.

In terms of agent utility, the offline and the online algorithm without suggestions achieve 100 % utility of the EVs that have been serviced, as their needs, and constraints are fully covered. Now, the online algorithm with suggestions achieves an average utility of about 88–90 % as despite the fact that more EVs are charged, some of their initial constraints are relaxed. This small deficit on average agent utility is unavoidable due to the fact that the initial incremental demand-response problem is unsolvable. In order to measure the utility, for every agent that will finally charge, we compute the Euclidean distance between its initial preferences and what it finally gets. Later, this value is normalized to $[0, 1]$. We notice that, at 30 to 60 EVs the utility is high, at 60 EVs it drops and then it continuously increases. This can be attributed to the fact that at 30 EVs not many suggestions have to be made as initial EV preferences can be fulfilled, thus the utility is high. At 60 to 120 EVs the utility drops, as in this window, the station is neither too empty, nor too congested, and therefore many EVs accept offers during the negotiation procedure. From 120 to 150 EVs, the station is already too congested with EVs charging within their initial preferences and therefore, less offers are being made to EVs.

Now, regarding the online algorithm with suggestions, its performance is directly related to the attitude of the agents during the negotiation procedure. In other words, the more cooperative the agents are, the more successful, the

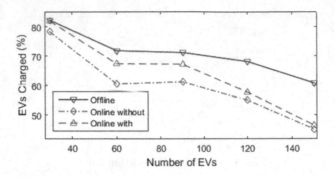

Fig. 3. EVs charged

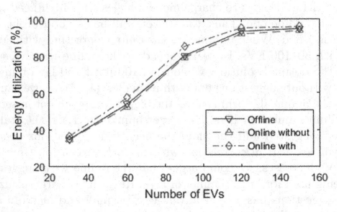

Fig. 4. Energy used

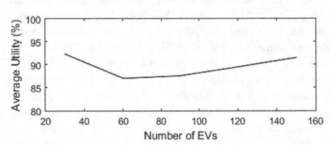

Fig. 5. Average utility

negotiation is. Therefore, we conducted a set of experiments where different levels of agent cooperation is assumed to exist. A cooperative agent is defined as an agent which has a high probability of accepting an offer (80 % to 90 %), while a non-cooperative agent is an agent with low probability of accepting offers (25 % to 30 %). As can be seen from Figs. 6, 7, 8, when the majority of the agents are cooperative higher number of them are serviced and energy is better utilized,

Table 1. Algorithms comparison - 5 chargers

		Number of Evs		
		60	90	150
EVs charged	On-Line vs Off-Line	−15.48 %	−14.63 %	−25.79 %
	Strategy vs On-Line	11.43 %	9.80 %	2.88 %
Energy utilization	On-Line vs Off-Line	−2.95 %	−1.19 %	−1.18 %
	Strategy vs On-Line	9.59 %	7.54 %	2.29 %
Agents' utility	On-Line vs Off-Line	0.0 %	0.0 %	0.0 %
	Strategy vs On-Line	−12.95 %	−12.4 %	−8.45 %

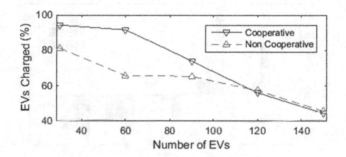

Fig. 6. Number of serviced EVs

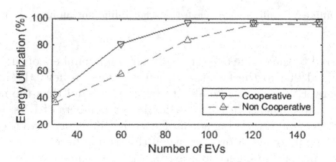

Fig. 7. Energy utilization

however the performance is worse in a setting where the majority of the agents are non-cooperative. Also, as expected, the utility of the cooperative agents is lower, as they accept more changes to their initial preferences.

4.3 Sensitivity Analysis

Here we further evaluate our algorithms, in a setting where the number of chargers varies but infinite amount of energy exists. We can observe (see Fig. 9) that for settings with up to 90 EVs the online algorithm with suggestions performs

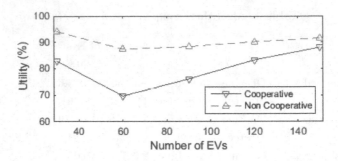

Fig. 8. Average utility

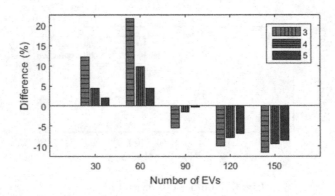

Fig. 9. Offline VS online with suggestions with different number of chargers

better compared to the offline one especially for small numbers of chargers. This can be explained due to the fact that when chargers are few, the initial preferences of many EVs may not be able to be covered, and thus the negotiation procedure is more efficient. In contrast, for larger numbers of EVs, full knowledge of future demand gives a big advantage to the offline one, and therefore it is better than the online one. Moreover, when the station becomes too congested, minimal space for feasible suggestions exists. Thus, we can conclude that overall, the offline algorithm is less sensitive to the change of the number of chargers.

5   Conclusions and Future Work

In this paper, we propose a number of algorithms for the problem of scheduling EV charging at a single station. In more detail, we present an offline optimal algorithm, and two online ones which incrementally call the optimal one when an EV arrives at the station. Moreover, we use agent-based negotiation techniques between the charging station and the EV-agents. Through an in depth empirical evaluation, we show that the performance of our solutions depends on the number of EVs, the energy they need to charge, the time of the day they need to charge, and the number of chargers that exist at the charging station. Moreover, we show that such negotiation techniques can prove to be efficient in increasing the number of serviced EVs and the utilization of the available energy, with only a small decrease in the average utility of the EVs. In this way, EVs that otherwise would not charge, now the can be charged either a smaller amount of energy or in a different time window.

Future work will look at applying learning techniques so as EVs' profiles to be modeled [10]. In this way, personalized suggestions can be made from the station to the EVs during the negotiation procedure in order to increase the probability of an EV accepting an offer. Moreover, mechanism design techniques will be applied so as to force EVs to always report their preferences truthfully (currently, truthfulness is assumed). Finally, sophisticated load balancing techniques will be investigated so as the integration of the charging station and the EVs to the smart grid to take place in the most smooth and efficient manner.

References

1. Bayram, I., Michailidis, G., Devetsikiotis, M., Granelli, F.: Electric power allocation in a network of fast charging stations. IEEE J. Sel. Areas Commun. **31**(7), 1235–1246 (2013)
2. Funke, S., Nusser, A., Storandt, S.: Placement of loading stations for electric vehicles: no detours necessary! In: Twenty-Eighth AAAI Conference on Artificial Intelligence (2014)
3. Gan, L., Topcu, U., Low, S.: Optimal decentralized protocol for electric vehicle charging. IEEE Trans. Power Syst. **28**(2), 940–951 (2013)
4. Gerding, E.H., Robu, V., Stein, S., Parkes, D.C., Rogers, A., Jennings, N.R.: Online mechanism design for electric vehicle charging. In: International Foundation for Autonomous Agents and Multiagent Systems, AAMAS 2011, Richland, SC, vol. 2, pp. 811–818 (2011)
5. Lam, A., Leung, Y.W., Chu, X.: Electric vehicle charging station placement. In: 2013 IEEE International Conference on Smart Grid Communications (SmartGrid-Comm), pp. 510–515, October 2013
6. Lopes, J.P., Soares, F.J., Almeida, P., da Silva, M.M.: Smart charging strategies for electric vehicles: enhancing grid performance and maximizing the use of variable renewable energy resources. In: EVS24 International Battery, Hybrid and Fuell Cell Electric Vehicle Symposium, Stavanger, Norveška (2009)
7. Rahwan, I., Ramchurn, S.D., Jennings, N.R., Mcburney, P., Parsons, S., Sonenberg, L.: Argumentation-based negotiation. Knowl. Eng. Rev. **18**(04), 343–375 (2003)
8. Ramchurn, S.D., Vytelingum, P., Rogers, A., Jennings, N.R.: Putting the 'smarts' into the smart grid: a grand challenge for artificial intelligence. Commun. ACM **55**(4), 86–97 (2012)
9. Rigas, E., Ramchurn, S., Bassiliades, N.: Managing electric vehicles in the smart grid using artificial intelligence: a survey. IEEE Intell. Transp. Syst. **16**(4), 1619–1635 (2015)
10. Webb, G., Pazzani, M., Billsus, D.: Machine learning for user modeling. User Model. User-Adap. Inter. **11**(1–2), 19–29 (2001)

Agreement Technologies Applied to Transmission Towers Maintenance

Pablo Chamoso[1(✉)], Fernando De la Prieta[1],
Juan Francisco De Paz Santana[1], Javier Bajo Pérez[2],
and Ignacio Belacortu Arandia[3]

[1] Department of Computer Science and Automation Control,
University of Salamanca, Plaza de la Merced s/n,
37008 Salamanca, Spain
{chamoso, fer, fcofds}@usal.es
[2] Faculty of Informatics, Department of Artificial Intelligence,
Technical University of Madrid, Campus Montegancedo,
Boadilla del Monte, 28660 Madrid, Spain
jbajo@fi.upm.es
[3] Normalización Técnica (Technical Standardization),
Iberdrola Distribución Eléctrica S.A.,
San Adrián Etorbidea, 48, 48003 Bilbao, Bizkaia, Spain
ibelakortu@iberdrola.es

Abstract. In the context of Smart Cities, one of the main indispensable elements required by a city is the electric power, for which electric towers are used to distribute it. Transmission towers have electrodes which need to be reviewed on a regular basis by controlling its resistance in order to assure avoidable malfunctions not to appear. From the point of view of Smart Cities, it is possible to address this maintenance task by trying to minimize the cost of operation through the estimation of values and the reduction of the size of the population sample. To do so, the use of an intelligent-agent virtual-organization based architecture is proposed within this working environment, which by using mathematical estimation models and agreement based negotiations it is capable of maximizing the estimations, minimizing the associated cost. The proposed model is evaluated in a simulator through a real case study, which allows validating the proposed approach.

1 Introduction

One of the main areas of Information Technology (IT) focuses on the application of emerging techniques and technologies in different everyday objects. The aim is to interconnect these objects and provide them with the ability to acquire some degree of knowledge and/or intelligence, which allows obtaining new benefits and features. This new paradigm is known as the Internet of Things (IoT). One of the main fields of research and application of IoT are cities. Using IoT techniques can make them smarter, Smart Cities. Generally, Smart Cities are associated with the pursuit of benefits for citizens. These benefits may affect the society directly by offering new or improved skills; or indirectly, by using the application of IT to achieve savings.

© Springer International Publishing Switzerland 2016
M. Rovatsos et al. (Eds.): EUMAS 2015/AT 2015, LNAI 9571, pp. 172–187, 2016.
DOI: 10.1007/978-3-319-33509-4_15

At present, the tendency is to transform a portion of the assets of the city into intelligent entities, interconnecting them by using large-scale networks to provide data practically automatically and instantaneously. However, there are different assets of the cities that are not suitable for this transformation to IoT, either because of their nature or the cost that adapting the existing infrastructure would entail. Among these assets is the focus of this article: the Transmission Towers (TT) that transport electricity. Many are located in isolated points, where even communication through mobile technologies is limited and the cost of the required equipment to monitor and control them is too high to be included or placed on every TT. However, it is important for the TT to benefit from smart city features, which will undoubtedly result in an economic benefit.

The main benefit of IoT, in this case, is the reduction of maintenance costs, which in this type of infrastructure is complex because these costs are necessary to guarantee periodic revisions in each TT, which include measuring different parameters to ensure the security basics of the installation. In addition, such revisions are imposed by law in most developed countries [4], although the specific processes to be followed are defined in each country. The threshold value of the observable parameters in each revision is also defined, which guarantees the safety of the electric line. Undoubtedly, having to revise all TT represents a high cost, mainly due to the great distance they cover, their inaccessibility and the need for specialized equipment and personnel. However, this cost can be reduced if the number of TT to check is minimized. Obviously, there must be a high level of confidence that the TT that are not reviewed are not going to fail.

Therefore, the problem consists of predicting the TT that should be physically checked. The complexity is determined by the large amount of TT. In fact, in Spain alone there are over 42,000 km of high voltage power lines [14], many of them, supported by more than 600,000 TTs. The solution is approached from a perspective of Artificial Intelligence (AI), through the use of Virtual Organizations (VO) of intelligent agents. These autonomous entities use distributed decision making processes and incomplete information, features that cater to the proposed problem. The VO create stratified sampling to analyze the state of the lines, the samples are used to analyze the condition of similar tower over ground with similar resistivity. Taking this into consideration, the system will determine the number of TT requiring review. Agents will then have to cooperate, negotiating with each other in order to determine the final sample of TT to be reviewed. To this end, we propose a framework for negotiations based on Agreement Technologies (AT), which provides the organizational system with the capability of finding and learning solutions when the problem to solve involves reaching an agreement among the agents, with autonomy and interactions between stakeholders being the main keys. The agents incorporate a neural network to predict resistance depending on several parameters. The proposed model is evaluated in a simulation environment, which, by using real data from TTs in Spain, allows validating the results of the samples and predictions obtained.

The following section presents the problem in greater detail, as well as existing related works. In Sect. 3 the proposed multi-agent system is detailed, followed by the model of argumentation in Sect. 4. The evaluation of the system is presented in Sect. 5. Finally, Sect. 6 presents the detailed conclusions.

2 Problem Description

A TT is a structure, usually made of steel, acting as a support for aerial electric conductors which are used to transport electrical energy. Each TT has (i) an associated configuration set, defining the model, the location and other static aspects; a (ii) state, which will group a set of observable magnitudes that vary over time; and (iii) revision history, which stores the evolution of data (static and dynamic).

One of the main drawbacks and the main reason that TT must be regularly reviewed is their exposure to people, who can walk around them or even touch them. A malfunction can cause that person to suffer serious or fatal electrical shock, in addition to causing other problems with energy distribution. In order to guarantee that situations like this never happen, and for additional security reasons, the regulations of each country forces a revision of the elements involved in the distribution of electricity through high voltage power lines (in the case of Spain, the legislation is published in [4]). The revision of a TT involves a high cost when having to manage the displacement of technical equipment and specialized machinery to each TT. Furthermore, the process requires previous preparation, since the towers are active high voltage lines. Definitively, by reducing the number of supports to be measured, the value and time of completion of the operation is decreased.

Most of the problems that can arise in a TT depend on their earth leakage. To achieve a good earth leakage, each TT has a number of buried or partially buried electrodes. These electrodes are conductors that remain in contact with the ground to (i) assure the grounding of static charges or atmospheric electrical discharges; (ii) limit the flow and contact voltages in the vicinity of the support; or (iii) limit the unintentional contact voltage with higher voltage systems. Flow and contact tensions are two magnitudes with complex measurements, but they are related to the grounding voltage. Therefore, the electrodes must be properly maintained to ensure they have a resistance that is preferably low, offering sufficient capacity for current conduction.

In general, a material resistivity (!) is defined as the ratio of the magnitudes of the electric field and current density, given that a perfect conductor would have a resistivity equal to zero, while a perfect insulator would have infinite resistivity. Based on this value, it is possible to determine the ability of a conductor to act as grounded electrodes, that is, its ability to derive the current can flow from the TT.

In particular, soil resistivity depends on the materials used in the floor where the support is located, relative humidity and ambient temperature. The transmission lines should not exceed a maximum value of grounding resistance of 20 Ω, although it may vary according to the soil resistivity. It must be clear that flow and contact tensions are two magnitudes with complex measurements compared to the grounding resistance, and there there is a relationship among the three of them; therefore, the parameter with the most essential measurement is is the grounding resistance.

Wenner method [18] is used to measure resistivity, which defines the soil resistivity as:

$$\rho = Resistance/K_R \tag{1}$$

This paper attempts to speed up the measurement task by estimating the most appropriate TT and designing a sample of different lines in order to validate the state of the towers. To do so, it is necessary to begin with information (locations) on a set of TTs in Spain, allowing us to know (i) the type of terrain over which it has been raised, including its (approximate) resistivity (ρ_p) and the distance to the rest of towers (d); (ii) the type of each tower, which in turn has its own coefficient of resistivity, K_R; and (iii) the line they belong to, which is important because ideally each line consists of towers of the same type; although this may not be the case with older facilities. With this information, samples are carried out to validate the state of the towers, and new configurations of towers are designed.

2.1   Transmission Tower Maintenance, Measurement and Related Works

The problem of maintenance on power lines is required mainly because of security reasons. There are different types of maintenance [2], which are presented below. First, the (i) **corrective maintenance** consists of fixing existing bugs for the system to start working correctly again. This type of maintenance can be divided, according to its required planning, into planned or unplanned maintenance. The planned corrective maintenance is a technique that ensures a reduction in costs and duration of the repair. So, classification algorithms [10] or neural networks [16, 17] have been applied to address problems of ice accumulation [9, 19] as well as the prediction of physical deterioration of machinery (generators and transformers) [13, 21]. Next, the (ii) **preventive maintenance** consists of reducing equipment failures by seeking solutions to problems before they happen. During the process, the service may be interrupted to carry out conservation work, which must be planned [1, 5]. The (iii) **predictive maintenance** arises as a complement to preventive and corrective maintenance. It consists of monitoring a number of parameters for further analysis, looking for possible anomalies. Finally, the (iv) **proactive maintenance** is a preventive maintenance strategy used to stabilize the reliability of the machinery or equipment. Within this maintenance, the work proposed in [3] stands out, where the authors manage to model the impact of proactive maintenance work theoretically. Later, thanks to the concepts of residual useful life and the models of each phase of failure, an optimal planning from the economic point of view is provided.

Although there is previous work in the maintenance of TT, there are no known jobs trying to predict the magnitudes that guarantee the safety of the line. This pioneering work makes it possible to predict and sample the number of TTs to revise through the use of intelligent agents. The system tries to predict the state of the lines by sampling the towers according to several parameters such as ground resistivity and type electrode, and other parameters such as the last revision and information taken from other towers. A VO is designed to include a specific module of ATs, whose power of argumentation is based on the use of a CBR (Case Based Reasoning), thus making it capable of learning as it is used. The VO designs the stratum and the final towers are selected through a negotiation process according to same parameters.

3 Multiagent System Description

Once the problem to be addressed has been detailed, namely, the reduction of operational costs in the maintenance of TTs, the solution is posed by an innovative approach where the set of TT to review is developed by using statistical sampling. Statistical samplings are used to estimate which resistance values are closest to a value with a maximum error and with known confidence levels, which makes it possible to avoid performing a complete analysis of a line with TT having similar features.

The problem can be addressed by a VO, which makes use of information gathered during the inspections and reviews of electrical lines. Using this information, it is possible to (i) predict the status of each TT and to (ii) determine what TT should be measured when companies have to make revisions in an area or line.

To create the model of interaction it is first necessary to analyze the motivation for potential users to use the system. Externally, there are two interest groups identified through an analysis of requirements. First, the user is the client of the application, which is used to manage the tasks related to the power lines and their maintenance. And, secondly, the provider is dedicated to updating the system information, adding new data as inspections or reviews are conducted. The VO can be framed in a dynamic but simple environment, since although new elements appear in the system, the output will always have the same format and meaning.

From this initial analysis of roles and external environment, the VO designed as part of this work can be seen in Fig. 1 and consists of the following roles:

- **User.** Represents the potential user of the system, which will use the prediction tool for optimal maintenance of power lines. Has access to the entire information repository. Finally, it is also responsible for starting a process of prediction for a set of high voltage power lines.
- **Provider.** Represents external entities that perform actual measurements in the TT; the system provides reliable information.
- **Tower.** Represents each TT and is in charge of storing each individual state. Therefore, contains information on the configuration, status, position, revision histories, etc. In addition to the agents representing the real TTs, the fictitious tower agents represent nonexistent TTs whose values have been estimated by using the final software tool.
- **Predictor.** This agent represents the predictability of the state of a TT in the system. It must have access to the repository revision histories of the TTs, as well as its information, to incorporate extra information on the estimation. The agent incorporates neural networks to predict the resistance and is used during the sample to predict the resistance of the tower.
- **Neighborhood.** Responsible for neighbor discovery of the tower agents. Able to access its information and exchange it with those agents who can know about it. The agent provides information about which TTs have the closest value to a specified distance or resistivity value.

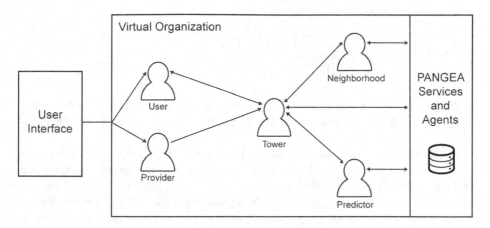

Fig. 1. MAS schema

- **Sample.** Retrieves the information of the selected towers and designs a sample over them. The agent retrieves the towers of the selected lines and designs a stratified sampling in order to reduce the number of towers reviews to carry out and perform a statistical analysis over the whole line.

  In the next section the interactions between these agents are described through the model of argumentation, detailing the way they autonomously agree on the necessary revisions.

4   Argumentation Model

The proposed negotiation model is presented throughout this section. In the first subsection a required previous step is explained; in the next subsection a general overview of it is also presented; then the various designed argumentation mechanisms are presented, and finally the negotiator agent architecture is presented.

4.1   Initial Step

One of the objectives of this work is to develop a stratified sampling to carry out a statistical analysis of the lines. The samples are stratified according to the K_R and the ground resistivity in order to analyze similar towers for each stratum. Ground resistivity should not change considerably, because it depends to a greater degree on the composition of the terrain. The size of the sample is calculated for each stratum, and is defined to calculate the average resistance with a level of confidence and error. The population is divided into three groups according to the kind of electrodes and the K_R associated. Additionally, the system calculates the deciles for each group of three. The size of the sample is then calculated for every decile. The Eq. (2) define the size of the sample, the error value is defined according to Eq. (3).

$$n = \frac{z^2 \sigma_i^2 N_i}{e_i^2 (N_i - 1) + z^2 \sigma_i^2} \tag{2}$$

$$e = Max\{(\rho_{i+1} + \rho_i)/2 \cdot k, (\rho_{i+1} - \rho_i) \cdot k\} \tag{3}$$

Where $z = 1.96$, σ is the variance, N is the population size, k is a constant defined by 0.15, ρ_i is the lower value of the resistibility in the decile i, ρ_{i+1} the upper value of the resistivity in the decile i.

For each decile we have to select the n_i elements with which the negotiation of this process is carried out. One of the desirable properties of a negotiation mechanism is flexibility, which is based on the ability of operators to refine their decision making processes and calculation of preferences during the negotiation. Since a rational agent has the ability to change its preferences if its information about the environment is updated, it seems logical to design negotiation models based on the exchange of information, which allows influencing mental attitudes and beliefs of the other agents. Therefore, an argument can be understood as a piece of meta-information that aims to make a more attractive or acceptable proposal [8]. Thus, compared to traditional cooperative models, argument-based negotiations are intended to cover this limitation.

4.2   Negotiation Description

The negotiations begin the moment the user agent requires the system to measure the sample of the TTs within a region. At that time, each TT within the territory is associated with a tower agent which checks its current Trust Percentage (TP). If TP equals 100, it means that the state of its parameters is reliable and does not require review, and therefore the agent does not participate in the negotiation. Otherwise, it does will participate by exchanging the arguments with its peers until a valid proposal is found.

During the negotiation process, all agents are connected and collaborate in pursuit of a common goal, which is to achieve the best solution based on their experiences. Thus, agents may have opposite interests:

- **Safe:** agents that promote this value will select those solutions that increase their TP.
- **Economic:** agents that promote this value will select those solutions involving the lowest revisions.
- **Neutral:** agents seeking to maximize their TP and reduce costs as much as possible, with a more relaxed posture than the others.

Each tower has a type of individual proposal (safe or economic) for the TT they represent.

Initially, to argue the individual proposal, it is necessary to obtain from the Predictor Agent the TP in the worst case of not being revised: Worst TP (WTP) (should be revised means its TP would be 100). Once this value is known, the Tower Agent determines its role in the negotiation, evaluating its history and checking two situations: (i) if the tower previously had a TP lower than the WTP (Previous TP, PTP); and (ii) consulting the Neighborhood Agent TP of its neighbors (NTP).

If there has not been a situation where $TP < WTP$, the position that the Tower Agent will adopt will be the safe one. On the other hand, if it is true that $WTP > \frac{\sum_{i=1}^{n} NTP_i}{n}$, where n is the number of neighbors, it will adopt an economic position, prioritizing the revision of its neighbors. Otherwise, its position will be neutral.

Thus, different situations may occur during the negotiation:

(a) Agents involved accept the proposal because they coincide, so the TT represented is added to the sample to be reviewed.
(b) Agents involved do not accept because more than one wishes the TT they represent to be revised.
(c) Agents involved do not accept because none wants the TT represented to be revised.
(d) The agents involved have a neutral perspective.

In situation a, because there is no agreement, the TT represented by the Tower Agent is added to the sample to review. In case b, c and d, the agents with the safe solution must negotiate to determine which TT are finally reviewed; an exchange of arguments supporting each position will use a CBR model, as detailed in subsequent sections.

4.3 Negotiation Mechanism

As previously noted, when defining a model of negotiation based on agreements in which arguments are used, it is first necessary to determine a number of mechanisms that support the negotiation process itself. The most important mechanisms are communication language and domain language.

To begin, the FIPA ACL (Foundation for Intelligent Physical Agents' Agent Communication Language) [6] is selected as the language of communication primarily because of its semantic capacity, as it includes locutions to express acceptance, rejection, proposal applications, requests, inquiries, statements, declarations, etc. Communication was made through the use of PANGEA [15, 20], which allows for a cross-platform distributed development and disengages the specific functionality of the application of basic functions, such as access to data or norms of communication between agents. For this negotiation, 4 types of locution on FIPA ACL are to be used: (i) inform: desire_to_revise (L3), desire_not_to_revise (L4), prefer_to_revise (L5), prefer_not_to_revise (L6), withdraw_dialogue (L11); (ii) propose: open_dialogue (L1); agree_to_revise (L9); (iii) accept-proposal: enter_dialogue (L2), agree_not_to_revise (L10); (iv) refuse: refuse_to_revise (L7), refuse_not_to_revise (L8).

Once the language of communication is defined, it is necessary to define a domain language, allowing the passage of meta-information separately or together with other locutions. To this end, we must define an ontology compatible with IFAP in order to carry out the decision-making process that will determine which TT are reviewed. Its class structure is defined in the Table 1.

Table 1. Negotiation ontology

Concept
AgentAction
■ Open_dialogue: area (String)
■ Agree_to_revise: proposal (Tower instance)
■ Revise: proposal (Tower instance)
■ Not_revise: proposal (Tower instance)
AgentID: agent identifier (String)
Tower: attributes (String)
Revision Requirement: constraints (String)
Revision Requirement Valuation: constraints (String): valuation (String)
Predicate
Desire_to_revise: tower (Tower instance): revision requirement (Revision Requirement instance)
Desire_not_to_revise: tower (Tower instance): revision requirement (Revision Requirement instance)
Prefer_to_revise: tower (Tower instance): revision requirement validation (Revision Requirement Validation instance)
Prefer_not_to_revise: tower (Tower instance): revision requirement validation (Revision Requirement Validation instance)
Withdraw_dialogue: area (String)

The structure is composed of two abstract classes (Concept and Predicate). The other classes are defined in the way shown in the diagram. For a better understanding, the type attributes *Attributes*, *Constraint* and *Valuation*, must be defined. First, (i) *attributes* reflects parameters that are associated with the TTs and which the Tower Agent already knows. They are needed when estimating the TP of the neighbors in the CBR. In particular, they are the model of the TT (predefined), the type of terrain on which the tower stands, the UTM (*Universal Transverse Mercator*) coordinates where the tower is located, and the number of neighbors (provided by the Neighborhood Agent). The value reflected by (ii) *constraints*, refers to its current TP and the TP it would adopt if each of its neighbors were revised. If the safe role was initially taken, it means that its WTP is the smallest one of the values sent and there are no lower values in its history. In the case of playing an economic role, it means that its WTP is larger than the smallest one of the values. Finally, (iii) *valuation* provides the level of interest of an agent in the review of each of the possibilities (it and its neighbors). In the case of adopting a safe role, the value that is associated to its current TP would take the maximum value (1), while the neighbor with the worst TP after the review would take the minimum (0). If taking an economic role, it will not be to be revised, so it will choose to take the minimum value (0) and the neighbor with the highest CP value will take the maximum value (1).

4.4   Negotiator Agent Model

Having presented a description of the model of negotiation and support mechanisms, this section will now present the structure of the negotiation agents. Figure 2 represents the structure of the Tower agent, an Argumentation-based Negotiator (ABN) which is a fundamental trait. As shown, the agents have the possibility of explicitly exchanging meta-information.

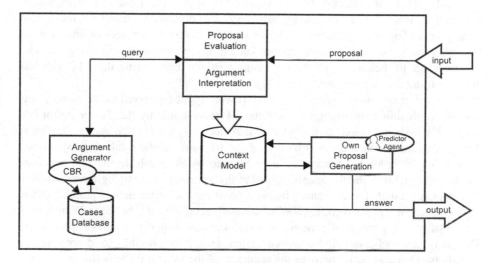

Fig. 2. ABN structure

The most important elements of the proposed ABN structure, starting with the context model, will now be presented, followed by a description of how the system is able to make predictions, and finally the argumentation model, which is where the CBR system resides.

4.4.1   Context Model

When establishing the negotiation, the TP value is important, but the arguments must also consist of other parameters such as the type of support, the type of terrain, the position of the tower and the number of neighbors. Thus, the (i) *type of support* ensures that K_r values vary in the threshold range, guaranteeing that the resistances of the electrodes are similar. Resistance grounding (ρ_p) also depends on the soil resistivity, so the terrain is another parameter whose influence is similar to that of K_r; however, it is a variable parameter that depends on environmental conditions, so it is less influential than the type of support. The (ii) *position of the tower* is important because it indicates the distance to each tower. In nearby distances of less than 5 km, and given the same type of terrain, the resistance value of the electrodes should be similar. Each Tower Agent contains information about the position of the support represented by UTM coordinates. Then, the (iii) *number of neighbors* parameter influences the negotiations, because the greater the influence over its neighbors, the higher the priority of measuring the tower.

4.4.2 Prediction

The system has two different functionalities. On the one hand the system helps to determine the model of the tower to install in a position according to the K_r and the ground resistivity, where the ground resistivity has to be calculated based on the nearest towers. On the other hand, the system has to predict the resistance for the selected towers during the sampling.

To identify the ground resistivity, a series of steps are followed. First we need to find and identify the nearest Tower Agents, for which the Delaunay triangulation method [12] is used. According to the algorithm, it is possible to generate a mesh from these points (Tower Agents) where all elements involved are vertices of one or more Delaunay triangles. Once the triangles are known, it is necessary to check the triangles to which the TT belongs, with the remaining vertices representing the TTs with less distance to the known support.

If the information corresponds to a real Tower Agent registered in the system, it is enough to obtaining the triangles where the TT represented by the Tower Agent is a vertex. If it does not belong to the system, there are two possible options: (i) the Tower Agent is within the area covered by any of the triangles of the mesh (Fig. 3); (ii) the Support Agent is located outside the area covered by the mesh. In the first situation, the nearest neighbors are the agents located in the vertexes of the triangle within which the tower is located. To determine whether a point lies on a triangle it is possible to use vector calculation or barycentric coordinate based techniques. In the second situation, it is necessary to regenerate the mesh to include the new support as part of the system. This way, the necessary links are generated and it is possible to determine the neighbors. This approach improves the accuracy of the system if the fictitious supports are consolidated as real ones.

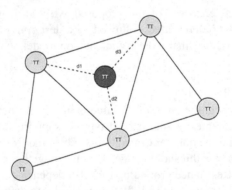

Fig. 3. TT fictitious positioning (black)

From the calculation of the mesh, the prediction is calculated as follows. First, the estimated ground resistivity $\bar{\rho}$ is calculated for a TT:

$$\bar{\rho} = \sum_1^n \rho(TT_i) * \frac{D_{max}/d_i}{\sum_1^n D_{max}/d_i} \qquad (4)$$

With an estimated error of σ, where:

$$\sigma = \sqrt{\frac{1}{n}\sum_{1}^{n}(\rho_i - \bar{\rho})^2 \frac{D_{max}/d_i}{\sum_1^n D_{max}/d_i}} \tag{5}$$

In addition to predicting the resistivity, the system has to predict the resistance for new towers and for the selected towers during the sampling. To predict the resistance, a CBR model is implemented by the agents. The case is defined with (6)

$$C = \{R, \rho, K_r, h, t\} \tag{6}$$

where h is the ground humidity and t is the temperature.

The cases are divided into three groups according to the K_r and a multilayer perceptron (MLP) is trained for each subset. During the retrieve phase the agent selects the MLP based on the K_r which is used in the reuse phase to predict the resistance. The new measure is introduced in the system in the revise and retain phases. The retraining of the neural network is carried out when the number of new measures reaches a value.

The MLP networks are defined according to this structure: four input (ρ, K_r, h, t), 9 neurons in the hidden layer, 1 output with the resistance. The activation functions are sigmoid.

4.4.3   Argumentation Model

Once each of the supports has a position within the negotiations, it is necessary share them with their peers. During this process, each individual agent shares its information with its peers. If several agents have a safe position, they must negotiate with each other in order to determine the agent whose TT will finally be reviewed.

The arguments developed in the argumentation are built through a CBR. Thus, firstly the case C is established based on information provided by the opponent where, in addition to the information of each of the supports benefited from the opponent's position T_i, its current TP_i and future TP are stored (in case of revising the opponent). In other words, TP_i'.

$$C = \left\{ T_i = \{K_r, d, n\} \quad TP_i \quad TP_i' \right\} \tag{7}$$

From this description of the problem, the cases that are similar in terms of K_r and position d are recovered from the cases base. Along with these cases the real TP', previously observed during a real revision, will be recovered, with two possible situations:

- If $TP_i \leq TP_i'$, then experience shows that the opponent is right and therefore the contrary position has to be accepted.
- If $TP_i > TP_i'$, then it is argued according to the recovered case or cases, where a real revision showed the error in predictions. In this case the opponent must provide new information or accept the position.

Once the negotiation is finished, those TT with the safe position are added to the revision list. Once the case has been reviewed and its parameters measured, the cases base is updated with the actual values, making it easier to deliver better results in the future.

5 Results

A tool was developed to help check the validity of the proposed system. With it, the user can ask the system for information on the TTs to be reviewed. It boasts a database of approximately 80,000 TTs with actual measurements distributed throughout Spain.

In the tool, the first step that the user must take is to define the lines or TTs that require revision, as seen in Fig. 4a. Subsequently, a detailed map of existing TTs is presented and can run the system.

Fig. 4. Final application. (a) Line & TT filtering; (b) Fictitious TT definition; (c) TT to be reviewed

It offers added functionality such as the ability to define new measurements which are recorded in the system through the provider agent, thus becoming part of the knowledge of the agents and specially of the CBR. It also allows the definition of fictitious TTs, which are represented in the system with their respective agent and the estimated value according to the methodology explained. An example can be seen in Fig. 4b, where the red marker is the fictitious TT and the closest neighbors (three in this case) are represented with a blue marker.

The output provided to the user consists of the list of TTs that the system has resolved to propose for reviewing. The system provides different visualizations which allow consulting the TTs separately or together over the field, as shown in Fig. 4c, where a simple listing view is shown.

The accuracy of the system when predicting the resistivity of fictitious TT is mainly affected by the distance between the TTs and the truthfulness of the previously gathered data. Some of the provided existing data has been proved to be wrong because of different errors on the measurement process, so these tests have been carried out, taking into consideration the correct data gathered with this purpose. With these data, high accuracy levels were achieved as shown in Table 2.

Table 2. Accuracy percentage on the estimation according to the mean distance.

Mean distance (km)	Accuracy of the estimation (%)
~1	98.85 %
~5	97.74 %
~50	94.41 %
~300	90.15 %

These results show that the accuracy of the estimation achieved by the software tool is more efficient the lower the distance of the TT considered. This is logical, as the resistivity is a parameter directly related to the type of the terrain, so considering widely spaced TT could have a negative influence on the result even if they have a lower relevance in the algorithm. As for reducing the number of TT that should be reviewed by the technicians, the system offers a significant reduction percentage as can be seen in Table 3.

Table 3. Percentage on the estimation according to the distance with fictitious TTs.

TTs	Mean distance (km)	Proposed TTs	Reduction (%)
100	~50	27	73
200	~50	35	82.5
500	~50	64	87.2
800	~50	83	89.625
800	~300	154	80.75

The most significant reduction is achieved as a greater number of TT is preselected for review. However, a lower level reduction is achieved when TT are far apart, even when the number of TT is high. Obviously, the farther TT are located from other TT, the more different their values are. For this work, the reduction only makes sense when working on a specific area or power line, so this problem is never going to be faced.

6 Conclusions

This paper proposes a model of artificial intelligence that allows predicting and sampling the number of TT to review. With this prediction system, it is possible to reduce the maintenance cost of the power transport infrastructure. By using VO and AT it is possible to propose a system capable of reducing the number of measurements in TT, although there are factors that cannot be controlled, such as undetectable environmental changes that alter the soil resistivity.

In addition, the system presented is able to decide autonomously which TT must be reviewed. The reduction amount of the initial sample depends directly on parameters such as the distance between them, the similarity of the resistance, soil resistivity and K_r values.

In addition, sampling is useful only when correct data is available. If predicted values or previous values are significantly different to those obtained when measured, more TT are likely to be wrong, so all the initial sample should be reviewed in order to solve more errors.

Acknowledgements. TABÓN Project is a research project sponsored by the companies Iberdrola Distribución de Energía S.A., Iberdrola S.A. and ATISAE, and funded by the EEA Grants and Norway Grants (IDI-20140885).

References

1. Badri, A., Niazi, A.N., Hoseini, S.M.: Long term preventive generation maintenance scheduling with network constraints. Energy Procedia **14**, 1889–1895 (2012)
2. de Faria, H., Costa, J.G.S., Olivas, J.L.M.: A review of monitoring methods for predictive maintenance of electric power transformers based on dissolved gas analysis. Renew. Sustain. Energy Rev. **46**, 201–209 (2015)
3. Do, P., Voisin, A., Levrat, E., Iung, B.: A proactive condition-based maintenance strategy with both perfect and imperfect maintenance actions. Reliab. Eng. Syst. Safe. **133**, 22–32 (2015)
4. España. Real Decreto-ley 1955/2000, de 1 de diciembre, por el que se regulan las actividades de transporte, distribución, comercialización, suministro y procedimientos de autorización de instalaciones de energía eléctrica. Boletín Oficial del Estado, 27 de diciembre de 2000, núm. 310. http://www.boe.es/buscar/pdf/2000/BOE-A-2000-24019-consolidado.pdf. Accessed 10 Sept. 2015
5. Feng, Y., Wu, W., Zhang, B., Gao, J.: Transmission line maintenance scheduling considering both randomness and fuzziness. J. Uncertain Syst. **5**(4), 243–256 (2011)
6. FIPA: Communicative Act Library Specification (2002). http://www.fipa.org. Accessed 10 Sept. 2015
7. Heras, S.: Case-based argumentation framework for agent societies. Ph.D. thesis, Universitat Politècnica de València (2011). http://hdl.handle.net/10251/12497
8. Jennings, N.R., Faratin, P., Lomuscio, A.R., Parsons, S., Wooldridge, M.J., Sierra, C.: Automated negotiation: prospects, methods and challenges. Group Decis. Negot. **10**(2), 199–215 (2001)
9. Ji, K., Rui, X., Li, L., Leblond, A., McClure, G.: A novel ice-shedding model for overhead power line conductors with the consideration of adhesive/cohesive forces. Comput. Struct. **157**, 153–164 (2015)
10. Krishnanand, K.R., Dash, P.K., Naeem, M.H.: Detection, classification, and location of faults in power transmission lines. Int. J. Electr. Power Energy Syst. **67**, 76–86 (2015)
11. Lee, D.T., Schachter, B.J.: Two algorithms for constructing a Delaunay triangulation. Int. J. Comput. Inform. Sci. **9**(3), 219–242 (1980)
12. Mayfield, J., Labrou, Y., Finin, T.: Evaluation of KQML as an agent communication language. In: Tambe, M., Müller, J., Wooldridge, M.J. (eds.) IJCAI-WS 1995 and ATAL 1995. LNCS, vol. 1037, pp. 347–360. Springer, Heidelberg (1996)
13. Murugan, R., Ramasamy, R.: Failure analysis of power transformer for effective maintenance planning in electric utilities. Eng. Fail. Anal. **55**, 182–192 (2015)
14. Ree.es: Gestor de la red y transportista | Red Eléctrica de España (2015). http://www.ree.es/es/actividades/gestor-de-la-red-y-transportista. Accessed 10 Sep. 2015

15. Sánchez, A., Villarrubia, G., Zato, C., Rodríguez, S., Chamoso, P.: A gateway protocol based on FIPA-ACL for the new agent platform PANGEA. In: Bajo Pérez, J., et al. (eds.) Trends in Practical Applications of Agents and Multiagent Systems. AISC, vol. 221, pp. 41–51. Springer, Heidelberg (2013)
16. Taher, S.A., Sadeghkhani, I.: Estimation of magnitude and time duration of temporary overvoltages using ANN in transmission lines during power system restoration. Simul. Model. Pract. Theory **18**(6), 787–805 (2010)
17. Trappey, A.J., Trappey, C.V., Ma, L., Chang, J.C.: Intelligent engineering asset management system for power transformer maintenance decision supports under various operating conditions. Comput. Ind. Eng. **84**, 3–11 (2015)
18. Wenner, F.: A method for measuring earth resistivity. J. Franklin Inst. **180**(3), 373–375 (1915)
19. Zarnani, A., Musilek, P., Shi, X., Ke, X., He, H., Greiner, R.: Learning to predict ice accretion on electric power lines. Eng. Appl. Artif. Intell. **25**(3), 609–617 (2012)
20. Zato, C., Villarrubia, G., Sánchez, A., Barri, I., Rubión, E., Fernández, A., Rebate, C., Cabo, J.A., Álamos, T., Sanz, J., Seco, J., Bajo, J., Corchado, J.M.: PANGEA – Platform for Automatic coNstruction of orGanizations of intElligent Agents. In: Omatu, S., Paz Santana, J.F., González, S.R., Molina, J.M., Bernardos, A.M., Rodríguez, J.M. (eds.) Distributed Computing and Artificial Intelligence. AISC, vol. 151, pp. 229–240. Springer, Heidelberg (2012)
21. Zhou, D., Zhang, H., Weng, S.: A novel prognostic model of performance degradation trend for power machinery maintenance. Energy **78**, 740–746 (2014)

TugaTAC Broker: A Fuzzy Logic Adaptive Reasoning Agent for Energy Trading

Thiago R.P.M. Rúbio[✉], Jonas Queiroz, Henrique Lopes Cardoso,
Ana Paula Rocha, and Eugénio Oliveira

LIACC/DEI, Faculdade de Engenharia, Universidade do Porto,
Rua Dr. Roberto Frias, 4200-465 Porto, Portugal
{reis.thiago,jonas.queiroz,hlc,arocha,eco}@fe.up.pt

Abstract. Smart Grid technologies are changing the way energy is generated, distributed and consumed. With the increasing spread of renewable power sources, new market strategies are needed to guarantee a
more sustainable participation and less dependency of bulk generation.
In PowerTAC (Power Trading Agent Competition), different software
agents compete in a simulated energy market, impersonating broker companies to create and manage attractive tariffs for customers while aiming to profit. In this paper, we present TugaTAC Broker, a PowerTAC
agent that uses a fuzzy logic mechanism to compose tariffs based on
its customers portfolio. Fuzzy sets allow adaptive configurations for brokers in different scenarios. To validate and compare the performance of
TugaTAC, we have run a local version of the PowerTAC competition. The
experiments comprise TugaTAC competing against other simple agents
and a more realistic configuration, with instances of the winners of previous editions of the competition. Preliminary results show a promising
dynamic: our approach was able to manage imbalances and win the competition in the simple case, but need refinements to compete with more
sophisticated market.

Keywords: PowerTAC · Energy trading agents · Smart electricity
market · Smart grids · Fuzzy logic · Power tariffs

1 Introduction

The management of energy consumption and production is not only a customer
concern, but however, a new trend characterised by the wide presence of distributed renewable power sources in low voltage grids. This factor is imposing new
challenges for main energy generation and distribution companies. In this new
scenario companies are not able anymore to predict energy demand, given limited visibility (small and distributed generator units are unknown), production
volatility (weather uncertainty affects renewable energy generation) and consumption flexibility (caused by smart grid and home automation technologies
that can control and shift loads to improve customer efficiency).

© Springer International Publishing Switzerland 2016
M. Rovatsos et al. (Eds.): EUMAS 2015/AT 2015, LNAI 9571, pp. 188–202, 2016.
DOI: 10.1007/978-3-319-33509-4_16

Electricity markets at retail level can help to address grid energy generation and load balance challenges, providing economical incentives for customers
to control and shift loads. Moreover, the available information also enables the
consumption and production forecasts [1]. As a result of liberalisation programs,
the new dynamics of electricity markets allow more complex market approaches,
competition and indirect supply-demand regulation through energy tariffs [2].
Figure 1 shows the different layers of a smart grid, highlighting tariff as the element which enables brokers to act on the customers layer and provide customer's
access to energy plans.

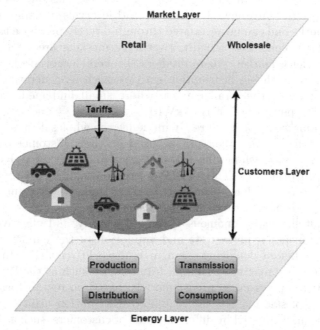

Fig. 1. Tariffs as the link element between Market and Customers

The energy *brokers* represent companies, intermediary trading entities
responsible for providing tariffs to customers. Aiming to achieve higher market shares and profit, brokers compete for offering attractive tariffs based on the
negotiated energy and prices. Electricity market simulation frameworks comprise important tools to test and validate different approaches and algorithms
for brokers in a simulated and controlled environment. In this sense, this work
presents an approach based on fuzzy logic to define competitive strategies for
energy brokers in the market. The proposed approach was defined and tested on
the PowerTAC simulation framework.

The paper is organised as follows. Section 2 gives an overview of the challenges
on the Electricity Markets area and related work regarding the PowerTAC competition. Section 3 presents our approach to create a competitive broker agent
named TugaTAC and Sect. 4 describes the preliminary results, obtained from
running competition experiments, comparing our model with other approaches.

We conclude Sect. 5 pointing the advantages of using fuzzy logic in the tariff creation process and looking for improvements in future work.

2   Electricity Markets and Power Trading Agent Competition

Electricity markets comprise commercial environments where energy is traded by several entities, such as generator companies, retailers, intermediary utilities, households, small and medium enterprises, electric vehicles owners and others. Energy is negotiated for different time slots and intervals, ranging from several minutes to months and can be negotiated through directly purchase transactions, auctions, or tariff contracts. Usually, electricity markets are separated in the wholesale electricity market, where retailers (brokers) negotiate large amounts of energy (MWh) with big distribution entities, such as generation companies or power plants, and the retail market, where small and medium customers negotiate small quantities of energy (kWh).

The retail market dynamics directly influence the wholesale market and vice-versa, since retailers define their prices based on their customer portfolio and wholesale market price, while wholesale market define their prices based on supply and demand principles. These features create dynamic environments with high financial risks that have been leveraged by the advent of smart grid and the use of all kinds of smart appliances and metering.

Creating intelligent autonomous systems to safely and effectively operate in such environments requires tests and validation of the employed strategies and algorithms, before deploying them in real world scenarios. In this sense, there exist electricity market simulation frameworks, such as the PowerTAC [3]. The PowerTAC employs many robust models, based on real historical data, to simulate the wholesale market, the regulated distribution utility, and the customer population, composed by different kinds of customers, such as households, electric vehicles, and a variety of commercial and industrial entities. Some of them can also have energy production capabilities through solar panels or wind turbines, for example. The regulated distribution utility uses a market-based mechanism for balancing the energy supply and demand.

2.1   PowerTAC Broker Agents

PowerTAC also comprises an electricity market competition[1], where different teams are challenged to develop fully autonomous broker agents to operate between wholesale and retail markets. In order to simulate a more realistic environment, the simulation relies in different constraints, such as fees and periodic payments [4]. The broker agents act as self-interested companies, aiming to make high profits from energy negotiations on both supply and demand sides. In the real world, brokers would represent energy retailers, commercial or municipal utilities or even energy cooperatives [5].

---

[1] http://powertac.org/.

As retailers, brokers need to define profitable tariff contracts to achieve bigger market share. Thus, brokers indirectly compete in the energy market by offering specific tariffs contracts for each kind of customers (production, consumption, storage) and specific type of energy source (solar, wind, thermal, etc.). Moreover, brokers should try to reach a balanced portfolio, i.e. trying to keep the amount of energy produced by customers close to the demanded energy, in order to reduce the dependency from wholesale-coming energy.

Agents can use different tariff features in order to draw the customers' attention, including fixed or dynamic price for kWh along the day, incentives for energy saving, bonus for sign-up, early withdrawal penalties, and monthly distribution fees. In fact, brokers can analyse information from different sources, such as customers, wholesale market and even weather. Such information enables predicting subscribers' production and consumption, which can lead to the necessary actions to keep reduced imbalances, through tariffs for complementary types of customers.

In simulation environments it is easy to analyse values and compose binary solutions as "if variable is greater than some value then do that". This approach limits brokers coverage, creating crisp sets of possible actions. In real decision making scenarios, human brokers compose their solutions based on both numbers and conceptual analysis. Humans often interpret concepts, such as "high", "low", or "interested", enabling a richer set of combination values for actions [6]. In energy markets and also in the PowerTAC competition, many of these conceptual values could be combined to design a tariff generator mechanism.

2.2 Tariff Selection Problem

Since we are dealing with tariff composition, an important problem is how to design competitive and interesting tariffs that provide the conditions required by customers and yet, be profitable to brokers [3]. Customers want to select the best tariff based on self interest. For example, some customers prefer tariffs with time-of-use price while others could prefer fixed prices, and so on. Customers actively participate in the market by choosing new tariffs through periodic evaluation of publicly offered tariffs. In PowerTAC, customers are utility-based, which means that they choose the next action based on the calculated gain on doing so. Nevertheless, the utility function used in customer models include an aversion of change and complexity that can retard the changing for better tariff offers [7]. Accordingly to the PowerTAC specification [8], customers in the competition evaluate new offers with a higher frequency at the beginning of the simulation. They use a inertia model for the probability of not evaluating tariffs, calculated as I_a that depend on the number of tariff publication cycles (n) and a factor $I \in [0,1]$ as seen in Eq. 1.

$$I_a = (1 - 2^{-n})I \tag{1}$$

The key part of customer evaluation is the calculation of the expected gain over maintaining the current contract. Our intention is to find a good approach that can attract customers' attention and also have high utility. If no broker achieve this goal, customers will use default tariffs provided by the *default_broker*, an agent that assure at least one option for customers.

In PowerTAC, the utility of a given tariff T_i is computed as a function of per-kWh payments pv_i, periodic payments pp_i, a one-time sign-up payment $psignup_i$, a potential one-time withdrawal payment $pwithdraw_i$ in case the customer withdraws its subscription before the tariff's contract minimum duration, and an inconvenience factor x_i to account for inconvenience of switching subscriptions, and of dealing with time-of-use or variable prices or capacity controls. The Eq. 2 describes this utility.

$$u_i = f(pv_i, pp_i, psignup_i, pwithdraw_i, x_i) \tag{2}$$

On the other hand, the cost of using a default_broker tariff depends on the consumption amount $Ct_{default}$, the cost per-kWh ($Pv_{default}$) and the periodic payment $Pp_{default}$, as seen in Eq. 3. More details about PowerTAC models can be found in [8].

$$cost_{default} = \sum_{t=0}^{d_e} (Ct_{default} * Pv_{default} + Pp_{default}) \tag{3}$$

Many PowerTAC related works address this problem with different approaches, depending on the market type and tariff features focus, as seen in Table 1. Reddy et al. [9] created a model to predict the attraction probability of a specific tariff, given the broker's portfolio. Liefers et al. [10] uses a Tit-For-Tat strategy, copying and improving opponent's tariffs. The CrocodileAgent [11] in the other hand, uses market properties as scarcity, balance and oversupply to generate the "most needed" tariffs at a given time.

Table 1. Comparison of PowerTAC broker agents

Broker	Approach	Market
AgentUDE [12]	Agressive fee manipulation	Retail
CwiBroker [13]	Equilibrium in continuous markets	Wholesale
CrocodileAgent [11]	Maximize profitability	Wholesale
Mertacor [14]	PSO to estimate relevant features	Wholesale
TacTex [15]	MDP to minimize costs	Wholesale
Default broker [16]	Fixed (high) prices	Retail

Although some of the related works on PowerTAC retail market describe conceptual characteristics, none have considered modelling conceptual values in the calculations. We have seen that mapping features to values only helped competitors to interpret the market in a simplistic and rigid way. This motivates addressing the tariff creation problem with a different paradigm, the conceptual analysis. The goal is to create a tariff generator that could interpret and adapt linguistic concepts helping to easily define efficient tariffs.

3   TugaTAC Broker Agent

In this work, we propose a strategy for developing PowerTAC agents based on fuzzy models. The proposed approach is called TugaTAC. It consists on updating tariffs using a conceptual model for agent's interest on selling or buying energy. Depending on the production and consumption quantities coming from the customers who are subscribed to TugaTAC's tariffs (portfolio), a fuzzy model determines the broker intentions and what it needs to do in order to improve the tariffs and attract the best profile of clients (consumers or producers) that could help reducing imbalances. Figure 2 shows a simplified scheme of the TugaTAC reasoning mechanism, in which the market prices are combined with the values of energy production and consumption from the broker's customer portfolio.

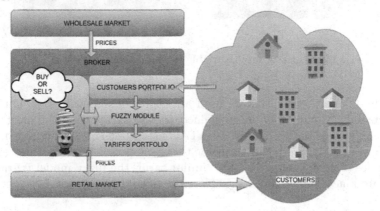

Fig. 2. TugaTAC tariff composition and interactions with the environment

3.1   Fuzzy Conceptual Tariff Strategy for Retail Market

The reasoning mechanism described in Fig. 2 is highly conceptual and connects numerical values to abstract interest. Fuzzy systems are suitable models for this kind of approach. Fuzzy is an alternative for the traditional binary logic in which variables can present more than two values (true or false), usually presenting a continuous range between 0 (completely false) to 1 (completely true) [17]. In fuzzy logic instead of a complex mathematical formulation, the variables are described using conceptual values, e.g. a temperature variable could be specified as "cold", "normal", and "hot".

Our approach for tariffs is based on a fixed price tariff model, where customers pay the same price along the day for the kilowatt-hour. Therefore, this strategy focuses on the price value definition. For this, it is considered the fluctuation of the wholesale market price (clear price), which varies along the day according to demand and production. This way the tariff price is always above the clear price or otherwise the broker would lose money. Thus, we have defined two fuzzy models: one for selling energy and the other for buying, implemented and tested using the jFuzzyLogic API[2].

---

[2] http://jfuzzylogic.sourceforge.net/.

The fuzzy models are illustrated in Fig. 3 for *buy-interest* and in Fig. 4 the *sell-interest* model. The *fuzzification* process establishes the correspondence between the input and output models. A set of IF-THEN fuzzy rules are defined in terms of the concepts defined. This comprises one of the advantages of using fuzzy logic, allowing adaptive configurations for brokers in different scenarios by easily changing rules as observed in Algorithm 1.

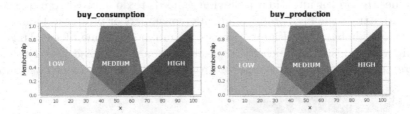

Fig. 3. Fuzzy input variable for model *buy-interest*

Finally, to create the tariffs we used an approach similar to [11]. On initial rounds customers tend to be more opened to new tariffs. Besides, most of the tariffs are published in this period. TugaTAC uses a Tit-For-Tat approach, copying competitors' tariffs when a tariff for the same power type does not exist in its portfolio. If there is already some similar tariff, the fuzzy model is triggered to calculate a new value, in order to beat the offered conditions.

IF buy-production **IS** high **THEN** definitely-interested
IF buy-production **IS** high **AND** buy-consumption **IS** high **THEN** interested
IF buy-production **IS** low **AND** buy-consumption **IS** high **THEN** not-interested
IF buy-production **IS** medium **OR** buy-consumption **IS** high **THEN** not-interested
IF buy-production **IS** medium **AND** buy-consumption **IS** medium **THEN** interested

---

Algorithm 1. Fuzzy rule set example: *buy-interest* variable

The resulting value of the fuzzy represent a multiplying factor for the prices (per-kWh) called interest, which represent the willingness to perform the action, as $interest \in [0, 1]$. When the interest is high, then multiplication will make the prices rise, otherwise the price will decrease. The evaluation of the new price values are verified in two equations, one for buying (to producers, Eq. 4) and other for selling (to consumers, Eq. 5).

$$buying : price_{new} = price_{last} - (price_{last} * buy_{interest}) \qquad (4)$$

$$selling : price_{new} = price_{last} + (price_{last} * sell_{interest}) \qquad (5)$$

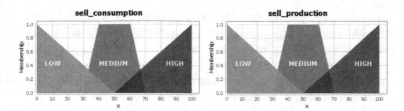

Fig. 4. Fuzzy input variable for model *sell-interest*

3.2   Tariff Composition Mechanism

The tariff composition module is responsible for creating and updating tariffs that are offered to customers. We used a similar approach as in [11]. The fuzzy model is triggered hourly for each energy type in order to calculate the updated tariff prices, as seen in Sect. 3.1. We also considered generic tariffs, such as *production*, *consumption*, and *storage* types. With this approach, the broker can cover more market possibilities offering a wide range of tariffs.

4   Evaluation

Experiments on a competition environment bring some challenges regarding evaluation metrics and how to evaluate the performance of the broker. PowerTAC, as an open source distributed Multi-Agent System simulation platform, allows to configure a local server to run the simulation. In this work we have used the 2015 version for both server and client.

The best way to evaluate the performance of TugaTAC is facing well consolidated agents, winners of the last competitions. If it presents good results under such scenarios, then it could be considered a competitive broker for real tournaments. Since the binary code for the ultimate PowerTAC finalists are available online, we could run the simulation with this exciting configurations. In fact, besides downloading the real PowerTAC competitors we instantiated another broker and called it ZucaTAC. ZucaTAC shares the same code of TugaTAC but has the fuzzy module disabled, updating the tariff prices with a random interest factor, useful for increasing the number of competitors without introducing other complex strategies as those presented by real competitors. Being a preliminary work, our broker is not yet tuned in order to fairly compete with the big ones, which have very complex reasoning architectures and include many other factors to tariff creation, as seen in Sect. 2.2. However, we wanted to check whether TugaTAC was able to win the competition in three evaluation experiments:

1. *Experiment 1 - 1 vs DF:* only one broker vs the default
2. *Experiment 2 - 2 vs DF:* 2 agents plus the default broker
3. *Experiment 3 - 3 or more:* 3 or more agents competing.

The experiments consisted on running one complete simulated tournament and evaluate the results. The winner of the competition is the broker agent with the highest total profit. Our validation metrics are: the energy traded both in wholesale market and retail market, and the total profit at the end of the game. We analyse each one of the experiments and their results regarding these metrics and the dynamics through the simulations.

4.1 Experiment 1 - TugaTAC Against the Default Broker

Firstly, we ran the simplest test: competing against the default broker. As explained on Sect. 2, the default broker guarantees that customers have at least one tariff option. In this case, if TugaTAC wins against the default broker, it means that our strategy at least makes sense. If something is wrong, e.g., if prices are not competitive, the results would show a big deficit with the bank.

Figure 5 presents the profit evolution during the simulation. TugaTAC won the competition with more than 2 million euros in cash, a significant difference against default broker's profits. It seems that initially, the default broker had some advantage in the tariff publication period, being overcame in less than 10 h. Although it seemed to gather customers attention in the moment our tariffs were being adjusted. TugaTAC refinements in future versions will try to reduce this time.

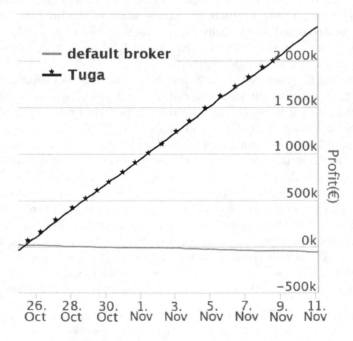

Fig. 5. Experiment 1 - Profit results

Table 2. Experiment 1 - Results of the simplistic competition scenario

Broker Agent	Wholesale trades	Retail trades	Profit
TugaTAC	23 MWh	−47575 kWh	2364911 €
default-broker	0 MWh	0 kWh	59019 €

In Table 2 we see the ranking results of the simulation. The energy traded with wholesale and retail markets are described on the respective columns and represent the total amount of traded energy through the competition in each market. Negative values represent energy sold. Although the default broker had not traded any energy, it made some profit because initial customers paid fees when they changed to TugaTAC tariffs. In the end of the game TugaTAC had 95 % of the customers subscribed, corroborating that TugaTAC is suitable for the competition.

4.2   Experiment 2 - 2 Brokers Against the Default Broker

Results from Experiment 1 have shown that TugaTAC seems to be a good broker, taking a big part of the market share and winning the competition against the default broker. However, the results of the first experiment do not give us much information about how good our fuzzy model performed. In Sect. 2 we have seen that in the cost formula (Eq. 3), customers have a penalty when subscribing to default broker tariffs. This could be a reason why TugaTAC gathered so many subscriptions and won the competition in Experiment 1.

The second step for validating this approach is to compare TugaTAC fuzzy mechanism to another broker, similar in complexity. For that, we ran the competition including the ZucaTAC agent. Figure 6 shows the profit dynamics throughout the game. It seems that in a more competitive scenario, TugaTAC slowly increases its participation on the market, trying to adjust the needs on buying and selling energy.

TugaTAC achieved positive profit. The cumulative balance chart in Fig. 7 corroborates that the strategy seeks somehow for wholesale independence, by showing a more squared shape in TugaTAC's balances meaning equilibrated participation on the markets. Finally, Fig. 8 shows the trading prices on this simulation. It is easy to see that the fuzzy model guaranteed a good adjustment on competitiveness. TugaTAC was able to negotiate less energy with a better relation of customers prices when compared to the prices paid on wholesale. In fact, TugaTAC has demonstrated to be good competing with other agents. The experiments have shown that the profit margin is very similar to the values achieved on the real competition [18].

4.3   Experiment 3 - 3 or More Agents

In a software competition things can change drastically from year to year. We wanted to compare our approach with the most advanced broker available.

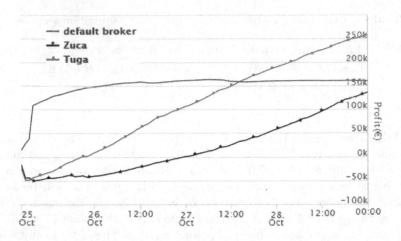

Fig. 6. Experiment 2 - Profit competition dynamics

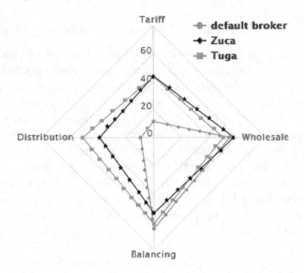

Fig. 7. Experiment 2 - Balance competition dynamics

Nothing better than competing with the current champion, serving as a benchmark. We have downloaded the binaries of AgentUDE, winner of the 2014 PowerTAC. This test scenario consisted on putting three agents to compete. In one side, ZucaTAC, with its simple mimic mechanism for tariffs generation. In the middle, TugaTAC, our novice competitor with its powerful fuzzy adjustment system. And, in the other side, AgentUDE.

AgentUDE's strategy relies on contract withdraw fees. The broker publishes highly competitive (low price) tariffs with big penalties for the customers and then, increasing prices at the same time that the other competitors react to draw market attention, customers start to move to others' tariffs and are penalised with high fees.

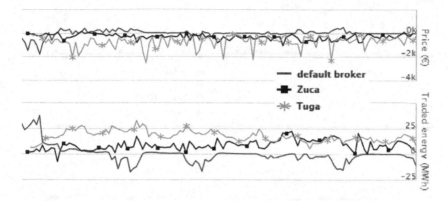

Fig. 8. Experiment 2 - Evolution of price dynamics

In Fig. 9 we can clearly observe through the evolution of the game that AgentUDE had a flawless victory against TugaTAC. We observe the impact of the low price strategy directly related to TugaTAC profit drop. We highlight AgentUDE stayed in owe a long time, having negative profits. In some way, this could represent that our TugaTAC resisted well to competitor's attacks. Another interesting behaviour was noticed when comparing the tariff evolution dynamics. AgentUDE not only recovered from the owe, but yet gained much of the market share, as seen in Fig. 10. With the greatest market share assured, it increased tariff prices and got the revenue recovered.

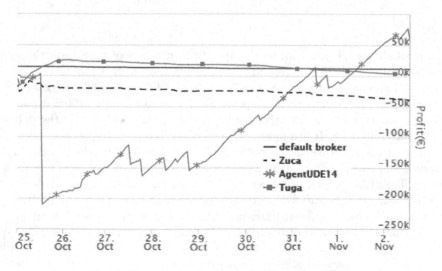

Fig. 9. Experiment 3 - AgentUDE vs TugaTAC

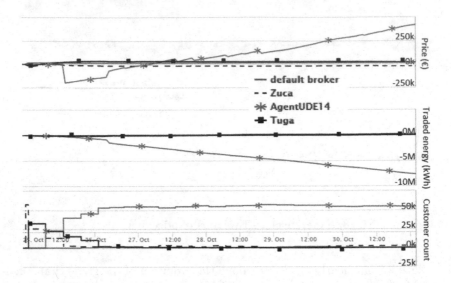

Fig. 10. Experiment 3 - Tariff analysis: price, energy and subscribers count

Table 3. Experiment 3 - Results of the realistic competition scenario

Broker Agent	Wholesale trades	Retail trades	Profit
AgentUDE14	42 MWh	−47793 kWh	70497 €
TugaTAC	31 MWh	−27485 kWh	11311 €
ZucaTAC	4 MWh	2246 kWh	2790 €
default-broker	0 MWh	0 kWh	59 €

Table 3 shows the result of the competition in terms of each broker's accumulated profit. TugaTAC is second after AgentUDE, with a profit of 11311 €. AgentUDE made approximately 600 % more profit with 70490 €. ZucaTAC appears third, without having much presence in this game, only 2790 € explained by its simplicity and not adaptive tariff prices. In the last place is the default broker, with only 59 €. It is interesting to see that in more complex scenarios the default broker loses expressiveness also. Although AgentUDE achieved the highest score, we believe that its strategy is not a fair comparison for our preliminary work on TugaTAC, which is not sensitive to that kind of strategy.

It is clear that AgentUDE outperforms TugaTAC in terms of profit and energy traded amount. AgentUDE is a very consolidated broker, with many optimisations, using more competition information to compose the tariffs. We already expected that our simple tariff generation mechanism could be insufficient to defeat more complex broker strategies. Current work in TugaTAC consist in analysing and considering other information sources to enhance its ability to manage market information as weather forecast to predict production, learning other players' strategies or optimising its participation on the wholesale part. As a preliminary work, we know that TugaTAC agent lacks some implementation in these aspects and we envisage to present an improved version in future work.

5   Conclusions and Future Work

This work outlines how fuzzy systems can be employed for composing tariff contracts in the electricity retail market. The inherent features of fuzzy models enable a rather more conceptual interpretation of the market information, than a traditional complex mathematical rearrangement. This enables market experts and managers to define suitable tariff policies. The PowerTAC framework demonstrated to be a powerful simulation engine for developing and testing new strategies for energy markets.

Our experiments have shown that TugaTAC is not the most optimised broker for trading energy at lower prices in the smart grid market but it is still highly competitive. When compared to the 2014 champion, the fuzzy strategy showed great potential leading the competition in market share and profit for a long time, just losing in the end affected to the drop-pricing fee penalisation approach. As a preliminary work, we observe that the models proposed in TugaTAC are promising, but need to be refined. TugaTAC is not very sensitive to other competitors' strategies and should be extended, integrating more market information, such as consumption and production forecasts that could improve profits. A balanced participation is a very good goal for agents in this scenario, where learning mechanisms could also be considered to improve agent's decisions. As future work we envisage to extensively test and tune the fuzzy models. Finally, we intend to apply fuzzy to support trading in wholesale market.

Acknowledgements. This work is partially funded through IBRASIL, a Full Doctorate programme under Erasmus Mundus, Action 2 – STRAND 1, Lot 16.

References

1. Jackson, M.O.: Networks and economic behavior. Annu. Rev. Econ. **1**(1), 489–511 (2009)
2. Joskow, P.L.: Lessons learned from electricity market liberalization. Energy J. **29**(2), 9–42 (2008)
3. Ketter, W., Collins, J., Reddy, P.: Power TAC: a competitive economic simulation of the smart grid. Energy Econ. **39**, 262–270 (2013)
4. Ketter, W., Collins, J., Block, C.A.: Smart grid economics: policy guidance through competitive simulation (2010)
5. Tykhonov, D.: Designing Generic and Efficient Negotiation Strategies. Delft University of Technology, TU Delft (2010)
6. Stango, V., Zinman, J.: Fuzzy math, disclosure regulation, and market outcomes: evidence from truth-in-lending reform. Rev. Finan. Stud. **24**(2), 506–534 (2011)
7. Kuate, R.T., He, M., Chli, M., Wang, H.H.: An intelligent broker agent for energy trading: an MDP approach. In: Proceedings of the Twenty-Third International Joint Conference on Artificial Intelligence, pp. 234–240. AAAI Press (2013)

8. Ketter, W., Collins, J., Reddy, P.P., Weerdt, M.D.: The 2015 Power Trading Agent Competition. ERIM Report Series Reference No. ERS-2015-001-LIS (2015)

9. Reddy, P.P., Veloso, M.M.: Negotiated learning for smart grid agents: entity selection based on dynamic partially observable features. In: AAAI (2013)

10. Liefers, B., Hoogland, J., Poutré, H.L.: A successful broker agent for power TAC. In: Ceppi, S., David, E., Podobnik, V., Robu, V., Shehory, O., Stein, S., Vetsikas, I.A. (eds.) AMEC/TADA 2013 and 2014. LNBIP, vol. 187, pp. 99–113. Springer, Heidelberg (2014)

11. Matetic, S., Babic, J., Matijas, M., Petric, A., Podobnik, V.: The Crocodileagent 2012: negotiating agreements in smart grid tariff market. In: AT, pp. 203–204 (2012)

12. Özdemir, S., Unland, R.: The broker strategies of a winner agent in power TAC

13. Hoogland, J.: Power TAC cwiBroker2014 (2014)

14. Diamantopoulos, T.G., Symeonidis, A.L., Chrysopoulos, A.C.: Designing robust strategies for continuous trading in contemporary power markets. In: David, E., Kiekintveld, C., Robu, V., Shehory, O., Stein, S. (eds.) AMEC 2012 and TADA 2012. LNBIP, vol. 136, pp. 30–44. Springer, Heidelberg (2013)

15. Urieli, D., Stone, P.: Tactex'13: A champion adaptive power trading agent. In: Proceedings of the 2014 International Conference on Autonomous Agents and Multi-agent Systems, AAMAS 2014, pp. 1447–1448. International Foundation for Autonomous Agents and Multiagent Systems, Richland (2014)

16. Ketter, W., Collins, J., Reddy, P.P., Flath, C.M., Weerdt, M.D.: The power trading agent competition. ERIM Report Series Reference No. ERS-2011-027-LIS (2011)

17. Novák, V., Perfilieva, I., Močkoř, J.: Mathematical Principles of Fuzzy Logic. Springer, New York (1999)

18. Babic, J., Podobnik, V.: An analysis of power trading agent competition 2014. In: Ceppi, S., David, E., Podobnik, V., Robu, V., Shehory, O., Stein, S., Vetsikas, I.A. (eds.) AMEC/TADA 2013 and 2014. LNBIP, vol. 187, pp. 1–15. Springer, Heidelberg (2014)

A Dialectical Approach to Enable Decision Making in Online Trading

Wei Bai[1,2]([✉]), Emmanuel Tadjouddine[2], and Terry Payne[1]

[1] Department of Computer Science, University of Liverpool,
Liverpool, England, UK
{Wei.Bai,T.R.Payne}@liverpool.ac.uk
[2] Department of Computer Science and Software Engineering,
Xi'an Jiaotong-Liverpool University, SIP, Suzhou, China
Emmanuel.Tadjouddine@xjtlu.edu.cn

Abstract. Software agents, acting on behalf of humans, have been identified as an important solution for future electronic markets. Such agents can make their own decisions given prior preferences and the market environment. These preferences can be described using web ontology languages (OWL), while the market can be represented in a machine-understandable way by utilizing the technique of Semantic Web Services (SWS). Besides, SWS enables agents to automatically discover, select, compose and invoke services. To extend the dependability and interactivity of SWS, we have utilized dialogue games and the proof-carrying code to enable buyers interact with sellers, so that interest properties for an online auction market can be automatically certified. Our decision making framework combines formal proofs with informal evidence collected by web services in a dialogue game between a seller and a buyer. We have implemented our approach and experimental results have demonstrated the feasibility as well as the validity of this framework as an enabler for a buyer agent to enter or not an online auction.

Keywords: Dialogue games · Decision making · Online auction · Semantic web services

1 Introduction

We consider e-commerce scenarios wherein software agents can buy or sell goods on behalf of their owners. To enable software agents to participate in such online trading, the trading mechanism should be presented in a machine understandable way. The Semantic Web provides an approach to enable agents to read and interpret a trading mechanism as an online service for which static and dynamic information can be explicitly described using ontology languages. For example, the Web Ontology Language (OWL) [12], which is based on description logic, can be used to express classes and relationships among them. The Semantic Markup for Web Services (OWL-S) [9], which is focused on the process description of a service, can be used to describe the procedures of the trading mechanism.

© Springer International Publishing Switzerland 2016
M. Rovatsos et al. (Eds.): EUMAS 2015/AT 2015, LNAI 9571, pp. 203–218, 2016.
DOI: 10.1007/978-3-319-33509-4_17

However, the message exchange in the architecture of semantic web services is restricted as a client-server or request-response pattern. To extend the inter-activity of the semantic web services, argumentation is introduced to support message exchanges via dialogues. By using dialogue games, agents can assert, challenge and justify their arguments according to their knowledge [16].

Dialogue games are rule-governed interactions among software agents [11], wherein each agent presents its ideas by making "moves" based on a set of rules. Since the common agent communication languages, such as FIPA ACL [7], lack certain locutions to express justifications for statements, additional locutions are proposed to extend the FIPA ACL so that argumentation can be supported in a dialogue [10]. Argumentation via dialogue games permit agents to carry out various types of interactions, such as information seeking, inquiry, persuasion or negotiation. Agents can construct a dialogue by dynamically adjusting the content and sequences of utterances as the discussion ensues. In our framework, we have used an inquiry dialogue to make two agents take turns in asserting, questioning, accepting, or rejecting statements. The goal of an inquiry dialogue is to find out whether a statement is true or false or show that there is insuffi-cient evidence to accept a statement [17]. In our work, evidence can be formal proof or an informal statement (e.g., statistical evidence) for a desirable prop-erty of the trading mechanism. An example of a desirable property of an auction mechanism could be that the highest buyer wins or that bidding its true valua-tion is the optimal strategy for a buyer. Formal proofs are constructed using the CoQ [6] theorem prover within the PCC (Proof-Carrying Code) paradigm [13]. In our online auction scenario, PCC enables the auctioneer to develop proofs for properties of interest and the buyer to check the correctness of a given proof [3]. By considering the set of evidences collected in a dialogue for a set of desirable properties, a buyer agent as a service consumer can evaluate the quality of a service and make decision as to whether to enter or leave a service.

The contributions in this paper are three-fold:

- We have integrated dialogue games within the PCC paradigm so as to increase trust in an agents-mediated online auction. As a consequence, we have extended the interactivity of agents communication wherein formal proofs can be used as arguments in a dialogue.
- Since, not all desirable properties of an online auction mechanism will have asso-ciated formal proofs, we have allowed for informal or empirical evidence related to the QoS (Quality of Service). For example, an auctioneer may claim that it does not have a proof that its mechanism is free from cheating, but 98 % of its consumers never complained about being cheated. We have designed a dialogue game wherein formal and informal evidence can be used as arguments.
- We have constructed a decision model over the formal and empirical evidences allowing a buyer agent, with predefined expectations, to decide whether to join or not an auction.

The proposed dialogue game framework is implemented in JADE [4], which is a widely used tool to implement multi-agent systems. It provides mechanisms to create agents, enable agents to execute tasks and make agents communicate with each other.

The remainder of this paper is organised as follows: In Sect. 2, we will introduce the technique of Semantic Web Service and give an example of an English Auction which is written in the language of OWL-S. The proposed dialogue framework is presented in Sect. 3. In Sect. 4, we present an example that implement our framework, followed by related work in Sect. 5 and conclusion in Sect. 6.

2   Semantic Web Services

The Semantic Web [5] not only enables greater access to content but also to services on the Web. Semantic Web Services (SWS) is a technology that combines semantic web and web services to develop new web applications. OWL-S [9] is one standard for the SWS technology. OWL-S is composed of three main parts: the service profile for advertising and discovering services; the process model, which gives a detailed description of a service operation; and the grounding, which provides details on how to interoperate with a service via messages. Current SWS technique can help us build a system that enables agents to publish, discover and invoke services in an open environment (the Internet).

2.1   A Scenario: An English Auction

In this paper, we use OWL-S to build up the web service. OWL-S can be used together with other Semantic Web languages, such as OWL DL [12] and SWRL [8], to describe the properties and capabilities of a Web service in unambiguous, computer-interpretable form. To set up a semantic web service, the first step is to build the ontology of the specific area. The ontology can be used to formally describe the semantics of terms representing an area of knowledge and give explicit meaning to the information, which enables automated reasoning, semantic search and knowledge management of the specific area. For example, the ontology of auction domain can contain the constructs of classes, relations, axioms, individuals and assertions. More details can be found in Sect. 4. After the construction of domain ontology, the trading mechanism should be described using the OWL-S ontology. In the trading mechanism, functional description should be defined: inputs, outputs, preconditions and results (IOPEs).

In OWL-S, a process represents a specification of the approaches a buyer use to interact with a service. In our scenario, we have used two kinds of processes: one is *atomic process*, which corresponds to a single interchange of a request message and a response message; the other is *composite process*, which consists of a series of processes linked together by control flows and data flows. The control flow describes the relations between the executions of different sub-processes. The control constructs include *sequence, split, if-then-else, iterate* etc. Data flow specify how information is transferred from one process to another. In our example of an English auction, we can define one *if-then-else* branch to describe that when a new bid is greater than current bid (a local variable), we update the value of current bid with the new bid. This process can be simply described as follows.

```
<process:CompositeProcess>
 <process:composedOf>
        <process:If−Then−Else rdf:ID="CompareBid">
              <process:ifCondition>
                   <expr:SWRL−Condition>
                   swrlb:lessThan(#currentBid,#newBid)
                   </expr:SWRL−Condition>
              </process:ifCondition>
              <process:then>
 <!−− Update the value of #currentBid −−>
     ...
              </process:then>
              <process:else>
 <!−− Keep the value of #currentBid as usual−−>
     ...
              </process:else>
        </process:If−Then−Else>
 </process:composedOf>
</process:CompositeProcess>
```

In our setting, we consider the scenario that a buyer communicate with an auctioneer to decide whether or not to join an online auction. Therefore, we do not need to define the grounding of the service. OWL-S can be used to build complex business solutions by describing the functional, non-functional properties of a service, so that agents can perform automatic reasoning on these descriptions. Dialogue games, which can help software agents interact rationally by providing support or counterexample for a conclusion, make this reasoning more flexible for greater interaction between an auctioneer and a buyer.

3   Our Dialogue Game Framework

Online auction web sites, such as eBay, have attracted millions of users around the world to sell, bid and buy goods. In our specific scenario, software agents are assumed to be capable of buying or selling goods through online auction houses. In this scenario, how can buyer agents choose the appropriate auction house? A buyer agent will have properties of interest. These properties need to hold in the auction for the agent to join, bid, and buy items. Our framework is aimed at enabling a participant (e.g., software agent) to interact with the auctioneer before deciding whether or not to join the auction. These interactions between the auctioneer and a buyer are carried out within a dialogue game wherein the buyer agent can query whether desirable properties hold and request associated evidences. An auctioneer needs to convince buyers that its service has some desirable properties, which can be proved formally [2,3]. For that purpose, an auctioneer specifies some desirable properties and develops formal proofs for them by using a theorem prover such as Coq in our case. Buyers use a proof checker to check that these proofs are valid and hence the service really has these characteristics. This process illustrates the PCC paradigm. Thus, trust can be established between auctioneers and buyers. Buyers can object to the auctioneer under the condition that a counterexample is found by the proof checker. In our framework, Coq is the interactive theorem prover used to specify and generate proofs, while Coq proof checker is used as the checker.

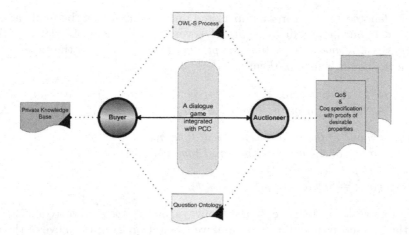

Fig. 1. The dialectical approach framework. A buyer agent uses a dialogue to communicate with the auctioneer and the checking of proofs of desirable properties can be integrated within the dialogue using PCC paradigm.

We have integrated the PCC paradigm within our dialogue model as illustrated by the framework in Fig. 1. In this framework, both the auctioneer and the buyer share the same question ontology for general online auction services. An OWL-S process ontology which provides a machine understandable description of the auction mechanism can be visited by both the participants. In the case of properties with formal proofs, the related specification of this OWL-S description can be translated into COQ specifications so that proofs of these properties can be developed from within COQ. These kind of sound language translation is described in our previous work [1]. The proof certificates for the established desirable properties and QoS information are local to the auctioneer. This strengthens the interactivity between a buyer and an auctioneer and reduce knowledge disclosing. The proofs will be disclosed to a buyer when related questions are proposed in a dialogue game. The dialogue game is used to enable a buyer agent to find out about properties and certificates. This dialogue is a two-person game, which means that only one buyer can communicate with the auctioneer at a time.

3.1   The Formal Dialogue Model

The proposed inquiry dialogue consists of a number of *locutions* or *moves*, *pre-conditions* that indicate the rules that must be satisfied before a move, and the *post-conditions* that describe the actions that will occur after a move. We have restricted the number of participants in the inquiry dialogue to two. Let P be the set of participants in the dialogue. A participant is either a sender or a recipient.

A dialogue D is simply defined by a sequence of moves between the participants. One move represents a message exchange made from one participant to the other. As the dialogue progresses, each move is indexed by a timepoint, which is denoted by a natural number, and only one move can be made at each timepoint. In our inquiry dialogue model, seven types of moves are defined. They are *open, assert, question, justify, accept, reject* and *close*, and the type of each legal move should be one of them.

Definition 1. *A **dialogue**, denoted D, is a sequence of moves $[m_r, ..., m_t]$, where $r, t \in \mathbb{N}, r < t$, involving two participants $P_i \in P, i = \{1, 2\}$, such that:*

1. *the first move of the dialogue, m_r is of type open,*
2. *the last move of the dialogue, m_t is of type close,*
3. *$Sender(m_s) \in P(r \leq s \leq t)$*
4. *$Sender(m_s) \neq Sender(m_{s+1})(r \leq s < t)$.*

The first move of a dialogue D must always be an *open* move (condition 1), while the last move should be a *close* move (condition 2). Each move of the dialogue must be performed by a participant of the dialogue (condition 3). Finally, participants take turns to make moves (condition 4).

    The dialogue assumes that each participant holds a commitment store that records its statements in a dialogue. The commitment store of participant P_i is defined as a private-write, public-read record containing all the commitments incurred by P_i. Both of the participants can read the commitment store of P_i, but the content of this commitment store can only be written using the moves made by P_i.

Definition 2. *A **commitment store** is a set of beliefs denoted as CS_x^t, where $x \in P$ is an agent and $t \in \mathbb{N}$ is a timepoint.*

The commitment store of P_i is created when the agent enters into a dialogue and persists until the dialogue terminates.

Definition 3. *A **proof** is an argument from hypotheses to a conclusion and each step of the argument follows the laws of logic.*

Definition 4. *A **counterexample** is a special kind of example that disproves a statement or proposition.*

Definition 5. *An **argumentation framework** is a pair $AF = <AR, attacks>$, where AR is a set of arguments, and attacks is a binary relation on AR.*

    In our dialogue model, a *counterexample* can be used to attack the statement proposed by an *auctioneer*, which means that a *counterexample* denies a statement. Attacks are represented in the dialogue as *reject* moves. A buyer responds with *reject* when a formal proof justification provided by an auctioneer is unsuccessfully checked.

    The state diagram of the dialogue is given in Fig. 2. A buyer can open a dialogue by using the *open* move. Then, the auctioneer can give an assertion to the buyer. The buyer can choose to close the dialogue on the condition that she

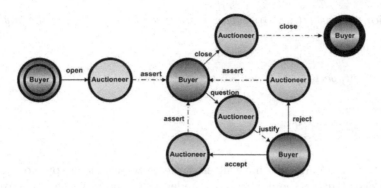

Fig. 2. The state diagram of the dialogue. Nodes indicate the agent whose turn is to utter a move. Moves uttered by the auctioneer are labeled with a dashed line, while those uttered by the buyer are labelled with a solid line.

does not have any issues to raise with the auctioneer. Otherwise, the buyer can give a move of type *question* to query on the issues that she is concerned about. The auctioneer must give a justification to the buyer for each specific question. There are three cases in the justification process: (1) the auctioneer has a formal proof for the answer to the question at hand; (2) the auctioneer has an informal evidence for the answer; or (3) the auctioneer does not know the answer for the question. In the first case, the buyer can check the correctness of the formal proof. If this proof is certified, then the buyer gives an *accept* move; otherwise, the proof checker will generate a counterexample and refuse the property at hand by making the *reject* move. In the second case, the buyer will compare the informal evidence with a reasonable expected value for the issue of interest and will accept it with some score. In the last case, the buyer will give a *reject* move to the auctioneer. Besides, the auctioneer can give assertions to the buyer, so that the dialogue can carry on until both participants agreed to close the dialogue.

The locutions used in the dialogue model are defined as follows.

Definition 6. *open(b): buyer b opens a dialogue.*

– *Pre-conditions:*
   1. $b \notin P$, where P is the set of dialogue participants.
– *Post-conditions:*
   1. $P' = P \cup \{b\}$
   2. $CS^b = \emptyset$
   3. $\rho = b$.

An buyer b can open a dialogue. The precondition of this locution is that the buyer is not a participant of this dialogue. The postcondition is that buyer b becomes a participant of the dialogue (post-condition 1) and his commitment store is created (post-condition 2).

Definition 7. $assert(a, b, \phi)$: auctioneer a gives an assertion to the buyer.

– *Pre-conditions:*
 1. $a \neq \rho$
 2. $locutiontype(l_{s-1}) \in \{open, accept, reject\}$
 3. $\phi \in \Sigma^a$
– *Post-conditions:*
 1. $CS^{a'} = \{\phi\} \cup CS^a$
 2. $\rho = a$.

The *auctioneer* should not have uttered the previous move (pre-condition 1) and the *assert* move should be given under the conditions that a buyer has open a dialogue. The justification is accepted or rejected by the buyer (pre-condition 2). A belief ϕ from the beliefs store of the auctioneer will be asserted by the auctioneer to ask the buyer to propose a question (pre-condition 3). Once the assertion has been uttered, the belief ϕ will be added to the commitment store of the auctioneer (post-condition 1).

Definition 8. $question(b, a, \phi)$: buyer b asks a question about property ϕ to the auctioneer a.

– *Pre-conditions:*
 1. $b \neq \rho$
 2. $locutiontype(l_{s-1}) \in \{assert\}$
 3. $\phi \notin \Sigma^b$
 4. $\phi \notin CS^b$
– *Post-conditions:*
 1. $\phi \notin \Sigma^b$
 2. $\phi \in CS^b$
 3. $\rho = b$.

A buyer can ask questions to the auctioneer after the auctioneer has uttered an assertion (pre-conditions 1 and 2). The property ϕ does not contain the knowledge base of b (pre-condition 3) and the buyer has not proposed questions about this property (pre-condition 4). Once b has uttered the question, the knowledge base of b does not change (post-condition 1), and the commitment store of b has been updated (post-condition 2).

Definition 9. $justify(a, b, \phi)$: auctioneer a justifies the property ϕ for buyer b.

– *Pre-conditions:*
 1. $a \neq \rho$
 2. $locutiontype(l_{s-1}) \in \{question\}$
 3. $\phi \in CS^b$
 4. $\phi \notin \Sigma^b$
– *Post-conditions:*
 1. $\phi \notin \Sigma^b$
 2. $\phi \in CS^a$
 3. $\rho = a$.

After receiving a question about property ϕ (pre-condition 2 & 3), the auctioneer a should provide a justification to this property. The knowledge base of the buyer and commitment store remains the same in this move (post-condition 1). The justification of this property is added to the commitment store of the auctioneer (post-condition 2).

Definition 10. $accept(b, a, \phi)$: *buyer b accepts the justification of property ϕ.*

- *Pre-conditions:*
  1. $b \neq \rho$
  2. $locutiontype(l_{s-1}) \in \{justify\}$
  3. $\phi \notin \Sigma^b$
  4. $\phi \in CS^a$
- *Post-conditions:*
  1. $\phi \in \Sigma^b$
  2. $\phi \in CS^a$
  3. $\rho = b$.

The *accept* move is used to accept the justification for property ϕ in the preceding *justify* move (pre-condition 2). The property ϕ is not contained in the knowledge base of the buyer before the move of *accept* (pre-condition 3), and the auctioneer has provided the justification for this property (pre-condition 4). Property ϕ becomes the element of the knowledge base of b after this move (post-condition 1). The commitment store of a does not change in the move of *accept* (post condition 2).

Definition 11. $reject(b, a, \phi^{att}, \phi)$: *buyer b rejects the property ϕ using ϕ^{att}.*

- *Pre-conditions:*
  1. $b \neq \rho$
  2. $locutiontype(l_{s-1}) \in \{justify\}$
  3. $attack(\phi^{att}, \phi)$
  4. $\phi \notin \Sigma^b$
  5. $\phi \in CS^a$
- *Post-conditions:*
  1. $\phi \notin \Sigma^b$
  2. $\phi \in CS^a$
  3. $\rho = b$.

Buyer can raise an rejection by giving an evidence ϕ^{att} to previously declared property ϕ in response to the move *justify* (pre-condition 2). There is an evidence ϕ^{att} which attacks ϕ (pre-condition 3). The knowledge base of b and commitment store of a does not change (pre-condition 4 & 5 and post-condition 1 & 2).

Definition 12. $close(p)$: *participant p closes a dialogue.*

- *Pre-conditions:*
  1. $p \neq \rho$
  2. $locutiontype(l_{s-1}) \in \{assert, close\}$

3. $\forall \phi \in \Sigma^b, \phi \in CS^b$
– *Post-conditions:*
   1. if matched-close $P = \emptyset$.

The participant can only close a dialogue after an *assert* or *close* (pre-condition 2). The buyer chooses to close the dialogue when all the questions in his knowledge base have been proposed (pre-condition 3). When both participants have agreed to close the dialogue, they will be removed from the dialogue (post-condition 1).

3.2   Decision Model and Processes of the Dialogue

In our setting, both the auctioneer and the buyer agents share the same knowledge base, which includes the ontologies of the online auction and related specifications. Both agents can understand each other's messages but have a private knowledge base. The set of questions are private to the buyer and the set of answers associated to the questions are private to the auctioneer. However, when a question or answer is proposed, it becomes public to both participants. Each question is associated with a *preference level*, which determines the order in which the questions are proposed by the buyer. The preference level $E = \{strong, average, weak\}$ is then used to drive the dialogue forward.

A *Weighted Sum* model is used in the dialogue game. The output of the *Weighted Sum* model is a binary set of O, whose elements are $\{Yes, No\}$. Decision is made by evaluating a bunch of properties, which are represented as the set of H. We assume that every property is bind with a score s_i and a relative weight w_i, which indicates the importance of a property. The value of s_i is determined by a function which depends on the type of evidence provided. If we have formal evidence, then the scoring function will return either negative value in the case of the proof cannot be accepted by the proof-checker, or a full score otherwise. If the evidence is empirical, then the scoring function is in the form of intervals, see Sect. 4 for more details. The summation of weights equals to 1, such that $\sum_{i=1}^{n} w_i = 1$ wherein n is the number of elements in H. The final score fs is calculated as follows:

$$fs = \sum_{i=1}^{n} w_i s_i,$$

where n is also the number of elements in H.

The buyer has an reasonable expectation in the form of an *admissibility threshold* ε beyond which the final score will lead the buyer to join the auction. In other words, if $fs \geq \varepsilon$, then the buyer will choose Yes to join the auction at hand. The threshold ε may come from experience or be derived from historical data.

The inquiry dialogue is described by Algorithm 1. A dialogue starts with a move opening an inquiry dialogue, that has a matched-close to terminate the dialogue and whose moves conform to the rules for each locution described in

---

Algorithm 1. The processes of an inquiry dialogue

1: buyer opens an inquiry dialogue uses an *open* move
2: auctioneer gives an *assert* to ask buyer to propose a question
3: **while** buyer has question(s) that has(have) not been proposed **do**
4:     buyer selects a question which with the highest preference level
5:     buyer asks this question using the move whose type is *question*
6:     auctioneer gives a justification using the move whose type is of *justify*
7:     **if** the justification is unknown or has failed to be checked **then**
8:         buyer gives a *reject* move
9:     **else**
10:        buyer gives an *accept* move
11:    **end if**
12:    auctioneer gives an *assert* to ask buyer to propose a question
13: **end while**
14: buyer gives a *close* move
15: auctioneer gives a *close* move to terminate the dialogue

---

Sect. 3.1. The *buyer* starts an inquiry dialogue by giving an *open* move, then the auctioneer propose an *assert* move to ask *buyer* to propose questions. The *buyer* chooses an unproposed question which with the highest preference level from his knowledge base and then uses the move of *question* to propose it. After receiving a question, the auctioneer should respond by a *justify* move. If the content of a justification is unknown, or a formal proof that is failed to be checked. The *buyer* will give a *reject* move, otherwise he should accepts the justification use an *accept* move. The *auctioneer* should give an assertion to ask *buyer* to propose a new question in the end of the loop. A dialogue can be closed when both of the participants agree to terminate it. All of the proposed questions and related justifications are stored in the commitment store of the dialogue. Besides, each question can only be asked once.

4 Inquiry Dialogue Example

We have illustrated the proposed inquiry dialogue by means of an example where a *buyer* talks to an *auctioneer* to decide whether or not to join an online auction service. The shared question ontology contains three types of questions: (1) questions about those properties whose answers could be formal proofs of a service; (2) questions about the functional properties (e.g. inner operation of a service) of a service; and (3) questions about the non-functional properties (e.g. QoS) of a service. In this example, four questions are proposed as listed in Table 1[1].

In Table 1, each question is marked by an ID, and the related type and content of each question are defined use the OWL *objectProperty* relationship. Users can extend this ontology by adding questions as the classification of types.

The *buyer* holds a private knowledge base that contains the questions to inquire about. The preference level and weight of each question are shown in

---

[1] The ontology files are available upon request.

Table 1. Questions in the shared ontology

QuestionID	hasType	hasContent
Q1	FormalProperty	Can you prove that the payment is the highest bid?
Q2	FunctionalProperty	What's the payment method?
Q3	nonFunctionalProperty	What's the Reputation of your service?
Q4	FormalProperty	Can you prove that the winner has the highest bid?

Table 2. As mentioned above the *buyer* will choose the questions in order on the basis of the preference level and calculate the scores of the justifications using the variable weight. The summation of all the weights in this table equals one.

Table 2. Questions of the buyer

QuestionID	Preference level	Weight
Q1	Strong	0.3
Q2	Average	0.2
Q3	Strong	0.3
Q4	Weak	0.2

Table 3. Justifications of the auctioneer

QuestionID	Justification
Q1	FormalProof_PEquHB
Q2	Visa DEBIT
Q3	0.85
Q4	FormalProof_WhatsHB

The *auctioneer* uses Table 3 to search for the answers for each query, a *buyer* can not directly visit this table unless she queries the *auctioneer*. All the questions in the shared ontology should be contained in this table, though there may exist questions that do not have related answers. Table 4 shows the grading standards of the *buyer* for the justifications. As this grading table is subjective, a buyer can grade the justification based on his own preference. However, for the question whose justification is a formal proof, the buyer should give full marks to it when the proof is successfully checked.

An example dialogue between *buyer* and *auctioneer* is presented as in Fig. 3. The turn order in the above dialogue is deterministic, the buyer should open a dialogue in **Move 1**. Then the *auctioneer* and *buyer* give assertions one by one.

Moves 2–5: The *auctioneer* asks *buyer* to ask a question. *buyer* searches in his knowledge base of questions and find out the question with the highest preference, say *Q1*. Then the auctioneer searches the justification for the question from Table 3. This justification is a formal proof, so the *auctioneer* should send a proof checker(in the case that the *buyer* does not have the proof checker) and related proof files to the *buyer*. The *buyer* then uses the proof checker to check the correctness of the proof and gets positive feedback. Finally, the *buyer* accepts the justification.

Table 4. Grading table of the buyer

QuestionID	Justification	Score
Q1	Formal proof successes	100
	Formal proof fails	−50
	Do not have formal proof	0
Q2	Alipay	100
	Visa DEBIT	80
	Others	0
Q3	[0.90,1.00]	100
	[0.70,0.90)	80
	[0.50,0.70)	50
	[0.00,0.50)	0
	UNKNOWN	0
Q4	Formal proof successes	100
	Formal proof fails	−50
	Do not have formal proof	0

(1) *buyer → auctioneer: open(buyer)*
(2) *auctioneer → buyer: assert(auctioneer, buyer, You can ask a question.)*
(3) *buyer → auctioneer. question(buyer,auctioneer,Q1)*
(4) *auctioneer → buyer: justify(auctioneer,buyer,FormalProof_PEquHB)*
(In the justification process, the *auctioneer* sends the proof to the *buyer*
and the proof is successfully checked by using the COQ proof checker.)
(5) *buyer → auctioneer: accept(buyer,auctioneer,FormalProof_PEquHB)*
(6) *auctioneer → buyer: assert(auctioneer, buyer, You can ask a question.)*
(7) *buyer → auctioneer: question(buyer,auctioneer,Q3)*
(8) *auctioneer → buyer: justify(auctioneer,buyer,0.85)*
(9) *buyer → auctioneer: accept(buyer,auctioneer,0.85)*
(10) *auctioneer → buyer: assert(auctioneer, buyer, You can ask a question.)*
(11) *buyer → auctioneer: question(buyer,auctioneer,Q2)*
(12) *auctioneer → buyer: justify(auctioneer,buyer,Visa DEBIT)*
(13) *buyer → auctioneer: accept(buyer,auctioneer, Visa DEBIT)*
(14) *auctioneer → buyer: assert(auctioneer, buyer, You can ask a question.)*
(15) *buyer → auctioneer: question(buyer,auctioneer,Q4)*
(16) *auctioneer → buyer: justify(auctioneer,buyer,FormalProof_WhasHB)*
(In the justification process, the *auctioneer* sends the proof to the buyer. The *buyer*
failed to checked the proof by using the COQ proof checker, which meansthe proof
provided by the *auctioneer* is wrong. The *buyer* finds an attack to this property.)
(17) *buyer → auctioneer: reject(buyer,auctioneer,FormalProof_WhatsHB)*
(18) *auctioneer → buyer: assert(auctioneer, buyer, You can ask a question.)*
(19) *buyer → auctioneer: close(buyer)*
(20) *auctioneer → buyer: close(auctioneer)*

Fig. 3. An example of the inquiry dialogue

Moves 6–9: The *auctioneer* asks *buyer* to ask another question. The *buyer* finds question *Q3*, which has the highest preference level within the remaining questions. The *auctioneer* gives the justification with value *0.85* and *buyer* accepts it.

Moves 10–13: After the *auctioneer* requests the *buyer* to ask a question. The *buyer* proposes question **Q2** and receives the justification with value of *Visa DEBIT*. The *buyer* accepts the justification in this round.

Moves 14–17: The *auctioneer* asks *buyer* to ask a question. The *buyer* proposes the last question from his knowledge base, which is *Q4*. Then the auctioneer sends the proof to the *buyer*. The *buyer* uses the proof checker to check the correctness of the proof and gets a counterexample, which means the proof provided by the auctioneer is wrong. In this case, the *buyer* find an attack of this property. Finally, the *buyer* rejects the justification.

Moves 18–20: The *auctioneer* asks the *buyer* to propose a new question. However, all the questions in the *buyer*'s knowledge base have been raised. The *buyer* chooses to close the dialogue in move 19 and the *auctioneer* agrees to close the dialogue.

After the termination of the dialogue, the *buyer* calculates the scores for each justification. The final score fs is calculated as: $fs = 0.3 * 100 + 0.2 * 80 + 0.3 * 80 + 0.2 * (-50) = 60$. We assume that the *admissibility threshold*, ε, of the *buyer* is 70. As $fs < \varepsilon$, the *buyer* decides to not join the auction house.

5   Related Work

In the work of [14], an inquiry dialogue is proposed to enable agents to negotiate over ontological correspondences. In this dialogue, agents can not only make *assert* moves to assert beliefs, they also can *object* to a belief by providing an attack and *accept* or *reject* beliefs. In the ArguGRID [15] project, Web service, agents and argumentation techniques are combined to support decision making and negotiations inside Virtual Organizations. ArgSCIFF [16] is a project that aims to make Web service reasoning more visible to potential users by using dialogues for service interaction. The difference between their work and our approach is that we have incorporated the PCC paradigm into the dialogue to enable agents to automatically check formal proofs that are provided by the service provider.

6   Conclusion

In this paper, we have proposed a dialogue game to enable buyer agents to automatically query an auctioneer before deciding whether or not to join an online auction. We have formally described this inquiry dialogue model by defining the rules of locutions and commitments. The auctioneer and the buyer share a common knowledge enabling them to communicate and make sense of each other's arguments. But they also have private knowledge. For example, the questions related to properties of interest to the buyer are not known to the auctioneer until they are revealed through the dialogue. The buyer has a ranking function over the questions in the form of a preference level, which is used to drive the dialogue forward. A decision model over possible answers in line with predefined expectations is used to decide whether to join or not an auction. This framework is implemented from within JADE and formal proofs are developed using Coq. Experimental results have demonstrated the feasibility as well as the validity of this framework. Future work includes the extension of the range of desirable properties to be proven in the system and extensive evaluation of our approach.

References

1. Bai, W., Tadjouddine, E.M.: Automated program translation in certifying online auctions. In: ETAPS/VpPT 2015, 11–18 April, London, UK (2015)
2. Bai, W., Tadjouddine, E.M., Guo, Y.: Enabling automatic certification of online auctions. arXiv preprint arXiv:1404.0854 (2014)
3. Bai, W., Tadjouddine, E.M., Payne, T.R., Guan, S.U.: A proof-carrying code approach to certificate auction mechanisms. In: Fiadeiro, J.L., Liu, Z., Xue, J. (eds.) FACS 2013. LNCS, vol. 8348, pp. 23–40. Springer, Heidelberg (2014)
4. Bellifemine, F., Caire, G., Greenwood, D.: Developing Multi-agent Systems with JADE. Wiley series in agent technology. Wiley, Chichester (2007)
5. Berners-Lee, T., Hendler, J., Lassila, O., et al.. The semantic web. Sci. Am. **284**(5), 28–37 (2001)
6. Dowek, G., Felty, A., Herbelin, H., Huet, G., Werner, B., Paulin-Mohring, C., et al.: The coq proof assistant user's guide: version 5.6 (1991)
7. FIPA ACL: FIPA ACL message structure specification. Foundation for Intelligent Physical Agents (2002). http://www.fipa.org/specs/fipa00061/SC00061G.html. Accessed 30 June 2004
8. Horrocks, I., Patel-Schneider, P.F., Boley, H., Tabet, S., Grosof, B., Dean, M., et al.: SWRL: a semantic web rule language combining OWL and RuleML. W3C Member Submission **21**, 79 (2004)
9. Martin, D., Burstein, M., Hobbs, J., Lassila, O., McDermott, D., McIlraith, S., Narayanan, S., Paolucci, M., Parsia, B., Payne, T., et al.: OWL-S: semantic markup for web services. W3C Member Submission **22**, 2007–04 (2004)
10. McBurney, P., Parsons, S.: Locutions for argumentation in agent interaction protocols. In: van Eijk, R.M., Huget, M.-P., Dignum, F.P.M. (eds.) AC 2004. LNCS (LNAI), vol. 3396, pp. 209–225. Springer, Heidelberg (2005)
11. McBurney, P., Parsons, S.: Dialogue games for agent argumentation. In: Simari, G., Rahwan, I. (eds.) Argumentation in Artificial Intelligence, pp. 261–280. Springer, Heidelberg (2009)
12. McGuinness, D.L., Van Harmelen, F., et al.: OWL web ontology language overview. W3C Recommendation **10**(10), 2004–03 (2004)
13. Necula, G.C.: Proof-carrying code. Design and implementation. In: Schwichtenberg, H., Steinbrüggen, R. (eds.) Proof and System-Reliability. Springer, Heidelberg (2002)
14. Payne, T.R., Tamma, V.: Negotiating over ontological correspondences with asymmetric and incomplete knowledge. In: Proceedings of the 2014 International Conference on Autonomous Agents and Multi-agent Systems, pp. 517–524. International Foundation for Autonomous Agents and Multiagent Systems (2014)

15. Toni, F., Grammatikou, M., Kafetzoglou, S., Lymberopoulos, L., Papavassileiou, S., Gaertner, D., Morge, M., Bromuri, S., McGinnis, J., Stathis, K., Curcin, V., Ghanem, M., Guo, L.: The ArguGRID platform: an overview. In: Altmann, J., Neumann, D., Fahringer, T. (eds.) GECON 2008. LNCS, vol. 5206, pp. 217–225. Springer, Heidelberg (2008)
16. Torroni, P., Gavanelli, M., Chesani, F.: Argumentation in the semantic web. IEEE Intell. Syst. **22**(6), 66–74 (2007)
17. Walton, D.N., Krabbe, E.C.: Commitment in Dialogue. Basic Concepts of Interpersonal Reasoning. State University of New York Press, Albany (1995)

What Should an Agent Know
Not to Fail in Persuasion?

Shizuka Yokohama and Kazuko Takahashi[(⊠)]

School of Science and Technology, Kwansei Gakuin University,
2-1, Gakuen, Sanda 669-1337, Japan
{yokohama-shizuka,ktaka}@kwansei.ac.jp

Abstract. This paper presents a strategy and conditions for non-failing persuasion using a dialogue model using argumentation. A concept of the predicted knowledge of the other agent participating in the dialogue is introduced. In the dialogue model, an agent's knowledge is updated as the dialogue proceeds; an argumentation framework is constructed from the current knowledge; and only the content of an acceptable argument can be offered as the next move. In this paper, a modified dialogue model is proposed in which the next move is determined using predicted knowledge and a strategy that navigates a non-failing persuasive argumentation is presented. Conditions under which persuasion never fails using this strategy when the prediction is equivalent to the actual knowledge of an opponent are described. Moreover, what the predicted knowledge should contain for non-failing persuasion are discussed. The introduction of predicted knowledge improves the formulation of real dialogue.

Keywords: Argumentation · Persuasion · Dialogue · Predicted knowledge base

1 Introduction

To achieve agreement during a dialogue between agents, it is important to resolve existing conflicts by exchanging protocols; persuasion is one dialogue type that has such characteristics. Each agent participating in a dialogue has their own knowledge, which changes as the dialogue proceeds. If dialogue is regarded as a game, then each agent is a player who determines their next move by considering the effect of the move based on a dialogue protocol. The agent's knowledge is updated with the utterance of an opponent, which may add knowledge that is inconsistent with their current belief. As an argumentation framework can handle inconsistency or nonmonotonicity of knowledge bases, it is useful for creating a dialogue model.

Amgoud et al. proposed a dialogue model using argumentation [2]. In their model, an agent's knowledge is updated as the dialogue proceeds; an argumentation framework is constructed from the current knowledge, and only the content of an acceptable argument can be asserted as the agent's beliefs. This approach

© Springer International Publishing Switzerland 2016
M. Rovatsos et al. (Eds.): EUMAS 2015/AT 2015, LNAI 9571, pp. 219–233, 2016.
DOI: 10.1007/978-3-319-33509-4_18

models argumentative agents who behave rationally; however, it lacks the viewpoint of predicting the opponent's inner states. On the other hand, in an actual dialogue, especially in the case of persuasion, we usually predict the opponent's knowledge or beliefs and create a strategy to succeed in persuasion.

Consider the following situation of students selecting their research laboratory. Alice and Bob want to apply to the same laboratory. Alice, who prefers a strict professor's laboratory, wants to apply to Charlie's laboratory. She knows that Charlie is generous as well as strict. On the other hand, Bob wants to apply to a generous professor's laboratory, but does not want to apply to a strict professor's laboratory. Bob does not know about the reputation of Charlie. In this example, if Alice has no idea about Bob's knowledge, then she may first say, "Let's apply to Charlie's laboratory because he is strict," which will fail to persuade Bob to accept Alice's proposal. However, if she knows that Bob does not like strict professors, then she could say, "Let's apply to Charlie's laboratory because he is generous," which will successfully persuade Bob to accept the proposal. This choice of utterance is based on the key knowledge that Bob does not want to apply to a strict professor's laboratory and on Alice having the correct key knowledge as her prediction.

In this paper, we revisit the dialogue model proposed by Amgoud et al. and enhance it to lead to non-failing persuasion by creating a strategy based on predicted knowledge. We propose a dialogue model in which each agent has predicted knowledge of their opponent as well as their own knowledge. In this strategy, an agent does not present an argument that s/he predicts will lead the opponent to refuse the proposal, and positively presents an argument that s/he predicts will lead the opponent to accept it. These decisions are made using an argumentation framework constructed from predicted knowledge.

We investigate the conditions under which persuasion succeeds, or at least does not fail using this strategy, when a prediction is equivalent to the actual knowledge of an opponent. Moreover, we discuss what the predicted knowledge should contain for persuasion not to fail.

This dialogue model using predicted knowledge, improves the formulation of real dialogue and can be extended to handle dialogues including a lie.

The rest of the paper is organized as follows. Section 2 describes the argumentation framework on which our model is based. Section 3 formalizes our dialogue model and proposes a persuasion strategy. Section 4 gives an example of a persuasive dialogue. Section 5, discusses the properties of this strategy. Section 6 compares our approach with other approaches. Finally, Sect. 7 presents our conclusions.

2   Argumentation Framework

Dung's abstract argumentation framework is defined as a pair of a set and a binary relation on the set [6]. We instantiate each argument by a set of formulas generated from a given knowledge base. In addition, *preference* is introduced to give relative strength to arguments.

Definition 1 (Argument). *Let Σ be a set of propositional formulas, called* knowledge base. *Σ may be inconsistent and not deductively closed. An argument on Σ is defined as a pair of support H and a conclusion h, (H, h), where either of the following conditions are satisfied: (i) $H = \emptyset$ and $h \in \Sigma$, or (ii) H is a consistent minimal subset of Σ in the sense of set inclusion, $H \vdash h$, and $\forall h' \in H$; $h' \not\equiv h$ where $\equiv$ represents logical equivalence.*

For an argument $A = (H, h)$, $supp(A)$ and $concl(A)$ denote H and h, respectively. $fml(A)$ denotes a set of formulas in A, that is, $fml(A) = H \cup \{h\}$. For a set of arguments Arg, $Fml(Arg)$ denotes $\bigcup_{A \in Arg} fml(A)$.

In an argumentation framework for a persuasive dialogue, it is often necessary to give relative strength to arguments to determine which formula is acceptable [1,4,8]. Similar to existing approaches, we define an argumentation framework with preferences.

The strength of each formula is assigned in advance, such that a higher level is more strong than a lower one. As a result, Σ is partially ordered with respect to strength. The preference of an argument is calculated depending on this strength, such that it depends on the least strong formula included in support of an argument. We do not discuss how to assign strength here, since it is out of the focus of this paper.

Definition 2 (Preference). *Let Σ be a set of formulas and str be a function that returns a natural number for an element of Σ. For each argument A, generated from Σ, $Pref(A)$ is defined as $min_{F \in supp(A)} str(F)$ if $supp(A) \neq \emptyset$, and $str(concl(A))$ if $supp(A) = \emptyset$.*

Let A_1 and A_2 be arguments. If $Pref(A_1) \leq Pref(A_2)$, it is said that A_2 is preferable to A_1.

Definition 3 (Attack). *For a pair of arguments $A_1 = (H_1, h_1)$ and $A_2 = (H_2, h_2)$, if $h_2 \equiv \neg h_1$, then it is said that A_2 rebuts A_1 ; if there exists $h \in H_1$ such that $h_2 \equiv \neg h$, then it is said that A_2 undercuts A_1; A_2 either rebuts or undercuts A_1 and A_2 is preferable to A_1, then it is said that A_2 attacks A_1.*

Definition 4 (Argumentation Framework). *An argumentation framework for a knowledge base Σ under strength str, denoted by $AF(\Sigma, str)$, is defined as a pair $\langle AR, AT \rangle$ where AR is the set of arguments generated from Σ and AT is the set of attacks on AR based on str. If str is fixed throughout the discussion, then we denote $AF(\Sigma)$ in the form where str is omitted.*

Definition 5 (Acceptable). *Let $\langle AR, AT \rangle$ be an argumentation framework. For a set of arguments $S \subseteq AR$ and an argument A_1, for any argument $A_2 \in AR$ that attacks A_1, there exists an argument $A_3 \in S$ that attacks A_2; it is said that A_1 is acceptable with respect to S.*

Definition 6 (Grounded Extension). *Let $\mathcal{AF} = \langle AR, AT \rangle$ be an argumentation framework. For a set of arguments $S \subseteq AR$, let F be a function:*
$F(S) = \{ A \in AR \mid A$ *is acceptable with respect to S* $\}$. *Let S' be the least fixedpoint of F. Then S' is said to be the grounded extension of $\mathcal{AF}$, and denoted by $Ext(\mathcal{AF})$.*

Note that there exists a unique grounded extension for any argumentation framework [6]. Hereafter, we use the term "extension" to mean a grounded extension, unless there is any confusion.

In addition to these well-known concepts, a few more new concepts are defined.

Definition 7 (Belief). *Let $\mathcal{AF}$ be an argumentation framework. A set of formulas appearing in arguments in the extension is said to be* a belief of $\mathcal{AF}$, *that is, $Bel(\mathcal{AF}) = \bigcup_{A \in Ext(\mathcal{AF})} fml(A)$.*

Definition 8 (NBA-Argument). *Let $\mathcal{AF} = \langle AR, AT \rangle$ be an argumentation framework. For an argument $A_1 \in AR$, if there does not exist an argument $A_2 \in AR$ that attacks A_1, then A_1 is said to be* not-being-attacked-argument *of $\mathcal{AF}$,* NBA-argument *in short.*

3 Dialogue Model

3.1 Dialogue Model Based on an Argumentation

Amgoud et al. proposed a dialogue model based on an argumentation [2]. An agent's knowledge and belief were distinguished by setting them as formulas in a knowledge base, and in an extension of an argumentation framework constructed from the knowledge base and an opponent's utterances, respectively. We modify this model by introducing a predicted knowledge base.

A dialogue is a sequence of utterances by agents along the protocol. Each agent constructs an argumentation framework from an initial knowledge base and the set of formulas provided so far. When an opponent makes an utterance, and new formulas are provided, then the argumentation framework is revised. First, s/he calculates the extension of the argumentation framework, that represents the consistent set of formulas that s/he currently believes. These are the formulas allowed for use as the next utterance. Next, s/he selects the best move from these allowed moves using a predicted knowledge base of an opponent.

Let X be a participant of a dialogue. Let Σ_X be X's initial knowledge base, Σ_Y be her opponent Y's initial knowledge base, and Π_Y be Y's initial knowledge base on X's prediction. That is, X has two knowledge bases Σ_X and Π_Y. It is usually assumed that common sense or widely prevalent facts on the subject are also known by the opponent. On the other hand, there is knowledge that only the opponent knows, or that the agent is not sure that the opponent knows. Therefore, we assume that the predicted knowledge base is a subset of the opponent's real knowledge base, that is, $\Pi_Y \subseteq \Sigma_Y$.

We consider acts of an agent.

Definition 9 (Act). *An act is either assert(p), assert(S, p), assertS(S, p), challenge(p) or pass, where p is a formula and S is a set of formulas.*

An act *assert* is asserting the statement with or without its ground, and an act *assertS* is asserting the ground itself. An act *challenge* is asking the reason for the assertion. An act *pass* is passing on the turn, without giving any information.

Let T be an act. We define the function *formula* that returns a set of formulas for an act.

$$formula(T) = \begin{cases} \{p\} & \text{if } T = assert(p) \\ \{p\} \cup S & \text{if } T = assert(S, p) \\ S & \text{if } T = assertS(S, p) \\ \emptyset & \text{otherwise.} \end{cases}$$

Definition 10 (Move). *A move is a pair of (X, T), where X is an agent, and T is an act.*

Definition 11 (Dialogue). *When $\Sigma_P, \Sigma_C, \Pi_P$ and Π_C are given, a dialogue d_k between a persuader P and their opponent C on a subject $\rho \in \Sigma_P$ is a finite sequence of moves $[m_0, \ldots, m_{k-1}]$ where each m_i $(0 \le i \le k-1)$ is in the form of (X_i, T_i) and the following conditions are satisfied:*

(i) $X_0 = P$ and T_0 is either $assert(\rho)$ or $assert(S, \rho)$.
(ii) For each i $(0 \le i \le k-1)$, $X_i = P$ if i is even, $X_i = C$ if i is odd.
(iii) For each i $(0 \le i \le k-1)$, m_i is one of allowed moves.

An allowed move is a move that obeys a dialogue protocol which is defined later.

Definition 12 (Complete Dialogue). *For a dialogue $[m_0, \ldots, m_{k-1}]$ between a persuader P and its opponent C on a subject ρ, if $m_{k-2} = (X, pass)$ and $m_{k-1} = (Y, pass)$, then it is said to be a complete dialogue.*

As a dialogue proceeds, formulas in each agent's knowledge base are disclosed. An agent's commitment store is a set of formulas which s/he has provided so far.

Definition 13 (Commitment Store). *For a dialogue $d_k = [m_0, \ldots, m_{k-1}]$ where each m_i $(i = 0, \ldots, k-1)$ is in the form of (X_i, T_i), X's commitment store for d_k, which is denoted by $CS_X^{d_k}$, is defined as $\emptyset$ if $k = 0$, and $\bigcup_{i=0, \ldots, k-1, X_i = X} formula(T_i)$ if $k \ne 0$.*

Definition 14 (Argumentation Framework for a Dialogue). *For a dialogue $d_k = [m_0, \ldots, m_{k-1}]$, an argumentation framework of agent X for d_k is defined as $AF(\Sigma_X \cup CS_Y^{d_k})$, which is denoted by $\mathcal{AF}_X^{d_k}$. A predicted argumentation framework of agent Y by X for d_k is defined as $AF(\Pi_Y \cup CS_X^{d_k} \cup CS_Y^{d_k})$, which is denoted by $\mathcal{PAF}_Y^{d_k}$.*

A dialogue protocol is a set of rules for each act. For example, $assertS(S, p)$ is allowed if an agent has asserted p but not asserted S as its ground, $challenge(p)$ is allowed if p has been asserted by the opponent but its support has not. An agent is basically allowed to assert a proposition contained in the extension of the current argumentation framework, and not allowed to give a repetitive assertion. *An allowed move is a move that obeys the rules.*

Definition 15 (Allowed Move). *Let X, Y be agents, and $d_k = [m_0, \ldots, m_{k-1}]$ be a dialogue. The preconditions of each act of agent X for d_k are formalized as follows. If a move m_k satisfies the precondition, then m_k is said to be* an allowed move *for d_k.*

- *$assert(p)$:*

  - *if $k = 0$ and $\exists A \in Ext(\mathcal{AF}_X^{d_k})$; $p = concl(A)$.*
  - *if $k \neq 0$ and $\neg p \in CS_Y^{d_k}$ and $\exists A \in Ext(\mathcal{AF}_X^{d_k})$; $p = concl(A)$.*

- *$assert(S, p)$:*

  - *if $k = 0$ and $\exists A \in Ext(\mathcal{AF}_X^{d_k})$; $p = concl(A), S = supp(A)$.*
  - *if $k \neq 0$ and $\neg p \in CS_Y^{d_k}$ and $(X, assert(p)) \neq m_i$ $(0 \leq i \leq k-1)$ and $\exists A \in Ext(\mathcal{AF}_X^{d_k})$; $p = concl(A), S = supp(A)$.*

- *$assertS(S, p)$: if $p \in CS_X^{d_k}, (X, assert(S, p)) \neq m_i$ $(0 \leq i \leq k-1)$ and $\exists A \in Ext(\mathcal{AF}_X^{d_k})$; $S = supp(A), p = concl(A)$.*
- *$challenge(p)$: if $p \in CS_Y^{d_k}$ and $(Y, assert(S, p)), (Y, assertS(S, p)) \neq m_i$ $(0 \leq i \leq k-1)$.*
- *$pass$: if $k \neq 0$.*

There are two additional preconditions for m_k:

- *for every act: if not both of the acts of m_{k-2} and m_{k-1} are pass.*
- *for an act other than pass: if $m_k \neq m_i$ $(0 \leq i \leq k-1)$.*

After the move $m_k = (X, T)$, the following updates are undertaken: d_{k+1} is obtained from d_k by adding (X, T) to its end, $CS_X^{d_{k+1}} = CS_X^{d_k} \cup formula(T)$ and $CS_Y^{d_{k+1}} = CS_Y^{d_k}$.

Definition 16 (Win/Lose). *For a complete dialogue d_k between a persuader P and their opponent C on a subject ρ, the dialogue is said to be* win *by P if $\rho \in Bel(\mathcal{AF}_C^{d_k})$,* strongly win *by P if $\rho \in Bel(\mathcal{AF}_P^{d_k}) \cap Bel(\mathcal{AF}_C^{d_k})$, and* lost *by P if $\neg\rho \in Bel(\mathcal{AF}_C^{d_k})$.*

Definition 17 (Dialogue Tree). *A* dialogue tree *between P and C on ρ is a finite tree of which each node corresponds to a dialogue, and constructed in the following manner.*

1. *The root node corresponds to ϵ (an empty sequence).*
2. *For a node N corresponds to dialogue $d_i = [m_0, \ldots, m_{i-1}]$,*
   (a) if the act of m_{i-2} and that of m_{i-1} are both pass, N has no child node;
   (b) otherwise, its child nodes $N_1 \ldots, N_l$ are the nodes corresponding to $[m_0, \ldots, m_{i-1}, m_{i_j}]$ $(1 \leq j \leq l)$, respectively, where $\{m_{i_1} \ldots m_{i_l}\}$ are the set of all allowed moves at N.

A dialogue tree is a finite tree of which each leaf is a complete dialogue, and in which the depth of a node corresponding to dialogue d_k is k. It surveys all possible dialogues between P and C on ρ. Therefore, different branches may include the same move whereas a single branch never includes the same move with the exception of the *pass* act.

Definition 18 (Failure Tree). *Let Tr be a subtree of a dialogue tree. If all leaves of Tr are dialogues lost by P, then Tr is said to be a failure tree.*

Definition 19 (Fatal Move). *For a dialogue tree, let N be a node from which outgoing edges are P's moves and $N_1, \ldots, N_l$ be its child nodes. If there exists N_i $(1 \le i \le l)$ that is a root node of a failure tree, and there exists N_j $(1 \le j \le l)$ that is not a root node of a failure tree, then the move from N to N_i is said to be P's fatal move at N.*

Once a fatal move is taken, there is no possibility of P's winning a dialogue whatever move s/he makes afterwards. Therefore, strategy should be constructed in such a way that makes P avoid selecting a fatal move.

3.2   Strategy

Strategy is a function of $\mathcal{AF}_X^{d_k}$, $\mathcal{PAF}_Y^{d_k}$ and a set of allowed moves that returns a move $m_k = (X, T)$.

Definition 20 (Never Lose). *Let S be an arbitrary strategy. If P does not lose in all possible dialogues between P and C on ρ taken by S, then it is said that P never loses by S.*

We propose a strategy $\mathcal{S}_{\mathcal{NF}}$. This strategy is based on the principle that an agent will not make a risky move. An agent avoids making a move that causes their opponent to believe $\neg\rho$, whereas s/he positively makes a move that causes their opponent to believe ρ. S/he gives no more information if the goal is satisfied.

Strategy $\mathcal{S}_{\mathcal{NF}}$: Let $\mathcal{AF}_P^{d_k}$ and $\mathcal{PAF}_C^{d_k}$ be an argumentation framework of P for d_k and a predicted argumentation framework of C by P for d_k, respectively. Then the move $m_k = (P, T)$ is selected by the following rules.

The following rule 1 is prior to rule 2, and rule 2 is prior to rule 3.

1. If $\rho \in Bel(\mathcal{AF}_P^{d_k}) \cap Bel(\mathcal{PAF}_C^{d_k})$ where $d_k \ne d_0$, then $(P, pass)$ is selected.
2. For all possible actions where $d_k = d_0$, if $\neg\rho \in Bel(\mathcal{PAF}_C^{d_1})$, then $m_0 = (P, assert(\rho))$ is selected.
3. The descending order of priority on taking actions is $assert(p)$, $assert(S, p)$, $assertS(S, p)$, $challenge(p)$ and $pass$, that is, $assert(p)$ has the highest priority. If T is either $assert(p)$, $assert(S, p)$ or $assertS(S, p)$, then the following rules are applied.
   (a) If $\neg\rho \in Bel(\mathcal{PAF}_C^{d_{k+1}})$, then (P, T) is not selected.
   (b) If $\rho \in Bel(\mathcal{PAF}_C^{d_{k+1}})$, then (P, T) is selected.

If multiple moves that satisfy all of the above rules exist, then one of them is selected nondeterministically.

4   Example

We show the formalization of the example of selecting a laboratory discussed in Sect. 1. Let a, g and s represent propositions that applying to Charlie's laboratory, Charlie is generous, and Charlie is strict, respectively. In this dialogue, P (Alice) tries to persuade C (Bob) to believe a (to apply to Charlie's laboratory).

Assume that the strength of the formulas are given as follows: $str(g) = str(s) = str(s \to \neg a) = 3$, $str(g \to a) = str(s \to a) = 2$ and $str(a) = str(\neg a) = 1$. We show the case in which the predicted knowledge base of C by P is equivalent to C's actual knowledge base, that is, $\Pi_C = \Sigma_C$. Assume that knowledge bases are given as follows.

$$\Sigma_P = \{g, s, g \to a, s \to a, a\} \qquad \Pi_P = \{g \to a\}$$
$$\Sigma_C = \{g \to a, s \to \neg a, \neg a\} \qquad \Pi_C = \{g \to a, s \to \neg a, \neg a\}$$

Below we show relevant arguments from given knowledge bases. The number attached to each argument is its preference. More arguments can be constructed, but here we show only related ones to simplify an explanation.

$$A_1 = (\emptyset, g)[3] \qquad\qquad A_6 = (\emptyset, a)[1]$$
$$A_2 = (\emptyset, s)[3] \qquad\qquad A_7 = (\emptyset, \neg a)[1]$$
$$A_3 = (\{s, s \to \neg a\}, \neg a)[3] \qquad A_8 = (\{g \to a, \neg a\}, \neg g)[1]$$
$$A_4 = (\{g, g \to a\}, a)[2] \qquad A_9 = (\{s \to a, \neg a\}, \neg s)[1]$$
$$A_5 = (\{s, s \to a\}, a)[2] \qquad A_{10} = (\{s \to \neg a, a\}, \neg s)[1]$$

We show three possible dialogues in Table 1.

Let $\mathcal{PAF}_C^{d_{k+1}} = \langle PAR_C^{d_{k+1}}, PAT_C^{d_{k+1}} \rangle$ be a predicted argumentation framework of C by P for d_{k+1}, that is, obtained as a result of the move m_k in a dialogue $d_{k+1} = [m_0, \ldots, m_k]$. Here, $\mathcal{PAF}_C^{d_{k+1}} = AF(\Pi_C \cup CS_P^{d_{k+1}} \cup CS_C^{d_{k+1}})$. In these dialogues, $CS_C^{d_i}$ is $\emptyset$ for any i $(0 \leq i \leq k+1)$. Important transitions $PAR_C^{d_{k+1}}$, $Ext(\mathcal{PAF}_C^{d_{k+1}})$ and $CS_P^{d_{k+1}}$ are shown in the table, and the graph representation corresponding to $\mathcal{PAF}_C^{d_{k+1}}$ in each state is shown in Fig. 1(a)~(e). In the figure, nodes represent arguments and edges represent attacks.

Initially, there is no attack, $PAR_C^{d_0} = \{A_7, A_8\}$, $Ext(\mathcal{PAF}_C^{d_0}) = \{A_7, A_8\}$, and $CS_P^{d_0} = \emptyset$ hold, represented in a graph AF1 (Fig. 1(a)). There are three allowed moves at the initial state. That is, P can give three acts: $assert(a)$, $assert(\{g, g \to a\}, a)$ or $assert(\{s, s \to a\}, a)$.

Dialogue1 shows the dialogue along the strategy $\mathcal{S}_{\mathcal{NF}}$. P first gives $assert(\{g, g \to a\}, a)$ from rules 3(a) and (b) (Fig. 1(c)). In this case, $a \in fml(A_4) \subseteq Bel(\mathcal{PAF}_C^{d_1})$. Next, C can provide only $challenge(g)$, $challenge(g \to a)$ or $pass$. The case in which $challenge(g)$ is given is shown in the table. P gives $pass$ along the strategy $\mathcal{S}_{\mathcal{NF}}$ against C's move. P continues to give $pass$ afterwards and finally wins. In case C gives $pass$ at any move, the result is the same.

If P does not have a strategy, she may make any one of three moves at the initial state. Dialogue2 and Dialogue3 are the ones P gives $assert(a)$ first (Fig. 1(b)). Next, C can provide only $challenge(a)$ except for $pass$. Next, P can

Table 1. Transitions of argumentation frameworks.

Dialogue1:

move m_k	$PAR_C^{d_k+1}$	$Ext(\mathcal{PAF}_C^{d_k+1})$	$CS_P^{d_k+1}$	graph
m_0: $(P, assert(\{g, g \to a\}, a))$	$\{A_7, A_8, A_6, A_{10},$	$\{A_1, A_4, A_6, A_{10}\},$	$\{a, g, g \to a\}$	AF3
m_1: $(C, challenge(g))$	$A_1, A_4\}$			
m_2: $(P, pass)$				
m_3: $(C, challenge(g \to a))$				
m_4: $(P, pass)$				
m_5: $(C, pass)$				

Dialogue2:

move m_k	$PAR_C^{d_k+1}$	$Ext(\mathcal{PAF}_C^{d_k+1})$	$CS_P^{d_k+1}$	graph
m_0: $(P, assert(a))$	$\{A_7, A_8, A_6, A_{10}\}$	$\emptyset$	$\{a\}$	AF2
m_1: $(C, challenge(a))$				
m_2: $(P, assertS(\{g, g \to a\}, a))$	$\{A_7, A_8, A_6, A_{10},$	$\{A_1, A_4, A_6, A_{10}\}$	$\{a, g, g \to a\}$	AF3
m_3: $(C, challenge(g))$	$A_1, A_4\}$			
m_4: $(P, pass)$				
m_5: $(C, challenge(g \to a))$				
m_6: $(P, pass)$				
m_7: $(C, pass)$				

Dialogue3:

move m_k	$PAR_C^{d_k+1}$	$Ext(\mathcal{PAF}_C^{d_k+1})$	$CS_P^{d_k+1}$	graph
m_0: $(P, assert(a))$	$\{A_7, A_8, A_6, A_{10}\}$	$\emptyset$	$\{a\}$	AF2
m_1: $(C, challenge(a))$				
m_2: $(P, assertS(\{s, s \to a\}, a))$	$\{A_7, A_8, A_6, A_{10},$	$\{A_2, A_3$	$\{a, s, s \to a\}$	AF4
m_3: $(C, challenge(s))$	$A_2, A_5, A_3, A_9\}$	$A_7, A_8\}$		
m_4: $(P, assertS(\{g, y \to a\}, a))$	$\{A_7, A_8, A_6, A_{10},$	$\{A_1, A_2$	$\{a, g, s,$	AF5
	A_2, A_5, A_3, A_9	$A_3, A_7\}$	$g \to a, s \to a\}$	
	$A_1, A_4\}$			

give either of $(assertS(\{g, g \to a\}, a)$ or $assertS(\{s, s \to a\}, a)$. If P gives the former one (Fig. 1(c)), $a \in fml(A_4) \subseteq Bel(\mathcal{PAF}_C^{d_3})$ holds. Dialogue2 shows this case. After that, if P gives $pass$, she finally wins. On the other hand, if P gives the latter one (Fig. 1(d)), $\neg a \in fml(A_3) \subseteq Bel(\mathcal{PAF}_C^{d_3})$ holds. Dialogue3 shows this case. Even if P gives $assertS(\{g, g \to a\}, a)$ afterwards (Fig. 1(e)), $\neg a \in fml(A_3) \subseteq Bel(\mathcal{PAF}_C^{d_5})$ holds, and P loses. In case C gives $pass$ at any move, the result is the same.

In this example, $assertS(a, \{s, s \to a\})$ is a fatal move.

5   Results

In this section, we discuss some properties of our model and what formulas should be included in a predicted knowledge base. All proofs are shown in the Appendix.

Note that hereafter N_i denotes a node in the depth i in a dialogue tree.

(a) AF1: initial state

(b) AF2: after $(P, assert(a))$ in Dialogue2 and Dialogue3

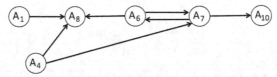

(c) AF3: after $(P, assert(\{g, g \to a\}, a))$ in Dialogue1,
after $(P, assertS(\{g, g \to a\}, a))$ in Dialogue2

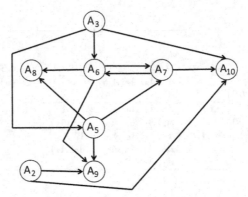

(d) AF4: after $(P, assertS(\{s, s \to a\}, a))$ in Dialogue3

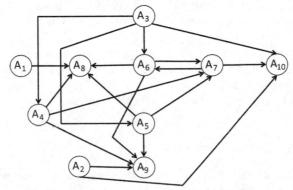

(e) AF5: after $(P, assertS(\{g, g \to a\}, a))$ in Dialogue3

Fig. 1. Predicted argumentation frameworks of C by P.

Lemma 1. *For a failure tree of which the root is N_i corresponding to a dialogue d_i, $\neg\rho \in Bel(\mathcal{AF}_C^{d_i})$ holds.*

Here, we introduce the concept of *changing move (c-move)*. It represents the turning point of the move from the state in which C does not accept $\neg\rho$, to the state in which C accepts $\neg\rho$.

Definition 21 (c-move). *For a dialogue $d_{k+1} = [m_0, \ldots, m_k]$, if $\neg\rho \notin Bel(\mathcal{AF}_C^{d_k})$ and $\neg\rho \in Bel(\mathcal{AF}_C^{d_{k+1}})$, then m_k is said to be* changing move, c-move *in short.*

The following theorem and its corollary show a condition for a non-failing dialogue.

Theorem 1. *If $\Pi_C = \Sigma_C$, then P does not give a c-move at N_k for any k $(1 \leq k)$ by the strategy $S_{\mathcal{NF}}$.*

Corollary 1. *If $\Pi_C = \Sigma_C$ and $\neg\rho \notin Bel(\mathcal{AF}_C^{d_k})$, then P can avoid a fatal move at N_k for any k $(1 \leq k)$ by the strategy $S_{\mathcal{NF}}$.*

When the predicted knowledge base is equivalent to the real knowledge base, if there exists such an initial move that P predicts that C will not believe $\neg\rho$ next, then P never loses. It means that there is a case in which we can judge that P never loses under the strategy $S_{\mathcal{NF}}$ simply from given knowledge bases.

Next, we consider the case in which the predicted knowledge base is a subset of the real knowledge base.

We show the condition in which P's strongly win can be judged only from an initially given C's real knowledge base. The following theorem shows that when the prediction is a subset of the real knowledge base, if there are no arguments which have $\neg\rho$ as its conclusion in C's initial argumentation framework, then X strongly wins by the strategy $S_{\mathcal{NF}}$.

Theorem 2. *Let $AF(\Sigma_C)$ be $\mathcal{AF}_C^{d_0} = \langle AR_C^{d_0}, AT_C^{d_0} \rangle$. If $\Pi_C \subseteq \Sigma_C$ and $\{A \mid A \in AR_C^{d_0} \wedge concl(A) = \neg\rho\} = \emptyset$, then $\rho \in Bel(\mathcal{AF}_P^{d_k}) \cap Bel(\mathcal{AF}_C^{d_k})$ holds for a complete dialogue d_k by the strategy $S_{\mathcal{NF}}$.*

Next, we discuss what formulas should be included in a predicted knowledge base Π_C.

The following theorem shows that it is insufficient to decide the condition for Π_C in order not to fail in P's persuasion simply from given knowledge bases, rather all dialogues must be surveyed.

Theorem 3. *Let S be the set of formulas in NBA-arguments of $AF(\Sigma_P \cup \Sigma_C)$, If $\Pi_C = S \cap \Sigma_C$, then P cannot always avoid the fatal move by the strategy $S_{\mathcal{NF}}$.*

We show a condition for Π_C using the concept of *NBA-only move*.

For a dialogue d_k, let $\mathcal{AF}_X^{d_k} = \langle AR_X^{d_k}, AT_X^{d_k} \rangle$ and $\mathcal{PAF}_X^{d_k} = \langle PAR_X^{d_k}, PAT_X^{d_k} \rangle$. Then $PAR_X^{d_k} \subseteq AR_X^{d_k}$ holds.

Definition 22 (NBA-Only Move). *Assume that* $\Pi_Y \subseteq \Sigma_Y$. *Let* m_k *be* X's *move,* $\mathcal{AF}_Y^{d_{k+1}} = \langle AR_Y^{d_{k+1}}, AT_Y^{d_{k+1}} \rangle$ *and* $\mathcal{PAF}_Y^{d_{k+1}} = \langle PAR_Y^{d_{k+1}}, PAT_Y^{d_{k+1}} \rangle$. *If there does not exist* $A \in AR_Y^{d_{k+1}} - PAR_Y^{d_{k+1}}$ *such that* $\exists C \in AR_Y^{d_{k+1}}; (C, A) \in AT_Y^{d_{k+1}}$ *holds, then the* m_k *is said to be* X's *NBA-only move.*

An intuitive meaning of an NBA-only move is as follows: when we compare Y's argumentation framework and the predicted argumentation framework of Y by X, let S be a set of arguments that are included in the former but not in the latter; there is no argument in S that is attacked by some argument in the former.

For a complete dialogue $d_k = [m_0, \ldots, m_{k-1}]$ between P and C on ρ, let m_i $(0 \leq i \leq k - 1)$ be a c-move, and SA_{d_k} be the set formulas in NBA-arguments in $\mathcal{AF}_C^{d_i+1}$. Let $SA = \bigcup_{d_k} SA_{d_k}$. It is clear that $SA \subseteq \Sigma_P \cup \Sigma_C$. Therefore, SA is divided into two disjoint subsets $SA_{P \setminus C}$ and SA_C, where $SA_{P \setminus C}$ is a set of formulas included in $\Sigma_P \setminus \Sigma_C$ and SA_C is a set of formulas included in Σ_C.

Theorem 4. *If* $\Pi_C = SA_C$ *and all* c-moves in a dialogue tree are P's NBA-only moves, then P does not give a c-move at N_k for any k $(1 \leq k)$ by the strategy $\mathcal{S}_{\mathcal{NF}}$.*

Corollary 2. *If* $\Pi_C = SA_C$, *all* c-moves in a dialogue tree are NBA-only and $\neg \rho \notin Ext(\mathcal{AF}_C^{d_k})$, then P can avoid a fatal move at N_k for any k $(1 \leq k)$ by the strategy $\mathcal{S}_{\mathcal{NF}}$.*

6   Discussion

There have been many studies on Dung's abstract argumentation framework [12]. Among them, a dialogue model using argumentation based on this framework has been proposed.

Our model is based on the one studied by Amgoud et al. The model is set out and applied to several types of dialogues [2]. The strategy is defined and the dialogue according to the strategy is shown [3]. There, the strategy is based on the level of acceptance, strength of the argument and attitude of the agents. The various relationships between sets of knowledge, including that between the joint knowledge of agents and the outcomes of dialogues, are investigated [10]. The most significant difference between our work and theirs is the use of the predicted knowledge base. We construct a strategy using the predicted knowledge base, whereas their strategy is constructed without considering the opponent's inner state. Moreover, we have given an explicit definition to the argumentation framework for the current state of a dialogue, whereas formalization of the current argumentation framework is ambiguous in their works.

It is essential to consider an opponent's beliefs, especially in handling a strategic dialogue, which may include a lie. Several works have been undertaken regarding on this issue. Thimm et al. studied a strategy that reflects an opponent's belief [16] but they did not relate belief to an extension of an argumentation framework. Rienstra et al. showed a strategy of selecting the best move from multiple opponent models with probability [14], and Hadjinikolis et al. showed an approach of augmenting opponent models from accumulated dialogues with an agent's likelihood [7]. They evaluated their approaches experimentally, whereas we focus on giving a strategy and investigate its validity theoretically. Black et al. formally investigated usage and maintenance of opponent models illustrating a simple persuasion dialogue with different types of persuaders [5]. However, the order of utterances is out of their focus. Sakama presented the treatment of untrusted argumentation [15]. Rahwan et al. discussed hiding and lying in argumentation [13]. In these works, abstract argumentation frameworks are used, that is, arguments are not constructed from logical deduction from knowledge base, whereas a structured framework is used in our model.

ASPIC+ is a structured argumentation framework that generates arguments from a knowledge base using logical entailment [11]. However, only static argumentation can be handled in that framework and dynamically changing structures are not available. Okuno and Takahashi proposed a dynamic structured argumentation [9]. In their proposed method, each agent's argument is generated from their own knowledge base and commitment store, and the argumentation structure dynamically changes. Their model did not operate at the dialogue level, whereas we propose here a dialogue model based on an argumentation framework that changes at every move.

7   Conclusion

We have proposed a dialogue model that utilizes a predicted knowledge base and a strategy of withholding moves predicted to fail and only providing moves that avoid failure to persuade. We have investigated the conditions under which a persuasive dialogue never fails using this strategy, when the predicted knowledge base is equivalent to the actual knowledge base of an opponent. The introduction of prediction provides a model that better simulates real dialogue.

Moreover, we have discussed what a predicted knowledge base should include for a persuasive dialogue not to fail. Our main contribution is to set out the formalization of a dialogue using prediction and to propose a strategy for non-failing persuasion.

There are several issues that should be addressed in future work. The conditions presented herein for non-failing persuasion are relatively loose and inefficient and, therefore, more rigorous and efficient conditions should be explored. The next step is to determine conditions for successful persuasion rather than for non-failing persuasion. In addition, we will investigate a case in which a predicted knowledge base is not a subset of an actual one.

Because it is necessary to have an opponent's predicted knowledge base to construct a lie or to reveal it, our final goal is to develop a strategy to handle dialogue that includes a lie, and to investigate conditions of a predicted knowledge base that support the validity of the strategy.

Appendix

We show the sketch of the proofs because of the space limit.

Proof for Lemma 1. For any dialogue $d_i = [m_0, \ldots, m_{i-1}]$, if P can proceed with the dialogue just by giving *pass* as acts of $m_i, \ldots, m_k$, then P does not add any information to C. Therefore, a complete dialogue $[m_0, \ldots, m_{i-1}, m_i, \ldots, m_k]$ exists that satisfies $Bel(\mathcal{AF}_C^{d_{k+1}}) = Bel(\mathcal{AF}_C^{d_i})$. Thus, such a leaf node N_{k+1} exists that satisfies $Bel(\mathcal{AF}_C^{d_{k+1}}) = Bel(\mathcal{AF}_C^{d_i})$ in a subtree of which the root node is N_i. As N_i is the root node of a failure tree, $\neg\rho \in Bel(\mathcal{AF}_C^{d_{k+1}})$ holds. Therefore, $\neg\rho \in Bel(\mathcal{AF}_C^{d_i})$ holds. □

Proof for Theorem 1. For any dialogue d_k, an agent must not give a move at N_k if $\neg\rho \in Bel(\mathcal{PAF}_C^{d_{k+1}})$ holds by rule 3(a) of the strategy $\mathcal{S}_{\mathcal{NF}}$. It follows that $\neg\rho \notin Bel(\mathcal{AF}_C^{d_{k+1}})$ holds, since $\Pi_C = \Sigma_C$. It means that a move other than *c-move* should have been selected by the strategy $\mathcal{S}_{\mathcal{NF}}$. □

Proof for Corollary 1. If a fatal move is selected at N_k, there exists a failure tree of which the root is N_{k+1}. From Lemma 1, $\neg\rho \in Bel(\mathcal{AF}_Y^{d_{k+1}})$ holds. It means that this move is a *c-move*. It is a contradiction from Theorem 1. Therefore, an agent can avoid the fatal move by the strategy $\mathcal{S}_{\mathcal{NF}}$. □

Proof for Theorem 2. In this case, according to the strategy $\mathcal{S}_{\mathcal{NF}}$, agent P first gives $assert(\rho)$, and repeats *pass* against any move given by C afterwards. C cannot attack ρ since s/he cannot construct an argument of which a conclusion is $\neg\rho$. In this case, $\rho \in Bel(AF(\Sigma_C \cup \{\rho\})) = Bel(\mathcal{AF}_C^{d_k})$. □

Proof for Theorem 3. We show an example. Assume that the strength of each formula is given as follows: $str(a) = str(a \to \rho) = 5$, $str(b) = str(c) = str(b \to \neg\rho) = 4$, $str(b \to \rho) = str(c \to \rho) = 3$, $str(\neg\rho) = 2$ and $str(\rho) = 1$. Assume that knowledge bases are given as follows: $\Sigma_P = \{\rho, b, b \to \rho, c, c \to \rho, a\}$, $\Sigma_C = \{\neg\rho, b \to \neg\rho, a \to \rho\}$. Then, Π_C is defined as $\{a \to \rho\}$.

In this case, a dialogue in which P behaves according to the strategy $\mathcal{S}_{\mathcal{NF}}$ proceeds as follows. P gives $assert(\rho)$ as an initial move m_0. Then, C can give either $assert(\neg\rho)$, $challenge(\rho)$ or *pass*. Assume that C gives $assert(\neg\rho)$ as m_1. Then P can gives either $m_2 = assertS(\{b, b \to \rho\}, \rho)$ or $m_2' = assertS(\{c, c \to \rho\}, \rho)$. Let d_3 and d_3' dialogues $[m_0, m_1, m_2]$ and $[m_0, m_1, m_2']$, respectively. If P gives m_2, it causes C to make a new argument $(\{b, b \to \neg\rho\}, \neg\rho)$, which is an NBA-argument in $\mathcal{AF}_C^{d_3}$. Therefore, C believes $\neg\rho$ at the state. Since this argument is not attacked other than by $(\{a, a \to \rho\}, \rho)$ which never appears in any dialogue, $\neg\rho \in Bel(\mathcal{AF}_C^{d_k})$ holds for $d_k = [m_0, m_1, m_2, \ldots, m_{k-1}]$. On the other hand, if P gives m_2', it causes C to make a new argument $(\{c, c \to \rho\}, \rho)$, which attacks an argument $(\emptyset, \neg\rho)$ in $\mathcal{AF}_C^{d_3'}$. Therefore, C believes ρ at that state. Thus, m_2 is a fatal move. However, the strategy $\mathcal{S}_{\mathcal{NF}}$ cannot determine which is the best move between m_2 or m_2'. We should have $b \to \neg\rho$ in Π_C, instead of $a \to \rho$. □

Proof for Theorem 4. If $AR_C^{d_{k+1}} - PAR_C^{d_{k+1}} = \emptyset$, then *c-move* is never selected at N_k by the strategy $\mathcal{S}_{\mathcal{NF}}$, by the same reason with that of Theorem 1.

Therefore, there should exist an argument $A \in AR_C^{d_k+1} - PAR_C^{d_k+1}$. Assume that P gives a c-move at N_k.

Since A is an NBA-argument in $\mathcal{AF}_C^{d_k+1}$ from the assumption that all c-moves in a dialogue tree are P's NBA-only moves, $fml(A) \subseteq SA_C \cup SA_{P \setminus C}$. On the other hand, $fml(A) \cap SA_C \subseteq SA_C = \Pi_C$ and $fml(A) \cap SA_{P \setminus C} \subseteq CS_P^{d_k+1}$. Therefore, $fml(A) \subseteq \Pi_C \cup CS_P^{d_k+1}$. On the other hand, $\Pi_C \cup CS_P^{d_k+1} \subseteq \Pi_C \cup CS_P^{d_k+1} \cup CS_C^{d_k+1} = Fml(PAR_C^{d_k+1})$. It follows that $A \in PAR_C^{d_k+1}$, which is a contradiction.

Therefore, P never gives a c-move at N_k. $\qquad\qquad\qquad\qquad\qquad\qquad$ □

Proof for Corollary 2. It is proved from Theorem 4 using similar logic to the proof of Corollary 1. $\qquad\qquad\qquad\qquad\qquad\qquad\qquad\qquad\qquad\qquad\qquad\qquad\qquad\qquad$ □

References

1. Amgoud, L., Cayrol, C.: On the acceptability of arguments in preference-based argumentation. In: UAI 1998, pp. 1–7 (1998)
2. Amgoud, L., Maudet, N., Parsons, S.: Modeling dialogues using argumentation. In: ICMAS 2000, pp. 31–38 (2000)
3. Amgoud, L., Maudet, N.: Strategical considerations for argumentative agents (preliminary report). In: NMR 2002, pp. 399–407 (2002)
4. Bench-Capon, T.: Persuasion in practice argument using value-based argumentation frameworks. J. Logic Comput. **13**(3), 429–448 (2003)
5. Black, E., Hunter, A.: Reasons and options for updating an opponent model in persuasion dialogues. In: TAFA 2015 (2015)
6. Dung, P.M.: On the acceptability of arguments and its fundamental role in non-monotonic reasoning, logic programming and n-person games. Artif. Intell. **77**, 321–357 (1995)
7. Hadjinikolis, C., Siantos, C., Modgil, S., Black, E., McBurney, P.: Opponent modelling in persuasion dialogues. In: IJCAI 2013, pp. 164–170 (2013)
8. Modgil, S.: Reasoning about preferences in argumentation frameworks. Artif. Intell. **173**(9–10), 901–934 (2009)
9. Okuno, K., Takahashi, K.: Argumentation system with changes of an agent's knowledge base. In: IJCAI 2009, pp. 226–232 (2009)
10. Parsons, S., Wooldridge, M., Amgoud, L.: On the outcomes of formal inter-agent dialogues. In: AAMAS 2003, pp. 616–623 (2003)
11. Prakken, H.: An abstract framework for argumentation with structured arguments. Argum. Comput. **1**(2), 93–124 (2010)
12. Rahwan, I., Simari, G. (eds.): Argumentation in Artificial Intelligence. Springer, Heidelberg (2009)
13. Rahwan, I., Lason, K., Tohmé, F.: A characterization of strategy-proofness for grounded argumentation semantics. In: IJCAI 2009, pp. 251–256 (2009)
14. Rienstra, T., Thimm, M., Oren, N.: Opponent models with uncertainty for strategic argumentation. In: IJCAI 2013, pp. 332–338 (2013)
15. Sakama, C.: Dishonest arguments in debate games. In: COMMA 2012, pp. 177–184 (2012)
16. Thimm, M., García, A.J.: On strategic argument selection in structured argumentation systems. In: McBurney, P., Rahwan, I., Parsons, S. (eds.) ArgMAS 2010. LNCS, vol. 6614, pp. 286–305. Springer, Heidelberg (2011)

Argumentation-Based Hybrid Recommender System for Recommending Learning Objects

Paula Rodríguez[1]([⊠]), Stella Heras[2], Javier Palanca[2],
Néstor Duque[1], and Vicente Julián[2]

[1] Universidad Nacional de Colombia, Bogotá, Colombia
{parodriguezma,ndduqueme}@unal.edu.co
[2] Universitat Politècnica de València, Valencia, Spain
{sheras,jpalanca,vinglada}@dsic.upv.es

Abstract. Recommender Systems aim to provide users with search results close to their needs, making predictions of their preferences. In virtual learning environments, Educational Recommender Systems deliver learning objects according to the student's characteristics, preferences and learning needs. A learning object is an educational content unit, which once found and retrieved may assist students in their learning process. In previous work, authors have designed and evaluated several recommendation techniques for delivering the most appropriate learning object for each specific student. Also, they have combined these techniques by using hybridization methods, improving the performance of isolated techniques. However, traditional hybidization methods fail when the learning objects delivered by each recommendation technique are very different from those selected by the other techniques (there is no agreement about the best learning object to recommend). In this paper, we present a hybrid recommendation method based on argumentation theory that combines content-based, collaborative and knowledge-based recommendation techniques and provides the students with those objects for which the system is able to generate more arguments to justify their suitability. This method has been tested by using a database with real data about students and learning objects, getting promising results.

1 Motivation

According to the IEEE, a learning object (LO) can be defined as a digital entity involving educational design characteristics. Each LO can be used, reused or referenced during computer-supported learning processes, aiming at generating knowledge and competences based on student's needs [1]. LOs have functional requirements such as accessibility, reuse, and interoperability. The concept of LO requires understanding of how people learn, since this issue directly affects the LO design in each of its three dimensions: pedagogical, didactic, and technological [2]. In addition, LOs have metadata that describe and identify the educational resources involved and facilitate their searching and retrieval. Learning Objects Repositories (LORs), composed of thousands of LOs, can be defined

© Springer International Publishing Switzerland 2016
M. Rovatsos et al. (Eds.): EUMAS 2015/AT 2015, LNAI 9571, pp. 234–248, 2016.
DOI: 10.1007/978-3-319-33509-4_19

as specialized digital libraries storing several types of heterogeneous resources. LORs are currently being used in various e-learning environments and belong mainly to educational institutions [2,3]. Also, federations of LORs provide educational applications to search, retrieve and access specific LO contents available in any LOR [4].

Recommender Systems aim to provide users with search results close to their needs, making predictions of their preferences [5]. In virtual learning environments, Educational Recommender Systems (ERS) deliver LOs according to the student's characteristics, preferences and learning needs. In order to improve recommendations, ERS must perform feedback processes and implement mechanisms that enable them to obtain a large amount of information about users and how they use the LOs. ERS can be classified into several types [6]:

- Content-based ERS: in this kind of systems, recommendations are performed based on the user's profile and created from the content analysis of the LOs that the user has already assessed in the past. The content-based systems use "item-by-item" algorithms generated through the association of correlation rules among those items.
- Collaborative ERS: these systems hold great promise for education, not only for their purposes of helping learners and educators to find useful educational resources, but also as a means of bringing together people with similar interests and beliefs, and possibly as an aid to the learning process itself. In this case, the recommendations are based on a similarity degree among users. Collaborative filtering algorithms aim at suggesting new items or predicting the utility of a certain item for a particular user profile based on the choices of other similar user profiles.
- Knowledge-based ERS: these systems attempt to suggest LOs based on inferences about the user's needs and preferences. Knowledge-based approaches use knowledge about how a particular item meets a particular user need, and can therefore reason about the relationship between a need and a possible recommendation. In addition, these systems are based on the user's browsing history and his/her previously selected LOs.
- Hybrid Recommender Systems: the hybrid approach combines several ERS techniques in order to maximize the advantages of each one and, thus, make better recommendations. To make the hybridization of recommendation techniques –using at least two of them– Burke [6] describes different methods that could be applied (e.g. weighted, switching, mixed, cascade, feature combination, feature augmentation, and meta-level).

In previous work, authors have proposed a Student-Centered Hybrid ERS, designing and evaluating several recommendation techniques for delivering the most appropriate LO for each specific student [7,8]. Also, they have combined these techniques by using hybridization methods, improving the performance of isolated techniques. The ERS proposed follows a hybrid recommendation technique that combines content-based, collaborative and knowledge-based approaches. In the system, LOs are retrieved from LORs and federations of LORs, using the stored descriptive *metadata* for these objects. Concretely, our

ERS follows the *IEEE-LOM*[1] standard to represent the metadata about the LOs. This is a hierarchical data model that defines around 50 metadata fields clustered into 9 categories. Figure 1 shows the fields used in our ERS (highlighted in green). Also, *student profiles*, including their personal information, language, topic and LO's format preferences, educational level, and learning style (aural, kinesthetic, reader, or visual), are used by the system to generate recommendations.

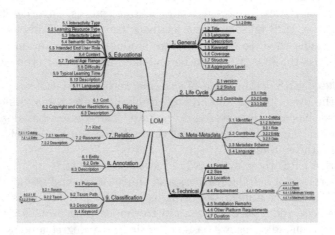

Fig. 1. IEEE-LOM metadata used in the ERS.

Therefore, as shown in Fig. 2, the ERS is composed by six modules: three recommendation modules (one for each recommendation technique); a module that performs the hybridization (integration) process, which follows a cascade method to provide recommendations results in strict priority[2]; and, finally, two modules that handle information about student profiles and LOs metadata.

The content-based recommendation module generates its recommendations by applying inference rules among LOs metadata and the student's learning style. The collaborative recommendation module seeks similar user profiles to deliver items that have been assessed by students with similar profiles. The knowledge-based recommendation module searches some LOs similar to those that the student has previously assessed. Then, the integration module performs the hybridization process to provide the student with the most relevant and appropriate LOs. This is done by selecting LOs that have been proposed by 2 or 3 of the recommendation modules. Figure 3 shows the specific LOs metadata and students' profile data that each recommendation modules uses.

---

[1] 1484.12.1-2002 - Institute of Electrical and Electronics Engineers (IEEE) Standard for Learning Object Metadata: https://standards.ieee.org/findstds/standard/1484.12.1-2002.html.

[2] Several hybridization methods, as proposed in [6], were tested, and the cascade approach achieved the best recommendation results [8].

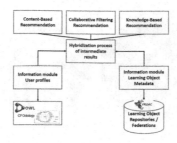

Fig. 2. Student-Centered Hybrid ERS.

Fig. 3. LOs metadata and students' profile data used by the recommendation modules.

However, this hybidization method has several disadvantages. On the one hand, it does not take the relevance of the LOs into account to encourage the use of a specific LO over another (considering that a LO is relevant for a student if it matches his/her learning objectives and profile). On the other hand, it fails when the LOs delivered by each recommendation technique are very different from those selected by the other techniques (there is no agreement about the best LO to recommend). To analyze the incidence of this problem, we performed some experiments to determine the dispersion degree between the LOs proposed by each recommendation technique (to determine how different are the top 5 or the top 10 LOs proposed by the three recommendation modules). Dispersion tests were performed as follows:

1. A student with a visual learning style was selected.
2. A search on the federation of repositories was performed to retrieve LOs about the topic (keyword) *Algorithms*.
3. The top 5 and top 10 results provided by each recommendation module (content, collaborative and knowledge-based) were saved for analysis.
4. The process was repeated with other keywords (*Programming* and *Audit*).
5. The process was repeated with other students with auditory and kinesthetic learning styles.

Finally, the amount of LOs that overlap between the three recommenders for each iteration of the tests was computed. The average of the results are shown in Fig. 4.

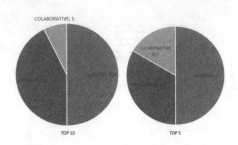

Fig. 4. Results of the dispersion tests.

Results show that, in many cases, the traditional hybridization method cannot deliver any recommendation, since there is no intersection between the recommendations provided by the three recommendation modules. For instance, knowledge-based recommendations (coloured in red) on the Top 5 tests, result in an average dispersion of 0.8 LOs. This means that for each 5 LOs delivered by this recommendation module, on average, only 0.8 overlap with the results of the other techniques (there is no agreement among them).

To overcome this problem, in this paper we present a new hybrid recommendation method based on argumentation theory. Among the wide range of agreement technologies proposed in the last years [9], argumentation provides a natural means of dealing with conflicts and knowledge inconsistencies with a high resemblance with the way in which humans reach agreements. Our method combines content-based, collaborative and knowledge-based recommendation techniques, and provides students with those LOs for which the system is able to generate more arguments to justify their suitability.

The rest of the paper is structured as follows: Sect. 2 reviews related work, Sect. 3 presents our argumentation-based hybrid recommendation method, in Sect. 4 we provide a validation proof for our proposal, and finally, Sect. 5 presents conclusions and future work.

2   Related Work

Over the last years, the literature on ERS reports a growing interest in the area. In [5, Chapter 12], discuss the need of support tools for learners based on contextualised recommender systems. According to the authors, it is very important to take into account pedagogical aspects, like prior knowledge, learning goals or study time in the recommendation process. In addition, they argue that the development of concrete evaluation frameworks that follow a layered approach is still an open reseach issue. These frameworks may focus on incorporating as many evaluation dimensions as possible, on addressing pedagogical dimensions, or on combining a variety of evaluation methods, metrics, and instruments.

In this regard, in [10] a recommendation system based on genetic algorithms that performs two recommendation processes was proposed. The first one uses explicit characteristics represented in a matrix of student's preferences, while the second assigns implicit weights to educational resources that are considered as chromosomes in a genetic algorithm that optimises them by using historical values. However, compared with out proposal, this work does not perform hybrid recommendation, but combines the characteristics of the student profile. Following a hybrid approach similar to ours, Zapata et al. deliver educational materials adapted to the user profile by combining several types of filtering methods with the available information about LOs and users [11]. However, although this work combines several filtering criteria (content-based, collaborative activity, and demographics), it is aimed at helping teachers rather than students. By contrast, the research presented by Sikka et al. [3], whichs presents an e-learning environment to recommend learning materials by using web mining techniques and software agents, implements just a unique collaborative recommendation filter rather than using a hybrid approach. However, in [12] a review of some hybrid recommendation systems was performed, concluding that the hybrid filter obtained by integrating collaborative and content-based filtering approaches improves the predictions made by the recommender. We share this view and extend it to recommend educational materials recovered from LORs.

Traditional recommender systems base their recommendations on quantitative measures of similarity, but fail at using the qualitative data available to empower recommendations [13]. Usually, recommender systems do not provide an explanation about the reasoning process that has been followed to come up with specific recommendations. However, people rely more on recommendations when the system can also show the reasons behind the recommendations [14], and when they can understand the reasons why these recommendations are presented [15]. Moreover, even when users already know the recommendations presented, the latter work demonstrated that they prefer recommender systems that are able to justify their suggestions. Thus, what is understood as a good recommendation is changing from the one that minimises some error evaluation to the one that is really able to *persuade* people and make them happier.

Recently, some argument-based recommender systems and recommendation techniques have been proposed to recommend music [16], news [17], movies [18], or restaurants [19], to perform content-based web search [20] or to formalize and structure user opinions in online recommender systems [21]. Among them, we share the approach of the movie recommender system based on defeasible logic programming proposed in [22]. In this work, authors define a preset preference criteria between rules to resolve argument attacks. However, as will be explained in Sect. 3, we use a probabilistic method to compute the likelihood that an argument prevails over another, which makes the system more adaptive. In educational domains, argumentation theory and tools have a large history of successful applications, specially to teach critical thinking skills in law courses [23]. However, to the best of our knowledge, the application of argumentation theory to enhance ERS is a new area of research.

There are a number of open challenges for the application of argumentation theory to recommender systems [20], such as *exposing underlying assumptions behind recommendations, approaching trust and trustworthiness* from the perspective of backing recommendations and *providing rationally compelling arguments for recommendations*. Our work involves a contribution in this latter area.

3 Formal Framework

In this section, we provide an overview on the argumentation formalism used for our proposal. As pointed out in Sect. 1, the original Student-Centered Hybrid ERS proposed uses several sources of knowledge to generate LOs recommendations for the students, namely information about the *student profile* and *metadata* about the LOs to recommend. In this paper, we present a hybrid recommendation method based on argumentation theory that uses these sources of knowledge and provides the students with those LOs for which the system is able to generate more arguments to justify their suitability. Concretely, we use a defeasible argumentation formalism based on logic programming (*DeLP*, see [24] for details) to encode information about the *facts* (metadata and profiles data) and the *rules* that determine the allowed inferences that can be done in our system.

Definition 1 (DeLP). *A defeasible logic program (DeLP) $P = (\Pi, \Delta)$, models strict (Π) and defeasible (Δ) knowledge about the application domain. In our system, the set Π includes strict inference rules with empty body that represent facts. Correspondingly, the set Δ includes defeasible rules of the form $P \leftarrow Q_1, ..., Q_k$, which represent the defeasible inference that literals $Q_1, ..., Q_k$ may provide reasons to believe P.*

For instance, $auditory(jose)$ represent the fact that a student named *'jose'* has an auditory learning style and prefers materials with sounds, and auditory formats such as mp3, mp4, or avi. Facts are assumed to be non-contradictory (e.g., if $\sim$ represents default logic negation, $auditory(jose)$ and $\sim auditory(jose)$ cannot be inferred). Also, we show below the main defeasible rules of our argumentative framework[3]. These rules are divided on 4 groups, 3 to represent the knowledge used by each recommendation technique (content-based, collaborative or knowledge-based), and 1 to represent general domain knowledge. Section 4 provides an example to clarify their meaning and use.

General Rules
G1: $\sim recommend(user, LO) \leftarrow cost(LO) > 0$
G2: $\sim recommend(user, LO) \leftarrow quality\_metric(LO) < 0.7$

Content-Based Rules
C1: $recommend(user, LO) \leftarrow$
$educationally\_appropriate(user, LO) \wedge generally\_appropriate (LO)$

C1.1: $educationally\_appropriate(user, LO) \leftarrow$
$appropriate\_resource(user, LO) \wedge appropriate\_interactivity(user, LO)$

C1.1.1: $appropriate\_resource(user, LO) \leftarrow user\_type(user, type) \wedge resource\_type(LO, type)$

---

[3] The complete rule set is not provided due to space limitations.

C1.1.2: appropriate_interactivity (user, LO) ← user_type(user, type) ∧ interactivity_type(LO, type)

C1.2: generally_appropriate(LO) ← structure(OA, atomic) ∧ state(LO, final)

C2: recommend(user, LO) ←

educationally_appropriate(user, LO) ∧ generally_appropriate(LO)) ∧ technically_appropriate(user, LO)

C2.1: technically_appropriate(user, LO) ← appropriate_language(user, LO) ∧ appropriate_format(LO)

C2.1.1: appropriate_language(user, LO) ← language_preference(user, language) ∧ object_language(LO, language)

C2.1.2: appropriate_format(LO) ← format_preference(user, format) ∧ object_format(LO, format)

C3: recommend(user, LO) ← educationally_appropriate(user, LO) ∧ generally_appropriate (LO) ∧ updated(OA)

C3.1: updated(LO) ← date(LO, date) < 5 years

C4: recommend(user, LO) ← educationally_appropriate(user, LO) ∧ generally_appropriate(LO) ∧ learning_time_appropriate(LO)

C4.1: learning_time_appropriate(LO) ← hours(LO) < γ

Collaborative Rules
O1: recommend(user1, LO) ← similarity(user1, user2) > α ∧ vote(user2, LO) ≥ 4

Knowledge-Based Rules
K1: recommend(user1, LO) ← similarity(LO1, LO2) > β ∧ vote(user1, LO2) ≥ 4
    Given a DeLP, the program can be queried to resolve if a ground literal can be derived from the program, and hence supported by an argument(s) based on the rules of Δ. Concretely, for our hybrid recommendation method to recommend a LO to a specific user, we need to be able to derive any of the *recommend(user, LO)* defeasible rules from our DeLP.
    Arguments in this framework are defined as follows:

Definition 2 (Argument). *An argument $\mathcal{A}$ for h (represented as a pair $\langle \mathcal{A}, h \rangle$) is a minimal non-contradictory set of facts and defeasible rules that can be chained to derive the literal (or conclusion) h.*

    Then, arguments are generetad by backward chaining of both facts and defeasible rules, a mechanism similar to the *Selective Linear Definite (SLD)* derivation of standard logic programming. Therefore, recommendations are computed by chaining arguments in a recursive process that creates a *dialectical tree* (see [24]) whose root node is the original argument under discussion (i.e. whether to recommend or not a LO for a particular user), and whose children nodes are arguments that defeat their parents.

Arguments can be *attacked* by other arguments that *rebut* them (i.e. propose the opposite conclusion) or *undercut* them (i.e. attack clauses of their body).

Definition 3 (Attack). *An argument $\langle \mathcal{B}, q \rangle$ attacks another argument $\langle \mathcal{A}, h \rangle$ if we can derive $\sim h$ from $\mathcal{B}$ or if q implies that one of the clauses of $\mathcal{A}$ no longer holds (there are a sub-argument $\langle \mathcal{A}_1, h_1 \rangle$ from $\langle \mathcal{A}, h \rangle$ such that $\Pi \cup \{h_1, q\}$ is contradictory).*

Therefore, an argument for not recommending a LO can be generated if an argument for recommending is attacked. Note that we assume negation as failure, so an argument for not recommending a LO can be generated by chaining rules whose literals cannot be derived (we do not have information to resolve them). For instance, by using the rule *O1*, which recommends a LO for a *user1* if other similar *user2* likes that object (i.e. *user2* has voted the LO with a score greater than 4), we can derive an argument for not recommending the LO: 1) if the system cannot find a similar user (negation as failure); or 2) if there is a similar user and he/she does not like the LO (undercut).

To resolve attacks between arguments, each rule has an associated probability measure that estimates the probability that an argument (generated by using the rule) succeedes based on the aggregated probability of the clauses that form the body of the rule. In doing so, we use a simplified *probabilistic argumentation* framework [25] that assigns probability values to arguments and aggregates these probabilites to compute a suitability value to rank and recommend LOs.

Definition 4 (Argumentation Framework). *In our ERS, an argumentation framework is a tuple (Arg, P_{Arg}, D) where Arg is a set of arguments, $D \subseteq Arg \times Arg$ is a defeat relation, and $P_{Arg} :\rightarrow [0 : 1]$ is the probability that an argument holds.*

The probability of an argument $Arg = \langle \mathcal{A}, h \rangle$ is calculated as follows:

$$P_{Arg} = \begin{cases} 1, \ if \ \mathcal{A} \subseteq \Pi \\ \dfrac{\sum_{i=1}^{k} P_{Q_i}}{k}, \ if \ \mathcal{A} \subseteq \Delta \mid h \leftarrow Q_1, ..., Q_k \end{cases} \tag{1}$$

Facts are assumed to have probability 1. The probability of defeasible rules is computed as the average of the probabilities of the literals $Q_1, ..., Q_k$ that form their body (i.e. 1 if they are facts, 0 if they cannot be resolved, or P_{Q_i} if they are derived from other defeasible rules).

Definition 5 (Defeat). *In our ERS, an argument $\langle \mathcal{B}, q \rangle$ defeats another argument $\langle \mathcal{A}, h \rangle$ if $\mathcal{B}$ attacks $\mathcal{A}$ and $P_B > P_A$.*

4   Validation

Students query our ERS to get LO recommnendations that may fit their learning objectives and preferences. With this aim, the system has a search engine that allows a student to find LOs by using keywords that express the educational skills that they want to achieve. This search results in a list of LOs that match the keywords. After that, our ERS starts the recommendations proccess to rank and deliver LOs of this list: the content-based recommendation module triggers its inference rules by using the LOs metadata and the student's learning style; the collaborative recommendation module seeks similar user profiles to deliver items that have been evaluated by similar students; and the knowledge-based recommendation module determines whether any LO in the list is similar to another LO that the student has already used and assessed positively. Then, the new argumentation-based hybridization method is used to combine these three sets of LOs and deliver those for which the system can generate better arguments to justify their suitability for the search performed by the student.

To illustrate the operation of our method, in this section we show the results of a validation experiment that we have performed using the LOs stored in the FROAC[4] repository (the Federation of Learning Objects Repositories of Colombia) [2]. FROAC has 637 LOs indexed, stored in different repositories. The main topics of the LOs stored are: Analysis and design of algorithms and information systems, audit, databases, software engineering, artificial intelligence, programming, natural sciences, social sciences, computing, and mathematics. FROAC was developed at the *Universidad Nacional de Colombia*, as a result of a research project entitled *ROAC, Creación de un modelo para la Federación de OA en Colombia que permita su integración a confederaciones internacionales* of *COLCIENCIAS*. FROAC also stores information about its user's profiles (students). For each student, FROAC stores explicit features such as personal information (e.g. full name, date of birth, email, gender, and language), LO preferences (language, topic, and format), and psycho-pedagogical information (learning style). The students' learning style is obtained through a test with 24 questions that determine how the student processes the information that he/she receives and turns it into knowledge. The students of the National University of Colombia make an intensive use of FROAC. However, they have difficulties in specifying a query string that meets what they really want to find. Therefore, our ERS was implemented to help those students to find materials to support their learning. Furthermore, students also reported difficulties to understand why the system selects a specific LO over the list of potential candidates as the one that best fits their learning objectives. Thus, we have designed the new argumentation-based hybridization module not only with the objective of improving the quality of recommendations, but also with the aim of being able to provide the students with justifications for those recommendations.

In what follows, we report the results of one of the validation experiments that we performed. We selected a student with an *auditory* learning style

---

[4] FROAC: http://froac.manizales.unal.edu.co.

(he prefers auditory LOs with formats such as mp3, mp4, avi, etc.), has queried the ERS to find LOs that can help him to improve his *programming* skills (he has used the keyword 'programming'). After retrieving the list of LOs that match this query, the ERS executed its recommendations proccess and got the following results[5]: the content-based recommendation module delivered the LO with ID *LO262*; the collaborative recommendation module proposed a different LO, with ID *LO269*; and finally, the knowledge-based recommendation module delivered again the LO with ID *LO269*.

The ERS selected from these three proposals the LO that should be more relevant for the studen learnig objectives. The relevance is understood as the suitability of a LO in view of the student's preferences and profile. Therefore, a LO delivered by our ERS can be considered as 'relevant' if it matches the student's learning objectives (determined by the keywords) and profile (his/her learning style, format, language, and learning time preferences). For this example, the traditional hybridization method that our ERS used to date [8] will select and provide the *LO269* to *Jose*, since it has been recommended by two out of the three recommendation modules.

To evaluate recommendation results according to their relevance for the student, we can use the usual precision formula:

$$Precision = \frac{RelevantLOs \cap RetrievedLOs}{RetrievedLOs} \tag{2}$$

Therefore, according to our relevance definition, we get the following results:

– LO262 Precision = 1 content-based recommendation
– LO269 Precision = 0 collaborative recommendation and knowledge-based recommendation

which shows how the traditional hybridization method failed to deliver the most relevant LO in this case. In fact, although LO269 is *educationally appropriated* (its type fits the user's learning style) and it is *updated* (it has been updated within the last 5 years), it does not meet other user's preferences. It is not *generally appropiated* (its structure is not atomic and its state is not final, which means that it can be a LO under review), not *technically appropiated* (its language and format do not match the preferences of the user), and not *learning time appropiated* (it exceeds the maximum learning time preferred by the user).

Alternatively, our new argumentation-based hybridization method will trigger the following rules[6] for LO262 and LO269 with their associated probabilities:

Content-Based Rules
$C1_{LO262}$ $P = 1$: *recommend(user, LO262)* ←
    educationally_appropriate(user, LO262) ∧ *generally_appropriate (LO262)*
$C1_{LO269}$ $P = 0.5$: *recommend(user, LO269)* ←

---

[5] For the sake of simplicity, we only provide the top 1 recommendation results of each module.
[6] Only a selection of these rules are presented due to space restrictions.

$educationally\_appropriate(user,\ LO269) \wedge generally\_appropriate\ (LO269)$
$C2_{LO262}\ P = 1:\ recommend(user,\ LO262) \leftarrow$
$educationally\_appropriate(user,\ LO262) \wedge generally\_appropriate(LO262)) \wedge$
$technically\_appropriate(user,\ LO262)$
$C2_{LO269}\ P = 0.33:\ recommend(user,\ LO269) \leftarrow$
$educationally\_appropriate(user,\ LO269) \wedge generally\_appropriate(LO269)) \wedge$
$technically\_appropriate(user,\ LO269)$
$C3_{LO262}\ P = 1:\ recommend(user,\ LO262) \leftarrow$
$educationally\_appropriate(user,\ LO262) \wedge generally\_appropriate\ (LO262) \wedge$
$updated(LO262)$
$C3_{LO269}\ P = 0.66:\ recommend(user,\ LO269) \leftarrow$
$educationally\_appropriate(user,\ LO269) \wedge generally\_appropriate(LO269) \wedge$
$updated(LO269)$
$C4_{LO262}\ P = 1:\ recommend(user,\ LO262) \leftarrow$
$educationally\_appropriate(user,\ LO262) \wedge generally\_appropriate(LO262) \wedge$
$learning\_time\_appropriate(LO262)$
$C4_{LO269}\ P = 0.33:\ recommend(user,\ LO269) \leftarrow$
$educationally\_appropriate(user,\ LO269) \wedge generally\_appropriate(LO269) \wedge$
$learning\_time\_appropriate(LO269)$

Collaborative Rules
$O1_{LO262}\ P = 1:\ recommend(user,\ LO262) \leftarrow similarity(user,\ 'juan') > \alpha \wedge$
$vote('juan',\ LO262) \geq 4$
$O1_{LO269}\ P = 1:\ recommend(user,\ LO269) \leftarrow similarity(user,\ 'pablo') > \alpha \wedge$
$vote('pablo',\ LO269) \geq 4$

Knowledge-Based Rules
$K1_{LO262}\ P = 1:\ recommend(user,\ LO262) \leftarrow similarity(LO262,\ LO258) > \beta \wedge$
$vote(user,\ LO258) \geq 4$
$K1_{LO269}\ P = 1:\ recommend(user,\ LO269) \leftarrow similarity(LO269,\ LO274) > \beta \wedge$
$vote(user,\ LO274) \geq 4$

The collaborative recommendation module was able to find two similar users *'juan'* that liked LO262, and *'pablo'* that liked LO269, but recommended LO269 since *'pablo'* is more similar to the actual user than *'juan'*. These inferences are also encoded in rules $O1_{LO262}$ and $O1_{LO269}$. Similarly, the knowledge-based recommendation module was able to find a LO258 similar to LO269 and another LO274 similar to LO269 that were successfully recommended in the past to the actual user, but LO274 received a highest vote, and hence, LO269 was recommended. These inferences are also encoded in rules $K1_{LO262}$ and $K1_{LO269}$. All these requirements were also met by LO262. However, while for LO262 all literals hold and all rules have an associated probability of 1, some literals do not hold for LO269 (those that represent the unfulfilled user preferences encoded in the content-based rules), which decreases the probability associated with their rules.

Table 1. Explanation schemes.

Rule	Explanation	Description
$C1$	$E1$	The learning object LO fits the topic T, is suitable for your LS learning style, and it is atomic and stable
$C2$	$E2$	The learning object LO fits the topic T, is suitable for your LS learning style, and fits your L language and F format preferences
$C3$	$E3$	The learning object LO fits the topic T, is suitable for your LS learning style, fits your L language and F format preferences, and it is updated
$C4$	$E4$	The learning object LO fits the topic T, is suitable for your LS learning style, and fits your L language, F format preferences and learning time < T preferences
$O1$	$E5$	The system has found a user that whose profile is similar to yours who liked LO
$K1$	$E6$	The system has found that you liked LOx, which is similar to LOy

Therefore, as the new argumentation-based hybridization method is able to generate more arguments to justify the recommendation of LO262, the system would succeed in selecting the most relevant LO for this specific user. Furthermore, we have also designed a module for constructing explanations (arguments) based on these rules. Since the number of rules of our ERS is finite and small, this is a simple module that associates each rule with a scheme of explanation (see Table 1).

For instance, with the rule $C1_{LO262}$ the ERS can use the explanation scheme $E1$ and provide the user with an argument to justify the recommendation of $LO262$: *'The learning object LO262 fits the topic 'Programming', is suitable for your 'auditory' learning style, and it is atomic and stable'.*

5   Conclusions and Future Work

This paper has proposed the employment of an argumentation-based formalism for modeling a hybrid recommender system which recommends LOs for specific students. In addition, an initial validation using real data from a LO repository of the *Universidad Nacional de Colombia* has been done with better results than previously implemented approaches. The proposed argument-based hybridization method is able to select the most relevant and suitable LOs to recommend, among those delivered previously by three recommendation modules (content-based, collaborative and knowledge-based). Also, by using this method, the recommender system can generate arguments to justify its recommendations. The whole system is still being implemented to be integrated in the Federation of Learning Objects Repositories of Colombia. As future work, we plan to enhance the simple explanation module with and advanced human-computing interaction module integrated in a conversational agent. Also, comprehensive evaluation tests will be performed.

Acknowledgements. This work was partially developed with the aid of the doctoral grant offered to Paula A. Rodríguez by 'Programa Nacional de Formación de Investigadores - COLCIENCIAS', Colombia and partially funded by the COLCIENCIAS project 1119-569-34172 from the Universidad Nacional de Colombia. It was also supported by the projects TIN2015-65515-C4-1-R and TIN2014-55206-R of the Spanish government and by the grant program for the recruitment of doctors for the Spanish system of science and technology (PAID-10-14) of the Universitat Politècnica de València.

References

1. Learning Technology Standards Committee: IEEE Standard for Learning Object Metadata. Institute of Electrical and Electronics Engineers, New York (2002)
2. Duque, N.D., Ovalle, D.A., Moreno, J.: Objetos de aprendizaje, repositorios y federaciones... conocimiento para todos. Universidad Nacional de Colombia, Bogotá (2015)
3. Sikka, R., Dhankhar, A., Rana, C.: A survey paper on e-learning recommender system. Int. J. Comput. Appl. **47**(9), 27–30 (2012)
4. Van de Sompel, H., Chute, R., Hochstenbach, P.: The adore federation architecture: digital repositories at scale. Int. J. Digit. Libr. **9**(2), 83–100 (2008)
5. Manouselis, N., Drachsler, H., Vourikari, R., Hummel, H., Koper, R.: Recommender Systems in Technology Enhanced Learning. Recommender Systems Handbook **54**, 479–510 (2011)
6. Burke, R.: Hybrid recommender systems: survey and experiments. User Model. User-Adap. Inter. **12**(4), 331–370 (2002)
7. Rodríguez, P.A., Duque, N.D., Ovalle, D.A.: Multi-agent system for knowledge-based recommendation of learning objects using metadata clustering. In: Bajo, J., Hallenborg, K., Pawlewski, P., Botti, V., Sánchez-Pi, N., Duque Méndez, N.D., Lopes, F., Vicente, J. (eds.) PAAMS 2015 Workshops. CCIS, vol. 524, pp. 356–364. Springer, Heidelberg (2015)
8. Rodríguez, P.A., Ovalle, D.A., Duque, N.D.: A student-centered hybrid recommender system to provide relevant learning objects from repositories. In: Zaphiris, P., Ioannou, A. (eds.) LCT 2015. LNCS, vol. 9192, pp. 291–300. Springer, Heidelberg (2015)
9. Ossowski, S.: Agreement Technologies, vol. 8. Springer Science & Business Media, Heidelberg (2012)
10. Salehi, M., Pourzaferani, M., Razavi, S.A.: Hybrid attribute-based recommender system for learning material using genetic algorithm and a multidimensional information model. Egypt. Inf. J. **14**(1), 67–78 (2013)
11. Zapata, A., Menendez, V.H., Prieto, M.E., Romero, C.: A hybrid recommender method for learning objects. IJCA Proc. Des. Eval. Digit. Content Educ. (DEDCE) **1**, 1–7 (2011)
12. Vekariya, V., Kulkarni, G.R., Hybrid recommender systems: survey and experiments. In: 2012 2nd International Conference on Digital Information and Communication Technology and It's Applications (DICTAP), pp. 469–473. IEEE, May 2012

13. Palanca, J., Heras, S., Jorge, J., Julian, V.: Towards persuasive social recommendation: knowledge model. SIGAPP Appl. Comput. Rev. 15(2), 41–49 (2015)
14. Linden, G., Hong, J., Stonebraker, M., Guzdial, M.: Recommendation algorithms, online privacy, and more. Commun. ACM 52(5), 10–11 (2009)
15. Sinha, R., Swearingen, K.: The role of transparency in recommender systems. In: CHI 2002 Extended Abstracts on Human Factors in Computing Systems, pp. 830–831. ACM (2002)
16. Briguez, C.E., Budán, M., Deagustini, C., Maguitman, A.G., Capobianco, M., Simari, G.R.: Towards an argument-based music recommender system. COMMA 245, 83–90 (2012)
17. Briguez, C.E., Capobianco, M., Maguitman, A.G.: A theoretical framework for trust-based news recommender systems and its implementation using defeasible argumentation. Int. J. Artif. Intell. Tools 22(04), 1350021 (2013)
18. Recio-García, J.A., Quijano, L., Díaz-Agudo, B.: Including social factors in an argumentative model for group decision support systems. Decis. Support Syst. 56, 48–55 (2013)
19. Heras, S., Rebollo, M., Julián, V.: A dialogue game protocol for recommendation in social networks. In: Corchado, E., Abraham, A., Pedrycz, W. (eds.) HAIS 2008. LNCS (LNAI), vol. 5271, pp. 515–522. Springer, Heidelberg (2008)
20. Chesñevar, C.I., Maguitman, A.G., González, M.P.: Empowering recommendation technologies through argumentation. Argumentation in Artificial Intelligence, pp. 403–422. Springer, Heidelberg (2009)
21. Heras, S., Atkinson, K., Botti, V., Grasso, F., Julián, V., McBurney, P.: Research opportunities for argumentation in social networks. Artif. Intell. Rev. 39(1), 39–62 (2013)
22. Briguez, C.E., Budán, M., Deagustini, C., Maguitman, A.G., Capobianco, M., Simari, G.R.: Argument-based mixed recommenders and their application to movie suggestion. Expert Syst. Appl. 41(14), 6467–6482 (2014)
23. Kirschner, P.A., Buckingham-Shum, S.J., Carr, C.S.: Visualizing Argumentation: Software Tools for Collaborative and Educational Sense-Making. Springer Science & Business Media, Heidelberg (2012)
24. García, A.J., Simari, G.R.: Defeasible logic programming: an argumentative approach. Theor. Pract. Logic Program. 4(1+2), 95–138 (2004)
25. Li, H., Oren, N., Norman, T.J.: Probabilistic argumentation frameworks. In: Modgil, S., Oren, N., Toni, F. (eds.) TAFA 2011. LNCS, vol. 7132, pp. 1–16. Springer, Heidelberg (2012)

How to Share Knowledge by Gossiping

Andreas Herzig$^{(\boxtimes)}$ and Faustine Maffre

IRIT, Université de Toulouse,
IRIT, 118 Route de Narbonne, 31062 Toulouse Cedex 9, France
Faustine.Maffre@irit.fr
http://www.irit.fr/~Andreas.Herzig

Abstract. Given n agents each of which has a secret (a fact not known to anybody else), the classical version of the gossip problem is to achieve shared knowledge of all secrets in a minimal number of phone calls. There exist protocols achieving shared knowledge in $2(n-2)$ calls: when the protocol terminates everybody knows all the secrets. We generalize that problem and focus on higher-order shared knowledge: how many calls does it take to obtain that everybody knows that everybody knows all secrets? More generally, how many calls does it take to obtain shared knowledge of order k? This requires not only the communication of secrets, but also the communication of knowledge about secrets. We give a protocol that works in $(k+1)(n-2)$ steps and prove that it is correct: it achieves shared knowledge of level k. The proof is presented in a dynamic epistemic logic that is based on the observability of propositional variables by agents.

Keywords: Gossip · Epistemic logic · Shared knowledge · Common knowledge

1 Introduction: The Gossip Problem and Its Generalization

The original version of the gossip problem goes as follows [1,13].

> There are six agents each of which knows some secret not known to anybody else. Two agents can make a telephone call and exchange all secrets they know. How many calls does it take to share all secrets, i.e., how many calls have to take place until everybody knows all secrets?

The problem can be generalized from six to arbitrary numbers of agents n. In the literature one can find various protocols achieving the goal in $2(n-2)$ calls. It has been proved that they are optimal: no protocol exists achieving the goal with less calls [4,9,14].

There are contexts where agents have to achieve higher-order knowledge, typically in order to coordinate some joint action. While after $2(n-2)$ calls all secrets are shared knowledge, they fail to be common knowledge. Unless everybody knows the protocol and there is a global clock, such common knowledge cannot be attained. More modestly, the agents may want to achieve second-order shared knowledge: they may have the goal that everybody *knows* that everybody

© Springer International Publishing Switzerland 2016
M. Rovatsos et al. (Eds.): EUMAS 2015/AT 2015, LNAI 9571, pp. 249–263, 2016.
DOI: 10.1007/978-3-319-33509-4_20

knows all secrets. This paper investigates how such higher-order knowledge can be achieved.

Let Agt be the set of all agents. Let us denote the secret of agent i by s_i. To simplify things we suppose that s_i is a proposition that is true. Let us write $K_i\varphi$ to express that agent i knows that the formula φ is true. The initial situation before the agents start gossiping is expressed by

$$\bigwedge_{i\in Agt}\left(s_i\wedge K_is_i\wedge\bigwedge_{j\in Agt, j\neq i}\left(\neg K_js_i\wedge\neg K_j\neg s_i\right)\right)$$

and the formula

$$\bigwedge_{i\in Agt}K_i\left(\bigwedge_{j\in Agt}s_j\right)$$

expresses the goal that every agent knows every secret. Let us abbreviate the conjunction $\bigwedge_{j\in Agt}s_j$ of all secrets by All. Furthermore, let $EK_J\varphi$ abbreviate the conjunction $\bigwedge_{i\in J}K_i\varphi$, where $J\subseteq Agt$ is an arbitrary nonempty subset of Agt. So $EK_{Agt}All$ expresses that all secrets are shared knowledge: every agent knows every secret. $EK_{Agt}EK_{Agt}All$ expresses the goal that every agent knows that all secrets are shared knowledge. The formula

$$\underbrace{EK_{Agt}\ldots EK_{Agt}}_{k\text{ times}}All$$

expresses that all secrets are shared knowledge up to depth $k\geq 1$.

The result of a phone call between two agents is that their knowledge increases. Let us model this by means of modal operators of action: the formula $[Call_j^i]\varphi$ expresses that φ is true after i and j talked to each other. Then $[Call_j^i]EK_{\{i,j\}}(s_i\wedge s_j)$ expresses that the result of $Call_j^i$ is that i and j know their secrets. When we say that during a call the agents communicate all they know then this not only concerns secrets, but also knowledge about secrets and more generally higher-order knowledge. Therefore calls achieve common knowledge between the calling agents:

$$[Call_j^i]EK_{\{i,j\}}\ldots EK_{\{i,j\}}(s_i\wedge s_j)$$

is the case for arbitrary nestings of $EK_{\{i,j\}}$. Furthermore, the formula

$$\underbrace{[Call_{j_1}^{i_1}]\ldots[Call_{j_{2(n-2)}}^{i_{2(n-2)}}]}_{2(n-2)\text{ times}}EK_{Agt}All$$

expresses that the protocol where i_1 calls j_1 first, then i_2 calls j_2, ..., and finally $i_{2(n-2)}$ calls $j_{2(n-2)}$ achieves shared knowledge.

We note (k,n) the instance of the generalized gossip problem with $n\geq 2$ agents and the goal to achieve depth $k\geq 1$ of shared knowledge. So the original problem corresponds to the instance $(1,6)$. We are going to introduce a protocol achieving shared knowledge of depth k in $(k+1)(n-2)$ calls. Our proofs are formally rigorous: they are couched in a dynamic epistemic logic that is called DEL-PAO (Dynamic Epistemic Logic of Propositional Assignment and Observation), with epistemic operators K_i, for $i \in Agt$, and dynamic operators $[Call^i_j]$, for $i, j \in Agt$. We had introduced and studied that logic in [10], building on previous work by van der Hoek and colleagues [11,12] and with further developments reported in [5]. We do not address the question whether our protocol is optimal and leave that to future work.

The paper is organized as follows. Section 2 presents our algorithm. Section 3 recalls syntax and semantics of our dynamic epistemic logic DEL-PAO. In Sect. 4 we show how to capture the algorithm as a DEL-PAO program. In Sect. 5 we prove in DEL-PAO that the algorithm is correct. Section 6 concludes.

2 An Algorithm Achieving Higher-Order Shared Knowledge

The following algorithm generates a sequence of calls for a given instance (k, n) of the generalized gossip problem, for $k \geq 1$ and $n \geq 4$. Throughout the algorithm two of the agents, which we call *left* and *right*, will have a central, fixed role: each of the other agents only communicates with either *left* or *right*. The $n-2$ remaining agents will be numbered $0, 1, \ldots, n-3$.

The algorithm is made up of *turns*. During each turn, *left* and *right* collect the secrets of other agents. Together with the last agent they talked to in that turn, they thereby become what we call 'semi-experts'. A further call between complementary semi-experts turns them into full experts. The last agents *left* and *right* talked to play a crucial role. These two further semi-experts are permuted at each turn in a way that will guarantee that the goal is reached.

Algorithm 1. *For $t = 0..k$ do*

   agent left calls agent $0-t$ (mod $n-2$);
   agent left calls agent $1-t$ (mod $n-2$);

   $\vdots$

   agent left calls agent $n-3$;
   agent left calls agent 0;
   agent left calls agent 1;

   $\vdots$

   agent left calls agent $n-4-t$ (mod $n-2$);
   agent right calls agent $n-3-t$ (mod $n-2$).

At the first turn (turn 0), agent *left* calls agent 0, then 1, ..., then $n-4$, and finally agent *right* calls agent $n-3$; at the second turn (turn 1), agent *left* calls agent $n-3$, then 0, then 4, ..., then $n-5$; and finally agent *right* calls agent $n-4$; and so on. So each turn involves $n-2$ calls, and overall the algorithm produces a sequence of $(k+1)(n-2)$ calls. In the rest of the paper, we assume that every index of agent is taken modulo $n-2$ and we omit "(mod $n-2$)".

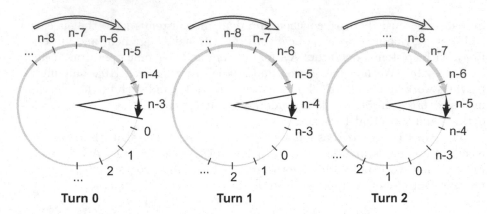

Turn 0   **Turn 1**   **Turn 2**

Fig. 1. Graphical represention of the first three turns of Algorithm 1. (Color figure online)

Figure 1 gives a visual representation of Algorithm 1: agents $0, 1, \ldots, n{-}3$ are put on a wheel which, between each turn, rotates clockwise. Agent *left* (in orange) calls everyone in ascending order, except the agent at the rightmost position of the wheel, then *right* (in blue) calls this agent.

Theorem 1. *The instance (k, n) of the generalized gossip problem can be solved in at most $(k{+}1)(n{-}2)$ calls.*

The rest of the paper is devoted to the proof of the above theorem: we prove that the sequence of calls produced by the algorithm is indeed a solution. Our proof will be done in the formal language of DEL-PAO that we introduce first.

3   Dynamic Epistemic Logic of Propositional Assignment and Observation DEL-PAO

Dynamic Epistemic Logic of Propositional Assignment and Observation DEL-PAO is grounded on the notion of observability of propositional variables. It refines a logic that was proposed and studied in a series of papers by van der Hoek, Wooldridge and colleagues under the names Epistemic Coalition Logic of Propositional Control with Partial Observability ECL-PC(PO) [12] and Logic of Revelation and Concealment LRC [11]. The idea is that each agent has a set of propositional variables she can observe: no different truth value is possible for her. The other way round, any combination of truth values of the non-observable variables is possible for her. We recall this logic now; more details are in [10].

3.1   Observability Atoms

The atomic formulas of DEL-PAO are called *visibility atoms* and take the form $S_{i_1} S_{i_2} \ldots S_{i_m} p$, where p is a propositional variable from a countable non-empty set *Prop* and $i_1, i_2, \ldots, i_m$ are agents from a finite non-empty set *Agt*. When

$m=0$ then we have nothing but a propositional variable. For $m=1$, the atom $\mathsf{S}_{i_1} p$ reads "agent i_1 sees the value of the variable p", and for $m=2$, the second-order observation $\mathsf{S}_{i_1} \mathsf{S}_{i_2} p$ reads "agent i_1 sees whether i_2 sees the value of p"; and so on. Beyond individual observability the language of DEL-PAO also accounts for joint observability: the atom $\mathsf{JS}p$ reads "all agents jointly see the value of p". Metaphorically, joint attention about p is the case when there is eye contact between the agents when observing p. Joint visibility implies individual visibility: when $\mathsf{JS}\,p$ is true then $\mathsf{S}_i\,p$ should also be true.

One can define first- and higher-order knowledge about literals by means of conjunctions of visibility atoms. Indeed, for a propositional variable p we have that agent i knows that p is true when p is true and i sees p. Similarly i knows that p is false when p is false and i sees p. The list below collects some equivalences that will be valid:

$$K_i p \leftrightarrow p \wedge \mathsf{S}_i\, p$$
$$K_i \neg p \leftrightarrow \neg p \wedge \mathsf{S}_i\, p$$
$$\neg K_i p \wedge \neg K_i \neg p \leftrightarrow \neg \mathsf{S}_i\, p$$
$$K_j K_i p \leftrightarrow p \wedge \mathsf{S}_i\, p \wedge \mathsf{S}_j\, p \wedge \mathsf{S}_j\, \mathsf{S}_i\, p$$
$$K_j K_i \neg p \leftrightarrow \neg p \wedge \mathsf{S}_i\, p \wedge \mathsf{S}_j\, p \wedge \mathsf{S}_j\, \mathsf{S}_i\, p$$

Formally, the set of *observability operators* is

$$OBS = \{\mathsf{S}_i : i \in Agt\} \cup \{\mathsf{JS}\},$$

where S_i stands for individual visibility of agent i and JS stands for joint visibility of all agents. The set of all sequences of visibility operators is noted OBS^* and the set of all non-empty sequences is noted OBS^+. We use $\sigma, \sigma', \ldots$ for elements of OBS^*. Finally, the set of atomic formulas is

$$ATM = \{\sigma\, p : \sigma \in OBS^*, p \in Prop\}.$$

The elements of ATM are also called *visibility atoms*, or atoms for short. For example, $\mathsf{JS}\,\mathsf{S}_2\, q$ reads "all agents jointly see whether agent 2 sees the value of q"; in other words, there is joint attention in the group of all agents concerning 2's observation of q. The elements of ATM are noted $\alpha, \alpha', \ldots, \beta, \beta', \ldots$.

3.2 Complex Formulas

Beyond atomic formulas the language of DEL-PAO has epistemic operators as well as actions, alias programs, assigning truth values to visibility atoms. It is defined by the following grammar:

$$\varphi ::= \alpha \mid \neg\varphi \mid \varphi \wedge \varphi \mid K_i\varphi \mid CK\varphi \mid [\pi]\varphi$$
$$\pi ::= +\alpha \mid -\alpha \mid \pi;\pi \mid \pi \sqcup \pi \mid \varphi?$$

where α ranges over ATM and i over Agt.

Our atomic programs are assignments of truth values to atoms from ATM: $+\alpha$ makes α true and $-\alpha$ makes α false. Complex programs are constructed with dynamic logic operators: $\pi; \pi'$ is sequential composition, $\pi \sqcup \pi'$ is nondeterministic choice, and $\varphi?$ is test. Just as in dynamic logic, the formula $[\pi]\varphi$ reads "after every execution of π, φ is true". The formula $K_i\varphi$ reads "i knows that φ is true on the basis of what she observes", and $CK\varphi$ reads "all agents jointly know that φ is true on the basis of what they jointly observe". These epistemic operators account for forms of individual and common knowledge that are respectively obtained via individual observation and joint observation of facts. They therefore differ conceptually from the classical operators of individual and common knowledge as studied in the area of epistemic logic [8].

The other boolean operators $\top, \bot, \vee, \rightarrow$ and $\leftrightarrow$ are defined as abbreviations, and $\widehat{K}_i\varphi$ abbreviates $\neg K_i \neg\varphi$. For $J \subseteq Agt$, the shared knowledge modality is defined by

$$EK_J\varphi \overset{\text{def}}{=} \bigwedge_{i \in J} K_i\varphi$$

and the iteration of that operator is defined inductively for $k \geq 0$ by $EK_J^0\varphi = \varphi$ and $EK_J^{n+1}\varphi = EK_J EK_J^n\varphi$. We sometimes drop set parentheses and, e.g., write $EK_{i,j}\varphi$ instead of $EK_{\{i,j\}}\varphi$. Moreover, $skip$ abbreviates $\top?$ and $fail$ abbreviates $\bot?$. We also use the abbreviation π^k, for $k \geq 0$, inductively defined by $\pi^0 = skip$ and $\pi^{k+1} = \pi^k; \pi$. Finally, **if** φ **then** π abbreviates $(\varphi?; \pi) \sqcup \neg\varphi?$; it therefore does nothing when φ is false.

3.3 Introspective Valuations

The models of **DEL-PAO** are simply sets of visibility atoms. In order to guarantee positive and negative introspection we have to ensure that agents are always aware of what they see: for every agent i and propositional variable p, $\mathsf{S}_i \mathsf{S}_i p$ has to be in every valuation. More generally, a valuation V is introspective when it contains every visibility atom having two consecutive S_i, such as $\mathsf{S}_j \mathsf{S}_i \mathsf{S}_i \mathsf{S}_k p$. So in an introspective valuation an agent is aware of what she sees, every agent sees this, and every agent sees that every agent sees this, etc.

Formally, a valuation $V \in 2^{ATM}$ is *introspective* if and only if the following hold, for every $\alpha \in ATM$ and $i \in Agt$:

$$\mathsf{S}_i \mathsf{S}_i \alpha \in V \tag{C1}$$

$$\mathsf{JS} \, \mathsf{JS} \, \alpha \in V \tag{C2}$$

$$\mathsf{JS} \, \mathsf{S}_i \mathsf{S}_i \alpha \in V \tag{C3}$$

$$\text{if } \mathsf{JS} \, \alpha \in V, \text{ then } \mathsf{S}_i \alpha \in V \tag{C4}$$

$$\text{if } \mathsf{JS} \, \alpha \in V, \text{ then } \mathsf{JS} \, \mathsf{S}_i \alpha \in V \tag{C5}$$

The set of all introspective valuations is noted $INTR$.

(C1) is about introspection of individual sight: an agent always sees whether she sees the value of an atom. (C2) requires the same for joint sight; indeed, if $\mathsf{JS}\,\alpha$ is true then $\mathsf{JS}\,\mathsf{JS}\,\alpha$ should be true by introspection, and if $\mathsf{JS}\,\alpha$ is false then all agents jointly see that at least one of them has broken eye contact. (C3) forces the first to be common knowledge. (C4) guarantees that joint visibility implies individual visibility. Together with (C2), (C5) guarantees that $\mathsf{JS}\,\alpha \in V$ implies $\mathsf{JS}\,\sigma\,\alpha \in V$ for $\sigma \in OBS^*$.

Constraints (C4) and (C5) guarantee that $\mathsf{JS}\,\alpha \in V$ implies $\sigma\,\alpha \in V$ for $\sigma \in OBS^+$. This motivates the following relation of *introspective consequence* between atoms: $\alpha \rightsquigarrow \beta$ iff either $\alpha = \beta$, or $\alpha = \mathsf{JS}\,\alpha'$ and $\beta = \sigma\,\alpha'$ for some σ.

Closure under introspective consequence characterizes introspective valuations.

Proposition 1 [10]. *A valuation $V \subseteq ATM$ is introspective if and only if, for every $\alpha, \beta \in ATM$ and $i \in Agt$:*

$$\sigma\,\mathsf{S}_i\,\mathsf{S}_i\,\alpha \in V \text{ for every } \sigma \in OBS^* \tag{1}$$

$$\sigma\,\mathsf{JS}\,\alpha \in V \text{ for every } \sigma \in OBS^+ \tag{2}$$

$$\text{if } \alpha \in V \text{ and } \alpha \rightsquigarrow \beta \text{ then } \beta \in V \tag{3}$$

An atom $\alpha \in ATM$ is *valid in INTR* if and only if α belongs to every valuation in *INTR*. By Proposition 1, α is valid in *INTR* if and only if α is of the form either $\sigma\,\mathsf{S}_i\,\mathsf{S}_i\,\alpha$ with $\sigma \in OBS^*$, or $\sigma\,\mathsf{JS}\,\alpha$ with $\sigma \in OBS^+$.

Indistinguishability Relations Between Valuations. Two valuations are related by the indistinguishability relation for agent i, noted $\sim_i$, if every α that i sees has the same value. Similarly, we have a relation $\sim_{Agt}$ for joint indistinguishability. They are defined as follows:

$$V \sim_i V' \text{ iff } \mathsf{S}_i\,\alpha \in V \text{ implies } V(\alpha) = V'(\alpha)$$

$$V \sim_{Agt} V' \text{ iff } \mathsf{JS}\,\alpha \in V \text{ implies } V(\alpha) = V'(\alpha)$$

where we write $V(\alpha) = V'(\alpha)$ when α has the same truth value in V and V', i.e., when either $\alpha \in V$ and $\alpha \in V'$, or $\alpha \notin V$ and $\alpha \notin V'$.

It is proven in [10] that the binary relations $\sim_i$ and $\sim_{Agt}$ are equivalence relations on the set of introspective valuations *INTR* and that valuations in *INTR* are not related to valuations outside of *INTR* by $\sim_i$ and $\sim_{Agt}$.

Truth Conditions and Validity. Given an introspective valuation V, update operations add or remove atoms from V. This requires some care: the resulting valuation should also be introspective. For example, removing $\mathsf{S}_i\,\mathsf{S}_i\,p$ should be impossible. Another example is when V does not contain $\mathsf{S}_i\,p$: then $V \cup \{\mathsf{JS}\,p\}$ would violate (C4). So when adding an atom to V one also has to add all its *positive consequences*. Symmetrically, when removing an atom one also has to remove its *negative consequences*. Let us define the following:

$$Eff^+(\alpha) = \{\beta \in ATM : \alpha \rightsquigarrow \beta\}$$

$$Eff^-(\alpha) = \{\beta \in ATM : \beta \rightsquigarrow \alpha\}$$

Clearly, when V is introspective then both $V \cup \textit{Eff}^+(\alpha)$ and $V \setminus \textit{Eff}^-(\alpha)$ are so, too (unless α is valid).

Now the truth conditions are as follows:

$$
\begin{aligned}
V &\models \alpha && \text{iff } \alpha \in V \\
V &\models \neg\varphi && \text{iff } V \not\models \varphi \\
V &\models \varphi \wedge \psi && \text{iff } V \models \varphi \text{ and } V \models \psi \\
V &\models K_i\varphi && \text{iff } V' \models \varphi \text{ for all } V' \text{ such that } V \sim_i V' \\
V &\models CK\varphi && \text{iff } V' \models \varphi \text{ for all } V' \text{ such that } V \sim_{Agt} V' \\
V &\models [\pi]\varphi && \text{iff } V' \models \varphi \text{ for all } V' \text{ such that } V R_\pi V'
\end{aligned}
$$

where R_π is a binary relation on valuations that is defined (by mutual recursion with the definition of $\models$) by:

$$
\begin{aligned}
V R_{+\alpha} V' \quad & \text{iff } V' = V \cup \textit{Eff}^+(\alpha) \\
V R_{-\alpha} V' \quad & \text{iff } V' = V \setminus \textit{Eff}^-(\alpha) \text{ and } \alpha \text{ is not valid in } \textit{INTR} \\
V R_{\pi_1;\pi_2} V' \quad & \text{iff there is } U \text{ such that } V R_{\pi_1} U \text{ and } U R_{\pi_2} V' \\
V R_{\pi_1 \sqcup \pi_2} V' \quad & \text{iff } V R_{\pi_1} V' \text{ or } V R_{\pi_2} V' \\
V R_{\varphi?} V' \quad & \text{iff } V = V' \text{ and } V \models \varphi
\end{aligned}
$$

The relation R_π is defined just as in PDL for the program operators ;, $\sqcup$ and ?. The interpretation of assignments is designed in a way such that we stay in $\textit{INTR}$: the program $+\alpha$ adds all the positive consequences of α; the program $-\alpha$ fails if α is valid in $\textit{INTR}$ and otherwise removes all the negative consequences of α. For example, we never have $V R_{-\mathsf{S}_1 \mathsf{S}_1 p} V'$, i.e., the program $-\mathsf{S}_1 \mathsf{S}_1 p$ always fails. In contrast, the program $-\mathsf{S}_1 \mathsf{S}_2 p$ always succeeds, and we have $V R_{-\mathsf{S}_1 \mathsf{S}_2 p} (V \setminus \{\mathsf{S}_1 \mathsf{S}_2 p, \mathsf{JS}\,\mathsf{S}_2 p, \mathsf{JS}\, p\})$ because the only atoms—beyond $\mathsf{S}_1 \mathsf{S}_2 p$ itself—whose consequence is $\mathsf{S}_1 \mathsf{S}_2 p$ are $\mathsf{JS}\,\mathsf{S}_2 p$ and $\mathsf{JS}\, p$. Therefore $V \not\models [-\mathsf{S}_1 \mathsf{S}_2 p]\mathsf{JS}\, p$ for every V.

Like $\sim_i$ and $\sim_{Agt}$, it is proven in [10] that valuations in $\textit{INTR}$ are only related to valuations in $\textit{INTR}$ by R_π. Therefore there is no risk to "go out" of the set of introspective valuations with modal operators.

A *model* of φ is a valuation V such that $V \models \varphi$. A formula φ is *satisfiable in* $\textit{INTR}$ if φ has an introspective model. For example, $\mathsf{JS}\, p \wedge \neg\mathsf{S}_i p$ has a model, but does not have an introspective model and is therefore unsatisfiable in $\textit{INTR}$. A formula φ is *valid in* $\textit{INTR}$ if every introspective valuation is a model of φ. We also say that φ is a *validity* of DEL-PAO. For example, $\neg[-\mathsf{S}_1 \mathsf{S}_2 p]\mathsf{JS}\, p$ is valid in $\textit{INTR}$, and $\neg\beta \rightarrow [+\alpha]\neg\beta$ is valid in $\textit{INTR}$ if and only if $\alpha \not\rightsquigarrow \beta$.

4   Expressing Calls in the Language of DEL-PAO

Our logic provides a suitable framework to model calls between agents and to reason about the evolution of their knowledge. Before the proof of correctness of our algorithm, we show how to express calls and we give some of their properties.

In the standard version of the gossip problem, agents only communicate their factual knowledge during a call. In order to achieve higher-order knowledge they also have to tell what they know about others: for shared knowledge of level k they have to exchange all their knowledge up to depth $k-1$.

Formally, let the level k of intended shared knowledge be given. Let i and j be two agents. For a given integer m, let the set all nonempty sequences of visibility operators S_i and S_j of length at most $k-m$ be $\{\sigma_1, \ldots, \sigma_l\}$. For example, for $k = 3$ and $m = 1$ that set is $\{S_i, S_j, S_i S_i, S_i S_j, S_j S_i, S_j S_j\}$. Then $Call_j^i$ is the sequential composition of programs of the form

$$\textbf{if } K_i K_{y_1} \cdots K_{y_m} s \vee K_j K_{y_1} \cdots K_{y_m} s \textbf{ then } +\sigma_1 S_{y_1} \cdots S_{y_m} s; \ldots; +\sigma_l S_{y_1} \cdots S_{y_m} s$$

for secret s in $\{s_i : i \in Agt\}$, integer $m \leq k-1$, and agents $\langle y_1, \ldots, y_m \rangle \in Agt^m$. For example, for $k = 3$ the following is an element of the sequence:

$$\textbf{if } K_i K_y s \vee K_j K_y s \textbf{ then}$$
$$+S_i S_y s; +S_j S_y s; +S_i S_i S_y s; +S_i S_j S_y s; +S_j S_i S_y s; +S_j S_j S_y s$$

That piece of program tests whether $K_y s$ is known by i or j and if so makes $S_y s$ visible for both i and j and i's observation of $S_y s$ visible for j, and vice versa. We observe that the additions $+S_i S_i S_k s$ and $+S_j S_j S_k s$ are trivial because they are introspectively valid.

Some properties of the program $Call_j^i$ and its interaction with the shared knowledge operator will be useful in our proofs.

First of all, the dynamic operators $[Call_j^i]$ and the shared knowledge operators EK_J are normal modal operators. So in particular $[Call_j^i]\varphi \wedge [Call_j^i]\psi \leftrightarrow [Call_j^i](\varphi \wedge \psi)$ and $(EK_J \varphi \wedge EK_J \psi) \leftrightarrow EK_J(\varphi \wedge \psi)$ are DEL-PAO valid. Moreover, we can put coalitions together: the schema

$$(EK_{J_1} \varphi \wedge EK_{J_2} \varphi) \leftrightarrow EK_{J_1 \cup J_2} \varphi$$

is valid for every $J_1, J_2 \subseteq Agt$. (To see this reduce EK according to its definition.) Finally, calls preserve positive knowledge and produce shared knowledge, which is a property that we state formally:

Proposition 2. *Let* $s \in \{s_i : i \in Agt\}$ *and* $m \geq 0$. *Let* φ *be of the form either* $K_{i_1} \ldots K_{i_m} s$ *or* $EK_{J_1} \ldots EK_{J_m} s$. *Then:*

1. $\varphi \rightarrow [Call_j^i]\varphi$ *is* DEL-PAO *valid;*
2. $K_i \varphi \rightarrow [Call_j^i] EK_{i,j}^{k-m} \varphi$ *is* DEL-PAO *valid.*

Proof. (1) is due to calls never decreasing knowledge. (2) is obvious from the definition of calls. $\square$

Finally, the program corresponding to the turn t of Algorithm 1 is:

$$\mathsf{turn}_t = Call_{n-2-t}^{left}; \ldots; Call_{n-3}^{left}; Call_0^{left}; \ldots; Call_{n-4-t}^{left}; Call_{n-3-t}^{right}.$$

5   Correctness of the Algorithm

We now prove that the algorithm returns a solution.

Let $Agt = \{left, right, 0, \ldots, n-3\}$ be the set of agents and $Prop = \{s_i : i \in Agt\}$ the set of propositional variables. The initial state is modeled by the valuation

$$w_0 = \{s_i : i \in Agt\} \cup \{S_i\, s_i : i \in Agt\} \cup \{\alpha : \alpha \text{ is valid in } INTR\}.$$

So all secrets are true, each agent knows her own secret, and moreover the introspectively valid atoms are true. We have:

$$w_0 \models \bigwedge_{i \in Agt} K_i \Big(s_i \wedge \bigwedge_{j \in Agt, j \neq i} \neg K_j s_i \Big).$$

An agent is an *expert for depth* t if her personal goal for depth t is reached. Precisely, agent i is an expert for depth $t \geq 1$ if and only if we have:

$$K_i EK_{Agt}^{t-1} All.$$

The dynamic modalities of **DEL-PAO** nicely allow to express that a further call would turn an agent i into an expert, i.e., that i is a semi-expert. Indeed, two agents i and j are *complementary for depth* t ('semi-experts'), noted $\mathsf{compl}_t(i,j)$, if a call between i and j would make them both experts for depth t. More formally:

$$\mathsf{compl}_t(i,j) \stackrel{\text{def}}{=} [Call_j^i] EK_{i,j} EK_{Agt}^{t-1} All.$$

Furthermore, two pairs of agents (i_1, i_2) and (j_1, j_2) are complementary for depth t if and only if we have:

$$\mathsf{compl}_t(i_1, j_1) \wedge \mathsf{compl}_t(i_1, j_2) \wedge \mathsf{compl}_t(i_2, j_1) \wedge \mathsf{compl}_t(i_2, j_2).$$

We will prove that at each turn, two pairs of agents are complementary: the first pair is agent *left* along with the last agent she called at this turn, and the second is agent *right* along with the last (and only agent) she called at this turn.

The first turn is a special case where semi-experts of depth 1 are produced.

Lemma 1. *We have:*

$$w_0 \models [\mathsf{turn}_0]\big(EK_{left, n-4}(s_{left} \wedge s_0 \wedge \ldots \wedge s_{n-4}) \wedge EK_{right, n-3}(s_{right} \wedge s_{n-3}) \big).$$

Proof. Let us write ij for the call between i and j. The first turn (turn 0) of Algorithm 1 produces the following sequence of calls:

$$left0, left1, \ldots, left(n-4), right(n-3).$$

By Proposition 2.2 we have $w_0 \models [Call_0^{left}] EK_{left, 0}(s_{left} \wedge s_0)$ and therefore $w_0 \models [Call_0^{left}] K_{left}(s_{left} \wedge s_0)$. We do the same for the next call:

$$w_0 \models [Call_0^{left}][Call_1^{left}]EK_{left,1}(s_{left} \wedge s_0 \wedge s_1)$$
$$\Rightarrow \ w_0 \models [Call_0^{left}][Call_1^{left}]K_{left}(s_{left} \wedge s_0 \wedge s_1).$$

And so on until:

$$w_0 \models [Call_0^{left}][Call_1^{left}] \ldots [Call_{n-4}^{left}]EK_{left,n-4}(s_{left} \wedge s_0 \wedge s_1 \wedge \ldots \wedge s_{n-4}).$$

In the same vein we also have $w_0 \models [Call_{n-3}^{right}]EK_{right,n-3}(s_{right} \wedge s_{n-3})$.
By Proposition 2.1 we then obtain:

$$w_0 \models [Call_0^{left}] \ldots [Call_{n-4}^{left}][Call_{n-3}^{right}] \big(EK_{left,n-4}(s_{left} \wedge s_0 \wedge \ldots \wedge s_{n-4}) \ \wedge$$
$$EK_{right,n-3}(s_{right} \wedge s_{n-3}) \big)$$

which is the same as

$$w_0 \models [\mathsf{turn}_0] \big(EK_{left,n-4}(s_{left} \wedge s_0 \wedge \ldots \wedge s_{n-4}) \wedge EK_{right,n-3}(s_{right} \wedge s_{n-3}) \big).$$

□

Lemma 2. *For $t \geq 1$, we have:*

$$w_0 \models [\mathsf{turn}_0; \ldots; \mathsf{turn}_t] \big(EK_{left,n-4-t}EK_{left,0-t,\ldots,n-4-t}EK_{Agt}^{t-1}All \ \wedge$$
$$EK_{right,n-3-t}EK_{right,n-3-t}EK_{Agt}^{t-1}All \big).$$

Proof. We use induction on t. Both cases resemble the proof of Lemma 1.
Base case: $t = 1$. The turn 1 of Algorithm 1 produces the following sequence:

$$left(n{-}3), left0, left1, \ldots, left(n{-}5), right(n{-}4).$$

By Lemma 1 and Proposition 2.2 we have:

$$w_0 \models [\mathsf{turn}_0][Call_{n-3}^{left}]EK_{left,n-3}EK_{left,n-3}All$$
$$\Rightarrow \ w_0 \models [\mathsf{turn}_0][Call_{n-3}^{left}]K_{left}EK_{left,n-3}All.$$

Then again by Proposition 2.2:

$$w_0 \models [\mathsf{turn}_0][Call_{n-3}^{left}][Call_0^{left}]EK_{left,0}EK_{left,n-3,0}All$$
$$\Rightarrow \ w_0 \models [\mathsf{turn}_0][Call_{n-3}^{left}][Call_0^{left}]K_{left}EK_{left,n-3,0}All,$$

and for the next call:

$$w_0 \models [\mathsf{turn}_0][Call_{n-3}^{left}][Call_0^{left}][Call_1^{left}]EK_{left,1}EK_{left,n-3,0,1}All$$
$$\Rightarrow \ w_0 \models [\mathsf{turn}_0][Call_{n-3}^{left}][Call_0^{left}][Call_1^{left}]K_{left}EK_{left,n-3,0,1}All,$$

and so on until:

$$w_0 \models [\mathsf{turn}_0][Call_{n-3}^{left}][Call_0^{left}][Call_1^{left}] \ldots [Call_{n-5}^{left}]EK_{left,n-5}EK_{left,n-3,0,1,\ldots,n-5}All.$$

Similarly we have:

$$w_0 \models [\text{turn}_0][Call_{n-4}^{right}]EK_{right,n-4}EK_{right,n-4}All.$$

Finally we obtain the result by Proposition 2.1:

$$w_0 \models [\text{turn}_0][Call_{n-3}^{left}][Call_0^{left}]\dots[Call_{n-5}^{left}][Call_{n-4}^{right}]\big(EK_{left,n-5}EK_{left,n-3,0,1,\dots,n-5}All$$
$$\wedge\ EK_{right,n-4}EK_{right,n-4}All\big)$$
$$\Leftrightarrow\ w_0 \models [\text{turn}_0][\text{turn}_1]\big(EK_{left,n-5}EK_{left,n-3,0,1,\dots,n-5}All$$
$$\wedge\ EK_{right,n-4}EK_{right,n-4}All\big).$$

Inductive case. The reasoning is similar, but generalized to turn $t+1$. Suppose the formula is true for turn t. The turn $t+1$ is:

$$left(n-3-t),\, left(0-t),\,\dots,\, left(n-5-t),\, right(n-4-t).$$

By our induction hypothesis and Proposition 2.2 we have:

$$w_0 \models [\text{turn}_0;\dots;\text{turn}_t][Call_{n-3-t}^{left}]EK_{left,n-3-t}EK_{left,n-3-t}EK_{Agt}EK_{Agt}^{t-1}All,$$

that is:

$$w_0 \models [\text{turn}_0;\dots;\text{turn}_t][Call_{n-3-t}^{left}]EK_{left,n-3-t}EK_{left,n-3-t}EK_{Agt}^{t}All,$$

which implies:

$$w_0 \models [\text{turn}_0;\dots;\text{turn}_t][Call_{n-3-t}^{left}]K_{left}EK_{left,n-3-t}EK_{Agt}^{t}All.$$

Then by Proposition 2.1:

$$w_0 \models [\text{turn}_0;\dots;\text{turn}_t][Call_{n-3-t}^{left}][Call_{0-t}^{left}]EK_{left,0-t}EK_{left,n-3-t,0-t}EK_{Agt}^{t}All$$
$$\Rightarrow\ w_0 \models [\text{turn}_0;\dots;\text{turn}_t][Call_{n-3-t}^{left}][Call_{0-t}^{left}]K_{left}EK_{left,n-3-t,0-t}EK_{Agt}^{t}All,$$

...and so on until:

$$w_0 \models [\text{turn}_0;\dots;\text{turn}_t][Call_{n-3-t}^{left}][Call_{0-t}^{left}]\dots[Call_{n-5-t}^{left}]$$
$$EK_{left,n-5-t}EK_{left,n-3-t,0-t,\dots,n-5-t}EK_{Agt}^{t}All.$$

Moreover, by Proposition 2.2:

$$w_0 \models [\text{turn}_0;\dots;\text{turn}_t][Call_{n-4-t}^{right}]EK_{right,n-4-t}EK_{right,n-4-t}EK_{Agt}EK_{Agt}^{t-1}All,$$

that is:

$$w_0 \models [\text{turn}_0;\dots;\text{turn}_t][Call_{n-4-t}^{right}]EK_{right,n-4-t}EK_{right,n-4-t}EK_{Agt}^{t}All.$$

We end as usual with Proposition 2.1:

$$w_0 \models [\mathsf{turn}_0; \ldots; \mathsf{turn}_t][Call^{left}_{n-3-t}] \ldots [Call^{left}_{n-5-t}][Call^{right}_{n-4-t}]$$
$$\left(EK_{left,n-5-t} EK_{left,n-3-t,\ldots,n-5-t} EK^t_{Agt} All \; \wedge \right.$$
$$\left. EK_{right,n-4-t} EK_{right,n-4-t} EK^t_{Agt} All \right)$$
$$\Leftrightarrow \; w_0 \models [\mathsf{turn}_0; \ldots; \mathsf{turn}_t][\mathsf{turn}_{t+1}]$$
$$\left(EK_{left,n-5-t} EK_{left,n-3-t,\ldots,n-5-t} EK^t_{Agt} All \; \wedge \right.$$
$$\left. EK_{right,n-4-t} EK_{right,n-4-t} EK^t_{Agt} All \right),$$

which is our result for $t+1$.   □

Lemma 3. *After turn $t-1$ of Algorithm 1, the pairs $(left, n-3-t)$ and $(right, 0-t)$ are complementary for depth t.*

Proof. From Lemma 2 we can deduce:

$$w_0 \models [\mathsf{turn}_0, \ldots, \mathsf{turn}_{t-1}]\left(K_{left} EK_{left,1-t,\ldots,n-3-t} EK^{t-2}_{Agt} All \; \wedge \right.$$
$$\left. K_{right} EK_{right,0-t} EK^{t-2}_{Agt} All \right).$$

Applying Proposition 2.2 we obtain:

$$w_0 \models [\mathsf{turn}_0, \ldots, \mathsf{turn}_{t-1}][Call^{left}_{right}] EK_{left,right} EK_{Agt} EK^{t-2}_{Agt} All,$$

that is:

$$w_0 \models [\mathsf{turn}_0, \ldots, \mathsf{turn}_{t-1}][Call^{left}_{right}] EK_{left,right} EK^{t-1}_{Agt} All,$$

which is equivalent to:

$$w_0 \models [\mathsf{turn}_0, \ldots, \mathsf{turn}_{t-1}] compl_t (left, right).$$

By the same reasoning for $left$ and $0-t$, $right$ and $n-3-t$, and finally $n-3-t$ and $0-t$, we obtain that each of them are complementary, hence the result.   □

Lemma 4. *The goal for depth t, $EK^t_{Agt} All$, is reached after the turn t of Algorithm 1.*

Proof. Turn t of Algorithm 1 is:

$$left(0-t), left(1-t), \ldots, left(n-4-t), right(n-3-t).$$

By Lemma 3, after turn $t-1$ and the first call $left(0-t)$ of turn t, agents $left$ and $0-t$ become experts for depth t. (Thus $EK_{left,0-t} EK^{t-1}_{Agt} All$.) Then after the $n-4$ calls $left(1-t), \ldots, left(n-4-t)$ we get by Proposition 2.2:

$$K_{1-t} EK^{t-1}_{Agt} All \; \wedge \ldots \wedge \; K_{n-4-t} EK^{t-1}_{Agt} All,$$

that is, $1-t$, ..., $n-4-t$ are all experts for depth t. Finally, after the last call $right(n-3-t)$, and also by Lemma 3, agents $right$ and $n-3-t$ become experts for depth t. (Thus $EK_{right,n-3-t} EK^{t-1}_{Agt} All$.) Therefore after the $n-2$ calls of turn t we have $EK_{Agt} EK^{t-1}_{Agt} All$, which is equivalent to $EK^t_{Agt} All$.   □

Proposition 3. *The sequence resulting from Algorithm 1 gives a solution to the generalized gossip problem.*

Proof. By Lemma 4, the goal for depth t is reached after turn t of Algorithm 1. Thus the goal for depth k is reached after turn k ($k+1$ turns), i.e., at the end of the algorithm. □

6   Conclusion

We have provided a logical analysis of the gossip problem, focusing on how higher-order shared knowledge can be obtained. We did so in a particular dynamic epistemic logic: Dynamic Epistemic Logic of Propositional Assignment and Observation DEL-PAO. Its integration of knowledge modalities and dynamic modalities provides a handy language in order to reason about concepts such as an agent being a semi-expert, which is pivotal in our algorithm.

The gossip problem recently attracted quite some attention in the dynamic epistemic logic community [2,3,7]. We believe that our generalization—as well as further variations where e.g. calls can only be made according to some graph structure—provide interesting, canonical multiagent planning problems that can be compared to the blocksworld in classical planning. This is the subject of ongoing work; first steps are reported in [6].

Acknowledgements. We would like to acknowledge several discussions about the gossip problem at the inspiring August 2015 workshop "To be announced" in Leiden, in particular with Hans van Ditmarsch, Jan van Eijck, Malvin Gattinger, Louwe Kuijer, Christian Muise, Pere Pardo, Rahim Ramezanian and Francois Schwarzentruber. We are also grateful to Davide Grossi, Emiliano Lorini and Martin Cooper.

References

1. Akkoyunlu, E.A., Ekanadham, K., Hubert, R.V.: Some constraints and tradeoffs in the design of network communications. In: Proceedings of the 5th ACM Symposium on Operating Systems Principles, pp. 67–74. ACM Press (1975)
2. Attamah, M., van Ditmarsch, H., Grossi, D., van der Hoek, W.: A framework for epistemic gossip protocols. In: Bulling, N. (ed.) EUMAS 2014. LNCS, vol. 8953, pp. 193–209. Springer, Heidelberg (2015). doi:10.1007/978-3-319-17130-2_13
3. Attamah, M., van Ditmarsch, H., Grossi, D., van der Hoek, W.: Knowledge and gossip. In: Proceedings of 21st ECAI pp. 21–26 (2014)
4. Baker, B., Shostak, R.: Gossips and telephones. Discrete Math. **2**(3), 191–193 (1972)
5. Charrier, T., Herzig, A., Lorini, E., Schwarzentruber, F.: Building epistemic logic from observations and public announcements. In: International Conference on Principles of Knowledge Representation and Reasoning (KR), CapeTown. AAAI Press (2016). http://www.aaai.org/Press/press.php, http://www.irit.fr/~Andreas.Herzig/P/Kr16.html

6. Cooper, M., Herzig, A., Maffre, F., Maris, F., Régnier, P.: A simple account of multiagent epistemic planning. In: Maris, F. (ed.) Journées Francophones sur la Planification, la Décision et l'Apprentissage (JFPDA), Rennes, 1 May 2015–3 July 2015, p. (online). AFIA (Juillet 2015). http://www.afia.asso.fr/, http://pfia2015. inria.fr/actes/index.php?procpage=jfpda

7. van Ditmarsch, H., van Eijck, J., Pardo, P., Ramezanian, R., Schwarzentruber, F.: Dynamic gossip. CoRR abs/1511.00867 (2015). http://arxiv.org/abs/1511.00867

8. Fagin, R., Halpern, J.Y., Moses, Y., Vardi, M.Y.: Reasoning About Knowledge. MIT Press, Cambridge (1995)

9. Hajnal, A., Milner, E.C.B., Szemerédi, E.: A cure for the telephone disease. Can. Math. Bull. 15(3), 447–450 (1972)

10. Herzig, A., Lorini, E., Maffre, F.: A poor man's epistemic logic based on propositional assignment and higher-order observation. In: van der Hoek, W., Holliday, W.H., Wang, W.-F. (eds.) LORI 2015. LNCS, vol. 9394, pp. 156–168. Springer, Heidelberg (2015). http://www.irit.fr/Andreas.Herzig/P/Lori15.html

11. van der Hoek, W., Iliev, P., Wooldridge, M.: A logic of revelation and concealment. In: van der Hoek, W., Padgham, L., Conitzer, V., Winikoff, M. (eds.) Proceedings of the 11th International Conference on Autonomous Agents and Multiagent Systems, IFAAMAS, pp. 1115–1122 (2012)

12. van der Hoek, W., Troquard, N., Wooldridge, M.: Knowledge and control. In: Sonenberg, L., Stone, P., Tumer, K., Yolum, P. (eds.) Proceedings of the 10th International Conference on Autonomous Agents and Multiagent Systems, IFAAMAS, pp. 719–726 (2011)

13. Hurkens, C.A.J.: Spreading gossip efficiently. Nieuw Archief voor Wiskunde 5/1(2), 208–210 (2000)

14. Tijdeman, R.: On a telephone problem. Nieuw Archief voor Wiskunde 19(3), 188–192 (1971)

Norms, Trust, and Reputation

Identifying Malicious Behavior in Multi-party Bipolar Argumentation Debates

Dionysios Kontarinis$^{(\boxtimes)}$ and Francesca Toni

Department of Computing, Imperial College London, London, UK
denniskont@gmail.com, f.toni@imperial.ac.uk

Abstract. Lately, several works have analyzed potential uses of argumentation in multi-party debates. Usually, the focus of such works is the computation of a collectively "correct" outcome, a challenging task even when the debate's users truthfully express their beliefs. This work focuses on debates where some users may exhibit specific types of "malicious" behavior: they may lie (by making statements they do not believe to hold) and they may hide valuable information (by not making relevant statements they believe to hold). Our approach is the following: firstly, we define "user attributes" which capture different aspects of a user's behavior in a debate (how active, how opinionated and how classifiable a user has been); then, we build and test experimentally hypotheses that, from the values of these attributes, can predict whether a user has lied and/or hidden valuable information.

1 Introduction

Several works, e.g. [4,10,12,13], have analyzed potential uses of argumentation in multi-party debates. Some focus on computing a "correct" collective outcome [10], given the users' claims, a challenging task even when users truthfully express their opinions. Others, e.g. [12,13,15], focus on user strategies.

In [12] concepts from game theory are used for the analysis of argumentation debates where some users, in order to satisfy their preferences, may exhibit "malicious" behavior: they may lie (by making claims they do not believe to hold) and they may hide (by not making claims they believe to hold).

In this work we attempt the analysis of argumentation debates in order to estimate which users have exhibited malicious behavior. We assume that there is an issue, which is an argument, being debated, as for example in [11]. We also assume that each user has a viewpoint over that issue, in the form of a (private) bipolar argumentation framework [1,5], which has two types of relations over arguments: an attack relation and a support relation. Users engage in a debate, by progressively stating new attacks and supports. These debates can be seen as abstractions of opinion exchanges in social networks, in general, and in argumentation-inspired social networks such as www.convinceme.net and www.quaestio-it.com [8]. In these settings, users have no access to the private argumentation frameworks of other users, and therefore no way to assess the truthfulness of information contributed to the debate. Our work aims at helping users and debate administrators estimate user truthfulness.

© Springer International Publishing Switzerland 2016
M. Rovatsos et al. (Eds.): EUMAS 2015/AT 2015, LNAI 9571, pp. 267–278, 2016.
DOI: 10.1007/978-3-319-33509-4_21

Our approach is the following: firstly, we define several *user attributes* which capture different aspects of a user's behavior. Then, we build and test experimentally *hypotheses* that, from the values of these attributes, predict whether a user may have lied and/or hidden valuable information. The experimental evaluation is in Java and simulates and analyzes a large number of debates. Albeit preliminary, the results seem to suggest that user attributes may indeed be good indicators of lying and hiding.

The paper is organized as follows. In Sect. 2 we present background on bipolar argumentation. In Sect. 3 we define our general debate framework. In Sect. 4 we define user attributes. In Sect. 5 we define lying and hiding in our debate setting, and we propose two hypotheses for identifying malicious behavior, which are experimentally tested in Sect. 6. In Sect. 7 we conclude.

2 Background on Bipolar Argumentation

A *Bipolar Argumentation Framework* (BAF) [1,5] is a tuple $\langle Arg, Att, Sup \rangle$ where: Arg is a set, whose elements are referred to as *arguments*, $Att \subseteq Arg \times Arg$, referred to as *attack relation* over arguments, and $Sup \subseteq Arg \times Arg$, referred to as *support relation* over arguments. We will represent BAFs as graphs whose nodes are elements of Arg and whose edges are of two types: simple arrows, to represent attack in Att, and double arrows, to represent support in Sup, as illustrated in the following example.

Example 1. Three users take part in a debate about global warming. The issue being debated is argument a = "global warming should be addressed now, because it already affects our ecosystems". User u_2 introduces the attack (b,a) with b = "there is no conclusive proof of global warming taking place", and then user u_3 introduces the support (c,a) with c = "recent studies show that global warming effects are real". User u_1 observes the debate but, when he is able to intervene, he refuses to contribute. The debate gives rise to the BAF $\langle Arg, Att, Sup \rangle$ with $Arg = \{a,b,c\}$, $Att = \{(b,a)\}$ and $Sup = \{(c,a)\}$, represented graphically in Fig. 1:

Fig. 1. BAF for Example 1.

Arguments in BAFs may be evaluated using a number of different methods (known as "semantics"), falling broadly within two classes: (1) methods for determining *acceptable sets of arguments*, e.g. as in [3], and (2) methods for determining a *numerical strength*, e.g. as in [2,5]. We shall focus on the latter approach, but we will not commit to any specific method until Sect. 6. Until then, we will use a generic evaluation function $\sigma : Arg \rightarrow [0,1]$ but assume that the addition to a BAF of a support for (attack against) an argument x increases (resp. decreases) $\sigma(x)$. In Sect. 6 we will choose σ from [2], for which this assumption holds.

3   A General Debate Framework

The starting point for our work is a general framework for multi-party argumentation debate focused on the evaluation of a specific argument, the *issue* of the debate, and involving users with different viewpoints with respect to that issue, represented by *private BAFs*. The evaluation of the issue, after the aggregation of all users' opinions, can be deemed a *collective goal*, shared by all users. We assume that each user pursues a *personal goal*, which is either the maximization or the minimization of the issue's evaluation by σ.

Definition 1. *Let a be the* (debate) *issue. Let $\mathcal{U}$ be a set of* users. *Each $u \in \mathcal{U}$ has a* private BAF, *denoted $AS_u = \langle Arg_u, Att_u, Sup_u \rangle$, such that $a \in Arg_u$, and a* personal goal, *which is either $max\sigma(a)$ or $min\sigma(a)$.*

A debate takes place in discrete timesteps. At each timestep, users introduce attacks against and/or supports for arguments, or pass (introducing no attack or support).

Definition 2. *A debate is a tuple $\mathcal{D} = \langle a, \mathcal{U}, IntroAtt, IntroSup, IntroPass \rangle$ such that: $IntroAtt \subseteq \{\langle t, u, (x,y) \rangle \mid t \in \mathbb{N}, u \in \mathcal{U}\}$, $IntroSup \subseteq \{\langle t, u, (x,y) \rangle \mid t \in \mathbb{N}, u \in \mathcal{U}\}$, $IntroPass \subseteq \{\langle t, u, pass \rangle \mid t \in \mathbb{N}, u \in \mathcal{U}\}$ where pass is a constant.*

In the remainder of the paper, unless otherwise indicated, we will assume as given a debate $\mathcal{D}=\langle a, \mathcal{U}, IntroAtt, IntroSup, IntroPass \rangle$. The *first timestep* of a debate is 0, the *last timestep* is defined as follows:

Definition 3. *The* last timestep *of $\mathcal{D}$ is $lastTs(\mathcal{D})$ such that:
if $IntroAtt = IntroSup = IntroPass = \{\}$, then $lastTs(\mathcal{D}) = 0$;
otherwise $lastTs(\mathcal{D}) = t$ such that:*

1. $\exists \langle t, u, (x,y) \rangle \in IntroAtt \cup IntroSup$ or $\exists \langle t, u, pass \rangle \in IntroPass$, and
2. $\nexists \langle t', u', (x',y') \rangle \in IntroAtt \cup IntroSup$ and $\nexists \langle t', u', pass \rangle \in IntroPass$, with $t' > t$.

All users' introductions in a debate lead to the emergence of a collective opinion in the form of a common BAF, that we call *gameboard* as in [4,10]. The fact that a debate "remembers" all the introductions that users made, and when they made them, means that it is possible to compute the gameboard at every timestep, up to and including the last, as follows:

Definition 4. *Let $t \in \mathbb{N}$ be such that $0 \le t \le lastTs(\mathcal{D})$. The* gameboard *of $\mathcal{D}$, at timestep t, is the BAF $GB_t^{\mathcal{D}} = \langle Arg_t^{\mathcal{D}}, Att_t^{\mathcal{D}}, Sup_t^{\mathcal{D}} \rangle$, such that:*
  $Arg_t^{\mathcal{D}} = \{a\} \cup \{x, y \mid \exists \langle t', u, (x,y) \rangle \in IntroAtt \cup IntroSup, 0 \le t' \le t\}$,
  $Att_t^{\mathcal{D}} = \{(x,y) \mid \exists \langle t', u, (x,y) \rangle \in IntroAtt, 0 \le t' \le t\}$,
  $Sup_t^{\mathcal{D}} = \{(x,y) \mid \exists \langle t', u, (x,y) \rangle \in IntroSup, 0 \le t' \le t\}$.

As an illustration, the BAF of Example 1 is the gameboard $GB_3^{\mathcal{D}}$ at the last timestep of the following debate:
  $\mathcal{D} = \langle a, \{u_1, u_2, u_3\}, \{\langle 1, u_2, (b,a) \rangle\}, \{\langle 2, u_3, (c,a) \rangle\}, \{\langle 3, u_1, pass \rangle\} \rangle$
Debates and gameboards are motivated by and provide abstractions of a number of currently available online debate platforms, as for example www.convinceme.net and

www.quaestio-it.com. In these platforms, users are able to make claims and back them up with relevant arguments, expressed in natural language, as well as introduce relations between arguments, such as attacks and supports, or simply observe.

In the remainder, we will use the following notations. Firstly, $Intro_u^{\mathcal{D}} = \{ \langle t, u, obj \rangle \mid \langle t, u, obj \rangle \in IntroAtt \cup IntroSup \cup IntroPass \}$ denotes all the introductions by user u in $\mathcal{D}$ (similarly for $IntroAtt_u^{\mathcal{D}}$, $IntroSup_u^{\mathcal{D}}$, $IntroPass_u^{\mathcal{D}}$). Moreover, for an introduction $i = \langle t, u, obj \rangle$, where $obj = (x, y)$ or $obj = pass$, the function $ts(i)$ returns its timestep t, while the function $rel(i)$ returns (x, y) or $pass$, respectively. Furthermore, $\sigma_t^{\mathcal{D}}(x)$ denotes the evaluation, using σ as in Sect. 2, of argument x in $GB_t^{\mathcal{D}}$. For all notations, if $\mathcal{D}$ is clear from the context, we will drop the $\mathcal{D}$ superscript. Finally, we refer to the set of all possible debates as Δ, and to the union of all $Arg_t^{\mathcal{D}}$ for all $t \in \mathbb{N}$ and $\mathcal{D} \in \Delta$ as $Arg_{\mathbb{N}}^{\Delta}$.

4   User Behavior Analysis

In order to analyze user behavior in multi-party argumentation debates, we define three *(user) attributes*, each capturing a specific aspect of user behavior. The first two attributes measure how active and opinionated a user has been in a debate. Thus, they describe a user's *general stance* in a debate. The third attribute estimates how similar a user's *beliefs* are to those of some known user classes.

The *activity attribute* indicates the quantity of a user's contribution in a debate. Roughly, the fewer pass introductions a user makes, the more active he is considered.

Definition 5. *The* activity evaluation *of a user in a debate is given by the function* $active : \mathcal{U} \times \Delta \to [0, 1]$: *if* $|Intro_u| = 0$, *then* $active(u, \mathcal{D}) = 0$, *else*

$$active(u, \mathcal{D}) = \frac{|IntroAtt_u \cup IntroSup_u|}{|Intro_u|}$$

Next, the *opinionatedness attribute* indicates how one-sided a user's impact has been on an argument's evaluation (with respect to σ). Roughly, the more a user has increased (or decreased) an argument's evaluation, the more opinionated he is deemed on that argument.

Definition 6. *The* opinionatedness evaluation *of a user on an argument in a debate is given by the function* $opinionated : \mathcal{U} \times Arg_{\mathbb{N}}^{\Delta} \times \Delta \to [0, 1]$:
if $\sum_{i \in Intro_u} |\sigma_{ts(i)}(x) - \sigma_{ts(i)-1}(x)| = 0$, *then* $opinionated(u, x, \mathcal{D}) = 0$, *else*

$$opinionated(u, x, \mathcal{D}) = \frac{|\sum_{i \in Intro_u} \sigma_{ts(i)}(x) - \sigma_{ts(i)-1}(x)|}{\sum_{i \in Intro_u} |\sigma_{ts(i)}(x) - \sigma_{ts(i)-1}(x)|}$$

In the fraction above, the numerator reflects how one-sided u's impact has been on $\sigma(x)$ (either increasing it, or decreasing it), while the denominator reflects how large u's overall impact has been on $\sigma(x)$.

Example 2. Let us assume that in debate $\mathcal{D}$, user u has made two relation introductions and three pass introductions. So, $active(u, \mathcal{D}) = \frac{|IntroAtt_u \cup IntroSup_u|}{|Intro_u|} = \frac{2}{2+3} = \frac{2}{5} = 0.4$.

Moreover, let us assume that u's first relation introduction had increased $\sigma(a)$ from 0.2 to 0.7 and u's second relation introduction had decreased $\sigma(a)$ from 0.5 to 0. Thus, $opinionated(u, a, \mathcal{D}) = \frac{|(0.7-0.2)+(0-0.5)|}{|0.7-0.2|+|0-0.5|} = \frac{0}{1} = 0$. Notice that this is the lowest possible opinionatedness value, indicating that u is not opinionated at all towards a. This is sensible, since u has equally increased and decreased a's evaluation.

In order to define the third user attribute, we introduce the notion of *user class*. In practice, if some users think in a similar way about a topic, then we may say that they *belong to the same class*. For example, there may be a class of users who believe global warming is a threat, and another class who believe it is not. Most probably, users of the same class will agree on many points, though not on everything. For example, a scientist may consider an elaborate argument that another user will not. We define user classes as BAFs:

Definition 7. *Let C be a set of* classes. *For each $\kappa \in C$, $AS_\kappa = \langle Arg_\kappa, Att_\kappa, Sup_\kappa \rangle$ is a BAF such that $Att_\kappa \cup Sup_\kappa \neq \{\}$.*

Users have personal BAFs which may be similar, but not identical, to classes, as illustrated next.

Example 3. For some class $\kappa \in C$, and two users $u_1, u_2 \in \mathcal{U}$, let the BAFs AS_κ, AS_{u_1} and AS_{u_2} be as given in Fig. 2.

Both u_1 and u_2 may be deemed to *belong to* κ, even though AS_{u_2} is not identical to AS_κ.

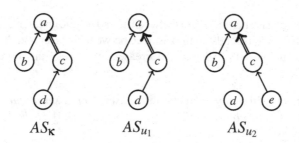

Fig. 2. The BAF of class κ (left) and the private BAFs of users u_1 and u_2 (middle and right) for Example 3.

The *classifiability attribute* estimates how *distant* a user is from classes in some given set. The notion of distance we use is inspired by the *edit distance*, used e.g. in [6], to measure the similarity of argumentation systems, albeit in our case it depends on a class, on introductions by the user alone, and on those by the other users.

Definition 8. *The function distance:* $\mathcal{U} \times C \times \Delta \rightarrow [0,1]$ *is defined as distance$(u, \kappa, \mathcal{D}) = \frac{dsg_{u,\kappa}}{agr_{u,\kappa} + dsg_{u,\kappa}}$, with $agr_{u,\kappa}$ ($dsg_{u,\kappa}$), the number of agreements (resp. disagreements) between u and κ, computed as follows:*

1. Set $agr_{u,\kappa} := 0$, $dsg_{u,\kappa} := 0$.
2. For every (x,y) such that either $(x,y) \in Att_\kappa \cup Sup_\kappa$ or $\exists \langle t,u,(x,y)\rangle \in IntroAtt_u \cup IntroSup_u$, find the corresponding case in the following table, where Rel is one of Att or Sup:

Case for (x,y)	$\exists \langle t,u,(x,y)\rangle$ $\in IntroRel_u$	$(x,y) \in Rel_\kappa$	$\exists \langle t',u',(x,y)\rangle \in IntroRel_{u'}$ with $u' \neq u$	Considered
1	Yes	Yes	Yes	Agreement
2	Yes	Yes	No	Agreement
3	Yes	No	Yes	Disagreement
4	Yes	No	No	Disagreement
5	No	Yes	Yes	Agreement
6	No	Yes	No	Disagreement
7	No	No	Yes	Agreement
8	No	No	No	Agreement

If the column "Considered" gives "Agreement", then $agr_{u,\kappa} := agr_{u,\kappa} + 1$, else $dsg_{u,\kappa} := dsg_{u,\kappa} + 1$.

Since the BAF of a class cannot (by definition) be without attacks and without supports, it can be proven that the denominator of $\frac{dsg_{u,\kappa}}{agr_{u,\kappa}+dsg_{u,\kappa}}$ is always different from zero. According to the above definition of distance, a disagreement between u and κ can take place in three cases: in cases 3 and 4, where u has introduced a relation (x,y) which κ does not have, and in case 6, where u has not introduced a relation (x,y) which κ has, and no other user has introduced it either. We consider case 5 as an agreement, because it is redundant for u to reintroduce (x,y), since this introduction will not change the gameboard.

The more disagreements there are between u and κ, the greater their distance is. Then, user classifiability depends on the distance between the user and the class which is "closest" to him. The more their distance decreases (increases), the more classifiability increases (resp. decreases).

Definition 9. *The* classifiability evaluation *of a user w.r.t. a set of classes in a debate is given by the function classifiable* : $\mathcal{U} \times 2^C \times \Delta \to [0,1]$ *such that classifiable* $(u,K,\mathcal{D}) = 1 - \min_{\kappa \in K} distance(u,\kappa,\mathcal{D})$.

Example 4. Let $\mathcal{D} = \langle a, \{u_1,u_2,u_3\}, \{\langle 1,u_1,(b,a)\rangle\}, \{\langle 2,u_2,(c,a)\rangle\}, \{\langle 3,u_3,pass\rangle\}\rangle$. Here, $IntroAtt_{u_1} = \{\langle 1,u_1,(b,a)\rangle\}$ and $IntroSup_{u_1} = \{\}$. Moreover, the gameboard of $\mathcal{D}$ at 3 is the BAF in Example 1. Let κ be as in Example 3. To determine $distance(u_1,\kappa)$ we consider, in turn, all the attacks and supports either introduced by u_1 or belonging in AS_κ. u_1 has introduced the attack (b,a) and it belongs to Att_κ, so we have an agreement (case 2). There is no other introduction by u_1, so we now check the relations of κ. The support (c,a) belongs to Sup_κ, u_1 has not introduced it, but another user (u_2) has introduced it, so we have another agreement (case 5). Finally, the attack (d,c) belongs to Att_κ, u_1 has not introduced it, and neither has any other user, so we have a disagreement (case 6). In total, $agr_{u_1,\kappa} = 2$ and $dsg_{u_1,\kappa} = 1$, thus $distance(u_1,\kappa,\mathcal{D}) = \frac{1}{3}$. As a result, $classifiable(u_1,\{\kappa\},\mathcal{D}) = 1 - \frac{1}{3} = \frac{2}{3}$.

5   Malicious User Behavior

In the context of multi-party debates, *malicious* user behavior could be defined in various ways, e.g. in terms of aggressivity. In this work, we shall call a user malicious if he undermines the satisfaction of the collective goal (of evaluating the issue after aggregating all users' opinions, see Sect. 3), More specifically, we assume that this can happen in two ways: (1) the user may avoid to contribute towards the satisfaction of the collective goal by *hiding* attacks and supports which would affect the issue's evaluation; (2) the user may mislead the satisfaction of the collective goal by *lying* (e.g. as studied in [14]); in our setting, this amounts to stating attacks and supports he does not believe (i.e. they are not in his private BAF). Formally:

Definition 10. $\langle t, u, (x,y) \rangle \in$ *IntroRel (such that Rel is one of Att, Sup) is a lie if and only if $(x,y) \notin Rel_u$; $\langle t, u, pass \rangle$ is a hide if and only if $\exists (x,y) \in Rel_u$ (such that Rel is one of Att, Sup) such that, given $\mathcal{D}'$ obtained from $\mathcal{D}$ after deleting $\langle t, u, pass \rangle$ (from IntroPass$_u^{\mathcal{D}}$) and adding $\langle t, u, (x,y) \rangle$ (to IntroRel$_u^{\mathcal{D}}$): $\sigma_t^{\mathcal{D}'}(a) \neq \sigma_t^{\mathcal{D}}(a)$; $\langle t, u, obj \rangle$ is a malicious action if and only if it is a lie or a hide.*

A user may decide to perform a malicious action if this may help him achieve his personal goal (see Definition 1). From now on, users who adopt the goal of maximizing (minimizing) the issue's evaluation are said to be *PRO* (resp. *CON*). Let us give an example of strategic lying and hiding in our setting:

Example 5. Let u_2 be a *CON* user, whose private BAF AS_{u_2} is illustrated in Fig. 3:

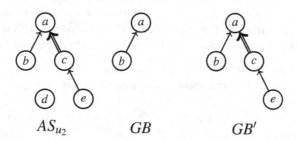

AS_{u_2} GB GB'

Fig. 3. The private BAF of user u_2 (left) and two different gameboards (middle and right) for Example 5.

Firstly, we analyze the case where the gameboard of the dialogue is GB above. The only relation in AS_{u_2} whose introduction can change a's evaluation in GB is the support (c,a). By introducing it, a's evaluation increases (by the assumptions at the end of Sect. 2). But, since u_2 is *CON*, he may decide to pass instead. This would be a hide. Secondly, let us analyze the case where the gameboard is GB' above. User u_2 cannot introduce any relation from his private BAF to change a's evaluation, but he may decide to introduce attack (d,c) and decrease the issue's evaluation. Since attack (d,c) is not in AS_{u_2}, that would be a lie.

Let us underline that, in the following, in addition to assuming that every user is either *PRO* or *CON*, we will also assume that there exists a set of classes K, and each debating user will be said to belong to one of these classes.

We now formulate two hypotheses about the relation between the three user attributes defined in Sect. 4 and the malicious actions of lying and hiding.

Let z_u denote the evaluation of an attribute, for user u, and let $z_u \uparrow (z_u \downarrow)$ indicate that the evaluation of that attribute for u is higher (resp. lower) than the average evaluation of that attribute for all users. Also, let $\mathcal{L}_u^{\mathcal{D}} (\mathcal{H}_u^{\mathcal{D}})$ denote the percentage of introductions made by u in $\mathcal{D}$ which were lies (resp. hides). Finally, let $\mathcal{L}_u^{\mathcal{D}} \uparrow (\mathcal{L}_u^{\mathcal{D}} \downarrow)$ indicate that the percentage of lies by u in $\mathcal{D}$ is higher (resp. lower) than the average percentage of lies by all users. Similarly, let $\mathcal{H}_u^{\mathcal{D}} \uparrow (\mathcal{H}_u^{\mathcal{D}} \downarrow)$ indicate that the percentage of hides by user u in $\mathcal{D}$ is higher (resp. lower) than the average percentage of hides by all users.

Hypothesis 1. $active(u, \mathcal{D}) \uparrow$ and $opinionated(u, a, \mathcal{D}) \uparrow$ and $classifiable(u, K, \mathcal{D}) \downarrow \Longrightarrow \mathcal{L}_u^{\mathcal{D}} \uparrow$

Hypothesis 1 says that a combination of high activity, high opinionatedness on the issue, and low classifiability indicates a liar. The intuition behind it is as follows. Firstly, a higher-than-average activity may indicate a liar, since a liar is not only introducing relations appearing in his private BAF (as honest users do), but he also "makes-up" introductions (lies) when they are useful to him. Secondly, a higher-than-average opinionatedness on the issue may indicate a liar, since lies are always introduced strategically in order to increase or decrease the issue's evaluation. Thirdly, a lower-than-average classifiability may indicate a liar. Indeed, since we have assumed that every user belongs to some class, their private BAFs are somewhat similar to the BAF of that class. When a user "disagrees" with every class (and has a lower-than-average classifiability), there are two possibilities: either (i) the "disagreement" is honest, or (ii) the user is lying. Finally, a combination of such values for all three attributes is an even stronger indication of a liar.

Hypothesis 2. $active(u, \mathcal{D}) \downarrow$ and $opinionated(u, a, \mathcal{D}) \uparrow \Longrightarrow \mathcal{H}_u^{\mathcal{D}} \uparrow$

Hypothesis 2 says that a combination of low activity and high opinionatedness on the issue indicates a hider. The intuition behind it is as follows. Firstly, a lower-than-average activity may indicate a hider, since a hider refrains from introducing relations which do not help achieve his personal goal (contrary to honest users). Secondly, a higher-than-average opinionatedness may indicate a hider, for the same reason. Finally, a combination of such values for the two attributes is an even stronger indication of a hider.

We do not claim that these hypotheses lead to the definite identification of liars and hiders. Nonetheless, they may be valuable to debate system administrators and to users, as they can raise "red flags" about potentially malicious users.

6   Experimental Evaluation

In order to test hypotheses 1 and 2 we conducted an experimental evaluation. To the best of our knowledge, no repository exists of debates for which the maliciousness of participants is known. Therefore, we opted for simulating debates, as follows.

- **Generation of BAFs**. Since many existing platforms model debates as trees, all BAFs in the simulation (for classes, users, gameboards) were trees, all with the issue as root. We chose for these trees to have a maximum branching factor of 4 and to contain at most 20 arguments and thus 19 relations.
- **Argument evaluation**. We used the function σ defined as the final score of [2].
- **Generation of user classes**. For each debate, we randomly generated 3 user classes (with their BAFs).
- **Generation of users**. From each user class, we randomly generated 4 users, as follows: we replicated with a 90 % probability each relation (and its arguments) from the class' BAF into the user's BAF. Thus each user was structurally "similar", but possibly not identical, to one class. The 4 users comprised of
  - one *honest user* who could never lie nor hide;
  - one *liar user* who could lie as many times as he wanted, but could never hide; the possible lies of a user u were restricted to a randomly generated set of attacks and supports $PossLies_u$;
  - one *hider user* who could hide as many times as he wanted, but could never lie;
  - one *malicious user* who could lie, restricted to $PossLies_u$, and hide, as many times as he wanted.

For each experiment, the 12 users (4 × 3 classes) were partitioned into *PRO* and *CON*, as follows: a user u was *PRO* if and only if the issue's evaluation $\sigma(u)$ in AS_u was at least 0.5, and *CON* otherwise.
- **Debate protocol**.
  - users took *turns* following an order over $\mathcal{U}$ and introducing a single relation or pass per turn;
  - users were *not allowed* to introduce an attack or support already in the debate gameboard;
  - each debate *terminated* after $|\mathcal{U}|$ passes in a row.
- **User strategies**. Each user u followed the strategy described informally below, with $t = lastTs(\mathcal{D})$:
  1. u computes the set P of all his *possible relation introductions* at $t+1$, i.e. $\langle t+1, u, (x,y) \rangle$ such that $(x,y) \in Att_u \cup Sup_u$ and $\sigma_t^{\mathcal{D}}(a) \neq \sigma_{t+1}^{\mathcal{D}'}(a)$, where $\mathcal{D}'$ is $\mathcal{D}$ after introducing any member of P;
  2. if u is a *liar user* or a *malicious user* then u computes the set M of all *possible lie relation introductions* at $t+1$, i.e. $\langle t+1, u, (x,y) \rangle$ such that $(x,y) \in PossLies_u$ and $\sigma_t^{\mathcal{D}}(a) \neq \sigma_{t+1}^{\mathcal{D}'}(a)$ where $\mathcal{D}'$ is $\mathcal{D}$ after introducing any member of M; all elements of M are then added to P;
  3. if $P = \{\}$ then the strategy returns $\langle t+1, u, pass \rangle$; else let $\mathcal{D}^{pass}$ be $\mathcal{D}$ after pass introduction $\langle t+1, u, pass \rangle$ and let $\mathcal{D}^i$ be $\mathcal{D}$ after relation introduction i;
     (a) if u is *PRO*:
         let $i^* = \operatorname*{argmax}_{i \in P} \sigma_{t+1}^{\mathcal{D}^i}(a)$; if $\sigma_{t+1}^{\mathcal{D}^{i^*}}(a) > \sigma_{t+1}^{\mathcal{D}^{pass}}(a)$ then the strategy returns i^*;
     (b) if u is *CON*:
         let $i^* = \operatorname*{argmin}_{i \in P} \sigma_{t+1}^{\mathcal{D}^i}(a)$; if $\sigma_{t+1}^{\mathcal{D}^{i^*}}(a) < \sigma_{t+1}^{\mathcal{D}^{pass}}(a)$ then the strategy returns i^*;
     (c) if $P \setminus PossLies_u = \{\}$ then the strategy returns $\langle t+1, u, pass \rangle$;
     (d) if u is a *hider* or *malicious user* then the strategy returns $\langle t+1, u, pass \rangle$;
     (e) otherwise, the strategy returns a random member of $P \setminus PossLies_u$.

Intuitively, the user first tries to (greedily) choose the relation introduction which is best (or tied for best) for him (cases 3.(a) and 3.(b)). But, if all possible relation introductions are bad for him, then: if they are all lies, then he "honestly" passes (case 3.(c)), whether he is a liar, a hider, both or neither. Otherwise, there exist some truthful moves, and in this case a hider or malicious user will pass (hiding), whereas a user who cannot hide will be forced to play a bad move.

We implemented this debate setting in Java, and we generated and analyzed a number of debates as follows. For each debate, for each of the 12 users in it, we calculated whether he had lied more than the average user (or not), and whether he had hidden more than the average user (or not). Then, for each user u, we tested the prediction given by the two hypotheses: if the attribute values of u were as indicated on the left-hand side of Hypothesis 1 (Hypothesis 2), then we estimated that u was an above-average liar (resp. hider). We also tested the predictions obtained by inverting the hypotheses: if the attribute values of u were *not* as indicated on the left-hand side of Hypothesis 1 (Hypothesis 2), then we estimated that u was *not* an above-average liar (resp. hider). This led to the following types of estimations:

- *Correct estimations*:
  - **true positive**: u was predicted to be a liar (resp. hider), and he was;
  - **true negative**: u was predicted not to be a liar (resp. hider), and he was not.
- *Erroneous estimations*:
  - **false positive**: u was predicted to be a liar (resp. hider), but he was not.
  - **false negative**: u was predicted not to be a liar (resp. hider), but he was.

We generated 100,000 debates, with $100,000 \times 12 = 1,200,000$ users, and the results are summarized in Table 1.

Table 1. Summary of the results of the hypotheses' experimental evaluation.

Malicious action	True positives	False positives	True negatives	False negatives
Lying	163,408	73,829	726,681	236,082
Hiding	211,514	193,378	613,497	181,611

Albeit preliminary, these results seem to confirm our hypotheses: as far as lying is concerned, there were approximately 2.2 times more true positives than false positives, and approximately 3 times more true negatives than false negatives; as far as hiding is concerned, the number of false positives was relatively high (compared to lying), though still lower than the number of true positives, while there were approximately 3.5 times more true negatives than false negatives.

7   Conclusion

Malicious user behavior analysis in on-line debates has recently caught the attention of researchers, e.g. in the case of *trolls* or *flamers* [9]. At the same time, interest in multi-party debates has grown steadily. Argumentation-based debate platforms offer their users the possibility of expressing their thoughts in a structured way, e.g. by introducing arguments and relations among them. This paper is a first step towards undertaking the analysis of malicious user behavior in multi-party argumentation debates. We have identified and evaluated empirically, in a simulated debate setting, two hypotheses providing indications of potential malicious behavior, in the form of lying and hiding. The hypotheses are formulated in terms of three user attributes, computed by observing users debate and measuring their activity, opinionatedness and classifiability. Albeit preliminary, the evaluation shows promise.

Our work has several limitations and opens the way to many directions for future work. It would be interesting to evaluate our approach in a real debate setting, rather than a simulated environment. Other user attributes, e.g. focus on specific arguments, may also provide useful information. Moreover, in addition to general-stance and belief attributes of the kinds we considered, we could consider a third category of attributes describing the relations a user has with others, for example his popularity. Our analysis focused on single debates, but it may be useful to compare the behavior of users across debates (potentially in different platforms). We have programmed agents to follow a specific strategy, but other strategies, e.g. the ones overviewed in [15], may be interesting. Other hypotheses may provide further indications of maliciousness, and it may be interesting to *learn*, rather than guess as in this paper, relationships between user attributes and malicious behavior. Our evaluation was restricted to a specific semantics for bipolar argumentation: it would be interesting to study the impact of different choices of semantics for prediction of maliciousness. The argumentation framework used throughout this work was just an example and it is possible to use other, more elaborate, argumentation frameworks instead, e.g. allowing for votes as in [7,8]. Another direction for future research includes the identification of additional types of malicious users, such as trolls, flamers, or even users simply searching for "friends" and neglecting the collective goal of a debate. Also, it may be interesting to draw insights from existing work on lying [14] in order to further characterise malicious behavior.

Acknowledgments. This research has been supported by the EU project *DesMOLD (FP7/2007-2013-314581)*.

References

1. Amgoud, L., Cayrol, C., Lagasquie-Schiex, M.C., Livet, P.: On bipolarity in argumentation frameworks. Int. J. Intell. Syst. **23**, 1062–1093 (2008)
2. Baroni, P., Romano, M., Toni, F., Aurisicchio, M., Bertanza, G.: Automatic evaluation of design alternatives with quantitative argumentation. Argument Comput. **6**(1), 24–49 (2015). special issue: applications of logical approaches to argumentation
3. Boella, G., Gabbay, D., van der Torre, L., Villata, S.: Support in abstract argumentation. In: Proceedings of the 3rd International Conference on Computational Models of Argument (COMMA 2010), pp. 111–122 (2010)
4. Bonzon, E., Maudet, N.: On the outcomes of multiparty persuasion. In: Proceedings of the Tenth International Conference on Autonomous Agents and Multiagent Systems (AAMAS 2011), pp. 47–54 (2011)

5. Cayrol, C., Lagasquie-Schiex, M.C.: Gradual valuation for bipolar argumentation frameworks. In: Godo, L. (ed.) ECSQARU 2005. LNCS (LNAI), vol. 3571, pp. 366–377. Springer, Heidelberg (2005)
6. Coste-Marquis, S., Devred, C., Konieczny, S., Lagasquie-Schiex, M.C., Marquis, P.: On the merging of dung's argumentation systems. Artif. Intell. **171**, 740–753 (2007)
7. Eğilmez, S., Martins, J., Leite, J.: Extending social abstract argumentation with votes on attacks. In: Black, E., Modgil, S., Oren, N. (eds.) TAFA 2013. LNCS, vol. 8306, pp. 16–31. Springer, Heidelberg (2014)
8. Evripidou, V., Toni, F.: Quaestio-it.com: a social intelligent debating platform. J. Decis. Syst. **23**(3), 333–349 (2014)
9. Hardaker, C.: Trolling in asynchronous computer-mediated communication: from user discussions to academic definitions. J. Politeness Res. Lang. Behav. Cult. **6**, 215–242 (2010)
10. Kontarinis, D., Bonzon, E., Maudet, N., Moraitis, P.: Picking the right expert to make a debate uncontroversial. In: Proceedings of the Fourth International Conference on Computational Models of Argument (COMMA 2012), pp. 486–497 (2012)
11. Prakken, H.: Coherence and flexibility in dialogue games for argumentation. J. Logic Comput. **15**(6), 1009–1040 (2005)
12. Rahwan, I., Larson, K.: Argumentation and game theory. In: Rahwan, I., Larson, K. (eds.) Argumentation in Artificial Intelligence, pp. 321–339. Springer, Heidelberg (2009)
13. Riveret, R., Prakken, H., Rotolo, A., Sartor, G.: Heuristics in argumentation: a game theory investigation. In: Proceedings of the Second International Conference on Computational Models of Argument (COMMA 2008), pp. 324–335 (2008)
14. Sakama, C., Caminada, M., Herzig, A.: A logical account of lying. In: Janhunen, T., Niemelä, I. (eds.) JELIA 2010. LNCS, vol. 6341, pp. 286–299. Springer, Heidelberg (2010)
15. Thimm, M.: Strategic argumentation in multi-agent systems. Künstliche Intelligenz **28**(3), 159–168 (2014)

Probabilistic Argumentation, a Small Step for Uncertainty, a Giant Step for Complexity

Xin Sun[1]([✉]) and Beishui Liao[1,2]

[1] Faculty of Science, Technology and Communication,
University of Luxembourg, Esch-sur-Alzette, Luxembourg
xin.sun@uni.lu
[2] Center for the Study of Language and Cognition,
Zhejiang University, Hangzhou, China
baiseliao@zju.edu.cn

Abstract. In this paper we study how the restrictions of probability function affects the complexity in probabilistic argumentation. Our results show that the complexity of computing the probability of acceptance can only become tractable when we impose very strong restrictions on the probability function. Even a tiny relaxation of the restriction dramatically increases the complexity.

Keywords: Probabilistic argumentation · Computational complexity

1 Introduction

In the past two decades, argumentation has been a very active research area in the field of knowledge representation and reasoning, as a nonmonotonic formalism to handle inconsistent and incomplete information by means of constructing, comparing and evaluating arguments. In 1995, Dung proposed a notion of abstract argumentation framework [4], which can be viewed as a directed graph (called *argument graph*, or defeat graph) $G = (A, R)$, in which A is a set of arguments and $R \subseteq A \times A$ is a set of attacks. Given an argument graph, a fundamental problem is to determine which arguments can be regarded as justified. According to [4], extension-based semantics is a formal way to answer this question. Here, an extension represents a set of arguments that are considered to be acceptable (i.e. able to survive the conflict) together, under a certain semantics which is defined according to a set of evaluation criteria [2].

However, in classical argumentation theory, the uncertainty of arguments and/or attacks is not considered. So, it could be regarded as a purely qualitative formalism. But, in the real world, arguments and/or attacks are often uncertain. So, in recent years, the importance of combining argumentation and uncertainty has been well recognized, and probability-based argumentation is gaining momentum [3,5,6,9,11,13,15,17].

In a *probabilistic argument graph* (or PrAG in brief), each argument is assigned with a probability, denoting the likelihood of the argument appearing in the graph. Similar to classical argumentation theory, given a PrAG,

© Springer International Publishing Switzerland 2016
M. Rovatsos et al. (Eds.): EUMAS 2015/AT 2015, LNAI 9571, pp. 279–286, 2016.
DOI: 10.1007/978-3-319-33509-4_22

a basic problem is to define the status of arguments. Given a PrAG with n nodes, 2^n subgraphs are constructed (each subgraph corresponds to a possible world of arguments appearing in the graph). Then, the extensions of each subgraph is computed according to classical argumentation semantics. Since in many cases, computing the extensions of a subgraph is computationally intractable, restrictions have to be imposed to the probabilistic argument graph in order to make the computation task tractable. Such restrictions can either be on the argument graph or the probability function. In this paper we study how restrictions on the probability function affect the computational complexity.

The rest of this paper is organized as follows. In Sect. 2, we review the notions of abstract argumentation and probabilistic abstract argumentation. In Sect. 3 we present our main results. We conclude this paper in Sect. 4.

2   Preliminaries

The notions of (classical) abstract argumentation are originally introduced in [4], including abstract argumentation framework (called *argument graph*, or *classical argument graph*, in this paper) and extension-based semantics. An argument graph is a directed graph $G = (A, R)$, in which A is a set of nodes representing arguments and R is a set of edges representing attacks between the arguments.

Definition 1. *An argument graph is a tuple* $G = (A, R)$, *where* A *is a set of arguments, and* $R \subseteq A \times A$ *is a set of attacks. For convenience, sometimes we use* $args(G)$ *to denote* A.

As usual, we say that argument $\alpha \in A$ attacks argument $\beta \in A$ iff $(\alpha, \beta) \in R$. If $E \subseteq A$ and $\alpha \in A$ then we say that α attacks E iff there exists $\beta \in E$ such that α attacks β, that E attacks α iff there exists $\beta \in E$ such that β attacks α, and that E attacks E' iff there exist $\beta \in E$ and $\alpha \in E'$ such that β attacks α. Given an argument graph, according to certain evaluation criteria, sets of arguments (called *extensions*) are identified as acceptable together. Two important notions for the definitions of various kinds of extensions are *conflict-freeness* and *acceptability* of arguments.

Definition 2. *Let* $G = (A, R)$ *be an argument graph, and* $E \subseteq A$ *be a set of arguments.*

– E *is* conflict-free *iff* $\nexists \alpha, \beta \in E$, *such that* $(\alpha, \beta) \in R$.
– *An argument* $\alpha \in A$ *is* acceptable *w.r.t. (defended by)* E, *iff* $\forall (\beta, \alpha) \in R$, $\exists \gamma \in E$, *such that* $(\gamma, \beta) \in R$.

Based on the above two notions, several classes of (classical) extensions can be defined as follows.

Definition 3. *Let* $G = (A, R)$ *be an argument graph, and* $E \subseteq A$ *a set of arguments.*

- E is admissible *iff E is conflict-free, and each argument in E is acceptable w.r.t. E.*
- E is preferred *iff E is a maximal (w.r.t. set-inclusion) admissible set.*
- E is complete *iff E is admissible, and each argument that is acceptable w.r.t. E is in E.*
- E is grounded *iff E is the minimal (w.r.t. set-inclusion) complete extension.*
- E is stable *iff E is conflict-free, and each argument in $A\backslash E$ is attacked by E.*

In this paper, for convenience, we use $\sigma \in \{ad, co, pr, gr, st\}$ to represent a semantics (admissible, complete, preferred, grounded or stable). An extension under semantics σ is called a σ-extension. The set of σ-extensions of G is denoted as $\mathcal{E}_\sigma(G)$.

Example 1. Let $G_1 = (A_1, R_1)$ be an argument graph illustrated as follows.

$$a \longleftrightarrow b \longrightarrow c \longleftrightarrow d \circlearrowright$$

According to Definition 3, G_1 has four admissible sets: $\varnothing$, $\{a\}$, $\{b\}$ and $\{a, c\}$, in which $\varnothing$, $\{b\}$ and $\{a, c\}$ are complete extensions, $\{b\}$ and $\{a, c\}$ are preferred extensions, $\{a, c\}$ is the only stable extension, $\varnothing$ is the unique grounded extension.

2.1 Probabilistic Argumentation

The notions of probabilistic abstract argumentation are defined by combining the notions of classical abstract argumentation and that of probability theory, including probabilistic argument graph and its semantics. According to [10], we have the following definition.

Definition 4. *A probabilistic argument graph (or PrAG for short) is a triple $G^p = (A, R, p)$ where $G = (A, R)$ is an argument graph and $p : A \rightarrow [0, 1]$ is a probability function assigning to every argument $\alpha \in A$ a probability $p(\alpha)$ that α appears (and hence a probability $1 - p(\alpha)$ that α does not).*

In existing literature, the semantics of a PrAG is defined according to the notion of possible world. Given a PrAG, a possible world represents a scenario consisting of some subset of the arguments and attacks in the graph. So, given a PrAG with n nodes, there are 2^n subgraphs. A subgraph induced by a set $A' \subseteq A$ is represented as $G' = (A', R')$, in which $R' = R \cap (A' \times A')$. Under a semantics $\sigma \in \{ad, co, pr, gr, st\}$, the extensions of each subgraph are computed according to the definition of classical argumentation semantics. Then, the probability that a set of arguments $E \subseteq A$ is a σ-extension, denoted as $p(E^\sigma)$, is the sum of the probability of each subgraph for which E is a σ-extension.

In order to calculate the probability of each subgraph, it is desirable to assume independence of arguments. In [10], the reason why independence can be assumed is provided. For an argument α in a graph G^p, $p(\alpha)$ is treated as the probability that α is a justified point (i.e. each is a self-contained, internally valid, contribution) and therefore should appear in the graph, and $1 - p(\alpha)$ is the probability that α is not a justified point and so should not appear in the graph. So, one may assume that the probability of one argument appearing in a graph is independent of the probability of some other arguments appearing.

Throughout this paper, we assume the independence of arguments appearing in a graph. In [14], the authors proposed an approach to relax independence assumptions in probabilistic argumentation. However, this aspect of research is out of the scope of the present paper.

For simplicity, let us abuse the notation, using $p(\bar{\alpha})$ to denote $1 - p(\alpha)$. Then, the probability of subgraph G', denoted $p(G')$, can be defined as follows.

$$p(G') = (\Pi_{\alpha \in A'}\, p(\alpha)) \times (\Pi_{\alpha \in A \setminus A'}\, p(\bar{\alpha})) \tag{1}$$

Given a PrAG $G^p = (A, R, p)$, let $Q_\sigma(E)$ denote the set of subgraphs of G^p, each of which has an extension E under a given semantics $\sigma \in \{ad, co, pr, gr, st\}$. Based on formula (1), $p(E^\sigma)$ is defined as follows [10].

$$p(E^\sigma) = \Sigma_{G' \in Q_\sigma(E)}\, p(G') \tag{2}$$

Example 2. Let $G_1^p = (A_1, R_1, p)$ be a PrAG (illustrated as follows), where $p(a) = 0.5$, $p(b) = 0.8$, $p(c) = 0.4$ and $p(d) = 0.5$.

$$a \longleftrightarrow b \longrightarrow c \longleftrightarrow d \,\circlearrowleft$$
$$0.5 \qquad 0.8 \qquad 0.4 \qquad 0.5$$

The subgraphs of G_1^p are presented in Table 1. According to formula (2), there are 5 preferred extensions with non-zero probability:

$$p(\varnothing^{pr}) = p(G_1^{15}) + p(G_1^{16}) = 0.06$$
$$p(\{a\}^{pr}) = p(G_1^3) + p(G_1^4) + p(G_1^7) + p(G_1^8) = 0.3$$
$$p(\{b\}^{pr}) = p(G_1^1) + p(G_1^2) + p(G_1^3) + p(G_1^4) + p(G_1^9) + p(G_1^{10})$$
$$+ p(G_1^{11}) + p(G_1^{12}) = 0.8$$
$$p(\{c\}^{pr}) = p(G_1^{13}) + p(G_1^{14}) = 0.04$$
$$p(\{a, c\}^{pr}) = p(G_1^1) + p(G_1^2) + p(G_1^5) + p(G_1^6) = 0.2$$

This example shows that according to the existing possible world-based approach, in order to compute the probability of a set of arguments being an extension, we have to compute the extensions of each subgraph, which in many cases is computationally expensive.

3   Complexity of Probabilistic Argumentation

Complexity theory [1,18] is the theory to investigate the time, memory, or other resources required for solving computational problems. We assume the readers

Table 1. Subgraphs of G_1^p

	Subgraphs	Probability of subgraph	Preferred extensions
G_1^1	$a \leftrightarrow b \rightarrow c \leftrightarrow d \circlearrowleft$	0.08	$\{b\}, \{a,c\}$
G_1^2	$a \leftrightarrow b \rightarrow c$	0.08	$\{b\}, \{a,c\}$
G_1^3	$a \leftrightarrow b \quad d \circlearrowleft$	0.12	$\{a\}, \{b\}$
G_1^4	$a \leftrightarrow b$	0.12	$\{a\}, \{b\}$
G_1^5	$a \quad c \leftrightarrow d \circlearrowleft$	0.02	$\{a,c\}$
G_1^6	$a \quad c$	0.02	$\{a,c\}$
G_1^7	$a \quad d \circlearrowleft$	0.03	$\{a\}$
G_1^8	a	0.03	$\{a\}$
G_1^9	$b \rightarrow c \leftrightarrow d \circlearrowleft$	0.08	$\{b\}$
G_1^{10}	$b \rightarrow c$	0.08	$\{b\}$
G_1^{11}	$b \quad d \circlearrowleft$	0.12	$\{b\}$
G_1^{12}	b	0.12	$\{b\}$
G_1^{13}	$c \leftrightarrow d \circlearrowleft$	0.02	$\{c\}$
G_1^{14}	c	0.02	$\{c\}$
G_1^{15}	$d \circlearrowleft$	0.03	$\{\}$
G_1^{16}		0.03	$\{\}$

are familiar with notions like Turing machine and the complexity class P, NP and coNP. A counting problem f is a function from strings over a finite alphabet into integers. $\sharp P$ is the complexity class of the functions f such that f counts the number of accepting paths of a non-deterministic polynomial-time Turing machine [20].

We study the following computing problem, which computes the probability of acceptance for a given probabilistic argument graph and a subset of arguments:

Given a finite PrAG $G^p = (A, R, p)$, a finite set $E \subseteq A$, compute $p(E^\sigma)$.

In Fazzinga *et al.* [8], the authors show that without any restrictions on the probability function, computing $p(E^\sigma)$ for $\sigma \in \{ad, st\}$ is done in polynomial time and for other semantics the computation is $\sharp P$-hard. In this paper we investigate the complexity of computing $p(E^\sigma)$ when restrictions are imposed to the probability function p. The following are the main results of this paper:

Theorem 1. *If for all $\alpha \in A$, $p(\alpha) \in \{0, 1\}$, then*

1. for $\sigma \in \{ad, st, co, gr\}$, $p(E^\sigma)$ can be computed in polynomial time.
2. for $\sigma \in \{pr\}$, computing $p(E^\sigma)$ is coNP complete.

Proof. Since $p(\alpha)$ is restricted to $\{0, 1\}$, we only need to consider the unique subgraph, say G', which contains and only contains those nodes which are assigned probablity 1. Then we test if E is a σ extension of G'. If yes, then $p(\alpha) = 1$, otherwise $p(\alpha) = 0$. Therefore we only have to solve a extension verification problem. Dunne and Wooldridge [7] show that the extension verification problem for $\sigma \in \{ad, st, co, gr\}$ is in P and for $\sigma \in \{pr\}$ is coNP complete.   ⊣

Theorem 2. *If for all* $\alpha \in A$, $p(\alpha) \in \{0, \frac{1}{2}, 1\}$, *then*

1. *for* $\sigma \in \{ad, st\}$, $p(E^\sigma)$ *can be computed in polynomial time.*
2. *for* $\sigma \in \{co, gr, pr\}$, *computing* $p(E^\sigma)$ *is* $\sharp P$-*hard.*

Proof

1. Fazzinga *et al.* [8] show that even when the attack relation is assigned with probabilities, the problem is still computable in polynomial time. Our problem assigns probability 1 to each attack relation. Therefore it is a specific case of the problem studied in [8]. Which meas it must be computable in polynomial time.

2. We prove by providing a reduction to our problem from a $\sharp P$-hard problem $\sharp PP2DNF$ (Partitioned Positive 2DNF [16]), that is, the problem of counting the number of satisfying assignment of a DNF formula $\phi = C_1 \vee \ldots \vee C_k$ whose propositional variables are positive and can be partitioned into two sets $X = \{x_1, \ldots, x_m\}$ and $Y = \{y_1, \ldots, y_n\}$, and each clause C_i has the form $x_j \wedge y_k$ with $x_j \in X, y_k \in Y$. Given such a $PP2DNF$ ϕ, we construct a PrAG $G_\phi^p = (A, R, p)$ as follows:

   (a) A contains two arguments x, x' (resp. y, y') for each propositional variable x (resp. y) in ϕ, an argument c_i for each clause C_i in ϕ, and an additional argument s.
   (b) R contains defeats $(x_i, c_k), (x'_i, c_k), (y_j, c_k)$ and (y'_j, c_k) for each clause $C_k = x_i \wedge y_j$ of ϕ, the defeats $(s, x_i), (x_i, x_i), (x'_i, x'_i)$ for each variable x_i of ϕ, and the defeats $(s, y_j), (y_j, y_j), (y'_j, y'_j)$ for each variable y_j of ϕ.
   (c) p assigns probability 0.5 to each x'_i, y'_j and 1 to all other arguments.

   Let $G = (A, R)$. For every valuation V, let $G_V = (A_V, R_V)$ where A_V is obtained by deleting from A all x' (resp. y') if $V(x) = 1$ (resp. $V(y) = 1$), $R_V = R \cap (A_V \times A_V)$. Then there is a bijection between the set of all valuations of ϕ and the set of all such G_V.

   Claim: for every valuation V, $V(\phi) = 1$ iff $G_V \notin \rho^{co}(\{s\})$.
   Proof of claim:
   - Assume $V(\phi) = 1$. Then there is a clause $C_k = x_i \wedge y_j$ such that $V(x_i) = 1 = V(y_j)$. Therefore $x'_i, y'_j \notin A_V$. So we know c_k is only attacked by x_i and y_j, which means c_k is defended by s. Therefore $\{s\}$ is not a complete extension of G_V.
   - Assume $V(\phi) = 0$. Then for all clause $C_k = x_i \wedge y_j$, either $V(x_i) = 0$ or $V(y_j) = 0$. Without loss of generality, assume $V(x_i) = 0$. Then $x'_i \in A_V$. From x'_i attacks $x_i \wedge y_j$ we know that c_k is not defended by s. Then we can further infer that $\{s\}$ is a complete extension of G_V.

   From the above claim we know that $|\{V | V(\phi) = 1\}| = |\{G_V | G_V \notin \rho^{co}(\{s\})\}|$. Now, for each $A' \subseteq A$, $p(A') = \frac{1}{2^{m+n}}$ if A' is some A_V, otherwise $p(A') = 0$. Therefore $Pro^{co}(G^p, \{s\}) = \Sigma\{p(G_V) | \{s\}$ is a complete extension of

$G_V\} = \Sigma\{p(G_V)|V(\phi) = 0\} = \frac{1}{2^{m+n}} \times |\{V|V(\phi) = 0\}|$. Therefore $|\{V|V(\phi) = 0\}| = 2^{m+n} \times Pro^{co}(G^p, \{s\})$, $|\{V|V(\phi) = 1\}| = 2^{m+n} - 2^{m+n} \times Pro^{co}(G^p, \{s\})$. This finishes the reduction from $\sharp PP2DNF$ to compute $Pro^{co}(G^p, E)$. The $\sharp P$ hardness for $Pro^{pr}(G^p, E)$ and $Pro^{gr}(G^p, E)$ can be proved similarly.   ⊣

Theorem 1 tells us that if we make extremely strong restrictions on the probability function, then most computation of acceptance become tractable. Fazzinga et al. [8] show that without any restrictions on the probability function, computing $p(E^\sigma)$ for $\sigma \in \{co, gr, pr\}$ is $\sharp P$-hard. Therefore Theorem 2 shows that restricting the probability of argument to $\{0, \frac{1}{2}, 1\}$ has no substantial effect on the complexity of computing the probability of acceptance. Theorems 1 and 2 together show that the only possible restriction on the probability function to reduce the complexity is to make extreme restrictions.

4   Conclusions and Future Work

In this paper we study how the restrictions of probability function affects the complexity in probabilistic argumentation. Our results show that the complexity of computing the probability of acceptance can only become tractable when we impose very strong restrictions on the probabilistic function. Even a tiny relaxation of the restriction dramatically increases the complexity.

In the future we will investigate how restrictions on the argument graph will affect the complexity in probabilistic argumentation. Another future work of interest to us is to study the complexity of fuzzy argumentation framework [12,19], which is another approach to extend classical argumentation theory with the uncertainty of arguments and attacks, and compare it with the results of this paper.

References

1. Arora, S., Barak, B.: Computational Complexity: a Modern Approach. Cambridge University Press, New York (2009)
2. Baroni, P., Giacomin, M.: On principle-based evaluation of extension-based argumentation semantics. Artif. Intell. **171**(10–15), 675–700 (2007)
3. Doder, D., Woltran, S.: Probabilistic argumentation frameworks – a logical approach. In: Straccia, U., Calì, A. (eds.) SUM 2014. LNCS, vol. 8720, pp. 134–147. Springer, Heidelberg (2014)
4. Dung, P.M.: On the acceptability of arguments and its fundamental role in non-monotonic reasoning, logic programming and n-person games. Artif. Intell. **77**(2), 321–357 (1995)
5. Dung, P.M., Thang, P.M.: Towards (probabilistic) argumentation for jury-based dispute resolution. In: Proceedings of the COMMA, pp. 171–182. IOS Press (2010)
6. Dunne, P.E., Hunter, A., McBurney, P., Parsons, S., Wooldridge, M.: Weighted argument systems: basic definitions, algorithms, and complexity results. Artif. Intell. **175**(2), 457–486 (2011)

7. Dunne, P.E., Wooldridge, M.: Complexity of abstract argumentation. In: Simari, G., Rahwan, I. (eds.) Argumentation in Artificial Intelligence, pp. 85–104. Springer, Boston (2009)
8. Fazzinga, B., Flesca, S., Parisi, F.: On the complexity of probabilistic abstract argumentation. In: Proceedings of the Twenty-Third International Joint Conference on Artificial Intelligence, pp. 898–904. AAAI Press (2013)
9. Gabbay, D.M., Rodrigues, O.: Probabilistic argumentation: an equational approach. Log. Univers. **9**(3), 345–382 (2015)
10. Hunter, A.: Some foundations for probabilistic abstract argumentation. In: Proceedings of the 4th International Conference on Computational Models of Argument, pp. 117–128. IOS Press (2012)
11. Hunter, A.: Probabilistic qualification of attack in abstract argumentation. Int. J. Approximate Reasoning **55**(2), 607–638 (2014)
12. Janssen, J., De Cock, M., Vermeir, D.: Fuzzy argumentation frameworks. In: Information Processing and Management of Uncertainty in Knowledge-based Systems, pp. 513–520 (2008)
13. Li, H., Oren, N., Norman, T.J.: Probabilistic argumentation frameworks. In: Modgil, S., Oren, N., Toni, F. (eds.) TAFA 2011. LNCS, vol. 7132, pp. 1–16. springer, Heidelberg (2012)
14. Li, H., Oren, N., Norman, T.J.: Relaxing independence assumptions in probabilistic argumentation. In: Proceedings of Argumentation in Multi-Agent Systems (ArgMAS) (2013)
15. Liao, B., Huang, H.: Formulating semantics of probabilistic argumentation by characterizing subgraphs. In: van der Hoek, W., Holliday, W.H., Wang, W.-F. (eds.) LORI 2015. LNCS, vol. 9394, pp. 243–254. Springer, Heidelberg (2015)
16. Provan, J.S., Ball, M.O.: The complexity of counting cuts and of computing the probability that a graph is connected. SIAM J. Comput. **12**(4), 777–788 (1983)
17. Rienstra, T.: Towards a probabilistic dung-style argumentation system. In: Proceedings of the AT, pp. 138–152 (2012)
18. Sipser, M.: Introduction to the Theory of Computation, 3rd edn. Cengage Learning, Boston (2012)
19. Tamani, N., Croitoru, M.: Fuzzy argumentation system for decision support. In: Laurent, A., Strauss, O., Bouchon-Meunier, B., Yager, R.R. (eds.) IPMU 2014, Part I. CCIS, vol. 442, pp. 77–86. Springer, Heidelberg (2014)
20. Valiant, L.G.: The complexity of computing the permanent. Theor. Comput. Sci. **8**, 189–201 (1979)

Modeling Social Deviance in Artificial Agent Societies

J. Octavio Gutierrez-Garcia[1]([✉]) and Emmanuel Lopez-Neri[2]

[1] Department of Computer Science, Instituto Tecnológico Autónomo
de México, 1 Río Hondo St., Progreso Tizapán, 01080 Mexico, DF, Mexico
octavio.gutierrez@itam.mx
[2] CIDETEC-UVM, Universidad del Valle de México, Guadalajara Sur Campus,
8077 Periférico Sur, Santa María Tequepexpan,
45601 Tlaquepaque, Jalisco, Mexico
emmanuel.lopezne@uvmnet.edu

Abstract. Rule-governed artificial agent societies consisting of autonomous members are susceptible to rule violations, which can be seen as the acts of agents exercising their autonomy. As a consequence, modeling and allowing deviance is relevant, in particular, when artificial agent societies are used as the basis for agent-based social simulation. This work proposes a belief framework for modeling social deviance in artificial agent societies by taking into account both endogenous and exogenous factors contributing to rule compliance. The objective of the belief framework is to support the simulation of social environments where agents are susceptible to adopt rule-breaking behaviors. In this work, endogenous, exogenous and hybrid decision models supported by the event calculus formalism were implemented in an agent-based simulation model. Finally, a series of simulations was conducted in order to perform a sensitivity analysis of the agent-based simulation model.

Keywords: Artificial agent societies · Social deviance · Agent-based social simulation · Rule-breaking behaviors

1 Introduction

Artificial agent societies (also known as computational societies [2]) consist of a set of members whose interaction among each other may cause emerging social dynamics [10]. In addition, artificial agent societies are regulated by rules [8] that lead agent interaction to attain individual and common goals of the society. Intentional deviations from such rule-governed interaction are regarded as violations [4]. However, an intentional deviation can also be seen as the act of an agent exercising its autonomy. As a consequence, modeling (and allowing) deviance is relevant, in particular, when artificial agent societies are used as the basis for agent-based social simulation [6].

This work proposes modeling social deviance in artificial agent societies by taking into account both endogenous and exogenous factors to support the simulation of environments where individuals are susceptible to adopt rule-breaking behaviors. Endogenous and exogenous factors that may influence an individual's motivation to

© Springer International Publishing Switzerland 2016
M. Rovatsos et al. (Eds.): EUMAS 2015/AT 2015, LNAI 9571, pp. 287–302, 2016.
DOI: 10.1007/978-3-319-33509-4_23

break a rule consist of (i) intrinsic characteristics of his/her formation [7] and (ii) his/her environment [5], e.g., the perception about rule compliance of other agents, respectively. In this work, three decision models for rule compliance are proposed: an endogenous model, an exogenous model, and a hybrid model. In the endogenous model, agents make use of a belief framework that enables the formalization of the context of rules with respect to rule compliance. The context is defined by means of (i) a set of beliefs encouraging an agent to follow a given rule and (ii) another set of beliefs encouraging the agent to break the rule. Agents compare both sets of beliefs and determine whether to follow or break a given rule. In the exogenous model, agents make use of beliefs about the perception of rule compliance by their neighbors within a perception scope. If an agent believes that its neighboring agents break rules, then the agent tends to break rules (as indicated by the social studies conducted by Cialdini et al. [5]). In the hybrid decision model for rule compliance, both the endogenous and the exogenous models are merged. Finally, an artificial agent society with an underlying digraph as its social network is used to support an agent-based simulation model. By using the simulation model, a sensitivity analysis was conducted.

The structure of the paper is as follows. Related work is discussed in Sect. 2. The endogenous, exogenous and hybrid decision models are defined in Sect. 3. The agent-based simulation model is described in Sect. 4. Simulation results and their analysis are presented in Sect. 5, and some concluding remarks and future work directions are presented in Sect. 6.

2 Related Work

There have been different approaches to model social deviance, ranging from deontic logic [16] and game theory [12] to agent-based simulation [11] and cellular automata simulation [7].

van der Torre [16] introduced reasoning contexts for violations based on deontic logic (which is concerned with normative aspects such as rights and obligations) to enable agents to reason about the consequences of violating a norm. However, van der Torre's approach is focused on agents' individuality and there is a lack of considerations about artificial agent societies.

Hammond [12] makes use of an agent-based model supported by game theory to define the transition of agents from rule compliance to rule-breaking. In Hammond's model, agents (i) have a randomly determined predisposition to break or follow rules and (ii) are capable of keeping track of previous encounters with other agents. Hammond concluded that the decision to break rules is endogenous, i.e., it depends on agents' beliefs, unlike other research efforts [5, 7], which state that the agents' environment plays an important role.

In the same vein as Hammond et al. [15] designed an agent-based model involving two types of agents: honest agents that follow rules and devious agents that try to persuade honest agents to break rules. Honest agents decide whether to break or follow rules on a probability of being punished for breaking rules. Situngkir and Khanafiah concluded that the higher the probability of being caught, the fewer the number of times honest agents brake a rule. Situngkir and Khanafiah implicitly take into account external factors, e.g., breaking a rule may result in a punishment, however, no context of an artificial agent society can be established.

Deguchi [7] makes use of game theory to model agents' decision making regarding following or breaking a rule. However, instead of using an agent-based model like Hammond [12] and Situngkir and Khanafiah [15], Deguchi makes use of a cellular automaton model to represent the underlying social structure of an artificial agent society. In Deguchi's model, a cell has two behaviors: *rule-following* and *rule-breaking*, which are updated based on predefined game-theory rules. The rules indicate how much a cell should be affected by the influence of neighboring cells that brake rules. The game-theory rules are based on the assumption that an individual perceiving rule-breaking behaviors of other individuals (with respect to a rule) tends to break the rule. Deguchi concluded that a cell, i.e., a person, brake rules based on both internal and external factors. Nonetheless, the individuality of Deguchi's cells is reduced to a limited number of profiles, e.g., obedient and deviant.

Gutierrez-Garcia and Rodríguez [11] propose an agent-based simulation model supported by a belief-desire-intention cognitive architecture defined by means of fuzzy logic and functional event calculus. The formal framework allows defining rule-based plans whose rules can be broken by agents based on the degree of belief in the truth of corruption related beliefs. By conducting simulations, Gutierrez-Garcia and Rodríguez concluded that agents are prone to ignore some rules stated in their plans when their beliefs discourage following rules, e.g., when agents believe that there will not be any punishment for breaking rules and they will make a profit as a result of breaking them.

It is acknowledged that the proposed exogenous decision model is based on Deguchi's game-theory rules [7]. However, in Deguchi's model, directly adjacent cells (to a given cell) represent the neighborhood whereas in this work the neighborhood of agents is determined randomly and there is no relation of physical proximity. Moreover, in Deguchi's model the perception about the rule compliance of neighboring cells is modeled by using a set of binary variables, whereas in the present work, the perception is modeled by using a set of real-valued beliefs.

3 Decision Model for Rule Compliance

In the present framework, determining whether an agent follows or breaks a given rule depends on two types of beliefs: (i) beliefs about potential effects of either following or breaking a rule, and (ii) beliefs about the perception of rule compliance.

The beliefs about potential effects support an endogenous decision model, whereas the beliefs about the perception of rule compliance support an exogenous decision model. In addition, both the endogenous and the exogenous decision models are merged to form a hybrid decision model for rule compliance.

3.1 Endogenous Decision Model for Rule Compliance

In an artificial agent society, agents interact with each other, and from their interactions and other external events, agents may change their beliefs about the potential effects of either breaking or following a rule. In fact, agents should be assumed to be uncertain (or at least certain to some extent) about the effects of breaking rules because they may not control rule-enforcing mechanisms.

A supporting belief about a potential effect of either following or breaking a rule is denoted as a compound Boolean fluent $\beta(r, d)$ with r and $d \in [0...1]$, where (i) r denotes the relevance of belief β about a positive or negative potential effect of either following or breaking a rule; and (ii) d denotes the degree of belief in the actual occurrence of the effect with respect to following or breaking the rule. For instance, a police agent may believe that accepting a bribe is relevant to be dismissed from the police department. However, the degree of belief of the police agent regarding the actual occurrence of such negative effect (at least from its point of view) may be low or high according to its perception of the police department's disciplinary measures.

Supporting beliefs (Eq. 1) for either following or breaking a rule k of a given *individual* are defined as follows:

$$\mathfrak{B}^k_{individual} = \mathfrak{B}^k_P \cup \mathfrak{B}^k_N. \tag{1}$$

Where $\mathfrak{B}^k_P$ is a disjunction of conjunctions that contains supporting beliefs for following a given rule (Eq. 2).

$$\mathfrak{B}^k_P = \vee\{\wedge \text{HoldsAt}(\beta_i(r_i, d_i), \tau) \wedge \neg \text{HoldsAt}(\beta_j(r_j, d_j), \tau)|\ i \neq j\}. \tag{2}$$

Event calculus predicate *HoldsAt(fluent, time point)* indicates that a fluent (e.g., a belief $\beta(r, d)$) holds at time point τ, i.e., the belief is true at a given moment. The event calculus was selected because it is a temporal action formalism that allows reasoning about the effects of actions using linear and discrete time points, which has been used to specify artificial agent societies, see for instance [1].

$\mathfrak{B}^k_N$ is a disjunction of conjunctions that contains supporting beliefs for breaking a given rule (Eq. 3).

$$\mathfrak{B}^k_N = \vee\{\wedge \text{HoldsAt}(\beta_m(r_m, d_m), \tau) \wedge \neg \text{HoldsAt}(\beta_n(r_n, d_n), \tau)|\ m \neq n\}. \tag{3}$$

Both $\mathfrak{B}^k_P$ and $\mathfrak{B}^k_N$ are disjunctions of conjunctions of beliefs that support following and breaking a given rule, respectively. Nevertheless, for each set of disjunctions, only the conjunction of beliefs with the highest support for a given rule is taken into account because it is assumed that each conjunction refers to the same rule, but in a different context.

It should be noted that a domain expert in the context of a given artificial society should define the supporting beliefs for each one of the rules that lead the interaction.

Transforming Beliefs into Vectors in a Cartesian System. Each belief contained in $\mathfrak{B}^k_{individual}$ at a given time point τ is transformed into a vector in a Cartesian system (see Fig. 1 for an example) in order that beliefs supporting rule compliance ($\mathfrak{B}^k_P$) can be contrasted with beliefs supporting rule breaking ($\mathfrak{B}^k_N$) by using vector addition. By contrasting beliefs in such manner, a decision vector indicating whether a given rule is broken or followed at a given time point τ is obtained.

On the one hand, beliefs contained in $\mathfrak{B}_P^k$ that support compliance of a given rule must be in quadrant I, i.e., the coordinates of a belief β that supports rule compliance are characterized as follows ($|r|$, $|d|$). On the other hand, beliefs contained in $\mathfrak{B}_N^k$ that support breaking a rule must be in quadrant III, i.e., the coordinates of a belief β that supports rule breaking are characterized as follows ($-|r|$, $-|d|$). By using quadrants I and III, beliefs that support rule compliance are set against beliefs that support rule breaking in terms of both relevance and the degree of belief in the actual occurrence of the potential effect of either following or breaking a rule.

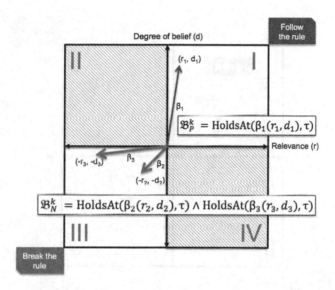

Fig. 1. Transforming beliefs into vectors: an example.

In addition, it should be taken into account that, as indicated by Deguchi [7], individuals (i.e., agents) may have different attitudes toward breaking rules even under the same context due to intrinsic characteristics of their formation. Then, for some agents the weight of the beliefs supporting rule compliance ($\mathfrak{B}_P^k$) may be greater than the weight of the beliefs supporting rule breaking ($\mathfrak{B}_N^k$) or vice versa. For this reason, in order to incorporate agents' individual attitudes toward rule compliance, the addition of beliefs should be affected by a weight $\alpha \in [0...1]$. α's values of 0.0, 0.5, and 1.0 mean that (i) there is an attitude toward following a rule, (ii) there is no attitude toward either breaking or following rule, and (iii) there is an attitude toward breaking a rule, respectively.

The result of transforming beliefs into vectors in a Cartesian system is represented by a decision point $\Delta = (\Delta_r, \Delta_d)$ extracted from the components of a decision vector

$(\Delta_r)\hat{x} + (\Delta_d)\hat{y}$, which is obtained by addition of beliefs (see Fig. 2 for an example) as follows:

$$\Delta_r = (1 - \alpha)\Sigma_{i=1}^{m}|r_i| - (\alpha)\Sigma_{j=1}^{n}|r_j|. \tag{4}$$

$$\Delta_d = (1 - \alpha)\Sigma_{i=1}^{m}|d_i| - (\alpha)\Sigma_{j=1}^{n}|d_j|. \tag{5}$$

such that $\beta_i \in \mathcal{B}_P^k$, $\beta_i = (|r_i|, |d_i|)$, $m = |\mathcal{B}_P^k|$, $\beta_j \in \mathcal{B}_N^k$, $\beta_j = (-|r_j|, -|d_j|)$, and $n = |\mathcal{B}_N^k|$.

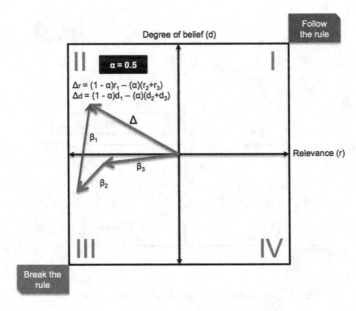

Fig. 2. Addition of beliefs: an example.

Interpreting the Resultant Decision Point. The Cartesian plane is diagonally divided into two areas by using a line $y = -x$. On the one hand, if the resultant point $\Delta = (\Delta_r, \Delta_d)$ falls in the area including quadrant I and the right half of quadrants II and IV, the rule is followed. On the other hand, if point Δ falls in the area including quadrant III, and the left half of quadrants II and IV, the rule is broken (see Fig. 3 for an example). If point Δ lies on the division line, determining whether the rule is followed or broken is based on a uniform random number h between 0.0 and 1.0, if h is greater than 0.5, the rule is followed, otherwise the rule is broken. The algorithm is as follows:

```
1: If −1·Δ_r < Δ_d Then 'follow the rule'
2: ElseIf −1·Δ_r > Δ_d Then 'break the rule'
3: ElseIf random number h > 0.5 Then 'follow the rule'
4: Else 'break the rule'
```

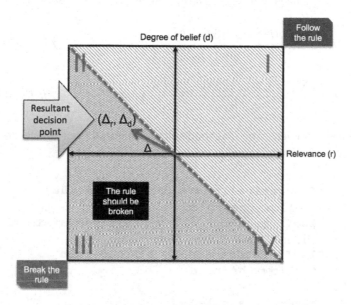

Fig. 3. Resultant decision point: an example.

3.2 Exogenous Decision Model for Rule Compliance

As indicated in [5, 7], an individual perceiving rule-breaking behaviors of other individuals (with respect to a rule) tends to break the rule. In a similar manner, an individual tends to follow a rule when he/she perceives that the majority of other individuals follow the rule. To model the influence (with respect to rule compliance) of other members within the same artificial society, agents are provided with beliefs about the perception of rule compliance by its neighbors.

A belief about rule compliance by a member m of an artificial society S is a compound Boolean fluent represented by $\beta(m, l)$ where $l \in [0 \ldots 1]$ denotes the degree of belief with respect to the rule compliance of member m. For instance, a belief of an agent a regarding the rule compliance of an agent m can be defined as $\beta(m, l = 0)$ meaning agent a believes that agent m follows a given rule. A value of $l = 1$ means agent a believes that agent m does not follow a given rule.

Each agent of an artificial society has a set of beliefs χ about the perception of rule compliance by its neighbors (Eq. 6).

$$\chi = \wedge \text{HoldsAt}(\beta_i(m_i, l_i), \tau) \forall m_i \text{ within a perception scope} \mid m_i \in S. \qquad (6)$$

Assuming that an artificial agent society has a social network structure represented by a digraph, the perception scope of an agent is defined as its number of neighbors represented by n. The negative (Eq. 7) and positive (Eq. 8) influence exercised by neighbors regarding rule compliance is determined by the number of neighbors that are believed to have a tendency to break and follow a given rule, respectively.

$$negative \; inf = \frac{\sum_{i=1}^{|\rho|}(l_i - 0.5)\forall\beta_i(m_i, l_i) \in \rho}{|\rho|}|\beta_i(m_i, l_i) \in \rho \subseteq \chi \; if \; l_i > 0.5. \qquad (7)$$

$$positive \; inf = \frac{\sum_{i=1}^{|\sigma|}(0.5 - l_i)\forall\beta_i(m_i, l_i) \in \sigma}{|\sigma|}|\beta_i(m_i, l_i) \in \sigma \subseteq \chi \; if \; l_i \leq 0.5. \qquad (8)$$

Based on the influence of neighbors, determining whether an agent breaks or follows a rule is as follows:

```
1: If negative inf < positive inf Then
2:    'follow the rule'
3: ElseIf negative inf > positive inf Then
4:    'break the rule'
5: ElseIf random number h > 0.5 Then
6:    'follow the rule'
7: Else
8:    'break the rule'
```

As in the endogenous decision model, when the negative influence is equal to the positive influence determining whether the rule is followed or broken is based on a uniform random number h between 0.0 and 1.0.

3.3 Hybrid Decision Model for Rule Compliance

Both the endogenous and the exogenous decision models are merged to form a hybrid decision model for rule compliance. However, to the best of the authors' knowledge, there is no evidence indicating that individuals are more inclined to break or follow rules based on either endogenous or exogenous factors. In fact, in this regard, Asch [3] and Deguchi [7] argue that sometimes individuals make decisions based on endogenous factors and sometimes based on exogenous factors. For this reason, in this present work, the uncertainty of individuals regarding making decisions based on either endogenous or exogenous factors is determined by the *probability of using the exogenous decision model* denoted by κ. In the hybrid decision model, probability κ is taken into account only when the outcome of the endogenous model indicates to break a given rule and the outcome of the exogenous model indicates to follow the rule. On the other hand, when the outcome of the exogenous model is equal to the outcome of the endogenous model, the individual either follows or breaks the rule according to the outcome of the models. The hybrid decision model is defined as follows.

```
1: If (−1·Δr < Δd) & (negative inf < positive inf) Then
2:  'follow the rule'
3: ElseIf (−1·Δr > Δd) & (negative inf > positive inf) Then
4:  'break the rule'
5: ElseIf random number h ≤ κ Then
6:  Make use of the exogenous decision model
7: Else
8:  Make use of the endogenous decision model
```

4 Agent-Based Simulation Model

In this work, an artificial agent society with an underlying digraph as its social network is used to support an agent-based simulation model. In the digraph, agents are represented by nodes and edges (a, b) indicate that an agent a is able to perceive whether agent b either breaks or follows a given rule.

The agent-based model was implemented using NetLogo [17]. Figure 4 shows an instance of the model representing an artificial agent society composed of 10 agents, two of which broke a rule (depicted by a red cross) and the remaining agents followed the rule (depicted by a white sphere).

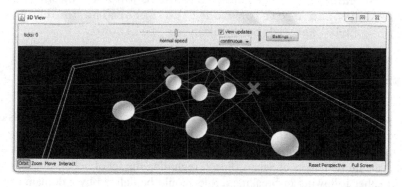

Fig. 4. Netlogo model for the study of rule compliance (Color figure online).

4.1 Model Parameters

The model parameters of the agent-based simulation model consist of:

- *Parameters of the endogenous decision model*: (i) agents' decision points ($Δ_r$, $Δ_d$) supported by a set of beliefs about potential effects of either following or breaking a rule, and (ii) agents' attitude toward either breaking or following a rule (denoted by $α$).
- *Parameters of the exogenous decision model*: (i) a set of beliefs denoting the degree of belief with respect to the rule compliance of neighboring agents, and (ii) number

of neighboring agents (denoted by n), i.e., the number of agents connected to a given agent by means of edges.

* *Parameters of the hybrid decision model*: (i) a probability of using the exogenous decision model (denoted by κ), and (ii) all the parameters of both the endogenous and exogenous decision models.
* *Other parameters include*: (i) number of days simulated, (ii) overall number of agents, (iii) a probability of an agent to be a rule breaker at the beginning of the simulation, and (iv) distribution of agent types per simulation.

It should be noted that agents adopting the endogenous, exogenous, and hybrid decision models are called endogenous, exogenous and hybrid agents, respectively. So, the distribution of agent types indicates the number of endogenous, exogenous and hybrid agents involved in the simulation.

The agent-based simulation algorithm is discrete in time and is as follows:

```
1:  Set the initial state of agents
2:  Set the initial beliefs of agents
3:  Create a random social network
4:  While (counter ≤ number of days to be simulated) Do
5:    For Each agent of the artificial society Do
6:      - Update the agent's beliefs
7:      - Make use of either the endogenous, exogenous or
          hybrid decision model to determine whether a
          rule should be broken or followed.
8:    End For Each
9:    Increase counter
10: End While
```

The setup of the simulation model is as follows. The initial state of agents as either *rule breakers* or *rule followers* is determined based on a given *probability of an agent to be a rule breaker at the beginning of the simulation* (line 1). In addition, it should be noted that the initial beliefs of agents (line 2) regarding the set of beliefs about potential effects of either following or breaking a rule should be defined by a domain expert in the context of an artificial society. Afterward, the social network of agents (line 3) is generated using as input the number of neighbors (n) defined for each agent. Then, each agent is connected to n randomly selected agents.

After the setup phase, the simulation is run for a discrete number of days (lines 4–9). For each day, each agent of the artificial society (line 5) updates its beliefs (line 6) about the rule compliance of its neighbors and about the potential effects of either following or breaking a rule. Once the beliefs are updated, each agent decides whether or not to break a rule based on its current beliefs and its decision model (line 7). It should be noted that even though the current version of the simulation model supports the update of beliefs about the potential effects of either following or breaking a rule, the update of such beliefs is conducted randomly. A system and/or rules for belief update are out of the scope of this work.

5 Simulations and Results

Objective. A series of simulations was conducted using the model settings reported in Table 1 in order to conduct a sensitivity analysis of the agent-based simulation model using the endogenous, exogenous and hybrid decision models.

Model settings. For the purpose of generality, the degrees of belief in the truth as well as the relevance of beliefs about the potential effects of either following or breaking a rule were determined randomly based on a uniformly distributed number on the interval [0, 1]. In doing so, the simulation model was detached from a specific context.

The agents involved in the simulation had no attitude toward either breaking or following a rule as denoted by an α value of 0.5 (see Sect. 3.1). In addition, when the exogenous and endogenous factors perceived by a hybrid agent resulted in different outcomes, the probability of using the exogenous decision model κ was set to 0.5 (see Sect. 3.3). In doing so, hybrid agents were prevented from being biased toward exogenous or endogenous factors.

The distributions of agent types (reported in Table 1) were defined in order to analyze the agent-based simulation model in the presence (and absence) of different types of agents. Both the number of neighbors and the overall number of agents were set to 10 and 300 agents, respectively. This was with the aim of having a relatively large artificial society, and when agents of different types were involved, having a good chance to connect them as the result of the random generation of the social network.

Different values for the probability of an agent to be a rule breaker at the beginning of the simulation were chosen in order to explore the emergent behavior of the model when it was subject to a different number of rule breakers.

Table 1. Model settings for the simulation.

Input parameter	Values
Agents' decision points (Δ_r, Δ_d)	(Δ_r, Δ_d) where Δ_r and Δ_d are chosen to be independent and uniformly distributed on the interval [−1, 1]
Attitude toward either breaking or following a rule (α)	0.50
Probability of using the exogenous decision model (κ)	0.50
Number of neighbors (n)	10
Overall number of agents	300
Probability of an agent to be a rule breaker at the beginning of the simulation	{0.25, 0.50, 0.75}
Distribution of agent types (number of endogenous agents, number of exogenous agents, number of hybrid agents)	{(0, 0, 300), (0, 300, 0), (300, 0, 0), (100, 100, 100), (150, 150, 0), (150, 0, 150), (0, 150, 150)}
Number of days simulated	100

Finally, the number of days simulated was set to 100 to observe the outcome of the model for a relatively long simulation time.

For each setting of the agent-based model reported in Table 1, 5 independent simulation runs were conducted. Figures 5 and 6 show the average percentage of rule breakers for each time point. From these results, a total of three observations are drawn.

Observation 1. Regardless of the initial configuration, the simulation model reached a relatively steady state after a few simulation time steps, e.g., up to 15 discrete time points (see Figs. 5 and 6).

Analysis. The stable long-term behavior of the simulation model is due to the fact that the social network of the artificial society is a strongly connected graph (i.e., where each node is connected to at least 10 nodes). This facilitates the spread of either rule-breaking behaviors or rule-following behaviors. In addition, a strongly connected graph prevented the creation of isolated groups, which may have had different and periodic behaviors.

Observation 2. The artificial society consisting of only endogenous agents were equally divided into rule breakers and rule followers (Fig. 5c). However, when the artificial society consisted of only exogenous agents, all the agents became either rule breakers or rule followers (Fig. 5b). Finally, when the artificial society consisted of only hybrid agents, most of the agents tended to be rule breakers (Fig. 5a).

Analysis. In the case of the simulations involving only exogenous agents (Fig. 5b), who are only influenced by their neighbors' behaviors, the initial number of rule breakers highly determined whether the entire society becomes or not a rule-breaking society due to its strongly connected social network. In contrast, the simulations involving only endogenous agents (Fig. 5c), who make decision based on their own beliefs and do not take into account their neighbors, the initial number of rule breakers had no influence on whether the entire society becomes or not a rule-breaking society. This was because, the agents' beliefs were set randomly and changed every simulation step resulting in a fully divided society with respect to whether the agents followed or broke the rules. In the simulations involving only hybrid agents (Fig. 5a) with an initial number of rule breakers set to approximately 50 % and 75 %, the long-term percentage of rule breakers resulted in 75 %, which can be explained as the average percentage of rule breakers obtained from the simulations involving only endogenous agents (50 %, Fig. 5c) and only exogenous agents (100 %, Fig. 5b).

In the simulations involving only hybrid agents (Fig. 5a) with an initial number of rule breakers set to approximately 25 %, the members of the society increasingly became rule breakers due to the influence of their randomly determined beliefs. In addition, once more agents broke rules, the transmission rate of the rule-breaking behaviors increased. With respect to the 25 % of agents that followed the rules, this is due to the random nature of their beliefs that were used for the endogenous model.

Observation 3. The average percentage of rule breakers of artificial societies consisting of heterogeneous agents varied according to the agent types that composed the society.

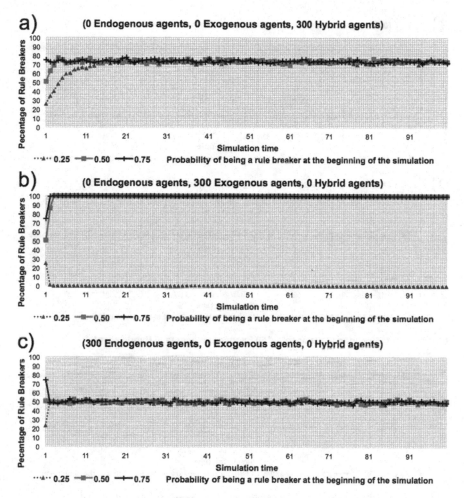

Fig. 5. Simulation results using homogeneous artificial agent societies (Color figure online).

Analysis. As shown in Fig. 6, the composition of the artificial society highly influenced the percentage of rule breakers from a long-term average of 10 % of rule breakers (see Fig. 6a with an initial number of rule breakers set to 25 %) to an approximately long-term average of 90 % of rule breakers (see Fig. 6a with an initial number of rule breakers set to 50 %). This is due to the fact that endogenous and exogenous agents made decisions based on different factors and hybrid agents sometimes behaved like endogenous agents and sometimes behaved like exogenous agents.

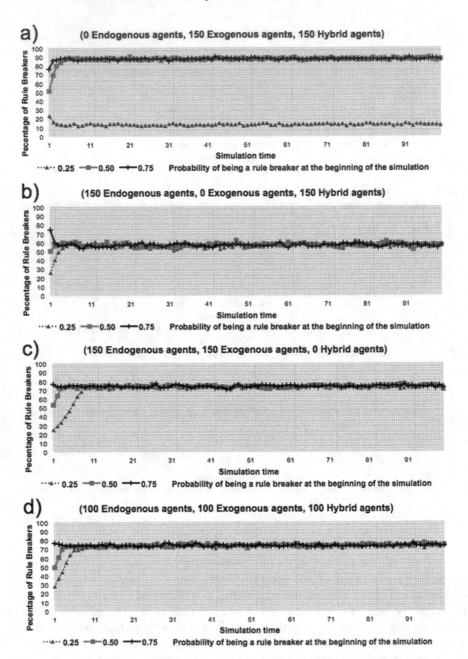

Fig. 6. Simulation results using heterogeneous artificial agent societies (Color figure online).

6 Conclusion and Future Work

This work contributes a belief framework for modeling social deviance in artificial agent societies that takes into account both endogenous and exogenous factors. Endogenous, exogenous and hybrid decision models were implemented in an agent-based simulation model. Simulation results show that:

- Artificial agent societies reach a steady state with respect to the percentage of rule breakers regardless of their initial configuration.
- Societies consisting of only endogenous agents with random beliefs tend to be equally divided into rule breakers and rule followers.
- When a society consists of only exogenous agents, after a few simulation steps, all the members adopt either a rule-breaking behavior or a rule-following behavior permanently based on the initial configuration of the model.
- In societies consisting of heterogeneous agents, the average percentage of rule breakers varies according to the agent types that compose the society.

It should be noted that the present work assumes that agents break rules intentionally, however, agents may also break rules unintentionally. In this regard, unintentional rule breaking can be seen as an agent's *mistake* [9], which is not based on beliefs. As a consequence, unintentional rule breaking should be modeled separately, for instance, by using agents' *mistakes* as triggers for rule-enforcing mechanisms. In addition, in the future, work will be conducted to attach probabilities to rules to model uncertain environments as in [13]. Furthermore, work will be focused on exploring the relationship between social deviance and trust models [14] where perceived social deviance may be used as a source for trust calculation.

Acknowledgments. The first author acknowledges the support provided by Asociación Mexicana de Cultura, A.C. and CONACYT under grant 216101. The second author wishes to thank UVM Laureate International Universities for their support.

References

1. Artikis, A., Pitt, J., Sergot, M.: Animated specifications of computational societies. In: International Joint Conference on Autonomous Agents and Multiagent Systems: Part 3, pp. 1053–1061. ACM Press (2002)
2. Artikis, A., Sergot, M., Pitt, J.: Specifying norm-governed computational societies. ACM Trans. Comput. Logic **10**(1), 1 (2009)
3. Asch, S.E.: Effects of group pressure upon the modification and distortion of judgements. In: Guetzkow, H. (ed.) Groups, Leadership, and Men, pp. 222–236. Carnegie Press, Pittsburgh (1951)
4. Boella, G., Van der Torre, L.: Fulfilling or violating obligations in normative multiagent systems. In: IEEE/WIC/ACM International Conference on Intelligent Agent Technology, pp. 483–486. IEEE Press (2004)

5. Cialdini, R.B., Kallgren, C.A., Reno, R.R.: A focus theory of normative conduct: a theoretical refinement and reevaluation of the role of norms in human behavior. Adv. Exp. Soc. Psychol. **24**(20), 1–243 (1991)
6. Davidsson, P.: Agent based social simulation: a computer science view. J. Artif. Soc. Soc. Simul. **5**(1) (2002). http://jasss.soc.surrey.ac.uk/5/1/7.html. Accessed 28 March 2016
7. Deguchi, T.: A simulation of rule-breaking behavior in public places. Soc. Sci. Comput. Rev. **32**(4), 439–452 (2014)
8. Dignum, V., Dignum, F.P.: Modelling agent societies: co-ordination frameworks and institutions. In: Brazdil, P.B., Jorge, A.M. (eds.) EPIA 2001. LNCS (LNAI), vol. 2258, pp. 191–204. Springer, Heidelberg (2001)
9. Freeman, J., McMaster, M., Rakotonirainy, A.: An exploration into younger and older pedestrians' risky behaviours at train level crossings. Safety **1**(1), 16–27 (2015)
10. Gerber, C.: An artificial agent society is more than a collection of "social" agents. Technical report, AAAI Fall Symposium (1997)
11. Gutierrez-Garcia, J.O., Rodríguez, L.F.: Corruptible social agents. Comput. Anim. Virtual Worlds (2014). doi:10.1002/cav.1613
12. Hammond, R.: Endogenous transition dynamics in corruption: an agent-based computer model. Working paper no. 19, Center on Social and Economic Dynamics, pp. 1–18 (2000)
13. Riveret, R., Rotolo, A., Sartor, G.: Probabilistic rule-based argumentation for norm-governed learning agents. Artif. Intell. Law **20**(4), 383–420 (2012)
14. Sabater, J., Sierra, C.: Review on computational trust and reputation models. Artif. Intell. Rev. **24**(1), 33–60 (2005)
15. Situngkir, H., Khanafiah, D.: Theorizing corruption through agent-based modeling. In: Joint International Conference on Information Sciences, pp. 1–4. Atlantis Press, Paris (2006). doi:10.2991/jcis.2006.183
16. van der Torre, L.: Contextual deontic logic: normative agents, violations and independence. Ann. Math. Artif. Intell. **37**(1–2), 33–63 (2003)
17. Wilensky, U.: NetLogo. Center for Connected Learning and Computer-Based Modeling, Northwestern University, Evanston, IL (1999). http://ccl.northwestern.edu/netlogo/

Modeling and Enforcing Semantic Obligations for Access Control

Fabio Marfia[(⊠)], Nicoletta Fornara, and Truc-Vien T. Nguyen

Università della Svizzera italiana, via G. Buffi 13, 6900 Lugano, Switzerland
{fabio.marfia,nicoletta.fornara,thi.truc.vien.nguyen}@usi.ch

Abstract. We describe a model in this paper for defining and enforcing obligations in Multiagent Systems for access control purposes, provided that information exchanged between agents is in the form of logical statements. Axioms are expressed in order to annotate the conditions according to which obligations are activated. Reasoning is used in order to correctly infer, for each piece of information involved in a user request, what obligations apply between all the ones specified. We describe the different architectural modules needed for storing and enforcing obligations, while monitoring their fulfillment in the system. An implementation of the model is presented with the use of OWL technology and OWL reasoning. It is applied, in particular, to a real case scenario of eBay auctions.

1 Introduction

Norms are a widespread approach for protecting users' privacy and security, and for allowing or enforcing agents to abide by different policies and laws. Usual functionalities related to norms in systems include editing, storing, evaluation, harmonization, and enforcement. As described by researches in deontic logic, every norm expression can be reduced to the form of a combination of one or more permission, prohibition or obligation statements [20].

In an Access Control context, where an agent (*data consumer*) sends an information request to another agent (*data provider*), a *permission* can express the conditions for which such information is released to the data consumer effectively. Otherwise, a denial of access can be returned. A *prohibition* can express the conditions for which such information is not released to the data consumer effectively. An *obligation* is able to represent a set of actions that have to be executed as a consequence of the information request, both by the data provider (*data provider obligations*) or the data consumer (*data consumer obligations*).

Acts that are a consequence of a permission, prohibition or data provider obligation statements can be executed by the data provider directly, and it can verify their execution effectiveness by itself. On the other hand, the task of

---

The work described in this paper is supported by Hasler Foundation project nr. 15014 within the COST Action IS1004 WEBDATANET.

M. Rovatsos et al. (Eds.): EUMAS 2015/AT 2015, LNAI 9571, pp. 303–317, 2016.
DOI: 10.1007/978-3-319-33509-4_24

checking whether data consumer obligations are fulfilled or not in a system represents a more complex matter, requesting the activation of a dedicated temporal engine for identifying the specific conditions in the system that determine the fulfillment of an activated obligation (see, e.g., [11]). Furthermore, in the case in which it is allowed by the context, additional modules can be activated in order to enforce one or more agents to perform some actions, as it can be requested by an obligation.

While permissions and prohibitions have been widely studied and formalized in Access Control literature (e.g., [2,13]), obligations have been modeled and applied more infrequently in the context of Access Control. Obligations may be used in that context for the definition of the actions that must be taken by the data provider for enforcing an access control decision. Also, they may be used for the definition of the actions that the data consumer must perform in order to gain access to certain resources [3,6]. In particular, data provider obligations may be used in two different cases:

1. for expressing the actions that must be performed before or after the access to certain data (for example, recording every granted or denied access for statistical purposes);
2. for editorial revisions that must be performed on the *content of the data* before the user get access to the data itself (for example, anonymizing the name of the participants of an online auction if certain conditions are satisfied).

In NorMAS (Normative Multiagent System) research obligations have been quite extensively studied [1]. Interesting approaches, where decidable description logics (OWL) have been used for the formalization and enforcement of obligations, are: the KAoS Policy Services Framework [19], the OWL-POLAR Framework for Semantic Policy Representation and Reasoning [15], the OCeAN meta-model for the specification of artificial institutions and, in particular, obligations [8,9]. We think that applying NorMAS models and techniques, in particular obligations, to the problem of managing and regulating Access Control to data expressed in the form of semantic statements will improve the existing models and frameworks and it can advance the state of the art.

Therefore, we present a model in this paper in which formal axioms are expressed for specifying both data provider and data consumer obligations, with the specific aim of regulating access to information that is represented in the general form of a collection of logical statements. We decided to focus on that specific type of information because we can show that obligations can not only be specified formally using axiomatic descriptions, but the same descriptions can be also used for enforcing the obligations directly with the use of reasoning techniques, which are used for identifying which pieces of logical information the obligations apply on.

We present how data provider obligations can be used for modifying the data before returning it as a consequence of a request, for abiding by specific norms. Data can be, e.g., deleted or anonymized according to specific directives (as presented in Sect. 4.1). We also explain how data consumer obligations can be monitored by a dedicated module for checking whether they are fulfilled or not, according to time constraints, referring to the work that has already been done on the subject by Fornara [8]. For example, a data consumer obligation may impose to an agent to pay for a received service or an access to certain data, and the monitoring module would control the effectiveness of such payment (see Sect. 4.2).

As far as we know, this is the first attempt to describe a model for formalizing and enforcing axiomatic obligations in the context of Access Control, when information exchanged between agents is in the form of logical statements, and the axiomatic expression of the obligations is evaluated on the data itself with the use of automatic reasoning techniques.

The paper proceeds as follows: we define a general framework for managing and enforcing semantic obligations in Sect. 2. We describe an obligation formally in Sect. 3; distinguishing, in particular, between data provider and data consumer obligations, and explaining their role during the whole data request workflow. We present an implementation of the model using OWL technology in Sect. 4. The results of our experiments are described in Sect. 5. Related work is presented in Sect. 6. Conclusion and future work are described in Sect. 7.

2   Reasoning-Based Obligation Framework

We identified the different modules that are needed for the data provider for editing and evaluating obligations regarding logical data, enforcing them eventually and monitoring their fulfillment during time. They are represented in Fig. 1.

The presented framework refers to the standard XACML security architecture[1]. XACML is a standard for the specification of a security framework, defining protocols for transmitting credentials, requesting resources, defining and storing access norms; together with the definition of a general security layer, made up of different and specialised software components [21]. Such a layer deals with the tasks of allowing administrators to edit and store norms, handling conflicts between contradictory decrees, and evaluate norms.

While obligation expression and enforcement represents the core concept of the present work, obligations are barely supported by the XACML standard, describing a general syntax for obligation specification only, focusing its core functionalities on permissions and prohibitions. So, we redefined the single modules for adapting them to the present context. They are described subsequently.

- **Enforcement Point:** The module that intercepts data consumer's request for information and moves it to the system. As a response from the system, it receives the data requested, enriched with the information about what obligations are active on each datum, and enforces each data provider obligation before returning the data to the consumer. It also enforces data consumer obligations in the system, if requested by the monitoring engine.

[1] OASIS eXtensible Access Control Markup Language (XACML) – https://www. oasis-open.org/committees/xacml/.

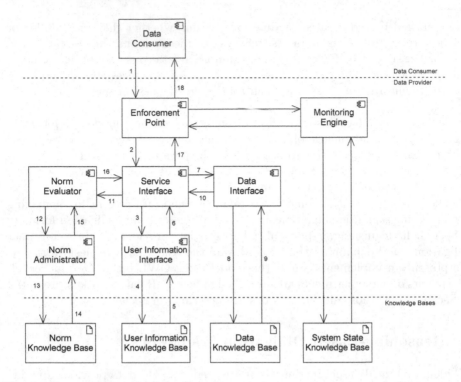

Fig. 1. Reasoning-based obligation framework – components and data request workflow.

- **Monitoring Engine:** The module which deals with the tasks of monitoring whether data consumer obligations are fulfilled or not. The system is monitored and its status is constantly annotated into the **System State Knowledge Base** (KB). If there are data consumer obligations that have to be enforced by the data provider, it notifies such information at the right time to the **Enforcement Point** that will enforce the obligations in the system.
- **Service Interface:** The module which deals with the coordination of the communications between **Norm Evaluator**, **Enforcement Point**, **User Information Interface** and **Data Interface**. In particular, it acts in order to return the output of the **Norm Evaluator** to the **Enforcement Point** as a response for a data request.
- **User Information Interface:** The interface that retrieves the information about the requesting agent (that is conceptualized by the data provider as a generic user of the service) in the **User Information KB** and returns it to the **Service Interface**.
- **Data Interface:** the interface that retrieves the requested information in the **Data KB** and returns it to the **Service Interface**.
- **Norm Evaluator:** The component that evaluates what are the pieces of data on which each obligation must be enforced. The module is provided with a

reasoning engine, in order to use inference for deducing the right conditions for the application of the obligations, starting from their formal definition.

- **Norm Administrator:** Module which manages access to the stored norms (in the **Norm KB**) and their editing.

3 Obligation Expression and Enforcement

An obligation, in its most general form, can be defined as a couple $o_i = \langle \alpha_i, \Gamma_i \rangle$, where α_i is an axiom that is used for describing the information about what conditions are to be verified for the obligation to apply on a datum, so we call it the *activation condition* of the obligation o_i. Γ_i is a generic algorithm operating on logical statements, that is able to modify the knowledge status in the framework. Such algorithm is the one that has to be executed whether the conditions expressed in α_i are satisfied. So, we call Γ_i the *content* of the obligation o_i. When there is at least one piece of data on which an obligation o_i apply, we say that such obligation is an *active* obligation.

The collection of all the norm axioms $A = \langle \alpha_1, \alpha_2, \ldots, \alpha_n \rangle$ represents the **Norm KB** in our framework, once every obligation o_i is expressed. It is a matter, instead, of the **Enforcement Point** to store each algorithm Γ_i associated to each axiom α_i and execute it at the right time.

As presented in Sect. 2, when a request is sent by the data consumer, the data provider retrieves the result of the request from the **Data KB**. In such a context, a data provider obligation can be represented, therefore, by a couple $o_i = \langle \alpha_i, \Gamma_i \rangle$, where α_i is a generic axiom that is able to identify the specific pieces of data on which the obligation applies among the retrieved ones. Γ_i represents the actions to be performed on the identified pieces of data, before returning them to the data consumer, as a consequence of the enforcement of the obligation. For example, a data provider obligation may impose to anonymize the name of under-age inpatients in a hospital system. The activation condition of the obligation would be represented by the axiom that identifies the name of any inpatient that is under age. The content of the obligation would be the set of actions that are to be executed in order to anonymize the identified data, before returning it to the data consumer.

In the framework, the *obligation enforcement* is done in the following way: the **Enforcement Point** receives an information request from a **Data Consumer**, it passes the request to the **Service Interface** that collects the necessary information about the data consumer from the **User Information Interface**. Then, it obtains the information requested by the **Data Consumer** from the **Data Interface** and enriches it with the information obtained from the **User Information Interface**. At this point, the data is passed to the **Norm Evaluator** that retrieves from the **Norm Administrator** the set A of norm axioms and uses it to enrich the data retrieved. The reasoning engine, included into the **Policy Evaluator**, can then infer, for every individual into the data to be returned, which activation conditions apply, and register such information. The so-enriched KB is passed, then, to the **Service Interface** and back to the **Enforcement Point**.

At this point, every algorithm Γ_i is executed on the identified data for each activation condition α_i that is active, in order to fulfill each obligation o_i. The obtained KB is returned to the **Data Consumer**, finally.

Regarding data consumer obligations, they can be represented again as a couple $o_i = \langle \alpha_i, \Gamma_i \rangle$, with the difference that the data on which the activation conditions apply are not the ones returned to the data consumer, but the information stored in the **System State KB**. Activation conditions are again used for finding the pieces of data on which the algorithm to be executed, specified as the content of the obligation, apply. A content activity is represented by the action of adding a set of new axioms to the **System State KB**, in order to allow the **Monitoring Engine** to correctly deduce the correct state (*activated, fulfilled, violated*) of each obligation o_i in the system, as it has been already described in [8].

4   Implementing the Obligation Framework Using OWL 2 Technology

An implementation of the presented model can be developed using the Web Ontology Language 2 (OWL 2) technology[2], for annotating and reasoning on Description Logics (DL) statements. There are different reasons for preferring OWL 2 in respect to other technologies for annotating logical statements, in particular:

- DL is a decidable subset of First Order Logic (FOL);
- OWL 2 is a standard since 2009, for annotating statements with DL semantics;
- Free tools are available for annotating knowledge in the OWL standard (e.g., JAVA Jena[3] and OWL API tools[4]) and reasoning on the available knowledge (e.g., Pellet [18] and Hermit [16] reasoners).

In such an implementation, every framework knowledge base can be represented by an OWL ontology. An activation condition can be defined with an OWL class axiom, identifying each piece of data on which an activation condition α_i is active as a member of a named class c_i. The **System State KB** can express temporal axioms, between the others, for checking the fulfillment of the data consumer obligations, using the OWL Time Ontology[5].

The choice of formalizing the activation conditions of obligations using OWL classes, moreover, has many advantages. First, defining the activation condition class, it is possible to use the rich set of OWL operators available for defining classes, as, for example, the intersection of classes or properties restriction. Therefore, it is possible to exploit the reasoning capability of an OWL reasoner

---

[2] OWL 2 Web Ontology Language Document Overview – http://www.w3.org/TR/owl-overview/.

[3] Apache Jena – https://jena.apache.org/.

[4] The OWL API – http://owlapi.sourceforge.net/.

[5] OWL Time Ontology – http://www.w3.org/TR/owl-time.

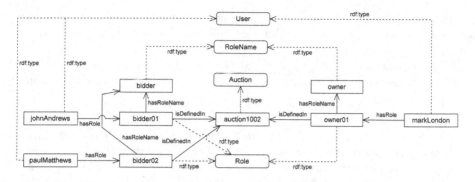

Fig. 2. eBay Auctions ontology – example of roles. The users *paulMatthews* and *johnAndrews* are two *bidders* in *auction1002*, while the user *markLondon* is the *owner* of the same auction.

and deducing new knowledge from the data in the **Data KB** and **System State KB**, that is necessary to perform or verify the fulfillment of the obligations correctly. Another advantage is that the activation condition is written in an ontology, so it is possible to change it by simply using and ontology editor without the need to re-code a software. Moreover, specific individuals can be added to special classes in the ontology at runtime for each request, for identifying specific roles assumed by users in the context of a single request, as, e.g., identifying the requesting user in the knowledge base by assigning her/him to a specific class.

We present a data provider obligation implementation example in Sect. 4.1, with a reference to the real life scenario of eBay auctions. We describe in Sect. 4.2 data consumer obligations instead, explaining how they can be defined, verified and monitored using OWL technology.

4.1 A Case Study and Data Provider Obligation Example: eBay Anonymization of Bidders

The company eBay Inc. releases information about its auctions since 2011 through its API[6] to external agents, in the form of different standard structures (e.g., XML, JSON). We took as an example the case in which the same data would be released by the eBay API in the form of logical statements (never supported, in fact, up to the present day). We described the main concepts that are involved in such context in an OWL TBox, and we collected some sample auctions in an OWL ABox. The most relevant concepts are presented in Fig. 2, together with some sample individuals.

As it can be seen in Fig. 2, the role of each user in an auction is modeled as an individual itself (`bidder01` is an example, in Fig. 2), as it has already been done in other ontological models (e.g., [10]). That allows to model the different

---

[6] eBay Developers Program – https://go.developer.ebay.com/.

interactions between the users in the auctions according to their role correctly, allowing the same user to cover different roles in different institutional spaces (auctions).

eBay presents a policy between its data access terms that requests some information to be anonymized, before it is released, according to specific conditions[7]:

> To keep certain info private, we limit how bid history information is displayed. When the highest bid, reserve price, or Buy It Now price reaches or exceeds a certain level, members can't view or search for member-specific information, such as user IDs, on the Bid History page. Though the Bid History: Details page has information on bidders, each bidder is assigned an anonymous name (x***y, for example). Only the seller can see a bidder's user ID. Note: eBay determines when user IDs are no longer viewable based on the price or bid amount, and this varies by country.

It can be noticed that the presented policy can be modeled as a data provider obligation, according to what is presented in Sect. 3. Such policy is based on the role of the requesting user, as well as the content of the data requested.

According to such policy, we tried to specify as an example, according to our model, the fact that in the case that the data consumer is not the owner of an auction, the identity of a bidder that made any offer is anonymized.

We gave to the condition class c_1 the name ActivationCondition01. So, the axiom α_1 results[8]:

```
Class: ActivationCondition01
    EquivalentTo: Role and hasRoleName value bidder and
                  isDefinedIn some (inverse(isDefinedIn) some
                  (hasRoleName value owner and (inverse(hasRole)
                  some (not CurrentUser))))
```

Where CurrentUser is a special class including the individual representing the data consumer in the ontology. So, the presented class axiom definess any role of any user that is a bidder of an auction whose owner $\notin$ CurrentUser as a member of the class ActivationCondition01.

We can imagine, then, a request for information of the user paulMatthews, as the data consumer, about the data of some auctions. The requested data is retrieved by the **Data Interface**, and information about paulMatthews is obtained from the **User Information Interface**, allowing the **Service Interface** to enrich the ontology with such information, and to add the axiom CurrentUser = {paulMatthews} to the ontology. Data is then passed to the **Norm Evaluator**, which adds the available collection of norms to the information and applies reasoning, deducing, among all the theorems, which individuals are included into the ActivationCondition01 class.

The so-enriched ontology, then, can be returned to the **Enforcement Point** that can apply a set of defined actions Γ_1 to each individual of

---

[7] eBay Bidding Overview – http://pages.ebay.com/help/buy/bidding-overview.html.
[8] The syntax in which all DL axioms are presented in this paper is the Manchester OWL Syntax http://www.w3.org/TR/owl2-manchester-syntax/.

ActivationCondition01. Referring to the ontology shown in Fig. 2, in order to anonymize a user, we propose the subsequent procedure. A new individual is created that is an anonymized version of such user. Then, the original hasRole relation between the user and its bidder role in an auction is removed, and a new hasRole relation is created between the generated anonymous individual and the bidder role. So, Γ_1 can be described as the collection of actions that, for every role $\rho_j \in$ ActivationCondition01:

1. Generates a new user in the ontology, that represents an anonymized version of the user ι_k: hasRole(ι_k, ρ_j), if and only if that has not been done before.
2. Deletes the hasRole property between ι_k and ρ_j.
3. Connects the anonymous user to ρ_j with the hasRole property.
4. Deletes ι_k, if and only if it has no more hasRole connections in the ontology.

4.2   Modeling and Monitoring Data Consumer Obligations

The **System State KB** represents a collection of concepts and observable facts about the system state and temporal constraints. As described in [8], time can be modeled with OWL technology importing the necessary knowledge from the OWL Time Ontology. That is done in order to correctly represent the state of the system for each instant and perform a dynamic monitoring of the state of interaction between different agents with respect to the specified set of obligations. The state of each obligation o_i can be checked in the system by applying in the **System State Ontology** the Γ_i set of actions generated by the activation of the data consumer obligation o_i, as already described in Sect. 3.

It has to be noticed that different facts registered in the **System State KB** can activate different obligations, and also a single obligation different times, being that the conditions for the activation of a single obligation can hold multiple times. For each instance of a single activation of an obligation, its status can be one between three:

- *Activated*: the activation condition of the obligation has been verified, but the content of the obligation has not been fulfilled by the data consumer.
- *Fulfilled*: the activation condition of the obligation has been verified, and the content of the obligation has been fulfilled before the specified deadline.
- *Violated*: the activation condition of the obligation has been verified, and the content of the obligation has not been fulfilled before the specified deadline.

As an example, the obligation o_2 may request to a user who asks for a specific datum delta to pay € 5.00 after the response by the data provider, no later than the time instant1. We can say, for example, that the user johnAndrews asks for the datum delta at the time instant2. The fact relative to such response is registered by the monitoring engine in the **System State KB** with the subsequent axioms:

```
Individual: request01
  Types: DataRequest
  Facts: hasAgent johnAndrews,
         hasObject delta,
         hasResponseTime instant2,
         hasPaymentDeadline instant1
```

That creates in the **System State KB** a new record of a request `request01` by `johnAndrews` for the datum `delta`, with the correct response that came at the time `instant2` by the data provider. The activation condition `ActivationCondition02` of the obligation o_2 can be modeled with the subsequent axiom:

```
Class: ActivationCondition02
  EquivalentTo: DataRequest and hasObject value delta
```

That puts every request for the datum `delta` in the class `Activation Condition02`. When it is noticed by the monitoring engine that `request01` $\in$ `ActivationCondition02`, the Γ_2 content of the obligation is applied to the **System State KB**. It must be a collection of actions that adds the knowledge that is necessary and sufficient for monitoring the state of the obligation in the **System State KB**. For the present example it can be represented by the subsequent class axiom for the class `Content02`:

```
Class: Content02
  EquivalentTo: Pay and hasActor value johnAndrews
                and hasService value request01
                and hasImport some integer[>=5]
                and hasCurrency some string["euro"]
```

At this point, the monitoring engine can infer the state of the obligation: if `Content02` $= \emptyset$ and `instant1` is in the future, the obligation is *activated*, being that the payment has still not been done, but the deadline has not been reached. If `Content02` $= \emptyset$ and `instant1` is in the past, the obligation is *violated*, being that the payment has still not been done, and the deadline has been reached. If `Content02` $\neq \emptyset$ and the payment time is after `instant1`, the obligation is again *violated*, being that the payment has been done, but that did not happen within the specified deadline. If `Content02` $\neq \emptyset$ and `instant1` is after the payment time, the obligation is *fulfilled*, being that the payment has been done within the specified deadline.

After the evaluation, as a consequence of specific obligation states by the **Monitoring Engine**, the **Enforcement Point** can then apply specific actions in the system eventually, as enforcing specific actions or apply penalties for certain agents, as described, e.g., by [4].

5   Experiments

We focused on the development of a framework for the enforcement of data provider obligations, while considering the modeling of data consumer

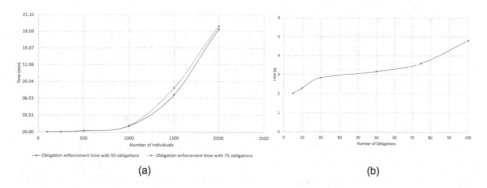

Fig. 3. (a) Obligation enforcement time (min) as a function of the number of individuals in the request response, for 50 and 75 obligations – (b) Obligation enforcement time (s) as a function of the number of obligations, with 250 individuals in the request response

obligations and the monitoring engine component as future work. The framework was developed with JAVA, using JAVA OWL API for annotating statements and Pellet [18] as DL reasoner. We measured the time for enforcing the obligations on the data to be returned to the data consumer by the data provider, as a function of the number of individuals in the response data (Fig. 3(a)) and the number of obligations to be applied (Fig. 3(b)). Tests were made with a PC with an Intel Core i7 2.7 GHz processor, 8 GB DD3 RAM.

The enforcement time is about 2 s for both 50 and 75 obligations when the number of individuals in the response data is 100. The enforcement time is about 3 s for both 50 and 75 obligations when the number of individuals in the response data is 250. However, the function increases exponentially and, for example, the enforcement time is 6 min and 38 s for 1500 individuals and 50 obligations. That suggests that the higher is the expected value for the number of individuals in the response, the more such reasoning-based framework results an inconvenient choice for enforcing obligations.

The graph in Fig. 3(b) shows that the number of obligations seems not to influence the enforcement time as much significantly. For example, enforcement time for 5 obligations and 250 individuals is 2.01 s, while enforcement time for 20 obligations and 250 individuals is 2.8 s. A 4× number of obligations raised the enforcement time of 28.21 %.

In conclusion, scenarios in which usual responses contain few individuals (e.g., a query for requesting information about a single eBay auction, see Sect. 4.1) present a high usability for the approach with ordinary software technologies and hardware. Scalability problems coming from higher expected values of the number of individuals in the response should be tackled with better hardware solutions or optimized algorithms.

6   Related Work

Fornara [8] models an ontology for specifying and monitoring obligations in Open Multiagent Systems. Her approach for monitoring the status of the system is proposed in the present work for implementing the Monitoring Engine module of data consumer obligations. We improve Fornara's work proposing a way to specify and enforce data provider obligations on ontological statements that have to be released as a consequence of a data consumer request.

Bettini et al. [4] present a model for specifying and evaluating provisions and obligations in a pioneering work in the context of Access Control. It is based on the expression of Datalog Rules and reasoning for evaluating norms. They use the word "provision" to refer to the conditions that have to be met before data is released after a request. However, any expression of such type can be reduced syntactically to the form of a permission or a prohibition. We differ from the work of Bettini et al. in the fact that reasoning is applied to the data in order to infer what pieces of information are to be altered according to the application of each obligation. Also, they do not describe any monitoring engine.

Gama and Ferreira [11] present a platform for specifying, monitoring and enforcing obligations in open systems. The language for expressing obligations is an arbitrary extension of the non-standard language SPL (Security Policy Language) [14]. Their monitoring engine includes the modeling of time constraints, obligation statuses and actions of enforcement. We differ from such a work in defining norms using logical statements and using reasoning for inferring the consequence of data provider obligations, and the status of each data consumer obligation.

Irwin et al. [12] describe an abstract metamodel for the obligation management. They start from the consideration that obligations are not to be assigned blindly to agents. Instead, a system should only allow obligations to be assigned when the receiving subject has sufficient privileges to fulfill them. They continue, then, describing how to monitor and verify such conditions. Furthermore, they describe an environment in which, in the case that an obligation goes unfulfilled, it is always possible to clearly identify whose fault it is (*accountability*). While our metamodel presents simpler constraints, it is applied to semantic pieces of information and presents a framework and an implementation, while Irwin et al.'s work represents a much more abstract definition of a normative system.

OWL-Polar [15] is a framework for the semantic definition and enforcement of permission, prohibition and obligation statements. While their definition of an obligation fits well in our own definition involving activation conditions and contents, they do not foresee the enforcement of data provider obligations to logical data directly for access control purposes. Furthermore, while considering the possibility to use SPARQL-DL [17] queries for checking the fulfillment of data consumer obligations using reasoning, activation conditions are translated into standard SPARQL[9] queries in fact, with poor or no use of reasoning. Such approach, while improving performances, lowers the expressiveness of the whole method significantly in respect to allowing the chance to add arbitrary axioms to the state of facts, for deducing new knowledge on the basis of a larger expressivity.

KAoS [5] is another framework for the definition of permissions, prohibitions and obligations. A norm is not defined with logical axioms in such a framework,

---

[9] SPARQL Query Language for RDF – http://www.w3.org/TR/rdf-sparql-query/.

but it is modeled as an individual in an ontology (corresponding to our **Norm KB**). Reasoning can not be used in order to apply obligations to data directly in that way, as it is done in the present work.

Chen et al. [7] define a model of obligations in the environment of risk-aware access control. Obligations are combined with a specific measure of how much risk is incurred by allowing or denying access to specific resources. Obligations are enforced effectively if and only if the measured risk for enforcing them is lower than a specified threshold.

7   Conclusions and Future Work

We presented a model for defining and enforcing data provider and data consumer obligations in a system, expressing such norms as logical statements. We explained how such model can be implemented using the standard OWL technology and standard DL reasoning, with, in particular, an example of application taken from the real-life world of eBay auctions. We developed a framework for defining and enforcing data provider obligations, presenting the performances of such environment in enforcing obligations.

We think that the present work can be considered an interesting advance of the actual state of the art, in modeling obligations, for the subsequent reasons:

- This is the first time, as far as we know, that obligations are defined as axioms that can be enforced directly on the available data, with the use of reasoning.
- The model for defining and enforcing such obligations can be implemented using available, standard technologies.
- Obligations expressed as logical statements can be read by other agents of a normative system, allowing them to change their behaviour accordingly to what they can infer starting from the expressed norms. Therefore, they are able to apply reasoning activities, in their turn, on the available normative state.
- Both data provider and data consumer obligations can be expressed in the same standard way, while they are, however, enforced in different manners, as it is requested by the system. Previous works usually focused on data provider or data consumer obligations only, as presented in Sect. 6, describing a non-necessarily standard way to define them and a hard-coded software to enforce them. We think to have presented a more general and standard model for the definition of both data provider and data consumer obligations.

Future work can include the development of a monitoring engine for checking the status of data consumer obligations. Furthermore, usability tests can be done to measure the OWL implementation applicability to real life cases, in order to consider the possibility to introduce different approaches for the development of the different modules, in the case that usability problems are noticed.

References

1. Andrighetto, G., Governatori, G., Noriega, P., van der Torre, L.W.N.: Normative Multi-agent Systems. Dagstuhl Follow-Ups, vol. 4. Schloss Dagstuhl-Leibniz-Zentrum fuer Informatik, Dagstuhl, Germany (2013)
2. Ardagna, C., De Capitani di Vimercati, S., Paraboschi, S., Pedrini, E., Samarati, P.: An XACML-based privacy-centered access control system. In: Proceedings of the 1st ACM Workshop on Information Security Governance (WISG 2009), Chicago, Illinois, USA, November 2009
3. Bettini, C., Jajodia, S., Wang, X.S., Wijesekera, D.: Provisions and obligations in policy management and security applications. In: VLDB 2002, Proceedings of 28th International Conference on Very Large Data Bases, 20–23 August 2002, Hong Kong, China, pp. 502–513. Morgan Kaufmann (2002)
4. Bettini, C., Jajodia, S., Wang, X.S., Wijesekera, D.: Provisions and obligations in policy management and security applications. In: VLDB, pp. 502–513. Morgan Kaufmann (2002)
5. Bradshaw, J., Uszok, A., Breedy, M., Bunch, L., Eskridge, T., Feltovich, P., Johnson, M., Lott, J., Vignati, M.: The KAoS policy services framework. In: Proceedings of the Eighth Cyber Security and Information Intelligence Research Workshop (CSIIRW 2013). Oak Ridge National Labs, Oak Ridge, TN (2013)
6. Chen, L., Crampton, J., Kollingbaum, M.J., Norman, T.J.: Obligations in risk-aware access control. In: Cuppens-Boulahia, N., Fong, P., García-Alfaro, J., Marsh, S., Steghöfer, J. (eds.) Tenth Annual International Conference on Privacy, Security and Trust, PST , Paris, France, 16–18 July 2012, pp. 145–152. IEEE (2012)
7. Chen, L., Crampton, J., Kollingbaum, M.J., Norman, T.J.: Obligations in risk-aware access control. In: Proceedings of the Tenth Annual International Conference on Privacy, Security and Trust (PST), PST 2012, Washington, DC, USA, pp. 145–152. IEEE Computer Society (2012)
8. Fornara, N.: Specifying and monitoring obligations in open multiagent systems using semantic web technology. In: Elçi, A., Koné, M.T., Orgun, M.A. (eds.) Semantic Agent Systems: Foundations and Applications. SCI, vol. 344, pp. 25–45. Springer, Heidelberg (2011). Chap. 2
9. Fornara, N., Colombetti, M.: Representation and monitoring of commitments and norms using OWL. AI Commun. 23(4), 341–356 (2010)
10. Fornara, N., Tampitsikas, C.: Semantic technologies for open interaction systems. Artif. Intell. Rev. 39, 63–79 (2013)
11. Gama, P., Ferreira, P.: Obligation policies: an enforcement platform. In: Sixth IEEE International Workshop on Policies for Distributed Systems and Networks, 2005, pp. 203–212, June 2005
12. Irwin, K., Yu, T., Winsborough, W.H.: On the modeling and analysis of obligations. In: Juels, A., Wright, R.N., di Vimercati, S.D.C. (eds.) ACM Conference on Computer and Communications Security, pp. 134–143. ACM (2006)
13. Kolovski, V., Hendler, J., Parsia, B.: Analyzing web access control policies. In: Proceedings of the 16th International Conference on World Wide Web, WWW 2007, pp. 677–686. ACM, New York (2007)
14. Ribeiro, C., Zquete, A., Ferreira, P., Guedes, P.: SPL: an access control language for security policies with complex constraints. In: Proceedings of the Network and Distributed System Security Symposium, pp. 89–107 (1999)

15. Şensoy, M., Norman, T.J., Vasconcelos, W.W., Sycara, K.: OWL-POLAR: semantic policies for agent reasoning. In: Patel-Schneider, P.F., Pan, Y., Hitzler, P., Mika, P., Zhang, L., Pan, J.Z., Horrocks, I., Glimm, B. (eds.) ISWC 2010, Part I. LNCS, vol. 6496, pp. 679–695. Springer, Heidelberg (2010)
16. Shearer, R., Motik, B., Horrocks, I.: HermiT: a highly-efficient OWL reasoner. In: Dolbear, C., Ruttenberg, A., Sattler, U. (eds.) OWLED, CEUR Workshop Proceedings, vol. 432. CEUR-WS.org (2008)
17. Sirin, E., Parsia, B.: SPARQL-DL: SPARQL query for OWL-DL. In: Golbreich, C., Kalyanpur, A., Parsia, B. (eds.) Proceedings of the Third International Workshop on OWL: Experiences and Directions (OWLED 2007), Innsbruck, Austria (2007)
18. Sirin, E., Parsia, B., Grau, B.C., Kalyanpur, A., Katz, Y.: Pellet: a practical OWL-DL reasoner. Web Semant. **5**(2), 51–53 (2007)
19. Uszok, A., Bradshaw, J.M.: Demonstrating selected W3C policy languages interest group use cases using the KAoS policy services framework. In: POLICY, pp. 233–234. IEEE Computer Society (2008)
20. Wright, G.: Deontic logics. Am. Philos. Q. **4**(2), 136–143 (1967)
21. OASIS XACML Version 3.0 Specification, Data-flow model, pp. 19–20 (2013). http://docs.oasis-open.org/xacml/3.0/xacml-3.0-core-spec-cs-01-en.pdf

Coupling Regulative and Constitutive Dimensions in Situated Artificial Institutions

Maiquel de Brito[1(✉)], Jomi Fred Hübner[1], and Olivier Boissier[2]

[1] Federal University of Santa Catarina, Florianópolis, SC, Brazil
maiquel.b@posgrad.ufsc.br, jomi.hubner@ufsc.br
[2] Laboratoire Hubert Curien UMR CNRS 5516, Institut Henri Fayol,
MINES Saint-Etienne, Saint-Etienne, France
Olivier.Boissier@emse.fr

Abstract. Artificial Institutions are often considered as systems where the regulation defined through norms is based on an interpretation of the concrete world where the agents are situated and interacting. Such interpretation can be defined through constitutive rules. Although the literature proposes independent approaches for the definition and management of both norms and constitutive rules, they are usually not connected to each other. This paper investigates how to make such a connection, that raises problems of representations and of coupling of independent dynamics (norms and constitutive rules). Our main contribution in this paper is an approach and a formal apparatus to base the regulation provided by the norms on the institutional interpretation of the world provided by constitutive rules as defined in the Situated Artificial Institutions model.

Keywords: Institutions · Status functions · Constitutive rules · Situatedness · Norms

1 Introduction

Like human societies, agents' ones may require some regulation of the behaviour of the possibly heterogeneous individuals. This paper refers to the element that represents such regulation in Multi-Agent Systems (MAS) as *artificial institution* (or simply *institution*). The regulation provided by institutions is usually expressed through regulative norms (henceforth referred just as *norms*) based on deontic concepts such as obligations, prohibitions, and permissions. Institutions are often viewed as systems where the norms perform their regulative tasks based on an interpretation (also referred in the literature as *constitution* or *classification*) of the concrete world (or the *environment*) where the agents are immersed [2,17]. Thus, for example, norms regulate *payments* and *bids* rather than exchanging of paper bills or raising hands. Constitution is usually specified through constitutive norms (henceforth referred as *constitutive rules*). They specify, for example, that the raising of hands counts as a bid in an auction.

Institutions have thus a *constitutive state* and a *normative state* with their specific representations and dynamics. The constitutive state is the institutional

© Springer International Publishing Switzerland 2016
M. Rovatsos et al. (Eds.): EUMAS 2015/AT 2015, LNAI 9571, pp. 318–334, 2016.
DOI: 10.1007/978-3-319-33509-4_25

view of the current state of the world. The normative state is the institutional view regarding the expected behaviour of the agents. Basing the normative state (i.e. defining norm activations, violations, fulfilments, etc.) on the constitutive one is a key issue in MAS institutions [5, 7, 8]. Although the literature proposes specialized approaches for norms and for constitutive rules, they are usually not connected to each other [3]. Challenges of connecting them are related to conceive how the environmental elements of different natures, abstracted under the notion of constitution, are taken into account in the norm lifecycle. For example, considering the norm *"a bidder is obliged to place a bid"*, it is necessary to define (i) how to monitor the norm taking into account all the agents considered as bidders, (ii) how to proceed when obliged agents are no longer considered as bidders or (iii) how to verify its compliance when many actions are considered as a bid (is the norm compliance conditioned to the performance of all of these actions or of at least one of them?).

This paper addresses the coupling between normative and constitutive states departing from normative and constitutive models already proposed in the literature. The constitutive model comes from the Situated Artificial Institution (SAI) approach [11], that defines representations and dynamics for the constitutive state [10]. The normative model is the one proposed in [16], that formalizes the deontic aspects of norms and defines the operational semantics for their monitoring. As the main contribution, we define an approach and a formal apparatus to monitor and reason about the norms of [16] based on the SAI constitutive state.

This paper is organized as follows: Sects. 2 and 3 describe, respectively, the considered normative and constitutive models; Sect. 4 describes how normative and constitutive representations are linked; Sect. 5 presents our approach to couple the normative dynamics in the constitutive one. This approach is illustrated in Sect. 6, discussed in Sect. 7 and compared with some related works in the Sect. 8, that also presents some conclusions and perspectives.

2 Normative Model

This section briefly describes the model of [16], firstly defining norms that compose a normative specification and then defining norm instances (i.e. norms enacted in the real world) and their dynamics. The focus is on the essential elements to our proposed coupling. More details about the normative model can be found in [16].

2.1 Normative Specification

Definition 1 (Norm). *A norm n is a tuple $n = \langle \alpha, c_a, c_m, c_d, c_r, c_t \rangle$ where (i) α is the agent obliged to comply with the norm, (ii) c_a is the activation condition of the norm, (iii) c_m is the maintenance condition, (iv) c_d is the deactivation condition, (v) c_r is the repair condition, and (vi) c_t is the timeout condition. The set of all norms of an institution, noted $\mathcal{N}$, is called a normative specification.*

As proposed by [16], the element α is an agent identifier and the remainder c elements are expressed in first order predicate language with connectives $\{\neg, \wedge, \vee, \rightarrow\}$ and quantifiers $\{\forall, \exists\}$. Informally, a norm expresses that if, at some point, c_a holds, then the agent α is obliged to see to it that c_m is maintained at least until c_d holds; otherwise, α is obliged to see to it that c_r holds before the timeout c_t. For example, the norm

$$\langle Ag, driving(Ag), \neg cross\_red(Ag, LightID), \neg driving(Ag), fine\_paid(Value), time(500)\rangle$$

expresses that, when an agent Ag is driving, he is obliged to not cross the red traffic light $LightID$ until he is not driving; otherwise it has to pay $Value$ before the time 500 (words starting with upper case letters are variables).

2.2   Normative Dynamics

The activation of the norms leads to the creation of instances, defined as follows.

Definition 2 (Norm Instance). *Given a norm n and a substitution of variables θ^1, a norm instance is represented by $n' = \langle \alpha', c_a', c_m', c_d', c_r', c_t'\rangle$ s.t α' is an agent, $c_a' = c_a\theta$, $c_m' = c_m\theta$, $c_d' = c_d\theta$, $c_r' = c_r\theta$, and $c_t' = c_t\theta$.*

The set of all norm instances, noted N, is called the normative state of the institution. It is defined as follows.

Definition 3 (Normative State). *The normative state of the institution is $N = AS \cup VS \cup DS \cup FS$ s.t. (i) AS is the set of active instances, (ii) VS is the set of violated instances, (iii) DS is the set of deactivated instances, and (iv) FS is the set of failed instances.*

As shown in Fig. 1, a norm instance n' is activated as soon as its activation condition c_a' is satisfied, getting then into AS. If at some point the maintenance condition c_m' is not satisfied, the norm instance is violated, getting into VS. If the norm instance is active and the deactivation condition c_d' is satisfied, the norm instance gets deactivated (DS). If it is violated, either (i) fulfilling its reparation condition c_r' leads it to deactivated state (DS) or (ii) the occurrence of the timeout condition c_t' leads it to the failure state (FS).

The predicates *active*, *viol*, *deactivated*, and *failed* are defined to check a norm instance with respect to the normative state N as follows:

$$N \models active(n') \text{ iff } n' \in AS \tag{1}$$

$$N \models viol(n') \text{ iff } n' \in VS \tag{2}$$

$$N \models deactivated(n') \text{ iff } n' \in DS \tag{3}$$

$$N \models failed(n') \text{ iff } n' \in FS \tag{4}$$

---

[1] In this paper, a *substitution* is always represented by θ. A *substitution* is a finite set of pairs $\{\alpha_1/\beta_1, \cdots, \alpha_n/\beta_n\}$ where α_i is a variable and β_i is a term. If ρ is a literal, then $\rho\theta$ is the literal resulting from the replacement of each α_i in ρ by the corresponding β_i [6].

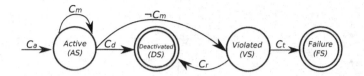

Fig. 1. Lifecycle of norm instances (based on [16])

In [16], a *normative monitor* is defined as a tuple $M_N = \langle \mathcal{N}, AS, VS, DS, FS, s \rangle$ where (i) $\mathcal{N}$ is the set of considered norms, (ii) AS, VS, DS, and FS are the sets of active, violated, deactivated, and failed norm instances, and (iii) s indexes the current state of the normative monitor. The transition system for a normative monitor M_N is $TS_{M_N} = \langle \Gamma_{M_N}, \triangleright \rangle$ where Γ_{M_N} is the set of all possible configurations of the normative monitor and $\triangleright \subseteq \Gamma_{M_N} \times \Gamma_{M_N}$ is a transition relation between configurations. The operational semantics of the normative monitor follows the transition rules (5) to (9).

$$\frac{\langle \alpha, c_a, c_m, c_d, c_r, c_t \rangle \in \mathcal{N} \qquad c_a\theta \qquad \neg c_d\theta}{M_N \triangleright \langle \mathcal{N}, AS \cup \langle \alpha', c_a\theta, c_m\theta, c_d\theta, c_r\theta, c_t\theta \rangle, VS, DS, FS, s_{i+1} \rangle} \quad (5)$$

$$\frac{n' = \langle \alpha', c_a', c_m', c_d', c_r', c_t' \rangle \qquad n' \in AS \qquad \neg c_m'}{M_N \triangleright \langle \mathcal{N}, AS \setminus n', VS \cup n', DS, FS, s_{i+1} \rangle} \quad (6)$$

$$\frac{n' = \langle \alpha', c_a', c_m', c_d', c_r', c_t' \rangle \qquad n' \in AS \qquad c_d'}{M_N \triangleright \langle \mathcal{N}, AS \setminus n', VS, DS \cup n', FS, s_{i+1} \rangle} \quad (7)$$

$$\frac{n' = \langle \alpha', c_a', c_m', c_d', c_r', c_t' \rangle \qquad n' \in VS \qquad c_r'}{M_N \triangleright \langle \mathcal{N}, AS, VS \setminus n', DS \cup n', FS, s_{i+1} \rangle} \quad (8)$$

$$\frac{n' = \langle \alpha', c_a', c_m', c_d', c_r', c_t' \rangle \qquad n' \in VS \qquad c_t'}{M_N \triangleright \langle \mathcal{N}, AS, VS \setminus n', DS, FS \cup n', s_{i+1} \rangle} \quad (9)$$

The sets $\mathcal{N}, AS$, VS, DS, and FS are those of the M_N. The conditions c_a, c_d, c_m', c_d', c_r', and c_d' are evaluated against the state of the world to manage the normative state N as illustrated in Fig. 1. For example, by the transition rule (5), if the state of the world satisfies the activation condition but does not satisfies the deactivation condition of a norm – both of them under some substitution θ – then the monitor adds a norm instance $n' = \langle \alpha', c_a\theta, c_m\theta, c_d\theta, c_r\theta, c_t\theta \rangle$ into the set AS.

3 Constitutive Model

As defined in [11], SAI considers that the dynamics of the normative state (i.e. the activation, fulfilment, violation, etc. of the norms) is based on a *constitutive*

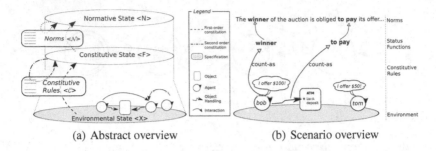

(a) Abstract overview   (b) Scenario overview

Fig. 2. SAI overview

state, that is the institutional view about the environmental state (Fig. 2(a)). For example, the norm *"the winner of an auction is obliged to pay its offer"* is fulfilled when, in the environment, an agent considered by the institution as *winner* performs an action considered by the institution as a *payment* (Fig. 2(b)). Section 3.1 describes how such interpretation is specified in SAI through constitutive rules. Section 3.2 describes the dynamics of such interpretation.

3.1 Constitutive Specification

The constitutive specification defines how the elements that *may* be part of the environment, defined below, are viewed from the institutional perspective.

Definition 4 (Environmental Elements). *The environmental elements are represented by $\mathcal{X} = \mathcal{A}_\mathcal{X} \cup \mathcal{E}_\mathcal{X} \cup \mathcal{S}_\mathcal{X}$ where $\mathcal{A}_\mathcal{X}$ is the set of agents possibly acting in the system, $\mathcal{E}_\mathcal{X}$ is the set of events that may happen in the environment, and $\mathcal{S}_\mathcal{X}$ is the set of properties used to describe the possible states of the environment.*

Agents in $\mathcal{A}_\mathcal{X}$ are represented by atoms (e.g. *bob*). Events in $\mathcal{E}_\mathcal{X}$ are pairs (e, a) where e is a first-order logic predicate identifying the event with its possible arguments and a identifies the element that has triggered the event e. Properties in $\mathcal{S}_\mathcal{X}$ are represented by first-order logic predicates. From the institutional point of view, the environmental elements may carry some *status functions* [18].

Definition 5 (Status Function). *The status functions of a SAI are represented by $\mathcal{F} = \mathcal{A}_\mathcal{F} \cup \mathcal{E}_\mathcal{F} \cup \mathcal{S}_\mathcal{F}$ where $\mathcal{A}_\mathcal{F}$ is the set of agent-status functions (i.e. status functions assignable to agents), $\mathcal{E}_\mathcal{F}$ is the set of event-status functions (i.e. status functions assignable to events), and $\mathcal{S}_\mathcal{F}$ is the set of state-status functions (i.e. status functions assignable to states).*

For example, in an auction, an agent may have the agent-status function of *winner*, the utterance "I offer $100" may have the event-status function of *bid*, and "more than 20 people placed in a room at Friday 10 am" may have the state-status function of *minimum quorum* for its realization. Agent-status functions are represented by atoms. Event- and state-status functions are represented by first-order logic predicates.

The previously described elements are used to write e-formulae $w_\mathcal{X} \in W_\mathcal{X}$ and sf-formulae $w_\mathcal{F} \in W_\mathcal{F}$ following the BNF grammar rules (10) and (11). Their semantics is given in Sect. 3.2.

$$w_\mathcal{X} ::\ = e_\mathcal{X}\,|\,s_\mathcal{X}\,|\,\neg w_\mathcal{X}\,|\,w_\mathcal{X} \vee w_\mathcal{X}\,|\,w_\mathcal{X} \wedge w_\mathcal{X}\,|\,\bot\,|\,\top \tag{10}$$

$$w_\mathcal{F} ::\ = e_\mathcal{F}\,|\,s_\mathcal{F}\,|\,\neg w_\mathcal{F}\,|\,w_\mathcal{F} \vee w_\mathcal{F}\,|\,w_\mathcal{F} \wedge w_\mathcal{F}\,|\,x \text{ is } y\,|\,\bot\,|\,\top \tag{11}$$

s.t. $e_\mathcal{X} \in \mathcal{E}_\mathcal{X}, s_\mathcal{X} \in \mathcal{S}_\mathcal{X}, e_\mathcal{F} \in \mathcal{E}_\mathcal{F}, s_\mathcal{F} \in \mathcal{S}_\mathcal{F}$, and x and y are logical literals.

The assignment of status functions of $\mathcal{F}$ to the environment elements of $\mathcal{X}$ is specified through *constitutive rules*.

Definition 6 (Constitutive Rule). *A constitutive rule $c \in \mathcal{C}$ is a tuple $\langle x, y, t, m \rangle$ where $x \in \mathcal{F} \cup \mathcal{X} \cup \{\varepsilon\}$, $y \in \mathcal{F}$, $t \in \mathcal{E}_\mathcal{F} \cup \mathcal{E}_\mathcal{X} \cup \top$, $m \in W$, and $W = W_\mathcal{F} \cup W_\mathcal{X}$.*

A constitutive rule $\langle x, y, t, m \rangle$ specifies that x counts as y when t has happened while m holds. If $x = \varepsilon$, then there is a *freestanding assignment* of the status function y, i.e. an assignment where there is not a concrete environmental element carrying y [11,18]. When x actually counts as y (i.e. when the conditions t and m declared in the constitutive rule are true), we say that there is a *status function assignment* (SFA) of the status function y to the element x. The establishment of a SFA of y to some x is the *constitution* of y.

3.2 Constitutive Dynamics

Status functions are dynamically assigned to the actual environmental elements by the interpretation of constitutive specifications [10]. This section introduces the elements involved on this dynamics that are relevant to couple normative and constitutive states.

Definition 7 (Environmental State). *The environmental state is represented by $X = A_X \cup E_X \cup S_X$ where (i) A_X is the set of agents participating in the system, (ii) E_X is the set of events occurring in the environment and (iii) S_X is the set of environmental properties describing the environmental state.*

Agents in A_X are represented by their names. States in S_X are represented by first order logic atomic formulae. Events in E_X are represented by pairs (e, a) where e is the event, represented by a first order logic atomic formula, triggered by the agent a. Events can be triggered by actions of the agents (e.g. the utterance of a bid in an auction, the handling of an environmental artifact, etc.) but can be also produced by the environment itself (e.g. a clock tick). In this case, events are represented by pairs (e, ε). The e-formulae (10) allow us to check if an event $e_\mathcal{X}$ or a state $s_\mathcal{X}$ are actually occurring in the environment according to the following semantics:

$$X \models e_\mathcal{X} \text{ iff } \exists \theta : e_\mathcal{X}\theta \in E_X \tag{12}$$

$$X \models s_\mathcal{X} \text{ iff } \exists \theta : s_\mathcal{X}\theta \in S_X \tag{13}$$

Definition 8 (Constitutive state). *The constitutive state of a SAI is represented by* $F = A_F \cup E_F \cup S_F$ *where (i)* $A_F \subseteq A_X \times \mathcal{A}_{\mathcal{F}}$ *is the set of agent-status function assignments, (ii)* $E_F \subseteq E_X \times \mathcal{E}_{\mathcal{F}} \times A_X$ *is the set of event-status function assignments and (iii)* $S_F \subseteq S_X \times \mathcal{S}_{\mathcal{F}}$ *is the set of state-status function assignments.*

Elements of F are *status-function assignments* (SFA), i.e. relations between environmental elements and status functions. Elements of A_F are pairs $\langle a_X, a_{\mathcal{F}} \rangle$ meaning that the agent a_X has the status function $a_{\mathcal{F}}$. Elements of E_F are triples $\langle e_X, e_{\mathcal{F}}, a_X \rangle$ meaning that the event-status function $e_{\mathcal{F}}$ is assigned to the event e_X produced by the agent a_X.[2] Elements of S_F are pairs $\langle s_X, s_{\mathcal{F}} \rangle$ meaning that the state s_X carries the status function $s_{\mathcal{F}}$. The constitutive state F allow us to define the semantics of sf-formulae (11) considering a model $M = \langle F, X, \mathcal{F} \rangle$:

$$
\begin{aligned}
M \models x \text{ is } y \quad & \text{iff } (x \in A_X \wedge y \in \mathcal{A}_{\mathcal{F}} \wedge \langle x, y \rangle \in A_F) \vee \\
& (x \in E_X \wedge x = (e, a) \wedge y \in \mathcal{E}_{\mathcal{F}} \wedge \langle e, y, a \rangle \in E_F) \vee \\
& (x \in S_X \wedge y \in \mathcal{S}_{\mathcal{F}} \wedge \langle x, y \rangle \in S_F) & (14)
\end{aligned}
$$

$$
M \models e_{\mathcal{F}} \text{ iff } \exists e_X : e_X \text{ is } e_{\mathcal{F}} \tag{15}
$$

$$
M \models s_{\mathcal{F}} \text{ iff } \exists s_X : s_X \text{ is } s_{\mathcal{F}} \tag{16}
$$

By Expression (14), the formula x **is** y is implied by the model M either (i) if x is an agent that participates in the system (i.e. $x \in A_X$) and that carries the agent-status function y (i.e. if $\langle x, y \rangle \in A_F$) or (ii) if $x = (e, a)$ is an event occurring in the environment carrying the event-status function y; or (iii) if y is an state holding in the environment carrying the state-status function y. By Expression (15), if $e_{\mathcal{F}}$ an event-status function assigned to some environmental event, then this event-status function follows from M. By Expression (16), if there is some assignment involving a state-status function $s_{\mathcal{F}}$, then this state-status function follows from M.

3.3   Example of SAI Constitutive Specification

A language to specify the constitution of status functions is proposed in [11]. Figure 3 shows the constitutive specification for the use case addressed in [12], where agents collaborate to manage crisis such as floodings, car crashes, etc. They act in an environment composed by geographic information systems (GIS) and by tangible tables [15] where they put objects equipped with RFID tags on to signal their intended actions. The constitutive rules assign institutional meaning to the environment elements. For example, putting a *launch_object* on the coordinates (15, 20) of a table signals the evacuation of the downtown (constitutive rule 3).

---

[2] As events are supposed to be considered at the individual agent level in normative systems (i.e. they can be related to a triggering agent) [13], it is important to record the agent that causes an event-status function assignment.

```
status_functions:
  agents: mayor, firefighter.
  events: evacuate(Zone).
  states: secure(Zone), insecure(Zone).
constitutive_rules:
                 /*** Agent-Status Functions constitutive rules ***/
      /*Actors carry the status functions according to their check in the tables*/
      1: Actor count-as mayor
              when checkin(table_mayor,Actor) while not(Other is mayor)|Other==Actor.
      2: Actor count-as firefighter
              when checkin(table_fire_brigade,Actor).
                 /*** Event-Status Functions constitutive rules ***/
      /*Putting a ''launch_object'' on (15,20) means the evacuation of the downtown*/
      3: put_tangible(launch_object,15,20,Actor) count-as evacuate(downtown).
      /*Sending a message with the proper arguments means the evacuation of the downtown*/
      4: send_message(evacuation,downtown,Actor) count-as evacuate(downtown).
                 /*** State-Status Functions constitutive rules ***/
      /*A zone in preventive phase is secure if it has at most 500 inhabitants */
      5: security_phase(Zone,preventive) count-as secure(Zone)
              while nb_inhabit(Zone,X) & X<=500
      /*A zone in emergency phase is insecure*/
      6: security_phase(Zone,emergency) count-as insecure(Zone).
```

Fig. 3. Constitutive specification

4 Linking Normative and Constitutive Representations

Normative models look to the "state of the world" to check agents' expected behaviour. Introducing SAI makes this "state of the world" as being the constitutive state. Basing the normative regulation on the constitutive state requires to define (i) how the "world" represented by the constitutive elements is captured by the representations of norms and norm instances and (ii) how the different components of the norms are evaluated considering the different nature of the constituted elements in the different states of the lifecycle of the norm instances. The first point is addressed in this section. The second point is addressed in Sect. 5, that explains our approach to couple the normative model of [16] in the SAI constitutive state.

4.1 Linking Norms to Constitutive State

To link the representation of norms presented in Sect. 2 to the constitutive state presented in Sect. 3, we need to introduce status functions in the norms. For a norm $n \in \mathcal{N}$, where $n = \langle \alpha, c_a, c_m, c_d, c_r, c_t \rangle$, we explicitly define that $\alpha \in \mathcal{A}_\mathcal{F}$, $c_a \in W_\mathcal{F} \cup W_N$, $c_m \in W_\mathcal{F} \cup W_N$, $c_d \in \mathcal{E}_\mathcal{F} \cup \mathcal{S}_\mathcal{F}$, $c_r \in \mathcal{E}_\mathcal{F} \cup \mathcal{S}_\mathcal{F}$, and $c_t \in W_\mathcal{F} \cup W_N$. The reasons for these decisions are:

- a norm is not directed to a concrete agent, but to the agents carrying the status function α.
- deactivation and repair conditions are anchored to event- and state-status functions as, from the institutional perspective, all that the agents can do to behave as prescribed by the norms is to produce, in the environment, events and states that carry event- and state-status functions.
- activation, maintenance, and timeout refer to the whole constitutive and normative states. Conditions over the whole constitutive state are expressed

1 : ⟨mayor, secure(downtown), secure(downtown), evacuate(downtown), ⊥, ¬secure(downtown)⟩
2 : ⟨firefighter, insecure(downtown), insecure(downtown), evacuate(downtown), ⊥, ¬insecure(downtown)⟩

Fig. 4. Norms using status functions

through sf-formulae $w_{\mathcal{F}} \in W_{\mathcal{F}}$. To express conditions over all the normative state, we introduce *n-formulae* $w_N \in W_n$, whose syntax follows the grammar (17) and whose semantics follows the expressions (1) to (4).

$$w_N := active(n')|viol(n')|deactivated(n')|failed(n')|w_N \wedge w_N|w_N \vee w_N|\bot|\top \tag{17}$$

Fig. 4 shows the norms as conceived in [16] using the status functions of Fig. 3 to specify that (i) the *mayor* is obliged to evacuate secure zones and (ii) *firefighters* are obliged to evacuate insecure zones.

4.2 Linking Normative and Constitutive States

While norms are referring to agent-status functions (i.e. $\alpha \in \mathcal{A}_{\mathcal{F}}$), their instances prescribe the behaviour of the concrete agents acting in the environment. The obligation of an agent a_X to follow a norm instance n' is conditioned by its carry of the status function α as prescribed in the norm n. As detailed later in the expressions (19) to (22), to check this condition considering individually the agents, norm instances must record both the agent to whom the norm is directed and the status function carried by that agent when the instance was created. Thus, in an instance $n' = \langle \alpha', c'_a, c'_m, c'_d, c'_r, c'_t \rangle$, we consider $\alpha' = (a_X, \alpha)$ where $a_X \in A_X$ points to the concrete agent targeted by the norm instance and $\alpha \in \mathcal{A}_{\mathcal{F}}$ is the status function carried by that agent when the instance was created.

5 Coupling Normative and Constitutive Dynamics

Having defined how normative and constitutive representations are linked, this section explains how the dynamics of the normative and constitutive states are coupled. Section 5.1 explains when, given the constitutive and normative states, norm instances are considered activated, deactivated, violated, and failed. These definitions can be used by the normative monitors that implement the operational semantics of the normative model, as shown in Sect. 5.2.

5.1 Norm Activation, Deactivation, Violation and Failure

Activation. Given a normative specification $\mathcal{N}$, a constitutive state F and a normative state N, the set of norms instances to be created is given by the function *activated* defined below:

$$activated(\mathcal{N}, F, N) = \{n'|\exists\theta\exists\langle\alpha, c_a, c_m, c_d, c_r, c_t\rangle \in \mathcal{N} :$$
$$F \cup N \models c_a\theta \wedge (a_X \text{ is } \alpha\theta) \wedge n' \notin AS\} \tag{18}$$
$$\text{s.t.} \quad n' = \langle(a_X, \alpha\theta), c_a\theta, c_m\theta, c_d\theta, c_r\theta, c_t\theta\rangle$$

The creation of norm instances is conditioned by the constitutive and norma-tive states satisfying the activation condition c_a for some substitution θ (i.e. $F \cup N \models c_a\theta$). The evaluation of c_a with respect to N follows the expres-sions (1) to (4). Its evaluation with respect to F follows the expressions (14) and (16). By the function *activated*, a norm directed to an agent-status function α produces an instance for *every* concrete agent a_X carrying α. For example, considering the specification in Fig. 3, if the agents *bob* and *tom* carry the sta-tus function of *firefighter* (i.e. $\{\langle bob, firefighter\rangle, \langle tom, firefighter\rangle\} \subseteq A_F$) and the *downtown* is in emergency phase of crisis, being thus insecure (i.e. $\langle security\_phase(downtown, emergency), insecure(downtown)\rangle \in S_F$), then (i) $F \models insecure(downtown)$, (ii) $F \models bob$ **is** $firefighter$, and (iii) $F \models tom$ **is** $firefighter$. Thus, the following instances of the norm 2 are created:

$$\langle(bob, firefighter), insecure(downtown), insecure(downtown),$$
$$evacuate(downtown), \bot, \neg insecure(downtown)\rangle$$
$$\langle(tom, firefighter), insecure(downtown), insecure(downtown),$$
$$evacuate(downtown), \bot, \neg insecure(downtown)\rangle$$

Deactivation. Deactivations are considered separately according to the nature of the deactivation condition (event or state). The functions *f-deactivated^e* and *f-deactivated^s* deal respectively with deactivations of active instances condi-tioned by events and by states.

$$f\text{-}deactivated^e(F, N) = \{\langle n'|\exists(e_X, a_X) \in E_X : n' \in AS \land c_d' \in \mathcal{E}_{\mathcal{F}} \land$$
$$F \models ((e_X, a_X) \text{ is } c_d' \lor \neg(a_X \text{ is } \alpha)) \land F \cup N \models c_m'\}$$
$$(19)$$

$$f\text{-}deactivated^s(F, N) = \{\langle n'|n' \in AS \land c_d' \in S_{\mathcal{F}} \land$$
$$F \models (c_d' \lor \neg(a_X \text{ is } \alpha)) \land F \cup N \models c_m'\} \quad (20)$$

$$\text{s.t. } n' = \langle(a_X, \alpha), c_a', c_m', c_d', c_r', c_t'\rangle$$

The function *f-deactivated^e* captures the notion of events as being considered at the individual agent level. The obligation of an agent a_X with respect to the occurrence in the environment of an event that counts as the event-status function c_d' is only fulfilled when c_d' is assigned to an event e_X really produced by the agent a_X. This is expressed by the element $F \models ((e_X, a_X) \text{ is } c_d')$, evaluated according to the Expression (14). By the function *f-deactivated^s* an agent fulfils an obligation to achieve a state when it *sees to it* that such state holds, no matter by whom it has been produced. This achievement is detected when there is an assignment to the state-status function c_d', evaluated according to the Expression (16).

The functions *f-deactivated^e* and *f-deactivated^s* capture the idea of norm instances being directed to the concrete agents but being conditioned by the agent-status function assignments. If an instance is assigned to the agent a_X because it carries the agent-status function α, then it is deactivated if a_X ceases to carry α. For example, we can imagine that the agent *bob* is obliged to evacuate the downtown because he carries the agent-status function of firefighter. As the obligation was directed to the *firefighter* rather than to *bob*, it should be deactivated as soon *bob* looses this function.

While active norm instances are deactivated when the deactivation condition c'_d is satisfied, violated instances are deactivated by the satisfaction of the repair condition c'_r. Deactivations by reparation of violated instances are also considered at the individual agent level when they are conditioned by events (function *r-deactivated^e*). Reparations conditioned by states are achieved when the agents see to them that such state holds (function *r-deactivated^s*). Different of deactivations of active instances, the maintenance condition is not considered in the reparations of violated ones. An instance, to be repaired, must be in the violated state, reached when the maintenance condition c'_m ceased to hold in the past. If the c'_m holds while the reparation condition of a violated instance is reached, it has started to hold again while the instance was violated, having thus no influence on such instance.

$$r\text{-}deactivated^e(F,N) = \{n'|\exists (e_X, a_X) \in E_X : n' \in VS \wedge c'_r \in \mathcal{E}_\mathcal{F} \wedge$$
$$F \models ((e_X, a_X) \text{ is } c'_r \vee \neg(a_X \text{ is } \alpha))\} \tag{21}$$

$$r\text{-}deactivated^s(F,N) = \{n'|n' \in VS \wedge c'_r \in \mathcal{S}_\mathcal{F} \wedge$$
$$F \models (c'_r \vee \neg(a_X \text{ is } \alpha))\} \tag{22}$$

$$\text{s.t.} \quad n' = \langle (a_X, \alpha), c'_a, c'_m, c'_d, c'_r, c'_t \rangle$$

Violation. Active norm instances are considered violated when the constitutive and normative states do not satisfy the maintenance condition (function *violated* below).

$$violated(F,N) = \{n'|n' \in AS \wedge F \cup N \not\models c'_m\} \tag{23}$$

$$\text{s.t.} \quad n' = \langle (a_X, \alpha), c'_a, c'_m, c'_d, c'_r, c'_t \rangle$$

Failure. An instance is failed if (i) it is violated and (ii) the current constitutive and normative states satisfy the timeout condition (function *failed* below).

$$failed(F,N) = \{n'|\exists \theta : n' \in VS \wedge F \cup N \models c_t\prime\} \tag{24}$$

$$\text{s.t.} \quad n' = \langle (a_X, \alpha), c'_a, c'_m, c'_d, c'_r, c'_t \rangle$$

5.2   Monitoring Norms Based on the Constitutive State

To base the operational semantics of the norm monitor proposed in [16] on the SAI constitutive state, we redefine below the transition rules presented in Sect. 2.

$$\frac{n' \in activated(\mathcal{N}, F, N) \qquad n' \notin f\text{-}deactivated^e(F, N) \cup f\text{-}deactivated^s(F, N)}{M_N \rhd \langle \mathcal{N}, AS \cup n', VS, DS, FS, s_{i+1}\rangle} \tag{25}$$

$$\frac{n' \in AS \qquad n' \in violated(F, N)}{M_N \rhd \langle \mathcal{N}, AS \setminus n', VS \cup n', DS, FS, s_{i+1}\rangle} \tag{26}$$

$$\frac{n' \in AS \qquad n' \in f\text{-}deactivated^e(F, N) \cup f\text{-}deactivated^s(F, N)}{M_N \rhd \langle \mathcal{N}, AS \setminus n', VS, DS \cup n', FS, s_{i+1}\rangle} \tag{27}$$

$$\frac{n' \in VS \qquad n' \in r\text{-}deactivated^e(F, N) \cup r\text{-}deactivated^s(F, N)}{M_N \rhd \langle \mathcal{N}, AS, VS \setminus n', DS \cup n', FS, s_{i+1}\rangle} \tag{28}$$

$$\frac{n' \in VS \qquad n' \in failed(F, N)}{M_N \rhd \langle \mathcal{N}, AS, VS \setminus n', DS, FS \cup n', s_{i+1}\rangle} \tag{29}$$

6   Example

Considering the proposed coupling, we illustrate the evolving of the normative regulation in the scenario introduced in Sect. 3.3. The constitutive specification is illustrated in Fig. 3. The norms are those illustrated in Fig. 4. We consider 5 steps of the environmental dynamics. In each step, the environmental state changes causing changes in the constitutive state and, as consequence, changing the normative state. These dynamics are described below and summarized in the Tables 1 and 2:

– **Step 1.** GIS indicate that the properties *security_phase(downtown,preventive)* and *(nb_inhabit(downtown,200)* hold in the environment, meaning that (i) the downtown is on preventive phase of the crisis management and (ii) the downtown has 200 inhabitants. By the constitutive rule 5, the institution considers the downtown as a secure zone. At this moment, the actor *bob* checks in the *table_mayor* and the actors *tom, jim,* and *ana* check in the *table_fire_brigade*. By the constitutive rules 1 and 2, *bob* is considered by the institution as the *mayor* while *tom, jim* and *ana* are considered *firefighter*. As the downtown is considered secure, *bob* is obliged to evacuate it.

– **Step 2.** *Bob* puts the *launch_object* on the coordinates $(15, 20)$. By the constitutive rule 3, this means, from the institutional perspective, the evacuation of the downtown, deactivating the previously created obligation.

– **Step 3.** After the evacuation performed by *bob*, for some reason, the downtown has 50 inhabitants. The security phase of the crisis changes from preventive to emergency, and, from the institutional perspective, the downtown is insecure (constitutive rule 6). Thus, new norm instances are created directed to the *firefighters*.

– **Step 4.** *Tom* puts the *launch_object* on the coordinates $(15, 20)$ of the table while *jim* sends a message. Both the actions count as the evacuation of the downtown (constitutive rules 3 and 4). Thus, *tom* and *jim* fulfil their obligations.

– **Step 5.** The security phase of the crisis becomes again preventive, and, from the institutional perspective, the downtown is again secure (constitutive rule 5). The agent *ana* violated its obligation as it has not evacuated the downtown while it was insecure.

Table 1. Evolution of environmental and constitutive states

Step	Environmental state (X)	Constitutive state (F)
1	$A_X = \{bob, tom, jim, ana\}$ $E_X = \{(checkin(table\_maior), bob),$ $\quad (checkin(table\_fire\_brigade), tom),$ $\quad (checkin(table\_fire\_brigade), jim),$ $\quad (checkin(table\_fire\_brigade), ana)\}$ $S_X = \{security\_phase(downtown, preventive),$ $\quad nb\_inhabit(downtown, 200)\}$	$A_F = \{\langle bob, mayor \rangle, \langle tom, firefighter, \rangle,$ $\quad \langle jim, firefighter \rangle, \langle ana, firefighter \rangle\}$ $S_F = \{\langle security\_phase(downtown, preventive),$ $\quad secure(downtown) \rangle\}$
2	$A_X = \{bob, tom, jim, ana\}$ $E_X = \{(putTangible(launch\_object, 15, 20), bob)\}$ $S_X = \{security\_phase(downtown, preventive),$ $\quad nb\_inhabit(downtown, 200)\}$	$A_F = \{\langle bob, mayor \rangle, \langle tom, firefighter, \rangle,$ $\quad \langle jim, firefighter \rangle, \langle ana, firefighter \rangle\}$ $E_F = \{(putTangible(launch\_object, 15, 20),$ $\quad evacuate(downtown), bob)\}$ $S_F = \{\langle security\_phase(downtown, preventive),$ $\quad secure(downtown) \rangle\}$
3	$A_X = \{bob, tom, jim, ana\}$ $S_X = \{security\_phase(downtown, emergency),$ $\quad nb\_inhabit(downtown, 50)\}$	$A_F = \{\langle bob, mayor \rangle, \langle tom, firefighter, \rangle,$ $\quad \langle jim, firefighter \rangle, \langle ana, firefighter \rangle\}$ $S_F = \{\langle security\_phase(downtown, emergency),$ $\quad insecure(downtown) \rangle\}$
4	$A_X = \{bob, tom, jim, ana\}$ $E_X = \{(putTangible(launch\_object, 15, 20), tom),$ $\quad (send\_message(evacuation, downtown), jim)\}$ $S_X = \{security\_phase(downtown, emergency),$ $\quad nb\_inhabit(downtown, 50)\}$	$A_F = \{\langle bob, mayor \rangle, \langle tom, firefighter, \rangle,$ $\quad \langle jim, firefighter \rangle, \langle ana, firefighter \rangle\}$ $E_F = \{(putTangible(launch\_object, 15, 20),$ $\quad evacuate(downtown), tom),$ $\quad (send\_message(evacuation, downtown),$ $\quad (evacuate(downtown), jim))\}$ $S_F = \{(security\_phase(downtown, emergency),$ $\quad insecure(downtown) \rangle\}$
5	$A_X = \{bob, tom, jim, ana\}$ $S_X = \{security\_phase(downtown, preventive),$ $\quad nbInhabit(downtown, 50)\}$	$A_F = \{\langle bob, mayor \rangle, \langle tom, firefighter, \rangle,$ $\quad \langle jim, firefighter \rangle, \langle ana, firefighter \rangle\}$ $S_F = \{\langle security\_phase(downtown, preventive),$ $\quad secure(downtown) \rangle\}$

7   Discussion

While [16] considers that activation, maintenance, deactivation, reparation, and failures of norms are evaluated with respect to the "state of the world", our proposed coupling explicitly defines, following the SAI approach, that such "world" is composed of the constitutive and normative states of the institution.

Norms are based on the *interpretation* of the environment provided by the constitutive state, but they regulate the elements *under such interpretation*. It is necessary, thus, to define how the elements abstracted under the constitution are considered in the management of the normative state. Our proposed coupling explicitly defines that (i) regarding to the addressee α, norms govern all the agents under the same constitution of agent-status function and (ii) the

Table 2. Evolution of the normative state

Step	Normative state
1	$AS = \{\langle(bob, mayor), secure(downtown), secure(downtown), evacuate$ $(downtown), \bot, \neg secure(downtown)\}\rangle$
2	$DS = \{\langle(bob, mayor), secure(downtown), secure(downtown), evacuate$ $(downtown), \bot, \neg secure(downtown)\rangle\}$
3	$AS = \{\langle(tom, firefighter), insecure(downtown), insecure(downtown),$ $evacuate(downtown), \bot, \neg insecure(downtown)\rangle, \langle(jim, firefighter),$ $insecure(downtown), insecure(downtown), evacuate(downtown),$ $\bot, \neg insecure(downtown)\rangle, \langle(ana, firefighter), insecure(downtown),$ $insecure(downtown), evacuate(downtown), \bot, \neg insecure(downtown)\rangle\}$ $DS = \{\langle(bob, mayor), secure(downtown), secure(downtown), evacuate$ $(downtown), \bot, \neg secure(downtown)\rangle\}$
4	$AS = \{\langle(ana, firefighter), insecure(downtown), insecure(downtown),$ $evacuate(downtown), \bot, \neg insecure(downtown)\rangle\}$ $DS = \{\langle(bob, mayor), secure(downtown), secure(downtown), evacuate$ $(downtown), \bot, \neg secure(downtown)\rangle, \langle(tom, firefighter), insecure$ $(downtown), insecure(downtown), evacuate(downtown), \bot, \neg insecure$ $(downtown)\rangle, \langle(jim, firefighter), insecure(downtown), insecure$ $(downtown), evacuate(downtown), \bot, \neg insecure(downtown)\rangle\}$
5	$DS = \{\langle(bob, mayor), secure(downtown), secure(downtown), evacuate$ $(downtown), \bot, \neg secure(downtown)\rangle, \langle(tom, firefighter), insecure$ $(downtown), insecure(downtown), evacuate(downtown), \bot, \neg insecure$ $(downtown)\rangle, \langle(jim, firefighter), insecure(downtown), insecure$ $(downtown), evacuate(downtown), \bot, \neg insecure(downtown)\rangle\}$ $VS = \{\langle(ana, firefighter), insecure(downtown), insecure(downtown),$ $evacuate(downtown), \bot, \neg insecure(downtown)\rangle\}$

activation, maintenance, deactivation, repair, and timeout conditions c_a, c_m, c_d, c_r, and c_t, differently, point to (at least) a single constitution of event- and state-status function. For example, considering a norm stating that firefighters are obliged to evacuate an insecure zone (Fig. 4 – norm 2), we can imagine a situation where many agents count as firefighter and two events count as an evacuation (Fig. 3 – constitutive rules 3 and 4). When instantiated, this norm stands to all the agents counting as *firefighter* but its fulfilment requires that every firefighter produces at least one event interpreted as *evacuation*. They can either put a tangible in the table or send a message (Fig. 3 – constitutive rules 3 and 4).

When the normative regulation is based on the constitutive state, the expected agents' behaviour is attached to the status functions instead of to the agents themselves. That is why we consider a norm instance as deactivated when the responsible agents are no longer carrying the target status function (expressions (19) to (22)). But other coupling approaches can be conceived where, for example, obligations and prohibitions remain active even if the agent-status functions are revoked. These decisions are related to the management of the social meanings of the agents in a society that, as noted in [19], is a complex question that can be addressed in different ways.

8   Related Work, Conclusions and Perspectives

Some works, such as [1,9], consider that regulative norms can be reduced to constitutive ones such that environmental states count as norm violations and fulfilments [14]. In these cases, constitution *determines* changes in the state of the norms instead of, as considered in this work, to *constitute* the conditions taken by the normative machinery to determine these changes. More similar to our direction, the work of [4,5] deals with environmental elements constituting the conditions that activate obligations to the agents. Following the SAI approach, however, we base the *whole* normative lifecycle – activation, fulfilment, violation, etc. – on the constituted elements. In [1], the constitution, that affects the whole normative lifecycle, results in predicates added to the knowledge base accessed by the normative reasoner. In our approach, differently, norms are coupled in meaningful institutional elements constituted from environmental ones.

This work firstly contributes by defining how the dynamics of the normative model of [16] is related to the SAI constitutive dynamics. We focused on the reasoning about the normative and constitutive states to define when instances should be activated, deactivated, violated, and failed. Such reasoning can be exploited in many ways. We shown how it can be used by a normative monitor that manages the regulation on top of the constitutive state. But it can be useful for the agents to plan their actions in the environment as they can reason about the normative impact of the environmental facts in the constitutive state and, then, in the normative one.

Our contribution can be related to the very notion of coupling between regulative norms and constitutive rules. Such coupling is here applied to a specific normative model. Applying a similar coupling to other normative models is one of the future works. We also plan to work (i) on agents using the proposed coupling to reason about the normative consequence of their actions in the environment, (ii) on a deeper analysis of implicit changes in the normative state due to revocations of agent-status functions, and (iii) on the analysis of the proposed coupling considering group norms.

Acknowledgements. The authors thanks the financial support given by CAPES (PDSE 4926-14-5) and CNPq (grants 448462/2014-1 e 306301/2012-1).

References

1. Aldewereld, H., Álvarez Napagao, S., Dignum, F., Vázquez-Salceda, J.: Making norms concrete. In: van der Hoek, W., Kaminka, G.A., Lespérance, Y., Luck, M., Sen, S. (eds.) Proceedings of the 9th International Conference on Autonomous Agents and Multiagent Systems (AAMAS 2010), vol. 1–3, pp. 807–814, Richland, SC. IFAAMAS (2010)
2. Balke, T., Pereira, C.C., Dignum, F., Lorini, E., Rotolo, A., Vasconcelos, W., Villata, S.: Norms in MAS: definitions and related concepts. In: Andrighetto, G., Governatori, G., Noriega, P., van der Torre, L.W.N. (eds.) Normative Multi-agent Systems. Dagstuhl Follow-Ups, vol. 4, pp. 1–31. Schloss Dagstuhl-Leibniz-Zentrum fuer Informatik, Dagstuhl, Germany (2013)

3. Boella, G., van der Torre, L.W.N.: Constitutive norms in the design of normative multiagent systems. In: Toni, F., Torroni, P. (eds.) CLIMA 2005. LNCS (LNAI), vol. 3900, pp. 303–319. Springer, Heidelberg (2006)
4. Boella, G., van der Torre, L.W.N.: A logical architecture of a normative system. In: Goble, L., Meyer, J.-J.C. (eds.) DEON 2006. LNCS (LNAI), vol. 4048, pp. 24–35. Springer, Heidelberg (2006)
5. Boella, G., van der Torre, L.W.N.: Regulative, constitutive norms in normative multiagent systems. In: Dubois, D., Welty, C.A., Williams, M.-A. (eds.) Principles of Knowledge Representation, Reasoning: Proceedings of the Ninth International Conference (KR 2004), pp. 255–266. AAAI Press (2004)
6. Brachman, R., Levesque, H.: Knowledge Representation and Reasoning. Morgan Kaufmann Publishers Inc., San Francisco (2004)
7. Broersen, J.M., Cranefield, S., Elrakaiby, Y., Gabbay, D.M., Grossi, D., Lorini, E., Parent, X., van der Torre, L.W.N., Tummolini, L., Turrini, P., Schwarzentruber, F.: Normative reasoning and consequence. In: Andrighetto, G., Governatori, G., Noriega, P., van der Torre, L.W.N. (eds.) Normative Multi-agent Systems. Dagstuhl Follow-Ups, vol. 4, pp. 33–70. Schloss Dagstuhl-Leibniz-Zentrum fuer Informatik, Germany (2013)
8. Broersen, J., van der Torre, L.: Ten problems of deontic logic and normative reasoning in computer science. In: Bezhanishvili, N., Goranko, V. (eds.) ESSLLI 2010 and ESSLLI 2011. LNCS, vol. 7388, pp. 55–88. Springer, Heidelberg (2012)
9. Dastani, M., Grossi, D., Meyer, J.J.C., Tinnemeier, N.A.M.: Normative multi-agent programs and their logics. In: Boella, G., Noriega, P., Pigozzi, G., Verhagen, H. (eds.) Normative Multi-agent Systems. Dagstuhl Seminar Proceedings, vol. 09121. Schloss Dagstuhl - Leibniz-Zentrum für Informatik, Germany (2009)
10. de Brito, M., Hübner, J.F., Boissier, O.: Bringing constitutive dynamics to situated artificial institutions. In: Pereira, F., Machado, P., Costa, E., Cardoso, A. (eds.) EPIA 2015. LNCS, vol. 9273, pp. 624–637. Springer, Heidelberg (2015)
11. de Brito, M., Hübner, J.F., Boissier, O.: A conceptual model for situated artificial institutions. In: Bulling, N., van der Torre, L., Villata, S., Jamroga, W., Vasconcelos, W. (eds.) CLIMA 2014. LNCS, vol. 8624, pp. 35–51. Springer, Heidelberg (2014)
12. de Brito, M., Thevin, L., Garbay, C., Boissier, O., Hübner, J.F.: Situated artificial institution to support advanced regulation in the field of crisis management. In: Demazeau, Y., Decker, K.S., Bajo Pérez, J., De la Prieta, F. (eds.) PAAMS 2015. LNCS, vol. 9086, pp. 66–79. Springer, Heidelberg (2015)
13. De Vos, M., Balke, T., Satoh, K.: Combining event- and state-based norms. In: Gini, M.L., Shehory, O., Ito, T., Jonker, C.M. (eds.) International Conference on Autonomous Agents and Multi-agent Systems (AAMAS 2013), pp. 1157–1158. IFAAMAS (2013)
14. Grossi, D., Meyer, J.J.C., Dignum, F.: Modal logic investigations in the semantics of counts-as. In: Sartor, G. (ed.) 10th International Conference on Artificial Intelligence and Law (ICAIL 2005), pp. 1–9. ACM (2005)
15. Kubicki, S., Lepreux, S., Kolski, C.: RFID-driven situation awareness on tangisense, a table interacting with tangible objects. Pers. Ubiquit. Comput. **16**(8), 1079–1094 (2012)
16. Panagiotidi, S., Alvarez-Napagao, S., Vázquez-Salceda, J.: Towards the norm-aware agent: bridging the gap between deontic specifications and practical mechanisms for norm monitoring and norm-aware planning. In: Balke, T., Dignum, F., van Riemsdijk, M.B., Chopra, A.K. (eds.) COIN 2013. LNCS, vol. 8386, pp. 346–363. Springer, Heidelberg (2014)

17. Searle, J.: The Construction of Social Reality. Free Press, New York (1995)
18. Searle, J.: Making the Social World: The Structure of Human Civilization. Oxford University Press, Oxford (2009)
19. Tessop, R.K.: Gestion de l'ouverture au sein d'organisations multi-agents: une approche basée sur des artefacts organisationnels. Ph.D. thesis, École Nationale Supéurieure des Mines de Saint-Étienne (2011)

Trust-Based Multiagent Credit Assignment (TMCA)

Samira Nazari[1](✉) and Mohammad Ebrahim Shiri[2]

[1] Institute for Advanced Studies in Basic Sciences (IASBS), Zanjan, Iran
samira.nazari@gmail.com
[2] Faculty of Mathematics and Computer Sciences,
Amirkabir University of Technology, Tehran, Iran
shiri@aut.ac.ir

Abstract. In Multiagent Reinforcement Learning (MARL), a single scalar reinforcement signal is the sole reliable feedback that members of a team of learning agents can receive from the environment around them. Hence, the distribution of the environmental feedback signal among learning agents, also known as the *"Multiagent Credit Assignment"* (MCA), is among the most challenging problems in MARL.

In this paper, the authors propose an extended solution to the problem of MCA. In the proposed method, called *"Trust-based Multiagent Credit Assignment"* (TMCA), a trust and reputation based model is utilized to evaluate the trustworthiness of the learning agents. Unlike the existing methods, TMCA not only qualifies to benefit from the knowledge and expertise of the sole target agent (the agent for which the credit is being evaluated), but also from the knowledge and expertise of the whole as a team.

To evaluate this method, the effect of different task types (e.g. AND vs. OR) are studied. Our simulations show the superiority of the proposed method in comparison to the prior investigated methods even in noisy environments, despite a reduction (caused by the noise) in the performance.

Keywords: Credit assignment · Multiagent reinforcement learning · Trust and reputation

1 Introduction

"Multi Agent Systems" (MAS) [1] have been successfully used as bottom up approaches for a variety of complicated problems in computer science. Despite its myriad of challenges, *"Reinforcement Learning"* (RL) [3] in a multiagent domain is extensively used to achieve the expansion of a cooperative behaviour, by coordinating actions of multiple agents [14].

One important example of these challenges is that in many cases, each agent can only learn from the global (team level) reinforcement signal which is assigned

© Springer International Publishing Switzerland 2016
M. Rovatsos et al. (Eds.): EUMAS 2015/AT 2015, LNAI 9571, pp. 335–349, 2016.
DOI: 10.1007/978-3-319-33509-4_26

to the performance of the whole team, and not to individuals. This feature arises from the origin of RL in its definition that the learning group should learn from that single reinforcement signal. The environment around individual learning agents is usually, if not always, not intelligent enough to qualify the role and effectiveness of each agent in the success of a cooperative team. Hence, distribution of this feedback among individual reinforcement learners is a well-studied problem known as "*Interagent credit assignment*" or "*Multiagent Credit Assignment*" (MCA). This feedback should be distributed among the agents in a manner that ensures all agents have the ability of independent and individual learning [5].

Sutton and Barto have proposed a number of solutions based on RL for the problem of "*Temporal Credit Assignment*" (TCA), determining the contribution of a particular action to the quality of the full sequence of actions in time-extended single-agent systems [3]. In contrast those solutions, an optimal approach towards imposing rewards and penalties on multi-agent is the "*Knowledge Evaluation Based Credit Assignment*" (KEBCA) [5]. In this approach, an intelligent critic evaluates the actions of each agent and their effect on the performance of the team. The information that is fed to the critic agent (which is responsible for the distribution of reinforcement among agents) originates from the agents' learning histories, and acts as a measure of agents' knowledge. Such information along with the idea of team reinforcement is used to estimate the likelihood of the correctness of an agent's decision, as well as assigning suitable reinforcements. This solution is based on the knowledge and expertise of the sole target, and not the knowledge and expertise of the whole team members in every credit assignment round.

The modelling of trust is a popular yet distinct problem among scholars in various fields such as philosophy, sociology, psychology and economics. With respect to the ever increasing importance of trust in computer science [7,8], trust and reputation models are a means for providing information to help agents better deicide in their inter agent interactions [9]. To the best of our knowledge, there is no general solution for the credit assignment problem based on trust models. We use it for solving the problem of credit distribution.

In this paper, we introduce a extended approach to that of [5]. We use the knowledge of each agent, also known as its "*expertise*", to generate a trust value for that agent similar to [5]. But we also take into consideration the viewpoint of other agents towards the trustworthiness of the chosen action by the target agent (the agent for which the credit is being evaluated by the critic agent). In other words, in addition to the trust, the reputation is also used in decision making. Here, we provide a proof of concept in a simple environment.

The rest of this paper is structured as follows. In Sect. 2, we provide a short literature review of the previous works related to credit assignment and trust models. In Sect. 3, the assumptions and definitions are described in detail. Section 4 describes the proposed approach. The credit assignment method of the critic agent and the proposed trust model are fully investigated. The evaluation indexes and the results of our simulation in the proposed algorithm are then reported in Sect. 5. Finally, Sect. 6 will contain the conclusion and discussion.

2   Related Works

In this paper, we try to find a solution for an *Structural Credit Assignment* (SCA) problem which means determining the contributions of a particular agent to a common task in a MAS. Most of the existing algorithms for SCA are implemented for competitive RL with a single active agent at a time, such as the Learning Classifier System (LCS) in [11]. On the contrary, in [10] like us, the SCA is proposed for the collaborative reinforcement learning systems.

MCA can be used to create cooperative behavior in a MAS [12,14]. But in these works, the methods are case-based and they are not general solutions [12,13] or periodic communicating some information among robots is an essential factor [14].

In *Q-Learning* [4], as the most frequently used version of RL, a set of agent's actions and a set of possible states are considered and a state-action value table called *Q-Table* is assigned to each agent. This table estimates the long-term discounted reward for each state-action pair by assigning a *Q-Cell* to it. A Q-Learning agent in state s_i selects action a_i (with a method of action selection e.g. by Boltzmann distribution) and executes it, receives an immediate reward r, observes the next state s_{t+1}, and updates the state-action value function $Q(s, a)$ according to the following equation:

$$Q_{t+1}(s, a) \leftarrow (1 - \alpha)Q_t(s, a) + \alpha \times [r + \gamma V(y)] \tag{1}$$

where α is the learning rate ($0 \preceq \alpha \preceq 1$), y is the next state reached from x after taking the current action a, $V(y)$ is the maximum Q-value for state y on its possible actions, ($0 \preceq \gamma \preceq 1$) is a discount parameter. The authors of [17] in a Q-Learning cooperative MAS used an expertise measure for each agent as an indirect evaluation method. It is also assumed that a critic agent is responsible for receiving the feedback signal from the environment, and then assigning the proper credit to each agent according to their expertise levels. In [16], the authors have used many different notations of expertise to estimate the knowledge of the serial learners. The main idea of [16–18] (using the expertise measure in order to judge agents by critic agent) is interesting, But the critic agent in these works considers the expertness level of just the selector agent. Although the expertness level of other members of the team in that action-state tuple is available, it is not used.

Based on [6,15], the critic agent is equipped with a learning ability in order to solve the credit assignment problem. So the critic agent with learning capabilities is not a general solution.

As mentioned, no general solution for MCA based on trust models has been proposed. Here, we review some trust models that are simpler to analyze to present our applied trust model. These models are used to help agents to detect deceitful ones and to make decisions. The first attempt to model (formalize) trust for agents is due to Marsh [19] which only studies a trust dimension. The *"Spora"* model in [22] also only considers a reputation dimension. Some models such as *"Regret"*[9] calculate a degree of trustworthiness based on a mix of the two (Trust and Reputation). *"Regret"* [9] uses a reputation model that takes into account the information coming from other agents (the social dimension of the agents) in order to be merged with the personal experiences to calculate a more accurate final trustworthiness value. *"Regret"* defines the reputation measure that takes into account the social dimension as:

$$SR_{a \to b}(subject) = \xi_{ab} \cdot R_{a \to b}(subject) + \xi_{aB} \cdot R_{a \to B}(subject)$$
$$+ \xi_{Ab} \cdot R_{A \to b}(subject) + \xi_{AB} \cdot R_{A \to B}(subject), \tag{2}$$

where $\xi_{ab} + \xi_{aB} + \xi_{Ab} + \xi_{AB} = 1$, a is the agent that calculates reputation, and b is the agent being calculated. $R_{a \to b}(subject)$ as the individual dimension is the result of direct interaction between a and b. $R_{a \to B}(subject)$ represents the interaction with the other members of the group to which agent b belongs to. To represent the opinion of the members of the group about the agent being evaluated (b), it uses $R_{A \to b}(subject)$. At last, $R_{A \to B}(subject)$ is used to represent what the members of the group think about the other group. Hence, with regard to the results of [9], utilizing *"Regret"* model in embedded trust model seems a good idea.

In [20]'s approach, the agents can observe other agents' behavior and collect information for establishing an initial trust model, and learn almost twice as fast as those agents that only use their own information. It uses the Bayes' rule for combining the trust values to identify trustworthy parties in open systems. According to [20]'s idea, establishing a trust model leads to have more precise assessment of agents' role and then accelerated learning.

3   Definitions and Assumptions

As mentioned in [5], group behavior is affected by individuals' decisions, and is known as the group's *"Tasks Type"*. We also investigate the group task in two distinct type, being AND and OR. A team with an AND task type acts correctly if and only if all the team members act correctly, i.e. all agents execute correct actions. However in the OR task type, the correctness of task evaluation needs only one correct action from all agents. All tasks can be decomposed into a collection of these basic types.*"Team Configuration"* means how agents are activated (in turn or at the same time) to perform their task, serial or parallel.

In this paper, in order to easily study the credit assignment, we consider teamwork a single step deterministic task. We assume that agents have no prior knowledge of one another ahead of the task. The global problem state is set so that each agent can only partially see the task. The agents are activated independent of each other and synchronously (i.e. all at the same time). Therefore this parallel task activation is viewed from the environment as a single task. Hence the environment returns a single scalar value as the team reinforcement.

Without loss of generality, one can assume that a *critic agent* observes each agent, which is then responsible for the distribution of the feedback among reinforcement learner agents (similar to Q-learning). The critic agent as a part of learning system, is only aware of the group task type, and has no information regarding the tasks of the agents, and also performs no attempts to learn them. The critic only receives the team feedback along with a vector of selected actions of the agents (in addition to the uncertainty in the form of noise) in each round. Since the information content of the team reinforcement feedback signal from the environment is not solely enough, the critic agent needs an additional criterion to evaluate each learner agent. On the other side, it is safe to assume that more knowledgeable agents will have fewer errors. Hence, the critic can estimate each agent's role in the group outcome using the corresponding knowledge evaluation measure, which is then assigned to them. The way of knowledge evaluating is described later on in the paper.

4   TMCA: Trust-Based Multi Agent Credit Assignment

In this paper, unlike [5], the critic agent uses the knowledge of whole members of the team (collective knowledge) in order to perform the credit assignment in a MARL system. The knowledge and expertise of each agent can be utilized to create the trust model and assign a trustworthiness value to individual agents. We believe that using trust models helps improve the speed and trustworthiness of the credit assignment process to each individual learner agent according some trust model's idea like [20] (as mentioned in Sect. 2). We call this the "*Trust-based MultiAgent Credit Assignment*" algorithm, i.e. TMCA for short. TMCA provides a more reliable criterion for the critic agent that works on behalf of the multiagent learning system.

Our proposed algorithm works as follows: A one-step deterministic task is defined for the independent agents. After a learning step, the critic agent receives the feedback signal from the environment and the state-action tuples from the agents. If the team was rewarded in the AND task, or penalized in the OR task, all the agents will get a reward and a penalty correspondingly. Then, the critic agent and the learning agent update their Q-Tables and Visit-Tables. Hence, the learning step finished. Otherwise, if the team is penalized in the AND task, or if rewarded in the OR task, the critic agent should evaluate which agents are deserved rewarding or punishing. For this purpose, it calculates the trust-worthiness of each learner agent, according to the trust model which has been constructed based on the aggregated knowledge of all learner agents. The construction of this trust model is thoroughly investigated further in Sect. 4.2. Afterwards and based on the trust values that are assigned to each agent from the trust model (which are between 0 and 1), the algorithm continues according to the following method:

The Clustering Method: The agents are clustered, based on their trust values using an approximate K-Means [23], into 3 clusters of rewardable, punishable, and ignorable. There are many fast an accurate approximations for K-Means. Afterwards, and according to the cluster of which the agent is a member, A_i is either rewarded or penalized based on the regular Q-Leaning formula [4], or is exempted from trial.

TMCA is a heuristics algorithm in which the only resource is the trust level of the team in the correctness of the decision for each individual. This parameter might be less confident in some scenarios, and hence there is a need for the investigation of the learning convergence. The critic categorizes the agents into 3 groups in order to create a balance between rationality and performance. The agents in the middle group will then not be criticized. This approach might sound naive and nonoptimal, but can guarantee the rational decision of the criticism using proper thresholds. In Sect. 5, the experimental results show that TMCA is robust enough in the cases of rare wrong credit assignments.

4.1   Knowledge Evaluation Measure

In TMCA, the critic agent needs to use a knowledge measure in the trust value calculation process. The authors of [21] have proposed and compared multiple measures for knowledge, among which the *Certainty* measure has the best performance while not using any additional information. Here, Certainty is considered a measure of an agent's knowledge. It is defined based on Q-Values in the related action-state tuple (s, a) as follows:

$$Certainty(s,a) = \frac{e^{\frac{Q(s,a)}{T}}}{\sum_{a' \in Actions} e^{\frac{Q(s,a')}{T}}} \tag{3}$$

Where T is a scaling factor that is set according to the learning parameters and the uncertainty level. Q-Values will be updated according to formula (1). This formula presents that the more knowledgeable an agent be, the more certain it is. Thus, more certain actions have higher probability of correctness.

4.2   The Applied Trust Model

After much deliberation and comparison between trust and reputation models, we have decided to utilize the *Regret* model [9]. The Regret model provides a complete framework for interactive trust modelling, with high compatibility to different domains, due to a flexible rating system.

The agents would start the learning process without any knowledge about one another. The critic agent constructs a trust model for each target agent based on the trustworthiness of own target agent and on the others' trustworthiness about the correctness of target agent's action selection. Such trust model, as mentioned before, is constructed based on the Q-Tables and Visit-Tables [2].

According to [2], the level of an agent's expertness and depth of its awareness can be presented in a Visit-Table based on the number of visits of each state e.g. all visits of each state are counted, regardless of the results. The $Visit(s)$ relates to state s is updated according this formula in each round: $Visit_{t+1}(s) \leftarrow Visit_t(s) + 1$. Highly experienced areas of Visit-Table indicate the qualified knowledge of corresponding state of Q-Table.

Trust Information Sources. To construct a trust measure in a system of agents, one can use two disparate sources, namely the *Direct Trust*(i.e. Experience), and the *Witness Reputation* (Witness Information), hence building a *Composite Trust*.

Direct Trust models the direct interaction between the agent who is evaluating and the agent being evaluated. In our test bed, in the case of the Direct Experience, the critic agent uses the previous experience (Q-Tables and Visit-Tables) of the target learner agent TA, to calculate the trustworthiness of that agent. This type of trust is hence called the *Direct Trust* ($DT_{CriticAgent \rightarrow TA}(s, a)$).

Witness Reputation represents what the other members of the group think about the agent being evaluated. In our case study, for the Witness Information, and considering the fact that all agents share their experiences of the action-state with the critic agent prior to the team learning, the critic agent can then use the experiences of all agents to infer the trustworthiness with respect to a selected action for a target agent TA, in a specific state. This type can thus be called *Witness Reputation* ($WR_{A \rightarrow TA}(s, a)$), where A is the set of all agents and $TA \in A$.

Then TMCA aggregates these to construct the composite trust value. Since *in the previous credit assignment methods* [5], *the critic agent did not use the knowledge of other agents to evaluate the actions of the target agent*, our applied witness reputation would optimize the performance of TMCA compared to previous solutions through decreasing the probability of incorrect credit assignments. We believe that through an aggregation of disparate sources, the confidence in the assignments will increase. This is investigated in the experiments further.

We assume that the agents share their Q-Tables and Visit-Tables with the critic agent prior to the team learning phase and they act altruistically when communicating with the critic agent.

In order to better utilizing the information by the critic agent, we propose a rating, which is the target agent's correctness of the selected action in the current state. In other words, when a target agent performs an action, the critic agent evaluates the correctness of that action in that specific state through studying the trustworthiness of that action in that state. A degree will be assigned in the interval of $[0, 1]$, where 1 denotes a full confidence in the correctness of the action, and 0 a complete lack of confidence. The ratings are reevaluated based on the Q-Values within the critic agent's data base in an online fashion, using one of the knowledge evaluation measures (in this case the Certainty measure). Hence, since the MAS environment is dynamic and the ratings keep changing, the critic agent does not need to keep track of the ratings and can calculate them from the Q-Tables on demand.

The Trust Formula. To calculate the trust value of the target agent, the trust elements need to be formulated, so that the correctness probability of the target agent could be calculated. A trivial way to do so is to calculate it as the average of all collective ratings. Since these ratings are not at the same level of trustworthiness at the time of estimation, we use a weighted average which is then normalized in $[0, 1]$:

$$CompositeTrust_{CriticAgent \rightarrow TA}(s, a)$$

$$= \zeta_{DT} DT_{CriticAgent \rightarrow TA}(s, a) + \zeta_{WR} WR_{A \rightarrow TA}(s, a)$$

$$\zeta_{DT} + \zeta_{WR} = 1, \tag{4}$$

where ζ_k is the rating weight function which is application dependent. Now, we want to map the trust formula to our application domain by defining the trust formula's components as follows:

Direct Trust: Since the Direct Trust initiates from the direct experience of an agent, the history of the target agent for the previous actions, is studied in our model in the action-state. To do so, we use one of the expertise measures to model the Direct Trust between the critic and the target agent. In more details, the critic agent considers the expertise level (Certainty) of the target agent in selected action, as the Direct Trust of that agent:

$$DT_{CriticAgent \rightarrow TA}(s, a) = Certainty_{TA}(s, a) \tag{5}$$

Witness Reputation: The target agent is evaluated based on the point of view of the other agents about its selected actions in previous action-states. To do so, the critic agent uses the information (Certainty as expertise measure) from other agents about the selected action of the target agent. As we have assumed, the critic can calculate the Certainty of the correctness of the action from the point of view of other agents, using the tables of other agents:

$$WR_{A \rightarrow TA}(s, a) = \sum_{a_i \in A} W_{a_i} Certainty_{a_i}(s, a), \tag{6}$$

where A is the set of all agents except TA and W_{a_i} is the degree of trust of the critic agent to agent a_i's point of view regarding the target agent's selection of action a in the state s. In fact, this parameter is the function of the level of other agents' expertness and depth of their awareness in the state s and is calculated by the critic using the Visit-Tables of each agent as follows:

$$W_{a_i} = \frac{Visit_{a_i}(s)}{\sum_{a_i \in A} Visit_{a_i}(s)} \tag{7}$$

$Visit_{a_i}(s)$ is the number of times agent a_i has hit state s. The table assigns to each possible state for a_i, a number relevant to the number of hits. [2] has used a similar hit table.

Composite Trust: In TMCA, since the trust values are calculated from different information sources, we believe that the combination of the aforementioned components will lead to a better performance for the critic agent in evaluation of the trust, and thus the target agent. Therefore, we propose the use of a combination of trust values as a singular value, which creates a better picture of the correctness of the action of the target agent. We use a weighted average of the two components as follows:

$$CompositeTrust_{TA}(s,a) = W_{TA}Certainty_{TA}(s,a) + \sum_{a_i \in A} W_{a_i}Certainty_{a_i}(s,a),$$

(8)

where A is the set of agents except TA; W_{TA} is calculated by using Target Agent's Visit-Table. In fact, we can consider $\zeta_{DT} = W_{TA}$ and $\zeta_{WR} = \sum_{a_i \in A} W_{a_i}$.

5   Experimental Results

In this section, at first the evaluation indexes and the test bed are introduced. Then, the results of using TMCA are presented based on the Certainty as the knowledge evaluation measure. It would be compared with previous work in [5], in a noiseless and noisy environment (to study the effect of uncertainty on the performance of the proposed method). For this purpose, we use five evaluation indices for both AND and OR type task, for the MCA problem. The results are the average of 10 distinct simulations, and averaged on windows of 50 trials to filter high frequencies in the results (due to exploration of the agents).

5.1   Evaluation Indexes

To evaluate our proposed approach, we compare our results with those presented in [5,6], using the following measure:

Correctness: is the ratio of correct assignments to all assignments, for the learner agents, by the critic agent [5]. This Index demonstrates a comparison between the critic agent and an optimal critic with all correct assignments.

Performance: It is the ratio of correct actions (the actions that result rewards) to all of actions of agents [5].

Efficiency: shows the degree to which the learning chances have been incorporated, and it is the ratio of the agent receiving reinforcement signal, regardless of their correctness [6].

Group Success Ratio (GSR): is the percentage of trials in less than 100 attempts, which have led to a positive feedback [6].

Learning Ratio: is the average of learned tasks ratios by all learners [6].

5.2   The Testbed

As in [5], we use a team of five learner agents as a MAS with a parallel configuration in a single-step task. The agents are supposed to perform an addition task. In each learning episode, the team is presented with two 5-digit numbers.

Thus each agent acts in a 5*5 state space with 9 different actions to select (0–8). The agents do not know the result of addition and need to learn it. The environment (critic agent) assesses the team performance after the agents perform their selections.

During the simulation of the AND task, if all agents perform the addition correctly, the environment rewards the team, and otherwise, each agent's role should be evaluated. In the case of an OR task, the reward will be given when at least one agent has performed successfully, and the team will be penalized if all agents were wrong. For example, if 2 numbers (11111, 11111) were given to agents, they would be rewarded in AND type task if and only if their chosen actions were (22222) and otherwise it is necessary to decide about role of each agent in the team work and punishing or rewarding by the critic. In OR task type, if none of the agents do not choose action (2), the team will be punished, but if only one agent choose it, the critic agent must be make decision about Individual punishing or rewarding. We set the feedback function to output fixed values of +10 and -10 for reward and penalty, respectively.

To create a balance between the extraction of the best learned actions so far, and the exploring of unseen actions, the agents use a Boltzmann distribution for their selection step. Since the tasks are deterministic and single-step, the agents use a single-step Q-learning algorithm to update their tables ($discount factor = 0$ in formula(1)) [4]. To evaluate the algorithm the learning rate and the temperature are fixed at $\alpha = 0.7$ and $T = 0.5$, respectively.

Prior to the team learning, each learner is presented with individual learning opportunities of different number of steps (20, 30, 100, 100, 300). According to the experimental results in [5], each agent learns %37–38 of the task in this phase. Also it is assumed that the critic agent gets a copy of each team member's information, including the Q-Cell values and Visit-Tables [2]. The critic then receives the actions of all agents during the team learning phase, and updates the tables according to the assigned credits, for further use in the trust values calculation.

5.3   TMCA Vs. KEBCA

In order to investigate our approach, we add an artificial noise to the feedback signal to create a worst-case scenario, and to better evaluate our system. We study the results for MCA under the noise levels of 10 and 30 percent.

In the KEBCA algorithm [5], the critic agent receives in each trial the team feedback along with the knowledge measure of the learner agents. Using these values and two predetermined thresholds, the critic agent then estimates the role of each agent and assigns its individual feedback. In what follows, we discuss the results of MCA and KEBCA in the two major task types, according to the five evaluation indices.

And Tasks. In a non-noisy environment, the preliminary learning phase is a challenge for the critic, since there is no information about the knowledge of the learners. Hence, any judgement about their actions is far from trivial. Also, due to a high rate of failure in the first trials for the team, informative feedbacks are scarce. In fact, since the learner agents need to complement each other in the AND tasks, the team is always less successful than the individual. This is much worse in highly populated teams.

Noise has a negative effect on the team performance, but the degree to which this effect exists is dependent upon the method used in MCA and the task type. If there exists a reliable history of learning for agents, then TMCA can process the new information much better, since it acts as a noise filter. Upon the increase of uncertainty, the learning rates needs to be adjusted.

Correctness Index: The Correctness diagrams for TMCA, as illustrated in Fig. 1, show that as learning happens, the critic's judgement is more accurate. This is because of the fact that the critic agent uses the knowledge of the team for evaluation and credit assignment. TMCA is highly robust with a 10 percent noise, and the critic agent has a good judgement of the learners under a noise of 30 percent. Figure 1 shows that TMCA is superior to KEBCA in a non-noisy environment, as well as a noisy one with both levels of noise.

Performance Index: Figure 2 demonstrates an improvement in learning of the agents under both KEBCA and TMCA in both types of environments. However, the proposed algorithm is clearly superior to KEBCA in both the non-noisy and noisy environments. TMCA in a non-noisy environment has a performance of about %98, and in the noisy environment, we witness a decrease in the team performance as the noise level increases.

For the KEBCA algorithm, the noisy has more effects as the %30 noise leads into a distinguishable reduction in the performance as compared to the non-noisy environment, until the performance is stable at a %40 rate.

Efficiency Index: According to Fig. 3, in a non-noisy environment, the efficiency of TMCA reaches to %100 very quickly. It also operates very robustly in a noisy environment. The efficiency of TMCA is always better than or equal to KEBCA.

GSR Index: TMCA has a better group success rate in non-noisy environments, when compared to KEBCA, as illustrated in Fig. 4. However in noisy environments, this index decreases drastically.

Learning Ratio Index: After an increase in the learning ratio in the first trials of the learning, this index for the proposed algorithm will reach to 1, even for the %10 noisy environment. This is due to the convergence of Q-values of the learner team towards correct credits, using the feedback (Fig. 5).

As the pictures shown, there is a big difference between %10 noise and %30 noise in different evaluation indexes. This is due the fact that when there are relatively a large amount of noise, the agents' gained knowledge does not increase after some trials. The reason for this is that the learning rate is not small enough. Thus, the agent must use a smaller learning rate to handle uncertainty in the noisy environment.

Or Tasks. In a non-noisy environment, as the learning is initiated, the critic agent can use the team penalties to educate the learners, which will lead to the team reach a certain point of performance. Another important issue in the OR tasks is that the team, and not individuals, perform the task rationally. However, if all agents are needed to learn their tasks, another problem will arise: the fulfillment of learning for all agents in an OR tasks is non-trivial, since the information level of the critic decreases as the performance increase, and thus the team will not learn new cases very quickly. In such occasions, the critic can control the exploration ratio. In the initial steps of learning, the learners should start with a high the exploration ratio and then decrease it.

Using TMCA and after an increase in Correctness and Learning Ratio indices at the initial steps, the increase speed will diminish, and thus the superiority of TMCA versus KEBCA is evident. According to the results shown in Figs. 6, 7, 8, 9 and 10, the GSR and performance indices act quite similarly for both algorithms, while TMCA proves to be better in the efficiency index (Fig. 8).

These results clearly show that TMCA performs better when compared to KEBCA in both an OR and an AND task.

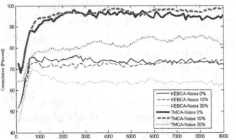

Fig. 1. Correctness in TMCA and KEBCA

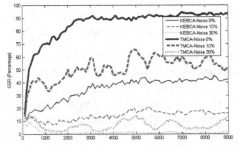

Fig. 2. Performance in TMCA and KEBCA

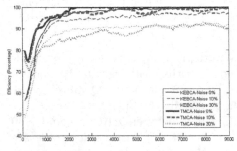

Fig. 3. Efficiency in TMCA and KEBCA

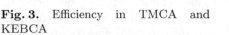

Fig. 4. GSR in TMCA and KEBCA

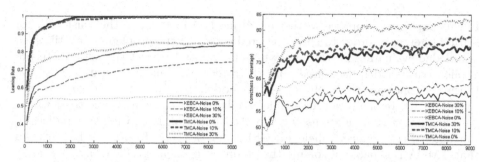

Fig. 5. LR in TMCA and KEBCA

Fig. 6. Correctness in TMCA and KEBCA (OR task type)

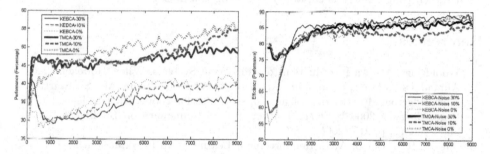

Fig. 7. Performance in TMCA and KEBCA (OR task type)

Fig. 8. Efficiency in TMCA and KEBCA (OR task type)

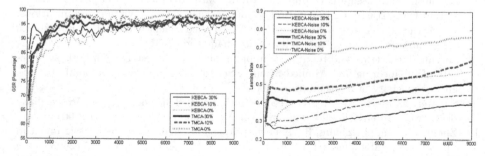

Fig. 9. GSR in TMCA and KEBCA (OR task type)

Fig. 10. LR in TMCA and KEBCA (OR task type)

6   Discussion and Conclusion

In this paper, we proposed a trust-based method to evaluate the trust value of learner agents, in order to solve the credit assignment problem. We utilized a knowledge evaluation measure known as Certainty to select the actions. In the applied trust model, have used both the direct trust and the reputation of the learners to increase the accuracy of the model, so that one could support the situations where one is not accessible or reliable for calculating the trust value.

The results of simulations was reported based on five evaluation indices of Certainty, Performance, Efficiency, GSR, and Learning Ratio. We have shown that TMCA is capable of solving the credit assignment problem in the studied cases, and also increases the speed and quality of the learning.

We mentioned that the task type affects the learning drastically. Usually MCA is a much harder problem in the parallel AND tasks, and thus prior knowledge is essential for an acceptable learning rate. The problem with OR tasks (Confining knowledge) can be solved using a exploration strategy. It has been shown that TMCA is capable of filtering the noise.

References

1. Wooldridge, M.: An Introduction to MultiAgent Systems. Wiley, Hoboken (2009)
2. Ahmadabadi, M.N., Imanipour, A., Araabi, B.N., Asadpour, M., Siegwart, R.: Knowledge-based extraction of area of expertise for cooperation in learning. In: Proceedings of 2006 IEEE/RSJ, International Conference on Intelligent Robots and Systems, p. 915 (2006)
3. Sutton, R.S., Barto, A.G.: Reinforcement Learning: An Introduction. MIT Press, Cambridge (1998)
4. Watkins, C.J.C.H., Dayan, P.: Q-learning. Mach. Learn. **8**(3–4), 279–292 (1992)
5. Harati, A., Ahmadabadi, M.N., Araabi, B.N.: Knowledge-based multi-agent credit assignment: a study on task type and critic information. IEEE Syst. J. **1**(1), 55–67 (2007)
6. Rahaie, Z., Beigy, H.: Expertness framework in multi-agent systems and its application in credit assignment problem. Intell. Data Anal. **18**(3), 511–528 (2014)
7. Patel, J.A.: Trust and reputation model for agent-based virtual organisations. Ph.D. thesis, Faculty of Engineering and Applied Science, School of Electronics and Computer Science, University of Southampton (2007)
8. Huynh, T.D.: Trust and reputation in open multi-agent systems. Ph.D thesis, Faculty of Engineering and Applied Science, School of Electronics and Computer Science, University of Southampton (2006)
9. Sabater, J., Sierra, C.: Regret: reputation in gregarious societies. In: Proceedings of the Fifth International Conference on Autonomous Agents. ACM (2001)
10. Zhong, Y., Gu, G., Zhang, R.: A new approach for structural credit assignment in distributed reinforcement learning systems. In: ICRA, pp. 1215–1220 (2003)
11. Holland, J.H.: Escaping brittleness: the possibility of general-purpose learning algorithms applied to rule-based systems. In: Michalski, R.S., Carbonell, J.G., Mitchells, T.M. (eds.) Machine Learning: An Artificial Intelligence Approach, vol. 2. Morgan Kaufmann, San Mateo (1986)

12. Kinny, D.N., Georgeff, M.P.: Commitment and effectiveness of situated agents. In: Proceedings of the 12th International Joint Conference on Artificial Intelligence, pp. 82–88 (1991)
13. Irwig, K., Wobcke, W.: Multi-agent reinforcement learning with vicarious rewards. Linkping Electron. Art. Comput. Inf. Sci. **4**(34) (1999)
14. Raghavan, S., Raghavan, S.V.: Learning the point gathering task using shared value function in mobile robots. In: International Conference on Advanced Computer Control, pp. 9–13 (2009)
15. Rahaie Z., Beigy, H.: Toward a solution to multi-agent credit assignment problem. In: Proceedings of the International Conference on Soft Computing and Pattern Recognition (SOCPAR 2009), Malacca, Malaysia, pp. 563–568, December 2009
16. Abbasi, M.A., Abbasi, Z.: Reinforcement distribution in a team of coopera- tive Q-learning agents. In: The Ninth ACIS International Conference on Soft- ware Engineering, IEEE Transactions on Artificial Intelligence, Networking, and Parallel/Distributed Computing (2008)
17. Harati, A., Ahmadabadi, M.N.: Certainty and expertness based credit assignment for cooperative Q-learning agents with and type task. In: Proceedings of the 9th International Conference on Neural Information Processing, ICONIP 2002, vol. 1, pp. 306–310 (2002)
18. Zaliamin, R,, Shiri, M.E.: Certainty and expertness based credit assignment for cooperative Q-learning agents with an and type task. Aust. J. Basic Appl. Sci. **2**, 1047–1054 (2010)
19. Marsh, S.: Formalising trust as a computational concept. Ph.D. thesis, University of Stirling, UK, pp. 271–293, March 1994
20. Schillo, M., Rovatsos, M., Funk, P.: Using trust for detecting deceitful agents in artificial societies. Appl. Artif. Intell. J. **14**, 825–848 (2000). Special Issue of the Deception, Fraud and Trust in Agent Societies
21. Harati, A., Ahmadabadi, M.N.: Experimental analysis of knowledge based mul- tiagent credit assign. In: Rajapakse, J.C., Wang, L. (eds.) Neural Information Processing: Research and Development. Studies in Fuzziness and Soft Computing, vol. 152, pp. 437–459. Springer, Heidelberg (2004)
22. Zacharia, G., Moukas, A., Maes, P.: Collaborative reputation mechanisms for elec- tronic marketplaces. Decis. Support Syst. **29**, 371–388 (2000)
23. Fung, G.: A comprehensive overview of basic clustering algorithms (2001)

Information Sources About Hydrogeological Disasters: The Role of Trust

Rino Falcone, Alessandro Sapienza[✉], and Cristiano Castelfranchi

Institute of Cognitive Sciences and Technologies ISTC-CNR of Rome, Rome, Italy
{rino.falcone,alessandro.sapienza,
cristiano.castelfranchi}@istc.cnr.it

Abstract. One issue particularly relevant in cases of risk of flooding and land-slides caused by specific conditions of the weather, is the ability of citizens to take the right decisions on the basis of different information sources to which they have access.

In this paper we describe some simulative experiments showing how a population of cognitive agents trusting in a different way three sources of information (institutional source, first neighbors source, their own perception), can make decisions more or less suited to the several weather patterns. The complexity of decisions is based on the fact that the agents differently trust the various sources of information which in turn may be differently trustworthy.

In our simulations we analyze some interesting case studies, with particular reference to social agents that need to wait others in order to make decision.

1 Introduction

One of the main problems in a world with various different information sources is to select the most reliable ones. However the reliability of each source has to be evaluated with respect its own scope of information. So the necessity of integrating sources on different scopes can be very useful in order to make a well-informed decision. In case of the weather forecast we can consider different sources like: official bulletin of authorities, the direct evaluation of some agents during the meteorological event, our own evaluation, and so on. Some of these sources are not correlated among them (a forecast is referred to mathematical model of the weather linked to its previous data, while a direct evaluation can be based on a current perception of the phenomenon). For this reason it is relevant to integrate these sources and at the same time to define their trustworthiness. For trusting an information source (S) we developed a cognitive model [3] based on the dimensions of competence and reliability/motivation of this source. These competence and reliability evaluations can derive from different reasons, basically:

- Our previous *direct experience* with S on that specific information content;
- *Recommendations* (other individuals Z reporting their direct experience and evaluation about S) or *Reputation* (the shared general opinion of others about S) on that specific information content [4, 7, 11, 12, 15]

© Springer International Publishing Switzerland 2016
M. Rovatsos et al. (Eds.): EUMAS 2015/AT 2015, LNAI 9571, pp. 350–362, 2016.
DOI: 10.1007/978-3-319-33509-4_27

– *Categorization* of S (it is assumed that a source can be categorized and that it is known this category), exploiting inference and reasoning (analogy, inheritance, etc.): on this basis it is possible to establish the competence/reliability of S on that specific information content [1, 2, 5, 6].

However in this paper we have simplified our trust model omitting the complex analysis that defines trust in the different sources. Our focus is on the integration of the information sources also based on their trustworthiness. In particular, we are interested to analyze how different populations of cognitive agents (composed by different percentage of agents who rely on various sources) react to the various weather situations and how many of them take the right decision (given the real weather).

2 The Trust Model

Given the complexity of simulations, we chose to use a relatively simple trust model, letting many parameters being unified in just one.

Trust decision in presence of uncertainty can be handle using uncertainty theory [8] or probability theory. We decided to use the second approach, as in this platform agents know a priori all the possible events that can happen and they are able to estimate how much it is plausible that they occur. In particular we exploit Bayesian theory, one of the most used approach in trust evaluation [9, 10, 13].

In this model each information source S is represented by a trust degree called *TrustOnSource*, with $0 \leq TrustOnSource \leq 1$, plus a Bayesian probability distribution PDF[1] (Probability Distribution Function) that represents the information reported by S.

The trust model allow the possibility of many events: it just split the domain in the corresponding number of interval. In this work we use three different events (described below), then the PDF will be divided into three parts.

The *TrustOnSource* parameters is used to smooth the information referred by S. This is the formula used for transforming the reported PDF:

$$NewValue = 1 + (Value - 1) * TrustOnSource$$

The output of this step is called Smoothed PDF (SPDF).
We will have that:

- The greater *TrustOnSource* is, the more similar the SPDF will be to the PDF; in particular if $TrustOnSource = 1 \Rightarrow$ SPDF = PDF;
- The lesser it is, the more the SPDF will be flatten; in particular if *TrustOnSource* = 0 $\Rightarrow$ SPDF is an uniform distribution with value 1.

The idea is that we trust on what S says proportionally to how much we trust it. In words, the more we trust S, the more we tend to take into consideration what it says; the less we trust S, the more we tend to ignore its informative contribution.

---

[1] It is modelled as a distribution continuous in each interval.

We define GPDF (Global PDF) the evidence that an agent owns concerning a belief P. Once estimated the SPDFs for each information source, there will be a process of aggregation between the GPDF and the SPDFs. Each source actually represents a new evidence E about a belief P. Then to the purpose of the aggregation process it is possible to use the classical Bayesian logic, recursively on each source:

$$f(P|E) = \frac{f(E|P) * f(P)}{f(E)}$$

where:

f(P|E) = GPDF (the new one)
f(E|P) = SPDF;
f(P) = GPDF (the old one)

In this case f(E) is a normalization factor, given by the formula:

$$f(E) = \int f(E|P) * f(P)dP$$

In words the new GPDF, that is the global evidence that an agent has about P, is computed as the product of the old GPDF and the SPDF, that is the new contribute reported by S.

As we need to ensure that GPDF is still a probability distribution function, it is necessary to scale down it to[2]. This is ensured by the normalization factor f(E).

3   The Platform

Exploiting NetLogo [14], we created a very flexible platform, where a lot of parameters are taken into account to model a variety of situations.

3.1   The Context

The basic idea is that, given a population distributed over a wide area, some weather phenomena happen in the world with a variable level of criticality.

The world is populated by a number of cognitive agents (citizens) that react to these situations, deciding how to behave, on the basis of the information sources they have and of the trustworthiness they attribute to these different sources: they can escape, take measures or evaluate absence of dangers.

In addition to citizens, there is another agent called authority. Its aim is to inform promptly citizens about the weather phenomena. Moreover the authority will be characterized by an uncertainty, expressed in terms of standard deviation.

---

[2] To be a PDF, it is necessary that the area subtended by it is equal to 1.

3.2   Information Sources

To make a decision, each agent can consult a set of information sources, reporting to it some evidence about the incoming meteo phenomena.

We considered the presence of three kind of information sources (whether active or passive) available to agents:

1. Their *personal judgment*, based on the direct observation of the phenomena. Although this is a direct and always true (at least in that moment) source, it has the drawback that waiting to see what happens could lead into a situation in which it is no more possible to react in the best way (for example there is no more time to escape if one realizes too late the worsening weather).
2. *Notification from authority*: the authority distributes into the world weather forecast with associated different alarm signals, trying to prepare citizens to what is going to happen. This is the first informative source that agents have.
3. *Others' behavior*: agents are in some way influenced by community logics, tending to partially or totally emulate their neighbors behavior.

The personal judgment and the notification from the authority are provided as clear signals: all the probability is focused on a single event.

Conversely, for others' behavior estimation the probability of each event is directly proportional to the number of neighbors making each kind of decision. If no decision is available, the PDF is a uniform distribution with value 1.

3.3   Agents' Description

At the beginning of the simulation, the world is populated by a number of agents belonging to four categories. The main difference between them lays in how much trust they have in their information sources:

1. *Self-trusting agents* prefer to rely on their own capabilities and direct experience, having a high level of trust in their self; they need to see the phenomena to make a decision, but as a consequence they need more time to take a decision. For this kind of agents the trust values are: self trust 0.9; authority trust 0.3; community trust 0.3.
2. *Authority-trusting agents* put trust mainly on what the authority says, so they are the first to make a decision (weather forecast are distributed in advance with respect to phenomena): self trust 0.3; authority trust 0.9; community trust 0.3;
3. *Social-trusting agents* model agents that are influenced by social dynamics; they need to see what other agents choose and then they follow the majority: self trust 0.3; authority trust 0.3; community trust 0.9;
4. *Equal-trusting agents* are just naïve agents that tend to believe to anything: self trust 0.9; authority trust 0.9; community trust 0.9;

These trust degrees are then used to apply the trust model above described.

3.4 World Description

The world is made by 32 × 32 patches, that wraps both horizontally and vertically. It is geographically divided in 4 quadrants of equal dimension, where agents are distributed in a random way (Fig. 1).

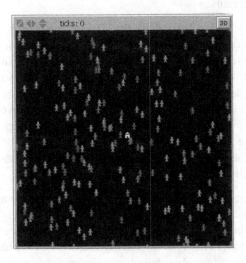

Fig. 1. A world example. There are 200 agents (50 per category) plus the authority, that is represented by the yellow house (Color figure online).

The quadrants differs in the possible weather phenomena that happens, modelled through the presence of clouds:

1. *No event*: there is just a light rain, from 1 to 29 clouds;
2. *Medium event*: there is heavy rain, that can make damages to agents or their properties; form 30 to 89 clouds;
3. *Critical event*: a tremendous event due to too high level of rain, with possible risks for the agents sake; from 90 clouds on.

These phenomena are not instantaneous, but they happens progressively in time. In particular, in each quadrant it will be added a cloud on each tick until the phenomena is completed (Fig. 2).

The four quadrants are independent from each other but there can be an indirect influence as agents can have neighbors in other quadrants.

These events are also correlated to the alarms that the authority raises. In fact, as previously said, the authority is characterized by a standard deviation. We use it to produce the alarm generated by the authority and from it depends the correctness of the prediction.

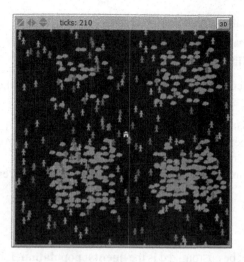

Fig. 2. An example of world after an event. Starting from the quadrants in the upper left and proceeding clockwise, we can see events 1, 2, 3 and 3.

3.5 Workflow

At the beginning, we start generating a world containing an authority and a given number of agents belonging to different categories.

At the time t_0 the authority gives forecast including an alarm signal, reporting the level of criticality of the event that is going to happen in each quadrant (critic $= 3$, mean $= 2$, none $= 1$). Being just a forecast, it is not sure that it is really going to happen. It will have a probability linked to the precision of the authority (depending from standard deviation). However, as a forecast, it allows agents to evaluate the situation in advance, before the possible event. Event that in fact starts randomly from t_{20} to t_{31}.[3]

During the decision making phase, agents check their own information sources, aggregating the single contributes according to the corresponding trust values. They estimate the possibility that each event happens and take the choice that minimize the risk. Then, accordingly to their own decision making deadlines, agents will choose how to behave.

While agents collect information they are considered as "thinking", meaning that they have not decided yet. When this phase reaches the deadline, agents have to make a decision, that cannot be changed anymore. This information is then available for the other agents (neighborhood), that can in turn exploit it for their decisions.

3.6 The Decision-Making Phase

Once consulted all the three sources of information, agents subjectively estimate the probability that each single event happens:

---

[3] This has been made in order to ensure that self-trusting agents cannot always see the whole critical event.

1. $P_{critical\_event}$ = probability that there is a critical event;
2. P_{medium_event} = probability that there is a medium event;
3. P_{no_event} = probability that there is no event;

They will react according to the event that is consider more likely to happen. There are three possible choices:

1. Escape: agents abandon their homes.
2. Take measures: agents take some measure (quick repairs) to avoid possible damages due to weather event;
3. Ignore the problem: agents continue doing their activities, regardless of possible risks.

3.7 Platform Input

The first thing that can be customized is the **agents' population**. It is possible to put any number of agents belonging to the 4 categories previously described. Also one can set agents' **decision-making deadline**, customizing their behavior. It is possible to change the **authority reliability**, modifying its standard deviation.

Then it is possible to determine the events that are going to happen on each quadrant configuring what we call the **event map**: it is the set of the four events relative to the four quadrants, starting from the one top left and proceeding clockwise.

A setting rather than another can completely change agents behavior.

3.8 Results Estimation

For each quadrant, it is possible to exploit a series of data to understand simulations' results (actually their average on 500 runs):

1. Kind of event that actually happens, kind of alarm raised by the authority and the corresponding absolute error: example 3(2.92/0.08);
2. Percentage of agents taking each kind of decision: this data is also available for each agent category;
3. Accuracy: how much the decisions taken by each agents' category are right.

4   Simulations

We decided to use the realized platform in order to understand how the decisions of agents preferring direct experience (self-trusting) or using trusted sources (authority-trusting) affect, positively or negatively agents that need others to decide (social-trusting).

We investigated a series of scenarios, populated by different percentages of agents belonging to those three categories, in order to verify the community behavior.

We started influencing social-agents with just another kind of agent. Then we tried using two kind. In fact, it is particularly interesting to observe what happen in presence of divergent sources.

4.1 First Scenario: Authority and Social

Simulation setting:

1. Agents population: we tried 7 different configurations of authority-trusting agents (AT) and social-trusting agents (SoT); (200, 0), (160, 40), (120, 80), (80, 120), (40, 160), (20, 180) and (0, 200).
2. Authority reliability: we used the value 0.3 to shape a very reliable authority and 0.9 to shape an incompetent one.
3. Event map: [1 3 3 2].
4. Decision making deadline (since the simulation starts): we decided to use this as a category parameters. As AT agents believe mainly in the authority and this kind of source is immediately available, they will quickly decide. Their deadline is fixed to 30 ticks. Conversely SoT agents need a lot of time to decide, as they first want to observe others. Their deadline is fixed to 115 ticks.

For sake of simplicity, we report just result of quadrants 1, 2 and 4, as quadrants 2 and 3 are quite the same. The following graphs represent the accuracy of the two population in each quadrant (Fig. 3).

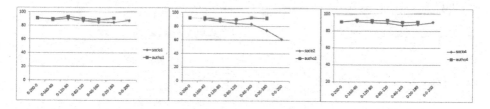

Fig. 3. Accuracy in quadrants 1, 2 and 4 when the authority standard deviation is 0.3.

As we can see, when the authority reports information correctly, AT agents perform well and they influence positively SoT agents, independently from the kind of event (Fig. 4).

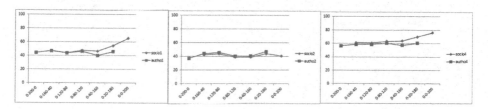

Fig. 4. Accuracy in quadrants 1, 2 and 4 when the authority standard deviation is 0.9.

Conversely, when the authority is not reliable AT agents perform badly, and this has a negative effect on SoT agents. Actually in the second quadrant, where the event is critical, SoT agents would have performed badly in any case, as in most cases they do not see the phenomena entirely.

4.2   Second Scenario: Self and Social

Simulation setting:

1. Agents population: we tried 7 different configurations of self-trusting agents (SeT) and social-trusting agents (SoT); (200, 0), (160, 40), (120,80), (80,120), (40,160), (20,180) and (0, 200).
2. Authority reliability: we used the value 0.3 to shape a very reliable authority and 0.9 to shape an incompetent one.
3. Event map: [1 3 3 2].
4. Decision making deadline (since the simulation starts): we wanted to use SeT agents as experts, able to understand what is going to happen. Therefore they can be good advisor about how to behave in the various situations. According to this, they need to see as much phenomena as they can, then their deadline is a randomly generated value, going from 105 to 125 ticks. Again SoT agents need first to observe others. But taking a decision needs time. We supposed that they need a temporal window of 10 ticks, from the moment they observe others to the moment in which they can actually accomplish their decision: So their deadline is fixed to 115 ticks (Figs. 5 and 6).

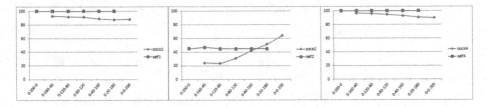

Fig. 5.   Accuracy in quadrants 1, 2 and 4 when the authority standard deviation is 0.3.

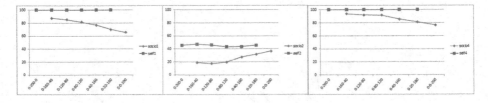

Fig. 6.   Accuracy in quadrants 1, 2 and 4 when the authority standard deviation is 0.9.

In quadrant 1 and 4 of both the cases, SeT agents perform perfectly (100 % of accuracy) as they are perfectly able to see the phenomena. This is no more true in quadrant 2, in which they are able to see the critical event just in about the 45 % of the cases. This bad result is due to the combination of two facts:

1. The event randomly starts from tick 20 to tick 31;
2. SeT agents have a variable deadline to make their decision.

When a critical event happens, their influence on SoT agents is always negative. Notice that SoT agents base their evaluation just on half of the SeT agents, those who decide until 115 ticks; it is quite probable that the reported information is not correct.

4.3 Third Scenario: Authority, Self and Social

Simulation setting:

1. Agents population: we tried 7 different configurations of authority-trusting agents (AT), self-trusting agents (SeT) and social-trusting agents (SoT); (100, 100, 0), (80, 80, 40), (60, 60, 80), (40, 40, 120), (20, 20, 160), (10, 10, 180) and (0, 200).
2. Authority reliability: we used the value 0.3 to shape a very reliable authority and 0.9 to shape an incompetent one.
3. Event map: [1 3 3 2].
4. Decision making deadline (since the simulation starts): 30 ticks for AT; a randomly generated value in the interval [105, 125] ticks for SeT; 115 for SoT (Figs. 7 and 8).

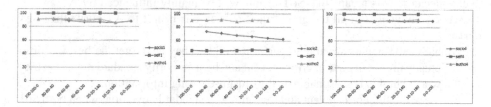

Fig. 7. Accuracy in quadrants 1, 2 and 4 when the authority standard deviation is 0.3.

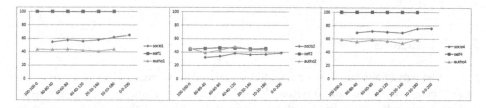

Fig. 8. Accuracy in quadrants 1, 2 and 4 when the authority standard deviation is 0.9.

This is the most interesting scenario, as SoT agents sometime have to deal with discording sources.

In order to better understand the experiment, let's analyze what happens when agents decide.

AT agents decide at time 30. Their decisions are influenced just by the authority, then they don't need extra time to see what is going to happen neither are interested in what other agents do. Their performance strictly depends on the authority accuracy. Plus the whole category will always take the same decision: there won't be an AT agent that decide differently from the others.

Concerning **SeT agents**, they are designed as the experts inside the population. They are able to understand the phenomena and decide accordingly. We assume that the last moment to make a decision is 125 ticks, but not all of them will take all this time to decide. Their deadline is randomly generated inside the interval [105, 125].

Their decision will always be true in case of no event or medium event, but just a few of them will be able to see completely a critical event. From the graph we can see it is about 45 % of them.

Finally, **SoT agents** need to see what others do, but this means that they will be slower. Supposing that they will need 10 ticks from the moment in which they decide to the moment in which they actually put into practice their decision, we decided to set their deadline to 115 ticks.

Practically, this means that at the moment they decide just half of SeT agents has decided, moreover it is the part that take the worst decision as, in case of critical event, it has the higher probability to do not see the whole phenomena. Conversely, all AT agents decided. This means that SoT agents will be mainly influenced by AT agents. This is clearly visible in all the graph: the SoT curve is nearer to AT curve than SeT curve.

Globally, SoT agents are able to perform well but they never get the best performance. Actually in case of case of critical event and high authority standard deviation they are the worst, but this is reasonable as they just use wrong information.

In case of medium or no event and low authority standard deviation, when both SeT and AT agents perform well and represent good sources, we notice that SoT agents perform a little worse than them. This is due to the fact that SoT agents are socially influenced also by agents in other quadrants, using information that are correct but in another context.

5   Conclusions

In the first part of this work we presented the platform we realized in order to study citizen behavior in case of different levels' weather phenomena. The platform is endowed with a Bayesian trust evaluation model that allows citizens to deduce information from their own information sources.

It is in fact interesting to study how different citizens react to different stimuli derived by their information sources.

This very complex platform can be populated by a number of agents/citizens belonging to a set of predefined categories. In this case categories are useful to differentiate the behavior of each agents, specifying how much trust they have in their information source.

In addition to agents, a lot of parameters can be customized, giving the possibility to recreate a lot of different simulation scenarios.

After that, we used the proposed platform with the aim of studying how agents that need to follow others behave. We put into the world three kind of agents weighing information sources differently (social trusting, authority trusting and self trusting) and we tried to understand the influence of these last two on social trusting agents.

Results clearly show that social agents are able to get good performance, following their information sources, but they never get optimal results.

We also showed that they are negatively influenced by the behavior of agents in other quadrants. Although not well studied, this phenomenon results to be quite interesting and it could become object of interest following this research line.

Acknowledgments. This work is partially supported by the Project PRISMA (PiattafoRme cloud Interoperabili per SMArt-government; Cod. PON04a2 A) funded by the Italian Program for Research and Innovation (Programma Operativo Nazionale Ricerca e Compctitività 2007–2013) and the project CLARA—CLoud plAtform and smart underground imaging for natural Risk Assessment, funded by the Italian Ministry of Education, University and Research (MIUR-PON).

References

1. Burnett, C., Norman, T., Sycara, K.: Bootstrapping trust evaluations through stereotypes. In: Proceedings of the 9th International Conference on Autonomous Agents and Multiagent Systems (AAMAS 2010), pp. 241–248 (2010)
2. Burnett, C., Norman, T., Sycara, K.: Stereotypical trust and bias in dynamic multiagent systems. ACM Trans. Intell. Syst. Technol. (TIST) 4(2), 26 (2013)
3. Castelfranchi, C., Falcone, R.: Trust Theory: A Socio-Cognitive and Computational Model. Wiley, Hoboken (2010)
4. Conte, R., Paolucci, M.: Reputation in Artificial Societies: Social Beliefs for Social Order. Kluwer Academic Publishers, Boston (2002)
5. Falcone, R., Castelfranchi, C.: Generalizing trust: inferencing trustworthiness from categories. In: Falcone, R., Barber, S.K., Sabater-Mir, J., Singh, M.P. (eds.) Trust 2008. LNCS (LNAI), vol. 5396, pp. 65–80. Springer, Heidelberg (2008)
6. Falcone, R., Piunti, M., Venanzi, M., Castelfranchi, C.: From manifesta to krypta: the relevance of categories for trusting others. In: Falcone, R., Singh, M. (eds.) Trust in Multiagent Systems (2013). ACM Trans. Intell. Syst. Technol. 4(2), March 2013
7. Jiang, S., Zhang, J., Ong, Y.S.: An evolutionary model for constructing robust trust networks. In: Proceedings of the 12th International Conference on Autonomous Agents and Multiagent Systems (AAMAS) (2013)
8. Liu, B.: Uncertainty Theory, 5th edn. Springer, Heidelberg (2014)
9. Quercia, D., Hailes, S., Capra, L.: B-trust: Bayesian trust framework for pervasive computing. In: Stølen, K., Winsborough, W.H., Martinelli, F., Massacci, F. (eds.) iTrust 2006. LNCS, vol. 3986, pp. 298–312. Springer, Heidelberg (2006)

10. Melaye, D., Demazeau, Y.: Bayesian dynamic trust model. In: Pěchouček, M., Petta, P., Varga, L.Z. (eds.) CEEMAS 2005. LNCS (LNAI), vol. 3690, pp. 480–489. Springer, Heidelberg (2005)
11. Sabater-Mir, J.: Trust and reputation for agent societies. Ph.D. thesis, Universitat Autonoma de Barcelona (2003)
12. Sabater-Mir, J., Sierra, C.: Regret: a reputation model for gregarious societies. In: 4th Workshop on Deception and Fraud in Agent Societies, Montreal, Canada, pp. 61–70 (2001)
13. Wang, Y., Vassileva, J.: Bayesian network-based trust model. In: Proceedings of the IEEE/WIC International Conference on Web Intelligence 2003 (WI 2003), pp. 372–378. IEEE, October 2003
14. Wilensky, U.: NetLogo. Center for Connected Learning and Computer-Based Modeling, Northwestern University, Evanston, IL (1999). http://ccl.northwestern.edu/netlogo/
15. Yolum, P., Singh, M.P.: Emergent properties of referral systems. In: Proceedings of the 2nd International Joint Conference on Autonomous Agents and MultiAgent Systems (AAMAS 2003) (2003)

Trust, Negotiations and Virtual Currencies for a Sharing Economy

Dave de Jonge[(✉)] and Carles Sierra

IIIA-CSIC, Bellaterra, Catalonia, Spain
{davedejonge,sierra}@iiia.csic.es

Abstract. We propose an application that allows users to request other users for help with every-day tasks. Users can pay each other for these tasks by issuing contracts in which the requester promises to return the favor in the future by performing some task for the other. Such contracts can be seen as an alternative currency, coined by the users themselves. Trust is an essential aspect of this system, as the issuer of a contract may fail to fulfill its commitments. Therefore, the application comes with a social network where users can leave comments about other users. Furthermore, our application includes a market place where users can exchange service contracts between each other, and a negotiation algorithm that can automatically trade these contracts on behalf of the user.

Keywords: Automated negotiation · Trust · Sharing economy · Virtual currency · Social networks

1 Introduction

Around the world traditional economies are converting more and more into what is known as a *sharing economy*: an economical system in which individuals share goods and services with each other, rather than buying them from official companies. Well-known examples of applications and communities based around sharing are Couch Surfing,[1] Airbnb[2] and BlaBlaCar.[3] Another important change in modern economy is the introduction of *virtual currencies*; currencies that are not regulated by governments or banks, but by informal communities and that only exist in digital form. The best known example of such currency is Bitcoin.[4]

In this paper we propose an extension of the u-Help application introduced in [2]. U-Help is a distributed community-based application that allows users to request help with every-day tasks from other community members. A user may for example request a babysitter for her child. This request is then propagated along the network so that any other user in the community may accept the request and voluntarily carry out the requested task. The original u-Help application however

---

[1] http://www.couchsurfing.org.
[2] http://www.airbnb.com.
[3] http://www.blablacar.com/.
[4] https://bitcoin.org/.

© Springer International Publishing Switzerland 2016
M. Rovatsos et al. (Eds.): EUMAS 2015/AT 2015, LNAI 9571, pp. 363–366, 2016.
DOI: 10.1007/978-3-319-33509-4_28

relies entirely on the willingness of people to help voluntarily. This may work in small communities where most people know each other, but it is less likely to succeed when used in larger communities with more anonymity because it would be tempting to act as a freerider. In this paper we therefore propose to extend u-Help with a virtual currency system that enables people to pay for the help they receive.

2   Alternative Currency

In our extension, when a user receives a request he or she may not only accept or reject that request, but may also ask for a favor in return. The requesting user can then pay the accepter by issuing a *service contract*, in which he promises to return the favor by helping the accepter with some task in the future.

Example: Bob asks Alice to pick up his child from school. In return Bob gives Alice a service contract in which he promises Alice to help her repair her computer, some time in the future whenever she needs it.

The users can negotiate on the terms of the contract, similar to a mechanism introduced in [3] in which agents may promise future rewards when negotiating a deal in the present. In the example above we say that Bob is the *issuer* of the contract. Such a service contract can then be used by Alice in two ways: she can *exercise* the contract, meaning that Alice requests Bob to fulfill his commitment and fix her computer, or she can *pass on* the contract to somebody else to make a payment, as if it were a sort of currency.

Example: Alice asks Charles to repair her car. As a payment Alice gives Charles the contract she earlier received from Bob. So whenever Charles' computer is broken, he can go to Bob and exercise the contract.

Note that this system is very similar to the original use of bank notes: they served as a proof that a bank owed a certain amount of gold to the holder of the bank note. In our case a service contract is a proof that another user still owes a certain favor to the holder of the contract.

We make a distinction between a *task* and a *service contract*. A task explicitly defines an activity that is going to take place at a specified time and place as a favor for a specific person. A service contract also specifies an activity but does not specify when, and does not specify who is the beneficiary. Exercising a service contract means to convert it into a task.

A service contract specifies:

- The type of activity.
- The person who is going to do the activity (the issuer of the contract).
- The duration of the activity.

A task specifies:

- The type of activity.
- The person who is going to do the activity (the issuer of the contract).
- The duration of the activity.
- The date, time and location of the activity.
- The beneficiary.

Of course it can always happen that the holder of a contract wants to exercise it on a moment inauspicious to the issuer. Therefore, the contract may include terms on how and when it can be exercised. For example: "Bob will fix your computer, but you have to request him to do so at least 2 days in advance".

3 Trust

The notion of trust is essential in this system. After all, Charles and Bob may not even know each other, so Charles does not know whether Bob is really handy enough with computers to solve his problem. If Charles does not trust Bob he will not accept any contract issued by Bob as a payment. Therefore, we propose a reputation system that helps users to decide whether to accept service contracts issued by unknown people. This reputation system consists of a database that stores for every user:

- His or her skills.
- Reviews of this user written by other users and their satisfaction levels for previous tasks executed by this user.
- A social graph, showing whether two users have common friends.
- His or her number of "outstanding" contracts (contracts that he or she has issued but that have not been exercised yet).

Every user has a profile where this information can be found. Other users can leave comments on this profile which cannot be removed. Of course, one should always consider the possibility that the issuer of a contract will not fulfill his commitment. In that case one can leave a negative comment on the issuer's profile, which will reflect badly on his reputation. This will strongly decrease his chances of receiving help from others in the future as they will consider contracts issued by him less valuable. Therefore, users have an incentive not to issue more contracts than they are actually able to fulfill. Again, this resembles the way that real monetary systems work: people accept payments in dollars because they trust that the Federal Reserve will not print dollars excessively and cause hyperinflation. In our proposed system every single user essentially acts as a central bank for his or her own currency.

4 Negotiations

When Alice requests Bob to execute some task for her, they need to agree on how Alice is going to repay this favor. These negotiations can become difficult if, for example, Alice does not have anything to offer in return that Bob is interested in. To solve this problem we propose an online *market place* where users can exchange service contracts. This market place has several advantages:

1. It enlarges the set of possible deals that can be made between users.
2. It enables users to exchange service contracts they do not need for contracts they do need.
3. It enables users to "buy back" contracts issued by themselves.

An example of the first case would be when Alice finds a contract on the market place that Bob is interested in. She can then agree with Bob to "buy" that contract in exchange for a contract issued by herself, so that she can give that contract to Bob, and Bob can help Alice with her computer. The second case applies when Bob has accepted a contract issued by Alice, but is not interested in exercising it. He can then trade that contract on the market place for another one that he is interested in. The third case applies if Alice has issued many contracts which have not yet been exercised, while she herself owns many contracts issued by others. If she is afraid she will not be able to fulfill all the contracts she issued she can take them off the market by trading them for the contracts she owns.

If there are thousands of users looking for contracts or offering contracts in the market place at the same time it may be very difficult to find the right deal. Therefore, we propose to incorporate an automated negotiating agent into the application based on the algorithm introduced in [1]. The user can then tell his agent the kinds of contracts he is looking for, the kinds of contracts he is willing to issue, and the contracts he currently owns (issued by others). The agent will then contact the market place to negotiate a deal with the agents of other users. The agent may propose deals to the other agents and may accept deals proposed by them. It determines the value of any such deal based on the terms of the contracts involved in it as well as on the reputations of the issuers of those contracts. Once several agents agree on a deal the users themselves will also be asked if they agree with that deal. If not, they can still reject it.

Acknowledgments. Supported by MILESS - Ministerio de economía y competitividad - TIN2013-45039-P, CollectiveMind - Ministerio de Economía y Competitividad, CONVOCATORIA 2013 - EXPLORA, TEC2013-49430-EXP and EU project 318770 PRAISE.

References

1. de Jonge, D., Sierra, C.: NB3: a multilateral negotiation algorithm for large, non-linear agreement spaces with limited time. Auton. Agent. Multi-Agent Syst. **29**(5), 896–942 (2015)
2. Koster, A., Madrenas, J., Osman, N., Schorlemmer, M., Sabater-Mir, J., Sierra, C., de Jonge, D., Fabregues, A., Puyol-Gruart, J., García, P.: u-Help: supporting helpful communities with information technology. In: Proceedings of the First International Conference on Agreement Technologies (AT 2012), vol. 918, pp. 378–392, Dubrovnik, Croatia, 15 October 2012
3. Ramchurn, S.D., Sierra, C., Godo, L., Jennings, N.R.: Negotiating using rewards. Artif. Intell. **171**, 805–837 (2007)

Logic and Games for Ethical Agents in Normative Multi-agent Systems

Xin Sun$^{(\boxtimes)}$ and Livio Robaldo

Faculty of Science, Technology and Communication,
University of Luxembourg, Luxembourg, Luxembourg
{xin.sun,livio.robaldo}@uni.lu

Abstract. In this paper we study how to characterize ethical agents in normative multi-agent systems. We adopt a proposition control game together with input/output logic. Norms create the normative status of strategies. Agents' preference in proposition control games are changed by the normative status of strategies. We distinguish four ethical types of agents: moral, amoral, negatively impartial and positively impartial. Agents of different ethical types use different input/output systems and different procedures to change their preference. Preference changes induce normative proposition control games and notions like normative Nash equilibrium are then introduced. We study some complexity issues related to normative reasoning/status and normative Nash equilibrium.

Keywords: Ethical type · Propositional control game · Norm · Input/output logic

1 Introduction

Norms prominently affected agent's behavior by creating obligations and permissions. Different agents have different reactions when there are conflicts between their obligations and preference. Intuitively, it seems acceptable that:

- A *moral agent* will consider fulfilling obligations to be more important that maximizing preference.
- An *amoral agent* will act in accordance with his preference and ignore obligations.
- An *impartial agent* will first classify his actions into legal and illegal categories according to norms, then rank his actions using preference within the two categories.

L. Robaldo—Received funding from the European Unions Horizon 2020 research and innovation programme under the Marie Sklodowska-Curie grant agreement No 661007 for the project "ProLeMAS: PROcessing LEgal language in normative Multi-Agent Systems".

© Springer International Publishing Switzerland 2016
M. Rovatsos et al. (Eds.): EUMAS 2015/AT 2015, LNAI 9571, pp. 367–375, 2016.
DOI: 10.1007/978-3-319-33509-4_29

Based on such intuition, our main research concern in this paper is to answer the following question: "How to formally characterize different ethical types of agents?"

This research question is understood in the setting of normative multi-agent system. Normative multi-agent system [3] is a new interdisciplinary academic area developed in recent years bringing together researchers from multi-agent system [16], deontic logic [8] and normative system [1,2,11]. In this paper we adopt a proposition control game together with input/output logic. Proposition control game, as a variant of Boolean game [4,10], is a class of games based on propositional logic. Input/output logic [12] appears as one of the new achievements in deontic logic in recent years [8].

Norms are social rules regulating agents' behavior by prescribing which actions are obligatory, forbidden or permitted. [15]'s early work on behavior change under norms has considered only a relatively simple view of norms, where some actions or states are designated as violations. [2] studies how conditional norms regulate agents' behaviors, but permissive norms plays no role in their framework. In this paper, agents' behavior are regulated by conditional norms including permissive norms.

In the proposition control game theoretical setting, norms classify strategies as moral, legal or illegal. Such classification transforms the game by changing the preference relation in the proposition control game. To represent norms in proposition control games, we make use of input/output logic. The preference relation in proposition control games are changed by the normative status of strategies. Agents of different ethical types use different input/output logic for normative reasoning and have different procedures of preference change. The input/output logic and the procedure of preference change characterizes different types of ethical agents.

The structure of this paper is the following: we present some background knowledge on proposition control game and input/output logic in Sect. 2. Normative status and ethical agents are introduced and its complexity issues are studied in Sects. 3 and 4. We summarize and conclude this paper with future work in Sect. 5.

2   Proposition Control Game and Input/Output Logic

2.1   Proposition Control Game

Proposition control game is a variant of Boolean game. Boolean game is super succinct in the sense that agents' strategy and utility function are represented implicitly. Such succinctness is reached with a cost: many decision problems in Boolean games are intractable. For example deciding whether there is a pure strategy Nash equilibrium in a given Boolean game is Σ_2^P hard [5]. To find a balance between succinctness and tractability, we introduce proposition control game.

In a proposition control game, the strategies available to each agent consist in assigning a truth value to each variable he can control. The goal of each agent is represented by a set of weighted formulas. Formally, let $\mathbb{P} = \{p_0, p_1, \ldots\}$ be a finite set of propositional variables and let $L_\mathbb{P}$ be the propositional language built from $\mathbb{P}$. $2^\mathbb{P}$ is the set of all valuations for $\mathbb{P}$, with the usual convention that for $V \in 2^\mathbb{P}$ and $p \in V$, V gives the value true to p if $p \in V$ and false otherwise. Let $X \subseteq \mathbb{P}$, 2^X is the set of X-valuations. A partial valuation (for $\mathbb{P}$) is an X-valuation for some $X \subseteq \mathbb{P}$. Partial valuations are denoted by listing all variables of X, with a "+" symbol when the variable is set to be true and a "−" symbol when the variable is set to be false: for instance, let $X = \{p, q, r\}$, then the X-valuation $V = \{p, r\}$ is denoted $\{+p, -q, +r\}$. If $\{\mathbb{P}_1, \ldots, \mathbb{P}_n\}$ is a partition of $\mathbb{P}$ and $V_1, \ldots, V_n$ are partial valuations, where $V_i \in 2^{\mathbb{P}_i}$, $(V_1, \ldots, V_n)$ denotes the valuation $V_1 \cup \ldots \cup V_n$.

Definition 1 (Proposition Control Game). *A proposition control game is a tuple* $(Agent, \mathbb{P}, \pi, S_1, \ldots, S_n, Goal)$*, where*

1. *$Agent = \{1, \ldots, n\}$ is a set of agents.*
2. *$\mathbb{P}$ is a finite set of propositional variables.*
3. *$\pi : Agent \mapsto 2^\mathbb{P}$ is a control assignment function such that $\{\pi(1), \ldots, \pi(n)\}$ forms a partition of $\mathbb{P}$.*
4. *For each agent i, $S_i \subseteq 2^{\pi(i)}$ is his strategy set.*
5. *$Goal = \{Goal_1, \ldots, Goal_n\}$ is a set of weighted formulas of $L_\mathbb{P}$. Each $Goal_i$ is a finite set $\{\langle x_1, m_1 \rangle, \ldots, \langle x_k, m_k \rangle\}$ where $x_j \in L_\mathbb{P}$ and m_j is a real number representing the weight of x_j.*

A strategy for agent i is a $\pi(i)$-valuation. Note that since $\{\pi(1), \ldots, \pi(n)\}$ forms a partition of $\mathbb{P}$, a strategy profile $s = (s_1, \ldots, s_n)$ is a valuation for $\mathbb{P}$. Agents' utilities are induced by their goals. For every agent i and every strategy profile s, $u_i(s) = \Sigma\{m_j : \langle \phi_j, m_j \rangle \in Goal_i, s \models \phi_j\}$. Agent's preference over strategy profiles is induced by his utility function: $s \leq_i s'$ iff $u_i(s) \leq u_i(s')$. Let $s = (s_1, \ldots, s_n)$ be a strategy profile, we use s_{-i} to denote the projection of s on $Agent - \{i\}$: $s_{-i} = (s_1, \ldots, s_{i-1}, s_{i+1}, \ldots, s_n)$ and s_i to denote the projection of s on i's strategy.

In a proposition control game, an agent's strategy set is a **subset** of the power set of the propositional variables he can control. This is why proposition control game are computational easier than Boolean game. For the sake of tractability, we sacrifice the super-succinctness of Boolean game and use proposition control game instead.

Example 1. *Let $G = (Agent, \mathbb{P}, \pi, S_1, S_2, Goal)$ where $Agent = \{1, 2\}$, $\mathbb{P} = \{p, q, r, s\}$, $\pi(1) = \{p, r\}$, $\pi(2) = \{q, s\}$, $S_1 = \{\{p, r\}, \{p\}, \{r\}\}$, $S_2 = \{\{q, s\}, \{q\}, \{s\}\}$, $Goal_1 = \{\langle p \leftrightarrow q, 1 \rangle, \langle s, 2 \rangle\}$, $Goal_2 = \{\langle p \wedge q, 2 \rangle, \langle \neg s, 1 \rangle\}$. This is depicted as:*

	$+q, +s$	$+q, -s$	$-q, +s$
$+p, +r$	$(3, 2)$	$(1, 3)$	$(2, 0)$
$-p, +r$	$(2, 0)$	$(0, 1)$	$(3, 0)$
$+p, -r$	$(3, 2)$	$(1, 3)$	$(2, 0)$

2.2   Input/Output Logic

In I/O logic, a norm is an ordered pair of formulas $(a, x) \in L_{\mathbb{P}} \times L_{\mathbb{P}}$. Two types of norms are used in I/O logic, obligatory norms and permissive norms. An obligatory norm $(a, x) \in O$ is read as "given a, x is obligatory". A permissive norm $(a, x) \in P$ is read as "given a, x is permitted". We further assume obligatory norms are attached with a priority relation $\geq$, which is reflexive, transitive and total. $(a, x) \geq (a', x')$ is understood as (a, x) has higher priority than (a', x'). We further extend the priority relation to permissive norms: every permissive norm has the same priority and it is strictly lower than any obligatory norm. We call $N = (O, P, \geq)$ a normative system.

Obligatory norms O can be viewed as a function from $2^{L_{\mathbb{P}}}$ to $2^{L_{\mathbb{P}}}$ such that for a set A of formulas, $O(A) = \{x \in L_{\mathbb{P}} : (a, x) \in O \text{ for some } a \in A\}$. [12] define the semantics of I/O logic from out_1 to out_4 for obligatory norms as follows:

- $out_1(O, A) = Cn(O(Cn(A)))$.
- $out_2(O, A) = \bigcap\{Cn(O(V)) : A \subseteq V, V \text{ is complete}\}$.
- $out_3(O, A) = \bigcap\{Cn(O(B)) : A \subseteq B = Cn(B) \supseteq O(B)\}$.
- $out_4(O, A) = \bigcap\{Cn(O(V)) : A \subseteq V \supseteq O(V), V \text{ is complete}\}$.

Cn is the classical consequence operator of propositional logic, and a set of formulas is complete if it is either maximal consistent or equal to $L_{\mathbb{P}}$. I/O logic is given a proof theoretic characterization. An ordered pair of formulas is derivable from a set O iff (a, x) is in the least set that extends $O \cup \{(\top, \top)\}$ and is closed under a number of derivation rules. The following are the rules used by [12] to define out_1 to out_4:

- SI (strengthening the input): from (a, x) to (b, x) whenever $b \vdash a$.
- WO (weakening the output): from (a, x) to (a, y) whenever $x \vdash y$.
- AND (conjunction of the output): from (a, x) and (a, y) to $(a, x \wedge y)$.
- OR (disjunction of input): from (a, x) and (b, x) to $(a \vee b, x)$.
- CT (cumulative transitivity): from (a, x) and $(a \wedge x, y)$ to (a, y).

The derivation system based on the rules SI, WO and AND is called $deriv_1$. Adding OR to $deriv_1$ gives $deriv_2$. Adding CT to $deriv_1$ gives $deriv_3$. The five rules together give $deriv_4$. In [12], $x \in out_i(O, a)$ iff $(a, x) \in deriv_i(O)$, for $i \in \{1, 2, 3, 4\}$ is proven.

[14] introduces a formation of prioritized I/O logic. In [14]'s, the priority relation over norms is lifted to priority over sets of norms. [14] uses the lifting originally introduced by [6]: $O_1 \succeq O_2$ iff for all $(a_2, x_2) \in O_2 - O_1$ there is $(a_1, x_1) \in O_1 - O_2$ such that $(a_1, x_1) \geq (a_2, x_2)$. Let $N = (O, P, \geq)$ be a normative system and A, C be two sets of formulas. [14] define prioritized I/O logic as follows: for $i \in \{1, 2, 3, 4\}$,

$$x \in out_i^p(O^{\geq}, A, C) \text{ iff } x \in \bigcap\{out_i(O', A, C) : O' \in preffamily_i^d(O^{\geq}, A, C)\}.$$

Here $preffamily_i^d(O^{\geq}, A, C)$ is defined via the following steps:

1. $maxfamily_i(O, A, C) = \{O' \subseteq O : out_i(O', A) \cup C$ is consistent, and $out_i(O'', A) \cup C$ is not consistent, for every $O' \subsetneq O''\}$.
2. $filterfamily_i(O^{\geq}, A, C)$ is the set of norms $O' \in maxfamily_i(O, A, C)$ that maximize the output, i.e., that are such that $out_i(O', A) \subsetneq out_i(O'', A)$ for no $O'' \in maxfamily_i(O, A, C)$.
3. $preffamily_i(O^{\geq}, A, C)$ is the set of $\succeq$-maximal elements of $filterfamily_i(O, A, C)$.
4. $preffamily_i^d(O^{\geq}, A, C)$ is the set of elements O' of $preffamily_i(O^{\geq}, A, C)$ stripped of all the pairs (a, x) such that $out_i(O', A) = out_i(O' - \{(a, x)\}, A)$.

We simplify [14]'s prioritized I/O logic as follows:

Definition 2.

$$x \in out_i^p(O^{\geq}, A, C) \; iff \; x \in \bigcap\{out_i(O', A) : O' \in preffamily_i(O^{\geq}, A, C)\}$$

Here $preffamily_i(O^{\geq}, A, C)$ is defined via the following two steps:

1. $maxfamily_i(O, A, C)$ is the same as in [14]'s definition.
2. $preffamily_i(O^{\geq}, A, C)$ is the set of $\succeq$-maximal elements of $maxfamily_i(O^{\geq}, A, C)$.

We drop $preffamily_i^d$ because our main concern is whether a formula x is in $out_i^p(O^{\geq}, A, C)$, $preffamily_i^d$ has no effect on whether $x \in out_i^p(O^{\geq}, A, C)$. We use the following example to illustrate why we delete $filterfamily_i$.

Example 2. *Let $O = \{(f, d), (d, a)\}$ where f means I have fever, d denotes that I go to my doctor, and a means I make an appointment with him. Let $(d, a) > (f, d)$. Put $A = \{f \wedge \neg a\}$ and $C = A$. Intuitively, I should go to an hospital and not to my doctor. Using [14]'s original definition, we have $d \in out_3^p(O^{\geq}, A, C)$, which prescribes me to go to my doctor without an appointment. Such behavior fulfills a lower obligation (f, d) meanwhile creates a violation of a higher obligation (d, a). Using our simplified definition, we have $d \notin out_3^p(O^{\geq}, A, C)$, which gives more socially acceptable prescription.*

In the setting of prioritized normative system, we choose negative and static positive permission from [13] and reformulate them as follows:

Definition 3. *Given a normative system $N = (O, P, \geq)$ and as set of input A,*

1. $NegPerm_i(N, A) = \{x \in L_{\mathbb{P}} : \neg x \notin out_i^p(O^{\geq}, A, \emptyset)\}$.
2. – If $P \neq \emptyset$, then $StaPerm_i(N, A) = \{x \in L_{\mathbb{P}} : x \in out_i^p((O \cup \{(a', x')\})^{\geq}, A, \emptyset)$, for some $(a', x') \in P\}$.
   – If $P = \emptyset$, then $StaPerm_i(N, A) = out_i^p(O^{\geq}, A, \emptyset)$.

We consider amoral agents as willing to commit as less obligations as possible. We choose the weakest out_1 to be the logic for amoral agents. Moral agents tends to accepts those slightly debatable rules of normative reasoning. We choose out_4 to be the logic for moral agents. Negatively/positively impartial agents classify actions according to whether they are negatively/positively permitted. Since the rule OR involves uncertainty and vagueness, out_2 seems to be not suitable for positively impartial agents. Thus, we choose out_3 for positively impartial agents and out_2 for negatively impartial agents.

3   Normative Status

We use a proposition control game to represent a multi-agent system.

Definition 4 (Normative Multi-agent System). *A normative multiagent system is a tuple (G, N, E, ρ) where*

- $G = (Agent, \mathbb{P}, \pi, S_1, \ldots, S_n, Goal)$ *is a proposition control game.*
- $N = (O, P, \geq)$ *is a finite normative system.*
- $E \subseteq L_{\mathbb{P}}$ *is the environment, which is a finite set of formulas representing facts.*
- $\rho : Agent \mapsto \{1, 2, 3, 4\}$ *is an agent type assignment function which assigns each agent a unique ethical type.*

Strategies are classified as moral, positively legal, negatively legal or illegal.

Definition 5 (Moral, Legal and Illegal Strategy). *Given a normative multi-agent system (G, N, E, ρ), a strategy $(+p_1, \ldots, +p_m, -q_1, \ldots, -q_n)$ is:*

- *moral: if $p_1 \wedge \ldots \wedge p_m \wedge \neg q_1 \wedge \ldots \wedge \neg q_n \in out_k^p(O^{\geq}, E, \emptyset)$.*
- *positively legal: if $p_1 \wedge \ldots \wedge p_m \wedge \neg q_1 \wedge \ldots \wedge \neg q_n \in StaPerm_k(N, E)$.*
- *negatively legal: if $p_1 \wedge \ldots \wedge p_m \wedge \neg q_1 \wedge \ldots \wedge \neg q_n \in NegPerm_k(N, E)$.*
- *illegal: if $\neg(p_1 \wedge \ldots \wedge p_m \wedge \neg q_1 \wedge \ldots \wedge \neg q_n) \in out_k^p(O^{\geq}, E, \emptyset)$.*

Example 3. *Let (G, N, E, ρ) be a normative multi-agent system as follows:*

- $G = (Agent, \mathbb{P}, S_1, S_2, \pi, Goal)$ *is a proposition control game with*
  - *$Agent = \{1, 2\}$, $\mathbb{P} = \{p, q\}$,*
  - *$\pi(1) = \{p\}$, $\pi(2) = \{q\}$, $S_1 = \{\{p\}, \emptyset\}$, $S_2 = \{\{q\}, \emptyset\}$,*
  - *$Goal_1 = \{\langle p \wedge q, 1 \rangle\}$, $Goal_2 = \{\langle p \vee q, 1 \rangle\}$,*
- $N = (O, P, \geq)$ *where $O = \{(\top, p)\}$, $P = \{(\top, q)\}$, $\geq = \emptyset$.*
- $E = \emptyset$, *and both 1 and 2 are type-1 agents.*

	$+q$	$-q$
$+p$	$(1, 1)$	$(0, 1)$
$-p$	$(0, 1)$	$(0, 0)$

$out_1(O, E) = Cn(\{p\}) = out_1^p(O^{\geq}, E, \emptyset)$, $StaPerm_1(N, E) = Cn(\{p, q\})$. *The normative status of $+p, +q, -q, -p$ is respectively moral, positively/negatively legal, illegal.*

Having defined the normative status of strategies, we now study the complexity of some decision problems related to normative reasoning and normative status.

Theorem 1. *Given a normative multi-agent system (G, N, E, ρ), deciding whether a type-k agent strategy $(+p_1, \ldots, +p_m, -q_1, \ldots, -q_n)$, is moral is Π_2^p complete.*

Corollary 1. *Given a normative multi-agent system* (G, N, E, ρ), *a type-k agent and his strategy* $(+p_1, \ldots, +p_m, -q_1, \ldots, -q_n)$,

1. *deciding whether this strategy is illegal is* Π_2^p *complete.*
2. *deciding whether this strategy is negatively legal is* Σ_2^p *complete.*

Theorem 2. *Given a normative multi-agent system* (G, N, E, ρ), *a type-k agent and his strategy* $(+p_1, \ldots, +p_m, -q_1, \ldots, -q_n)$ *deciding whether this strategy is positively legal is* Π_2^p *complete.*

Corollary 2. *Given a normative multi-agent system* (G, N, E, ρ), *a type-k agent and his strategy* $(+p_1, \ldots, +p_m, -q_1, \ldots, -q_n)$, *deciding the normative status of* $(+p_1, \ldots, +p_m, -q_1, \ldots, -q_n)$ *is* Σ_2^p *hard and in* $\Delta_3^p = P^{\Sigma_2^p}$.

4   Ethical Agents

Different types of agents change their preference in different ways. Informally:

1. Amoral agents prefer strategy profiles with higher utility; for two profiles of the same utility, the one containing the strategy of higher normative status is preferred.
2. Moral agents prefer strategy profiles containing the strategy of higher normative status; for two profiles of the same status, the with higher utility is preferred.
3. Negatively impartial agents classify strategies into negatively legal category and illegal category; then they rank the strategies using utility within the two categories.
4. Positively impartial agents classify strategies into positively and not-positevely legal category; then they rank the strategies using utility within the two categories.

Given a normative multi-agent system, it induces a normative proposition control game by changing the preference of agents.

Definition 6 (Normative Proposition Control Game). *Given a normative multi-agent system* (G, N, E, ρ) *where* $G = (Agent, \mathbb{P}, \pi, S_1, \ldots, S_n, Goal)$, *it induces a normative proposition control game* $G^N = (Agent, \mathbb{P}, \pi, S_1, \ldots, S_n, \prec_1, \ldots \prec_n)$ *where* $\prec_i$ *is the preference of i over strategy profiles such that*

1. *if i is type-1 (amoral), then* $s \prec_i s'$ *if*
   - $u_i(s) < u_i(s')$, *or*
   - $u_i(s) = u_i(s')$ *and the normative status of* s_i' *is higher than that of* s_i.
2. *if i is type-2 (negatively impartial), then* $s \prec_i s'$ *if*
   - s_i *is illegal (not negatively legal) and* s_i' *is negatively legal, or*
   - *both* s_i *and* s_i' *are illegal and* $u_i(s) < u_i(s')$, *or*
   - *both* s_i *and* s_i' *are negatively legal and* $u_i(s) < u_i(s')$.
3. *if i is type-3 (positively impartial), then* $s \prec_i s'$ *if*

374   X. Sun and L. Robaldo

- s_i is not positively legal and s_i' is positively legal, or
- both s_i and s_i' are not positively legal and $u_i(s) < u_i(s')$, or
- both s_i and s_i' are positively legal and $u_i(s) < u_i(s')$.

4. if i is type-4 (moral), then $s \prec_i s'$ if
    - the normative status of s_i' is higher than that of s_i, or
    - the normative status of s_i' is equal to s_i and $u_i(s) < u_i(s')$.

Theorem 3. *Given a normative multi-agent system (G, N, E, ρ), an agent i and two strategy profiles s and s', deciding whether $s \prec_i s'$ is in Δ_3^p.*

Definition 7 (Normative Nash Equilibrium). *Given a normative multi-agent system (G, N, E, ρ), a strategy profile s is a normative Nash equilibrium if it is a Nash equilibrium in the normative proposition control game G^N.*

Theorem 4. *Given a normative multi-agent system (G, N, E, ρ) and a strategy profile s, deciding whether s is normative Nash equilibrium is in Δ_3^p.*

5   Conclusion and Future Work

In this paper we adopt a proposition control game and I/O logic approach to normative multi-agent systems. We distinguish four ethical types of agents, which use different I/O logic for normative reasoning and different procedures to change their preference. Such preference change create normative proposition control games and notions like normative Nash equilibrium are then introduced. We study some complexity issues related to normative reasoning/status and normative Nash equilibrium.

The contribution of this paper is twofold: on the conceptual side, we give a formal characterization of four ethical types of agents. On the technical side, we present some complexity results of normative reasoning with respect to prioritized I/O logic. All the complexity results in this paper are intractable, we leave it as future work to find tractable fragments. We conjecture that if we restrict every formula that appears in I/O logic to be a conjunction of literals, then all decision problems studied in this paper is tractable. Such restricted prioritized I/O logic has similar expressive power to the logic of abstract normative systems [7], as well as defeasible deontic logic [9]. A detailed comparison between these logic is also left as future work.

References

1. Ågotnes, T., van der Hoek, W., Rodríguez-Aguilar, J.A., Sierra, C., Wooldridge, M.: On the logic of normative systems. In: Proceedings of the 20th International Joint Conference on Artificial Intelligence, Hyderabad, India (2007)
2. Alechina, N., Dastani, M., Logan, B.: Reasoning about normative update. In: Proceedings of the 23rd International Joint Conference on Artificial Intelligence, Beijing, China (2013)

3. Boella, G., van der Torre, L., Verhagen, H.: Introduction to the special issue on normative multiagent systems. Auton. Agents Multi-Agent Syst. **17**(1), 1–10 (2008)
4. Bonzon, E., Lagasquie-Schiex, M., Lang, J., Zanuttini, B.: Compact preference representation and boolean games. Auton. Agents Multi-Agent Syst. **18**(1), 1–35 (2009)
5. Bonzon, L., Lagasquie-Schiex, M., Lang, J., Zanuttini, B.: Boolean games revisited. In: Proceedings of 17th European Conference on Artificial Intelligence, Riva del Garda, Italy (2006)
6. Brass, S.: Deduction with supernormal defaults. In: Brewka, G., Jantke, K.P., Schmitt, P.H. (eds.) NIL 1991. LNCS, vol. 659, pp. 153–174. Springer, Heidelberg (1993)
7. Colombo Tosatto, S., Boella, G., van der Torre, L., Villata, S.: Abstract normative systems: semantics and proof theory. In: Principles of Knowledge Representation and Reasoning, pp. 358–368 (2012)
8. Gabbay, D., Horty, J., Parent, X., van der Meyden, R., van der Torre, L. (eds.): Handbook of Deontic Logic and Normative Systems. College Publications, London (2014)
9. Governatori, G., Olivieri, F., Rotolo, A., Scannapieco, S.: Computing strong and weak permissions in defeasible logic. J. Phil. Logic **42**(6), 799–829 (2013)
10. Harrenstein, P'., van der Hoek, W., Meyer, J., Witteveen, C.: Boolean games. In: Proceedings of the 8th Conference on Theoretical Aspects of Rationality and Knowledge. Morgan Kaufmann Publishers Inc (2001)
11. Herzig, A., Lorini, E., Moisan, F., Troquard, N.: A dynamic logic of normative systems. In: Proceedings of the 22nd International Joint Conference on Artificial Intelligence, Barcelona, Spain (2011)
12. Makinson, D., van der Torre, L.: Input-output logics. J. Philos. Logic **29**, 383–408 (2000)
13. Makinson, D., van der Torre, L.: Permission from an input/output perspective. J. Philos. Logic **32**, 391–416 (2003)
14. Parent, X.: Moral particularism in the light of deontic logic. Artif. Intell. Law **19**(2–3), 75–98 (2011)
15. Shoham, Y., Tennenholtz, M.: On social laws for artificial agent societies: Off-line design. Artif. Intell. **73**(1–2), 231–252 (1996)
16. Wooldridge, M.: An Introduction to MultiAgent Systems, 2nd edn. Wiley, New York (2009)

Agent-Based Simulation and Agent Programming

Human-in-the-Loop Simulation
of a Virtual Classroom

Jesper Nilsson and Franziska Klügl[✉]

School of Science and Technology, Örebro University, Örebro, Sweden
jrn1989.jn@gmail.com, franziska.klugl@oru.se

Abstract. As technology for virtual reality becomes more and more accessible, virtual reality based training becomes a hot topic as an application environment for multiagent systems. In this contribution, we present a system that connects a game engine with a BDI platform for simulating a group of listeners that may be believable enough for serving as a virtual audience for training gestures and body language while teaching.

1 Introduction

Virtual reality forms an interesting substrate for e-learning systems not just in distance learning applications or educational role-playing games. While military training systems were a kind-of early applications of risk-free and fully controllable environments, e-learning has discovered virtual environments enabling training experiences in a huge variety of domains (see [11] for a short review). In this contribution, we present a prototypical system for testing and training body language when speaking in front of an audience. The main addressees are teaching and research students who often have no chance to properly train their non-verbal behavior and style of presenting, experiencing how a group of listeners behaves differently in reaction to a particular posture or gestures. Rehearsing a talk in front of a simulated audience is without risk in the sense that the opinion or virtual agent is not important for the speaker. Also potential fatigue of the audience is not an issue. The group's reaction is fully controlled: if not wanted, there are no emergent group dynamics.

However, the audience behaviour cannot be trivial imposing challenges on the used agent architecture. When decoupling the simulation engine from the visualization game engine, we can integrate complex behaviour models that may generate required non-trivial agent behaviour with sophisticated visualization. Hereby, BDI agent architectures turned out to be a good starting point, offering a rather light-weight way of formulating flexible, and complex agent behaviour.

In the following, we will first discuss related work in more detail, also including a short analysis of requirements. After a description of the overall system, we indicate the particular way of using the BDI agent architecture integrating personality and abstract emotions in Sect. 5. Section 6 describes the set-up and results from a few initial experiments. The contribution ends with a short discussion of initial experiences and outlook to future work.

© Springer International Publishing Switzerland 2016
M. Rovatsos et al. (Eds.): EUMAS 2015/AT 2015, LNAI 9571, pp. 379–394, 2016.
DOI: 10.1007/978-3-319-33509-4_30

2   Virtual Reality-Based Training

Virtual Reality based training can be found in many variants, with commercial, academic and other applications. It is far beyond the scope of this contribution to attempt any form of a comprehensive review. Virtual reality may support training of special abilities or manoeuvres - such as in emergency medicine or for rescue operations. Even more than physical activities, Virtual Reality based training systems address behaviour. That means, a human immersed in the Virtual Reality system may train for example appropriate reactions in critical situations, e.g. when reacting to verbal attacks, managing a crowd or rescue management etc. In this contribution, we discuss a first prototype coupling agent-based simulation and a 3D game engine for training non-verbal aspects of lectures.

Also for this application area, one can find recent works. One example is *TeachLivE*[1]. It consists of a 3D virtual environment with "simulated" students which are actually controlled by human players invisible to the human interacting with them. Related studies are by Poeschl and Doering [22] and Slater et al. [25]. They deal with practising in front of virtual agents to overcome fear of public speaking. Poeschl and Doering discuss designing a realistic virtual audience based on observations of the behaviour of a real life audience. Slater et al. concentrate on the "presence response" as a metric for the efficiency of a virtual environment. Ideally the perceived level of presence should be equal to that of the real world. One interesting finding was that even with a low level of representational and behavioral fidelity in the virtual agents, the presence response was quite high. The training scenario in the TARDIS project [3] was a job interview. A human interacts with a virtual recruiter. The focus was not on an elaborated model of the recruiter agent, but on automated analysis of the test person's state so that a maximum of useful advice could be given. Tools for emotion detection and other signals, developed in this project, can be very helpful also in our scenario for enabling the virtual students to react to multi-modal signals from the human "teacher".

We did not find research that focused on modelling the simulated audience. Focus was put on how to use such a system, not how such a system can be built. In the following we concentrate on architectures to be used for human listener models as well as how to couple such an architecture to a visualization platform. We start by analysing requirements for the overall agent behaviour.

3   Human Behaviour Modelling

Considering artificial audiences, the following qualities can be postulated for believability partially derived from B. Hayes-Roth's [12] and others' discussion:

- There must be an intrinsic motivation for activities beyond reactions to external triggers. Believability of behaviour needs autonomy. A consequence is that agents need to possess pro-activity for behaviour without external trigger [5].

---

[1] http://teachlive.org.

- The virtual students exhibit heterogeneity. Behaviour should be typical and realistic for the situation. Consistent individual activities with different reactions by different agents to the same signal are necessary. An observer may attribute these differences to personality.
- Display of emotions forms an important feature for believability [7]. Heterogeneity not just concerns underlying personality types, but also relates to dynamism. Agents react in different ways to the same input over time. They shall possess some state that allows a situation to escalate. The overall dynamics shall emerge without being scripted. Emotions form a good basis for modelling this time-dependency and modifications of behaviour.
- The behaviour should not be fully predictable to a human observer. That means fully rational optimizing behaviour is not appropriate, but some reduced form of unpredictability might end up in interesting effects. So, simple variations related to for example how often a gesture is repeated or how fast the character moves, are not enough.
- The virtual characters shall also interact with each other and not just to the teacher. That means simply duplicating one agent is not enough.
- The behaviour just needs to appear believable for the experiments. The agents do not need to fully reproduce human behaviour and reasoning in other scenarios.
- The agents should be able to adapt their behaviour not just in reaction to what other agents did, but also with respect to the human "in the loop". If there is a human presenter or teacher, the virtual agents should react to his/her gestures, actions, etc. It is not sufficient to pre-define more or less sophisticated behaviour, but the agent should display some feedback to the involved human.

It may appear surprising that aspects related to graphics and life-like visualization are not listed. We assume that consistent believable behaviour forms the essential ingredient – given a sufficient level of realism in visualization. This is also supported by our experiments. None of the human subject remarked existing flaws in the visualization, although there were obvious problems with e.g. agents standing in tables; the actual behaviour in interaction with the human was decisive.

We assume that a simple rule- or script-based architecture of the individual agents is not sufficient to produce behaviour satisfying those characteristics with reasonable modelling effort. Inventing a new architecture was out of question considering the huge variety of existing ones. In the following, we discuss agent architectures, that have already been used for controlling virtual characters in computer games or Virtual-Reality based training.

3.1 Cognitive Agent Architectures

Cognitive Architectures are special in the overall landscape of agent architectures that has been traditionally coined more using terms like deliberative, reactive, social or hybrid (see [32]). Cognitive architectures as used in general artificial intelligence are not only used to build intelligent agents, but concretize theories of human cognition: "a cognitive architecture provides a concrete framework for more detailed modelling of cognitive phenomena, through specifying essential structures, divisions of modules, relations between modules and a variety of other essential aspects" [28]. That means they are based on assumptions and models how humans reason, organize memory etc. that are at least partially validated by experiments, interviews, etc.

Over the years, a number of those cognitive architectures have been suggested. In Soar cognitive processes as well as processes that determine behaviour are based on search in specific "problem spaces" that organize long-term memory in sets of rules. An elaborated decision making process either directly identifies rules relevant for the current context or selects another problem space to identify rule ranking, effect of actions, etc. This is combined with a learning process compiling new rules form solved problems.

Soar has been used for controlling virtual characters as opponents or collaborators for human players in virtual reality game and training settings for some time: QuakeBot [15] for controlling a non-player character in games and in later versions also for modelling opponents in military training scenarios [33] or TacAirSoar agents [29] for steering a plane in virtual manoeuvres with mixed human and agent formations.

To our knowledge, ACT-R [2] has not been used for virtual agents to the same extent as SOAR. ACT-R also forms a unified architecture aiming at human cognitive processes for reproducing phenomena known from cognitive psychology. Its overall set-up is modular reflecting hypotheses on modular brain functionality. It is based on hybrid approaches combining declarative and procedural knowledge processing, symbolic and sub-symbolic representations.

There are a number of other architectures for resembling human behaviour that are at least partially grounded in psychological literature. PSI developed by D. Dörner [10], as well as its implementation in MicroPSI [6], is based on sub-symbolic motive representation. OpenPSI [9] forms an implementation of the PSI theory based on OCP architecture combining uncertain logic representation and processing with approaches from computational linguistics, evolutionary learning and connectionist attention. CLARION [27] explicitly distinguishes between procedural knowledge that is represented sub-symbolically and declarative knowledge that is based on symbolic representation and explicit reasoning. A special focus is put on learning techniques to acquire these different knowledge types.

These cognitive architectures have in common that they combine various representations in different memory modules with complex reasoning processes to a unified architecture. However, for our aim it would have been not feasible to use one of those architectures given only limited resources. In the following, we will discuss architectures that are capable of producing believable behaviour of virtual characters without the claim to resemble real human cognition and reasoning.

Recently, more and more models involving social behaviour for capturing group dynamics have been published in agent-based simulation – an area in which there is a clear need for transparent, theoretically grounded but feasible agent architectures. Modelling and simulation frameworks as presented in [31] specifically aim at testing crowd behaviour models with emergent group-level behaviour patterns. It might be an interesting line of research to test the applicability of such frameworks also in the domain addressed here.

3.2 Elements and Architectures for Believable Agents

In the area of Intelligent Virtual Agents, many approaches exist for creating life-like characters that generate believable behaviour [24]. Clearly, a focus is on appearance and visualization-related aspects, generating realistic facial expressions or gestures coherent with emotions that the agents shall express. Already [7], Bates et al. illustrated how many and which components an architecture for a generally believable agent needs, even if it is "just" a virtual cat. Emotional dynamics are hereby based on a sort of reaction to success or not of its action (measured along some "standards"). Attitudes towards other agents and events as well planned behaviour are also captured. Similarly also *PMFserv* was prominently developed for behaviour generation of believable virtual characters combining diverse functionality. Due to the wealth of incorporated components, this architecture appears to be as sophisticated as the cognitive ones described above.

For emotions and personality rather established and psychologically grounded models exist: Already the virtual cat of J. Bates et al. was based on the OCC model ([20] after [26]). The main idea is that emotions result from mental reactions to consequences of events, actions of agents (others and own) and aspects of objects. The OCC model elaborates positive and negative emotions depending on whether the consequence, etc. was expected or not and whether the agent sees it positive or negative. The OCC model is meanwhile widely used for creating emotions in virtual characters.

Personality appears to be a good approach to systematically express heterogeneity between virtual agents. Instead of randomly chosen parameter settings or behavior details, it better to combine them into a consistent "personality". Due to its economic and coaching value, many basic concepts expressing traits that combine to a personality have been proposed. In virtual agents the model of the big five factors [18] appears to be prominent. This model assumes that five basic traits (Openness, Conscientiousness, Extraversion, Agreeableness and Neuroticism) make up the personality of a human. It is purely descriptive based on a large volume of empirical work. Yet, there are only few agent architectures that integrates personalities in generic way.

BDI architectures seem to be agent architectures that are also used for virtual characters. The central idea is that goals and the plans for achieving those goals are two separate categories in the reasoning of the agent. Most BDI architectures – mostly descendants of PRS [13] – do not plan from first principles, but select and configure pre-defined activity descriptions that may contain subgoals, actions, branching or loops explicitly capturing the procedural knowledge of the agents. There are many research works that use BDI architectures for controlling virtual agents, such as [19,30], also several extensions for emotions or personalities have been suggested (e.g. [21]).

L. Antunes et al. [4] recently published very interesting conceptual considerations on enhancing goal-driven behaviour as used in BDI. They suggested to use more elaborated desire acquisition processes for generating socially realistic behaviour of simulated agents. An operationalisation of their approach – when available – might form an interesting alternative to the BDI-based architecture we used in the following. Clearly, in agent-based social simulation, we will find a wider range of agent architectures that might be suitable in our project context. A thorough search and evaluation will be part of our future work.

For our first tests, we selected to start with a basic BDI architecture as it allows for pro-active behaviour based on intrinsic motivations. Heterogeneity can be easily expressed. The architecture is flexible enough to also embed variations in the behaviour of an individual agent, as well as simple interactions between agents. Another important reason for selecting an BDI-based approach was the availability of convenient tools for implementing. However, although we could produce reasonable agent behaviour within a rather short time, the level of its genericness appears to be too high and we will continue testing other architectures. A relevant element of future research will hereby focus on architecture that involve predictions of how the human might react to actions.

4 Classroom Scenario

4.1 Information Flow

Figure 1 illustrates the overall set-up and information flow. Agents behaviour is visualized in some virtual reality display. Such a display can be a sufficiently large screen, a Cave or some modern VR device like Oculus Rift or similar. A human is immersed in the set-up and his or her behaviour is detected using suitable sensors. The sensor abstract raw data to information that steers an avatar representing the human in an agent-based simulation. The avatar is interacting with other simulated agents during a running simulation which is coupled to real-time for producing an appropriate impression for the advance of time. Each of the simulated agents connects to a virtual character in visualization. With today's technology, one may assume that all involved systems are sufficiently fast including reaction time of the simulated agents. Latency for communication between different systems is not relevant as usually reaction times do not need to be as fast as possible, but just result in a realistic impression.

4.2 Architectural Concept

There are two general approaches to connect an agent control architecture to a game engine, in case one does not want to re-implement the behaviour control within the game engine loop. The main difference consists in the representation of the environment: either there is an explicitly simulated environment that is

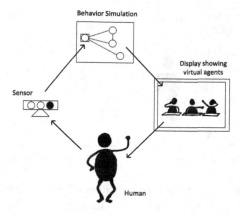

Fig. 1. Overall information flow in a system for training non-verbal behaviour with simulated listener agents

mapped to the virtual one including all agents that it contains being mapped to corresponding agents or there is just one representation of the environment in which complex agents with "external" reasoning capabilities are placed.

An elaborated middleware such as proposed by [16] or [30] transforms sensor data into percepts as input for the agent reasoning. The reasoning outputs high-level actions that are then transformed into control instructions for execution by the virtual characters' body situated in the virtual environment. Sensing, action and interactions happen in the Virtual World that is accessed by elaborated interfaces between intelligent behaviour generation and the virtual characters' body. Most systems mentioned in Sect. 3 use such a set-up. Those approaches are quite natural considering the analogy between physical and virtual reality environments and the physicalness of embodied agents.

We take a different approach that simplifies modelling interactions between agents and between agents and their environment keeping both on the same level of abstraction. Figure 2 illustrates the differences between both approaches. We basically double the environment and relevant entities for avoiding complex transformations in the interface between agents and their environment. The simulated agents interact with and in a simulated environment. All relevant events are triggered in the simulated environment. The virtual reality system serves merely for visualization purposes based on commands that inform the virtual character about what its corresponding agent is actually doing and translating that into gestures, facial expressions, etc. Clearly, those commands must be augmented with specific parameters for determining speed of a gesture, gazing directions, etc. Assuming that visualization can be created basically from existing 3d Object Models with given animations, handling behaviour within one system leads to simplified overall system development.

The commands for visual behaviour (movements, gestures, etc.) must contain specific symbols such as WaveRightHand or ExpressJoy triggering a particular

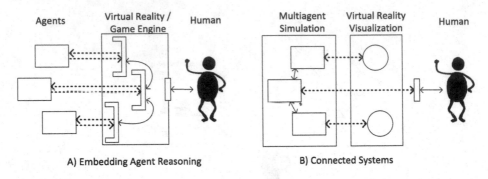

Agents | Virtual Reality / Game Engine | Human | Multiagent Simulation | Virtual Reality Visualization | Human

A) Embedding Agent Reasoning   **B) Connected Systems**

Fig. 2. Types of architectural for integrating multi-agent systems and virtual reality. The critical questionis where interaction between agents (as well as between agents and their environment) is actually happening.

gesture in a humanoid character model. The symbols must be understandable in a way that the visualization system can match it with a particular animation of the character model for e.g. raising the right arm and waving with it or setting up a facial expression for joy. Luckily, virtual characters and their animations are often reusable in the same domain. For example, the object models that we used in this work were developed at the University of Augsburg for a library of object models to be used in multiple projects.

In the overall system, the loop between visualization and simulation is not directly closed. Using a generic connection to the simulator for parsing strings sent to individual agents from software outside the simulator, we directly integrated sensor information into the simulation. Information form the sensor controls an avatar in the simulation, thus the simulated agents' perception of and interaction with the teacher happens completely within the simulated environment. The avatar does not decide about actions that then manipulate the environment itself, it simply displays what the user did.

Such a general set-up was previously suggested for advanced visualization with the vision to create a platform for "immersive" validation [17]. In this project, a rich environment was not as essential as flexible and intelligent agent programs. We selected JASON [8] which appears to be currently the most elaborated, documented and easy to use open source BDI system.

4.3   Tools and Technicalities: JASON

JASON[2] [8] is a JAVA-based multiagent system platform around an interpreter of AgentSpeak(L) programs. AgentSpeak(L) is a BDI architecture with clear logics-based semantics. The interpreter takes care of handling agent's belief and hierarchical plans and based on this, of action selection. A plan forms a piece of procedural knowledge consisting of specification of the triggering events (newly added/deleted percept, incoming messages or establishment or abandonment of

---

[2] http://jason.sourceforge.net.

```
/* Initial beliefs and rules */
posture(sit).
contentment(25).
mood(best) :-
    contentment(C) &
    C > 75.
mood(better) :-
    contentment(C) &
    C <= 75 &
    C > 50.
...
/* Initial goals */
/* Plans */
...
+spokenTo[source(Source)] : true
    <- .drop_all_intentions;
    !modifyContentment(25);
    .wait(500);
    lookAt(Source);
    .wait(2000);
    expressSadness(1);
    lookAtCamera.

+hitByObject : true
    <- .drop_all_intentions;
    !modifyContentment(25);
    .wait(1800);
    lookAtPaper;
    expressSurprise(1);
    scratchHead(1);
    .wait(2000);
    lookAtCamera.
...
```

Fig. 3. Excerpt from a behaviour program of a nervous student agent

goals), the context in which the plan is applicable and the actual sequence of
goals and actions that needs to be executed for achieving the plan. Goals can
be the achievement a particular state or testing whether a particular condition
holds. There is a number of built-in actions, for example for updating the belief
base or sending messages to other agents. Domain specific actions can be added
on the JAVA level elaborating the environmental model. Thus, an agent program
consists of initial beliefs and goals, belief update rules and a set of plans that
may be organized in multiple plan hierarchies. Figure 3 shows a snippet from an
example behaviour of one of our agents. Thus, JASON provided the possibility
to do fast prototyping of sophisticated agent behaviour in a human-readable
form. Technically it works as an Eclipse plugin which enables easy JAVA-related
extensions.

In contrast to full agent-based simulation platforms, predefined structures
for the environmental model and the embodiment of the agents in JASON are
quite rudimentary. Thus, we derived a specific environment class that manages
additional representations of agents' bodies containing the relevant "physical"
information such as position, orientation, current facial expression, gesture and
focus point. Domain specific actions are dispatched by the environment and
update the agents' body model. With a given frequency, updated information
about what animations to display, etc. is send to the agents' corresponding virtual agent in the game engine. The human teacher has a simple, corresponding

agent in JASON that regularly updates information about the gesture that the human performed last receiving it from the sensor. Depending on such a incoming belief, the teacher agent sends corresponding messages to the other audience agent.

4.4 Tools and Technicalities: Horde3D Game Engine and Connection Components

Visualization was done using the Horde3D Game Engine[3] with extensions that we developed previously for connecting to an agent-based simulation platform as sketched in [14]. The Horde3d Game Engine was and is developed at the University of Augsburg, Germany. It is an open source, light weight and conceptually clean game engine on top of a graphics engine with the same name. The component responsible for connecting the external behaviour control to the game engine's characters is based on proprietary strings sent via a socket connection containing information on what needs to be changed in the characters' display. The Horde3D component parses the string and executes the changes. Control of delays and parameters of execution (speed, repetitions of gestures, etc.) are determined by the behaviour control. Also the component that recognizes human gestures via the Kinect sensor is an existing component of the Game Engine.

5   Listener Behaviour

The central aspect of our research was not just doing a hardware and software set-up but actually creating believable audience behaviour using this for testing how far one can come with such simple means.

5.1   Action Repertoire and Interactions

In the agent plans, actions could be used that correspond to gestures and other actions displayed by the 3d characters in the visualizing Game Engine. Agents could stand up, turn, write, nudge or approach their neighbours, shake their heads, show a number of gestures such as pointing to the watch, move the hand to the head in a thinking gesture, etc. Also facial expressions for emotions were included, yet not really well recognizable in the visualization. Other students in the classroom however, could not miss-understand agents' actions and facial expressions as they perceived within the (high-level) simulation platform. Thus, no interpretation was necessary; they were transmitted as clear symbols in messages between agents. Only the human teacher could miss-interpret what the agents displayed.

In a similar way, a set of pre-defined gestures could be recognized via the Kinect sensor. Once the gesture was sent to the agent simulation system, all agents had the same understanding. There were a number of miss-interpretations

---

[3] http://www.hcm-lab.de/projects/GameEngine/.

of human gestures, as recognition was not perfect, but in those situations all audience members miss-understood what the human wanted to convey in the same way.

5.2 Emotions and Personalities

Two options were used to individualize the audience agents: emotions and personality. Inspired by the OCC model, we designed every agent to have a numeric variable expressing some general form of "contentment" with its individual situation. This can be basically seen as a one-dimensional appraisal model of emotion: Each event, that means each perception or incoming messages has an effect on the level of this variable, its value is increased or decreased. So for example, if an agent is approached by one of its neighbours, the contentment level is modified by certain number. The number, and actually whether it is increased or decreased depend on the agents' particular personality. The contentment forms both a modulator of how often a gesture action is done or also determining which gesture is selected as a reaction to an event. For our implementation in Jason, this means: The numeric variable is abstracted into a categoric statement like "mood(bad)", which is then used as context for plan selection.

Yet, integrating emotional behaviour alone does not produce sufficient individualism. Agents need to exhibit more particularities than what can be expressed by for example different start values for the contentment level. The interaction in this project is not rich enough for that compared to conversation-oriented scenarios as interaction is solely based on gestures and postures of the teacher, and on approaches or attacks from other agents. As discussed above, equipping the agents with personality appears to be the gold standard for individualism. We selected only a few personalities that we assumed to challenge a teaching situation. Without further elaboration, we choose to model agents on the positive and negative extreme of extraversion, neuroticism and non-agreeableness. Together they might form a "good" audience for training non-verbal reactions to student behaviour. Yet, this is clearly a decision that needs further grounding in pedagogical and psychological research. The personalities cause differences in the agent programs, formulated in a quite ad hoc way. Simulated students with different personalities react to different incoming events, for example a "timid" student reacts to hardly any gesture and also continues ignoring its neighbours approaching it. A nervous student will also not react to its neighbours in a meaningful way, but becomes more and more uneasy, the longer the teacher is inactive, eventually disturbing other agents. A hostile student agent shows aggression towards its neighbours and reacts with an angry expression to many interactions from other students, but also to most gestures of the human teacher. Extravert students were designed so that they interact frequently with their neighbours and are quite active especially when the human is inactive. We added more than one hostile and extravert personality making additional differentiation in parameters, durations but also in a few events that they react that others ignore. In the final scene there are one timid, one nervous, two hostile and four extravert students. If there is no activity from the teacher identified, the situation escalates.

A critical aspect in developing those agents' personality and behaviour was the parametrisation of the dynamics of the "contentment" variable. There are clearly a lot of ways to extend and improve the agent programs for the different agent personalities. Also the repertoire of gestures that the student agent react to can be extended as well as the reactions could be much more sophisticated. We see that as a starting point for further developments in collaboration of the pedagogic department in Örebro. Despite of the shortcomings in the behaviour definitions, we tested how human subjects would react to the virtual agents audience and conducted experiments for getting an impression how humans would rate the realism of the virtual audience.

6   Experiments

6.1   Experimental Set-Up

Using the configuration described above, we exposed 16 subjects to two sub-experiments. In the first one, the task was to observe a more and more escalating situation without teacher interaction (the sensor was not turned on, so the teacher agent was observed to be inactive by the student agents over the duration of that experiment). So, the subject could concentrate in observing and evaluating the behaviour of the simulated audience. Figure 4 shows how the situation looked like at the start of the experiment and how it could look like at the end. The behaviour of the agents is not scripted, so the final situation was slightly different in each of the experiments even without interactions with the human teacher. For the second experiment, the subjects were informed about the gestures that the system could recognize, yet not how the agents would react to those gestures. The subjects' task was to keep the groups' attention. Both experiments lasted 5 min.

a) Typical situation at the start of experiment 1   b) Typical situation after 5 minutes without "teacher" interaction

Fig. 4. Scenarios during the observation experiment. These are screenshots from two different runs; gender and cloth of the virtual agents were randomized.

After each sub-experiment the subjects were asked to fill a questionnaire. There were only slight variations between the two questionnaires: They contained three groups of questions: (1) General question on the perceived realism of the scenario; (2) questions on the experienced emotions during participating the experiment and (3) open questions for feedback. The idea behind those questions was first to get a general evaluation and to check whether the subjects would perceive variations between the simulated students in a way that could allow them to identify the students' personalities. Emotional reactions of the subjects indicate that they experienced some form of presence. The rationale behind giving twice almost the same questionnaire was to find out whether interaction changes the evaluation that the subject gives.

The experiment were performed with 16 subjects recruited mostly from PhD students, Postdocs and Lecturers at the computer science, mathematics and technology departments at Örebro University. 6 of the subjects were female, 10 male. All had teaching experience; 10 subjects stated experience with games involving some form of motion capturing.

6.2 Results

In the following we only show the most interesting results concerning overall believability (Fig. 5). There is a tendency that subjects find the audience more realistic when they just observe rather than interact. We observed that some of the subjects spent some time in "testing" gestures systematically.

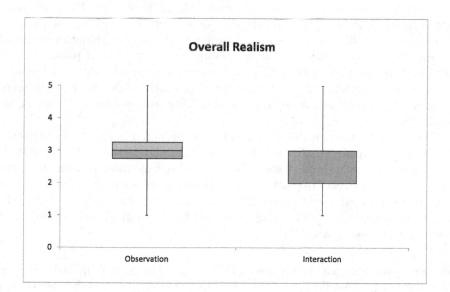

Fig. 5. Answers on the question "How would you rate the overall realism of the agents' behaviour?" with 1 as "Not realistic at all" to 5 as "very realistic".

Interestingly, some subjects also expressed emotional reaction in the first experiment in which they were told not to interact with the audience. So, some limited form of presence could be seen because the students reacted to the missing actions of the teacher - more and more interactions among the audience occurred, most of the agents turned away from the teacher which was what the subjects expected them to do as the teacher remained inactive. Some teachers felt stressed as they were not allowed to intervene. Despite of the limited gesture repertoire, the most subjects felt that they could influence the students and were in control of the situation. In the open questions, many subjects expressed the need for more modes of interaction.

Heterogeneity of student behaviour was well recognized - both between students as well as over time; yet hardly any subject could identify the particular personalities displayed.

7   Discussion and Future Work

The experiments – although far from providing us with statistically significant results – show that it is possible to set up such a human-in-the-loop system with a virtual audience using rather simple, existing technology. Clearly, we just tested for believability of agent behaviour. For actually testing potential training effects, much more has to be invested from improvements in the gesture recognition to visualization that is fine-grained enough for enabling the reliable perception of the characters' emotions. The behaviour and especially the reaction to the teachers' actions need to be improved to be more realistic; Currently only limited tuning was done. We did actually not expect that subjects rate realism higher than they did, yet we assumed positive effects of enabling interaction. The question remains, what is the minimum necessary level of plausibility of audience behaviour and interaction so that the non-verbal behaviour training for teachers is useful? Addressing this question must be clearly the next step. A better selection of gestures and actions that the teacher can do, would be an essential for that.

Whether more realistic group behaviour (as proposed in [23]) or augmenting BDI reasoning with reasoning about emotions (e.g. [1]) have to be integrated, is a consequence of this next step. Is it necessary to develop simulated students who not just react to gestures, but intentionally drive the human teacher mad? Technology-oriented research in this project has set a first step, but without a wealth of tests and extensions grounded in pedagogical and psychological research, it is done in vain.

Acknowledgement. The authors would like to thank Elisabeth André and her group at the University of Augsburg - in particular Michael Wissner - for their support with the Horde 3D Game Engine as well as with providing the 3d Object models for the virtual students and the scenario visualization.

References

1. Adam, C., Lorini, E.: A BDI emotional reasoning engine for an artificial companion. In: Corchado, J.M., et al. (eds.) PAAMS 2014. CCIS, vol. 430, pp. 66–78. Springer, Heidelberg (2014)
2. Anderson, J.R.: Rules of the Mind. Erlbaum, Hillsdale (1993)
3. Anderson, K., et al.: The TARDIS framework: intelligent virtual agents for social coaching in job interviews. In: Reidsma, D., Katayose, H., Nijholt, A. (eds.) ACE 2013. LNCS, vol. 8253, pp. 476–491. Springer, Heidelberg (2013)
4. Antunes, L., Nunes, D., Coelho, H.: The geometry of desire. In: Proceedings of the 13th International Conference on Autonomous Agents and Multiagent Systems, AAMAS 2014, Paris, France, pp. 1169–1172, May 2014 (2014)
5. Avradinis, N., Panayiotopoulos, T., Anastassakis, G.: Behavior believability in virtual worlds: agents acting when they need to. SpringerPlus 2, 246 (2013)
6. Bach, J.: MicroPsi 2: the next generation of the MicroPsi framework. In: Bach, J., Goertzel, B., Iklé, M. (eds.) AGI 2012. LNCS, vol. 7716, pp. 11–20. Springer, Heidelberg (2012)
7. Bates, J., Lyall, A.B., Reilly, W.S.: An architecture for action, emotion, social behavior. In: Castelfranchi, C., Werner, E. (eds.) MAAMAW 1992. LNCS, vol. 830, pp. 55–68. Springer, Heidelberg (1994)
8. Bordini, R.H., Hübner, J.F., Wooldridge, M.: Programming Multi-agent Systems in AgentSpeak using Jason: A Practical Introduction with Jason. Wiley, Chichester (2007)
9. Cai, Z., Goertzel, B., Zhou, C., Huang, D., Ke, S., Yu, G., Jiang, M.: OpenPsi: a novel computational affective model and its application in video games. Eng. Appl. Artif. Intell. 26, 1–12 (2013)
10. Dörner, D.: Bauplan für eine Seele. Rowohlt, Reinbeck (1999)
11. Eschenbrenner, B., Nah, F.F., Siau, K.: 3-d virtual worlds in education: applications, benefits, issues, and opportunities. J. Database Manag. 19(4), 91–110 (2008)
12. Hayes-Roth, B.: What makes characters seem life-like. In: Prendinger, H., Ishizuka, M. (eds.) Life-Like Characters, Cognitive Technologies, pp. 447–462. Springer, Heidelberg (2004)
13. Ingrand, F.F., Georgeff, M.P., Rao, A.S.: An architecture for real-time reasoning and system control. IEEE Expert Intell. Syst. Appl. 7(6), 34–44 (1992)
14. Klügl, F., Wissner, M., Timpf, S., Andre, E.: Bridging virtual world visualization and multiagent simulation (extended abstract). In: Proceedings of the 11th Scandinavian Conference on Artificial Intelligence, Trondheim, May 2011, pp. 191–192 (2011)
15. Laird, J.E., Duchi, J.C.: Creating human-like synthetic characters with multiple skill levels: a case study using the soar quakebot. In: AAAI 2000 Fall Symposium Series: Simulating Human Agents, November 2000 (2000)
16. Lee, J., Baines, V., Padget, J.: Decoupling cognitive agents and virtual environments. In: Dignum, F., Brom, C., Hindriks, K., Beer, M., Richards, D. (eds.) CAVE 2012. LNCS, vol. 7764, pp. 17–36. Springer, Heidelberg (2013)
17. Louloudi, A., Klügl, F.: Immersive face validation: a new validation technique for agent-based simulation. In: Federated Conference on Computer Science and Information Systems (FedCSIS), pp. 1255–1260 (2012)
18. McCrae, R.R., John, O.P.: An introduction to the five-factor model and its application. J. Personality 60(2), 175–215 (1992)

19. Norling, E.: On evaluating agents for serious games. In: Dignum, F., Bradshaw, J., Silverman, B., van Doesburg, W. (eds.) Agents for Games and Simulations. LNCS, vol. 5920, pp. 155–169. Springer, Heidelberg (2009)
20. Ortony, A., Clore, G.L., Collins, A.: The Cognitive Structure of Emotions. Cambridge University Press, Cambridge (1988)
21. Parunak, II.V.D., Bisson, R., Brueckner, S., Matthews, R., Sauter, J.: A model of emotions for situated agents. In: Proceedings of AAMAS, Hokodate, Japan, pp. 993–996 (2006)
22. Poeschl, S., Doering, N.: Virtual training for fear of public speaking–design of an audience for immersive virtual environments. In: Virtual Reality Short Papers and Posters (VRW), pp. 101–102. IEEE (2012)
23. Prada, L., Paiva, A.: Teaming up humans with autonomous synthetic characters. Artif. Intell. **173**, 80–103 (2009)
24. Prendinger, H., Ishizuka, M. (eds.): Life-Like Characters. Springer, Heidelberg (2004)
25. Slater, M., Pertaub, D.-P., Barker, C., Clark, D.: An experimental study on fear of public speaking using a virtual environment. Cyberpsychol. Behav. **9**(5), 627–633 (2006)
26. Steunebink, B.R., Dastani, M., Meyer, J.-J.C.: The OCC model revisited. In: Reichart, D. (ed.) Proceedings of the 4th Workshop on Emotion and Computing, KI 2009, Paderborn (2009)
27. Sun, R.: Learning, action and consciousness: a hybrid approach toward modelling consciousness. Neural Netw. **10**(7), 1317–1331 (1997)
28. Sun, R., Coward, L.A., Zenzen, M.J.: On levels of cognitive modeling. Philos. Psychol. **18**(5), 613–637 (2005)
29. Tambe, M., Johnson, W.L., Jones, R.M., Koss, F., Laird, J., Rosenbloom, P.S., Schwamb, K.: Intelligent agents for interactive simulation environments. AI Mag. **16**(1), 15–39 (1995)
30. van Oijen, J., Dignum, F.: Towards a design approach for integrating BDI agents in virtual environments. In: Vilhjálmsson, H.H., Kopp, S., Marsella, S., Thórisson, K.R. (eds.) IVA 2011. LNCS, vol. 6895, pp. 462–463. Springer, Heidelberg (2011)
31. Wijermans, N., Jorna, R., Jager, W., van Vliet, T., Adang, O.: CROSS: modelling crowd behaviour with social-cognitive agents. J. Artif. Soc. Soc. Simul. **16**(4), 1 (2013)
32. Wooldridge, M.: An Introduction to Multiagent Systems, 2nd edn. Wiley, Chichester (2009)
33. Wray, R.E., Laird, J.E., Nuxoll, A., Stokes, D., Kerfoot, A.: Synthetic adversaries for urban combat training. In: Proceedings of the 16th Conference on Innovative Applications of Artifical Intelligence, IAAI 2004, pp. 923–930. AAAI Press (2004)

Applying Agent Based Simulation to the Design of Traffic Control Systems with Respect to Real-World Urban Complexity

Andreea Ion, Cristian Berceanu, and Monica Patrascu[✉]

Department of Automatic Control and Systems Engineering,
University Politehnica of Bucharest, Bucharest, Romania
{andreea.ion,monica.patrascu}@acse.pub.ro

Abstract. The problem of reducing traffic congestion in a city has always been difficult to solve with monolithic control methods, which have both high costs and increased implementation complexity. This paper aims to minimize vehicle waiting time at stoplights by using a multi-agent system control technology. Moreover, the system is required to respond adequately to the presence of emergency intervention vehicles, allowing them quick and sure passage, but without significantly interrupting regular traffic. The solution designed in this paper allows for on demand synchronization of intersections, depending on the traffic context at any given time. In order to test this concept, an agent based simulation model has been developed, that offers real world traffic simulations on urban maps, and integrated complex road networks and traffic participant behaviour, with a possibility to measure the performance of the control system through parameters such as noise levels and emissions.

Keywords: Agent based simulation · Urban traffic congestion · Traffic control systems · Distributed control systems

1 Introduction and Related Work

Transportation and traffic systems represent a core element in the socio-economical development, dealing with the flow of persons and goods, on local as well as global level. The advance of technology has expanded into all areas of human activity and urban transport and traffic systems are no exception, but they come with both advantages and disadvantages. Intelligent Transport Systems (ITS) have been introduced to solve the latter, from minimizing pollution and congestion of roads, to increasing population safety. Emergency intervention vehicles [1] enter this category, bringing forth issues of optimal travel times [2] from their departure point to the affected areas [3]. In the often high traffic situations of urban environments, ensuring fast and easy access of such crews can become a matter of preserving human life [4]. Hence, a Smart City ITS is required to incorporate specifications related to emergency response systems.

To integrate emergency vehicles in ITS, different implementation strategies have been approached. An example of such a solution is based on Dijkstra algorithms [5]

© Springer International Publishing Switzerland 2016
M. Rovatsos et al. (Eds.): EUMAS 2015/AT 2015, LNAI 9571, pp. 395–409, 2016.
DOI: 10.1007/978-3-319-33509-4_31

and evolution strategies to find an optimal route within a given short time period, with the addition of a combined communication between cars by sending signals that could help avoiding collisions. Another approach presented in the project Emergency Vehicle Priority refers to overriding traffic lights in favor of response units [6].

Intelligent transportation systems vary, in what concerns the applied technologies they use, from basic management systems like vehicle navigation systems [7], traffic light control [8], management & monitoring systems, signs with dynamic message displays, applications for automatic recognition of registration number, video cameras for recording driving velocity (CCTV systems), to advanced systems which integrate real-time data and responses from a number of sources [9], such as parking guidance and information systems, meteorological information etc. Nevertheless, the considerable progress in telecommunications and information technology, with radio frequency identification, microchips, smart technologies in sensor networks [10], has strengthened the technical capabilities that facilitate the development of intelligent transportation systems.

In order to develop such systems, starting from design, and all the way to implementation and monitoring, a very important phase is testing and validation. Without it, the efficiency and viability of a proposed solution can not be quantified, and the development costs would climb exponentially. For this, proper modelling and simulation tools are necessary in order to ensure the most accurate representations of real world systems and in order to obtain relevant data for the problem at hand.

As such, since ITS are inherently complex systems, then complex models are the most natural choice. From this category, one of the most versatile technologies are agent based [11–13]. In this paper, we focus on applying agent based simulation models to the design of traffic control systems, taking into account the presence of emergency vehicles in urban traffic.

2 Problem Description

The importance of agent based technology has increased due to the ability of solving complex real-world problems in a flexible and modular way. The agent based perspective offers a strong and effective suite of tools for analysis, design, simulation, and implementation of simple or complex systems. Thus, Agent Based Simulation Models (ABSM) can describe complex systems by using agents that are relatively simple, and by constructing global behaviours through rules of interaction between them. This is a useful tactic for modelling traffic systems, which can have a high analytical and computational cost.

There are two issues that need to be considered here. First, for a distributed system like urban traffic, the most suitable model would be also implicitly distributed. Second, an ITS is decomposable, distributed geographically, with large amounts of data circulating between the component entities. Thus, the top-down control design approach is not feasible, requiring decentralized control strategies.

With these in mind, turning to ABSM in order to aid the design process of urban traffic control systems is beneficial.

An agent based model is a computational or simulation representation of a real world system or process, in which a series of entities (agents) placed in an environment interact based on a set of rules. In an ABSM, an agent is an open system defined by inputs (data from the environment and from other agents), outputs (actions toward the environment, and data to other agents), feedback (data used to regulate the agent internally, allowing it to change its state), internal state (the representation of the agent's behaviour), internal rules that govern the agent behaviour.

The ABSM is thus a multi-agent system, which in turn is defined by ABSM inputs (from designers/engineers/users, interface parameters), ABSM outputs (the results of the simulation, displaying either the effects of the system as it is left to operate in the given environment, or the effects of unexpected events inserted as disturbances during simulation), ABSM state (the cumulative state of the multi-agent system comprised of the states of all its component agents, but viewed from a higher observation point) and ABSM rules (interaction rules between component agents).

The problem considered in this paper deals with a traffic control system in an urban area which needs to be fluid and free of congestion. In addition, these requirements need to be fulfilled even when emergency vehicles appear in traffic, disturbing the regular flow due to increased priority. Increasing the complexity of the problem, we have also imposed that the emergency vehicles be let through intersections with minimal waiting time, meaning that the control system itself needs to re-adjust its behaviour in order to comply with this request.

3 Design Concept

To address these problems, this paper describes a simulation model based on cooperative agents. The aims of the agent based simulation are to reduce the waiting time at traffic lights in controlled intersections, increase the traffic flow in large areas. It is important that the proposed solution reduce (or at least not increase) greenhouse gases emissions and fuel consumption. The system must be able to detect and facilitate access of emergency vehicles avoiding problems that might arise. The probability of collisions, either due to rapid change of traffic light color from yellow to red or because of emergency vehicles, must be reduced.

For this, we have developed an ABSM that includes:

(a) a world model (environment) using real urban maps;
(b) the models of the traffic participants, both regular and emergency;
(c) a multi-agent control system based on cell agents.

All component agents, their behaviours and rules of interaction, along with implementation details are described in the following sections.

The cell agent concept is aligned with CitySCAPE, a framework for design of complex urban systems in Smart Cities. This agent structure is introduced in [14], where only its aggregation mechanism is presented. The novelty of this paper is the application of cell agents to the development of distributed control systems, taking into account specific issues of multi-agent systems, such as synchronization, negotiation and collaboration.

A cell agent is used for implementing or modelling control systems. When used for the former, its components are devices (sensors, actuators, microcontrollers etc.), while when used for the latter, its components are, in turn, virtual simple agents that emulate these devices. In simulation, a cell agent is a multi-agent system in itself, but through the interactions between its components, it can easily reproduce the behaviour of real world control systems.

A generic cell agent for simulation is defined as:

$$\langle \cdot \rangle = \{D_I, D_S, D_A, N\} \tag{1}$$

a set of inference entities D_I (either software agents or hardware devices), sensing entities D_S (either software agents or hardware devices), and acting entities D_A (either software agents or hardware devices), organized around a nucleus agent N.

Naturally, when using the cell in an ABSM, the sensing agents emulate sensors and transducers, the acting agents model actuators and effectors, while the inference agents run the control algorithms and elaborate commands and decisions. The nucleus is an agent that can aggregate cells (can compose the control system on demand), disintegrate them when they've served their purpose, assign tasks to the other agents in the cell, receive objectives to be accomplished by their cell, and communicate•with other nuclei for more complex operations like collaboration/cooperation/coordination (for example, synchronization of intersections).

Figure 1 illustrates the components of a cell agent for simulation, along with the data exchange between them: y_d environmental data, y processed data, u computed commands/decisions, m executed actions, O cell objective of controlling an intersection, $T_{1,2,3}$ desired tasks according to objectives (the task of a sensing agent is to collect traffic data, process it, and transmit it to the inference agent, whose task is in turn to elaborate control decisions based on the received data and transmit it to the acting agents, who in turn are tasked with executing the command).

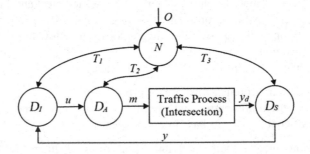

Fig. 1. Cell agent configuration

The entirety of cell agents in a considered urban area form part (c) of the ABSM, namely the control system part, which is organized on three levels, based on the complexity of the agents: (c.1) device level: cell components; (c.2) intersection control system level: cell agents; and (c.3) distributed traffic control system level: the collection of cell agents in a considered urban area.

With this structure, the traffic control system can be modelled and simulated for testing both the interactions within the local control loops in individual intersections, but also for testing the global behaviour of the entire system.

4 Preliminary Considerations for Implementation

To reduce waiting time in intersections and increase traffic flow in large areas a (co-operative) multi-agent system was designed. Each intersection will be modelled with a minimal cell agent [18] and they can cooperate when needed. The inference components of each cell will require a minimum time for yellow traffic light and a minimum time for green traffic light in order to reduce the probability of collisions. The designed agents are developed using JADE (Java Agents Development Environment) [15]. JADE is a software framework fully developed in Java programming language that simplifies the implementation of multi-agent systems through the offered features. Among them, JADE includes a set of software tools for troubleshooting and debugging. A system based on JADE can be distributed on several machines that do not have the same operating system and environment configuration can be changed at runtime [15].

The JADE environment has 3 types of special agents: (a) AMS (Agent Management System) - it can create or destroy agents, (b) DF (Directory Facilitator) - allows agents to register their services in 'Yellow pages', (c) RMA (Remote Agent Management) - interacts with AMS and DF to provide the user with useful data about the environment shown in a GUI.

From the many simulation solutions such as Aimsun [16], Matsui [17], or VisSim [18], for this approach we chose SUMO (Simulation of Urban Mobility) [19] because it is easy to use, it is open source, and has been used in various important projects such as: iTETRIS and COLOMBO [20], AIMTRAN [21], or DRIVE C2x [22].

SUMO is a free suite for traffic simulation and open source available since 2001, developed by the Institute of Transportation Systems in Berlin. The SUMO simulation platform offers a wide range of features including: microscopic simulation - vehicles, pedestrians and public transport; online interaction - control simulation with the TraCI interface; there are no artificial limitations in network size or the number of vehicles simulated.

Each SUMO simulation requires a map; the map can be either a map generated using SUMO with the *netgenerate* tool or a real map converted into a SUMO map type file. In this paper's traffic simulation model a real-world map is be used. The conversion is made by downloading and resizing the map of Romania or directly specifying geographic coordinates. Once downloaded, the map is edited using the JOSM application [23] and after editing, the *.osm* file is imported into the eWorld application [24] and from there exported in a SUMO map file format with the extension.*net.xml*. Traffic generation for a map is done using specific SUMO commands. Based on them, 500 random routes have been generated for the different vehicles and routes written and defined in an *.xml* file. This file contains simulation timestamps for every vehicle that appears on the map and follows the route assigned in file. The developed Java application communicates with the SUMO simulator through a TCP connection. Encoding and decoding the TCP packets sent and received by SUMO is done using TraCI4 J library. By choosing the above options, the proposed solution can have scalability (JADE allows distributing agents on multiple hosts as they communicate through TCP) and portability (Java can run on almost any platform) (Fig. 2).

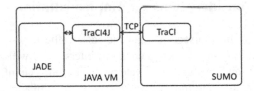

Fig. 2. Application structure and connections between components

The sampling period of the system is $T_e = 1$ s and, at every simulation step, useful data is stored and processed in MATLAB for analysis (graphic representation) and evaluation of the results.

5 Control System Development

5.1 Modelling Agents and Their Behaviours

Agents can be classified by their role in the implemented environment and their behaviours are described in what follows.

1. Type of agents with global simulation role

   - *Sim* (Simulator) - interacts with SUMO; it sends messages to Map agent in order to create the required agents for the simulation; it sends messages to sensors at each simulation step.
   - *Map* (Mapper) - sends a request to AMS agent to create other agents, whenever it receives a message from the *Sim* agent.
   - *Log* (Logger) - stores the simulation data received from *Sim* agent and exports the data at the end of the simulation.

2. Agents that can form cell agents

   As mentioned in Sect. 2, each cell agent part of the multi-agent system contains a nucleus agent N, a controller or inference agent D_I emulating the controller, an actuator agent D_A emulating the traffic lights ensemble, and at least one sensor agent D_S. Each intersection is mapped to a cell and each lane is mapped to a sensor agent. The cell can work independently or it can synchronize with other cells.

   Each agent can have multiple behaviours, and each behaviour runs on a thread. As shown in Fig. 3, each simulator agent thread interacts differently with other agents. For the *Sim* agent, there are three execution threads: Sim_T1 sends data d to sensor agents and to the logger agent every simulation step, Sim_T2 sends the traffic lights phases list pl to the controller agent on request, and Sim_T3 changes traffic lights colors upon actuator agent request (through command u).

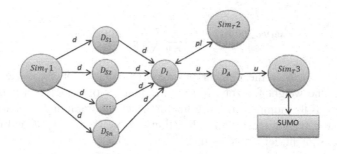

Fig. 3. Application structure and communication between components

5.2   Emergency Vehicles Management

In this ABSM, a phase is expressed as a (traffic lights state, time) pair and represents the amount of time the traffic lights at an intersection has a certain state. An intersection program is an ordered list of all phases at the intersection. Thus, any intersection has at least one program with at least 3 phases that changes cyclically. A primary phase is a phase for which all the traffic lights are green or red. A secondary phase is a phase for which there is at least one yellow traffic light.

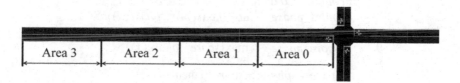

Fig. 4. Areas of a road

Figure 4 shows four areas of a street related to an intersection. The lengths of these areas are divided equally and are numbered from 0 to 3, counting from the closest area to intersection. Each sensor agent that corresponds to a lane sends to the inference agent the number and type of vehicles in each of the 4 areas of the lane. This approach will allow defining and computing a score for each phase setting as weights for each area of a road (Algorithm 1 presented in Fig. 5).

$$score\_sensor(x) = \sum_{i=0}^{N=3} w_i n_i(x) v_x \tag{2}$$

$$score\_phase(y) = \sum_{j=0}^{M} score\_sensor(x_j) \tag{3}$$

$$score\_phase(y) = \sum_{j=0}^{M} \left(\sum_{i=0}^{N=3} w_i n_i(x_j) v_{x_j} \right) \tag{4}$$

In Eqs. (2)–(4), N is the number of areas for each sensor, M is the number of sensors, W_i is the weight for zone i, $N_i(x)$ the number of vehicles in zone i for the x sensor and v_x is the number of directions for which the traffic light color is green. If $v_x = 0$ if traffic lights are red for all 4 directions, else $v_x = 2 \ [0, 4]\backslash \mathbf{Z}$ and the 4 travel directions are: straight, left, right or turn.

Data: k, t_{yellow}, $t_{min} \in \mathbf{Z}^+$, F_α, $f \in F_\alpha$
Input: $counter \in \mathbf{Z}$, $S(k)$
Result: $u(k) \in F_\alpha \cup F_\beta$

---

1 if *first u was not sent* then
2     $index\_phase \leftarrow \underset{x \in F_\alpha}{\arg\max}(score\_phase(x))$
3     $u(k) \leftarrow f \leftarrow phase(index\_phase) \in F_\alpha$
4     $counter \leftarrow t_{yellow}$
5     $send(u(k))$
6 else
7   if $counter = 0$ then
8        $index\_phase \leftarrow \underset{x \in F_\alpha}{\arg\max}(score\_phase(x))$
9        $score\_phase \leftarrow \underset{x \in F_\alpha}{\max}(score\_phase(x))$
10   if $score\_phase > score(f)$ then
11          $u(k) \leftarrow f \leftarrow phase(index\_phase) \in F_\beta$
12          $send(u(k))$
13   else
14          $counter \leftarrow -1$
15   else if $counter = t_{yellow}$ then
16       $u(k) \leftarrow f \in F_\alpha$
17       $send(u(k))$
18    $counter \leftarrow counter + 1$
19   if $counter > t_{min}$ then
20       $counter \leftarrow 0$

Fig. 5. Algorithm 1. Control algorithm for independent intersections

The algorithm developed to control an intersection is presented in Fig. 5, where k is the current simulation step, t_{yellow} the time that the traffic light should be yellow before changing to red expressed in seconds, t_{min} the minimum time to wait before changing the primary phase in seconds, $S(k)$ is the set of sensors in current cell at step k, F_α is the set of primary phases of the intersection, F_β is the set of secondary phases of the intersection, F is the last primary phase stage sent.

For example, for Fig. 4 there are 4 traffic lights that can have primary or secondary phases, for each road toward the intersection there is one sensor that measures the number of vehicles in each road area. Based on this measurement, a score is computed for each sensor (Eq. 2), which is the used to compute the score of the phase (Eqs. 3 and 4). At start, the phase is initialized and then sent to the actuator elements (Algorithm 1, lines 1–5). Then, it is checked if the phase needs to be changed (variable *counter* from algorithm 1) and, if the condition is met, a new set of phases is computed, the best is chosen and compared with the current one (Algorithm 1, lines 7–9). If the best computed phase is greater than the current one, the new phase is sent to the actuator elements.

5.3 Communication, Negotiation, and Synchronization

The communication between system components is very important. Reducing the network load is a current problem in networked control systems; therefore by using the cell agent concept, the impact of this problem is minimized. In this application, the communication is message based. The types of message that can exist within the network are based on FIPA communication messages. Their structure and definition are:

1. REQUEST: in Fig. 3, all interactions between agents (except the interaction between agents D_I and Sim_T2) are REQUEST type messages. The structure of the message, based on the sender and the receiver varies. This type of message can be sent between Simulator and D_S, Simulator and D_I, Simulator and *logger*, Simulator and *mapper*, D_I and leader, leader and D_I.
2. QUERY_REF: this type of message is sent by agent D_I to agent *Sim* in order to request the program of the intersection it controls.
3. INFORM_REF: at D_I agent's request, *Sim* agent replies with an INFORM_REF message containing the program of the controlled intersection (a list of intersection phases).
4. PROPOSE: message sent by a nucleus agent (*N*) to another nucleus agent (*N*) in order to propose cell synchronization.
5. ACCEPT_PROPOSAL: message sent by a nucleus agent (*N*) as a reply to another nucleus agent's synchronization request, if the request was accepted.
6. REJECT_PROPOSAL: message sent by a nucleus agent (*N*) as reply to another nucleus agent's synchronization request, if the request was rejected.
7. CONFIRM: message sent by a nucleus agent (*N*) to another nucleus agent (*N*) to confirm the synchronization.
8. INFORM: *DF* agent (from JADE environment) replies with an INFORM message as a reply to any agent's request concerning exposed services.

All messages are objects converted to strings for sending and strings converted to objects after receiving. Strings consist of field values separated by a colon character.

Sometimes, cell agents must synchronize with neighboring cells in order to avoid collisions. If each intersection is modelled through a cell agent, then the negotiation

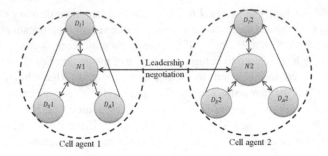

Fig. 6. Negotiation between two intersections (two cell agents)

process is realized between nuclei (Fig. 6), after which a leader is chosen. If the negotiation must be done between more than two cells, the CONFIRM message is sent to all cells in the synchronization group by the first nucleus that received an ACCEPT_PROPOSAL message.

After the negotiation is finished, each inference agent will compute the score of each phase in the intersection it controls and will sent the results to the leader controller. The leader cell agent evaluates the sum of scores for each phase and finds the index of the phase with the largest score using Eq. (5) and informs other cell agents about the result. In order to make the synchronization possible, all intersections must have the same number of phases in their program.

$$index = \arg\max_{i=\overline{0,N-1}} \left(\sum_{f \in F(i)} score\_phase(f) \right) \qquad (5)$$

where $F(i)$ is a set of all phases N from all cells i that participate to negotiation.

In this case, when the cells are synchronized, the control algorithm includes Eq. (5) in computing the *index_phase* (Fig. 7), where k is the current simulation step, t_{yellow} the time the traffic light color will be yellow before switching to red, t_{min} the minimum waiting time before switching the primary phase again, F_α is the set of primary phases of the intersection, F_β is the set of secondary phases of the intersection, f is the last primary phase stage sent. In this algorithm the *send*() function will send the command to the local actuator and to the other cells in the group.

Similar to Algorithm 1, in Algorithm 2 lines 1–5 represents the initialization of the traffic lights phases. It is checked if the phase needs to change (variable *counter*) and, if the condition is met, a new phase is computed for each cell agent (each intersection) that attended the negotiation process (Algorithm 2, lines 7–9). The best computed phase is compared with the current one and, if greater, the new phase is sent to the actuator elements (lines 10–12).

Considering the synchronization mode, the switching logic inside every inference component is represented in the Fig. 8.

In Algorithm 3 the data is the same as in algorithms 1 and 2. In addition, *leader_message* is the message received from the leader, *sensor_message* is the message received from a sensor. The *send()* function will send the command to the local actuator and the *update_data()* function will update the local data received from the sensors, will compute the current score for each phase and will inform the leader about the result.

Data: k, t_{yellow}, $t_{min} \in \mathbf{Z}^+$, F_α, $f \in F_\alpha$
Input: *counter* $\in \mathbf{Z}$
Result: $u(k) \in F_\alpha \cup F_\beta$

---

1 if *first u was not sent* then

2      $index\_phase \leftarrow \underset{x=0,N-1}{\arg\max} \left(\sum_{f \in F(i)} score\_phase(f) \right)$

3      $u(k) \leftarrow f \leftarrow phase(index\_phase) \in F_\alpha$
4      $counter \leftarrow t_{yellow}$
5      $send(u(k))$
6 else
7   if *counter = 0* then

8          $index\_phase \leftarrow \underset{x=0,N-1}{\arg\max} \left(\sum_{f \in F(i)} score\_phase(f) \right)$

9          $score\_phase \leftarrow \underset{x=0,N-1}{\max} \left(\sum_{f \in F(i)} score\_phase(f) \right)$

10   if *score_phase > score(f)* then
11             $u(k) \leftarrow f \leftarrow phase(index\_phase) \in F_\beta$
12             $send(u(k))$
13   else
14             $counter \leftarrow -1$
15   else if *counter = t_{yellow}* then
16         $u(k) \leftarrow f \in F_\alpha$
17         $send(u(k))$
18 $counter \leftarrow counter +1$
19 if *counter > t_{min}* then
20      $counter \leftarrow 0$

Fig. 7. Algorithm 2. Control algorithm for synchronized cells (leader)

Data: k, t_{yellow}, $t_{min} \in \mathbf{Z}^+$, F_α, F_β, $S(k)$
Input: *leader_message* $\in F_\alpha \cup F_\beta$, *sensor_message*

---

1 if *message_sender = leader* then
2     $send(leader\_message)$
3 else if *message_sender = sensor* then
4     $update\_data(S(k), sensor\_message)$

Fig. 8. Algorithm 3. inference agent cooperating with other cells

6   Case Study: University Politehnica of Bucharest Campus Map

The case study analyzed for this paper uses a real-world map (part of Bucharest) that includes University Politehnica of Bucharest, with an estimated area of 4.4 km^2.

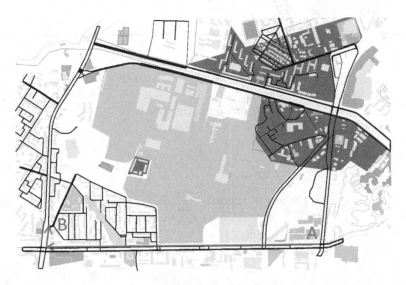

Fig. 9. Real-world map of University Politehnica of Bucharest campus and neighborhoods

For simulations some parameters were defined, the sampling time $T_e = 1$ s and the following model for vehicles: length 5 m, maximum speed 70 m/s, maximum acceleration 2.6 m/s^2, maximum braking deceleration 4.5 m/s^2, speed factor 1, HBEFA emissions model: "P_7_7". The speed factor is a multiplier for the maximum speed allowed on the street and the emissions model corresponds to a wide range of engines for vehicles [23].

Stored simulation data is exported to file at the end of simulation by the logger agent and the file data can be imported in MATLAB. The average noise emission of a vehicle at each simulation step is computed using Eq. (6) [25].

$$noise\_average[dB] = 10 \log_{10}\left(\frac{1}{N}\sum_{k=1}^{N} 10^{k/10}\right) \qquad (6)$$

In what follows the described simulation scenarios, the evaluation of the model is made by using a series of performance indicators (CO - carbon monoxide, CO_2 - carbon dioxide, HC - hydrocarbons, NOx - nitric oxides; PMx - particulate matter) particularly defined for SUMO. These indicators are evaluated relative to their measured values for the open loop system (without controllers). Thus, the effect that the control system has over the traffic process can be observed and quantified in terms of improvement (for instance emission reduction percentages), even if the indicators can be more or less true to life. In control engineering, this practice is common, as the dangers of simulation models of only approximately reflecting reality have to be always kept in mind during design. This is one of the well-known limitations of modelling in general and, by extent, of agent based models as well.

Scenario 1 – Reducing the Waiting Time for Vehicles at Traffic Lights. The simulation time is 3000 s. From start and until $t_0 = 1500$ s, a vehicle will appear every second on the map. Once the destination is reached by a vehicle it disappears from the map. All vehicle routes are written in an XML file previously generated, but the arrival time results from the simulation.

For this scenario, there are three groups of cells synchronized in order to avoid collisions. The other intersections are controlled independently. Controller parameter t_{yellow} is 4 s for all simulations using this map. The purpose of this scenario is to highlight the reduction of emissions and fuel consumption as an effect of reducing waiting time of vehicles at traffic lights (Table 1).

Table 1. Scenario 1 results: performance of controlled system vs. uncontrolled

	Fuel consumption	CO	CO_2	HC	NOx	PMx
$t_{min} = 10$ s reduction [%]	2.97	3.80	2.97	4.96	2.65	2.54
$t_{min} = 13$ s reduction [%]	3.18	4.07	3.18	5.27	2.86	2.78
$t_{min} = 18$ s reduction [%]	3.04	4.05	3.04	5.11	2.76	2.76
Average reduction [%]	3.06	3.97	3.06	5.11	2.76	2.69

Scenario 2 – Reducing Waiting Time for Emergency Vehicles. On the map, an ambulance will depart from point A to point B as shown in Fig. 9 at simulation step $k = 990$ and the travel distance is about 2100 m. The ambulance has the same model as the other vehicles, but it can exceed the maximum allowed speed on a street at most twice. The controller will no longer compute the phase score using Eq. (2); instead, it will force a primary phase change if needed, assigning a large number to the sensor score. The ambulance will be detected when it will be in zone 0 or zone 1.

Except in the case where $t_{min} = 18$ s, the emergency vehicle waiting time is significantly reduced. The exception has occurred because of the controller restriction to wait t_{min} seconds before changing the phase (Table 2).

Table 2. Reduced waiting time for the emergency vehicle

	Arrival time [s]	Average speed [km/h]
$t_{min} = 10$ s	123	61.5
$t_{min} = 13$ s	100	75.5
$t_{min} = 18$ s	142	53.3
Uncontrolled	134	56.4

Table 3. Results for scenario 2: performance of controlled system vs. uncontrolled

	Fuel consumption	CO	CO_2	HC	NOx	PMx
t_{min} = 10 s reduction [%]	2.90	3.60	2.90	4.87	2.56	2.40
t_{min} = 13 s reduction [%]	3.06	3.90	3.06	5.13	2.72	2.62
t_{min} = 18 s reduction [%]	3.23	4.13	3.23	5.32	2.91	2.84
Average reduction [%]	3.07	3.88	3.07	5.11	2.73	2.62

7 Conclusions

The environment is becoming more polluted, while the growing traffic congestion is making emergency vehicles travel difficult. These problems must be solved through a cheap and effective solution to be implemented at large scale.

In this paper, an agent based simulation model (ABSM) is presented for traffic control system design. The simulation results reveal that the waiting time of vehicles at traffic lights has been reduced, allowing them to arrive quicker at destinations, thus reducing emissions of greenhouse gases and fuel consumption. The results obtained are promising and the complexity of the inference components is reduced, as the implemented algorithms are simple and do not require floating-point operations. Reduced requirements for computation performance and recent advances in wireless sensor networks make possible a future implementation of such a system at low cost (Table 3).

The solution proposed in this paper can be improved by introducing new features like learning algorithms for inference components or adding pedestrian simulation scenarios.

References

1. de Boer, J.: An attempt at more accurate estimation of the number of ambulances needed at disasters in The Netherlands. Prehosp. Disaster Med. **11**(02), 125–128 (1996)
2. Blackwell, T.H., Kaufman, J.S.: Response time effectiveness: comparison of response time and survival in an urban emergency medical services system. Acad. Emerg. Med. **9**(4), 288–295 (2002)
3. Sladjana, A., Gordana, P., Ana, S.: Emergency response time after out-of-hospital cardiac arrest. Eur. J. Intern. Med. **22**(4), 386–393 (2011)
4. Pons, P.T., Haukoos, J.S., Bludworth, W., Cribley, T., Pons, K.A., Markovchick, V.J.: Paramedic response time: does it affect patient survival? Acad. Emerg. Med. **12**(7), 594–600 (2005)
5. Barrachina, J., Garrido, P., Fogue, M., Martinez, F.J., Cano, J.C., Calafate, C.T., Manzoni, P.: Reducing emergency services arrival time by using vehicular communications and evolution strategies. Expert Syst. Appl. **41**(4), 1206–1217 (2014)
6. White, J.: Emergency Vehicle Priority. In: The Queensland Surveying and Spatial Conference, Brisbane, Australia (2012)
7. Fiosina, J., Fiosins, M.: Resampling based modelling of individual routing preferences in a distributed traffic network. Int. J. Artif. Intell.™ **12**(1), 79–103 (2014)

8. de Oliveira, D., Bazzan, A.L.: Traffic lights control with adaptive group formation based on swarm intelligence. In: Dorigo, M., Gambardella, L.M., Birattari, M., Martinoli, A., Poli, R., Stützle, T. (eds.) ANTS 2006. LNCS, vol. 4150, pp. 520–521. Springer, Heidelberg (2006)
9. Wilkie, D., Sewall, J., Lin, M.C.: Transforming GIS data into functional road models for large-scale traffic simulation. IEEE Trans. Visual Comput. Graphics 18(6), 890–901 (2012)
10. Laitakari, J., Pakkala, D.: Dynamic context monitoring service for adaptive and context-aware applications. In: Eighth International Workshop on Applications and Services in Wireless Networks, 2008 ASWN 2008, pp. 11–19, October 2008
11. Jin, X., Jie, L.: A study of multi-agent based model for urban intelligent transport systems. Int. J. Adv. Comput. Technol. 4(6) (2012)
12. Chen, B., Cheng, H.H.: A review of the applications of agent technology in traffic and transportation systems. IEEE Trans. Intell. Transp. Syst. 11(2), 485–497 (2010)
13. Wang, N., Chen, Y., Zhang, L.: Design of multi-agent-based distributed scheduling system for bus rapid transit. In: 2011 International Conference on Intelligent Human-Machine Systems and Cybernetics (IHMSC), vol. 2, pp. 111–114. IEEE (2011)
14. Patrascu, M., Dragoicea, M., Ion, A.: Emergent intelligence in agents: a scalable architecture for smart cities. In: 18th International Conference on System Theory, Control and Computing (ICSTCC) 2014, pp. 181–186. IEEE (2014)
15. Jade. http://jade.tilab.com/, Accessed 01 Mar 2015
16. Casas, J., Ferrer, J.L., Garcia, G., Casas, J., Perarnau, J., Torday, A.: Traffic simulation with AIMSUN. In: Barceló, J. (ed.) ANTS 2006. International Series in Operations Research & Management Science, vol. 145, pp. 173–232. Springer, New York (2010)
17. Balmer, M., Rieser, M., Meister, K., Charypar, D., Lefebvre, N., Nagel, K., Axhausen, K.: MATSim-T: Architecture and simulation times. In: Multi-agent Systems for Traffic and Transportation Engineering, pp. 57–78 (2009)
18. Gomes, G., May, A., Horowitz, R.: Congested freeway microsimulation model using VISSIM. Transp. Res. Rec. J. Transp. Res. Board 1876, 71–81 (2004)
19. Krajzewicz, D., Erdmann, J., Behrisch, M., Bieker, L.: Recent development and applications of SUMO–simulation of urban mobility. Int. J. Adv. Syst. Meas. 5(3&4), 128–138 (2012)
20. Bellavista, P., Caselli, F., Foschini, L.: Implementing and evaluating V2X protocols over iTETRIS: traffic estimation in the COLOMBO project. In: Proceedings of the Fourth ACM International Symposium on Development and Analysis of Intelligent Vehicular Networks and Applications, pp. 25–32. ACM (2014)
21. Rodríguez, T., Urquiza, A., Klunder, G.A.: The Amitran project contribution to the validation of methodologies for assessment of Intelligent Transport Systems. In: Transport Research Arena (TRA) 5th Conference: Transport Solutions from Research to Deployment (2014)
22. Katsaros, K., Kernchen, R., Dianati, M., Rieck, D.: Performance study of a Green Light Optimized Speed Advisory (GLOSA) application using an integrated cooperative ITS simulation platform. In: 2011 7th International Wireless Communications and Mobile Computing Conference (IWCMC), pp. 918–923. IEEE (2011)
23. JOSM Project. https://josm.openstreetmap.de. Accessed 01 Nov 2015
24. eWorld Project. http://eworld.sourceforge.net. Accessed 01 Nov 2015
25. Goelzer, B., Hansen, C.H., Sehrndt, G.: Occupational Exposure to Noise: Evaluation, Prevention and Control. World Health Organisation, Geneva (2001)

Towards Smart Open Dynamic Fleets

Holger Billhardt[1], Alberto Fernández[1(✉)], Marin Lujak[1], Sascha Ossowski[1],
Vicente Julián[4], Juan F. De Paz[3], and Josefa Z. Hernández[4]

[1] CETINIA, University Rey Juan Carlos, Madrid, Spain
{holger.billhardt,alberto.fernandez,marin.lujak,
sascha.ossowski}@urjc.es
[2] DSIC, Universidad Politécnica de Valencia, Valencia, Spain
vinglada@dsic.upv.es
[3] BISITE, Universidad de Salamanca, Salamanca, Spain
fcofds@usal.es
[4] DIA, Universidad Politécnica de Madrid, Madrid, Spain
phernan@fi.upm.es

Abstract. Nowadays, vehicles of modern fleets are endowed with advanced devices that allow the operators of a control center to have global knowledge about fleet status, including existing incidents. Fleet management systems support real-time decision making at the control center so as to maximize fleet performance. In this paper, setting out from our experience in dynamic coordination of fleet management systems, we focus on fleets that are open, dynamic and highly autonomous. Furthermore, we propose how to cope with the scalability problem as the number of vehicles grows. We present our proposed architecture for open fleet management systems and use the case of taxi services as example of our proposal.

Keywords: Multiagent systems · Coordination · Open systems · Dynamic fleet management · Dynamic optimization

1 Introduction

The increase of human mobility and freight transportation in urban environments presents one of the challenges major urban cities in Europe and all over the world are faced with in today's society. It is one of the causes of congestion problems, inefficiencies in logistics and energy use, and air pollution in modern cities [1, 2]. To approach this challenge, innovative transportation solutions are required that allow for a more efficient use of resources (vehicles, energy resources, roads, etc.) but that assure at the same time flexible mobility solutions for both citizens and freight distribution. The idea of smart cities presents new challenges and requires new solutions related to traffic and transport. As a direct result, in the last years more and more systems that promote the shared use of vehicles have begun to emerge [3]. Solutions like public bicycle services, bike or car sharing systems, or applications like UBER, providing taxi services through "free" drivers, have the objective to improve human mobility and at the same time

© Springer International Publishing Switzerland 2016
M. Rovatsos et al. (Eds.): EUMAS 2015/AT 2015, LNAI 9571, pp. 410–424, 2016.
DOI: 10.1007/978-3-319-33509-4_32

reducing its cost. Also in the domain of freight distribution in the business sector the idea of "flexible" fleets that are composed on the fly by vehicles from possibly different owners has emerged. The goal is again to optimize the use of available resources but also to increase the flexibility in providing services with more and more demand fluctuations.

We call this type of solutions *open fleets*. Similar to the traditional fleet concept, an open fleet is operated by some entity that manages and coordinates the use of a limited set of resources in order to provide a specific transportation service. However, open fleets extend the traditional fleet concept towards a new dimension of openness: vehicles may join and leave the fleet at any time, and the capacity of the operator to control the fleet in its entirety may vary considerably. Both of those aspects imply the need for new solutions in the field of fleet management and fleet coordination.

In this paper we discuss the concept of open fleets and present preliminary work towards new solutions for management systems for these type of fleets. In Sect. 2 we specify our notion of open fleet as compared to static and dynamic fleets. Section 3 presents an initial proposal for an architecture for a management system for open fleets. Section 4 defines an algorithm for assigning service tasks in a fleet management system in an efficient manner. Due to its decentralized nature, we believe that this algorithm is especially applicable for (very) large open fleets with high service demands. Finally, Sect. 5 presents some conclusions and future work.

2 Fleet Coordination: From Static to Open Fleets

In this section we analyze different notions of fleets and discuss the requirements and possibilities for their efficient coordination. We proceed from simpler to ever more complex types of fleets, ending up with open fleets, which constitute the main focus of this paper.

In general, we conceive a fleet as a set of vehicles, possible of different types, that is used by some organization (*fleet operator*) with the aim of providing a specific transportation service. A transportation service comprises the fulfillment of several *service or transportation tasks*, in a given geographical region and distributed over time. And a transportation task consists in transporting objects (goods, humans, ...) from one geographical position to another.

Usually the objective of any fleet operator is to improve the efficiency of the fleet operation. In particular, the aim is to maximize the quality of the service that is provided while minimizing the operational costs.

Regarding the quality of service, the objective is usually to reduce waiting and transportation times. However, other aspects may also be important, like reducing traffic congestions, an equalitarian and fair usage of the resources, etc.

The operation cost of a fleet, is composed of two components: (i) a fixed cost of each vehicle, and (ii) a cost for each transportation service. The latter depends on the type of vehicle that has done the service and the required distance of movements.

The efficiency of a fleet based transportation service depends on long term strategic decisions (e.g., the fixed number of vehicles in the fleet; the distributions of vehicle bases in the geographical region, etc.) and on the coordination of the fleet at the operational level. And different types of fleets require different coordination mechanisms for assuring an efficient operation.

Fleet Management Systems (FMS) are usually used to implement such coordination mechanisms. They have been used in a wide range of vehicle fleet-related applications in the fields of transportation, distribution and logistics. They can either support operators at a control center to take decisions both, at long term and at the operational level, or they can implement control and coordination strategies directly, without human intervention. In general, the objective of such systems is to improve the efficiency through an efficient coordination of the fleet, adapted to the specific transportation service that is provided.

2.1 Static Fleets

Static fleets operate in situations, where the number of vehicles and also the number of transportation tasks is constant (or almost constant) during the normal operation of the fleet. Typical examples of this kind of fleets are traditional public transport systems, like bus fleets, trains, metro, airplanes, etc.

For such systems, the goal of FMSs is to support planning and scheduling of the fleet (at long term), maintain the performance of the system as close as possible to the preschedule plans (e.g. timetables) and monitoring and actuating in case of unexpected events.

A key problem is the design of a transit route network. It consists in optimizing the (fixed) routes and schedules of the service under constraints such as the number and length of public transportation routes, allowable service frequencies, and the number of available vehicles. Furthermore, at the tactical level, the challenges also include supporting decision-making regarding the modification of the routes and schedules in order to adapt to seasonality, changing trends, or changing customer demands.

Static route network planning has been studied widely in the past. Good reviews can be found in [4–6]. Typically, the approaches focus on the development of optimal or near-optimal plans using various types of effective vehicle routing algorithms. Fleet schedules designed a priori with *static route planning* assume the following: all relevant data is known before the planning starts, and the time required for creation, verification, and implementation of route plans is of minor importance (e.g., offline planning).

The use of an initially created fleet schedule, is usually not sufficient to assure efficient operation, since it may not cope adequately with unexpected events during execution like, e.g., traffic delays, vehicle breakdowns, road works, and other, which may cause fleet delays, unexpected costs, and poor customer service. Thus, at the operational and real-time level, the challenge is to respond to such events in an adequate way, i.e. to detect deviations from the initial dispatch plan and adjust the schedule accordingly by suggesting effective re-routing immediately.

We consider semi-static fleets as fleets that are used for transportation services where the planning of routes and schedules is repeated at certain time intervals. This occurs, for example, in many logistics scenarios, like fright distribution or parcel delivery services. There, routes for a given set of transportation tasks are planned on a daily basis.

The planning phase is still static since all service tasks are known beforehand, and exact routing algorithms can be applied. Usually, in such environments, the incidence of unforeseen events is greater, e.g. due to the cancellation of service tasks, time restrictions for delivery, etc. Therefore, real-time management systems that are able to treat such situations are of greater importance [7].

2.2 Dynamic Fleets

Dynamic fleets operate in an environment where transportation tasks appear on-the-fly and, thus, their operation cannot rely on pre-defined schedules. Usually, the objective is to provide transportation services "on demand". Typical examples for the application of such types of fleets are taxi services, certain commercial delivery services, courier fleets, fire trucks, police cars, emergency medical services, and so on. Thus, dynamic fleets are characterized by a fixed number of vehicles but a dynamically changing and a priori unknown number of transportation tasks.

For dynamic fleets, the management tasks focus mainly on the real-time operational level. The main goal of FMSs is to solve the allocation or dispatching of vehicles, that is, assigning vehicles to transportation tasks in an efficient way. Usually, efficiency means minimizing the global travel distance of the fleet (the sum of the required travel distances for all transportation tasks). Minimizing the global distance implies reducing the operational costs, as well as improving the service quality (by reducing the average time required to fulfill all service tasks). This problem, known as the dynamic vehicle routing problem, has been studied widely in the literature. Good surveys in this regard are [8–10]. Many approaches are based on an adaptation of static algorithms. Here the main challenge is a rather short time horizon for decision making: as the degree of dynamicity of the environment increases, usually time-consuming optimization algorithms are less applicable.

In addition to the allocation of vehicles, the problem of vehicle deployment and re-deployment is of importance. This problem refers to the task of distributing the available resources (vehicles) both at spatial (in the geographic area of influence) and temporal level. The underlying idea is to distribute vehicles in the area of interest based on the current and the expected demand, such that new appearing service tasks can be completed in a fast manner. Especially for services that require a quick response to certain events, effective deployment strategies can improve the service quality considerably. This is the reason why deployment approaches have been extensively studied in the area of emergency medical services where short response times are of foremost importance.

Some reviews of the research in the field emergency medical services are [11, 12], concentrating on covering models and optimization techniques for facility location, and [13] analysing the use of simulation models in emergency medical service operations. Early deployment approaches treated the problem in a static long-term way trying to find optimal distributions of vehicle base stations in the region of interest, according to observed or estimated demand patterns and possible changes in the environment (e.g. planned population variation or urban developments), e.g., [14, 15]. More recent approaches propose short-term dynamic deployment and redeployment models so as to adapt the fleet to the demands in any moment. Here, vehicles are either redeployed among a set of base stations (e.g., [16, 17]), or in a patrol like way without using fixed stations (e.g., [18, 19]).

Finally, in certain environments, dynamic allocation and re-deployment strategies may be combined with a priori planning. In such a context, timely close decisions are more important than the ones more remote in time.

2.3   Open (Dynamic) Fleets

During the last decades, vehicle sharing systems have proliferated. The main idea behind such systems is to maximize the utilization of vehicles for transportation tasks by reducing the times vehicles are idle. Instead of using private vehicles for a limited number of (private) transportation tasks, vehicles are used by different users, maximizing in this way their utilization.

Sharing systems may be of different types. On one hand, a number of vehicles, owned or operated by some organization, may be used by different users for their individual transportation needs, like it is the case in bicycle or car sharing services for human mobility. Here, the advantage is a reduction of the number of vehicles and, thus, of the operational costs, necessary for providing a transportation service. On the other hand, private users or organizations that own vehicles may offer a partial use of those vehicles to others, or may participate with their own vehicle in the provisioning of a given transportation service. This is for instance the case in "free" taxi or courier services, like UBER[1], where private people participate on an irregular basis in the provisioning of a certain service. In this case, the advantage is again a reduction of the number of vehicles exclusively dedicated to a transportation service. But also the possibility to have at disposal a "flexible" fleet that can adapt its size to varying service demands.

We call the type of fleets that are used in sharing systems *open fleets*. Open fleets are characterized by the following aspects:

- *Dynamic service demand:* Like dynamic fleets, open fleets are dynamic in the sense that service tasks may appear dynamically at any time and at any location (within the region of operation).
- *Dynamic number of vehicles:* The number of vehicles that participate in the fleet may also be dynamic. New vehicles may join or leave the fleet at any time and this should not affect normal fleet operation. It should be noted that also in sharing systems with an a priori fixed number of vehicles (like public bicycle services) the systems are conceived to operate regardless the actual number of vehicles in a given moment. Vehicles may be retained (e.g., for reparation) or new vehicles may be put into the system at any time, and this should not affect fleet coordination at the operational level.
- *Autonomy/limited control*: The capability of the fleet operator to regulate and control the fleet's behaviour may be limited. In open fleets, the usage of a particular vehicle, its availability in a given moment at a specific location does not only depend on the

---

[1]   https://www.uber.com/.

operator's decisions, but also on the user or owner of that vehicle. Here, individual preferences, objectives and needs of owners and users have to be balanced with the global objectives and goals of the system in its entirety. Depending on the particular application, there may be fleets that are more controllable, and others that allow only for very limited control, as it is the case, for instance, in a public bicycle service.

- *Size:* Whereas static and dynamic fleets typically operate in rather small environments with a limited size, open fleets are conceived to potentially work on a larger, maybe unlimited, scale.

Regarding long-term fleet management, at the tactical level, techniques that are applied in static and dynamic fleets may also be applied in open fleets, e.g., for calculating the adequate number of vehicles, or identifying good locations for base stations (where it applies). However, as for dynamic fleets, the efficiency of an open fleet depends much more on the coordination at the operational, real-time level. Here, however, we believe that the methods and techniques used in FMSs for static and dynamic fleets are not sufficient.

Operational management of open fleets must focus on coordination and regulation mechanisms that deal with the problem of balancing global and individual objectives. The aim is to maximize the achievement of individual needs and preferences but at the same time assuring an efficient operation with regard to some globally desirable parameters. Also, the type of global objectives may be different to static or dynamic fleets. Especially for public mobility services, parameters like energy efficiency, egalitarian and fair usage of resources, traffic reduction in a city, etc. will usually be of importance.

The basic decision tasks that have to be solved in operational management are the same as in dynamic fleets: (i) task or vehicle allocation, and (ii) vehicle (re-) deployment. However, due to the characteristics of open fleets, research on new solution approaches is required. We consider that there are essentially two new aspects that have to be considered.

The first aspect refers to the lack of control capabilities of the fleet operator and the autonomy of the vehicle drivers or users. Whereas in a dynamic fleet it is assumed that the orders regarding task assignment or re-deployment of vehicles are always fulfilled, in open fleets the autonomy (of greater or lesser degree) of the vehicles with respect to the fleet operator implies that the latter cannot impose a certain behavior. For instance, in a bicycle sharing system, a user will usually decide by himself which bike to take and he will return it at the station he likes to. In a "free" taxi service, where private drivers accomplish transportation tasks, the drivers may be able to reject task assignments and may also leave the fleet at their will, thus, not following a certain re-deployment strategy. Instead of using coercive strategies for imposing a certain behavior, fleet management should rely on soft, persuasion techniques. Or it may be necessary to combine both, coercive and soft enforcement mechanisms. Thus, the task of an FMS system consists not only in computing an optimal assignment and deployment solution in each particular moment (like for dynamic fleets), but also in convincing the drivers and/or users to adopt such a solution. In addition, the optimality criterion has to be changed to a utility criterion. Optimal solutions in the fleet context, usually involve the joint actions of several vehicles. This means that there are multiple possible points of failure (drivers not accepting the assigned task). In this sense, a best solution is not any more one that minimizes some global parameters, but a solution that has the highest utility; combing both the minimization of global parameters and the probability of being successfully executed.

Depending on the application domain, different persuasion techniques can be applied in order to convince users/driver to act in a specific way, such as incentives, argumentation, social reputation, etc. [23–25]. Furthermore, trust and reputation mechanisms may be used to estimate the future behavior of drivers/users based on an analysis of their historic behaviors. Such information may be helpful when deciding on how to persuade a specific person, or when estimating the probability of success of a given assignment and/or deployment solution.

With regard to the (re-)deployment task, a common problem in large scale vehicle sharing applications for human mobility is that the flow of vehicles is usually not the same between different areas and, thus, the vehicle distribution may become unbalanced with respect to the demand in the near future. There have been different proposals for supporting fleet operators with operational strategies for relocation and redistribution of vehicles in order to meet future demand [20–22]. In addition to such techniques, we believe that persuasion mechanisms may help to avoid unbalanced distributions of vehicles (at least partially) and even may be used to adopt a given distribution to a changing demand pattern. The idea is to use persuasion techniques (like recommendation, argumentation or incentives) to convince the users to adapt their travel routs slightly towards a situation that represents a better distribution of the vehicles with regard to future demand.

The second aspect we consider, that should be taken into account in an FMS for open fleets, is scalability. As we mentioned before, open fleets are often conceived for large-scale problems with potentially many transportation tasks and vehicles. Usually also the dynamicity of such systems, in term of the frequency of new service task demands, is quite high. Furthermore, the fleets should be robust with regard to the appearance or disappearance of vehicles as well as with regard to local incidents or problems. That is, such situations should not affect the global operation. In order to cope with this aspect, distributed and scalable coordination approaches that rely on local computations of assignment and (re-)deployment strategies should be used at the operational level.

In the next section we propose a preliminary architecture for management systems for open fleets that takes the above-mentioned aspects into account.

3   An Architecture for Smart Open Fleets

There are two main problems fleet operators are faced with: task allocation and redeployment. The *allocation* problem consists in determining which vehicle should be sent to serve a given task. *Redeployment* consists in relocating vehicles in the region of influence in a way that new tasks can be reached fast and/or with low costs. Both issues are particularly challenging in dynamic environments, as continuously upcoming new tasks may require attendance, and the current situation of the fleet may change due to external influences. In order to maximize vehicle utilization and to improve service quality in such environments, task allocation and vehicle redeployment should as well be accomplished in a dynamic manner, adapting the coordination of the fleet seamlessly to upcoming events and changing demands. In order to adequately capture the real-time requirements in such a scenario, we set out from an event-driven approach.

Figure 1 depicts our architecture for open fleet management. It contains three basic layers: the top layer contains the vehicles; the second layer represents the fleet coordination modules; while the third layer includes other components that are necessary for the normal operation of a fleet operator (e.g., components for monitoring, global fleet control, etc.).

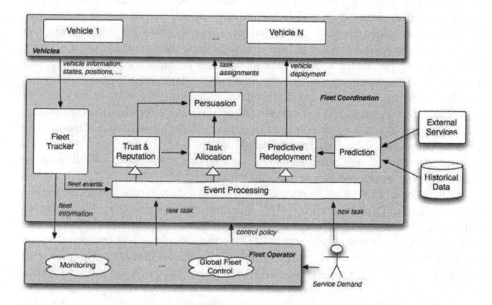

Fig. 1. Architecture for open fleets

In the fleet coordination layer, a *Fleet Tracker* follows the operational states and positions of the vehicles[2]. It informs the *Event Processing* module about any changes in the fleet that would require an adaptation of the task allocations and/or the deployment of idle vehicles. This module analyses the incoming events (state changes of vehicles and new task events) and determines whether or not a re-calculation of task assignments and/or deployment of idle vehicles should be done. If necessary, it triggers the execution of the task allocation and predictive redeployment modules. The *Task Allocation* module, when executed, re-calculates the optimal global assignment of all pending tasks (in the current moment) to vehicles, based on a set of assignment criteria (depending on the application domain). The *Predictive Redeployment* module, calculates adequate positions for all idle vehicles at the current moment taking into account predictions concerning the appearance of new tasks (based on historical data) and the current state of the fleet.

---

[2] We assume that vehicles have capabilities to send their current positions on a regular basis and to inform about changes in their operational states.

Prediction is carried out taking into account historical data and other external sources (e.g. weather forecast, leisure events, etc.). Depending on the application domain, new tasks can be triggered by fleet users (clients) by communicating with the fleet operators or directly with the fleet coordination layer.

In order to deal with the (possible high) autonomy of vehicles, we include persuasion and trust and reputation modules in the architecture. The *Persuasion* module is in charge of providing actions for inducing agents (vehicles) to carry out the actions that tend to improve the overall performance measure of the system.

Information about previous experience of vehicles within the system can be exploited so as to take better decisions. The *Trust and Reputation* module is in charge of modeling the expected behavior of agents[3] in the system using feedback provided by the *fleet tracker*. That information is used at least in two different though related ways: (i) what actions have to be chosen and (ii) how agents can be influenced accordingly. For instance, in a vehicle renting scenario, the information about liability of users to return vehicles at the expected time can be used for estimating the number of available resources, which is important for task allocation decision. Likewise, the information given to a particular user in the course of an explanation or persuasion dialogue can be different depending on his/her expected behavior.

It is important to note that, depending on each particular case, not all modules described in the architecture are necessarily implemented.

As the number of vehicles increases, an important aspect to take into account when designing an architecture for open fleet management is scalability. The approach followed to this respect highly depends on the application domain: coordinating a fleet of about ambulances (for instance, there are less than 30 advanced life support ambulances in the Spanish town of Madrid [19]) is obviously quite different from orchestrating taxis as open fleets (Madrid can count on 15000 registered taxis). To address scalability, in many approaches the environment is divided into (generally overlapping) areas, and the control is applied locally in each area. Coordination is needed in case there are conflicts for using shared resources or services. That kind of approaches has been used, for instance, for public transportation management [26]. In the next section, we present a distributed coordination algorithm for taxi service assignment.

4   Example: Taxi Fleet Coordination

In this section we apply the aforementioned architecture in a system for coordinating a fleet of "free" taxi services in a big city, where there are thousands of taxis (as mentioned before, some 15000 taxis in the case of Madrid). Usually, there are several taxi companies which taxis are affiliated to. They coordinate service calls, either assigning a taxi to the client or asking those taxis nearby who is interested in doing the service.

One of the main goals of the taxi company is to reduce the response time (e.g., the time between a client call and the moment a taxi arrives).

---

[3] Depending on the domain, agents can represent vehicles (e.g. taxi) or users/clients (person renting a bike).

This scenario has the main features we used to characterize open fleets: (i) taxis join and leave the fleet anytime during the day, and (ii) taxis are autonomous since they decide whether they take a service and it is not possible to enforce them to carry out their commitments. In this example, we focus on the task allocation part of the architecture. We assume that event management and fleet tracking are processed by the corresponding modules. We do not use predictive redeployment in this scenario.

A naïve method many companies use for taxi assignment is the closest method rule based on the first-come/first-served (FCFS) principle. That is, the first client in the system is assigned first, then the next client, and so on. In each case, a client is assigned to the closest available taxi (using GPS) in that particular moment.

Imagine the scenario shown in Fig. 2, where there are three available taxis, and two clients. $c1$ asked for a taxi a few seconds before $c2$. Figure 2a shows the locations of taxis and clients, numbers represent the distance[4] between them. Figure 2b shows the assignment resulting from applying the naïve strategy: when $c1$ entered the system the closest taxi ($t1$) was assigned, and then $t3$ was the closest to $c2$ (with a total distance $3 + 10 = 13$). However, there is a better assignment, as shown in Fig. 2c, where both clients get a taxi at distance 4 (total 8), which is better for a global point of view ($c1$ has a lightly worse taxi but there is a high improvement for $c2$).

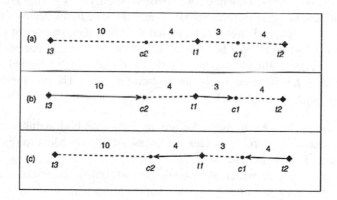

Fig. 2. Taxi assignment strategies: numbers represent distances, t1, t2 and t3 are available taxis, c1 and c2 are clients. (a) without assignment; (b) FCFS and shortest path with c1 appearing first; (c) optimal assignment

The situation (b) was due to the FCFS strategy although both clients arose very close in time. That could be avoided using time windows so that several clients could be considered together and a better global assignment could be obtained.

We follow a different approach for the assignment of taxis to clients (task allocation). Our proposal is inspired by Bertsekas' auction algorithm [27]. We already developed an extension of Bertsekas' auction algorithm for efficiently coordinating the fleet of ambulances of the Emergency Medical Assistance Service SUMMA112 in the Autonomous Region of Madrid in Spain [19].

---

[4] At this point it is not important the distance function used.

However, unlike the ambulances scenario, taxi drivers have higher autonomy. In particular, they have to accept the assignment proposed by the system. Furthermore, they might not fulfill the agreed service, so incentives/penalties are necessary to enforce their commitments.

The process of deciding which taxi is proposed to be assigned to a given client is based on the following idea. Clients bid for the available taxis in an auction process. Every taxi has a "virtual" price[5]. First, the prices of all taxis are initialized to 0. Then, the auction process starts. In each iteration, a bidding and an assignment phase take place. During the bidding phase, each client c that is not currently assigned to any taxi determines the taxis t_i and t_k with the least cost (p_1) and second least cost (p_2), respectively. The cost of a taxi t for a given client c is computed as proportional to the expected travel time for t to reach client c plus the current cost of t (other functions can be used). Then, client c issues a bid for its best taxi (t_i), where the bid value is the difference between the cost of the second best and the best taxi for c plus a constant ε. The rationale behind this bid value is that, at the current prices and up to a price increment of $p_2 - p_1$ for taxi t_i, client c would prefer this taxi with regards to its second choice (t_k), i.e. it represents how important for the client is to get that taxi compared to get the second choice. For instance, in the example of Fig. 2, if client $c2$ does not get taxi $t1$ its price increment would be 6 (10 – 4), while for $c1$ would be only 1 (4 – 3). ε is a (positive) constant (the minimum price increment), necessary to assure termination of the auction process. After all unassigned clients have issued their bids the assignment phase takes place. Each taxi t_i that received a bid is assigned to the client c that issued the highest bid for that taxi. If t_i was already assigned to another client, it is deassigned previously. Finally, the price of t_i is incremented by the highest bid value. The bidding and assignment phases are repeated until all clients are assigned to a taxi.

Dealing with Scalability. As discussed before, in fleets with high number of vehicles, scalability becomes a real problem. This is the case of taxi coordination in big cities, where thousands of taxis circulate daily.

Our proposal for coping with that problem is a distributed execution of the method described above. It consists of three type of components running in different devices: a taxi application that participate in the auction and finally accept or reject services, a client application that runs on the client device (e.g. smartphone) and a central server that manage a registry with basic information of taxis (such as location and cost).

The *central server*[6] is in charge of maintaining the location, price and status (available, occupied) of each taxi, and provides a set of functionalities such as calculating the closest taxis to a given location. Taxis send periodically their location to the server, and update their status and cost.

Figure 3 shows the algorithm running on the taxis. It basically manages the participation in the auction for deciding which taxi is in charge of accepting the service a client needs.

---

[5] Do not confuse with the price a client has to pay for a taxi service .

[6] We consider the server "conceptually" centralized, we do not focus in this paper on the distributed implementation of the registry.

```
1:    price = 0
2:    current_client = null
3:    Wait for bid<c, pc>
4:    tmp_client = c
5:    price = pc
6:    updatePrice(t, price)
7:    Start time window
8:    repeat Wait for bid<c, pc> or end_of_time_window
9:             if pc > price then
10:                     reject(tmp_client)
11:                     tmp_client = c
12:                     price = pc
13:                     updatePrice(t, price)
14:             else
15:                     reject(c)
16:             end if
17:    until end_of_time_window
18:    if taxi driver accepts then
19:             notifyAssignment(t,tmp_client)
20:    else
21:             reject(tmp_client)
22:    end if
```

Fig. 3. Taxi algorithm executed whenever a taxi *t* gets available

The algorithm is started when the taxi becomes available (it joins the fleet or finishes a service). Initially the *price* is established to 0 and waits for a bid from a client (line 3). The bid includes the client *c* issuing that bid and the price p_c it offers. After receiving the first bid, the taxi establishes a time window during which it will accept bids from other potential clients. The variable *tmp_client* stores the client that is temporally assigned to the taxi during the time window. Then, the taxi waits for a new bid or the end of the time window (lines 8-17). If a new bid is received, then there are two possibilities: (i) if the price of the new bid is lower than the current price then the client is rejected (line 15); (ii) if the price is higher then the client is temporally chosen, the price is updated and the previous temporal client is rejected (lines 10-13). When the time window finishes the temporal client is definitively chosen and, after receiving the confirmation from the taxi driver (line 18), a notification (line 19) or rejection (line 20) is sent to him/her. Assignment notification (*notify Assignment(t,c)*) and price update (*update Price(t,p)*) communicate with the central registry, which update the information of taxi *t* accordingly.

Figure 4 shows the algorithm executed when a client asks for a taxi service. It asks the central registry for the two taxis with lowest costs (line 2). The registry returns (function *search Cheapest Available Taxis*) basic information of such taxis including their current prices (according to the algorithm) and their "costs" (taxi *price* + *distance* to client).

Then, the client issues a bid to the cheapest taxi (line 3) and waits for an answer. If the bid is rejected, then the process is repeated until a bid is accepted. Functions *cost* and *price* return information of cost and price of taxis, respectively.

```
1:    repeat
2:              <t1,t2> = searchCheapestAvailableTaxis(c)
3:              Bid(t1, cost(t2) – cost(t1) + price(t1))
4:              Wait for answer
5:    until bid accepted
```

Fig. 4. Client algorithm

Persuasion. As mentioned previously, autonomy is a characteristic of this kind of systems. In particular, taxi drivers are free to accept or reject client assignments. As detailed in Fig. 3, at the end of the auction process the taxi driver has always the option to reject the assignment proposal.

However, it might be interesting to use mechanisms to foster taxis to follow the assignments recommended by the system, or even worst if they do not actually fulfill the service they committed. In Sect. 3 we pointed out this aspect by including trust and reputation and persuasion in the architecture.

Even though in the proposed algorithm we did not deal with the problem of convincing driver to accept the clients the system recommends, this aspect could be integrated by manipulating the prices of taxis in the auction process. In particular, a trust model could be used to determine "reliable" drivers. During the auction, the central server could increase the price of "unreliable" taxis such that clients will be less inclined to bid for such taxis (if they have other similar options).

5   Conclusions

In this paper we have discussed the coordination of transportation fleets. The main contributions of this work are (i) an analysis and classification of different types of fleets ending up with the introduction of the notion of *open fleets*, (ii) an architectural framework for the management of open fleets, and (iii) some preliminary work on a decentralized algorithm for vehicle assignment that could be applied, for instance, in a large "free" taxi service.

In the future, we plan to evaluate the proposed decentralized algorithm for taxi assignment. In particular, we will compare its efficiency against the approaches that are currently applied in real world applications (e.g. FCFS with shortest path). In addition, we will explore other decentralized options (for instance based on spatial division of the region).

Finally, we will also like to analyze in more detail the relation between the autonomy of taxi drivers and the system performance.

Acknowledgments. Work partially supported by Spanish Government through the projects iHAS (grant TIN2012-36586-C03) and SURF (grant TIN2015-65515-C4-X-R), the Autonomous Region of Madrid through grant S2013/ICE-3019 ("MOSI-AGIL-CM", co-funded by EU Structural Funds FSE and FEDER) and URJC-Santander (30VCPIGI15).

References

1. Dablanc, L.: Goods transport in large european cities: difficult to organize, difficult to modernize. Transp. Res. Part A: Policy Pract. **41**(3), 280–285 (2007)
2. Shaheen, S.A., Cohen, A.P.: Growth in worldwide carsharing: an international comparison. Transp. Res. Rec.: J. Transp. Res. Board **1992**(1), 81–89 (2007)
3. Mont, O.: Institutionalisation of sustainable consumption patterns based on shared use. Ecol. Econ. **50**(1), 135–153 (2004)
4. Kepaptsoglou, K., Karlaftis, M.: Transit route network design problem: review. J. Transp. Eng. **135**(8), 491–505 (2009)
5. Wren, A., Carr, J.D.: Computers in Transport Planning and Operation. Ian Allan Publishing, Limited, London (1971)
6. Chua, T.A.: The planning of urban bus routes and frequencies: a survey. Transportation **12**(2), 147–172 (1984)
7. Zeimpekis, V., Minis, I., Mamassis, K., Giaglis, G.M.: Dynamic management of a delayed delivery vehicle in a city logistics environment. In: Zeimpekis, V., Tarantilis, C.D., Giaglis, G.M., Minis, I. (eds.) Dynamic Fleet Management, pp. 197–217. Springer, Heidelberg (2007)
8. Gendreau, M., Potvin, J.Y.: Dynamic vehicle routing and dispatching. In: Crainic, T.G., Laporte, G. (eds.) Fleet Management and Logistic, pp. 115–226. Springer, Heidelberg (1998)
9. Ichoua, S., Gendreau, M., Potvin, J.Y.: Planned route optimization for real-time vehicle routing. In: Zeimpekis, V., Tarantilis, C.D., Giaglis, G.M., Minis, I. (eds.) Dynamic Fleet Management: Concepts, Systems, Algorithms & Case Studies. Operations Research/Computer Science Interfaces, vol. 38, pp. 1–18. Springer, Heidelberg (2007)
10. Pillac, V., Gendreau, M., Gueret, C., Medaglia, A.L.: A review of dynamic vehicle routing problems. Eur. J. Oper. Res. **225**(1), 1–11 (2013)
11. Brotcorne, L., Laporte, G., Semet, F.: Ambulance location and relocation models. Eur. J. Oper. Res. **147**(3), 451–463 (2003)
12. Li, X., Zhao, Z., Zhu, X., Wyatt, T.: Covering models and optimization techniques for emergency response facility location and planning: a review. Math. Methods Oper. Res. **74**(3), 281–310 (2011)
13. Aboueljinane, L., Sahin, E., Jemai, Z.: A review on simulation models applied to emergency medical service operations. Comput. Ind. Eng. **66**(4), 734–750 (2013)
14. Toregas, C., Swain, R., ReVelle, C., Bergman, L.: The location of emergency service facilities. Oper. Res. **19**(6), 1363–1373 (1971)
15. ReVelle, C., Hogan, K.: The maximum availability location problem. Transp. Sci. **23**(3), 192–200 (1989)
16. Naoum-Sawaya, J., Elhedhli, S.: A stochastic optimization model for real-time ambulance redeployment. Comput. Oper. Res. **40**(8), 1972–1978 (2013)
17. Ibri, S., Nourelfath, M., Drias, H.: A multi-agent approach for integrated emergency vehicle dispatching and covering problem. Eng. Appl. Artif. Intell. **25**(3), 554–565 (2012)
18. Andersson, T., Varbrand, P.: Decision support tools for ambulance dispatch and relocation. J. Oper. Res. Soc. **58**(2), 195–201 (2007)

19. Billhardt, H., Lujak, M., Sánchez-Brunete, V., Fernandez, A., Ossowski, S.: Dynamic coordination of ambulances for emergency medical assistance services. Knowl.-Based Syst. **70**, 268–280 (2014)
20. Nair, R., Miller-Hooks, E., Hampshire, R.C., Bušic, A.: Large-scale vehicle sharing systems: analysis of Vélib. Int. J. Sustain. Transp. **7**, 85–106 (2013)
21. Kek, A.G.H., Cheu, R.L., Meng, Q., Fung, C.H.: A decision support system for vehicle relocation operations in carsharing systems. Transp. Res. Part E: Logist. Transp. **45**(1), 149–158 (2009)
22. Nair, R., Miller-Hooks, E.: Fleet management for vehicle sharing operations. Transportation Science **45**(4), 524–540 (2011)
23. Modgil, S., et al.: The added value of argumentation. In: Ossowski, S. (ed.) Agreement Technologies, pp. 357–403. Springer, Netherlands (2012)
24. Koster, A., Sabater-Mir, J., Schorlermmer, M.: Argumentation and trust. In: Ossowski, S. (ed.) Agreement Technologies, pp. 441–451. Springer, Netherlands (2012)
25. Castelfranchi, C., Falcone, R.: Trust Theory: A Socio-Cognitive and Computational Model. Wiley, New York (2010)
26. Ossowski, S., Hernandez, J.Z., Belmonte, M.V., Fernandez, A., García-Serrano, A., Pérez-de-la-Cruz, J.L., Serrano, J.M., Triguero, F.: Decision support for traffic management based on organisational and communicative multiagent abstractions. Transp. Res. Part C **13**, 272–298 (2005)
27. Bertsekas, D.: The auction algorithm: a distributed relaxation method for the assignment problem. Ann. Oper. Res. **14**(1), 105–123 (1988)

A Concurrent Architecture for Agent Reasoning Cycle Execution in Jason

Maicon R. Zatelli[1]([✉]), Alessandro Ricci[2], and Jomi F. Hübner[1]

[1] Federal University of Santa Catarina (UFSC), Florianópolis, Brazil
xsplyter@gmail.com, jomi.hubner@ufsc.br
[2] University of Bologna, Bologna, Italy
a.ricci@unibo.it

Abstract. Reactiveness and performance are important features of Multi-Agent Systems (MAS) and the underlying execution platform has a direct impact on them. These features can be improved by properly exploiting the parallelism provided by multi-core architectures and related parallel hardware. In this paper, we take Jason as a reference for BDI agents and analyze its execution platform according to its concurrency features. Our aim is to modify the Jason reasoning cycle to introduce a concurrent architecture for individual agents. We experimentally evaluate the benefits and drawbacks of the new Jason reasoning cycle.

1 Introduction

A main desirable characteristic in an MAS application is that agents react promptly to changes in the environment, reply to messages fast, and process other high-cost activities, all at the same time [12]. A proper exploitation of parallel hardware, such as multi-core architectures, can help on this direction. However, most current MAS execution platforms implementing the BDI architecture (e.g. 2APL [6], JACK [8], Jadex [15], Jason [3], JIAC [17], simpAL [16]) exploit parallelism for executing multiple agents (using different strategies), but not for improving the execution for individual agents. An example is related to the agent reasoning cycle, where the reasoning cycle is implemented as a sequential execution of steps, resulting in lack of reactivity in some scenarios [5,11,18–20]. Experiments performed in [18] demonstrated that, according to the adopted concurrency configuration[1] to execute an MAS, we can obtain different results in terms of performance, reactivity, and scalability. While one configuration provides a faster response time in an MAS composed of few agents, another configuration provides a faster response time in an MAS composed of more agents.

The authors are grateful for the support given by CNPq and CAPES (PDSE), grants 140261/2013-3, 448462/2014-1, and 306301/2012-1.
[1] For concurrency configuration we mean the set of concurrency features, including their parameters, that are used to run the MAS.

© Springer International Publishing Switzerland 2016
M. Rovatsos et al. (Eds.): EUMAS 2015/AT 2015, LNAI 9571, pp. 425–440, 2016.
DOI: 10.1007/978-3-319-33509-4_33

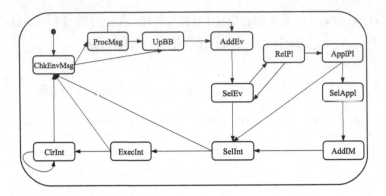

Fig. 1. Jason reasoning cycle [3].

Differently from our previous work [18], the aim of this paper is to exploit parallelism in the execution of the BDI agent reasoning cycle considering a *concrete MAS execution platform*. The structure of the reasoning cycle is slightly revisited, making it possible to introduce a concurrent architecture also for the execution of individual agents while, at the same time, the consistency and coherence of the agent reasoning can be preserved. We do it by considering the reasoning cycle as implemented in the Jason execution platform, however the results can be extended to other BDI platforms. We start by presenting the Jason reasoning cycle and its concurrent architecture (Sect. 2). In the following, we modify the Jason agent reasoning cycle to better exploit parallelism, guaranteeing a coherent and consistent execution for applications (Sect. 3). The proposed reasoning cycle is reified in an abstract concurrent BDI architecture (Sect. 4), which is used to extend the Jason execution platform, allowing an experimental evaluation (Sect. 5). Conclusions and further work are presented in Sect. 6.

2   The Jason Language

This section presents the Jason language and execution platform [3]², focusing on the reasoning cycle (Sect. 2.1) and the concurrent architecture (Sect. 2.2).

2.1   Jason Reasoning Cycle

The semantics of the agent execution is defined by the agent reasoning cycle, which is sketched in Fig. 1 by means of a state chart and discussed in details in [3]. Basically, the reasoning cycle can be divided in three main stages: the *sense*, the *deliberate*, and the *act*.

---

² More details about Jason can be also found at http://jason.sf.net/.

```
1. @p1 +pressure(P): P > 1024 <- ... .
2. @p2 +temperature(T): T < 10 <- ... .
3. @p3 +temperature(T): T >= 10 & T <= 20 <- ... .
4. @p4 +temperature(T): T > 20 <- ... .
5. @p5 +temperature(T): T > 30 <- ... .
```

Code 1: Example of plans in the plan library.

In the sense stage, the agent senses the environment and receives messages from other agents (ChkEnvMsg). As the result of the perception of the environment, the agent gets all percepts that represent the state of the environment. Each percept represents a particular property of the current environment state (e.g. the temperature). After the agent perceives the environment and gets its percepts, the belief base must be updated in order to reflect changes occurred in the environment. The belief update function can be customized and by default it follows two simple rules. (1) Each literal in the list of percepts and not currently in the belief base is added to the belief base; (2) each literal in the belief base and no longer in the list of percepts is removed from the belief base.

Messages received by the agent are processed according to the performative (ProcMsg). Thus, a message can refer to the addition or removal of plans, goals, or beliefs. The order in which messages are selected and processed can be also customized and by default messages are handled in the arrival order.

In both cases (changes in the belief base or messages received by the agent), events are produced and included in a queue (AddEv). In the deliberate stage, the agent handles such events. Only one pending event is selected to be handled in each reasoning cycle execution (SelEv). The selection of an event can be customized and by default it selects the first event among the pending ones.

After the agent selects an event to be handled, the next step is to find a plan that allows the agent to actually handle the event. The first step is to retrieve all plans from the plan library which are relevant for the event (RelPl). It is done by retrieving the plans that have a triggering event that can be unified with the selected event. For example, let Code 1 represents the current plan library of the agent. If an event +temperature(32) just happened, only plans @p2, @p3, @p4, and @p5 are relevant to handle it.

The agent can have several relevant plans to handle the same event, however not all relevant plans can be applied according to the current context of the system. Thus, the next step is to select from the relevant plans those which are applicable by checking the current context (ApplPl), that is, those that can be used to handle the event successfully given the agent's known-how and its current beliefs. Continuing with the example about the event +temperature(32), only two plans are applicable (@p4 and @p5). They are applicable because after the unification, the variable T contains 32, which is higher than 20 (@p4) and 30 (@p5).

The agent can still have several applicable plans and any of them could be chosen to (hopefully) handle the event successfully. The next step is to select one from the applicable plans to commit (SelAppl). After selecting the plan, the agent can finally have the intention of pursuing the course of deeds[3] determined by that plan. The selection can be customized and by default it selects the first applicable plan to commit. Among the two remaining plans to handle the event +temperature(32) (@p4 and @p5), the selected plan would be @p4, and an intention will be finally produced (AddIM).

Several intentions can be active at the same time and competing for the agent attention. In each reasoning cycle execution, only one intention among all current ready intentions for execution is selected to be executed (SelInt). Although the strategy to select intentions can be customized, by default they are selected using a round-robing scheduling mechanism, which means that in each turn *one* intention is selected and *only one* of its deeds is executed (ExecInt). A deed of an intention can be an environment action, which is an action that the agent performs to act in the environment; an instantiation of a new goal; an operation to add or remove beliefs; or an internal action, which is a Java/legacy code provided by the programmer. Thanks to these mechanisms that allow the execution of deeds of different intentions in each cycle, a concurrent execution of different intentions can be provided by interleaving their execution, avoiding the need of launching dedicated threads for each intention. Finally, empty intentions (finished ones) are removed (ClrInt).

2.2   Jason Concurrent Architecture

Currently, a concurrent architecture is adopted in the Jason execution platform for executing the set of agents of an MAS. The two first features are related to the distribution of threads among agents in the system, while the last three features are related to how Jason manages the execution of agent intentions.

By default, each Jason agent has one thread control for executing the reasoning cycle, which means that an MAS composed of 100 agents has 100 threads to execute them. Such strategy is widely adopted in current MAS execution platforms, such as JADE [2], Jadex [15], 2APL [6], JIAC [17]. Jason also allows the MAS developer to define a thread pool to execute all agents in the MAS. Thus, it is possible to execute an MAS composed of thousands of agents only using few threads (e.g. 10000 agents can be executed by the same 4 threads available in a thread pool). The use of thread pools is another feature adopted in some MAS execution platforms such as simpAL [16], GOAL [10], and JACK [8].

Intentions in Jason are executed concurrently without using a physical thread for each one (i.e. all agent intentions are executed by the agent thread). The MAS execution platform interleaves the execution of intentions, which is controlled by the agent reasoning cycle (Sect. 2.1). Thus, only part of each intention is executed each time. For example, if two intentions (α and β) are active, part of intention α is executed and then part of intention β is executed. Such feature allows to provide internal concurrency even without a high number of threads, which is useful for the agent to perform several activities *at the same time*. The same

---

[3] The term *deed* is used in the same form as in [7]. It refers to the kinds of formulae that appear in a plan body.

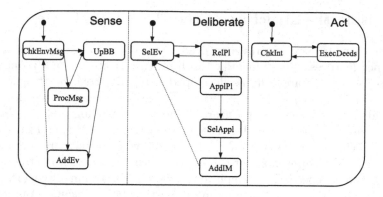

Fig. 2. New Jason reasoning cycle.

feature is provided by other MAS execution platforms such as Agent Factory Framework [13,14], JACK [8], and 2APL [6]. .

In order to avoid that an agent enters in an inconsistent state whether it must execute two or more intentions that can conflict (e.g. read and write the same belief), Jason allows to define plans as *atomic*. The execution of an atomic plan will not be interrupted by the execution of other current active intentions. A very simple example where such mechanism is necessary is when the agent must increase and decrease the value of the same belief (e.g. count) adopting two concurrent intentions. It is clear that if the value of count starts with 0 and the *increase intention* increases the count 100 times and the *decrease intention* decreases the count 100 times, the final result for count must be 0 again. Changes in the count belief must be done atomically. Similar constructions to guarantee the atomic execution of parts of the agent code are also present in languages like 2APL [6] and JIAC [17].

Finally, another mechanism provided by Jason to work with intentions is the capability to perform operations over intentions, such as suspend, resume, and inspect their current state (e.g. check if some intention is suspended). Such operations are especially useful to allow the agent to have a full control of all activities that are active in certain moment, which includes the capability to deal with possible interferences among the execution of two or more intentions concurrently. An example of application is when a robot has the goal to find gold and to keep the battery charged. In this example, as soon as the agent perceives that the battery charge is low, the agent must suspend the intention to find gold, start to charge the battery, and at the end resume the intention to find gold. Other MAS execution platforms that allow the agent to have this kind of control about the activities that it is carrying on are simpAL [16], JADE [2], and Jadex [15].

3   Revising the Structure of the Reasoning Cycle

Besides the concurrency features supported in Jason (Sect. 2.2), a series of other concurrency features, can be identified in literature related to MAS languages, platforms, and other applications developed using the concept of agents and MAS [18]. In this paper, our aim is to modify the Jason reasoning cycle to support a wider set of concurrency features. The new reasoning cycle for Jason is conceived based on the current Jason reasoning cycle (Sect. 2.1) and the concurrent agent architectures proposed in [5,11,19,20], where agents are composed of different internal components that run concurrently. However, while the focus of those works are on specific MAS applications, our focus is on modifying the agent reasoning cycle already implemented in an existing MAS execution platform to support any kind of MAS application.

The new Jason reasoning cycle (Fig. 2) is explicitly divided in three main stages: the *sense* (left), the *deliberate* (middle), and the *act* (right). Each stage can be executed independently and asynchronously in order to improve the reactivity of the agent and allows the agent to continuously deliberate and act without stop sensing.

The sense stage is executed almost in the same form as in Fig. 1. Thus, the agent starts by checking the environment and messages (ChkEnvMsg), then processing received messages (ProcMsg), updating belief base (UpBB), and producing events about belief changes and message exchanges (AddEv). However, at the end of the sense stage, instead of starting to deliberate, the agent checks new percepts and messages again. Once the sense stage can be executed as a non-terminating cycle, events for the deliberate stage can be produced as fast as possible ensuring that emergencies or other higher priority situations be handled promptly.

As in the sense stage, the deliberate stage is executed similarly as in Fig. 1. Thus, the deliberate stage starts by selecting an event from the set of pending events (SelEv), then retrieving all relevant plans (RelPl), checking which of those are applicable (ApplPl), selecting one particular applicable plan (SelAppl), and adding the selected one to the set of intentions (AddIM). However, at the end of the deliberate stage, instead of start acting, the agent proceeds by handling another pending event. The main gain with the cyclical execution of the deliberate stage is that intentions are added in the act stage continuously. Thus, that emergency or high priority situation previously handled by the sense stage continues being promptly handled also in the deliberate stage, guaranteeing that an intention will be instantiated to handle it as soon as possible.

In contrast to the sense and the deliberate stages, the act stage has a new proposal to cover the features stated in the beginning of this section. In the first step of the act stage, it is verified if there is any active intention to be executed (ChkInt). If so, the agent proceeds with the execution of the deeds of the active intentions. Like in the sense and the deliberate stages, the act stage also executes cyclically by continuously checking active intentions and executing deeds. Such cycle in the act stage is the final step to guarantee that the emergencies and more priority situations be effectively handled promptly.

The main challenge about supporting both asynchronous and synchronous execution for the reasoning cycle is to keep a coherent and consistent semantics. The critical part in the execution of the agent when executing an asynchronous version for the reasoning cycle are the interferences among threads used in different stages of the reasoning cycle (e.g. when accessing the belief base both for reading (deliberate stage) and writing (sense and act stages)). Due to the access to the same data structures by different stages of the reasoning cycle, concurrent access mechanisms must be used to avoid an inconsistent state of the system. For example, the addition (AddEv) and selection of events (SelEv) read and write in the same data structure (the pending events set), which cannot be done at the same time, as well as the addition of intentions (AddIM) and the verification of intentions (ChkInt), which access the set of active intentions. Other parts of the reasoning cycle also access structures like the belief base and they cannot be executed concurrently. For example, ApplPl and UpBB must be executed atomically, otherwise the agent could reason about partial updates of the belief base even in scenarios where it should not be done (e.g. in a game of chess, the agent must have the situation of the whole board updated in order to make the best decision). Moreover, updates in the belief base related to a single percept must be done atomically, otherwise, in the deliberate stage, the agent could see states of the belief base that do not correspond to any possible state of the world.

4   A Concurrent Architecture Based on the New Reasoning Cycle

Different architectures can be proposed based on the reasoning cycle presented in Sect. 3. This section presents one possible concurrent BDI architecture (Fig. 3), already introduced in [18], and that can support a wider set of concurrency features compared to current agent architectures. While *Beliefs*, *Plans*, *Threaded Intentions*, and *Suspended Intentions* are placed in data sets (represented by horizontal rectangles), *Messages*, *Percepts*, *Events*, and *Pooled Intentions* are placed in queues (represented by vertical rectangles) and processed by the threads in their respective components. These queues are priority queues in order to process emergencies promptly (e.g. an event notifying low battery in a robot). The steps of the reasoning cycle are defined by means of some functions (represented by octagons). Such functions are used, for example, to act in the environment or manipulate the data sets.

The agent is divided in three main components, which represent the stages of the reasoning cycle, that can run concurrently, depending on the configuration. The *Sense Component* (SC) is responsible for receiving inputs from the environment (*percepts*) and from other agents (*messages*), updating the belief base, and producing events. The *Deliberate Component* (DC) is responsible for reasoning about the events and producing new intentions to handle them. Finally, the *Act Component* (AC) is responsible for executing the intentions. Each component can have its own thread pool, named *Sense Threads* (ST), *Deliberate Threads* (DT), and *Act Threads* (AT). The three components can also be configured to

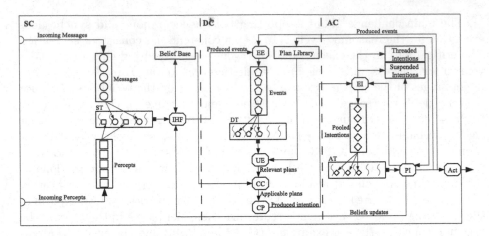

Fig. 3. Agent architecture.

share the same thread pool in order to reduce the number of threads in applications composed of more agents.

The reasoning cycle can be executed in two distinct forms: synchronous and asynchronous. In the synchronous form, each component finishes its execution before the other component starts its execution (i.e. the sense-deliberate-act cycle is executed sequentially). In the asynchronous form, the three components run concurrently and do not wait for the other components to finish their execution before doing something, whether they already have something to do. However, differently from the synchronous execution, where the reasoning cycle is explicit, in the asynchronous execution the reasoning cycle is implicit by a producer-consumer strategy, where each component produces inputs for the other components. For example, the SC produces events for the DC and the DC produces intentions for the AC. Thus, the reasoning cycle is ensured because for a stage be executed it will depend on the execution of the previous stage. A more detailed presentation of the agent architecture can be found at [18].

5   Evaluation

The aim of this section is to provide an evaluation of the extended version of Jason. The evaluation is made according to five characteristics of an MAS:

- *computation load.* While a light computation load means that an agent has a soft task to perform (e.g. to factor a 3 digit number), an heavy computation load means that an agent has a hard task to perform (e.g. to factor a 100 digit number);
- *intention load.* While an agent with few intentions has a light intention load, an agent with many intentions has a heavy intention load;

- *perception load.* An agent that receives few percepts from the environment has a light perception load, while an agent that receives many percepts from the environment has a heavy perception load;
- *communication load.* While few message exchanges mean a light communication load, a high number of message exchanges means a heavy communication load;
- *MAS population.* A low populated MAS means that the MAS is composed of few agents and a high populated MAS means that the MAS is composed of many agents.

We evaluate three different concurrency configurations ($C1$, $C2$, $C3$). The two first configurations are already supported in the traditional Jason execution platform, while the support for the third configuration is implemented in the extended version of the Jason execution platform. In $C1$, agents execute a sequential (*synchronous*) reasoning cycle and each agent has its own thread. In $C2$, agents also execute a sequential (*synchronous*) reasoning cycle, however all agents share the same thread pool. In $C3$, agents execute a parallel (*asynchronous*) reasoning cycle where each component is executed by its own thread. Each thread in $C3$ executes the same components of all agents (i.e. there is only one thread to execute the sense of all agents).

The evaluation is done by means of experiments, which consist on the implementation of very simple and small scenarios, each one focused on some of the aforementioned MAS characteristics. We start the experiments by considering some scenarios where the *computation load* (Sect. 5.1) and the *intention load* (Sect. 5.2) are evaluated. Then, agents are stressed according to the *perception load* (Sect. 5.3). Finally, agents are evaluated considering different *communication loads* (Sect. 5.4). The *MAS population* is evaluated through changing the number of agents in some scenarios. The experiments were performed on a computer Intel(R) Core(TM) 2 Duo @ 2.0 GHz (2 CPU cores), 4 GB DDR2, running Linux version 3.6.3-1.fc17.x86_64 and Java version 1.7.0_17.[4] Only the main

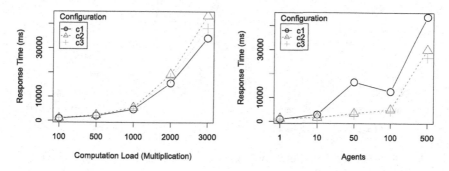

Fig. 4. Multiplication table: computation load (left) and MAS population (right).

---

[4] Experiment parameters are dimensioned according to the available computer hardware. More powerful computers will be used in the future.

results are presented, while a deeper analysis, other results, and source codes can be found at https://sourceforge.net/p/mrzatelli/code/HEAD/tree/trunk/2015/Experiment3/.

5.1   Computation Load

In this experiment, two simple applications are implemented aiming to give a heavy computation for the agents. In the first one, agents must print the multiplication table from 1 to k without creating any sub-goal, thus, once instantiated the intention, the only stage of the reasoning cycle that should be executed is the act stage. The implementation is done by means of a nestled loop (Code 3).

In order to evaluate the computation load, we fix the number of agents in *one* agent and vary k from 100 to 3000. The results depicted in Fig. 4(left) show that adopting a synchronous reasoning cycle with one thread per agent ($C1$) has the fastest response time[5], while adopting a synchronous reasoning cycle with a single thread pool ($C2$) has the worst response time. These results are expected due to the overhead caused by using thread pools ($C2$ and $C3$) to execute a single agent. Moreover, the asynchronous reasoning cycle ($C3$) showed a faster response time than $C2$. This is also an expected result and the reason for this behavior is that while the full reasoning cycle is executed in $C2$, the only reasoning cycle stage that remains active in $C3$ is the act stage.

In order to evaluate the MAS population, we vary the number of agents from 1 to 500. The results depicted in Fig. 4(right) show that adopting an asynchronous reasoning cycle ($C3$) has the fastest response time, while adopting a synchronous reasoning cycle with one thread per agent ($C1$) has the worst response time. These results are expected due to the context-switch overhead caused by the high number of threads in $C1$. Moreover, as also stated before, $C3$ has a faster response time than $C2$ due to only executing the act stage.

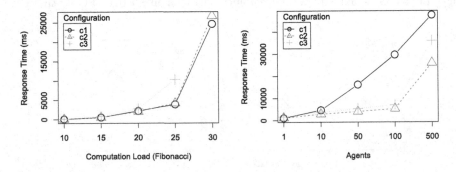

Fig. 5. Fibonacci: computation load (left) and MAS population (right).

---

[5] The response time is the elapse time for an agent to complete the execution of an intention.

```
1.  +?fib(0,0).
2.  +?fib(1,1).
3.  +?fib(K,X) <-
4.      ?fib(K-1,A);
5.      ?fib(K-2,B);
6.      X = A+B.
```
Code 2: Fibonacci Numbers.

```
1.  +!work(K) <-
2.      for (.range(X,1,K)) {
3.          for (.range(Y,1,K)) {
4.              .print(X * Y);
5.          };
6.      }.
```
Code 3: Multiplication Table.

In the second application, agents must compute the first k Fibonacci numbers (Code 2). The implementation of the plan to compute the first k Fibonacci numbers follows the traditional recursive approach, where each recursive call is a *sub-goal* (lines 4 and 5), which forces the execution of the deliberate stage of the reasoning cycle because the agent must select a plan to handle the adoption of the sub-goal.

In order to evaluate the computation load, we fix the number of agents in *one* agent and vary k from 10 to 30. The results depicted in Fig. 5(left)[6] show that as soon as the computation load increases, adopting a synchronous reasoning cycle with one thread per agent ($C1$) has the fastest response time, while adopting an asynchronous execution for the reasoning cycle ($C3$) has the worst response time. These results are expected due to the overhead caused by using thread pools ($C2$ and $C3$) to execute a single agent. Moreover, the concurrency control access mechanism necessary in the asynchronous reasoning cycle ($C3$) demonstrated to have a very high overhead in this scenario, where both deliberate and act stages must be executed constantly.

The MAS population is evaluated in the same form as in the multiplication table scenario. The results depicted in Fig. 5(right) show that adopting a synchronous reasoning cycle with a single thread pool ($C2$) has the fastest response time, while adopting a synchronous reasoning cycle with one thread per agent ($C1$) has the worst response time. Moreover, adopting an asynchronous reasoning cycle ($C3$) has a worse response time than adopting $C2$. While the worst response time for $C1$ is explained due to the high context-switch overhead caused by the high number of threads, the worse response time for $C3$ compared to $C2$ is caused by the overhead to handle the concurrent execution of the deliberate and act stages.

5.2 Intention Load

The intention load is evaluated based on the Fibonacci and the multiplication table scenarios by means of varying the number of intentions. Only *one* agent is used in the execution, but instead of only computing a single Fibonacci or printing a single multiplication table, the agent has from 10 to 1000 intentions (to compute Fibonacci numbers or to print the multiplication tables) being

---

[6] The response time for $fib(30)$ adopting the asynchronous reasoning cycle ($C3$) was 204117 ms, however we omitted from the graphic to let it readable to compare the other two configurations.

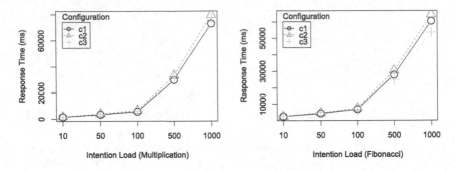

Fig. 6. Multiplication table (left) and Fibonacci (right): intention load.

executed concurrently. The results are depicted in Fig. 6. While adopting a synchronous reasoning cycle with one thread per agent (*C1*) showed the fastest response time in the multiplication table scenario, the fastest response time in the Fibonacci scenario happens when an asynchronous reasoning cycle (*C3*) is adopted. This result is expected because in the Fibonacci scenario, while one thread is deliberating about the sub-goals that are being produced by the act stage, another thread is executing intentions. Such advantage of the asynchronous reasoning cycle does not appear in the multiplication scenario because the only active reasoning cycle stage is the act stage. The overhead caused by the thread pool in the act stage of the asynchronous reasoning cycle is higher than the overhead of executing the sense and deliberate stages in the synchronous reasoning cycle with one thread per agent. Finally, the synchronous reasoning cycle with a single thread pool (*C2*) has the worst response time in both scenarios because of both the overhead of the thread pool and the overhead of executing the full reasoning cycle.

5.3 Perception Load

In this third experiment, we extend the multiplication table scenario (Code 2) to measure the agent reactivity, which consists on evaluating how long an agent takes to print the multiplication table from 1 to 100, while the environment is producing new percepts constantly. The environment basically consists on a set of counters that are updated everytime that an agent performs an `inc` action, thus producing percepts for agents that are observing the environment. All produced percepts are perceived by an agent in a *single shot*, which means that the state of the environment is given by the current value of all counters in a certain moment (i.e. all counters must have the same value since they are updated in the same operation). Thus, the belief update only finishes when all percepts have been processed. While one agent is responsible for performing the `inc` action, others simply observe the environment. The execution finishes when all agents finish to print the multiplication table.

In order to evaluate the perception load, we fix the number of agents in *one* agent and vary the number of counters from 100 to 3000. The results depicted in

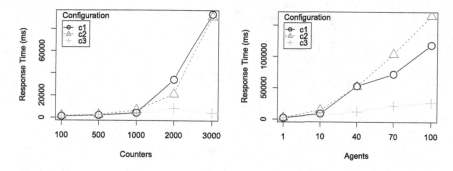

Fig. 7. Counting: perception load (left) and MAS population (right).

Fig. 7(left) show that adopting an asynchronous reasoning cycle has the fastest response time, while adopting a synchronous reasoning cycle, with one thread per agent (*C1*) or with a single thread pool (*C2*), have the worst response times. This is an expected result and important to highlight one benefit of adopting an asynchronous reasoning cycle. In the asynchronous execution, the agent can execute the act stage more than once before the sense or deliberate stages enter in a critical section (e.g. the deliberate stage starts to execute the belief update function). Thus, the act stage can be executed concurrently until it gets blocked because the concurrent access to some critical section. Moreover, the main reason for the worst response times for *C1* and *C2* is due to the execution of only *one* deed in each reasoning cycle. Thus, everytime that the cycle restarts, the agent needs to sense the environment and update the belief base, which has a huge computational cost as soon as the number of counters increases.

In order to see the impact of the MAS population, we vary the number of agents from 1 to 100. The results depicted in Fig. 7(right) show that adopting an asynchronous reasoning cycle (*C3*) has the fastest response time, while adopting a synchronous reasoning cycle with a single thread pool (*C2*) has the worst response time. The fastest response time for *C3* is again expected because the act stage can be executed concurrently while it does not get blocked due to the concurrent access to a shared structure with the sense or the deliberate stages.

5.4   Communication Load

The communication load is evaluated by means of a token-ring scenario. We implement a variation of the token-ring presented in [4]. The ring is made by means of linking each agent to another agent in a circular form. Each agent must pass the received tokens to its neighboring agent and each token must pass by each agent only once. The number of tokens in the system vary from 1 to t, in order to change the number of message exchanges. The initial configuration of the tokens is given by the formula: $a = i\, n/t$, where a is the current agent that will receive the token, i is the identifier of the current token that will be given for the agent, n is the number of agents in the ring (fixed in 500), and t is the

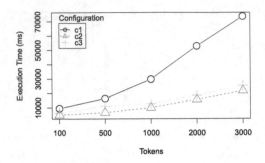

Fig. 8. Token ring: communication load.

number of tokens that must be given for the agents. The execution finishes when all tokens have been passed by all agents in the ring.

The results depicted in Fig. 8 show that adopting a synchronous reasoning cycle with a single thread pool ($C2$) has the fastest execution time, while adopting a synchronous reasoning cycle with one thread per agent ($C1$) has the worst execution time. The faster execution time for $C2$ compared to $C3$ is explained because all stages of the reasoning cycle must be executed for each received message. The agent receives messages (they are processed in the sense stage), selects a plan to forward the token (it is performed in the deliberate stage), and executes the intention to forward the token (it is performed in the act stage). In this scenario, all these activities have more or less the same computational cost. Thus, the asynchronous execution does not provide any advantage, because the overheads caused by the use of multiple thread pools (one for each reasoning cycle stage) and the concurrency control access mechanisms have a high impact on the execution. Finally, the reason for $C1$ has the worst execution time is again due to the context-switch overhead caused by the high number of threads.

6   Conclusion

In this paper, we enriched the Jason execution platform with a wider set of concurrency features. Our main contribution is the analysis of the Jason agent reasoning cycle and its concurrency architecture, as well as the integration of both synchronous and asynchronous reasoning cycles in a *concrete MAS execution platform*. It contrasts with other works like [5, 11, 19, 20] in the sense that we do not constrain our proposal to specific MAS applications. Instead, we allow the execution of any MAS application that can be developed using the Jason platform. The coherent and consistent execution of the agent reasoning cycle is ensured by controlling the concurrent access to certain data structures (e.g. the belief base). The same extensions done in the Jason execution platform can be integrated in other MAS execution platform, however always considering that each MAS platform has its own implementation, agent architecture, and agent reasoning cycle. For example, the 2APL and GOAL execution platforms can have their agent reasoning cycle revised in order to conceive a proper asynchronous version, as well as their agent architecture can be extended to support the use of different threads to execute each agent component separately.

Although the scenarios adopted to perform the experiments are very simple, they demonstrated that the extensions on the reasoning cycle not only allow the improvement of the overall MAS execution when adopted the most suitable configuration, but also the execution of individual agents, especially their reactivity, since agents can now perceive the environment, deliberate, and act concurrently. However, still more extensions must be integrated in the Jason platform in order to better exploit parallelism. Each agent could adopt a different concurrency configuration, e.g. while an agent can adopt a synchronous execution for the reasoning cycle, another agent can adopt an asynchronous reasoning cycle. Moreover, as stated in [9] (in the context of actors), different agents in the same MAS could have different demands, and balancing the CPU usage among the agents can make those with a heavier workload respond faster. The use of a different number of threads for each agent could help on this direction (e.g. the execution platform could use 3 threads for an agent and 5 threads for another agent). The number of threads could also be changed dynamically, supporting forms of self-adaptation, which is useful to improve the performance according to the current workload of each agent. Another direction could be the implementation of different scheduling strategies, thus agents with heavier workloads could be selected and executed more often.

In the future, besides integrating those features, new experiments will be performed considering more complex applications, where several characteristics can be combined at the same time (e.g. *communication load*, *MAS population*, and *perception load*), such as in the *Multi-Agent Programming Contest* (MAPC) scenarios [1]. Experiments will be also performed considering different number of computer cores, so that the effect of concurrency configurations can be evaluated according to the number of computer cores. The use of more powerful computers would allow to stress the parameters of the experiments, such as move from hundreds to thousands of agents.

References

1. Behrens, T., Dastani, M., Dix, J., Hübner, J., Koester, M., Novak, P., Schlesinger, F.: The multi-agent programming contest. AI Mag. **33**(4), 111–113 (2012)
2. Bellifemine, F., Bergenti, F., Caire, G., Poggi, A.: JADE - a Java agent development framework. In: Bordini, R.H., Dastani, M., Dix, J., El Fallah-Seghrouchni, A. (eds.) Multi-Agent Programming. Multiagent Systems, Artificial Societies, and Simulated Organizations, vol. 15, pp. 125–147. Springer, New York (2005)
3. Bordini, R.H., Hübner, J.F., Wooldridge, M.: Programming Multi-agent Systems in AgentSpeak Using Jason. Wiley, Liverpool (2007)
4. Cardoso, R.C., Zatelli, M.R., Hübner, J.F., Bordini, R.H.: Towards benchmarking actor- and agent-based programming languages. In: Proceedings of the Workshop on Programming Based on Actors, Agents, and Decentralized Control, AGERE! 2013, pp. 115–126. ACM, New York (2013)

5. da Costa, A.L., Bittencourt, G.: From a concurrent architecture to a concurrent autonomous agents architecture. In: Veloso, M.M., Pagello, E., Kitano, H. (eds.) RoboCup 1999. LNCS (LNAI), vol. 1856, pp. 274–285. Springer, Heidelberg (2000)
6. Dastani, M.: 2APL: a practical agent programming language. Auton. Agent. Multi-Agent Syst. **16**(3), 214–248 (2008)
7. Dennis, L.A., Fisher, M., Webster, M.P., Bordini, R.H.: Model checking agent programming languages. Autom. Softw. Eng. **19**(1), 5–63 (2012)
8. Evertsz, R., Fletcher, M., Frongillo, R., Jarvis, J., Brusey, J., Dance, S.: Implementing Industrial Multi-agent Systems Using JACK^{TM}. In: Dastani, M., Dix, J., El Fallah-Seghrouchni, A. (eds.) PROMAS 2003. LNCS (LNAI), vol. 3067, pp. 18–48. Springer, Heidelberg (2004)
9. Francesquini, E., Goldman, A., Méhaut, J.-F.: Improving the performance of actor model runtime environments on multicore and manycore platforms. In: Proceedings of the Workshop on Programming Based on Actors, Agents, and Decentralized Control, AGERE! 2013, pp. 109–114. ACM, New York (2013)
10. Hindriks, K.V.: Programming rational agents in GOAL. In: El Fallah Seghrouchni, A., Dix, J., Dastani, M., Bordini, R.H. (eds.) Multi-agent Programming, pp. 119–157. Springer, New York (2009)
11. Kostiadis, K., Hu, H.: A multi-threaded approach to simulated soccer agents for the RoboCup competition. In: Veloso, M.M., Pagello, E., Kitano, H. (eds.) RoboCup 1999. LNCS (LNAI), vol. 1856, pp. 366–377. Springer, Heidelberg (2000)
12. Lee, S.-K., Cho, M., Yoon, H.-J., Eun, S.-B., Yoon, H., Cho, J.-W., Lee, J.: Design and implementation of a multi-threaded TMN agent system. In: Proceedings of the 1999 International Workshops on Parallel Processing, pp. 332–337 (1999)
13. Muldoon, C., O'Hare, G.M.P., Collier, R.W., O'Grady, M.J.: Towards pervasive intelligence: reflections on the evolution of the agent factory framework. In: El Fallah Seghrouchni, A., Dix, J., Dastani, M., Bordini, R.H. (eds.) Multi-agent Programming, pp. 187–212. Springer, New York (2009)
14. O'Hare, G.M.P.: Agent factory: an environment for the fabrication of multi-agent systems. In: Distributed Artificial Intelligence, pp. 449–484 (1996)
15. Pokahr, A., Braubach, L., Lamersdorf, W.: Jadex: a BDI reasoning engine. In: Bordini, R.H., Dastani, M., Dix, J., El Fallah-Seghrouchni, A. (eds.) Multi-agent Programming. Multiagent Systems, Artificial Societies, and Simulated Organizations, vol. 15, pp. 149–174. Springer, New York (2005)
16. Ricci, A., Santi, A.: Programming abstractions for integrating autonomous and reactive behaviors: an agent-oriented approach. In: Proceedings of the 2nd Edition on Programming Systems, Languages and Applications Based on Actors, Agents, and Decentralized Control Abstractions, AGERE! 2012, pp. 83–94. ACM, New York (2012)
17. Wieczorek, D., Albayrak, Ş.: Open scalable agent architecture for telecommunication applications. In: Albayrak, Ş., Garijo, F.J. (eds.) IATA 1998. LNCS (LNAI), vol. 1437, pp. 233–249. Springer, Heidelberg (1998)
18. Zatelli, M.R., Ricci, A., Hübner, J.F.: Evaluating different concurrency configurations for executing multi-agent systems. In: Baldoni, M., Baresi, L., Dastani, M. (eds.) EMAS 2015. LNCS, vol. 9318, pp. 212–230. Springer, Heidelberg (2015). doi:10.1007/978-3-319-26184-3_12
19. Zhang, H., Huang, S.Y.: Are parallel BDI agents really better? In: Proceedings of the 17th European Conference on Artificial Intelligence (ECAI), Riva Del Garda, Italy, pp. 305–309. IOS Press, Amsterdam (2006)
20. Zhang, H., Huang, S.-Y.: A general framework for parallel BDI agents in dynamic environments. Web Intell. Agent Syst. Int. J. **6**, 327–351 (2008)

Hardware Architecture Benchmarking for Simulation of Human Immune System by Multi-agent Systems

Fábio Rodrigues Martins[1,2], Alcione de Paiva Oliveira[1,2(✉)],
Ricardo Santos Ferreira[1,2], and Fábio Ribeiro Cerqueira[1,2]

[1] Departamento de Informática, Universidade Federal de Viçosa,
Viçosa 365700-900, Brazil
frm.martins@gmail.com, alcione@gmail.com, cacauvicosa@gmail.com,
frcerqueira@gmail.com
[2] The University of Sheffield, Western Bank, Sheffield S10 2TN, UK

Abstract. The emergence of agent oriented systems has provided an alternative approach to address many complex problems that require distributed behavior, local decisions, and emerging global behavior from the interactions of their basic elements. There are several natural, artificial and social phenomena that present these features. However, despite providing a suitable tool for modeling complex distributed systems, implementations of multi-agent systems are limited by the available hardware architecture. A recent possibility to circumvent this problem is the use of graphics cards to implement such systems. Nevertheless, these devices reach the optimal performance when agents have homogeneous and simple behavior, which might not be the case of many problems. Systems such as simulators of the immune system, in addition to having a large number of agents with complex behavior, those agents communicate massively, indirectly, through dissemination of various substances in their environment. Diffusion of substances is something easily simulated in modern current graphics cards, but the problem is to provide the results of those simulations to thousands (or millions) of agents simultaneously. This paper presents a benchmarking conducted to determine a suitable software/hardware architecture to implement such a system. The results show that a heterogeneous system can have a better performance.

Keywords: Multi-agent systems · GPU benchmarking · Immune system simulators

1 Introduction

The emergence of agent oriented systems (Agent Oriented Software programming - AOP) [1] made available a new approach to cope with complex problems that require distributed behavior, local decisions, and emerging global behavior

A. de Paiva Oliveira—The author receives grant from capes, process n.0449/15-6.

M. Rovatsos et al. (Eds.): EUMAS 2015/AT 2015, LNAI 9571, pp. 441–448, 2016.
DOI: 10.1007/978-3-319-33509-4_34

from the interactions of their basic entities. Many natural, artificial and social phenomena fit these characteristics: Behavior of animal hordes, crowd behavior, or even the behavior of cells in an organism. Nonetheless, despite providing an appropriate means for modeling complex distributed systems, implementations of multi-agent systems are restricted by the available hardware architecture. Deployment of these systems requires massively distributed processing and the available hardware is essentially sequential. It can be argued that there are computer clusters available in research centers that may be used for this purpose. However, the clusters do not provide yet a number of nodes in the order of magnitude that is needed in complex systems concerning the number of their constituent elements. In addition, there is a limitation concerning the speed of communication between cluster nodes, which imposes severe restrictions for modeling systems with intense communication among agents. A recent possibility to avoid this issue is the use of graphics cards to implement such systems. However, these devices reach the optimal performance when agents present homogeneous and elementary behavior, which is not the case of many problems. This restriction is particularly striking in multi-agent systems (MAS) that seek to simulate the behavior of biological systems such as the human immune system. What makes them more troublesome, and further increases their complexity, is the fact that they have a large number of agents with complex behavior, and the agents communicate massively, indirectly, by diffusion of various substances in the environment. Diffusion of substances is something easily simulated in modern graphics cards. However, the crucial point is to present the consequences of this simulation to thousands (or millions) of agents simultaneously. To help making progress in these matters, it is necessary to develop a hardware and software architecture that is scalable in the number of agents that communicate intensively. The combination of the processing power of graphics cards with clusters equipped with high-performance processors seems to be the most promising approach. However, it is necessary to define the best way of distributing tasks and data communication among these two architectures. This paper presents a benchmarking performed in order to detect the best combination of architecture and distribution of tasks to be used in multi-agent systems targeted for modeling biological systems such as the immune system. The results presented in this paper show that using a multi-agent system in conjunction with the GPU leads to a better speedup when compared with version based purely on the CPU.

2   Related Works

There are several studies that analyze the use of GPU in multi-agent systems. However, the problem and the approach differ in some way from the problem we are dealing with. Chen et al. presented a simulation of the blood coagulation system [2]. They implemented the simulation using GPU and other three different platforms: NetLogo, Repast, and a direct C version, in order to perform comparisons. In their experiments, it was demonstrated that the computational speed of the GPU implementation of the million-level scale of agents was over

10 times faster than the direct C version, over 100 times faster than the Repast version, and over 300 times faster than the NetLogo simulation. The problem they simulated differs from ours in the sense that the substances do not undergo diffusion. Therefore the information that agents access remains static, i.e., there is no need to update the grid at each cycle. In addition, the behavior of the agents is simple, making it possible to be implemented efficiently with GPU.

Richmond et al. described an application of the flexible large-scale agent modelling environment framework on GPU (FLAME GPU) for simulation of biological systems on the cellular level. The authors stated that the limitations of the GPU for simulating cellular systems, such as the difficulty in including stochasticity and complex behavior, were addressed with FLAME GPU. The Simulation steps utilizing brute force computation were accelerated by approximately of 250 times when compared with FLAME (non GPU) simulation running on a single CPU. As before, the problem they simulated differs from ours in the sense that there are no substances that undergo diffusion. Therefore, it is not equivalent to the behavior of the immune system [3].

3   Materials and Methods

In order to perform the benchmarking a small multi-agent system, simulating bacteria, immune cells, as well as a set of cytokines (chemical signals) and antibiotics, was developed. The space is defined by a two-dimensional grid whose size varies in each test set. The regions are simulated as a discrete space in a two-dimensional grid in which each agent has a position (i, j). More than one agent can occupy the same position, which somehow simulates a 3D space. The agent is moved by changing its position to a new position in the *Moore neighborhood* [4]. Thus, an agent cannot skip positions, i.e., it needs to move one position at a time. In such two-dimensional-grid structure, the Moore neighborhood (of radius one) comprises the eight neighboring positions to a central position. Bacteria randomly move in this space and reproduce by division in a certain time interval. If a cell of the immune system finds a bacterium, the latter is eliminated. If the antibiotic concentration at bacteria location is greater than a certain threshold, no bacterium will reproduce. To model substance diffusion, we used Eq. 1, suggested by North et al. [5]. When a substance is released with a given value at an initial position (x, y), a diffusion gradient is generated based on the following equation:

$$newValue(x, y) = evap \times (oldValue(x, y) + diff \times (nghAvg - oldValue(x, y)))$$
(1)

In Eq. 1, *evap* is the evaporation constant, *diff* is the diffusion constant, *oldValue* returns the current value of the substance concentration at (x, y), and *nghAvg* is the average of substance concentrations in the Moore neighborhood around the point (x, y). This calculation is recomputed at every cycle and for every grid position for every substance layer. This procedure is performed intensely and is highly suitable to be performed by GPU hardware. In a simulation involving a grid of a certain size, it is not possible to keep a grid of each substance in GPU memory. It is then necessary, at each cycle, to copy each grid of each substance to GPU memory, perform calculations, and copy the values back to main memory, causing a substantial data traffic on the PCI bus.

The benchmarking results shows a comparison between an implementation using only the CPU and an implementation keeping agents in the CPU and performing the calculation of substance diffusion in the GPU. The reason for this implementation is to try to allocate to each computer architecture what is more suitable for processing. However, this distribution imposes a bottleneck in the processing, i.e., the data transfer between main memory and GPU memory. Therefore, the main focus of this benchmarking is analyzing the impact of data transfer via PCI bus in this distribution of tasks between the CPU and the GPU. To implement the multi-agent system in the CPU, we used the framework Flame [6]. Communication between FLAME and CUDA code was done through link-editing. The benchmarking was carried out in an i7-4790 CPU 3.60GHz microcomputer equipped with 16 GB RAM and a NVidia GeForce GTX 780 Ti with 2880 cuda cores. We used version 6.5 of the CUDA library.

4   Results

The parameter settings of our experiments were: (1) number of layers for calculating substance diffusion: 1, 5, 10, 15, and 20; (2) Number of agents: 100, 1000, and 10000; and (3) Matrix dimension of float datatypes: 1024×1024, 2048×2048, and 16384 × 16384. In each case, we performed 1000 cycles (ticks). The speedup shown in each table was calculated by the equation below:

$$S = \frac{T1 - T2}{T2} \times 100, \tag{2}$$

where T1 is the CPU runtime and T2 is the GPU runtime. The result is presented in percentage. For the matrix dimension of 16384 × 16384, the experiments with 15 and 20 layers were not executed due to the fact that the CPU has 16 GB of RAM, and each layer occupies about 1 GB. In the following, we analyze the results from different perspectives.

4.1   Number of Agents

When looking at the number of agents in relation to the number of layers, it can be identified that as the number of agents increases the speedup decreases. For just one layer, the biggest speedup occurred with matrix dimension of 16384 × 16384 and 100 agents, recording 81.03 % of speedup. Still for one layer the best speedups for 1000 agents and 10000 agents were 75.62 % and 1.19 %, respectively, also for a matrix dimension of 16384 × 16384. These variations can be observed in Table 1.

A similar behavior occurred with experiments for 5, 10, 15, and 20 layers, 100 agent and, a matrix dimension of 1024 × 1024, where it was obtained a greater speedup (Table 2). Initially, the speedup was 85.96 % for 100 agents. With 1000

Table 1. Number of layers= 1 - Varying number and matrix dimension (Time in seconds).

Dimension	Agents	CPU ONLY	CPU+GPU	Speedup %
1024 × 1024	100	23	13	**76.92**
2048 × 2048		75	42	**78.57**
16384 × 16384		4446	2456	**81.03**
1024 × 1024	1000	180	170	**5.88**
2048 × 2048		321	287	**11.85**
16384 × 16384		4726	2691	**75.62**
1024 × 1024	10000	679	671	**1.19**
2048 × 2048		4498	4464	**0.76**
16384 × 16384		31382	30965	**1.35**

agents it went to 37.55 %, and with 10000 the value went down to 13.61 %. This behavior was repeated in all the analysed situations: whenever the number of agents increased the speedup decreased.

Table 2. Number of layers= 10 - Varying number and matrix dimension (Time in seconds).

Dimension	Agents	CPU ONLY	CPU+GPU	Speedup %
1024 × 1024	100	212	114	**85.96**
2048 × 2048		732	401	**82.54**
16384 × 16384		44537	25502	**74.64**
1024 × 1024	1000	370	269	**37.55**
2048 × 2048		979	645	**51.78**
16384 × 16384		44798	26070	**71.84**
1024 × 1024	10000	868	764	**13.61**
2048 × 2048		5159	4829	**6.83**
16384 × 16384		71478	52052	**37.32**

Table 3 presents values for 20 layers. Despite missing values for matrices of dimension 16384 × 16384, the tendency described above is maintained.

4.2   Number of Layers

Table 4 shows the variation in speedup as the number of layers increases. The matrix dimension is fixed in 1024 × 1024, while the values for the number of agents are: 100, 1000, and 10000. In this simulation, we can highlight the example 1024 × 1024 − 100 agents, which resulted in 76.92 % of speedup for 1 layer,

446   F.R. Martins et al.

Table 3. Number of layers= 20 - Varying number and matrix dimension (Time in seconds).

Dimension	Agents	CPU ONLY	CPU+GPU	Speedup %
1024 × 1024	100	421	213	**97.65**
2048 × 2048		1464	795	**84.15**
16384 × 16384		-	-	**0.00**
1024 × 1024	1000	579	377	**53.58**
2048 × 2048		1710	1052	**62.55**
16384 × 16384		-	-	**0.00**
1024 × 1024	10000	1079	876	**23.17**
2048 × 2048		5925	5233	**13.22**
16384 × 16384		-	-	**0.00**

in 84.48 % for 5 layers, in 85.96 % for 10 layers, in 92.68 % for 15 layers, in 97.65 % for 20 layers. Therefore, as shown in Table 4, for 100 agents, the increase of layers has resulted in significant gains in speedup in all cases.

Table 4. Results varying number of layers and number of agents, while fixing the matrix dimension in 1024 × 1024. The results are shown in seconds.

Number of agents	1 layer	5 layers	10 layers	15 layers	20 layers
100 - CPU	23	107	212	316	421
100 - GPU	13	58	114	164	213
1000 - CPU	180	265	370	474	579
1000 - GPU	170	214	269	317	377
10000 - CPU	679	765	868	974	1079
10000 - GPU	671	713	764	822	876

Table 5 presents the results with matrix dimension of 2048 × 2048. The best improvements were, once more, observed for 100 agents: 78.57 % of speedup for 1 layer, 79.02 % of speedup for 5 layers, 82.54 % of speedup for 10 layers, 81.6 % of speedup for 15 layers, and 84.15 % of speedup for 20 layers. Note that in relation to the test with 10 layers, the test with 15 layers showed a decrease. However, in testing with 20 layers, the speedup were improved. In the case of 2048 × 2048 − 1000, the speedups were: 11.85 % of speedup for 1 layer, 42.89 % of speedup for 5 layers, 51.78 % of speedup for 10 layers, 57.56 % of speedup for 15 layers, and 62.55 % of speedup for 20 layers. The experiment 2048 × 2048 − 10000 resulted in similar gains. Therefore, for this dimension, the GPU implementation led to significant performance gains.

Table 6 presents the results with matrix dimension of 16384 × 16384, and varying number of layers and number of agents. The speedup values were: 75.62 %

Table 5. Results varying number of layers and number of agents, while fixing the matrix dimension in 2048 × 2048. The results are shown in seconds.

Number of agents	1 layer	5 layers	10 layers	15 layers	20 layers
100 - CPU	75	367	732	1097	1464
100 - GPU	42	205	401	604	795
1000 - CPU	321	643	979	1344	1710
1000 - GPU	287	450	645	853	1052
10000 - CPU	4498	4795	5159	5525	5925
10000 - GPU	4464	4632	4829	5036	5233

of speedup for 1 layer, 75.31 % of speedup for 5 layers, and 71.84 % of speedup for 10 layers. The experiments with 15 and 20 layers were not accomplished due to the limit of RAM installed. In this set of tests it is important to note that as the number of agents increases, the speedup decreases. However, with the setting $16384 \times 16384 - 10000$ the speedup was increased, presenting a significant improvement.

Table 6. Results varying number of layers and number of agents, while fixing the matrix dimension in 16384 × 16384. The results are shown in seconds.

Number of agents	1 layer	5 layers	10 layers	15 layers	20 layers
100 - CPU	4446	22228	44537	66660	–
100 - GPU	2456	12551	25502	–	–
1000 - CPU	4726	22505	44798	66904	–
1000 - GPU	2691	12837	26070	–	–
10000 - CPU	31382	49200	71478	93960	–
10000 - GPU	30965	40233	52052	–	–

It is important to notice that in all plots (Tables 4, 5 and 6), as the number of layers increases, the differences between the CPU version and the GPU version increases, i.e., the speedup for the same number of agents is improved, as the number of layers is increased, although occurs an increase of the amount of traffic between the main memory and the GPU memory.

5   Conclusion

This work presents performance tests to compare two approaches for the simulation of the immune system involving diffusion of substances. Both approaches adopt the agent-based simulation. One approach was based purely on the CPU, while the other used the GPU in the calculation of the diffusion of substances.

The results presented in this paper show that using a multi-agent system in conjunction with the GPU leads to a better speedup when compared with versions based purely on the CPU. The CPU+GPU version was superior in all tested cases, especially the test with 20 layers and matrix with dimension of 1024×1024, which achieved a speedup of 97.65 %. As the number of agents increases, the advantage of using GPU decreases naturally, due to the increase in processing time on the CPU. For systems with a large number of agents, one must seek ways to implement the agents on the GPU, as the case of frameworks like FLAME-GPU. This will be the next step in our research. Another option being investigated is the possibility of using multiple GPUs.

Acknowledgments. This research is supported in part by the funding agencies FAPEMIG, CNPq, and CAPES.

References

1. Shoham, Y.: Agent-oriented programming. Artif. Intell. **60**(1), 51–92 (1993)
2. Chen, W., Ward, K., Li, Q., Kecman, V., Najarian, K., Menke, N.: Agent based modeling of blood coagulation system: implementation using a gpu based high speed framework. In: 2011 Annual International Conference of the IEEE on Engineering in Medicine and Biology Society, EMBC, pp. 145–148. IEEE (2011)
3. Richmond, P., Walker, D., Coakley, S., Romano, D.: High performance cellular level agent-based simulation with flame for the gpu. Briefings Bioinform. **11**(3), 334–347 (2010)
4. Dewri, R., Chakraborti, N.: Simulating recrystallization through cellular automata and genetic algorithms. Modell. Simul. Mater. Sci. Eng. **13**(2), 173 (2005)
5. North, M.J., Collier, N.T., Ozik, J., Tatara, E.R., Macal, C.M., Bragen, M., Sydelko, P.: Complex adaptive systems modeling with repast simphony. Complex adapt. syst. model. **1**(1), 1–26 (2013)
6. Kiran, M., Richmond, P., Holcombe, M., Chin, L.S., Worth, D., Greenough, C.: Flame: simulating large populations of agents on parallel hardware architectures. In: Proceedings of the 9th International Conference on Autonomous Agents and Multiagent Systems, vol. 1, pp. 1633–1636. International Foundation for Autonomous Agents and Multiagent Systems (2010)

Automating Personalized Learning
Through Motivation

Patricia Gutierrez[✉], Nardine Osman, and Carles Sierra

IIIA-CSIC, Bellaterra, Spain
patricia@iiia.csic.es

Abstract. In this paper, we propose a model that personalises the learning experience of a student by automatically selecting the exercises that
best suit the student's competences and that also maintain the student's
motivation at a certain (high) level.

1 Motivation

Motivation is a big issue in learning theory and cognitive science [2,5,7,8]. It
is known that motivation is a trigger for eagerness, close attention, cognitive
development, personal growth and ultimately goal achievement. Most importantly, motivation is a key factor for keeping any learning experience pleasant
independently of its speed or success. If an experience is rewarding or pleasurable, one most likely would want to repeat it, with the expectation to obtain
more of that positive reward, and as we know, repetition and practice are very
strongly linked to learning.

The relationship between rewards and learning has been studied extensively
in fields such as psychology, neuroscience and pedagogy.[1] Studies such as [3] show
how the biological reward mechanism works in relation with reinforcement learning. It has been found that dopamine, which is a neurotransmitter associated
with the reward system of the brain, plays an important role in learning, choice
and belief formation. In the brain, dopamine functions as a neurotransmitter (a
chemical messenger), that is, a chemical released by neurons (nerve cells) to send
signals to other nerve cells. The brain includes several distinct dopamine path-
ways, one of which plays a major role in reward-motivated behavior. Most types

---

[1] The relations between expectations, rewards and dopamine release has also been
studied in the field of music. [9] discusses how we get from the perception of sound
patterns and the prediction of future sound patterns to reward and valuation. They
state that when listening to a new musical piece, one can expect a certain set sounds
to occur, based on one's history of listening to music. For instance, when we have
heard a certain set of patterns in music, we expect a certain set of sounds to occur
and we also know when they are supposed to occur in time. These expectations are
related to templates derived from one's individual history of listening. Thus, in some
way we are able to decode relationships and patterns in music, such that it generates
expectations about upcoming events based on past events.

© Springer International Publishing Switzerland 2016
M. Rovatsos et al. (Eds.): EUMAS 2015/AT 2015, LNAI 9571, pp. 449–454, 2016.
DOI: 10.1007/978-3-319-33509-4_35

of reward increase the level of dopamine in the brain, and also most addictive drugs increase dopamine neuronal activity.

The reward prediction error hypothesis says that neurons release levels of dopamine in proportion to the difference between a "predicted reward" and the actual "experienced reward" of a particular event. For instance, an unpredicted reward elicits activation (positive prediction error), a fully predicted reward elicits no response, and the omission of a predicted reward induces a depression (negative error). Reinforcement learning algorithms in computer science, where expected rewards can be estimated considering recently viewed rewards on sequential trials, are heavily inspired in these neuroscientific findings and behaviorist psychology approaches.

In this paper, we make the following analogy. Just like dopamine is released when reward is greater than expected leading to an increased desire or motivation towards the reward [1], we say when the mark a student gets is greater that his self-assessment this leads to an increased desire or motivation towards the subject the student is learning. And as we have pointed out before, motivation is key for any learning experience.

As a result of this analogy, we propose a model that personalises the learning experience of a student not only by selecting the exercises to suit the student's competences (as is currently common, e.g. knewton.com), but also to maintain the student's motivation at a certain (high) level.

2   eLearning and Feedback Expectations

In this paper, we want to estimate the level of reward of a student, and personalise his/her learning experience to maintain a certain level of reward. To achieve this, we will estimate the *expected reward* and the *actual reward* for a given student and a given assignment.

In a learning scenario, we understand marks as rewards. The marks that a student receives (whether from a tutor or from a learning community) can be understood as positive/negative rewards. Whether the reward is positive or negative for the student, as our analogy illustrates, depends on the difference between the *expected reward* of the student and the *actual reward* the student receives.

We can think of *expected rewards* as self-assessments (what a student may expect in terms of marking) and *actual rewards* as the actual assessment the student received. (whether it is the teacher's assessment or the community's assessment, where members of the learning community may assess the student and those would get aggregated into a final mark). The difference between these two values (expected and actual rewards) describes the level of reward obtained by the student. We refer to this difference as the student's *motivation* value.

We say receiving a mark higher than expected results in a positive motivation value, whereas receiving a mark lower than expected results in a negative motivation value. It is possible then to design a *sensor* for a class that would give us a hint of the motivational level of each student. This sensor could help the teacher to keep track of which students are fulfilling their expectations (have a high motivation value) and which users may feel discouraged (have a low motivation value) to take further actions for that students in the learning process. Such actions, as we will see shortly, can include the personalised selection of assignments for that particular student, according to its motivational levels.

We do not want students to stop making mistakes when solving assignments, of course, as mistakes are a necessary step in any learning process. What we are interested in, however, is to maintain a positive motivation level. In other words, we want the learning process to become a pleasurable experience (a dopamine release experience) which will motivate the student to repeat that experience, performing similar assignments to the one just performed. We believe that increasing the complexity of assignments while maintaining a good (positive) motivation level is the key to an optimal learning path.

We say this criteria should be tailored to every student since each individual has a different learning pace and capacity which impacts his/her motivational level. For instance, some students might not feel challenged enough by an assignment and hence get bored, while others may find the same assignment too complicated and get discouraged. In other words, there is no one ideal assignment for all students. Taking into consideration the individuality of each student is very important for effective teaching, as it is the need to propose assignments tailored to students' different performances.

As mentioned above, we want to design a sensor that can sense the motivation level of students. We can then take into account the individuality of students based on their history of motivation. The question that this paper tries to address is then: *Given a student and a selected assignment, what is the expected self-assessment and the expected actual assessment?* In other words, what is the expected motivation for a particular student being assigned with a particular assignment? Based on these expectations, we then need to decide *how to optimise the learning path for a particular student.* In other words, what is the sequence of assignments that should be assigned to the student to maintain a good level of challenge and motivation?

3   Formal Model

We assume there is a set of problems P to achieve an education competence c_P, a group G of students that have to achieve that capacity and a teacher t. Students solve problems from P and receive a mark in the range $E = [0, 10]$. Marks can be either self-assessed (when the student assess their own work) or externally assessed (e.g. by the teacher, colleagues, an automated software, etc.). We note by $se(\alpha, p_i) \in [0, 10]$ the self evaluation of student α over problem $p_i \in P$. Similarly, we note by $fe(\alpha, p_i) \in [0, 10]$ the final evaluation provided by some external entity (e.g. G's evaluation or t's evaluation) of α's performance over

p_i.[2] When one of the problems is solved and a final mark is provided with a 10, we consider the student has achieved competence c_P.

We conceptualise the *motivation* that α obtains from solving a problem $p \in P$ as the difference between the final assessment and α's self assessment, that is:

$$fe(\alpha, p) - se(\alpha, p).$$

We assume there is a history of evaluations:

$$H = \langle (se(\alpha,p), fe(\alpha,p)), (se(\beta,q), fe(\beta,q)), (se(\gamma,r), fe(\gamma,r)), \dots \rangle$$

that allows to compute expectations on se and fe via a learning procedure (e.g. via Bayesian inference). That is, we assume we can compute for all $X \in P$ and $Y \in [0, 10]$, the following expectation (or probabilities):

– $P(se(\alpha, X) = Y | H)$
– $P(fe(\alpha, X) = Y | H)$

We could also compute the following probability distribution, representing the *expected motivation* of a new problem p to be solved:

$$P(fe(\alpha, p) - se(\alpha, p) = Y | H)$$

Given these expectations, we can define different learning strategies to select new assignments for student α. In the following, EMD stands for earth mover's distance [6] between two probability distributions[3] and *Beta* stands for the beta distribution, where $Beta(1, 100)$ is a distribution totally skewed towards 0. Consider now the following different learning strategy functions, noted as $New(\alpha, H) \in P$.

MaxMotivation: Maximise motivation, which is achieved by looking for an assignment that will maximise the difference between the expected self-assessment and the expected final assessment:

$$New(\alpha, H) = \arg\max_{p} EMD(\mathbb{P}(fe(\alpha, p) = Y | H), \mathbb{P}(se(\alpha, p) = Y | H)) \quad (1)$$

---

[2] For G's evaluation, where one essentially calculates the community's assessments, the COMAS algorithm can be used [4]. COMAS calculates the final assessment by aggregating peer assessments in the community in such a way that more weight is given to those assessments whose assessors are more trusted by the tutor. To calculate the tutor's trust in students, a trust graph is built based on how similar are the students' assessments to those of the tutor.

[3] If probability distributions are viewed as piles of dirt, then the earth mover's distance measures the minimum cost for transforming one pile into the other. This cost is equivalent to the 'amount of dirt' times the distance by which it is moved, or the distance between elements of the probability distribution's support. The range of EMD is $[0, 1]$, where 0 represents the minimum distance and 1 represents the maximum possible distance.

MaxChallenge: Maximise learning speed, which is achieved by looking for an assignment that will maximise the expected final assessment:

$$New(\alpha, H) = \arg\max_{p} EMD(\mathbb{P}(fe(\alpha,p) = Y|H), Beta(1,100)) \qquad (2)$$

MaxSelfAssessment: Maximise student self's opinion, which is achieved by looking for an assignment that will maximise the expected self-assessment:

$$New(\alpha, H) = \arg\max_{p} EMD(\mathbb{P}(se(\alpha,p) = Y|H), Beta(1,100)) \qquad (3)$$

Balance: Maximise the balance between motivation and learning speed, which essentially combines MaxMotivation and MaxChallenge:

$$New(\alpha, H) = \arg\max_{p} EMD(\mathbb{P}(fe(\alpha,p) = Y|H), \mathbb{P}(se(\alpha,p) = Y|H)) \cdot$$
$$EMD(\mathbb{P}(fe(\alpha,p) = Y|H), Beta(1,100)) \qquad (4)$$

4   Position

We conjecture that *learning strategies that aim at increasing motivation (e.g. our MaxMotivation and Balance strategies) result in more effective learning.* This conjecture is inspired by research results that highlight the importance of motivation in enhancing learning [2,5,8].

To measure motivational levels and expectations, the model presented in this paper is designed based on the evidence that, when a reward is greater than expected, the level of dopamine release increases, which consequently increases reward-seeking behaviors and the desire or motivation towards the reward [1]. The model proposed in this paper assumes that *marks, in a learning environment, are a type of reward* and thus we interpret motivation as the difference between the expected mark of the student and the actual final mark the student receives.

We say that personalised learning paths tailored to individual students based on their motivation values and expectations are more suitable than providing the same assignment for all students to achieve a given competence or just selecting randomly an assignment that achieves that competence. Although this is not a novel approach in pedagogy, automating this process for the tutor is new and it is — to the best of out knowledge — not present in current online learning plattforms.This conjecture will be put to test with an implementation of the idea and experiments with real students.

Acknowledgments. This work is supported by the following projects: PRAISE (European Commission, grant # 388770), CollectiveMind (Spanish Ministry of Economy & Competitiveness (MINECO), grant # TEC2013-49430-EXP), and MILESS (MINECO, grant # TIN2013-45039-P).

References

1. Arias-Carrión, O., Pöppel, E.: Dopamine, learning, and reward-seeking behavior. Acta Neurobiol. Exp. (Wars) **67**(4), 481–488 (2007)
2. Boekaerts, M.: Motivation to learn. In: Educational Practices Series. International Bureau of Education (2002)
3. Glimcher, P.W.: Understanding dopamine and reinforcement learning: the dopamine reward prediction error hypothesis. Proc. Natl. Acad. Sci. U.S.A. **108**, 15647–15654 (2011)
4. Gutierrez, P., Osman, N., Sierra, C.: Trust-based community assessment. Pattern Recognit. Lett. **67**, 49–58 (2015)
5. Kyndt, E., Dochy, F., Struyven, K., Cascallar, E.: The direct and indirect effect of motivation for learning on students' approaches to learning through the perceptions of workload and task complexity. High. Educ. Res. Dev. **30**, 135–150 (2011)
6. Rubner, Y., Tomasi, C., Guibas, L.J.: A metric for distributions with applications to image databases. In: Proceedings of ICCV, pp. 59–66. IEEE Computer Society (1998)
7. Wise, R.A.: Dopamine, learning and motivation. Nat. Rev. Neurosci. **5**, 483–494 (2004)
8. Wlodkowski, R.J.: Enhancing Adult Motivation to Learn: A Comprehensive Guide for Teaching All Adults. Wiley, Chichester (2011)
9. Zatorre, R.J., Salimpoor, V.N.: From perception to pleasure: music and its neural substrates. Proc. Natl. Acad. Sci. U.S.A. **110**, 10430–10437 (2013)

Agent Based Simulation to Evaluate Adaptive Caching in Distributed Databases

Santhilata Kuppili Venkata[1]([✉]), Jeroen Keppens[1], and Katarzyna Musial[2]

[1] Department of Informatics, King's College London, London, UK
{santhilata.kuppili_venkata,jeroen.keppens}@kcl.ac.uk
[2] Faculty of Science and Technology, Bournemouth University, Poole, UK
kmusialgabrys@bournemouth.ac.uk

Abstract. Caching frequently used data is a common practice to improve query performance in database systems. But traditional algorithms used for cache management prove to be insufficient in distributed environment where groups of users require similar or related data from multiple databases. Repeated data transfers can become a bottleneck leading to long query response time and high resource utilization. Our work focuses on adaptive algorithms to decide on optimal grain of data to be cached and cache refreshment techniques to reduce data transfers. In this paper, we present agent based simulation to investigate and in consequence improve cache management in the distributed database environment. Dynamic grain size and decisions on cache refreshment are made as a result of coordination and interaction between agents. Initial results show better response time and higher data availability compared to traditional caching techniques.

Keywords: Cache management · Distributed databases · Agent based simulation

1 Introduction

Nowadays, large volumes of data are inseparably connected with scientific and commercial applications. Common query interface provides uniform access and allows a client to interact with multiple data stores seamlessly. Often user queries tend to get repeated when groups of users working on related projects, send their queries to multiple databases. Repeated queries need same data to be retrieved and processed several times causing repeated data transfers, high bandwidth utilisation and thus delayed responses.

The main focus of our research is to investigate the effectiveness of adaptive caching with sub-query fragmentation technique [1]. This work aims to reduce average query response time and reduction in data transfers. Adaptive caching in distributed cache system works on the aggregated information across groups of users related by a specified work-flow and need information at various stages of their work repeatedly from different locations. It is observed that when users are

© Springer International Publishing Switzerland 2016
M. Rovatsos et al. (Eds.): EUMAS 2015/AT 2015, LNAI 9571, pp. 455–462, 2016.
DOI: 10.1007/978-3-319-33509-4_36

distributed, often their queries are not repeated fully but overlap only partially. We utilise this feature to develop sub-query data caching based on the query information collected from multiple groups of users. Cache collects data needed across users and adapts itself to common data usage patterns.

Adaptive caching works by collaborating the knowledge gathered by independent cache units in the system. We have developed a query analysis tool (QA tool) to support distributed query decomposition in the distributed database environment. Each cache unit supply information about the query origination and usage of data locally. QA tool then analyzes the information to find associations between queries and finds patterns. QA tool predicts future requirements and takes a decision about the best way to cache data across multiple cache units.

It was expensive to obtain a dedicated real life distributed system to evaluate our cache techniques and their suitability. Adaptive cache system requires independent autonomous cache units to collect data about queries and forward information about their current and predicted needs. Hence the nature of this application makes an ideal model for agent based simulation. Our simulation has active agents such as users, cache units, query analyzer(s) that work together and coordinate their actions with static agents such as databases. This paper mainly is focused on two goals (i) reduction in response time, (ii) efficient cached data management as a result of cache grain modification and cache refreshment.

This paper is organised as follows: A brief context of caching in databases, adaptive caching is given in Sect. 2. A detailed application of the multi-agent system and implementation of agents for the successful cache maintenance is explained in Sect. 3. Evaluation of simulation and analysis of the results are presented in Sect. 4.

2   Background

A general background about caching in distributed database environment and a brief introduction to sub-query fragmentation is explained in this section.

Caching in Databases: Data caching is used to improve the performance of the database management system to achieve reduced query response time and thus lessen the burden of processing resources. The effectiveness of a cache depends on three important cache management techniques: *cache granularity, cache refreshment and cache coherence.* In client-server systems cache refreshment uses time based algorithms such as LRU (Least Recently Used), MRU (Most Recently Used), frequency based algorithms e.g. LFU (Least Frequently Used) or the combination of both [2]. Cache effectiveness is measured in terms of number of cache hits.

A distributed database environment consists of data distributed over multiple data stores across the globe. Distributed caching systems also need to consider the resource utilization such as network bandwidth, processing time at data servers and the heterogeneity of the data from multiple databases. Usually user queries are fragmented into smaller segments according to the data source from where the data can be retrieved to achieve query optimization [3]. Proxy caches are installed to improve optimization of network and processor resource utilization. General practice in the distributed caching is to cache all the data that comes from a single source and reuse for the future queries [5].

The usual grain of cache is a page/table/attribute in applications that query relational databases [2]. In web applications, queries are sent to retrieve information from text documents that reside in web servers. Hence, the grain for cache is often independent data item such as a frequently visited web page, an image or a multimedia item [6]. Extending any of these caching methods to distributed databases is difficult, as applications need to integrate data from multiple databases. Large data transfers, work loads at servers, network limitations and limited cache storage size are the general issues to consider while designing a cache [4].

Sub-query Fragmentation: A sub-query within a query is the smallest independent thread of execution generated as a part of the overall query plan [1]. For example, a *join* between tables or a standalone nested query is a sub-query. other words, a sub-query (q_k) of a query ($\mathcal{Q}$) is defined as the atomic query segment that stores an independent data block such that $\mathcal{Q} = q_1 \cup q_2 \cup .. \cup q_n \Rightarrow \bigcup_{k=1}^{n} q_k$. Here '$\cup$' represents aggregation such as *join* between two tables.

Adaptive cache learns data access patterns and finds the longest sub-query of common interest. Sub-query caching tool aids the data localization phase in distributed query processing. We define *cache grain* as the longest sequence of sub-queries accessed frequently together. Initially, a grain may be of the size equivalent to the smallest query segment recognized by the query optimizer. But the grain size can be refined depending on the user queries. Hence it is possible to store bigger patterns (sequences of sub-queries) as a whole as a single grain in the cache. Similarly, infrequent sub-queries are removed from the grain.

3   Multi-Agent System for Adaptive Caching

Multi-Agent system (MAS) modelling is a widely used approach to solve complex learning, planning, and decision making problems in distributed systems. Autonomous processing nodes (agents) contribute, communicate and coordinate to achieve common goals. For e.g., multi-agent system models developed for distributed health, power [7–9]. To develop a multi-agent system for adaptive caching, we follow an approach consisting of a flexible and generic MAS architecture that can use decision making (with the help of machine learning) and information gathering techniques. In our system, we have identified four main types of agents as shown in Fig. 1. Each of these agents is defined with one or many attributes (A) from the tuple: Object O, States S, Communication C, Domain knowledge K, Heuristics H.

$$\text{Hence, } A = \; < O, S, \; C, \; K, \; H >$$

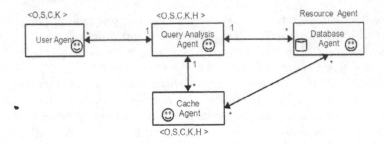

Fig. 1. Agent architecture with related agents

User Agents (UA) are the instigators of the querying process. Main responsibility for a user agent is to monitor the query response time.

User Agent	$A \Rightarrow <\ O,\ S,\ C,\ K\ >$
O= the query,	1. Coordinate with global clock time
S ={send, suspend, wait},	2. Set the query start time S_t
C= Communication with Query Analysis	3. t = send(Query, QAA)
Agent (QAA),	4. Set receive time (R) = t
K = Domain knowledge	5. Response time = R-S_t

Cache Agents (CA) manage the query pattern store at local level. They have the responsibility to share knowledge with QAA by recommending optimal place for the cached data unit.

Cache Agent	$A \Rightarrow <\ O,\ S,\ C,\ K,\ H\ >$
O = set of sub-queries,	1. Receive request for a sub-query
S = {search, acquire, cluster,	2. search &update the frequency for
contribute },	sub-query
C = {Contribute to QAA, acquire from	3. Apply association rules
Database agent},	4. Contribute to QAA knowledge base
K = Local knowledge about patterns,	5. If data not available, acquire
H = set of association rules to	data from database
modify cache grain	

Query Analysis Agent (QAA) is a central coordinating agent at the highest level to implement the decision making layer in the system. It plans the execution module and periodically gathers queried data patterns from all cache agents and user agents. QAA then consolidates information to perform cache refreshment.

Database agents (DA) are resource (static) agents. They understand database load characteristics of the data usage and periodically submits this information to QAA. For this paper, we have not implemented any functionality for this agent.

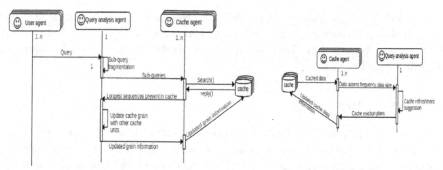

(a) Communication between agents to update cache grain using sequence diagram

(b) Communication between agents for cache refreshment using sequence diagram

Fig. 2. Communication between agents to perform adaptive caching activities

3.1   Task1: Cache Grain Modification

Is a part of periodical cache management. Deciding an optimal grain is achieved by sequence of interactions between user agents, query analysis agent and cache agents. From time to time, query analysis agent actively collects data access patterns across all groups of users (user agents) and then decides on the longest sequences that are queried frequently. Similarly, a grain is shrunk when a containing sub-query is accessed less frequently. Sequence diagram to achieve optimal grain is shown in Fig. 2(a).

Query Analysis Agent	$A \Rightarrow <\ O,\ S,\ C,\ K,\ H\ >$
O = set of sub-queries,	1. Receive request for a query
S = {send, update, maintain },	2. fragment and send query to CA
C = {communicate to UA, CA and	3. send or receive data requests to
Database agent},	databases
K = Global knowledge (query	4. Update knowledge base
patterns),	
H = association rules to modify	
cache grain, cache data mobility	

3.2   Task2: Cache Refreshment

A.k.a. cache eviction. Periodically, the query analysis agent collects data access frequency and the cached data size from cache agents. Less needed queries are removed from the cache. Owing to the distributed nature of caching we propose two distributed caching algorithms: (i) Distributed Least Recently Used (DLRU), (ii) Distributed Least Frequently Used (DLFU). Both these algorithms are based on the metadata about each cached grain indexed in the query index for the current period of time and it's historical information. A decision is made for each of the cached grain to store, delete or relocate from the current location to new location dynamically by collecting information from distributed cache units. Typical interactions between query analysis agent and cache agents is shown in Fig. 2(b).

4   Evaluation

In order to evaluate the efficiency of decisions taken by agents, we have implemented a discrete time step agent simulator using Java (JDK-1.7) programming language. A centralized common time thread (global clock) was implemented to run in an infinite loop of time steps that forwards itself by one tick with every iteration of the loop. Network elements, database servers, cache servers, and users were defined with a unit of work to be completed within one clock tick.

Experimental Setup: We generated input query traces using TPC-H benchmark[1] composite queries (Query number: 5, 7, 10). In order to measure and compare, we have generated synthetic workloads using known statistical distributions. Each experiment was repeated with identical query traces for multiple number of times. We made following assumptions: (i) maximum data size for each query is fixed (since our aim is to estimate the percentage of data transfer reductions, this assumption would not hamper any observation); (ii) transmission networks are congestion free (hence the data transfer delay consists of only transmission time over the network); and (iii) all tabulations show time in terms of number of ticks elapsed by the global clock. Goals to be achieved by the tasks above was divided into two distinct cases.

Case 1: Observation of Average Query Response Time. Comparison of average response time between different caching strategies is plotted in Fig. 3(a). We have compared average response time when (i) no cache is used, (ii) cache that stores only full query results as a whole is used, and (iii) cache with sub-query caching with grain modification is used.

To investigate the effectiveness of sub-query fragmentation for partially repeated data, we created query trace where sub-queries within the queries repeat in 40 % of cases. For a standard time window of cache refreshment, it is observed that sub-query caching with modified grain has considerably lower response times compared to the response time with no cache or cache that stores only full query results. Sub-query caching seems to be better as the complexity of queries increase. (The label "3_2500" on x-axis represents a query trace of 2,500 queries with each of these queries having three sub-queries). Figure 3(b) compares average query response time with sub-query caching with growing complexity. This figure compares two caching techniques: (i) full query result caching and (ii) sub-query caching for queries with two *joins* (2 sub-queries) and three *joins* (3 sub-queries).

Case 2: Observation of Average Data Transfers. The volume of data needed for a query is proportional to the amount of resources required. Figure 4

---

[1] http://www.tpc.org/tpch/.

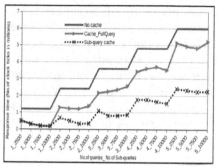
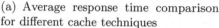

(a) Average response time comparison for different cache techniques

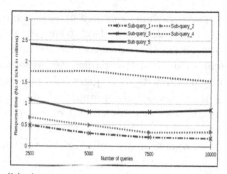

(b) Average response time for queries varying complexity

Fig. 3. Evaluation using average response time

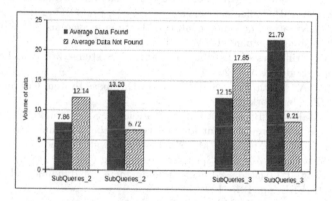

Fig. 4. Comparison of average data found in cache for full query search and sub-query search techniques

compares volume of data found within cache when user queries were repeated only partially.

Test input consists of four traces of 10,000 queries each with varying query complexity. The first two sets of columns on the left-hand side represent the volume of data found (in black) in the cache and volume of data needed (in checkered) to be brought from remote databases. Volume of data found within the cache and volume of data to be brought for full query caching is shown on the left hand side and sub-query caching on the right. Average data size found using sub-query caching technique is found 1.6 to 1.8 times more than the full query cache, suggesting less resource utilization and hence reduction in data transfers.

5   Conclusion and Future Work

This work is a part of research on mobile adaptive caching for distributed databases when query load consists of partially repeated queries from groups of users.

Adaptive caching is aimed at resource optimization by coordinating needs from users in the distributed environment. We have developed sub-query caching technique to be able to maximize the benefit of cached data, using sub-queries as cache grains. In this paper, we presented the evaluation of adaptive caching in comparison with full query caching using agent based simulation. As of now, we have checked the potency of our strategy for read-only queries. We need to extend this work for concurrent read-write queries. Also we intend to develop exchange of cached data with other cache units with the help of demand assessing mobile agents using sub-queries in future.

References

1. Kuppili Venkata, S., Keppens, J., Musial, K.: Adaptive Caching Using Subquery Fragmentation for Reduction in Data Transfers from Distributed Databases, ADASS XXV, ASP Conference Service, vol. TBD, pp. TBD (2016)
2. Elmasri, R., Navathe, S.: Fundamentals of Database Systems, 6th edn. Addison-Wesley Publishing Company, USA (2010)
3. Ozsu, M.T.: Principles of Distributed Database Systems, 3rd edn. Prentice Hall Press, Upper Saddle River (2007)
4. Silberschatz, A., Korth, H.F., Sudarshan, S.: Database System Concepts, 6th edn. McGraw-Hill, New York (2010)
5. Wang, X., Malik, T., Burns, R., Papadomanolakis, S., Ailamaki, A.: A workload-driven unit of cache replacement for mid-tier database caching. In: Kotagiri, R., Radha Krishna, P., Mohania, M., Nantajeewarawat, E. (eds.) DASFAA 2007. LNCS, vol. 4443, pp. 374–385. Springer, Heidelberg (2007)
6. Zhu, H., Yang, T.: Class-based cache management for dynamic web content. In: INFOCOM, IEEE, pp. 1215–1224 (2001)
7. Mahmoud, S., Tyson, G., Miles, S., Taweel, A., Staa, A., Tjeerd, V., Luck, M., Delaney, B.: Multi-agent system for recruiting patients for clinical trials. In: Proceedings of International Conference on AAMAS 2014, France, pp. 5–9 (2014)
8. Chuan-Jun, S., Chia-Ying, W.: JADE implemented mobile multi-agent based, distributed information platform for pervasive health care monitoring. Appl. Softw. Comput. **11**(1), 315–325 (2011)
9. Zhong, Z., McCalley, J.D., Vishwanathan, V., Honavar, V.: Multiagent system solutions for distributed computing, communications, and data integration needs in the power industry. In: Power Engineering Society General Meeting, 2004. IEEE (2004)

Analysing Incentive Strategies to Promote Participation in Crowdsourcing Systems

E. del Val[1]([✉]), G. Martínez-Cánovas[2], V. Botti[1], and P. Hernández[2]

[1] Dpto. de Sistemas Informaticos y Computación,
Universitat Politècnica de València, Valencia, Spain
{edelval,vbotti}@dsic.upv.es
[2] ERI-CES, Departamento de Analisis Economico,
Universitat de València, Valencia, Spain
{guillem.martinez,penelope.hernandez}@uv.es

Abstract. In this paper, we define two strategies for crowdsourcing systems to encourage users to participate at a cost that is close to the optimal cost for the system. In the scenario considered, the system has temporal constraints and potential participants have dynamic behaviors related to the expected rewards (i.e., users' expected rewards in exchange of their contributions change over time). We propose and evaluate two types of strategies that promote participation of users through monetary rewards that can change as time passes in order to adapt them to the population dynamic behaviors.

1 Introduction

Currently, there are many organizations that move towards participatory models. In order to develop a crowdsourcing application, there is a set of features to be considered: (i) the task should be modular; (ii) a community of interest must be engage; (iii) utilize the output from the crowd in a manner that creates value [8]. In this paper, we focus on the promotion of users' participation [1,5,7,10]. Users may provide their contribution free since they have intrinsic motivations or enjoyment [6] or, they may expect an economic reward in exchange of their contribution. Services based on crowdsourcing are usually related to real-time applications (i.e., citizens behavior monitoring [3], traffic monitoring [2], noise monitoring [4]) and periodically require a high number of contributions. For potential participants, each contribution may require resources. Therefore, it is important to ensure participation through the use of incentive mechanisms. In this paper, we consider two type of mechanisms that take into account the number of required samples, and time and budget constraints. Both mechanisms allow the adaptation of the reward per contribution to populations where individual behavior patterns evolve with time.

2 System Model

We consider a general model for crowdsourcing applications in which a system announces a task and calls for participation (cfp) to a potentially large

© Springer International Publishing Switzerland 2016
M. Rovatsos et al. (Eds.): EUMAS 2015/AT 2015, LNAI 9571, pp. 463–471, 2016.
DOI: 10.1007/978-3-319-33509-4_37

population of agents. Before recruiting any agents for fulfilling the task, the system decides the number of required samples for the task. The system will recruit N agents who are interested in the task. The process of collecting samples consists in one or several rounds until a deadline that is only known by the system. The participation in the task implies a cost to agents. For this reason, the system will provide a monetary incentive to agents that contribute with a sample. The monetary incentive may vary from one round to the next. Agents have the flexibility to contribute anytime after the call of participation is announced until the deadline established by the system.

In order to formalize the problem of promoting participation through incentives, we have defined a following model where there are two main entities: the system and the set of potential agents that may be interested in participating.

Definition 1 *(System). In this context, the system is characterize by a tuple of elements $S = (\rho, N, G, T, B, \mathbf{X}, \mathbf{P})$ where:*

- *ρ is the task that the system should fulfil in order to properly offer a service.*
- *$N = \{i, ..., n\}$ is a set of agents that are potential participants.*
- *$G \leq |N|$ number of samples required to properly offer its service.*
- *T is a time constraint to collect G samples. T is divisible in discrete rounds $(t = 1, 2, ..., T)$.*
- *B is the budget that the system can spend in monetary rewards for agents' contributions.*
- *$\mathbf{X} = \{x_1, x_2, ..., x_T\}$ is the set that contains the samples collected by the system in each round $t \leq T$.*
- *$\mathbf{P} = \{p_1, p_2, ..., p_T\}$ is the set that contains the rewards per sample provided in each round $t \leq T$.*

We consider a system S that needs to obtain G contributions (samples or data) in order to properly offer its service ρ. There is a set of agents N that are potential participants. Each agent chooses to participate (i.e., providing one piece of information), or to do nothing. For simplicity, we assume that the information provided by all agents is identical (i.e., we assume that data acquisition only requires simple periodic data reporting, therefore, it may be assumed that users contributions are homogeneous). An agent only can contribute with a sample in each task ρ.

Definition 2 *(Agent). In this context, an agent i is characterized by the following attribute $r_i : t \to \mathbb{R}$, that is the expected reward function (i.e., the monetary payment that agent i expects to receive in exchange of its sample). This function may vary from agent to agent. The expected reward function is private information.*

The system S requires $G \leq |N|$ samples to properly offer its service. There is a time constraint of T rounds to obtain G and S has budget B to spend in rewards. Considering the previous constraints, S tries to collect G samples minimizing the cost of the rewards offered to agents that decide to provide a sample. Therefore, the aim of the system is to approximately maximize the system utility. G, B, and T are private information of S.

The utility function for the system S is defined as follows:

$$u_S(\mathbf{P}, \mathbf{X}) = \begin{cases} B - \sum_{t=1}^{T} \mathbf{P}(t), \mathbf{X}(t) & \text{if } \sum_{t=1}^{T} x_t \geq G \\ 0 \end{cases}$$

where $\mathbf{P}$ and $\mathbf{X}$ are vectors of size T that contain the reward (p_t) and the number of samples collected (x_t), respectively, in each round t.

The utility function for an agent i is:

$$u_i(\mathbf{P_t}, t) = \begin{cases} p_t - r_i(t) & \text{if agent participates in one period } t \\ 0 & \text{otherwise} \end{cases}$$

Modelling the problem as a game, we find equilibrium strategies where solving ρ satisfying all constraints is profitable for the system and the agents. The Nash Equilibrium strategy for agent i is to participate in the first cfp where $p_t \geq r_i(t)$. The alternative strategy would be to wait for a $t' > t$ with a cfp where $p_{t'} > p_t$. Then, the agent has two options: (i) to participate in round t obtaining $p_t - r_i(t)$; or (ii) not participate in t obtaining $q(p_{t'} - r_i(t))$, where q is a probability that satisfies the following constraints: (i) the process continues and S makes at least one more cfp; (ii) the price that S offers in the following $cfps$ $p_{t'} > p_t$.

Since B, G and T are unknown for agents, the first condition cannot be assumed. Agents cannot know how many $cfps$ S will do, making them to perceive each round t as the last one that is going to happen. Therefore, $q = 0$ and $p_t - r_i(t) > 0$.

3   Adaptive Strategies

Taking into account that S has not knowledge about user expected rewards r_i, our goal is to determine how is the best strategy for S to deal with ρ at the nearest possible optimal cost before T. The worst case scenario would be $T = 1$, where S will set the maximum price per sample. The process will fail if $x_1 \leq G, x_1 \in \mathbf{X}$ or it will success with an extra cost. In other scenarios $T \geq 1$, it is possible to optimize the cost of S.

We propose two strategies to determine how many samples are required in each round t and which is the reward $p_t \in \mathcal{P}$ that is nearest to the optimal cost of users samples. The first strategy is *Adaptive System-Oriented* (ASO) does not consider information from the potential participants. The second strategy is *Adaptive User-Oriented* (AUO) that is based on the previous one but has information about the expected rewards of the potential participants (r_i). This information is used to estimate the reward that S will give to the participants that contribute in each round.

The process to obtain G samples is as follows. There is a set of rounds ($t < T$). Potential participant agents (N) do not know if the current round is the last one. In each round t, S calculates a unique public reward p_t and makes a call for participation (*cfp*). Each agent i receives the information about the reward proposed by S. If agent i has not already participated and $p_t \geq r_i$, it gives its data to S. Then, i receives p_t from S, and, finally, becomes inactive during the following rounds ($t' > t$). At the end of round t, S collects the samples provided by the participants (x_t) and calculates the price for the next round $p_{(t+1)}$. The process ends when the number of collected samples at round $t' < T$ ($\sum_{t=1}^{t'} x_t \geq G$) or when $t' = T$.

The key factor of the model for S is the strategy to decide the reward for participants. Note that if $T = 1$ the best strategy for S is $p_1 = \frac{B}{G}$. This price may not guarantee the required G samples, or would make S spends the whole budget and maybe get more samples than required ($x_1 > G$). With $T \geq 1$, S can establish a different price in each round t (p_t) to satisfy the expected rewards of agents. S can take into account the feedback from previous rounds (**P** and **X**) and modify the rewards in the following rounds to minimize the final cost. Therefore, from the point of view of S, the problem that arises is how to approximate the prices to pay to the *cumulative distribution function* (*cdr* hereafter) of the expected rewards of agents r_i considering T rounds.

Algorithm 1. Adaptive System-Oriented Strategy

1: **begin function**
2: Inputs: N potential participants; B Budget; G required samples; T time limit;
3: *expense* $\leftarrow 0$
4: $\mathbf{P} \in \mathbb{R}^N$
5: $\mathbf{X} \in \mathbb{R}^N$
6: $t \leftarrow 1$
7: $p_1 \leftarrow initial\_price\_estimation()$
8: $\mathbf{X} \leftarrow \{0, cfp(p_1)\}$
9: $\mathbf{P} \leftarrow \{0, p_1\}$
10: **while** $\sum_{j=0}^{j=t} x_j \in \mathbf{X} < G \wedge t \leq T \wedge expense < B$ **do**
11:     $f() \leftarrow cdr\_estimation(\mathbf{P}, \mathbf{X})$
12:     $samples \leftarrow \sum_{j=0}^{j=t} x_j \in \mathbf{X}$
13:     $\hat{x}_{t+1} \leftarrow (G - samples)/(T - t)$
14:     **if** $\sum_{j=t+1}^{T} f(samples + \hat{x}_{t+1} * ((t+1) - 2)) * \hat{x}_{t+1} \leq B - expense$ **then**
15:         $t \leftarrow t + 1$
16:         $p_t \leftarrow f(samples + \hat{x}_t)$ // number of samples that S expects to reach at the end of round t
17:         $x_t \leftarrow cfp(p_t)$
18:         $\mathbf{P} \leftarrow \mathbf{P} \cup \{p_t\}$
19:         $\mathbf{X} \leftarrow \mathbf{X} \cup \{x_t\}$
20:         $expense \leftarrow expense + x_t * p_t$
21:     **else**
22:         return FAIL
23:     **end if**
24: **end while**
25: return $\mathbf{P}, \mathbf{X}$
26: **end function**

3.1   Adaptive System-Oriented Strategy

Algorithm 1 describes the *Adaptive System-Oriented strategy* that estimates the reward p_t that G should give to participants in each round t. The process starts with *initial_price_estimation* that establishes the reward that S will give for the participants in the first round (p_1). *initial_price_estimation* considers a linear *cdr*, therefore, $p_1 = \frac{G}{T}$ as a result. Considering this reward (p_1), S starts a *cfp*. An agent i will participate providing its data to S, if the reward offered in the *cfp* is greater than its expected reward r_i ($r_i \leq p_1$). In that case, agent i will receive p_1. The number of agents that participate and the reward given by S in round $t = 1$ is stored in $\mathbf{X}$ and $\mathbf{P}$, respectively. Note that it is assumed that there is a previous round 0 where the reward is $p_0 = 0$ and nobody participates.

A similar process is repeated in the following rounds ($1 < t \leq T$). While the number of samples until current round t is lower than G (i.e., $\sum_{j=0}^{j=t} x_j < G$), and there is enough budget (*expense* $< B$), S continues the process and estimates the price for the next round.

Based on the information collected from previous rounds (i.e., $\mathbf{P}$ and $\mathbf{X}$), *cdr_estimation* creates a linear function f that establishes the relation between the expected number of contributions that S might obtain given a certain reward per contribution (i.e., an estimation of the *cdr* of the market at round t). We establish two estimation methods to generate f (see Fig. 1):

1. Short term memory (stm): that estimates *cdr* using a linear function that passes through the last two points in $\mathbf{P}$ and the last two cumulative samples $\sum_{j=0}^{j=t-2} x_j \in \mathbf{X}$ and $\sum_{j=0}^{j=t-1} x_j \in \mathbf{X}$.
2. Long term memory (ltm): is a more informed method than *stm*. *ltm* estimates *cdr* using the Least Squares method taking all the information from previous rounds into account (i.e., $\mathbf{P}$ and $\mathbf{X}$).

Once f is estimated for the following round, S calculates the number of samples collected until now (*samples*) and the total number of samples that S expects to obtain in round t+1 ($\hat{x}_{(t+1)}$). Taking into account $\hat{x}_{(t+1)}$, f, and the number of rounds until T, S estimates if there is enough budget to continue with the next round. If this cost is lower than the current budget, the system continues with the next *cfp*. The next price p_t is calculated using f. f receives as input parameter the cumulative number of samples that S expects to reach at the end of the round (*samples* + $\hat{x}_t$). Then, S starts a *cfp* protocol and the agents whose expected reward (r_i) is under the price proposed by S, will provide their sample to S. After that, S adds to $\mathcal{P}$ the price established and the number of samples obtained in round t to $\mathcal{X}$, and updates the expensed budget.

3.2   Adaptive User-Oriented Strategy

The *Adaptive System-Oriented strategy* (AUO) establishes the price per each sample without asking about the expected reward of the agents. This is a useful approximation when there are privacy concerns about this kind of information.

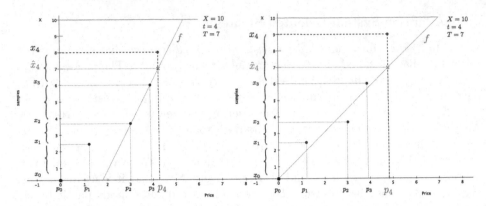

Fig. 1. Function f in round $t = 4$ using *ASO Strategy* and considering $G = 10$ and $T = 7$. X-axis represents the prices from previous rounds (i.e., $\mathbf{P} = \{p_0, p_1, p_2, p_3\}$). Y-axis represents the number of participations in previous rounds (i.e., $\sum_{j=0}^{j<t} x_j \in \mathbf{X}$). In the left figure, f in $t = 4$ is calculated with *stm* (i.e., (p_2, x_2) and (p_3, x_3)). In the right figure, f in $t = 4$ is calculated with *ltm* (i.e., $\mathbf{P}, \mathbf{X}$). S uses f to estimate the reward in the following round $t = 4$. S establishes the number of participations that it expects to obtain in round $t = 4$ (i.e., $\hat{x}_4$) and $f(\hat{x}_4)$ provides the reward p_4 that S will offer to obtain the expected number of participations.

However, there are scenarios where is possible to obtain this information. Therefore, we have considered a user-oriented approach that modifies the previous algorithm adding an initial process where S asks to potential participants N for the expected reward in exchange of their samples. Moreover, in this second strategy, we also consider that an agent not always provides the real value of the expected reward r_i. We have consider that an agent has two values related to the expected reward: r_i that is the real expected reward, and $\tilde{r}_i$ that is a value that can overrate or undervalue r_i.

Algorithm 2 describes the *Adaptive User-Oriented strategy* that estimates the reward p_t that S should give to participants in each round t. The process starts calculating the total samples that S expects to collect in round t ($\hat{x}_t$) taking into account the number of samples that S already has (i.e., $\frac{G-samples}{T-t}$). The function *get_expected_rewards* asks for the expected rewards of agents (i.e., $\tilde{r}_i$). Then, assuming that each potential participant a_i may contribute with one sample, S creates a partial ordered subset that contains the lowest $\tilde{x}_t$ expected rewards of agents $\mathbf{R} = \{(i, \tilde{r}_i), (j, \tilde{r}_j), \dots, (n, \tilde{r}_n)\} : r_i \leq r_j \leq r_n \wedge |\mathbf{R}| = \hat{x}_t$. From $\mathbf{R}$, S selects the highest expected reward ($\mathbf{R}[\hat{x}_t]$). Based on this reward, S starts a *cfp* protocol. In this protocol, S behaves differently depending on the agent that is interacting with. If an agent i was one of the agents with the lowest values of expected reward ($\tilde{r}_i \in \mathbf{R}$), S offers the expected reward $\tilde{r}_i$. Otherwise, S offers p_t to the rest of agents that expected a reward higher than p_t. Then, each agent decides to participate or not depending on their real expected reward (r_i). The algorithm returns the total number of samples (x_t), the rewards provided to agents that participated ($\mathbf{P}$), and calculates the expense in the current round t.

Algorithm 2. Adaptive User-Oriented Strategy

---

begin function
Inputs: N potential participants; B Budget; G required samples; T time limit;
$expense \leftarrow 0$
$\mathbf{P} \in \mathcal{M}_{N \times T}$
$\mathbf{X} \in \mathbb{R}^N$
$t \leftarrow 1$
while $\sum_{j=0}^{j=t} x_j \in \mathbf{X} < G \wedge t \leq T \wedge expense < B$ **do**
$\quad samples \leftarrow \sum_{j=0}^{j=t} x_j \in \mathbf{X}$
$\quad \hat{x}_t \leftarrow \frac{G - samples}{T - t}$
$\quad \mathbf{R} \leftarrow get\_expected\_rewards()$
$\quad p_t \leftarrow \mathbf{R}[\hat{x}_t]$
$\quad \{x_t, \mathbf{P}, expense_t\} \leftarrow cfp(p_t, \mathbf{R})$
$\quad \mathbf{X} \leftarrow \mathbf{X} \cup \{x_t\}$
$\quad expense \leftarrow expense + expense_t$
$\quad t \leftarrow t + 1$
end while
return $\mathbf{P}, \mathbf{X}$
end function

This process is repeated until the number of required samples G is reached, or the number of rounds exceeds T, or there is not enough budget to continue cfp for samples.

4 Experiments

The following tests focus on how the previous strategies are able to adapt the prices that S offers to the potential participants N in order to reach the number of required samples G minimizing the cost of S. To simulate the dynamic economic behaviors of potential participants, we consider rational and irrational behavior patterns (pattern 1 and pattern 5) from [9]. We evaluated the following configurations: Population 1 with 25 % rational and 75 % irrational users and Population 2 with 75 % rational and 25 % irrational users.

In the experiments, we considered that the potential number of participants was $N = 1000$, the number of samples that S required was $G = 800$, and the number of rounds was $T = 10$. Table 1 shows the results obtained with ASO strategy using stm and ltm methods and considering populations 1 and 2. It was observed that in populations where more than the 50 % of the population were irrational, in the last rounds, the mechanism stm estimated the rewards that potential participants expected better than ltm. This fact can be observed in the percentage error, the total expense, and the final number of samples. The results obtained using the AUO strategy that interacts with potential participants to ask for their expected reward values shows a similar performance independently of the behavior of the potential participants. The possibility of asking for the expected reward makes that the mechanism adjusts better the rewards and the final expense is lower than in stm and ltm. However, with population 1

Table 1. Comparison between ASO with *stm*, *ltm*, and *AUO*.

	Participation			Expense			Error	
	b2p	bls	Informed	b2p	bls	Informed	b2p	bls
Population 1	845	965	797	13173.3	16784.91	13161.6	23.7%	34.48%
Population 2	820	876	802	12038.18	13842	12326.26	6.03%	10.7%

(i.e., when there are irrational potential participants), S does not always collect the expected number of samples X.

5 Conclusions

The strategies described in the paper minimize the cost of the potential participants contributions and adapt the reward in each round considering that the expected rewards may change with time. The experiments show that for populations where the majority of potential participants follow an irrational pattern and it is not possible to obtain information from them, the best mechanism is ASO with *stm*. If there is information about the expected reward of the potential participants, the AUO strategy offers more accurate rewards than the other strategies independently of the behavior of the population.

Acknowledgements. This work was partially supported by the following projects: TIN2014-55206-R, TIN2012-36586-C03-01, and PROMETEOII/2013/019.

References

1. Del Val, E., Rebollo, M., Botti, V.: Promoting cooperation in service-oriented mas through social plasticity and incentives. JSS **86**(2), 520–537 (2013)
2. Koukoumidis, E., Peh, L.S., Martonosi, M.R.: Signalguru: leveraging mobile phones for collaborative traffic signal schedule advisory. In: MobiSys, pp. 127–140 (2011)
3. Liu, Y., Zhao, Y., Chen, L., Pei, J., Han, J.: Mining frequent trajectory patterns for activity monitoring using radio frequency tag arrays. TPDS **23**(11), 2138–2149 (2012)
4. Maisonneuve, N., Stevens, M., Niessen, M.E., Steels, L.: Noisetube: measuring and mapping noise pollution with mobile phones. In: ITEE, pp. 215–228 (2009)
5. Martínez-Cánovas, G., Del Val, E., Botti, V., Hernández, P., Rebollo, M.: A formal model based on game theory for the analysis of cooperation in distributed service discovery. INS **326**, 59–70 (2016)
6. Nov, O., Naaman, M., Ye, C.: What drives content tagging: the case of photos on flickr. In: Proceedings of the SIGCHI, pp. 1097–1100 (2008)
7. Reddy, S., Estrin, D., Srivastava, M.: Recruitment framework for participatory sensing data collections. In: Floréen, P., Krüger, A., Spasojevic, M. (eds.) Pervasive 2010. LNCS, vol. 6030, pp. 138–155. Springer, Heidelberg (2010)

8. Rowe, M., Poblet, M., Thomson, J.D.: Creating value through crowdsourcing: the antecedent conditions. In: Kamiński, B., Kersten, G.E., Szapiro, T. (eds.) GDN 2015. LNBIP, vol. 218, pp. 345–355. Springer, Heidelberg (2015)
9. Spann, M., Tellis, G.J.: Does the internet promote better consumer decisions? the case of name-your-own-price auctions. J. Mark. **70**(1), 65–78 (2006)
10. del Val, E., Rebollo, M., Botti, V.: Emergence of cooperation through structural changes and incentives in service-oriented mas. In: Proceedings of the AAMAS, pp. 1355–1356 (2012)

Author Index

Agrawal, Rahul   121
Angelidakis, Angelos   91

Bai, Wei   203
Bajo Pérez, Javier   172
Bassiliades, Nick   157
Belacortu Arandia, Ignacio   172
Berceanu, Cristian   395
Billhardt, Holger   410
Boissier, Olivier   318
Botti, V.   463
Botvich, Dmitri   65

Cardoso, Henrique Lopes   188
Castelfranchi, Cristiano   350
Cerqueira, Fábio Ribeiro   441
Chakraborti, Anirban   121
Chalkiadakis, Georgios   91
Chamoso, Pablo   172

Davidsson, Paul   82
Davy, Steven   65
de Brito, Maiquel   318
de Jonge, Dave   363
De la Prieta, Fernando   172
de Paiva Oliveira, Alcione   441
De Paz Santana, Juan Francisco   172
De Paz, Juan F.   410
del Val, E.   463
Duque, Néstor   234

El Guedria, Zina   50
Elshaafi, Hisain   65

Falcone, Rino   350
Fernández, Alberto   410
Ferreira, Ricardo Santos   441
Fornara, Nicoletta   303

Gutierrez, Patricia   449
Gutierrez-Garcia, J. Octavio   287

Haynes, Chris   3
Heras, Stella   234

Hernández, Josefa Z.   410
Hernández, P.   463
Herzig, Andreas   249
Hübner, Jomi Fred   318, 425

Ion, Andreea   395

Jakubův, Jan   21
Julián, Vicente   234, 410

Kalles, Dimitris   129, 137
Kambayashi, Yasushi   108
Keppens, Jeroen   455
Kiourt, Chairi   129, 137
Klügl, Franziska   379
Komenda, Antonín   21
Kontarinis, Dionysios   267
Kuppili Venkata, Santhilata   455

Liao, Beishui   279
Lopez-Neri, Emmanuel   287
Luck, Michael   3
Lujak, Marin   34, 410

Maffre, Faustine   249
Marfia, Fabio   303
Martínez-Cánovas, G.   463
Martins, Fábio Rodrigues   441
Mihailescu, Radu-Casian   82
Miles, Simon   3
Musial, Katarzyna   455

Nazari, Samira   335
Nguyen, Truc-Vien T.   303
Nilsson, Jesper   379
Nouha, Nouri   145

Oikawa, Ryotaro   108
Oliveira, Eugénio   188
Osman, Nardine   449
Ossowski, Sascha   34, 410

Palanca, Javier   234
Patrascu, Monica   395

Pavlidis, George   129
Payne, Terry   203
Persson, Jan   82

Queiroz, Jonas   188

Ramchurn, Sarvapali D.   157
Ricci, Alessandro   425
Rigas, Emmanouil S.   157
Robaldo, Livio   367
Rocha, Ana Paula   188
Rodríguez, Paula   234
Rúbio, Thiago R.P.M.   188

Sapienza, Alessandro   350
Sarangan, Venkatesh   121
Seitaridis, Andreas   157
Shiri, Mohammad Ebrahim   335
Shroff, Gautam   121

Sierra, Carles   363, 449
Singh, Karamjit   121
Sun, Xin   279, 367

Tadjouddine, Emmanuel   203
Takahashi, Kazuko   219
Takimoto, Munehiro   108
Talel, Ladhari   145
Toni, Francesca   267
Tošić, Predrag T.   74
Tožička, Jan   21

Vercouter, Laurent   50

Yokohama, Shizuka   219

Zatelli, Maicon R.   425

Printed in the United States
By Bookmasters